The Big Book of Special Education Resources

of Special Education Resources

Second Edition

George Giuliani • Roger Pierangelo

CARREL

BOOKS

This book is dedicated to my wife, Anita, and two children, Collin and Brittany, who give me the greatest life imaginable. The long hours it took to finish this book would never have been possible without the support of my loving wife. Her constant encouragement, understanding, and love provided me with the strength I needed to accomplish my goals. I thank her with all my heart.

I also dedicate this book to my parents, who have given me so much support and guidance throughout my life. Their words of encouragement and guidance have made my professional journey a very rewarding and successful experience.

—G. G.

This book is dedicated to my wife, Jackie, and my two children, Jacqueline and Scott, who provide me with the love and purpose for undertaking projects that will hopefully enhance the lives of others. The fact that they are such a loving presence in my life is the reason why my life has been blessed.

I also dedicate this book to my parents, who provided me with the secure and loving foundation from which to grow; my sister Carol, who has always made me smile and laugh; and my brother-in-law George, who has always been a very positive guiding light in my professional journey.

—R. P.

Carrel Books may be purchased in bulk at special discounts for sales promotion, corporate gifts, fund-raising, or educational purposes. Special editions can also be created to specifications. For details, contact the Special Sales Department, Carrel Books, 307 West 36th Street, 11th Floor, New York, NY 10018 or carrelbooks@skyhorsepublishing.com.

Carrel Books® is a registered trademark of Skyhorse Publishing, Inc.®, a Delaware corporation.

Visit our website at www.carrelbooks.com.

10 9 8 7 6 5 4 3 2 1

Library of Congress Cataloging-in-Publication Data is available on file.

ISBN: 978-1-63144-006-9
Ebook ISBN: 978-1-63144-013-7

Printed in the United States of America

Contents

Part 5. Additional Resources 353

Preface

The idea for writing The Big Book of Special Education Resources first came to us when we were looking for a comprehensive information source for members in The American Academy of Special Education Professional (AASEP) The National Association of Special Education Teachers (NASET), and The National Association of Parents With Children in Special Education (NAPCSE). As officers in all three organizations, we were looking for one particular resource book where we could find all necessary information for both parents and professionals in the field of special education. Nothing that we read seemed to have all the information in one all-inclusive directory.

That set us on a mission to write a practical, useful, and helpful book of special education resources. We interviewed numerous parents and professionals to find out what they would want in a comprehensive book of information on disabilities and special education. After months of research, we narrowed down areas that came up consistently as ones that were "absolutely necessary" for this type of book to be a practical resource tool.

The Big Book of Special Education Resources is subsequently broken down into 5 sections. Each section is alphabetized, A-Z, for your convenience.

We hope you find this book to be a tremendously valuable resource guide. It was designed to meet your everyday needs and help you in doing research in all areas of special education.

ACKNOWLEDGMENTS

In the course of writing this book, we have encountered many professional and outstanding sites. It has been our experience that those resources have contributed and continue to contribute enormous information, support, guidance, and education to parents, students, and professionals in the area of special education. Although we have accessed many worthwhile sites, we would especially like to thank and acknowledge the National Dissemination Center for Children and Youths With Disabilities (NICHCY). NICHCY is the center that provides information to the nation on disabilities in children and youth; programs and services for infants, children, and youth with disabilities; IDEA, the nation's special education law; No Child Left Behind, the nation's general education law; and research-based information on effective practices for children with disabilities. Its professional resources were critical to making this book a comprehensive information source for parents and professionals.

We both extend sincere thanks to Kylee Liegl at Corwin Press. Her constant encouragement and professionalism made this project a very worthwhile and *rewarding experience.*

I, Dr. George Giuliani, extend sincere thanks to all of my colleagues at Hofstra University in the School of Education and Allied Human Services. I am especially grateful to those who have made my transition to Hofstra University such a smooth one, including Dr. Penelope J. Haile (Associate Dean), Dr. Daniel Sciarra (Chairperson), Dr. Frank Bowe, Dr. Diane Schwartz (Graduate Program Director of Special Education), Dr. Darra Pace, Dr. Gloria Wilson, Dr. Laurie Johnson, Dr. Joan Bloomgarden, Dr. Tai Chang, Dr. Jamie Mitus, Dr. Estelle Gellman, Dr. Joseph Lechowicz, Dr. Ron McLean, Adele Piombino, Marjorie Butler, Eve Byrne, Sherrie Basile, and Linda Cappa.

I would also like to thank my brother and sister, Roger and Claudia, mother-in-law, Ursula Jenkeleit, sisters-in-law, Karen and Cindy, brothers-in-law, Robert and Bob, and grandfather, all of whom have provided me with the encouragement and reinforcement in all of my personal and professional endeavors.

I, Dr. Roger Pierangelo, extend thanks to the faculty, administration, and staff in the Department of Graduate Special Education and Literacy at Long Island University; the students and parents of the Herricks Public Schools that I have worked with and known over the past twenty-eight years; the late Bill Smyth, a truly gifted and "extraordinary ordinary" man; Helen Firestone, for her influence on his career and tireless support of him; and Ollie Simmons, for her friendship, loyalty, and great personality.

About the Authors

George Giuliani, J.D., PSY.D., FSICPP, FCICPP

Dr. George Giuliani is a full-time Associate Professor at Hofstra University's School of Education and former Director of the Graduate School programs in Special Education. He is also an Adjunct Professor at Hofstra University's Maurice A. Deane School of Law where he teaches the course, Special Education Law. Dr. Giuliani earned his B.A. from the College of the Holy Cross, M.S. from St. John's University, J.D. from City University of New York School of Law, and M.A. and Psy.D. from Rutgers University. He earned Board Certification as a Diplomate Fellow in Advanced Child and Adolescent Psychology, Board Certification as a Diplomate Fellow in Forensic Sciences from the International College of Professional Psychology, and Board Certification in Special Education from the American Academy of Special Education Professionals.

Dr. Giuliani is a member of the American Psychological Association, Education Law Association, New York State Psychological Association, American Bar Association, Suffolk County Psychological Association, Psi Chi, American Association of University Professors, and the Council for Exceptional Children. Dr. Giuliani is the Executive Director of The National Association of Special Education Teachers, Executive Director of the American Academy of Special Education Professionals, and President of the National Association of Parents with Children in Special Education. He has been a consultant for school districts and early childhood agencies, and has provided numerous workshops for parents, teachers and other professionals on a variety of special education and psychological topics.

Dr. Giuliani is the co-author of various articles in the New York State Family Law Review of the New York State Bar Association. He is the co-author of The Educator's Diagnostic Manual of Disabilities and Disorders (EDM), The Special Educators Comprehensive Guide to 301 Diagnostic Tests, and The Special Educator's Complete Guide to 109 Diagnostic Tests, all published by Jossey Bass; the co-author of college textbooks titled, Assessment in Special Education: A Practical Approach (4th ed.); Transition Services in Special Education: A Practical Approach; and Learning Disabilities: A Practical Approach to Foundations, Diagnosis, Assessment, and Teaching, all published by Allyn and Bacon; co-author of Why Your Students Do What They Do-and What to Do When They Do It-Grades K-5; Why Your Students Do What They Do-and What to Do When They Do It-Grades 6-12; Creating Confident Children in the Classroom: The Use of Positive Restructuring, and What Every Teacher Should Know about Students with Special Needs, all published by Research Press; co-author of The Big Book of Special Education Resources, Teaching Students With Learning Disabilities; Teaching in a Special Education Classroom; Teaching Students With Autism Spectrum Disorders; Classroom Management for Students With Emotional and Behavioral Disorders; Frequently Asked Questions

About Response to Intervention; Classroom Management Techniques for Students With ADHD; Understanding Assessment in the Special Education Process; Understanding, Developing, and Writing Effective IEPs; Special Education Eligibility: and 100 Frequently Asked Questions About the Special Education Process, all published by Corwin Press.

Dr. Giuliani recently completed his latest book with Jessica Kingsley Publishers, *The Comprehensive Guide to Special Education Law.*

Roger Pierangelo, Ph.D., FSICPP, FCICPP

Dr. Roger Pierangelo is a full-time Associate Professor in the Department of Special Education and Literacy at Long Island University. He has been an administrator of special education programs, served for 18 years as a permanent member of Committees on Special Education, has over 35 years of experience in the public school system as a general education classroom teacher and school psychologist, and a consultant to numerous private and public schools, PTA, and SEPTA groups. Dr. Pierangelo has also been an evaluator for the New York State Office of Vocational and Rehabilitative Services; a director of a private clinic; and a consultant to CNN News, US News, and World Report. He is a New York State licensed clinical psychologist and has been in private practice for over 30 years, is a certified school psychologist, and a Board Certified Diplomate Fellow in Child and Adolescent Psychology and Forensic Psychology. Dr. Pierangelo currently holds the office of Executive Director of the National Association of Special Education Teachers (NASET), Executive Director of The American Academy of Special Education Professionals (AASEP), and Vice-President of The National Association of Parents with Children in Special Education (NAPCSE).

Dr. Pierangelo earned his B.S. from St. John's University, M.S. from Queens College, Professional Diploma from Queens College, Ph.D. from Yeshiva University, and Diplomate Fellow in Child and Adolescent Psychology and Forensic Psychology from the International College of Professional Psychology. Dr. Pierangelo is a member of the American Psychological Association, New York State Psychological Association, Nassau County Psychological Association, New York State Union of Teachers, and Phi Delta Kappa.

Dr. Pierangelo is the author of the *Special Educator's Survival Guide* and the *Special Education Teacher's Book of Lists,* published by Jossey Bass, and *301 Ways to be a Loving Parent,* published by SPI Publishers. He is is the co-author of *The Educator's Diagnostic Manual of Disabilities and Disorders (EDM), The Special Educators Comprehensive Guide to 301 Diagnostic Tests,* and *The Special Educator's Complete Guide to 109 Diagnostic Tests,* all published by Jossey Bass; the co-author of college textbooks titled, *Assessment in Special Education: A Practical Approach (4th ed.); Transition Services in Special Education: A Practical Approach;* and *Learning Disabilities: A Practical Approach to Foundations, Diagnosis, Assessment, and Teaching,* all published by Allyn and Bacon; co-author of *Why Your Students Do What They Do-and What to Do When They Do It-Grades K-5; Why Your Students Do What They Do-and What to Do When They Do It-Grades 6-12; Creating Confident Children in the Classroom: The Use of Positive Restructuring,* and *What Every Teacher Should Know about Students with Special Needs,* all published by Research Press; co-author of *The Big Book of Special Education Resources,* and the co-author of *"The Educator's Step-by-Step Guide to…"* 10-book series, with the titles: *The Educator's Step-by-Step Guide to IEP Development, The Educator's Step-by-Step Guide to the 100 Most FAQ Asked by About Special Education the Special Education Process, The Educator's Step-by-Step Guide to Eligibility in Special Education, The Educator's Step-by-Step Guide to Assessment in Special Education, The Educator's Step-by-Step Guide to Working with Students with ADHD, The Educator's Step-by-Step Guide to Response to Intervention (RTI), The Educator's Step-by-Step Guide to Classroom Management for Students with Emotional and Behavioral Disorders, The Educator's Step-by-Step Guide to Setting Up*

Your Special Education Classroom, The Educator's Step-by-Step Guide to Classroom Management for Students with Autism, and *The Educator's Step-by-Step Guide to Classroom Management for Students with Learning Disabilities.* Dr. Pierangelo has also published 6 articles for the *New York State Bar Association's Family Law Review* on separation and divorce issues.

National Disability Resources

CLEARINGHOUSES

Center on Positive Behavioral Interventions and Supports

1761 Alder Street
1235 University of Oregon
Eugene, OR 97403-5262
(541) 346-2505
E-mail: pbis@oregon.uoregon.edu
Web: www.pbis.org
Materials available in Spanish

The Center has been established by the Office of Special Education Programs, U.S. Department of Education, to give schools capacity-building information and technical assistance for identifying, adapting, and sustaining effective schoolwide disciplinary practices. The Center operates as a consortium of researchers, advocates, family members, teacher educators, professional association leaders, and model developers and receives guidance from an external evaluation team. A network of researchers has been established to provide feedback on Center-related products and activities, receive and disseminate Center-related products and information, and participate in Center-sponsored events.

Clearinghouse on Disability Information

Office of Special Education and
*   Rehabilitative Services*
Communication and Media Services
Room 3132, Switzer Building
330 C Street SW
Washington, DC 20202-2524
(202) 205-8241 (Voice/TTY)

The Office of Special Education and Rehabilitative Services (OSERS) is committed to improving results and outcomes for people with disabilities of all ages. In supporting President Bush's No Child Left Behind agenda and the New Freedom Initiative, OSERS provides a wide array of supports to parents and individuals, school districts, and states in three main areas: special education, vocational rehabilitation, and research.

DB-LINK

National Information Clearinghouse on
    Children Who Are Deaf-Blind
345 N. Monmouth Avenue
Monmouth, OR 97361
(800) 438-9376 (Voice); (800) 854-7013 (TTY)
E-mail: info@nationaldb.org
Web: https:/nationaldb.org/
Materials available in Spanish

DB-LINK's extensive resources and personalized service are available to anyone needing information about or for deaf-blind children. Its goal is to help parents, teachers, and others by providing them with information to foster the skills, strategies, and confidence necessary to nurture and empower deaf-blind children. DB-LINK is a federally funded service that identifies, coordinates, and disseminates information related to children and youth from birth through 21 years of age, at no cost.

ERIC Clearinghouse on Disabilities and Gifted Education

Council for Exceptional Children
(Project is no longer in operation, but a substantial
    Web site of disability-related materials is still
    available)
Web: http://ericec.org

The Council for Exceptional Children (CEC) has been the largest international professional organization dedicated to improving educational outcomes for individuals with exceptionalities, students with disabilities, and the gifted. CEC has advocated for appropriate governmental policies, has set professional standards, provided continual professional development, advocated for newly and historically underserved individuals with exceptionalities, and helped professionals obtain conditions and resources necessary for effective professional practice.

ERIC System

Educational Resources Information Center
(800) 538-3742
Web: http://eric.ed.gov

The Education Resources Information Center (ERIC) is a digital library of education-related resources sponsored by the Institute of Education Sciences of the U.S. Department of Education. ERIC's mission is to provide a comprehensive, easy-to-use, searchable, Internet-based bibliographic and full-text database of education research and information that also meets the requirements of the Education Sciences Reform Act of 2002. A fundamental goal for ERIC's future is to increase the availability and quality of research and information for educators, researchers, and the general public.

Fetal Alcohol Spectrum Disorders Center for Excellence

Center for Substance Abuse Prevention
Substance Abuse and Mental Health Services
    Administration
E-mail: fasdcenter1@ngc.com
Web: http://www.fascenter.samhsa.gov/

Fetal alcohol spectrum disorders (FASD) is an umbrella term describing the range of effects that can occur in an individual whose mother drank alcohol during pregnancy. These effects may include physical, mental, behavioral, and learning disabilities, with possible lifelong implications. It refers to conditions such as fetal alcohol syndrome (FAS), fetal alcohol effects (FAE), alcohol-related neurodevelopmental disorder (ARND), and alcohol-related birth defects (ARBD). Each year, as many as 40,000 babies are born with FASD, costing the nation about $4 billion.

Genetic and Rare Diseases Information Center

P.O. Box 8126
Gaithersburg, MD 20898-8126
(888) 205-2311 (Voice); (888) 205-3223 (TTY)
E-mail: gardinfo@nih.gov
Web: http://rarediseases.info.nih.gov/

The goals of the Genetic and Rare Diseases Information Center, also known as the Office of Rare Diseases (ORD) are to stimulate and coordinate research on rare diseases and to support research to respond to the needs of patients who have any one of the more than 6,000 rare diseases known today. To leverage its resources, stimulate rare diseases research activities, and foster collaboration, ORD works with National Institutes of Health (NIH) Institutes or Centers to support grants, programs, conferences, workshops, information, and activities.

HEATH Resource Center (National Clearinghouse on Postsecondary Education for Individuals with Disabilities)

The George Washington University
2121 K Street NW, Suite 220
Washington, DC 20037
(800) 544-3284 (V/TTY); (202) 973-0904
E-mail: askheath@heath.gwu.edu
Web: www.heath.gwu.edu

The HEATH Resource Center of The George Washington University, Graduate School of Education and Human Development, is the national clearinghouse on postsecondary education for individuals with disabilities. Support from the U.S. Department of Education enables the clearinghouse to serve as an information exchange about educational support services, policies, procedures, adaptations, and opportunities at UNITED STATES campuses, vocational and technical schools, and other postsecondary training entities.

Health Resources and Services Administration Information Center (for publications and resources on health care services for low-income, uninsured individuals and those with special health care needs)

Health Resources and Services Administration
U.S. Department of Health and Human Services
Parklawn Building, 5600 Fishers Lane
Rockville, MD 20857
(888) 275-4772
E-mail Web Form: http://www.hrsa.gov/
    about/contact/hrsahelp.aspx
Web: http://www.hrsa.gov/index.html
Publications available in Spanish;
    Spanish speaker on staff

The Health Resources and Services Administration (HRSA) provides national leadership, program resources, and services needed to improve access to culturally competent, quality health care. HRSA envisions optimal health for all, supported by a health care system that assures access to comprehensive, culturally competent, quality care.

Laurent Clerc National Deaf Education Center and Clearinghouse

KDES PAS-6
800 Florida Avenue, NE
Washington, DC 20002-3695
(202) 651-5051 (V/TTY)
E-mail: infotogo@gallaudet.edu
Web: http://clerccenter.gallaudet.edu/
    InfoToGo

The Clerc Center has been mandated by Congress to develop, evaluate, and disseminate innovative curricula, instructional techniques and strategies, and materials to improve the quality of education for deaf and hard of hearing children and youth from birth through age 21.

National Center on Secondary Education and Transition

University of Minnesota
6 Pattee Hall, 150 Pillsbury Drive SE
Minneapolis, MN 55455
(612) 624-2097
E-mail: ncset@umn.edu
Web: www.ncset.org

The National Center on Secondary Education and Transition (NCSET) was established to create opportunities for youth with disabilities to achieve successful futures. NCSET provides technical assistance and disseminates information focused on four major areas of national significance for youth with disabilities and their families. The four areas are

1. Providing students with disabilities with improved access and success in the secondary education curriculum

2. Ensuring that students achieve positive post-school results in accessing postsecondary edu-

cation, meaningful employment, independent living, and participation in all aspects of community life

3. Supporting student and family participation in educational and postschool decision making and planning

4. Improving collaboration and system linkages at all levels through the development of broad-based partnerships and networks at the national, state, and local levels

National Digestive Diseases Information Clearinghouse

Two Information Way
Bethesda, MD 20892
(800) 891-5389; (301) 654-3810
E-mail Web Form: http://digestive
   .niddk.nih.gov/about/contact.htm
Web: http://digestive.niddk.nih.gov/about/
   index.htm
Materials available in Spanish

The National Digestive Diseases Information Clearinghouse (NDDIC) was established in 1980 to increase knowledge and understanding about digestive diseases among people with these conditions and their families, health care professionals, and the general public. To carry out this mission, NDDIC works closely with a coordinating panel of representatives from federal agencies, voluntary organizations on the national level, and professional groups to identify and respond to informational needs about digestive diseases.

National Health Information Center

P.O. Box 1133
Washington, DC 20013-1133
(800) 336-4797; (301) 565-4167
E-mail: info@nhic.org
Web: www.health.gov/nhic/
Materials available in Spanish; Spanish
   speaker on staff

The National Health Information Center (NHIC) is a health information referral service. NHIC puts health professionals and consumers who

have health questions in touch with those organizations that are best able to provide answers. The Health Information Resource Database includes 1,400 organizations and government offices that provide health information upon request. Entries include contact information, short abstracts, and information about publications and services the organizations provide.

National Institute of Arthritis and Musculoskeletal and Skin Diseases Information Clearinghouse

1 AMS Circle
Bethesda, MD 20892-3675
(877) 226-4267; (301) 495-4484 (Voice)
(301) 565-2966 (TTY)
E-mail: NIAMSinfo@mail.nih.gov
Web: www.niams.nih.gov
Materials available in Spanish; Spanish
   speaker on staff

The mission of the National Institute of Arthritis and Musculoskeletal and Skin Diseases is to support research into the causes, treatment, and prevention of arthritis and musculoskeletal and skin diseases, the training of basic and clinical scientists to carry out this research, and the dissemination of information on research progress in these diseases.

National Institute of Neurological Disorders and Stroke

NIH Neurological Institute
P.O. Box 5801
Bethesda, MD 20824
(800) 352-9424; (301) 496-5751; (301)
   468-5981(TTY)
E-mail Web Form: http://www.ninds.nih.gov/
   contact_us.htm
Web: www.ninds.nih.gov
Materials available in Spanish; Spanish
   speaker on staff

The National Institute of Neurological Disorders and Stroke (NINDS) conducts and supports research on brain and nervous system disorders. The mission of NINDS is to reduce the burden of neurological disease—a burden borne by every *age group, by every segment of society, by people all over the world.*

National Institute on Deafness and Other Communication Disorders Clearinghouse

31 Center Drive, MCS 2320
Bethesda, MD 20892-3456
(800) 241-1044 (V); (800) 241-1055 (TTY)
E-mail: nidcdinfo@nidcd.nih.gov
Web: www.nidcd.nih.gov
Materials available in Spanish;
    Spanish speaker on staff

The National Institute on Deafness and Other Communication Disorders (NIDCD) is one of the institutes that compose the National Institutes of Health (NIH). NIH is the Federal government's focal point for the support of biomedical research. Its mission is to uncover new knowledge that will lead to better health for everyone. Simply described, the goal of NIH research is to acquire new knowledge to help prevent, detect, diagnose, and treat disease and disability.

National Institute on Mental Health

Public Inquiries
6001 Executive Boulevard, Room 8184
MSC 9663
Bethesda, MD 20892-9663
(866) 615-6464; (301) 443-4513 (V)
    (301) 443-8431 (TTY)
E-mail: nimhinfo@nih.gov
Web: http://www.nimh.nih.gov/index.shtml
Materials available in Spanish;
    Spanish speaker on staff

The National Institute on Mental Health's (NIMH) mission is to reduce the burden of mental illness and behavioral disorders through research on mind, brain, and behavior. This public health mandate demands that powerful scientific tools be harnessed to achieve better understanding, treatment, and eventually, prevention of these disabling conditions that affect millions of Americans.

National Organization for Rare Disorders

P.O. Box 1968
Danbury, CT 06813-1968
(800) 999-6673; (203) 744-0100 (Voice)
(203) 797-9590 (TTY)
E-mail: orphan@rarediseases.org
Web: www.rarediseases.org

The National Organization for Rare Disorders (NORD), a 501(c)3 organization, is a unique federation of voluntary health organizations dedicated to helping people with rare "orphan" diseases and assisting the organizations that serve them. NORD is committed to the identification, treatment, and cure of rare disorders through programs of education, advocacy, research, and service.

National Rehabilitation Information Center

4200 Forbes Boulevard, Suite 202
Lanham, MD 20706
(800) 346-2742; (301) 459-5900
    (301) 459-5984 (TTY)
E-mail: naricinfo@heitechservices.com
Web: www.naric.com

The National Institute on Disability and Rehabilitation Research (NARIC) is one of three components of the Office of Special Education and Rehabilitative Services (OSERS) at the U.S. Department of Education. NIDRR operates in concert with the Rehabilitation Services Administration (RSA) and the Office of Special Education Programs (OSEP).

It is the mission of NIDRR to generate, disseminate, and promote new knowledge to improve the options available to disabled persons. The ultimate goal is to allow these individuals to perform their regular activities in the community and to bolster society's ability to provide full opportunities and appropriate supports for its disabled citizens.

Research and Training Center on Family Support and Children's Mental Health, Portland State University

P.O. Box 751
Portland, OR 97207-0751
(503) 725-4040 (Voice); (503) 725-4165 (TTY)
E-mail: gordon1@pdx.edu
Web: www.rtc.pdx.edu/
Materials available in Spanish;
    Spanish speaker on staff

The Research and Training Center on Family Support and Children's Mental Health was established in 1984 at Portland State University, Portland, Oregon, with funding from the National Institute on Disability and Rehabilitation Research (NIDRR), U.S. Department of Education, and the Center for Mental Health Services, Substance Abuse and Mental Health Services Administration, U.S. Department of Health and Human Services. The Center is dedicated to promoting effective community-based, culturally competent, family-centered services for families and their children who are or may be affected by mental, emotional, or behavioral disorders. This goal is accomplished through collaborative research partnerships with family members, service providers, policy makers, and other concerned persons.

Research and Training Center on Independent Living

University of Kansas
4089 Dole Building, 1000 Sunnyside Ave.
Lawrence, KS 66045-7555
(785) 864-4095 (Voice); (785) 864-0706 (TTY)
E-mail: rtcil@ku.edu
Web: www.rtcil.org
Materials available in Spanish

The Research and Training Center on Independent Living (RTC/IL) is made up of a team of people who are committed to research and training to enhance independent living for people with disabilities. Staff members work on projects that both interest them and address a need in the field. A project might be the sole activity under a grant; however, multiple projects are commonly funded under larger or "center" grants. Projects bridge local, state, and national levels.

DISABILITY ORGANIZATIONS

Alexander Graham Bell Association for the Deaf and Hard of Hearing

3417 Volta Place NW
Washington, DC 20007
(202) 337-5220 (Voice); (202) 337-5221 (TTY)
E-mail: info@agbell.org
Web: www.agbell.org
Materials available in Spanish; Spanish
    speaker on staff

The Alexander Graham Bell Association for the Deaf and Hard of Hearing (AG Bell) is a lifelong resource, support network, and advocate for listening, learning, talking, and living independently with hearing loss. Through publications, outreach, training, scholarships and financial aid, AG Bell promotes the use of spoken language and hearing technology.

Alliance for Technology Access

2175 East Francisco Boulevard, Suite L
San Rafael, CA 94901
(800) 455-7970; (415) 455-4575 (Voice)
(415) 455-0491 (TTY)
E-mail: atainfo@ataccess.org
Web: www.ataccess.org

The mission of the Alliance for Technology Access (ATA) is to increase the use of technology by children and adults with disabilities and functional limitations. The ATA is a growing national network of technology resource centers, organizations, individuals, and companies. ATA encourages and facilitates the empowerment of people with disabilities to participate fully in their communities.

The American Academy of Special Education Professionals (AASEP)

1201 Pennsylvania Avenue, NW, Suite 300
Washington, DC, 20004
(800) 754-4421
E-mail: contactus@aasep.org
Web: http://www.aasep.org/

The American Academy of Special Education Professionals (AASEP) is a national professional association that seeks to meet a critical need for many of America's special education professionals. AASEP develops and promotes professional excellence through the support of professionals who provide services to children with special needs. It seeks to help professionals stay abreast of current issues that are shaping the field, affecting the lives of students, and influencing professional careers. AASEP is committed to standards of excellence and innovation in educational research, practice, and policy. AASEP works to enhance professional practice for professionals in special education and to build public support for high-quality special education programs.

American Brain Tumor Association

2720 River Road
Des Moines, IA 60018
(847) 827-9910; (800) 886-2282 (Patient Services)
E-mail: info@abta.org
Web: www.abta.org/
One publication in Spanish

The American Brain Tumor Association is a not-for-profit, independent organization. Not affiliated with any one institution, it serves individuals globally and awards funds to researchers throughout the United States and Canada. The Association exists to eliminate brain tumors through research and to meet the needs of brain tumor patients and their families.

American Council of the Blind

1155 15th Street NW, Suite 1004
Washington, DC 20005
(800) 424-8666; (202) 467-5081
E-mail: info@acb.org
Web: www.acb.org

The American Council of the Blind is the nation's leading membership organization of blind and visually impaired people. It was founded in 1961 and incorporated in the District of Columbia. The Council strives to improve the well-being of all blind and visually impaired people by serving as a representative national organization of blind people; elevating the social, economic and cultural levels of blind people; improving educational and rehabilitation facilities and opportunities; cooperating with the public and private institutions and organizations concerned with blind services; encouraging and assisting all blind persons to develop their abilities; and conducting a public education program to promote greater understanding of blindness and the capabilities of blind people.

American Foundation for the Blind

11 Penn Plaza, Suite 300
New York, NY 10001
(800) 232-5463; (212) 502-7662 (TTY)
E-mail: afbinfo@afb.net
Web: www.afb.org
Materials available in Spanish; Spanish
  speaker on staff

The American Foundation for the Blind (AFB)—the organization to which Helen Keller devoted her life—is a national nonprofit whose mission is to ensure that the ten million U.S. residents who are blind or visually impaired enjoy the same rights and opportunities as other citizens. The American Foundation for the Blind promotes wide-ranging, systemic change by addressing the most critical issues facing the growing blind and visually impaired population—employment, independent living, literacy, and technology. In addition to its New York City headquarters, AFB maintains four national centers in cities across the United States and a Governmental Relations office in Washington, DC.

American Occupational Therapy Association

4720 Montgomery Lane
P.O. Box 31220
Bethesda, MD 20824-1220
(301) 652-2682 (Voice); (800) 377-8555 (TTY)
Web: www.aota.org

The American Occupational Therapy Association (AOTA) is the nationally recognized professional association of approximately 35,000 occupational therapists, occupational therapy assistants, and students of occupational therapy. AOTA advances the quality, availability, use, and support of occupational therapy through standard setting, advocacy, education, and research on behalf of its members and the public. The contributions of occupational therapy to health, wellness, productivity, and the quality of life are widely used, understood, and valued by society.

American Physical Therapy Association

1111 North Fairfax Street
Alexandria, VA 22314
(800) 999-2782; (703) 684-2782 (Voice)
(703) 683-6748 (TTY)
E-mail: practice@apta.org
Web: www.apta.org
Materials available in Spanish; Spanish
   speaker on staff

The American Physical Therapy Association (APTA) is a national professional organization representing more than 63,000 members. Its goal is to foster advancements in physical therapy practice, research, and education.

American Society for Deaf Children

P.O. Box 3355
Gettysburg, PA 17325
(800) 942-2732; (717) 334-7922 (V/TTY)
E-mail: ASDC1@aol.com
Web: www.deafchildren.org

The American Society for Deaf Children (ASDC) is a national organization of families and professionals committed to education and empowering and supporting parents and families to create opportunities for their children who are deaf and hard of hearing in gaining meaningful and full communication access in their homes, schools, and communities, particularly through the competent use of sign language.

American Speech-Language-Hearing Association

10801 Rockville Pike
Rockville, MD 20852
(800) 498-2071 (V/TTY); (301) 571-0457 (TTY)
E-mail: actioncenter@asha.org
Web: www.asha.org
Materials available in Spanish; Spanish
   speaker on staff

The American Speech-Language-Hearing Association (ASHA) is the professional, scientific, and credentialing association for more than 115,000 members and affiliates who are audiologists; speech-language pathologists; and speech, language, and hearing scientists. Its mission is "To promote the interests of and provide the highest quality services for professionals in audiology, speech-language pathology, and speech and hearing science, and to advocate for people with communication disabilities."

American Syringomyelia Alliance Project

P.O. Box 1586
Longview, TX 75606-1586
(800) 272-7282; (903) 236-7079
E-mail: info@asap.org
Web: www.asap.org

The American Syringomyelia Alliance Project, Inc. (ASAP), is a nonprofit, 501(c)(3), member-supported organization chartered in May 1988. Don and Barbara White started ASAP as a grassroots organization in their spare bedroom due to the frustration they encountered when

Barbara was first diagnosed. Since then, ASAP has become a nationwide support group serving thousands and sending tens of thousands of information packages.

American Therapeutic Recreation Association

1414 Prince Street, Suite 204
Alexandria, VA 22314
(703) 683-9420
E-mail: atra@atra-tr.org
Web: www.atra-tr.org

The American Therapeutic Recreation Association (ATRA) is the largest national membership organization representing the interests and needs of recreational therapists. Recreational therapists are health care providers using recreational therapy interventions for improved functioning of individuals with illness or disabling conditions. ATRA was incorporated in the District of Columbia in 1984 as a nonprofit, grassroots organization in response to growing concern about the dramatic changes in the health care industry.

Angelman Syndrome Foundation

414 Plaza Drive, Suite 209
Westmont, IL 60559
(800) 432-6435; (630) 734-9267
E-mail: info@angelman.org
Web: www.angelman.org
Materials available in Spanish

The Angelman Syndrome Foundation (ASF) is a national organization of families, caregivers, and professionals who care about those with Angelman syndrome. It is a member organization of the International Angelman Syndrome Organization (IASO).

As described in its by-laws, ASF's mission is to advance the awareness and treatment of Angelman syndrome through education and information, research, and support for individuals with Angelman syndrome, their families, and other concerned parties.

Anxiety Disorders Association of America

8730 Georgia Avenue, Suite 600
Silver Spring, MD 20910
(240) 485-1001
E-mail: AnxDis@adaa.org
Web: www.adaa.org

The Anxiety Disorders Association of America (ADAA) is the only national, nonprofit, membership organization dedicated to informing the public, healthcare professionals, and legislators that anxiety disorders are real, serious, and treatable. ADAA promotes the early diagnosis, treatment, and cure of anxiety disorders and is committed to improving the lives of the people who suffer from them.

The Arc (formerly the Association for Retarded Citizens of the U.S.)

1010 Wayne Avenue, Suite 650
Silver Spring, MD 20910
(301) 565-3842
E-mail: Info@thearc.org
Web: www.thearc.org

The Arc is the national organization of and for people with mental retardation and related developmental disabilities, and their families. It is devoted to promoting and improving supports and services for people with mental retardation and their families. The association also fosters research and education regarding the prevention of mental retardation in infants and young children.

ARCH National Respite Network and Resource Center

Chapel Hill Training-Outreach Project
800 Eastowne Drive, Suite 105
Chapel Hill, NC 27514
(800) 773-5433 (National Respite Locator Service)
Web: www.archrespite.org

Chapel Hill Training-Outreach Project (CHTOP) is a national provider of training and technical assistance services and audiovisual and print materials, as well as a provider of direct services to families and children, such as Head Start. CHTOP was established in 1969 with funding from the federal government as part of the nation's earliest attempts to provide educational services to young children with disabilities.

Asperger Syndrome Coalition of the United States

This group has joined forces with MAAP Services for Autism and Asperger Syndrome.

Autism Coalition

181 Westchester Avenue, 3rd Floor
Port Chester, NY 10573
(914) 935-1462
Web: http://www.autismcoalition.org/

The Autism Coalition works with and supports national, state, and local organizations working to accelerate biomedical and applied research to find the causes of autism to lead to a cure.

Autism Information Center

Web: http://www.cdc.gov/ncbddd/autism/index.html

The Autism Information Center is part of the National Center on Birth Defects and Developmental Disabilities, Centers for Disease Control.

Autism National Committee

Autism National Committee
P.O. Box 6175
North Plymouth, MA 02362-6175
(781) 648-1813
Web: www.autcom.org

The Autism National Committee is an advocacy organization dedicated to "Social Justice for All Citizens with Autism" through a shared vision

and a commitment to positive approaches. It was founded in 1990 to protect and advance the human rights and civil rights of all persons with autism, Pervasive Developmental Disorder, and related differences of communication and behavior.

Autism-PDD Resources Network

Autism-PDD.Net
P.O. Box 1596
Pleasanton, CA 94566
Web: www.autism-pdd.net/

Autism Society of America

7910 Woodmont Avenue, Suite 300
Bethesda, MD 20814-3015
(800) 328-8476; (301) 657-0881
E-mail: info@autism-society.org
Web: www.autism-society.org
Materials available in Spanish

The mission of the Autism Society of America (ASA) is to promote lifelong access and opportunity for all individuals within the autism spectrum, and their families, to be fully participating and included members of their community. Education, advocacy at state and federal levels, active public awareness, and the promotion of research form the cornerstones of ASA's efforts to carry forth its mission.

Beach Center on Disability

The University of Kansas
Haworth Hall, Room 3136
1200 Sunnyside Avenue
Lawrence, KS 66045-7534
(785) 864-7600 (V/TTY)
E-mail: beach@ku.edu
Web: www.beachcenter.org

Through excellence in research, teaching and technical assistance, and service in Kansas, the United States, and globally, and through collaborations with those individuals and entities dedicated to the same ends, the Beach Center on Disability makes a significant and sustainable difference in the quality of life of families and individuals affected by disability and of those who are closely involved with them.

Best Buddies International, Inc.

100 SE Second Street, Suite 1990
Miami, FL 33131
(800) 892-8339; (305) 374-2233
E-mail: info@bestbuddies.org
Web: www.bestbuddies.org

Best Buddies is a nonprofit organization dedicated to enhancing the lives of people with intellectual disabilities by providing opportunities for one-to-one friendships and integrated employment. In addition to the traditional, campus-based volunteer activities, and for those with limited personal time, Best Buddies helps people with intellectual disabilities connect with others through technology with its online friendship program, e-Buddies.

Blind Children's Center

4120 Marathon Street
Los Angeles, CA 90029-0159
(323) 664-2153; (800) 222-3566
E-mail: info@blindchildrenscenter.org
Web: www.blindchildrenscenter.org
Materials available in Spanish; Spanish
   speaker on staff

The Blind Children's Center is a family-centered agency which serves children with visual impairments from birth to school age. The Center-based and home-based programs and services help the children acquire skills and build their independence. The Center utilizes its expertise and experience to serve families and professionals worldwide through support services, education, and research.

Brain Injury Association of America

8201 Greensboro Drive, Suite 611
McLean, VA 22102
(703) 761-0750; (800) 444-6443
E-mail: FamilyHelpline@biausa.org
Web: www.biausa.org
Materials available in Spanish; Spanish
   speaker on staff

The Brain Injury Association of America was founded in 1980 by a group of individuals who wanted to improve the quality of life for their family members who had sustained brain injuries. Despite phenomenal growth over the past two decades, the Association remains committed to its grassroots. The Brain Injury Association of America encompasses a national network of more than 40 chartered state affiliates across the country as well as hundreds of local chapters and support groups.

CADRE (see Consortium for Appropriate Dispute Resolution in Special Education, Direction Service, Inc.)

Center for Effective Collaboration and Practice (Improving Services for Children and Youth with Emotional and Behavioral Problems)

1000 Thomas Jefferson Street, NW, Suite 400
Washington, DC 20007
(888) 457-1551; (202) 944-5300
   (877) 334-3499 (TTY)
E-mail: center@air.org
Web: http://cecp.air.org

It is the mission of the Center for Effective Collaboration and Practice (CECP) to support and promote a reoriented national preparedness to foster the development and the adjustment of children with or at risk of developing serious emotional disturbance. To achieve that goal, the

Center is dedicated to a policy of collaboration at federal, state, and local levels that contributes to and facilitates the production, exchange, and use of knowledge about effective practices.

Center for Universal Design

North Carolina State University,
   College of Design
Campus Box 8613
Raleigh, NC 27695-8613
(800) 647-6777; (919) 515-3082 (V/TTY)
E-mail: cud@ncsu.edu
Web: http://www.ncsu.edu/ncsu/design/cud/

The Center for Universal Design was established in 1989 under a grant from the National Institute on Disability and Rehabilitation Research as the Center for Accessible Housing, with a mission to improve the quality and availability of housing for people with disabilities, including disabilities that result from aging. Guided by the vision of founder Ronald L. Mace, FAIA, the Center developed a successful program of assembling and disseminating existing information and created new, landmark materials on accessible housing. The Center's mission is to improve the built environment and related products for all users by impacting change in policies and procedures through research, information, training, and design assistance.

Child and Adolescent Bipolar Foundation

1187 Wilmette Avenue, PMB #331
Wilmette, IL 60091
E-mail: cabf@bpkids.org
Web: www.bpkids.org
Materials available in Spanish; Spanish
   speaker on staff

The Child and Adolescent Bipolar Foundation (CABF) is a parent-led, not-for-profit, Web-based membership organization of families raising children diagnosed with or at risk for early-onset bipolar disorder. Its online community includes parents, researchers, medical doctors, neuroscientists, social workers, therapists, civic leaders, teachers, and others. Its Professional Advisory Council includes lead-

ing experts on bipolar disorder. An Honorary Advisory Board is being formed. Its sponsors are charitable organizations, individuals, corporations, and government agencies.

Childhood Apraxia of Speech Association of North America

123 Eisele Road
Cheswick, PA 15024
(412) 767-6589
E-mail: helpdesk@apraxia-kids.org
Web: www.apraxia-kids.org

Partnering together to work on the difficulties of childhood apraxia of speech, the Childhood Apraxia of Speech Association of North America (CASANA) and The Hendrix Foundation build quality programs and services for professionals and parents. Services include education programs, research symposiums, a comprehensive resource-oriented Web site, online discussion groups, and a phone help line. Serving well over 1,000 families and professionals monthly, it helps children struggling to overcome apraxia of speech.

Children and Adults with Attention-Deficit/ Hyperactivity Disorder

8181 Professional Place, Suite 201
Landover, MD 20785
(301) 306-7070
(800) 233-4050 (To request information packet)
Web: www.chadd.org
Materials available in Spanish; Spanish
   speaker on staff

Children and Adults with Attention-Deficit/ Hyperactivity Disorder (CHADD) is a national nonprofit organization founded in 1987 in response to the frustration and sense of isolation experienced by parents and their children diagnosed with AD/HD. Many individuals and families dealing with AD/HD turn to CHADD, the national organization representing individuals with AD/HD, for education, advocacy, and support. The organization is composed of dedicated volunteers from around the country who play an integral part in the association's success by providing resources and encouragement to parents, educators, and professionals on a grassroots level through CHADD chapters.

Children's Craniofacial Association

13140 Coit Road, Suite 307
Dallas, TX 75240
(800) 535-3643; (214) 570-9099
E-mail: contactCCA@ccakids.com
Web: www.ccakids.com

Children's Craniofacial Association (CCA) is a national, 501(c)3 nonprofit organization head-quartered in Dallas, Texas, dedicated to improving the quality of life for people with facial differences and their families. Nationally and internationally, CCA addresses the medical, financial, psychosocial, emotional, and educational concerns relating to craniofacial conditions. CCA's mission is to empower and give hope to facially disfigured children and their families.

Closing The Gap, Inc.
(for information on computer technology in special education and rehabilitation)

P.O. Box 68
526 Main Street
Henderson, MN 56044
(507) 248-3294
Web: www.closingthegap.com

Computers are tools that can provide solutions to many problems facing people with disabilities today. Closing The Gap, Inc., is a company that focuses on computer technology for people with special needs. Through its newspaper, annual conference, and new online service, "Solutions," Closing The Gap provides practical up-to-date information on assistive technology products, procedures, and best practices.

Consortium for Appropriate Dispute Resolution in Special Education

Direction Service, Inc.

P.O. Box 51360
Eugene, OR 97405-0906
(541) 686-5060; (800) 695-0285 (NICHCY)
E-mail: cadre@directionservice.org

Web: www.directionservice.org/cadre
Materials available in Spanish; Spanish
    speaker on staff

The Consortium for Appropriate Dispute Resolution in Special Education (CADRE), The National Center on Dispute Resolution is funded by the United States Department of Education, Office of Special Education Programs. CADRE uses advanced technology as well as traditional means to provide technical assistance to state departments of education on implementation of the mediation requirements under IDEA 1997. CADRE also supports parents, educators, and administrators to benefit from the full continuum of dispute resolution options that can prevent and resolve conflict and ultimately lead to informed partnerships that focus on results for children and youth.

Council for Exceptional Children

1110 N. Glebe Road, Suite 300
Arlington, VA 22201-5704
(888) 232-7733; (866) 915-5000 (TTY)
(703) 620-3660
E-mail: cec@cec.sped.org
Web: www.cec.sped.org/

The Council for Exceptional Children (CEC) is the largest international professional organization dedicated to improving educational outcomes for individuals with exceptionalities, students with disabilities, and the gifted. CEC advocates for appropriate governmental policies, sets professional standards, provides continual professional development, advocates for newly and historically underserved individuals with exceptionalities, and helps professionals obtain conditions and resources necessary for effective professional practice.

Craniofacial Foundation of America

975 East Third Street
Chattanooga, TN 37403
(800) 418-3223; (423) 778-9192
E-mail: terry.smyth@erlanger.org
Web: https://www.craniofacialfoundation.
    org/www

Materials available in Spanish; Spanish
  speaker on staff

Dedicated to creating better tomorrows for patients suffering from birth defects, tumors, and trauma-related injuries, the Craniofacial Foundation of America (CFA) supports the work of the Tennessee Craniofacial Center in Chattanooga while offering a variety of services for patients and health professionals.

Crohn's and Colitis Foundation of America

386 Park Avenue South, 17th Floor
New York, NY 10016
(800) 932-2423; (212) 685-3440
E-mail: info@ccfa.org
Web: www.ccfa.org
Materials available online only in Spanish;
  Spanish speaker on staff

The purpose of this foundation is to cure and prevent Crohn's disease and ulcerative colitis through research and to improve the quality of life of children and adults affected by these digestive diseases through education and support. Crohn's and Colitis Foundation of America (CCFA) sponsors basic and clinical research of the highest quality. It also offers a wide range of educational programs for patients and health-care professionals and provides supportive services to help people cope with these chronic intestinal diseases.

Cystic Fibrosis Foundation

6931 Arlington Road
Bethesda, MD 20814
(800) 344-4823; (301) 951-4422
E-mail: info@cff.org
Web: www.cff.org
Materials available in Spanish;
  Spanish speaker on staff

Established in 1955, the mission of the Cystic Fibrosis Foundation is to assure the development of the means to cure and control cystic fibrosis (CF) and to improve the quality of life for those with the disease.

Depression and Bipolar Support Alliance

730 N. Franklin Street, Suite 501
Chicago, IL 60610
(800) 326-3632; (312) 642-0049
E-mail: questions@dbsalliance.org
Web: www.dbsalliance.org
Spanish speaker on staff

The Depression and Bipolar Support Alliance (DBSA) is the nation's leading patient-directed organization focusing on the most prevalent mental illnesses—depression and bipolar disorder. The organization fosters an understanding about the impact and management of these life-threatening illnesses by providing up-to-date, scientifically based tools and information written in language the general public can understand. DBSA supports research to promote more timely diagnosis, develop more effective and tolerable treatments, and discover a cure. The organization works to ensure that people living with mood disorders are treated equitably.

Disabled Sports USA

451 Hungerford Drive, Suite 100
Rockville, MD 20850
(301) 217-0960 (Voice); (301) 217-0963
  (TTY)
E-mail: Information@dsusa.org
Web: www.dsusa.org

Disabled Sports USA (DS/USA) is a national nonprofit, 501(c)(3), organization established in 1967 by disabled Vietnam veterans to serve the war injured. DS/USA now offers nationwide sports rehabilitation programs to anyone with a permanent physical disability. Activities include winter skiing, water sports, summer and winter competitions, fitness, and special sports events. Participants include those with visual impairments, amputations, spinal cord injury, dwarfism, multiple sclerosis, head injury, cerebral palsy, and other neuromuscular and orthopedic conditions.

Easter Seals—National Office

230 West Monroe Street, Suite 1800
Chicago, IL 60606
(800) 221-6827; (312) 726-6200 (Voice)
(312) 726-4258 (TTY)
E-mail: info@easter-seals.org
Web: www.easter-seals.org
Materials available in Spanish;
   Spanish speaker on staff

Easter Seals has been helping individuals with disabilities and special needs, and their families, live better lives for more than 80 years. From child development centers to physical rehabilitation and job training for people with disabilities, Easter Seals offers a variety of services to help people with disabilities address life's challenges and achieve personal goals.

Epilepsy Foundation-National Office

4351 Garden City Drive, 5th Floor
Landover, MD 20785-4941
(800) 332-1000; (301) 459-3700
E-mail: ContactUs@efa.org
Web: www.epilepsyfoundation.org
Materials available in Spanish; Spanish
   speaker on staff

The Epilepsy Foundation is a national, charitable organization founded in 1968 as the Epilepsy Foundation of America. The only such organization wholly dedicated to the welfare of people with epilepsy, its mission is simple: To work for children and adults affected by seizures through research, education, advocacy, and service.

Exploring Autism

Web: www.exploringautism.org/

The Exploring Autism Web site is the collaborative effort of Autism Genetics Cooperative, a group of researchers and clinicians working with the help of families with children affected by autism to find the genetic causes of autism.

FACES: The National Craniofacial Association

P.O. Box 11082
Chattanooga, TN 37401
(800) 332-2372; (423) 266-1632
E-mail: faces@faces-cranio.org
Web: www.faces-cranio.org

FACES: The National Craniofacial Association is a nonprofit organization serving children and adults throughout the United States with severe craniofacial deformities resulting from birth defects, injuries, or disease. There is never a charge for any service provided by FACES. In addition to a quarterly newsletter, of which over 20,000 copies are mailed to client families, supporters, professional groups, and the medical community, FACES has an ever-growing national speaker's bureau of clients, clients' family members, and volunteers who speak to groups about the challenges and needs of those with craniofacial differences.

Families and Advocates Partnership for Education

This project is out of operation, but its Web site still provides information on IDEA legislation and its implications for parents.

Web: www.fape.org
Materials available in Spanish

The Families and Advocates Partnership for Education (FAPE) project was a partnership that aimed to improve the educational outcomes for children with disabilities. It linked families, advocates, and self-advocates to information about the Individuals with Disabilities Education Act (IDEA). The project was designed to address the information needs of the 6 million families throughout the country whose children with disabilities receive special education services.

Family Center for Technology and Disabilities Academy for Educational Development

1825 Connecticut Avenue, NW, 7th Floor
Washington, DC 20009-5721
(202) 884-8068
E-mail: fctd@aed.org
Web: www.fctd.info

The Family Center for Technology and Disabilities Academy for Educational Development (AED) is a resource designed to support organizations and programs that work with families of children and youth with disabilities. It offers a range of information and services on the subject of assistive technologies to organizations, parents, educators, and interested friends that supports efforts to bring the highest quality education to children with disabilities.

Family Empowerment Network: Support for Families Affected by FAS/E

772 S. Mills Street
Madison, WI 53715
(800) 462-5254; (608) 262-6590
E-mail: fen@fammed.wisc.edu
Web: www.fammed.wisc.edu/fen

The Family Empowerment Network (FEN) is a national resource, referral, support, and research program serving families affected by fetal alcohol syndrome (FAS) and fetal alcohol effects (FAE) and the providers who work with them. FEN's mission is simple: to empower families through education and support.

Family Resource Center on Disabilities

20 East Jackson Boulevard, Room 900
Chicago, IL 60604
(800) 952-4199 (Voice/TTY; toll-free in IL only)
(312) 939-3513 (Voice); (312) 939-3519 (TTY)
Web: www.frcd.org/
Materials available in Spanish; Spanish
  speaker on staff

The Family Resource Center on Disabilities (FRCD) was a pioneer coalition that covered all disabilities. Formerly known as the Coordinating Council for Handicapped Children, FRCD was organized in 1969 by parents, professionals, and volunteers who sought to improve services for all children with disabilities.

Family Village (a global community of disability-related resources)

Waisman Center
University of Wisconsin-Madison
1500 Highland Avenue
Madison, WI 53705-2280
Web: http://www.waisman.wisc.edu/

Family Village is a global community that integrates information, resources, and communication opportunities on the Internet for persons with cognitive and other disabilities, for their families, and for those that provide them services and support. The community includes informational resources on specific diagnoses, communication connections, adaptive products and technology, adaptive recreational activities, education, worship, health issues, disability-related media and literature, and much more.

Family Voices (a national coalition speaking for children with special health care needs)

3411 Candelaria NE, Suite M
Albuquerque, NM 87107
(888) 835-5669; (505) 872-4774
E-mail: kidshealth@familyvoices.org
Web: www.familyvoices.org
Materials available in Spanish

Family Voices, a national grassroots network of families and friends, advocates for health care services that are family-centered, community-based, comprehensive, coordinated, and culturally competent for all children and youth with special health care needs. It promotes the inclusion of all families as decision makers at all levels of health care and supports essential partnerships between families and professionals.

Federation of Families for Children's Mental Health

1101 King Street, Suite 420
Alexandria, VA 22314
(703) 684-7710
E-mail: ffcmh@ffcmh.com
Web: www.ffcmh.org
Materials available in Spanish

This national family-run organization is dedicated exclusively to helping children with mental health needs and their families achieve a better quality of life. It provides leadership to (a) develop and sustain a nationwide network of family-run organizations, (b) focus the passion and cultural diversity of its membership to be a potent force for changing how systems respond to children with mental health needs and their families, and (c) help policy makers, agencies, and providers become more effective in delivering services and supports that foster healthy emotional development for all children.

Forward Face (for children with craniofacial conditions)

317 East 34th Street, Suite 901A
New York, NY 10016
(212) 684-5860
E-mail: linda@forwardface.org

Forward Face's mission is to help children with craniofacial conditions and their families find immediate support that helps empower them to successfully manage the craniofacial condition. Knowing the overwhelming demands that craniofacial conditions place on the patient as well as the family, Forward Face provides comprehensive services: educational support, advocacy, networking, community organizing, and other forms of assistance when necessary. Forward Face strongly advocates educating members and the public in the quest for understanding and acceptance. The organization is totally committed to providing the necessary resources to enable every person to attain the highest quality of life.

Genetic Alliance

4301 Connecticut, NW, Suite 404
Washington, DC 20008
(800) 336-4363; (202) 966-5557
E-mail: info@geneticalliance.org
Web: www.geneticalliance.org

Genetic Alliance increases the capacity of genetic advocacy groups to achieve their missions and leverages the voices of millions of individuals and families living with genetic conditions. As a coalition of hundreds of genetic advocacy organizations, health professionals, clinics, hospitals, and companies, Genetic Alliance is at the crossroads of the genetics community.

Office of Head Start Administration on Children, Youth and Families

U.S. Department of Health & Human Services
P.O. Box 1182
Washington, DC 20013
Web: http://www.acf.hhs.gov/programs/ohs

The Administration for Children and Families (ACF), within the Department of Health and Human Services (HHS) is responsible for federal programs that promote the economic and social well-being of families, children, individuals, and communities.

Human Growth Foundation

997 Glen Cove Avenue
Glen Head, NY 11545
(800) 451-6434
E-mail: hgf1@hgfound.org
Web: www.hgfound.org
Materials available in Spanish

Today, with the advent of recombinant (synthetic) growth hormone for humans, the Human Growth Foundation (HGF) has broadened its services to encompass many disorders, including intrauterine growth retardation, Russell-Silver syndrome, Turner's syndrome, Prader-Willi syndrome, Noonan's syndrome, chondroplasias, and more. The Foundation has a membership of over 1,000, with approximately 30 chapters. It publishes a quarterly newsletter and many booklets and answers questions from the members and the public in support of its goals. HGF sponsors "starter grants" to encourage research in both physical and psychosocial areas of growth disorders and chondroplasias.

Huntington's Disease Society of America

158 West 29th Street, 7th Floor
New York, NY 10001-5300
(800) 345-HDSA; (212) 242-1968
E-mail: hdsainfo@hdsa.org
Web: www.hdsa.org
Materials available in Spanish

The Huntington's Disease Society of America is a national nonprofit voluntary health agency that is dedicated to finding a cure for Huntington's disease (HD) while providing vital services to improve the lives of those affected by HD and support and guidance for HD families, through a national network of volunteer-based chapters and affiliates as well as through its Centers of Excellence.

Hydrocephalus Association

870 Market Street #705
San Francisco, CA 94102
(415) 732-7040
E-mail: | FCO | Hyperlinkinfo@hydroassoc
   .org | FCC |
Web: www.hydroassoc.org
Materials available in Spanish

The Hydrocephalus Association was founded in 1983, incorporated as a nonprofit 501(c)(3) in 1986. Twenty prominent medical professionals actively serve on its Medical Advisory Board. Its mission is to provide support, education, and advocacy for individuals, families, and professionals. Its goal is to ensure that families and individuals dealing with the complex issues of hydrocephalus receive personal support, comprehensive educational materials and ongoing quality health care.

IBM Accessibility Center

11400 Burnet Road
Austin, TX 78758
(800) 426-4832 (Voice); (800) 426-4833 (TTY)
E-mail: via the Web site
Web: http://www-03.ibm.com/able/index.html

IBM's Accessibility Center offers services to make organizations more accessible to citizens, employees, and other businesses. Accessibility offers tremendous new business opportunities, and IBM believes in a holistic, end-to-end approach, going beyond compliance with disability regulations to create a better user experience and improving people's interaction with information technology.

Independent Living Research Utilization Project

The Institute for Rehabilitation and Research
2323 South Sheppard, Suite 1000
Houston, TX 77019
(713) 520-0232 (Voice); (713) 520-5136 (TTY)
E-mail: ilru@ilru.org
Web: www.ilru.org
Spanish speaker on staff

Independent Living Research Utilization Project (ILRU) is a program of The Institute for Rehabilitation and Research (TIRR) and is affiliated with Baylor College of Medicine. The Web site was developed and is supported in part by Baylor College of Medicine. ILRU is supported in part by public and private funding agencies, including the U.S. Department of Education—National Institute on Disability and Rehabilitation Research (NIDRR) and the Rehabilitation Services Administration (RSA)—and the Robert Wood Johnson Foundation. See individual project descriptions for further information on these organizations.

Indiana Resource Center for Autism

Indiana Institute on Disability
and Community
2853 E. 10th Street
Bloomington, IN 47408-2696
(812) 855-6508 (Voice)
(812) 855-9396 (TTY)
Web: www.iidc.indiana.edu/
irca/fmain1.html

International Dyslexia Association (formerly the Orton Dyslexia Society)

Chester Building #382
8600 LaSalle Road
Baltimore, MD 21286-2044
(800) 222-3123; (410) 296-0232
E-mail: info@interdys.org
Web: www.interdys.org
Materials available in Spanish

The International Dyslexia Association (IDA) is a nonprofit organization dedicated to helping individuals with dyslexia, their families, and the communities that support them. IDA is the oldest learning disabilities organization in the nation, founded in 1949 in memory of Dr. Samuel T. Orton, a distinguished neurologist. Throughout its history, its goal has been to provide the most comprehensive forum for parents, educators, and researchers to share their experiences, methods, and knowledge.

International Rett Syndrome Association

9121 Piscataway Rd., Suite 2B
Clinton, MD 20735-2561
(800) 818-7388; (301) 856-3334
E-mail: irsa@rettsyndrome.org
Web: www.rettsyndrome.org
Materials available in Spanish

The mission of the International Rett Syndrome Association (IRSA) is to support and stimulate
biomedical research that will determine the cause and find treatments and cures for Rett syndrome, to increase public awareness of the disease, and to provide informational and emotional support to families of children with Rett syndrome.

Internet Mental Health (Web site only)

Web: www.mentalhealth.com

Internet Mental Health is a free encyclopedia of mental health information created by a Canadian psychiatrist, Dr. Phillip Long.

Job Accommodation Network

West Virginia University
P.O. Box 6080
Morgantown, WV 26506-6080
(800) 526-7234 (Voice/TTY)
(800) 232-9675 (Voice/TTY, information
on the ADA)
E-mail: jan@jan.wvu.edu
Web: www.jan.wvu.edu
Materials available in Spanish; Spanish
speaker on staff

The Job Accommodation Network (JAN) is one of several projects of the Office of Disability Employment Policy (ODEP) of the U.S. Department of Labor. JAN's mission is to facilitate the employment and retention of workers with disabilities by providing employers, employment providers, people with disabilities, their family members, and other interested parties with information on job accommodations, self-employment and small business opportunities, and related subjects. JAN's efforts are in support of the employment of people with disabilities, including self-employment and small business ownership. It represents the most comprehensive resource for job accommodations available. It has provided information on job accommodations since 1984.

Kristin Brooks Hope Center

210 North 23rd Street, Suite 100
Purcelleville, VA 20132
(540) 338-5756
E-mail: reese@hopeline.com
Web: http://www.hopeline.com/

The Kristin Brooks Hope Center is a nonprofit organization dedicated to suicide prevention, intervention, and healing by providing a single point of entry to community-based crisis services through innovative telephony and Internet-based technologies, by bringing national attention and access to services for postpartum depression and other women's mood disorders, through education and advocacy, through formal research and evaluation of crisis line services, and by championing the need for national funding for community-based suicide prevention crisis services.

LD Online (Web site on learning disabilities)

Web: www.ldonline.org

LD OnLine is a national educational service of public television station WETA in Washington, DC. It is operated in association with the Coordinated Campaign for Learning Disabilities and is made possible by generous support from Lindamood-Bell Learning Processes®. LD OnLine offers online services and produces video programs dedicated to improving the lives of children and adults with learning disabilities and ADHD.

Learning Disabilities Association of America

4156 Library Road
Pittsburgh, PA 15234
(412) 341-1515
E-mail: info@ldaamerica.org
Web: www.ldaamerica.org

Learning Disabilities Association of America (LDA) is dedicated to identifying causes and promoting prevention of learning disabilities and to enhancing the quality of life for all individuals with learning disabilities and their families by encouraging effective identification and intervention, fostering research, and protecting their rights under the law. LDA seeks to accomplish this through awareness, advocacy, empowerment, education, service, and collaborative efforts.

Let's Face It USA (for information and support on facial differences)

P.O. Box 29972
Bellingham, WA 98228-1972
(360) 676-7325
E-mail: letsfaceit@faceit.org
Web: www.faceit.org

Let's Face It's vision since 1987 has been to educate the world to value the person behind every face and to bring resources to all who are dealing with and caring for people with facial difference.

Little People of America— National Headquarters

P.O. Box 65030
Lubbock, TX 79464
(888) LPA-2001
E-mail: LPADataBase@juno.com
Web: www.lpaonline.org
Spanish speaker on staff

Little People of America, Inc. (LPA) assists dwarfs with their physical and developmental concerns resulting from short stature. By providing medical, environmental, educational, vocational, and parental guidance, short-statured individuals and their families may enhance their lives and lifestyles with minimal limitations. Through peer support and personal example, members are supportive of all those who reach out to LPA. By networking with national and international growth-related and genetic support groups, LPA enhances knowledge and support of short-statured individuals.

MAAP Services for Autism and Asperger Spectrum

Web: http://www.aspergersyndrome.org/

Major Aspects of Growth Disorders in Children: MAGIC Foundation

6645 W. North Avenue
Oak Park, IL 60302
(708) 383-0808
E-mail: mary@magicfoundation.org
Web: www.magicfoundation.org

The Major Aspects of Growth Disorders in Children (MAGIC) Foundation is a national nonprofit organization created to provide support services for the families of children afflicted with a wide variety of chronic or critical disorders, syndromes, and diseases that affect children's growth. Some of the diagnoses are quite common while others are very rare. MAGIC continues and develops through membership fees, corporate sponsorship, private donations, and fundraising.

Mental Help Net (Web site only)

Web: http://mentalhelp.net

The Mental Help Net Web site exists to promote mental health and wellness education and advocacy. This Web site participates in the CenterSite Network of behavioral healthcare Web sites.

MUMS, National Parent-to-Parent Network

150 Custer Court, Green Bay, WI 54301-1243
(920) 336-5333; (877) 336-5333 (Parents only)
E-mail: mums@netnet.net
Web: www.netnet.net/mums/

MUMS is a national parent-to-parent network whose mission is to help parents who have a child with any disorder, medical condition, mental or emotional disorder, or rare diagnosis make connections with other parents whose children have the same or similar conditions. If possible, matches are made according to age, geographical location, gender, and severity of the symptoms. MUMS is a nonprofit, tax-exempt organization that runs on donations and subscription fees for their quarterly newsletters. Anyone wanting to be registered in the MUMS database for matching with other parents can download the MUMS' survey form or call and leave name, address, and phone number and the child's diagnosis on the answering machine. A sample newsletter will be sent with a survey form to fill out and return.

Muscular Dystrophy Association

3300 East Sunrise Drive
Tucson, AZ 85718
(800) 572-1717; (520) 529-2000
E-mail: mda@mdausa.org
Web: www.mdausa.org
Web site in Spanish: www.mdaenespanol.org
Materials available in Spanish; Spanish
    speaker on staff

The Muscular Dystrophy Association (MDA) is a voluntary health agency—a dedicated partnership between scientists and concerned citizens aimed at conquering neuromuscular diseases that affect more than a million citizens. MDA combats neuromuscular diseases through programs of worldwide research, comprehensive medical and community services, and far-reaching professional and public health education.

National Alliance for the Mentally Ill

Colonial Place Three, 2107 Wilson
Boulevard, Suite 300
Arlington, VA 22201-3042
(800) 950-6264; (703) 524-7600
(703) 516-7991 (TTY)
E-mail: info@nami.org
Web: www.nami.org
Materials available in Spanish

The National Alliance for the Mentally Ill (NAMI) is a nonprofit, grassroots, self-help, support and advocacy organization of consumers, families, and friends of people with severe mental illnesses, such as schizophrenia, schizoaffective disorder, bipolar disorder, major depressive disorder, obsessive-compulsive disorder, panic and other severe anxiety disorders, autism and pervasive

developmental disorders, attention deficit/hyper-
activity disorder, and other severe and persistent
mental illnesses that affect the brain. Local affiliates and state organizations identify and work on
issues most important to their community and
state. Individual membership and the extraordinary work of hundreds of thousands of volunteer
leaders is the lifeblood of NAMI's local affiliates
and state organizations. The national office, under
the direction of an elected board of directors, provides strategic direction to the entire organization;
support to NAMI's state and affiliate members;
governs the NAMI corporation; and engages in
advocacy, education, and leadership development nationally.

National Association for the Dually Diagnosed (mental illness and mental retardation)

132 Fair Street
Kingston, NY 12401
(800) 331-5362; (845) 331-4336
E-mail: info@thenadd.org
Web: www.thenadd.org

The National Association for the Dually
Diagnosed (NADD) is the leading North
American expert in providing professionals,
educators, policy makers, and families with
education, training, and information on mental
health issues relating to persons with intellectual or developmental disabilities. NADD is
recognized as the world's leading organization in providing educational services, training
materials, and conferences in this area of interest. NADD has been influential in the development of appropriate community-based policies,
programs, and opportunities in addressing the
mental health needs of persons with mental
retardation.

National Association of the Deaf

814 Thayer Avenue, Suite 250
Silver Spring, MD 20910
(301) 587-1788; (301) 587-1789 (TTY)
E-mail: nadinfo@nad.org
Web: www.nad.org

The National Association of the Deaf (NAD)
was established in 1880 in Cincinnati, Ohio.
NAD has a long history of defending the rights
of deaf and hard-of-hearing people. Throughout
its history, new challenges always rise, and
breakthroughs and achievements have created
a better life for deaf and hard-of-hearing people.

National Association of Hospital Hospitality Houses

P.O. Box 18087
Asheville, NC 28814-0087
(800) 542-9730; (828) 253-1188
E-mail: helpinghomes@nahhh.org
Web: www.nahhh.org

The National Association of Hospital Hospitality
Houses, Inc. (NAHHH) promotes and assists
not-for-profit programs that provide lodging
and supportive services in a caring environment
for families receiving medical care away from
home. The NAHHH vision is to be the resource
and voice for homes that help and heal by providing true hospitality in extraordinary ways to
patients and families receiving medical care.

National Association of Parents With Children in Special Education

1201 Pennsylvania Avenue, NW Suite 300
Washington DC, 20004
(800) 754-4421
E-mail: contact@napcse.org
Web: www.napcse.org

The mission of The National Association of
Parents with Children in Special Education
(NAPCSE) is to render all possible support
and assistance to parents with children in special education, both in and outside of school.
NAPCSE is dedicated to ensuring that all
children and adolescents with special needs
receive the most appropriate education possible. NAPCSE develops and promotes excellence
in special education through the support of parents who have children with special needs and
the professionals with whom they work.

National Association of Private Special Education Centers

1522 K Street NW, Suite 1032
Washington, DC 20005
(202) 408-3338
E-mail: napsec@aol.com
Web: http://www.napsec.org/

The National Association of Private Special Education Centers (NAPSEC) programs provide special education services for preschool, elementary, and secondary students and adults with mild to severe disabilities in over 60 different disability categories who need individualized education programs that address their unique needs.

National Disability Rights Network

820 1st Street NE, Suite 740
Washington, DC 20002
(202) 408-9514 (Voice); (202) 408-9521 (TTY)
E-mail: info@ndrn.org
Web: http://www.ndrn.org/index.php

The National Disability Rights Network (NDRN) is the voluntary national membership association of protection and advocacy systems and client assistance programs. It assumes leadership in promoting and strengthening the role and performance of its members in providing quality legally based advocacy services. NDRN has a vision of a society where people with disabilities exercise self-determination and choice and have equality of opportunity and full participation. NDRN believes this vision will be realized through the enactment and vigorous enforcement of laws protecting civil and human rights.

National Association of Special Education Teachers (NASET)

1201 Pennsylvania Avenue, NW, Suite 300
Washington, DC, 20004
(800) 754-4421
E-mail: contactus@naset.org
Web: www.naset.org

The National Association of Special Education Teachers (NASET) is a national membership organization dedicated to supporting and assisting teachers and future teachers of special education. It was founded to promote the profession of special education teachers and to provide a national forum for their ideas. NASET seeks to meet a critical need for many of America's special education teachers. It develops and promotes professional excellence through the support of teachers who provide services to children with special needs.

National Ataxia Foundation

2600 Fernbrook Lane, Suite 119
Minneapolis, MN 55447
(763) 553-0020
E-mail: naf@ataxia.org
Web: www.ataxia.org
Materials available in Spanish

The National Ataxia Foundation (NAF) is a nonprofit, membership-supported organization established in 1957 to help ataxia families. The Foundation is dedicated to improving the lives of persons affected by ataxia through support, education, and research. It supports research in dominant ataxia, recessive ataxia (including Friedreich's), and sporadic ataxia. In addition, the Foundation has developed an extensive library of NAF brochures, fact sheets, books, and other educational material relating to ataxia. Also available to its members is a quarterly news publication called Generations.

National Attention Deficit Disorder Association

P.O. Box 543
Pottstown, PA 19464
(484) 945-2101
E-mail: mail@add.org
Web: www.add.org

The Attention Deficit Disorder Association (ADDA) is designated as a 501(c)3 nonprofit organization by the Internal Revenue Service. This international organization has been in existence since 1989. The mission of ADDA is to provide information, resources, and networking to adults with AD/HD and to the professionals who work with them. In doing so, ADDA generates hope, awareness, empowerment, and connections worldwide in the field of AD/HD. Bringing together scientific perspectives and the human experience, the information and resources provided to individuals and families affected by AD/HD and professionals in the field focus on diagnoses, treatments, strategies, and techniques for helping adults with AD/HD lead better lives.

National Brain Tumor Foundation

414 13th Street, Suite 700
Oakland, CA 94612
(800) 934-2873; (510) 839-9777
E-mail: nbtf@braintumor.org
Web: www.braintumor.org
Materials available in Spanish; Spanish
   speaker on staff

The National Brain Tumor Foundation (NBTF) is a nonprofit health organization dedicated to providing information and support for brain tumor patients, family members, and health-care professionals, while supporting innovative research into better treatment options and a cure for brain tumors.

National Center for Learning Disabilities (NCLD)

381 Park Avenue South, Suite 1401
New York, NY 10016
(212) 545-7510; 1(888) 575-7373
Web: www.ld.org; www.getreadytoread.org

The National Center for Learning Disabilities (NCLD) works to ensure that the nation's 15 million children, adolescents, and adults with learning disabilities have every opportunity to succeed in school, work, and life.

NCLD provides essential information to parents, professionals, and individuals with learning disabilities, promotes research and programs to foster effective learning, and advocates for policies to protect and strengthen educational rights and opportunities.

The National Center for Learning Disabilities' (NCLD) Get Ready to Read! (GRTR!) is a national initiative to build the early literacy skills of pre-school-aged children. The initiative provides an easy-to-administer, research-based screening tool to early childhood educators, child care providers, and parents in order to help them prepare all children to learn to read and write.

GRTR!'s program vision is that all preschool children will have the skills they need to learn to read when they enter school. This Web site is a part of NCLD's initiative to provide parents, educators, health-care professionals, and advocates with information to help build early literacy skills by integrating emergent literacy screening and learning activities into routine early childhood education, child care, and parenting practices.

National Center for Post-Traumatic Stress Disorder

VA Medical Center (116D)
215 North Main Street
   White River Junction, VT 05009
(802) 296-6300
E-mail: ncptsd@va.gov
Web: http://www.ptsd.va.gov/

The National Center for Post-Traumatic Stress Disorder (PTSD) was created within the Department of Veterans Affairs in 1989, in response to a Congressional mandate to address the needs of veterans with military-related PTSD. Its mission was, and remains, to advance the clinical care and social welfare of America's veterans through research, education, and training in the science, diagnosis, and treatment of PTSD and stress-related disorders. This Web site is provided as an educational resource concerning PTSD and other enduring consequences of traumatic stress.

National Center on Physical Activity and Disability

1640 W. Roosevelt Road
Chicago, IL 60608-6904
(800) 900-8086 (V/TTY)
E-mail: ncpad@uic.edu

Web: www.ncpad.org
Materials available in Spanish; Spanish
   speaker on staff

The National Center on Physical Activity and Disability (NCPAD) is an information center concerned with physical activity and disability. Being physically active is good for every body. That's a message you will find many times on this site. Being active is an important part of getting and staying healthy. NCPAD's goal is to provide people with options and information to help them pursue whatever kinds of activities they would enjoy. The important thing is that everyone does something. Indoor or outdoor, recreational or competitive, solo or team, easy or intensive, NCPAD has resources, contacts, and assistance available.

National Chronic Fatigue Syndrome and Fibromyalgia Association

P.O. Box 18426
Kansas City, MO 64133
(816) 313-2000
E-mail: information@ncfsfa.org

National Council on Independent Living

1916 Wilson Boulevard, Suite 209
Arlington, VA 22201
(703) 525-3406; (703) 525-4153 (TTY)
E-mail: ncil@ncil.org
Web: www.ncil.org
Spanish speaker on staff

The National Council on Independent Living (NCIL) is the oldest cross-disability, grass-roots organization run by and for people with disabilities. Founded in 1982, NCIL represents over 700 organizations and individuals, including centers for independent living, statewide independent living councils, individuals with disabilities, and other organizations that advocate for the human and civil rights of people with disabilities throughout the United States.

National Down Syndrome Congress

1370 Center Drive, Suite 102
Atlanta, GA 30338
(800) 232-6372; (770) 604-9500
E-mail: info@ndsccenter.org
Web: www.ndsccenter.org
Parent packet available in Spanish

The mission of the National Down Syndrome Congress (NDSC) is to provide information, advocacy, and support concerning all aspects of life for individuals with Down syndrome. The vision of the NDSC is a world with equal rights and opportunities for people with Down syndrome. It is the purpose of the National Down Syndrome Congress to create a national climate in which all people will recognize and embrace the value and dignity of persons with Down syndrome.

National Down Syndrome Society

666 Broadway, 8th Floor
New York, NY 10012-2317
(800) 221-4602; (212) 460-9330
E-mail: info@ndss.org
Web: ndss.org
Materials available in Spanish; Spanish
   speaker on staff

The National Down Syndrome Society (NDSS) envisions a world in which all people with Down syndrome have the opportunity to realize their life aspirations. NDSS is committed to being the national leader in enhancing the quality of life and realizing the potential of all people with Down syndrome. The mission of NDSS is to benefit people with Down syndrome and their families through national leadership in education, research, and advocacy.

National Early Childhood Technical Assistance Center

Web: www.nectac.org/topics/autism/autism.asp

This group offers an online resource page on autism spectrum disorders and young children.

National Eating Disorders Association (formerly Eating Disorders Awareness and Prevention)

603 Stewart Street, Suite 803
Seattle, WA 98101
(800) 931-2237; (206) 382-3587
E-mail: info@National
*   EatingDisorders.org*
Web: www.nationaleatingdisorders.org
Materials available in Spanish

The National Eating Disorders Association (NEDA) is the largest not-for-profit organization in the United States working to prevent eating disorders and provide treatment referrals to those suffering from anorexia, bulimia, and binge eating disorder and those concerned with body image and weight issues. NEDA serves the needs of the national community by providing programs, products, and services of superior quality that support the elimination of eating disorders. To achieve its mission, it develops prevention programs for a wide range of audiences, publishes and distributes educational materials, and operates the nation's first toll-free eating disorders information and referral helpline.

National Federation for the Blind

1800 Johnson Street
Baltimore, MD 21230
(410) 659-9314
E-mail: nfb@nfb.org
Web: www.nfb.org
Materials available in Spanish; Spanish
*   speaker on staff*

The purpose of the National Federation of the Blind (NFB) is twofold—to help blind persons achieve self-confidence and self-respect and to act as a vehicle for collective self-expression by the blind. By providing public education about blindness, information and referral services, scholarships, literature and publications about blindness, aids and appliances and other adaptive equipment for the blind, advocacy services and protection of civil rights, development and evaluation of technology, and support for blind persons and their

families, members of the NFB strive to educate the public that the blind are normal individuals who can compete on terms of equality.

National Fragile X Foundation

P.O. Box 190488
San Francisco, CA 94119-0488
(800) 688-8765; (925) 938-9315
E-mail: NATLFX@FragileX.org
Web: www.fragilex.org
Materials available in Spanish

The National Fragile X Foundation unites the Fragile X community to enrich lives through educational and emotional support, promote public and professional awareness, and advance research toward improved treatments and a cure for Fragile X.

National Gaucher Foundation

5410 Edson Lane, Suite 260
Rockville, MD 20852-3130
(800) 428-2437; (301) 816-1515
E-mail: ngf@gaucherdisease.org
Web: www.gaucherdisease.org

The National Gaucher Foundation (NGF) was established in 1984 as a nonprofit, tax-exempt organization dedicated to supporting and promoting research into the causes of and a cure for Gaucher Disease. The mission of the NGF is to find a cure for Gaucher Disease by funding vital research programs, meet the ever-increasing needs of patients and families, as well as promote community and physician awareness and educational programs.

National Library Service for the Blind and Physically Handicapped

The Library of Congress
1291 Taylor Street NW
Washington, DC 20011
(800) 424-8567; (202) 707-5100 (Voice); (202)
*   707-0744 (TTY)*
E-mail: nls@loc.gov
Web: www.loc.gov/nls
Materials available in Spanish; Spanish speaker
*   on staff*

The National Library Service for the Blind and Physically Handicapped (NLS), Library of Congress, administers the free program that loans recorded and braille books and magazines, music scores in braille and large print, and specially designed playback equipment to residents of the United States who are unable to read or use standard print materials because of visual or physical impairment. NLS administers the program nationally while direct service to eligible individuals and institutions is the responsibility of cooperating libraries in the various states, the District of Columbia, Puerto Rico, Guam, and the Virgin Islands. Service is also extended to eligible U.S. citizens residing abroad.

National Mental Health Association

2001 N. Beauregard, 12th Floor
Alexandria, VA 22311
(800) 969-6642; (703) 684-7722
(800) 433-5959 (TTY)
E-mail: via the Web site
Web: www.nmha.org
Materials available in Spanish; Spanish
   speaker on staff

The National Mental Health Association (NMHA) is the country's oldest and largest nonprofit organization addressing all aspects of mental health and mental illness. With more than 340 affiliates nationwide, NMHA works to improve the mental health of all U.S. citizens, especially the 54 million individuals with mental disorders, through advocacy, education, research, and service.

National Mental Health Information Center (formerly the Knowledge Exchange Network)

P.O. Box 42557
Washington, DC 20015
(800) 789-2647; (866) 889-2647 (TTY)
Web: http://www.samhsa.gov/
Materials available in Spanish; Spanish
   speaker on staff

The Substance Abuse and Mental Health Services Administration's National Mental Health Information Center provides information about mental health via a toll-free telephone number (800-789-2647), their Web site, and more than

600 publications. The National Mental Health Information Center was developed for users of mental health services and their families, the general public, policy makers, providers, and the media.

National Multiple Sclerosis Society

733 Third Avenue
New York, NY 10017
(800) 344-4867
E-mail: via the Web site
Web: www.nationalmssociety.org
Materials available in Spanish; Spanish
   speaker on staff

Founded in 1946, the National Multiple Sclerosis Society supports more multiple sclerosis (MS) research, offers more services for people with MS, provides more professional education programs, and furthers more MS advocacy efforts than any other MS organization in the world. It does this through the extensive research it supports to find the cause, cure, and improved treatments of the disease; the comprehensive services we provide to people with MS and their families; the professional education programs we offer to assist health care providers better serve their MS patients; and through our advocacy efforts on state and federal levels to encourage public policies supportive of the needs of people with MS.

National Neurofibromatosis Foundation

95 Pine Street; 16th Floor
New York, NY 10005
(800) 323-7938; (212) 344-6633
E-mail: nnff@nf.org
Web: www.nf.org
Materials available in Spanish; Spanish
   speaker on staff

The Children's Tumor Foundation is a nonprofit 501(c)(3) medical foundation dedicated to improving the health and well-being of individuals and families affected by neurofibromatoses (NF). The mission of The Children's Tumor Foundation is to encourage and support research and the development of treatments and curesfor neurofibromatosis types 1 and 2, schwannomatosis, and related disorders (hereafter collectively referred to as "NF"); support persons with NF, their families and caregivers by providing thorough, accurate, current, and readily accessible information; assist in the development of clinical centers, best practices, and other patient support mechanisms (but not including direct medical care) to create better access to quality healthcare for affected individuals; and expand public awareness of NF topromote earlier and accurate diagnoses by the medical community, increase the nonaffected population's understanding of the challenges facing persons with NF, and encourage financial and other forms of support from public and private sources.

National Organization on Disability

910 16th Street NW, Suite 600
Washington, DC 20006
(202) 293-5960 (Voice); (202) 293-5968 (TTY)
E-mail: ability@nod.org
Web: www.nod.org
Spanish speaker on staff

The mission of the National Organization on Disability (NOD) is to expand the participation and contribution of the United States's 54 million men, women, and children with disabilities in all aspects of life. By raising disability awareness through programs and information, together it is possible to work toward closing the participation gaps.

National Organization on Fetal Alcohol Syndrome

900 17th Street NW, Suite 910
Washington, DC 20006
(800) 666-6327; (202) 785-4585
E-mail: information@nofas.org
Web: www.nofas.org
Materials available in Spanish; Spanish
    speaker on staff

NOFAS is a 501(c)(3) nonprofit organization founded in 1990 to address alcohol use during pregnancy, the leading known preventable cause of mental retardation and birth defects.
   NOFAS recognizes the importance of health education in order to reduce the number of alcohol-exposed births and fulfills its mission

by implementing innovativeideas in prevention, education, intervention, and advocacy. The organizational objectives include
   Increasing public awareness about the range of consequences associated with prenatal alcohol exposure
   Educating medical and allied health students and practitioners about the range of health effects related to alcohol and pregnancy
   Training youth as peer educators in their schools and communities
   Developing prevention and education messages and strategies for implementation among diverse populations nationwide
   Providing referrals, resources, and information on a broad range of alcohol and pregnancy services through a national clearinghouse
   Collaborating and partnering with prevention, education, advocacy, and research agencies, organizations, and universities to promote the awareness of FAS and to coordinate activities

National Patient Air Transport Hotline

c/o Mercy Medical Airlift,
4620 Haygood Road, Suite 1
Virginia Beach, VA 23445
(800) 296-1217
E-mail: mercymedical@erols.com
Web: www.patienttravel.org

PatientTravel.org is a third-generation site updated in April 2002, a continuation of the original National Patient Air Travel HELPLINE site which has been serving patients since 1998. This site now receives more than 3,000 visits per month. The availability of charitable, long-distance medical air transportation in the United States is growing rapidly. More than 41,500 patients and their escorts were served during calendar year 2002. This Web site is a service of the National Patient Travel Center—the facility housing all the programs of Mercy Medical Airlift, a national charity. The Center is in Virginia Beach, Virginia, and provides a variety of services to those seeking a way to travel long distances for specialized medical evaluation, diagnosis, and treatment.

National Resource Center for Family Centered Practice

University of Iowa
100 Oakdale Hall
Iowa City, IA 52242-5000
(319) 335-4965
Web: http://www.uiowa.edu/~nrcfcp/
Materials available in Spanish;
   Spanish speaker on staff

National Resource Center for Paraprofessionals in Education and Related Services

6526 Old Main Hill Utah State University
Logan, UT 84322-6526
(435) 797-7272
E-mail: info@nrcpara.org
Web: http://www.nrcpara.org/

National Resource Center on Supported Living and Choice

Syracuse University, Center on Human Policy
805 S. Crouse Avenue
Syracuse, NY 13244-2280
(800) 894-0826; (315) 443-3851; (315)
   443-4355 (TTY)
E-mail: thechp@sued.syr.edu
Web: http://thechp.syr.edu/nrc.html

National Reye's Syndrome Foundation

P.O. Box 829
Bryan, OH 43506
(800) 233-7393; (419) 636-2679
E-mail: nrsf@reyessyndrome.org
Web: www.reyessyndrome.org
Materials available in Spanish

Reye's syndrome, a deadly disease, strikes swiftly, and can attack any child or adult without warning. All body organs are affected, with the liver and brain suffering most seriously. While the cause and cure remain unknown, research has established a link between Reye's syndrome and the use of aspirin and other salicylate-containing medications. In 1974, the National Reye's syndrome Foundation was incorporated, becoming the first citizen group to generate a concerted, organized lay movement to eradicate Reye's syndrome.

National Spinal Cord Injury Association

6701 Democracy Boulevard Suite 300-9
Bethesda, MD 20817
(800) 962-9629; (301) 588-6959
E-mail: info@spinalcord.org
Web: www.spinalcord.org
Spanish speaker on staff

Founded in 1948, the National Spinal Cord Injury Association (NSCIA) is the nation's oldest and largest civilian organization dedicated to improving the quality of life for hundreds of thousands of Americans living with the results of spinal cord injury and disease and their families. This number grows by 30 newly injured people each day. NSCIA educates and empowers survivors of spinal cord injury and disease to achieve and maintain the highest levels of independence, health, and personal fulfillment. This mission is fulfilled by providing an innovative peer support network and by raising awareness about spinal cord injury and disease through education. Education programs are developed to address information and issues important to the Association's constituency, policy makers, the general public, and the media and include injury prevention; improvements in medical, rehabilitative, and supportive services; research; and public policy formulation.

National Stuttering Association

119 W. 40th Street, 14th Floor
New York, NY 10018
(800) 937-8888
E-mail: info@westutter.org
Web: www.westutter.org

The National Stuttering Association (NSA) is the largest self-help/support organization in the

United States for people who stutter. Its mission is to bring hope, dignity, support, education, and empowerment to children and adults who stutter and their families.

National Tay-Sachs and Allied Diseases Association

2001 Beacon Street, Suite 204
Brighton, MA 02135
(800) 906-8723
E-mail: info@ntsad.org
Web: www.ntsad.org
Materials available in Spanish

The National Tay-Sachs and Allied Diseases Association (NTSAD) is dedicated to the treatment and prevention of Tay-Sachs, Canavan, and related diseases and to provide information and support services to individuals and families affected by these diseases, as well as the public at large. Strategies for achieving these goals include public and professional education, research, genetic screening, family services, and advocacy.

Neurofibromatosis, Inc.

9320 Annapolis Road, Suite 300
Lanham, MD 20706-3123
(800) 942-6825; (301) 918-4600
E-mail: info@nfinc.org
Web: www.nfinc.org
Materials available in Spanish

Neurofibromatosis, Inc. (NF, Inc.) is a national, tax-exempt, charitable organization whose mission is to create a community of support for those affected by NF through education, advocacy, coalitions, raising public awareness, and supporting research for treatments and a cure.

NLD on the Web! (Web site only)

Web: www.NLDontheweb.org

NLD on the Web! was designed and developed in September, 1999, by Pamela Tanguay and Joan Scott, both mothers of daughters with nonverbal learning disorder (NLD). They met on a neuropsychology bulletin board and joined

forces as they headed down the same challenging path—researching the disorder at a time when NLD information was very hard to come by, especially on the Web. This site is a result of those efforts. Their goal was to create the kind of Web site they were hoping to find themselves . . . but never did.

Nonverbal Learning Disorders Association

2446 Albany Avenue
West Hartford, CT 06117
(800) 570-0217
E-mail: NLDA@nlda.org
Web: www.nlda.org

The Nonverbal Learning Disorders Association (NLDA) is an international nonprofit corporation committed to facilitating education, research, and advocacy for children and adults who manifest disabilities associated with the syndrome of nonverbal learning disorders. The NLDA volunteer workforce includes individuals with learning disabilities, their families and associates, and those who provide professional care and intervention. It strives to enhance the lives of all individuals with NLD by encouraging effective identification and intervention, fostering research, and protecting the rights of learning disabled individuals. NLDA seeks to accomplish this through awareness, advocacy, empowerment, education, and service.

OASIS—Online Asperger Syndrome Support and Information

Web: www.aspergersyndrome.org/

Obsessive-Compulsive Foundation, Inc.

676 State Street
New Haven, CT 06511
(203) 401-2070
E-mail: info@ocfoundation.org
Web: www.ocfoundation.org
Materials available in Spanish; Spanish speaker on staff

The Obsessive-Compulsive Foundation (OCF), with more than 10,000 members, is an international not-for-profit organization composed of people with obsessive-compulsive disorder (OCD) and related disorders, their families, friends, professionals, and other concerned individuals. Founded by a group of individuals with OCD in 1986, the mission of the OCF is to educate the public and professional communities about OCD and related disorders; to provide assistance to individuals with OCD and related disorders, their family and friends; and to support research into the causes and effective treatments of OCD and related disorders.

Osteogenesis Imperfecta Foundation

804 Diamond Avenue, Suite 210
Gaithersburg, MD 20878
(800) 981-2663; (301) 947-0083
E-mail: bonelink@oif.org
Web: www.oif.org
Materials available in Spanish

The Osteogenesis Imperfecta Foundation, Inc. (OI Foundation) is the only voluntary national health organization dedicated to helping people cope with the problems associated with osteogenesis imperfecta (OI). The Foundation's mission is to improve the quality of life for individuals affected by OI through research to find treatments and a cure, education, awareness, and mutual support. The OI Foundation began in 1970 when a small group of parents from around the United States met in Chicago to discuss OI and its problems. At that time, they banded together to stimulate public and professional interest, support families, and encourage research. Today, many of the people who serve on the board of directors and oversee the Foundation's operation have OI themselves or are parents of children with OI.

Parents Helping Parents: The Parent-Directed Family Resource Center for Children with Special Needs

3041 Olcott Street
Santa Clara, CA 95054
(408) 727-5775
E-mail: info@php.com
Web: www.php.com
Materials available in Spanish;
    Spanish speaker on staff

Parents Helping Parents (PHP) is a 28-year-old nonprofit, family resource center that benefits children with special needs. This includes children of all ages (birth through life) and all backgrounds who have a need for special services due to any special need, including but not limited to illness, cancer, accidents, birth defects, neurological conditions, premature birth, learning or physical disabilities, mental health issues, and attention deficit (hyperactivity) disorder. PHP's mission is to help children with special needs receive the resources, love, hope, respect, health care, education, and other services they need to reach their full potential by providing them with strong families, dedicated professionals, and responsive systems to serve them.

Parents of Galactosemic Children

885 Del Sol Street
Sparks, NV 89436
(775) 626-0885
E-mail: mesmeadow@aol.com
Web: www.galactosemia.org

Parents of Galactosemic Children, Inc. (PGC) is a nonprofit charitable organization. Founded in February 1985 by a small group of mothers in New York, PGC realizes the need for further information and networking between affected families and professionals. Metabolic clinics across the nation continue to assist PGC in researching families and information. Today its mailing list includes over 1,000 families and extended families, professionals and clinics, media groups, donors, and numerous international contacts. Objectives and functions are achieved by unpaid volunteers.

Parent to Parent of the United States (Web site only)

Web: http://www.p2pusa.org/p2pusa/
sitepages/p2p-home.aspx

Parent to Parent-USA (P2P-USA) is an alliance of parent-to-parent programs whose primary purpose is to help emerging or established parent-to-parent programs by: providing a clearinghouse of information and support on best practices, offering networking and peer mentoring experiences, mentoring future parent-to-parent leaders, nurturing and developing key relationships that enhance P2P programs' ability to support families, and effect policy change.

Pathways Awareness Foundation

150 N. Michigan Avenue, Suite 2100
Chicago, IL 60601
(800) 955-2445
E-mail: friends@pathwaysawareness.org
Web: www.pathwaysawareness.org
Brochure and video available in Spanish

Pathways Awareness Foundation is a national nonprofit organization dedicated to raising awareness about the benefit of early detection and early therapy for children with physical movement differences. Our Web site, designed for both parents and professionals, contains valuable information about children's physical development, including a growth and development chart where it is possible to track a child's physical, play, and speech milestones from 3 months to 15 months.

Patient Centers: The Autism Center

Web: www.patientcenters.com/autism/

Prader-Willi Syndrome Association

5700 Midnight Pass Road, Suite 6
Sarasota, FL 34242
(800) 926-4797; (941) 312-0400
E-mail: national@pwsausa.org
Web: www.pwsausa.org
Materials available in Spanish

Prader-Willi Syndrome Association (USA) [PWSA(USA)] is dedicated to serving individuals affected by Prader-Willi syndrome (PWS), their families, and interested professionals. Organized in 1975 to provide a resource for education and information about Prader-Willi syndrome and support for families, professionals and other interested citizens, PWSA(USA) was first headquartered in the Minneapolis/St. Paul area, then in St. Louis, Missouri, and currently in Sarasota, Florida since October of 1997. The association is governed by a 12-member Board of Directors who, together with an executive director and four officers, are responsible for directing the organization's operations and serving the twenty-seven state and regional chapters and their members.

Recording for the Blind and Dyslexic

The Anne T. Macdonald Center
20 Roszel Road
Princeton, NJ 08540
(800) 221-4792; (866) 732-3585; (609) 452-0606
E-mail: custserv@rfbd.org
Web: www.rfbd.org

Recording for the Blind and Dyslexic, a nonprofit volunteer organization, is the nation's educational library serving people who cannot effectively read standard print because of visual impairment, dyslexia, or other physical disability. Its mission is to create opportunities for individual success by providing and promoting the effective use of accessible educational materials.

Registry of Interpreters for the Deaf

333 Commerce Street
Alexandria, VA 22314
(703) 838-0030; (703) 838-0459 (TTY)
E-mail: info@rid.org
Web: www.rid.org

The philosophy of the Registry of Interpreters for the Deaf (RID) is that excellence in the delivery of interpretation and transliteration services among people who are deaf or hard of hearing and people who are hearing will ensure effective communication. As the pro-

fessional association for interpreters and trans-literators, RID serves as an essential arena for its members in their pursuit of excellence. It is the mission of RID to provide international, national, regional, state, and local forums and an organizational structure for the continued growth and development of the professions of interpretation and transliteration of American Sign Language and English. It is the goal of RID to promote the profession of interpreting and transliterating American Sign Language and English.

Rehabilitation Engineering and Assistive Technology Society of North America

*1700 N. Moore Street, Suite 1540
Arlington, VA 22209-1903
(703) 524-6686 (Voice); (703) 524-6639 (TTY)
E-mail: info@resna.org
Web: www.resna.org*

Rehabilitation Engineering and Assistive Technology Society of North America (RESNA) is an interdisciplinary association of people with a common interest in technology and dis-ability. Its purpose is to improve the potential of people with disabilities to achieve their goals through the use of technology. It serves that purpose by promoting research, development, education, advocacy, and provision of technol-ogy and by supporting the people engaged in these activities.

The International Rett Syndrome Foundation

*4600 Devitt Drive
Cincinnati, Ohio 45246
513/874.3020
Web: http://www.rettsyndrome.org/*

The International Rett Syndrome Foundation offers an electronic newsletter, which can be e-mailed about once a week with the latest research news, abstracts from new Rett publica-tions, treatment and drug information, scientific meetings, and fundraising events.

Schwab Learning

*1650 S. Amphlett Boulevard, Suite 300
San Mateo, CA 94402
(800) 230-0988; (650) 655-2410
E-mail: webmaster@schwablearning.org
Web: www.schwablearning.org
Portion of Web site in Spanish*

Schwab Learning is an operating program of the Charles and Helen Schwab Foundation, a private, nonprofit foundation that funds pro-grams in learning disabilities and human ser-vices. Schwab Learning aspires to help kids with learning and attention problems, such as learn-ing disabilities and attention-deficit/hyperactiv-ity disorder lead satisfying and productive lives in an environment that recognizes, values, and supports the unique attributes of every child. Schwab Learning provides free information, resources, publications, and support to parents of children who struggle with learning and to kids themselves through two Web sites and out-reach and community services.

Self Help for Hard of Hearing People, Inc.

*7910 Woodmont Avenue, Suite 1200
Bethesda, MD 20814
(301) 657-2248; (301) 657-2249 (TTY)
E-mail: information@hearingloss.org
Web: www.hearingloss.org*

Self Help for Hard of Hearing People (SHHH) is the nation's largest organization for people with hearing loss. SHHH exists to open the world of communication for people with hearing loss through information, education, advocacy, and support. Its primary purpose is to educate its members, their families, friends, coworkers, teachers, hearing health care providers, indus-try, government, and others about hearing loss.

Special Needs Advocate for Parents

*11835 W. Olympic Boulevard, Suite 65
Los Angeles, CA 90069
(888) 310-9889
E-mail: info@snapinfo.org*

What started as a frustrated but determined mother and five file drawers of information is now Special Needs Advocate for Parents (SNAP). The organization was founded by Nadine Vogel in 1993, two years after she had her first child, Gretchen, who was born with numerous health problems. Gretchen's younger sister, Rachel, was born in 1999, also with special needs. SNAP offers a number of services to parents who have children with special needs to help them make important decisions in planning for their child's well-being as well as to provide information, resources, and networking opportunities. Whether a child is 2 years old or 42, SNAP stands ready to offer support.

Special Olympics International

1325 G Street NW, Suite 500
Washington, DC 20005
(202) 628-3630
E-mail: info@specialolympics.org
Web: www.specialolympics.org/
Materials available in Spanish and French
Spanish and French speaker on staff

Special Olympics is an international organization dedicated to empowering individuals with intellectual disabilities to become physically fit, productive, and respected members of society through sports training and competition. Special Olympics offers children and adults with intellectual disabilities year-round training and competition in 26 Olympic-type summer and winter sports. There is no charge to participate in Special Olympics. Special Olympics currently serves almost 1.4 million persons with intellectual disabilities in more than 200 programs in more than 150 countries.

Spina Bifida Association of America

4590 MacArthur Boulevard, NW, Suite 250
Washington, DC 20007-4226
(800) 621-3141; (202) 944-3285
E-mail: sbaa@sbaa.org
Web: www.sbaa.org
Materials available in Spanish; Spanish
    speaker on staff

The mission of the Spina Bifida Association of America (SBAA) is to promote the prevention of spina bifida and to enhance the lives of all affected. SBAA serves the 70,000 adults and children who live with spina bifida. Since 1973, SBAA has served as the nation's only voluntary health agency dedicated to enhancing the lives of those with spina bifida and those whose lives they touch. Through its network of 57 chapters, SBAA has a presence in more than 125 communities nationwide and serves thousands of people each year.

Stuttering Foundation

3100 Walnut Grove Road #603
P.O. Box 11749
Memphis, TN 38111
(800) 992-9392
E-mail: stutter@stutteringhelp.org
Web: www.stutteringhelp.org
Materials available in Spanish

The Stuttering Foundation provides free online resources, services, and support to those who stutter and their families, as well as support for research into the causes of stuttering. It is the largest—and the first—nonprofit charitable organization in the world working towards the prevention and improved treatment of stuttering, reaching over a million people annually. It also offers extensive educational programs on stuttering for professionals.

TASH (formerly the Association for Persons with Severe Handicaps)

29 W. Susquehanna Avenue, Suite 210
Baltimore, MD 21204
(410) 828-8274 (Voice); (410) 828-1306 (TTY)
E-mail: info@tash.org
Web: www.tash.org

TASH is an international association of people with disabilities, their family members, other advocates, and professionals fighting for a society in which inclusion of all people in all aspects of society is the norm. TASH is an organization of members concerned with human dignity, civil rights, education, and independence for all individuals with disabilities.

Technical Assistance Alliance for Parent Centers PACER Center

8161 Normandale Boulevard
Minneapolis, MN 55437-1044
(888) 248-0822; (952) 838-9000
(952) 838-0190 (TTY)
E-mail: alliance@taalliance.org
Web: www.taalliance.org
Materials available in Spanish; Spanish
    speaker on staff

The Technical Assistance Alliance for Parent Centers (the Alliance) is an innovative project that supports a unified technical assistance system for the purpose of developing, assisting, and coordinating parent training and information projects and community parent resource centers under the Individuals with Disabilities Education Act (IDEA). The project is funded to strengthen the connections to the larger technical assistance network and fortify partnerships between parent centers and state education systems at regional and national levels.

Tourette Syndrome Association

42-40 Bell Boulevard
Bayside, NY 11361
(718) 224-2999
E-mail: ts@tsa-usa.org
Web: www.tsa-usa.org
Materials available in Spanish

The Tourette Syndrome Association's mission is to identify the cause of, find the cure for, and control the effects of Tourette syndrome (TS). It offers resources and referrals to help people and their families cope with the problems that occur with TS. It raises public awareness and counters media stereotypes about TS.

Trace Research and Development Center

1550 Engineering Drive, 2107 Engineering Hall
Madison, WI 53706
(608) 262-6966; (608) 263-5408 (TTY)
E-mail: info@trace.wisc.edu
Web: www.trace.wisc.edu/

The Trace Research and Development Center is a part of the College of Engineering, University of Wisconsin-Madison. Founded in 1971, Trace has been a pioneer in the field of technology and disability. The Trace Center mission statement is to prevent the barriers and capitalize on the opportunities presented by current and emerging information and telecommunication technologies, in order to create a world that is as accessible and usable as possible for as many people as possible.

Tuberous Sclerosis Alliance

801 Roeder Road, Suite 750
Silver Spring, MD 20910
(800) 225-6872; (301) 562-9890
E-mail: info@tsalliance.org
Web: http://www.tsalliance.org/

The Tuberous Sclerosis Alliance (TS Alliance)—the only national voluntary health organization for the genetic disorder known as tuberous sclerosis complex (TSC)—is a membership-based organization; members have voting privileges at the organization's annual meeting. It is also the lead organization for the funding of medical research related to TSC. Such medical research has included the breakthrough discovery of two genes (TSC1 and TSC2) that are known to cause the disorder.

United Cerebral Palsy Association, Inc.

1660 L Street, NW, Suite 700
Washington, DC 20036
(202) 776-0406; (800) 872-5827;
(202) 973-7197 (TTY)
E-mail: national@ucp.org
Web: www.ucp.org
Materials available in Spanish

The United Cerebral Palsy Association (UCP) is the leading source of information on cerebral palsy and is a pivotal advocate for the rights of persons with any disability. As one of the largest health charities in the United States, the UCP mission is to advance the independence, productivity, and full citizenship of people with disabilities through an affiliate network.

United Leukodystrophy Foundation

2304 Highland Drive
Sycamore, IL 60178
(800) 728-5483
E-mail: ulf@tbcnet.com
Web: www.ulf.org
Materials available in Spanish

The United Leukodystrophy Foundation (ULF), incorporated in 1982, is a nonprofit, voluntary health organization dedicated to providing patients and their families with information about their disease and assistance in identifying sources of medical care, social services, and genetic counseling; establishing a communication network among families; increasing public awareness and acting as an information source for health care providers; and promoting and supporting research into causes, treatments, and prevention of the leukodystrophies. Leukodystrophies are a group of genetic nervous system disorders affecting the myelin sheath, which insulates the axon through which nerve impulses are conducted.

U.S. Society of Augmentative and Alternative Communication

P.O. Box 21418
Sarasota, FL 34276
(941) 312-0992
E-mail: USSAAC@comcast.net
Web: www.ussaac.org

The U.S. Society of Augmentative and Alternative Communication (USSAAC) is the only national association specifically designed to address the needs of persons who are either severely speech impaired or unable to speak. Augmentative and alternative communication (AAC) refers to methods of communication that enhance (augment) or replace (provide alternative) conventional forms of expression. Members of USSAAC join together to improve the services, supports, and products used by children and adults in need of AAC. The main purpose of USSAAC is to enhance the communication effectiveness and ultimately, the independence of persons needing access to a communication system. USSAAC is the national chapter of the International Society for Augmentative and Alternative Communication.

Vestibular Disorders Association

P.O. Box 4467
Portland, OR 97208-4467
(800) 837-8428; (503) 229-7705
E-mail: veda@vestibular.org
Web: www.vestibular.org

Vestibular Disorders Association (VEDA) is a nonprofit organization that provides information to the public and health professionals about inner-ear balance disorders, such as Ménière's disease, BPPV, and labyrinthitis. VEDA now has over 70 publications on general and more specific topics related to vestibular balance disorders, and it also serves as a hub service to support groups located around the world. In addition, VEDA provides a listing service by state of the United States and regions of the world for health professionals who specialize in vestibular disorders.

Williams Syndrome Association, Inc.

P.O. Box 297
Clawson, MI 48017-0297
(800) 806-1871; (248) 244-2229
E-mail: info@williams-syndrome.org
Web: www.williams-syndrome.org
Materials available in Spanish

The Williams Syndrome Assocation (WSA) was formed in 1982 by and for families of individuals with Williams syndrome. WSA is the only group in the United States devoted exclusively to improving the lives of individuals with Williams syndrome and their families. It supports research into all facets of the syndrome and the development of the most up-to-date educational materials regarding Williams syndrome.

World Association of Persons with disAbilities

4503 Sunnyview Drive, Suite 1121
P.O. Box 14111
Oklahoma City, OK 73135
(405) 672-4440
E-mail: thehub@wapd.org
Web: www.wapd.org

World Association of Persons with disAbilities (WAPD) advances the interests of persons with disAbilities at national, state, local, and home levels. It is based on a belief that all are entitled to high quality of life. Over 15 years of grassroots planning and growth catapulted the association to a world leadership position, advancing the soundness and empowerment of the so-called "disAbled" everywhere. WAPD links the "disAbled" and supporters to current leading-edge disAbility information via the various mediums of communication.

Yale Developmental Disabilities Clinic

Web: http://info.med.yale.edu/
    chldstdy/autism/

The Yale Developmental Disabilities Clinic offers comprehensive, multidisciplinary evaluations for children with social disabilities, usually focusing on the issues of diagnosis and intervention. It is also conducting several large research projects on autism, AS, and other PDDs. The clinic is located in the Child Study Center at Yale University in New Haven, Connecticut.

2

National Toll-free Numbers

Americans With Disabilities Act (ADA)

ADA InfoLine—U.S. Department of Justice
1(800) 514-0301 (V, English/Spanish)
1(800) 514-0383 (TTY)

ADA National Access for Public Schools Project

1(800) 893-1225 (V/TTY)

Center for Universal Design

1(800) 647-6777 (V)

Disability & Business Technical Assistance Centers

1(800) 949-4232 (V/TTY)

Equal Employment Opportunity Commission

1(800) 669-4000 (V; English/Spanish)
1(800) 669-6820 (TTY)

Job Accommodation Network (Jan)

1(800) 526-7234 (V/TTY)
1(800) 232-9675 (V/TTY; ADA Information)

U.S. Access Board

1(800) 872-2253 (V)
1(800) 993-2822 (TTY)

U.S. Department of Housing and Urban Development—HUD User

1(800) 245-2691 (V)
1(800) 927-7589 (TTY)

Assistive Technology/Devices

ABLEDATA

1(800) 227-0216

AbleNet

1(800) 322-0956 (V)

Alliance for Technology Access

1(800) 455-7970

**Apple Computers
Disability Connection**

1(800) 692-7753

**IBM Accessibility Center
(formerly the Independence
Series Information Center)**

1(800) 426-4832 (V); 1(800) 426-4833 (TTY)

TechKnowledge

1(800) 726-9119 (V/TTY)

BLINDNESS AND VISUAL IMPAIRMENTS

American Council of the Blind

1(800) 424-8666 (V; English/Spanish)

American Foundation for the Blind

1(800) 232-5463 (V)

**American Printing
House for the Blind**

1(800) 223-1839

Blind Children's Center

1(800) 222-3566 (V)

Library Reproduction Service (LRS)

1(800) 255-5002

**Lighthouse National Center for Vision
and Child Development**

*1(800) 829-0500 (V)
1(212) 821-9713 (TTY)*

**National Association for Parents of
Children with Visual Impairments**

1(800) 562-6265

**National Library for the Blind
and Physically Handicapped**

1(800) 424-8567 (V)

Prevent Blindness America

1(800) 331-2020 (V)

Recording for the Blind and Dyslexic

1(800) 221-4792 (V)

The Foundation Fighting Blindness

*1(888) 394-3937 (V)
1(800) 683-5551 (TTY)*

CHILD ABUSE

National Child Abuse Hotline

1(800) 422-4453

**Clearinghouse on Child Abuse and
Neglect/Family Violence Information**

1(800) 394-3366 (V)

**National Center for Missing
and Exploited Children**

*1(800) 843-5678 (V)
1(800) 826-7653 (TTY)*

Prevent Child Abuse America

1(800) 244-5373

CHILD CARE

Child Care Aware

1(800) 424-2246

National Child Care Information Center

*1(800) 616-2242 (V; English/Spanish)
1(800) 516-2242 (TTY)*

National Resource Center for Health and Safety in Child Care

1(800) 598-5437

COMMUNICATION DISORDERS

Communication Aid Manufacturers' Association

1(800) 441-2262

National Institute on Deafness and Other Communication Disorders Clearinghouse

1(800) 241-1044 (V); 1(800) 241-1055 (TTY)

National Stuttering Association

1(800) 937-8888

Stuttering Foundation of America

1(800) 992-9392

CRANIOFACIAL SYNDROMES

Children's Craniofacial Association

1(800) 535-3643 (V)

Craniofacial Foundation of America

1(800) 418-3223

Faces—National Craniofacial Association

1(800) 332-2373 (V)

Foundation for Nager and Miller Syndromes

1(800) 507-3667 (V)

CRISIS INTERVENTION

National Hopeline Network

1(800) 999-9999

Nineline Crisis Hotline

1(800) SUICIDE (784-2433)

DEAFNESS AND HEARING IMPAIRMENTS

American Society for Deaf Children

1(800) 942-2732 (V/TTY)

Better Hearing Institute

1(800) 327-9355 (V/TTY)

Hear Now

1(800) 648-4327 (V/TTY)

Hearing Aid Helpline

1(800) 521-5247 (V/TTY)

John Tracy Clinic

1(800) 522-4582 (V/TTY; English/Spanish)
1(213) 748-5481 (V; in 213 area)
1(213) 747-2924 (TTY; in 213 area)

National Cued Speech Association

1(800) 459-3529

National Information Clearinghouse on Children Who are Deaf-Blind (DB-LINK)

1(800) 438-9376 (V); 1(800) 854-7013 (TTY)

National Institute on Deafness and Other Communication Disorders Clearinghouse

1(800) 241-1044 (V); 1(800) 241-1055 (TTY)

**Postsecondary Education Programs
Network Resource Center (PEPNet)**

1(888) 684-4695 (V/TTY)

DISABILITY AWARENESS

Kids on the Block

1(800) 368-5437 (V)

EDUCATION

**American Association for
Vocational Instructional Materials**

1(800) 228-4689 (V)

**Association for Career
and Technical Education**

1(800) 826-9972 (V/TTY)

**Association for Childhood
Education International**

1(800) 423-3563 (V)

**ERIC System (Educational
Resources Information Center)**

1(800) 538-3742

**HEATH Resource Center (for
information on post-secondary
education for individuals with
disabilities)**

1(800) 544-3284 (V/TTY)

**National Association
for the Education of
Young Children (NAEYC)**

1(800) 424-2460

**National Clearinghouse
for Comprehensive
School Reform (NCCSR)**

1(877) 766-4277

**National Clearinghouse for
English Language Acquisition
& Language Instruction
Educational Programs (NCELA)**

1(800) 321-6223

**National Information
Center for Educational Media**

1(800) 926-8328 (V/TTY)

National Institute for Literacy (NIFL)

1(800) 228-8813
1(800) 552-9097 (TTY)

National Library of Education (NLE)

1(800) 424-1616

National Middle School Association

1(800) 528-6672

No Child Left Behind (NCLB)

1(888) 814-6252 (V)
1(800) 437-0833 (TTY)

EMPLOYMENT

**Education, Career,
and Community Program**

1(800) 547-6339

**Equal Employment
Opportunity Commission**

1(800) 669-4000 (V; English/Spanish)
1(800) 669-6820 (TTY)

Job Accommodation Network

1(800) 526-7234 (V/TTY)
1(800) 232-9675 (V/TTY; ADA Information)

**National Center on
Workforce and Disability/Adult**

1(888) 886-9898 (V/TTY)

**National Collaborative on Workforce and
Disability/Youth**

1(877) 871-4748 (V/TTY)

FINANCIAL COUNSELING

**National Foundation
for Consumer Credit**

1(800) 388-2227 (V)
1(800) 682-9832 (Spanish)

HOSPICE

Children's Hospice International

1(800) 242-4453 (V/TTY)

**Hospice Education
Institute (formerly Hospicelink)**

1(800) 331-1620 (V)

INFORMATION CENTERS

**Abledata (for information on
assistive technology)**

1(800) 227-0216 (V/TTY)

Access Eric

1(800) 538-3742 (V)

**HRSA Information Center
(formerly National Maternal
and Child Health Clearinghouse)**

1(888) 275-4772

**National Dissemination
Center for Children with
Disabilities (NICHCY)**

1(800) 695-0285 (V/TTY; English/Spanish)

National Epilepsy Library

1(800) 332-4050

**National Health
Information Center**

1(800) 336-4797

**National Lead
Information Center**

1(800) 424-5323 (English/Spanish)

National Library of Medicine

1(888) 346-3656

LITERACY

National Literacy Hotline

1(800) 228-8813
1(800) 552-9097 (TTY)

**ProLiteracy Worldwide
(formerly Laubach Literacy International
and Literacy Volunteers of America)**

1(888) 528-2224

Reading is Fundamental

1(877) 743-7323

MEDICAL AND HEALTH DISORDERS

American Stroke Association

1(888) 478-7653 (V)

Aplastic Anemia and MDS International Foundation

1(800) 747-2820 (V)

Chronic Fatigue and Immune Dysfunction Syndrome Association (CFIDS)

1(800) 442-3437 (V)

Crohn and Colitis Foundation of America

1(800) 932-2423

Epilepsy Foundation

1(800) 332-1000

Family Voices: A National Coalition Speaking for Children with Special Health Care Needs

1(888) 835-5669 (V)

Foundation for Ichthyosis and Related Skin Types

1(800) 545-3286

International Foundation for Functional Gastrointestinal Disorders

1(888) 964-2001

Kennedy Krieger Institute

1(888) 554-2080

National Association of Hospital Hospitality Houses (NAHHH)

1(800) 542-9730

National Brain Tumor Foundation

1(800) 934-2873 (V; English/Spanish)

National Digestive Diseases Information Center

1(800) 891-5389

National Eating Disorders Association (formerly Eating Disorders Awareness and Prevention)

1(800) 931-2237

National Epilepsy Library

1(800) 332-4050

National Health Information Center

1(800) 336-4797

National Institute of Arthritis and Musculoskeletal and Skin Diseases Clearinghouse

1(877) 226-4267 (V)

National Patient Travel Helpline

1(800) 296-1217

Shriners Hospital for Children

1(800) 237-5055 (V)

United Ostomy Association

1(800) 826-0826 (V)

Vestibular Disorders Association

1(800) 837-8428

Williams Syndrome Association

1(800) 806-1871

MENTAL HEALTH

Anxiety Disorders Information, National Institute of Mental Health

1(888) 826-9438 (English/Spanish)

Mood and Anxiety Disorders Program, National Institute of Mental Health

1(866) 627-6464

National Alliance for the Mentally Ill

1(800) 950-6264 (V, English/Spanish)

National Association for the Dually Diagnosed

1(800) 331-5362

National Foundation for Depressive Illness

1(800) 239-1265

National Hopeline Network

1(800) Suicide (784-2433) (English/Spanish)

National Institute of Mental Health (NIMH) Hopeline

1(800) 784-2433

National Institute of Mental Health (NIMH) Information Line

1(866) 615-6464

National Mental Health Association

1(800) 969-6642 (V); 1(800) 433-5959 (TTY)

National Mental Health Consumer Self-Help Clearinghouse

1(800) 553-4539 (English/Spanish)

National Mental Health Information Center (formerly Knowledge Exchange Network)

1(800) 789-2647

PHYSICAL DISABILITIES

Christopher and Dana Reeve Paralysis Resource Center

1(800) 539-7309

Courage Center

1(888) 8INTAKE (846-8253)

Craniofacial Foundation of America

1(800) 418-3223

Easter Seals—National Office

1(800) 221-6827 (V); 1(312) 726-4258 (TTY)

Human Growth Foundation

1(800) 451-6434 (V)

Muscular Dystrophy Association

1(800) 572-1717

National Institute of Arthritis and Musculoskeletal and Skin Diseases Information Clearinghouse

1(877) 226-4267 (V)

National Library Services for the Blind and Physically Handicapped

1(800) 424-8567 (V)

National Spasmodic Torticollis Association

1(800) 487-8385

National Spinal Cord Injury Hotline

1(800) 962-9629 (V)

Pathways Awareness Foundation

1(800) 955-2445 (V)

RARE SYNDROMES

Genetic Alliance

1(800) 336-4363 (V)

**Genetic & Rare
Diseases Information Center**

*1(888) 205-2311
1(888) 205-3223 (TTY)*

**National Organization
for Rare Disorders (NORD)**

1(800) 999-6673 (V/TTY)

RECREATION

**Adventures in Movement
for the Handicapped**

1(800) 332-8210 (V)

Best Buddies

1(800) 892-8339 (V)

Girl Scouts of the USA

1(800) 478-7248

**National Center on
Physical Activity and Disability**

1(800) 900-8086 (V/TTY)

**National Lekotek Center's
Toy Resource Helpline**

1(800) 366-PLAY (V); 1(800) 573-4446 (TTY)

**North American Riding
for the Handicapped, Inc.**

1(800) 369-7433 (V)

REHABILITATION

Abledata

1(800) 227-0216 (V/TTY)

**ADED: Association for
Driver Rehabilitation Specialists**

1(800) 290-2344

**National Clearinghouse of Rehabilitation
Training Materials**

1(800) 223-5219 (V)

**National Rehabilitation
Information Center (NARIC)**

1(800) 346-2742

RESPITE CARE

**Arch National Resource Center, National
Respite Locator Service**

1(800) 773-5433 (V)

RURAL

Rural Institute on Disabilities

1(800) 732-0323

SPECIFIC DISABILITIES

**American Association
on Mental Retardation**

*1(800) 424-3688 (outside DC area)
(202) 387-1968 (in DC)*

American Behcet's Disease Association

1(800) 7-BEHCETS (723-42387)

Amyotrophic Lateral Sclerosis Association (ALSA)

1(800) 782-4747 (for Patients)

Angelman Syndrome Foundation

1(800) 432-6435

Aplastic Anemia and MDS International Foundation

1(800) 747-2820 (V)

Arthritis Foundation

1(800) 283-7800

Autism Society of America

1(800) 3-Autism (328-8476)

Beckwith Wiedemann Support Network

1(800) 837-2976

Brain Injury Association

1(800) 444-6443 (V)

Center for the Study and Treatment of Usher Syndrome

1(800) 835-1468 (V/TTY)

Children and Adults With Attention-Deficit/ Hyperactivity Disorder (CHADD)

1(800) 233-4050
(301) 306-7070 (in DC metro area)

Cleft Palate Foundation

1(800) 242-5338

Cornella de Lange Syndrome Foundation

1(800) 223-8355 (V); (860) 676-8166 (V; in CT)

Crohn's and Colitis Foundation of America

1(800) 932-2423

Cystic Fibrosis Foundation

1(800) 344-4823 (V)

Epilepsy Foundation— National Office

1(800) 332-1000 (V)

Family Empowerment Network: Support for Families Affected by FAS/E

1(800) 462-5254

Foundation for Ichthyosis & Related Skin Types

1(800) 545-3286

Huntington's Disease Society of America

1(800) 345-4372

International Dyslexia Association (formerly the Orton Dyslexia Society)

1(800) 222-3123

International Rett Syndrome Association

1(800) 818-7388

Little People of America

1(888) 572-2001

Lyme Disease Foundation

1(800) 886-5963

Malignant Hyperthermia Association of the U.S.

1(800) 986-4287

National Association for the Dually Diagnosed (NADD)

1(800) 331-5362

National Center for Learning Disabilities

1(888) 575-7373

National Down Syndrome Congress

1(800) 232-6372 (V)

National Down Syndrome Society

1(800) 221-4602 (V; English/Spanish)

National Eating Disorders Association (formerly Eating Disorders Awareness and Prevention)

1(800) 931-2237

National Fragile X Foundation

1(800) 688-8765 (V)

National Gaucher Foundation

1(800) 428-2437

National Lymphedema Network

1(800) 541-3259

National Marfan Foundation

1(800) 8-Marfan (862-7326)

National Multiple Sclerosis Society

1(800) 344-4867 (V; English/Spanish)

National Neurofibromatosis Foundation

1(800) 323-7938

National Niemann-Pick Disease Foundation

1(877) 287-3672

National Organization on Fetal Alcohol Syndrome

1(800) 666-6327

National Reye's Syndrome Foundation

1(800) 233-7393 (V)

National Scoliosis Foundation

1(800) 673-6922 (V)

National Stuttering Association

1(800) 937-8888

National Tay-Sachs & Allied Diseases Association, Inc.

1(800) 906-8723 (V)

Neurofibromatosis, Inc.

1(800) 942-6825

Nonverbal Learning Disorders Association

1(800) 570-0217

Osteogenesis Imperfecta Foundation

1(800) 981-2663 (V)

Prader-Willi Syndrome Association

1(800) 926-4797 (V)

Spina Bifida Association of America

1(800) 621-3141 (V; English/Spanish)

Sturge-Weber Foundation

1(800) 627-5482

Stuttering Foundation of America

1(800) 992-9392 (V)

Support Organization for Trisomy 17, 13, and Related Disorders

1(800) 716-7638

Tuberous Sclerosis Alliance (formerly National Tuberous Sclerosis Association)

1(800) 225-6872 (V)

United Cerebral Palsy Associations

1(800) 872-5827 (V)

United Leukodystrophy Foundation

1(800) 728-5483 (V)

Williams Syndrome Association

1(800) 806-1871

Wilson's Disease Association

1(800) 399-0266

SUICIDE PREVENTION

American Foundation for Suicide Prevention

1(888) 333-2377

National Hopeline Network

1(800) SUICIDE (784-2433)

Nineline Crisis Hotline

1(800) 999-9999

(See also Mental Health resources)

SUPPLEMENTAL SECURITY INCOME (SSI)

Social Security Administration

1(800) 772-1213 (V; English/Spanish)
1(800) 325-0778 (TTY)

TRAUMA

American Trauma Society

1(800) 556-7890 (V)
1(800) 735-2258 (TTY)

Brain Injury Association

1(800) 444-6443 (V)

National Spinal Cord Injury Association

1(800) 962-9629 (V)

WISHES FOR CHILDREN

Believe in Tomorrow National Children's Foundation (formerly the Grant-a-Wish Foundation)

1(800) 933-5470

Sunshine Foundation

1(800) 767-1976

3

Disability Publishers Offering Books, Videos, and Journals on Specific Disabilities, Special Education, Parenting, and Other Disability and Special Needs Topics

A

Academic Therapy Publications

Web: www.academictherapy.com/

This Web site offers books for all professionals working with children who have special needs. In addition, this publisher offers High Noon Books, which are written for high-interest/low-level readers. That is, students who are reading below their age level but prefer more age-appropriate subject matter.

ADD Warehouse

Web: www.addwarehouse.com

Developmental disorders, including attention deficit/hyperactivity disorder, are this publisher's specialty. Browse through the books by category: kids, adults, parents, and teachers. Don't miss the videos. Some products are also available in Spanish.

Albert Whitman and Company

Web: www.awhitmanco.com

This publisher specializes in children's books and features stories for kids on asthma, Down syndrome, learning disabilities, and more.

Allyn & Bacon/Longman

Web: www.ablongman.com/

This publisher produces tons of materials on a variety of disability-related topics for teachers, teachers in training, and parents. Search by keyword to pinpoint what you are looking for.

B

Brookline Books

Web: www.brooklinebooks.com

This publisher offers three categories of disability books: assistive technology, general disability, and self-advocacy. The materials are for teachers, families, and young adults with disabilities.

Butte Publications Resources

Web: www.buttepublications.com/

At this publisher's site, you'll find educational materials for students who are deaf or hard of hearing, their parents, teachers, and other professionals in the field.

C

Canter and Associates

Web: www.canter.net

Click on "Canter Store" when you get to this Web site, and you'll find a wealth of information. Products are broken down into categories for parents, teachers, and administrators. Or you can search by keyword.

Centering Corporation

Web: www.centering.org

This organization specializes in publications about grief and overcoming loss.

Childswork/Childsplay

Web: www.childswork.com

This publisher offers over 450 resources to address the social and emotional needs of children and adolescents. Their Web site has areas dedicated to disorders, research issues, teachers, parents, and mental health professionals.

Compact Clinicals

Web: www.compactclinicals.com

This publisher offers concise overviews on attention-deficit/hyperactivity disorder, aggressive and defiant behavior, depression, obsessive compulsive disorder, and other conditions.

Corwin Press, Inc.

Web: www.corwinpress.com

Educators, administrators, and counselors, this publisher has products for you! Check out the books and journals listed on the Web site. Request a free catalog.

Council for Exceptional Children (CEC)

Web: www.cec.sped.org

CEC publishes almost exclusively on issues related to exceptional children, which includes both children with disabilities and children who are gifted. You can find a lot of guidance here about educating exceptional students.

D

Delmar Learning/Thomson Learning

Web: www.earlychilded.delmar.com/

This Web site features early childhood education products. Browse through the categories of books to find books on assessment, inclusion, and much more.

E

Educators Publishing Service

Web: www.epsbooks.com/#XYZ

At this site you will find books and workbooks for students from kindergarten through high school as well as students who are home-schooled. This publisher focuses on teacher-developed literacy products.

F

Free Spirit Publishing

Web: www.freespirit.com

This publisher offers books and other learning materials on learning differences (or learning disabilities) for kids, teens, teachers, and parents. Browse by category to find what you are looking for.

Future Horizons

Web: www.futurehorizons-autism.com

This is the site to visit if you are looking for products on autism, PDD, or Asperger's syndrome. They offer books, videos, and a magazine, as well as medical resources, and conference information.

G

Gallaudet University Press

Web: http://gupress.gallaudet.edu

This site is a one-stop shop for books on deaf and hard of hearing topics, including American Sign Language, deaf culture, parenting, special education, and more.

GSI Publications

Web: www.gsi-add.com

This site is chock full of ADHD products for parents, teachers, children with ADHD, and their siblings. Some materials are also available in Spanish.

Guilford Press

Web: www.guilford.com

Click on "ADHD Resources" to find lots of books and videos on Attention Deficit/Hyperactivity Disorder. Also check the "Education" category for other disability-related resources. Some materials are also available in Spanish.

H

Heinle & Heinle/Thomson Learning

Web: www.heinle.com

This publisher specializes in ESL and ELT (English as a Second Language, and English Language Teaching) materials. Teachers and students can find products tailored to them.

J

Jason & Nordic Publishers

Web: www.jasonandnordic.com

This publisher offers an awesome series of children's books about what it's like to have a disability such as cerebral palsy, Down syndrome, or deafness. Some books are also available in an audio version.

John Wiley & Sons

Web: www.wiley.com

Check out the "Special Education" category (within the "Education" section) to find over 20 different books for teachers on teaching special-needs kids.

L

L&A Publishing

Web: www.lapublishing.com

This publisher offers tons of reader-friendly information on brain injury in children and adults. Check out the resources for survivors, parents, kids, siblings, teachers, advocates, and counselors.

LRP Publications

Web: www.lrp.com

LRP offers lots of legal information regarding special education. On their site, you can sign up for free Special Ed e-news—short e-mail newsletters giving you significant case decisions, important developments in the special education community, and updates on LRP's new products. Also visit their special education store to find resources on IDEA, inclusion and more.

Lawrence Erlbaum Associates

Web: www.erlbaum.com

Education professionals will find over 50 resources of interest at this publisher's site when they search by "special education." Topics covered include learning disabilities, multiculturalism, and educational placement.

Love Publishing

Web: www.lovepublishing.com

Click on "special education" at this publisher's Web site to find a categorical list of special-needs resources, including behavior, early intervention, special education law, and much more.

M

Magination Press

Web: www.maginationpress.com

This publisher features special books for children's special concerns. Written for ages 4 through 18 years, these books range in topic from autism and attention deficit/hyperactivity disorder to medical problems and self-esteem. This is a great site for hard-to-find children books.

Master Teacher

Web: www.masterteacher.com

This publisher has great special education resources for teachers, principals, administrators, and paraeducators (also called teacher aides).

N

Nolo Press

Web: www.nolo.com

This publisher offers easy-to-read legal information. Search by "special education" to find the products that would be of interest to you.

O

Open Minds

Web: www.openmindsinc.com

This publisher focuses on children's literature that celebrates differences and models inclusion. Materials are available in series sets that can easily be used in the classroom—fiction books, student journals, and parent and teacher guides.

P

Paul H. Brookes

Web: www.brookespublishing.com

This publisher is a gold mine of special needs materials, useful particularly to professionals, with some parent materials scattered throughout. They publish research-based resources in developmental and learning disabilities, early intervention, child development, language and literacy, special and inclusive education, community supports and services, mental health, and behavior.

Peachtree Publications

Web: www.peachtree-online.com

Check out the children and young adult's section of this publisher's Web site. You'll find great children's books covering topics such as deafness, getting a prosthetic hand, and using a wheelchair.

Peytral Publications

Web: www.peytral.com

This publisher has a great bunch of publications for parents, teachers, paraeducators and more on various disability and special education materials.

Prentice Hall/ Pearson Education

Web: http://vig.prenhall.com

Special educators in training will find tons of resources at this publisher's site. Select "special education" under the Discipline Finder and you'll get over 20 subcategories of special education topics, including behavior management, families in special education, special education law.

Pro-Ed, Inc.

Web: www.proedinc.com

Visit this site to find the resources this publisher provides on speech, language, and hearing; psychology and counseling; special education; early childhood intervention; and occupational and physical therapy.

Psy-Ed Corporation

Web: www.exceptionalparent.com

Psy-Ed Corporation publishes Exceptional Parent, a magazine published primarily for parents of children with special needs.

S

SAGE Publications

Web: www.sagepub.com

This publisher offers a wide range of publications geared toward teachers and teachers in training. Search by "special education" or "disability" to find books suited to your interests.

Scholastic, Inc.

Web: www.scholastic.com/index.asp

This site has numerous disability-related materials. Search by "disabilities" or "special needs," and you'll find tons of books, articles, and other products.

Sensory Resources

Web: www.sensoryresources.com/

Parents, teachers, and therapists will love the hard-to-find resources on sensory integration and sensory processing that are available through this site. Children with autism spectrum disorders often have sensory issues.

Sopris West

Web: www.sopriswest.com

Education professionals and parents: This publisher specializes in practical products aimed at helping students with their behavior, social skills, and academics. You'll find books, journals, curricula, and more on a variety of topics, including behavior management, inclusion, reading, and social skills. Search the online catalog or request a free publications catalog.

Special Kids

Web: www.specialkids1.com

Special Kids produces educational videotapes and picture books aimed at children who have autism, Down syndrome, PDD, Asperger's syndrome, or learning disabilities. This site also has tons of links to other good resources.

W

Woodbine House

Web: www.woodbinehouse.com/

You'll find a real treasure chest of special needs products here. This publisher offers "The Special-Needs Collection"—60 books on disabilities and related topics for parents, children, and professionals.

4

Disability-Related Resources of Agencies and Organizations in the United States That Address Disability-Related Issues, Listed by States

ABOUT THE AGENCIES AND ORGANIZATIONS

The agencies and organizations listed in this section provide assistance to people with disabilities and their families. Some are national, with offices in each state or territory. Others are organized by region, and yet others are unique to their communities. In the individual state listings, you'll find their names and addresses and, in many cases, the names of contact persons.

State Education Department

The State Department staff can answer questions about special education and related services in your state. Many states have special manuals explaining the steps to take. Check to see if one is available. State Department officials are responsible for special education and related services programs in their state for preschool, elementary-school , and secondary-school-aged children.

State Vocational Rehabilitation Agency

The state vocational rehabilitation agency provides medical, therapeutic, counseling, education, training, and other services needed to prepare people with disabilities for work. This state agency can provide you with the address of the nearest rehabilitation office where you can discuss issues of eligibility and services with a counselor. The state vocational rehabilitation agency can also refer you to independent living programs available in your state. Independent living programs provide services which enable adults with disabilities to live productively as members of their communities. The services might include, but are not limited to, information and referral, peer counseling, workshops, attendant care, and technical assistance.

Office of State Coordinator of Vocational Education for Students With Disabilities

States receiving federal funds used for vocational education must ensure that funding is used in programs which include students with disabilities. This office can tell you how your state funds are being used and provide you with information on current programs.

State Mental Retardation and Developmental Disabilities Agencies

The functions of state mental retardation and developmental disabilities agencies vary from state to state. The general purpose of these offices is to plan, administer, and develop standards for state and local mental retardation and developmental disabilities programs provided in state-operated facilities and community-based programs. These offices provide information about available services to families, consumers, educators, and other professionals.

State Developmental Disabilities Council

Assisted by the U.S. Department of Health and Human Services' Administration on Developmental Disabilities, state councils plan and advocate for improvement in services for people with developmental disabilities. In addition, funding is made available for time-limited demonstration and stimulatory grant projects.

State Mental Health Agencies

The functions of state mental health agencies vary from state to state. The general purposes

of these offices are to plan, administer, and develop standards for state and local mental health programs, such as state hospitals and community health centers. They can provide information to the consumer about mental illness and resource lists of contacts where you can go for help.

Protection and Advocacy Agency and Client Assistance Program

Protection and advocacy systems are responsible for pursuing legal, administrative, and other remedies to protect the rights of people who have developmental disabilities or mental illness, regardless of their age. Protection and advocacy agencies may provide information about health, residential, and social services in your area. Legal assistance is also available. The client assistance program provides assistance to individuals seeking and receiving vocational rehabilitation services. These services, provided under the Rehabilitation Act of 1973, include assisting in the pursuit of legal, administrative, and other appropriate remedies to ensure the protection of the rights of individuals with developmental disabilities.

Programs for Children With Special Health Care Needs

The U.S. Department of Health and Human Services' Maternal and Child Health Bureau provides grants to states for direct medical and related services to children with handicapping conditions. Although services will vary from state to state, additional programs may be funded for training, research, special projects, genetic disease testing, and counseling services. For additional information about current grants and programs in your state, contact

National Center for Education in Maternal
  and Child Health
Georgetown University
Box 571272
Washington, DC 20057
(202) 784-9770
E-mail: mchlibrary@ncemch.org
Web: www.ncemch.org

University Centers for Excellence In Developmental Disabilities

A national network of programs affiliated with universities and teaching hospitals, the University Centers for Excellence in Developmental Disabilities (formerly called University Affiliated Programs) engage in research, education, and service designed to further independence, productivity, and full community participation of people with developmental disabilities. The centers train professional leaders, individuals with disabilities, and family members in fields such as early intervention and education, health care, special education, and innovative housing and employment programs.

You can obtain information about the university centers, as well as a listing of them, by contacting

Association of University Centers on
    Disabilities (AUCD)
1010 Wayne Avenue, Suite 920
Silver Spring, MD 20910
(301) 588-8252
www.aucd.org

Parent Training and Information Centers

Each state has a parent training and information center (PTI) that is funded through our nation's special education law, the Individuals With Disabilities Education Act (IDEA). PTIs are a valuable resource for parents. They provide training and information on different disabilities, educational rights under the law, how to work with the schools, where to find resources in your state and community, and much more.

The following listings, state by state alphabetically, include specific information in five areas:

- *U.S. senators, governors, and official Web sites*
- *State agencies serving children and youth with disabilities*
- *State chapters of disability organizations and parent groups*
- *Parent training and information projects*
- *Other useful associations and organizations*

ALABAMA

Alabama—State Agencies and Organizations

United States Senators

Honorable Jeff Sessions (R)
335 Russell Senate Office Building
Washington, DC 20510
(202) 224-4124
(202) 224-3149 (Fax)
E-mail: senator@sessions.senate.gov
Web: http://sessions.senate.gov

Honorable Richard C. Shelby (R)
110 Hart Senate Office Building
Washington, DC 20510
(202) 224-5744
(202) 224-3416 (Fax)
E-mail: senator@shelby.senate.gov
Web: http://shelby.senate.gov

United States Representatives

To find the contact information for your representative in the House of the U.S. Congress, visit the House's Web site at: www.house.gov, or call (202) 224-3121; (202) 225-1904 (TTY).

Governor

Honorable Robert Bentley
State Capitol
600 Dexter Avenue
Montgomery, AL 36130-2751
(334) 242-7100
Web: www.governor.state.al.us/

Official State Web Site

Web: www.alabama.gov/

State Department of Education: Special Education

Crystal Richardson
Gordon Persons Building, Room 3346
50 North Ripley St.
Montgomery, AL 36104-3833
(334) 242-8114
E-mail: crystalr@alsde.edu
Web: www.alsde.edu/

*Alabama has been removed from the require-
ments of No Child Left Behind Act as of
2013.*

**Programs for Infants and Toddlers
With Disabilities: Birth–2 Years**

*Alabama's Early Intervention System
Department of Rehabilitation Services
Division of Early Intervention
Elizabeth Prince, Part C Coordinator
602 South Lawrence Street
Montgomery, AL 36104
(334) 293-7166
E-mail: betsy.prince@rehab.alabama.gov
Web: http://rehab.alabama.gov/individuals-
and-families/early-intervention/*

**Programs for Children With
Disabilities: Ages 3–5 Years**

*Contact State Department of Education:
Special Education
Jan Enstrom, Interim 619 Coordinator
Education Specialist
PO Box 302101
Montgomery, AL 36130-2101
(334) 242-8114
E-mail: jane@alsde.edu
Web: http://web.alsde.edu/home/Sections/
SectionInfo.aspx?SectionID=65*

Coordinator for Transition Services

*DaLee Chambers, Director of
Transition Initiative
Special Education Services
Alabama State Department of Education
P.O. Box 302101
Montgomery, AL 36130
(334) 242-8114
Web: www.alsde.edu/html/sections/
documents.asp*

**Office of State Career
and Technical Education**

*Career/Technical Education
Alabama State Department of Education
Nancy Beggs, Director
Gordon Persons Building, Room 5239
P.O. Box 302101
Montgomery, AL 36130-2101
(334) 242-9111*

*E-mail: nbeggs@alsde.edu
Web: www.alsde.edu/*

**State Mental
Health Representative
for Children and Youth**

*Steve Lafreniere, Director
Office of Children's Services
Alabama Department of Mental Health and
Mental Retardation
P.O. Box 301410
Montgomery, AL 36130-1410
(334) 353-7110
E-mail: slafreniere@mh.state.al.us
Web: www.mh.state.al.us*

State Mental Retardation Program

*Alabama Department of Mental
Health and Mental Retardation
Kathy E. Sawyer, Commissioner
RSA Union Building
P.O. Box 301410
Montgomery, AL 36130-1410
(334) 242-3107
E-mail: ksawyer@mh.state.al.us
Web: www.mh.state.al.us*

Council on Developmental Disabilities

*Alabama Council for
Developmental Disabilities
Elmyra Jones, Executive Director
RSA Union Building
100 N. Union Street, Suite 498
P.O. Box 301410
Montgomery, AL 36130-1410
(334) 242-3973; (800) 232-2158
E-mail: acdd@mh.state.al.us
Web: http://acdd.org*

Protection and Advocacy Agency

*Alabama Disabilities Advocacy
Program (ADAP)
Reuben Cook, Director
The University of Alabama
526 Martha Parham West
P.O. Box 870395
Tuscaloosa, AL 35487-0395
(205) 348-4928 (V/TTY); (800) 826-1675
E-mail: ADAP@law.ua.edu
Web: www.adap.net*

Client Assistance Program

Department of Rehabilitation Services
Jerry Norsworthy, Coordinator
2129 East South Boulevard
Montgomery, AL 36116
(334) 613-2209; (800) 228-3231
    (V/TTY in AL)
E-mail: sacap2000@yahoo.com

Programs for Children With
Special Health Care Needs

Alabama Department of
    Rehabilitation Services
Children's Rehabilitation Service
Dr. Cary Boswell, Assistant
    Commissioner
2129 East South Boulevard
P.O. Box 11586
Montgomery, AL 36111-0586
(334) 281-8780; (800) 441-7607
(800) 846-3697 (in AL)
E-mail: cboswell@rehab.state.al.us
Web: www.rehab.state.al.us

State CHIP Program
(health care for low-income,
uninsured children)

Children's Health Insurance Program
Gayle Lees Sandlin, Director
Alabama Department of Public Health
201 Monroe Street, Suite 250
Montgomery, AL 36104
(334) 206-5568; (877) 774-9521
Web: www.adph.org/allkids/

Programs for Children
and YouthWho Are
Blind or Visually Impaired, Deaf
or Hard of Hearing, or Deaf-Blind

Alabama Institute for Deaf and Blind
Michelle Jones, Regional Director
1050 Government Street
Mobile, AL 36604
(251) 432-7777 (V/TTY)
E-mail: mijone@aidb.state.al.us
Web: www.AIDB.org

Department of Rehabilitation Services
Division of Early Intervention
Steve Shivers, Commissioner
2129 East South Boulevard
Montgomery, AL 36116
(334) 281-8780
E-mail: sshivers@rehab.state.al.us
Web: www.rehab.state.al.us/vr.html

Telecommunications
Relay Services for Individuals
Who Are Deaf, Hard of Hearing,
or With Speech Impairments

(800) 548-2547 (V)
(800) 548-2546 (TTY); 711 (TTY)
(888) 229-5746 (Speech to
    Speech-English)
(866) 260-9470 (Speech to
    Speech-Spanish)

Regional ADA & IT
Technical Assistance Center

Southeast Disability and Business Technical
    Assistance Center
Shelley Kaplan, Project Director
Center for Assistive Technology
    and Environmental Access
Georgia Tech
490 10th Street
Atlanta, GA 30318
(404) 385-0636; (800)
    949-4232 (V/TTY)
E-mail: sedbtacproject@catea.org
Web: www.sedbtac.org

Alabama Department
of Rehabilitation Services

Assistant Attorney General, Graham Sisson
2129 East South Boulevard
Montgomery, AL 36111
(334) 613-3471 (Montgomery office)
(205) 290-4540 (Birmingham office)
(888) 574-2257 (TTY)
(800) 205-9986 (Alabama's Toll Free Hotline
    for ADA Information)
E-mail: gsisson@rehab.state.al.us
Web: www.rehab.state.al.us/ada

*University Center for Excellence
in Developmental Disabilities*

Civitan International Research Center
Michael J. Friedlander, Director
University of Alabama at Birmingham
1719 6th Avenue South
Birmingham, AL 35294-0021
(205) 934-8900; (800) 822-2472
Web: www.circ.uab.edu

Technology-Related Assistance

STAR (Statewide Technology Access and
    Response for Alabamians With Disabilities)
Ted Bridges, Executive Director
2125 East South Boulevard
P.O. Box 20752
Montgomery, AL 36120-0752
(334) 613-3480; (334) 613-3519 (TTY)
(800) 782-7656 (In AL)
Web: www.rehab.state.al.us/star

Technology Assistance for Special
    Consumers (TASC)
Lisa Snyder, Resource Center Coordinator
P.O. Box 443
Huntsville, AL 35804
(256) 532-5996
E-mail: tasc@hiwaay.net
Web: http://tasc.ataccess.org

State Mediation System

Alabama Department of Education
Doris McQuiddy, Coordinator
Gordon Persons Building
P.O. Box 302101
Montgomery, AL 36130-2101
(334) 242-8114; (800) 392-8020 (in AL)
E-mail: dorismc@alsde.edu
Web: www.alsde.edu

Respite Care

The Alabama Respite Resource Network
Linda Lamberth, Project Manager
2505 Inverness Lane
Birmingham, AL 35242
(205) 991-0927; (866) 737-8252
E mail: alabamarespite@aol.com
Web: http://alabamarespite.org

Special Format Library

Alabama Regional Library
    for the Blind and Physically
    Handicapped
Fara L. Zaleski, Librarian
6030 Monticello Drive
Montgomery, AL 36130-6000
(334) 213-3906, ext. 921; (800) 392-5671
(334) 213-3900 (TTY)
E-mail: fzaleski@apls.state.al.us
Web: http://apls.state.al.us/
    webpages/services

Alabama—Disability-Specific Organizations

Attention Deficit Disorder

    To identify an ADD group in Alabama, contact

Children and Adults With Attention-Deficit/
    Hyperactivity Disorder (CHADD)
8181 Professional Place, Suite 150
Landover, MD 20785
(301) 306-7070
(800) 233-4050 (Voice mail to request
    information packet)
Web: www.chadd.org

Autism

Autism Society of Alabama
Jennifer Muller, Executive Director
3100 Lorna Road, Suite 132
Birmingham, AL 35216
(205) 824-6734; (877) 4AUTISM
E-mail: director@autism-alabama.org
Web: www.autism-alabama.org

Blind/Visual Impairments

American Foundation for the Blind–National
    Literacy Center
Frances Mary D'Andrea, Director
100 Peachtree Street, Suite 620
Atlanta, GA 30303
(404) 525-2303
E-mail: literacy@afb.net
Web: www.afb.org

Cerebral Palsy

United Cerebral Palsy of Greater Birmingham
Hand In Hand: A Learning Environment
   for Children
Gary Edwards, Executive Director
120 Oslo Circle
Birmingham, AL 35211
(205) 944-3939; (800) 654-4483
E-mail: gedwards@ucpbham.com
Web: http://ucpbham.com

United Cerebral Palsy of Mobile, Inc.
Glenn R. Harger, President/CEO
3058 Dauphin Square Connector
Mobile, AL 36607
(251) 479-4900; (888) 630-7102
E-mail: info@ucpmobile.org
Web: http://www.ucpmobile.org/

Epilepsy

Epilepsy Foundation of North and Central Alabama
Judith Lindsay Adamson, Executive Director
701 37th Street South, Suite 8
Birmingham, AL 35222
(205) 324-4222; (800) 950-6662 (In AL)
E-mail: epilepsy@aol.com
Web: www.epilepsyfoundation.org/local/
   ncalabama

Epilepsy Foundation of South Alabama
F. Mitchell Garrett, Executive Director
Office Park 3 273 Azalea Rd #310
Mobile, AL 36609
(251) 341-0170; (800) 626-1582 (In AL)
E-mail: mgarrett@epilepsysouthalabama.org
Web: http://www.epilepsy.com/alabama

Head Injury

Alabama Head Injury Foundation
Charles Priest, Director
3100 Lorna Road, Suite 226
Hoover, AL 35216
(205) 823-3818; (800) 433-8002
E-mail: charlespriest@bellsouth.net
Web: www.ahif.org

Learning Disabilities

Learning Disabilities Association of Alabama
Mattie Ray, President
P.O. Box 11588
Montgomery, AL 36111
(334) 277-9151
Web: www.ldaal.org

Mental Health

NAMI Alabama
Jolene James, President
6900 6th Avenue South, Suite B
Birmingham, AL 35212-1902
(205) 833-8336; (800) 626-4199 (In AL)
E-mail: office@namialabama.org
Web: www.namialabama.org

Mental Retardation

The Arc of Alabama, Inc.
Thomas B. Holmes, Executive Director
300 S. Hull Street
Montgomery, AL 36104-6105
(334) 262-7688
E-mail: Tholmes@TheArcAlabama.org
Web: www.thearcofalabama.com/

Special Health Care Needs

Family Voices
Susan Colburn, State & Regional Coordinator
c/o Children's Rehabilitation Service
2129 E. South Boulevard
Montgomery, AL 36116
(334) 613-2284
E-mail: scolburn@rehab.state.al.us
Web: www.familyvoices.org

Family Voices
Dr. Gerald Oveson, State & Regional Coordinator
9800 Cascade Drive
Mobile, AL 36695
(251) 633-3756
E-mail: oveson@bellsouth.net

Speech and Hearing

Speech and Hearing Association of Alabama
Byron McCain, CAE Executive Director
P.O. Box 130220
Birmingham, AL 35213
(205) 802-7551
E-mail: bymccain@bellsouth.net
Web: www.alabamashaa.org

Spina Bifida

Spina Bifida Association of Alabama
P.O. Box 130538
Birmingham, AL 35213-0538
(205) 978-7287

Alabama—Organizations Especially for Parents

Parent Training and Information Center (PTI)
Mavis Smith, Director
Special Education Action Committee Inc.
    (SEAC)
600 Bel Air Boulevard, Suite 210
P.O. Box 161274
Mobile, AL 36616-2274
(251) 478-1208; (800) 222-7322 (In AL)
E-mail: seacofmobile@seacpac.com
Web: www.seacparentassistancecenter.com/

Partners in Policymaking of Alabama
100 N. Union Street
Montgomery, AL 36130-1410
(256) 765-3895; (800) 846-3735
Web: http://acdd.org

Parent Teacher Association (PTA)
Lori Farsheé, Executive Director
Alabama PTA
470 S. Union Street
Montgomery, AL 36104-4330
(334) 834-2501; (800) 328-1897
E-mail: al_office@pta.org

Alabama—Other Disability Organizations

Alabama Association for Persons in
    Supported Employment

Byron White, President
P.O. Box 11586
Montgomery, AL 36116
(334) 613-3527
E-mail: bwhite@rehab.state.al.us
Web: www.al-apse.org

Alabama Disability Action Coalition
Graham Sisson, President
206 13th Street South
Birmingham, AL 35233-1317

Alabama Institute for the Deaf and Blind
Terry Graham, President
P.O. Box 698
Talladega, AL 35161
(256) 761-3200
E-mail: tgrah@aidb.state.al.us
Web: www.aidb.org

Alabama Work Incentives Network
John Roberts, Director
2129 East South Boulevard
Montgomery, AL 36116
(334) 613-2241; (800) 441-7607
E-mail: jroberts@rehab.state.al.us
Web: www.alawin.org

Easter Seals Alabama
6005-A E. Shirley Lane
Montgomery, AL 36117-1935
(334) 395-4489; (800) 388-7325
Web: www.easter-seals.org

Lakeshore Foundation
Jeff Underwood, President/CEO
4000 Ridgeway Drive
Birmingham, AL 35209
(205) 313-7400; (888) 868-2303 (In AL)
Web: www.lakeshore.org

Start on Success Alabama
Donna Sargent, Director
United Cerebral Palsy of Greater
    Birmingham
2430 N. 11th Avenue
Birmingham, AL 35234
(205) 251-0165, ext. 227
E-mail: dsargent@ucpbham.com

VSA Arts of Alabama
Sherri Van Pelt, Executive Director
1116 S. 26th Street

Birmingham, AL 35205
(205) 322-4086
E-mail: vsaal@bellsouth.net
Web: www.vsartsalabama.org

ALASKA

Alaska—State Agencies and Organizations

United States Senators

Honorable Lisa Murkowski (R)
522 Hart Senate Office Building
Washington, DC 20510
(202) 224-3004
E-mail Web Form: http://murkowski
.senate.gov/webform.htm
Web: http://murkowski.senate.gov

Honorable Mark Begich (D)
322 Hart Senate Office Building
Washington, DC 20510
(202) 224-6665
E-mail Web Form: http://begich.senate.gov/
Web: http://begich.senate.gov

United States Representatives

To find the contact information for your representative in the House of the U.S. Congress, visit the House's Web site at: www.house.gov, or call (202) 225-3121; (202) 225-1904 (TTY).

Governor

Honorable Sean Parnell
Office of the Governor
P.O. Box 110001
Juneau, AK 99811-0001
(907) 465-3500
Web: www.gov.state.ak.us
Official State Web Site
Web: www.alaska.gov/

State Department of Education: Special Education

Office of Special Education
Alaska Department of Education
Donald Enoch, Director
801 W. Tenth Street, Suite 200
Juneau, AK 99801-1894
(907) 465-2800
E-mail: donald.enoch@alaska.gov
Web: www.eed.state.ak.us/tls/speed

Alaska received a waiver from the government in 2013 and no longer has a NCLB program.

Programs for Infants and Toddlers With Disabilities: Birth–2 Years

State of Alaska Department of
Health and Social Services
Laurie Thomas, Early Intervention Manager/
Part C Coordinator
Early Intervention/Infant Learning Programs
Office of Children's Services
323 East 4th Avenue
PO Box 240249
Anchorage, AK 99501
(907) 269-3423
E-mail: laurie.thomas2@alaska.gov
Web: http://dhss.alaska.gov/ocs/Pages/
infantlearning/default.aspx

Programs for Children With Disabilities: 3–5 Years

Cassidy Jones, 619 Coordinator
Education Specialist II
801 West 10th Street
PO Box 110500
Juneau, AK 99801-0500
(907) 465-8702
E-mail: cassidy.jones@alaska.gov
Web: http://www.eed.state.ak.us/tls/sped/

State Vocational Rehabilitation Agency

Division of Vocational Rehabilitation
Dave Quisenberry, Director
801 W. 10th Street, Suite A
Juneau, AK 99801
(907) 465-2814
E-mail: david_quisenberry
@labor.state.ak.us

Coordinator for Transition Services

Danny Frazier, Acting Director
State Improvement Grant -
Quality Education in the Last Frontier
801 W. 10th Street, Suite 200
Juneau, AK 99801-1894
(907) 465-2097
E-mail: danny_frazier
@eed.state.ak.us
Web: www.eed.state.ak.us

Office of State Coordinator
of Vocational Education for
Students With Disabilities

Office of Career and Technical Education
Helen Mehrkens, Program Director
800 W. 10th Street, Suite 200
Juneau, AK 99801-1894
(907) 465-8730
E-mail: Helen_Mehrkens
@eed.state.ak.us
Web: www.eed.state.ak.us

State Mental Health Agency

Division of Behavioral Health
Department of Health
and Social Services
P.O. Box 110620
Juneau, AK 99811-0620
(907) 465-3370; (907) 465-2225 (TTY)
Web: www.hss.state.ak.us/dbh

Alaska Mental Health Board
Richard Rainery, Executive Director
431 N. Franklin Street, Suite 200
Juneau, AK 99801
(907) 465-4765
E-mail: Richard_Rainery
@health.state.ak.us
Web: www.amhb.org

State Mental Health
Representative for Children and Youth

Brita Bishop, LCSW, Children's Behavioral
Health Specialist
Division of Behavioral Health
P.O. Box 110620
Juneau, AK 99811-0620
(907) 465-4994
E-mail: brita_bishop@health.state.ak.us
Web: www.hss.state.ak.us

State Mental Retardation
Program (for children 6 and under)

Division of Senior and Disabilities Services
Leanna Rein, Children With Complex Medical
Conditions Specialist III, RNC
3601 C Street, Suite 310
Anchorage, AK 99503
(907) 269-3666; (800) 478-9996
E-mail: leanna_rein@health.state.ak.us
Web: www.state.ak.us

State Mental Retardation
Program (for children 6 and older)

Developmental Disabilities Section
Rebecca Hilgendorf, Program Manager
Division of Senior and Disabilities Services
3601 C Street, Suite 310
Anchorage, AK 99503
(907) 269-3666; (800) 478-9996
E-mail: rebecca_hilgendorf@health.state.ak.us
Web: www.hss.state.ak.us

Council on Developmental Disabilities

Governor's Council on Disabilities
and Special Education
Millie Ryan, Executive Director
P.O. Box 240249
Anchorage, AK 99524-0249
(907) 269-8990; (888) 269-8990
E-mail: Millie_Ryan@health.state.ak.us
Web: www.hss.state.ak.us/gcdse

Protection and Advocacy Agency

Disability Law Center of Alaska
Dave Fleurant, Director
3330 Arctic Boulevard, Suite 103
Anchorage, AK 99503
(907) 344-1002; (907) 565-1002 (V/TTY)
E-mail: akpa@dlcak.org

Client Assistance Program

ASIST, Inc.
Pam Stratton, Director
2900 Boniface Parkway, Suite 100
Anchorage, AK 99504-3195
(907) 333-2211 (V/TTY); (800)
    478-0047 (V/TTY)
E-mail: akcap@alaska.com
Web: http://home.gci.net/~alaskacap/

Health Care Programs for
Children With Special Needs

State of Alaska Department
    of Health and Social Services
Special Needs Services Unit
3601 C Street, Suite 934
P.O. Box 240249
Anchorage, AK 99524-0249
(907) 269-3419; (800) 799-7570
Web: www.hss.state.ak.us

The Stone Soup Group
2401 E. 42nd Avenue, Suite 200
Anchorage, AK 99508
(907) 561-3701
E-mail: ssg@stonesoupgroup.org
Web: www.stonesoupgroup.org

State CHIP Program
(health care for low-income,
uninsured children)

Denali KidCare
P.O. Box 110601
Juneau, AK 99811-0801
(907) 465-1696
Web: www.hss.state.ak.us/dhcs/
    DenaliKidCare/default.htm

Programs for Children
and Youth Who Are
Deaf or Hard of Hearing

Alaska Division of Vocational Rehabilitation
Duane Mayes, Program Coordinator/
    Regional Manager
3600 Bragaw
Anchorage, AK 99508
(907) 269-2060
E-mail: duane_mayes
    @labor.state.ak.us
Web: www.state.ak.us

Telecommunications Relay Services
for Individuals Who Are Deaf, Hard
of Hearing, or With Speech Impairments

(800) 770-8255 (V)
(800) 770-8973 (TTY); 711 (TTY)
(866) 355-6198 (Speech to Speech)

Programs for Children and Youth
Who Are Blind or Visually Impaired

Alaska Division of Vocational Rehabilitation
Cheryl A. Walsh, Director
1016 W. 6th, Suite 102
Anchorage, AK 99501
(907) 269-3580; (888) 330-6468
E-mail: kent_ireton@labor.state.ak.us
Web: http://labor.alaska.gov/dvr/home.htm

Program for Children and
Youth Who Are Deaf-Blind

Alaska Dual Sensory Impairment Service
Sara Gaar, Project Director
Special Education Service Agency
2217 E. Tudor Road, Suite 1
Anchorage, AK 99507
(907) 562-7372; (907) 563-8284 (TTY)
E-mail: sesa@sesa.org
Web: www.sesa.org

Regional ADA Disability and
Business Technical Assistance Center

Northwest ADA & IT Center
Charles F. Davis, Center Coordinator
Oregon Health & Science University-CDRC
P.O. Box 574
Portland, OR 97207-0574
(503) 494-4001; (503) 418-0296 (TTY)
(800) 949-4232 (V/TTY)
E-mail: nwada@ohsu.edu
Web: www.nwada.org

University Center for Excellence
in Developmental Disabilities

University of Alaska Anchorage
Center for Human Development
Karen M. Ward, Director
2210 Arca Drive
Anchorage, AK 99508
(907) 272-8270
Web: www.alaskachd.org

State Mediation System

Office of Special Education
    and Early Development
Art Arnold, Director
Alaska Department of Education
801 W. 10th Street, Suite 200
Juneau, AK 99801-1894
(907) 465-2824
E-mail: art_arnold@eed.state.ak.us
Web: www.eed.state.ak.us/tls/sped/

Special Format Library

Alaska State Library
Talking Book Center
Patience Frederiksen, Librarian
344 W. Third Avenue, Suite 125
Anchorage, AK 99501
(907) 269-6575; (800) 776-6566
(907) 269-6575 (TTY)
E-mail: beverly_griffin@eed.state.ak.us
Web: www.library.state.ak.us/dev/tbc.html

Alaska—Disability-Specific Organizations

Attention Deficit Disorder

To identify an ADD group in Alaska,
contact either of the following
organizations:

Children and Adults With
    Attention-Deficit/Hyperactivity
    Disorder (CHADD)
8181 Professional Place, Suite 150
Landover, MD 20785
(301) 306-7070
(800) 233-4050 (Voice mail to request
    information packet)
Web: www.chadd.org

Attention Deficit
    Disorder Association (ADDA)
P.O. Box 543
Pottstown, PA 19464
(484) 945-2101
Web: www.add.org

Autism

To identify an autism group in Alaska, contact

Autism Society of America
7910 Woodmont Avenue, Suite 300
Bethesda, MD 20814
(301) 657-0881; (800) 3-AUTISM
Web: www.autism-society.org

Blind/Visual Impairments

For pertinent services in Alaska, contact

American Foundation for the Blind
Gil Johnson, Director
111 Pine Street, Suite 725
San Francisco, CA 94111
(415) 392-4845
E-mail: sanfran@afb.net
Web: www.afb.org

Cerebral Palsy

UCP of Alaska/Parents Inc.
4743 E. Northern Lights Boulevard
Anchorage, AK 99508
(907) 337-7678
E-mail: parents@parentsinc.org

Learning Disabilities

Learning Disabilities Association of Alaska
Barbara Lefler, President
P.O. Box 243172
Anchorage, AK 99524
(907) 345-7731

Mental Health

Alaska Youth and Family Network
Frances Purdy, Program Manager
801 Karluk, #1
P.O. Box 23-3142
Anchorage, AK 99523-3142
(907) 770-4979; (888) 770-4979
E-mail: ayfn@ayfn.org
Web: www.ayfn.org

NAMI Alaska
Tracy Barbee, Executive Director
144 W. 15th Avenue
Anchorage, AK 99501
(907) 277-1300; (800) 478-4462
E-mail: tbarbee@nami-alaska.org

Web: www.nami-alaska.org

Mental Retardation

The Arc of Anchorage
Gwendolyn Lee, Executive Director
2211 Arca Drive
Anchorage, AK 99508
(907) 277-6677
E-mail: glee@arc-anchorage.org
Web: www.arc-anchorage.org

Physical and Cognitive Disabilities

Easter Seals Alaska
V. Gutierrez-Osborne, Executive Director
126 W. 15th Avenue
Anchorage, AK 99501
(907) 277-7325
E-mail: vgosborne@gci.net
Web: www.easter-seals.org

Speech and Language

Alaska Speech-Language-Hearing Association
Kelly Scannell-Brewer, Member
3211 Starboard Lane
Anchorage, AK 99516
(907) 261-5800, ext. 4037
E-mail: Kbrewer@provak.org

Alaska—Organizations Especially for Parents

Parent Training and Information Project

PARENTS, Inc.
Sonja Bolling, Executive Director
4743 E. Northern Lights Boulevard
Anchorage, AK 99508
(907) 337-7678 (V/TTY); (800) 478-7678
   (in AK only)
E-mail: parents@parentsinc.org
Web: www.parentsinc.org

Community Parent Resource Center

LINKS Mat-Su Parent Resource Center
HC01 Box 6389
Palmer, AK 99645
(907) 373-3632; (907) 373-3652
E-mail: linksdf@gci.net

Web: www.linksprc.org

Parent Teacher Association (PTA)

Alaska Congress of Parents and Teachers
Suellen Appellof, President
P.O. Box 201496
Anchorage, AK 99520-1496
(907) 279-9345
E-mail: ak_office@pta.org
Web: www.alaskapta.org

Independent Living

For information about the Statewide Independent Living Council (SILC) in Alaska, contact

Independent Living Research Utilization Project
The Institute for Rehabilitation and Research
2323 South Sheppard, Suite 1000
Houston, TX 77019
(713) 520-0232 (V); (713) 520-5136 (TTY)
E-mail: ilru@ilru.org
Web: www.ilru.org

For information on centers for independent living (CILs) in Alaska, contact

National Council on Independent Living
1916 Wilson Boulevard, Suite 209
Arlington, VA 22201
(703) 525-3406; (703) 525-4153 (TTY)
E-mail: ncil@ncil.org
Web: www.ncil.org

ARIZONA

Arizona—State Agencies and Organizations

United States Senators

Honorable John McCain (R)
241 Russell Senate Office Building
Washington, DC 20510
(202) 224-2235
(202) 228-2862 (Fax)
E-mail: john_mccain
   @mccain.senate.gov
Web: http://mccain.senate.gov

Honorable Jeff Flake (R)
730 Hart Senate Office Building
Washington, DC 20510
(202) 224-4521
(202) 228-1239 (Fax)
E-mail Web Form: http://flake.senate.gov/
con_form.htm
Web: http://flake.senate.gov

United States Representatives

To find the contact information for your representative in the House of the U.S. Congress, visit the House's Web site at: www.house.gov, or call (202) 225-3121; (202) 225-1904 (TTY).

Governor

Honorable Jan Brewer
Governor of Arizona
1700 W. Washington
Phoenix, AZ 85007
(602) 542-4331
E-mail Web Form: www.governor.state.az.us/
post/feedback.htm
Web: www.governor.state.az.us

Official State Web Site
Web: www.az.gov/

State Department of Education: Special Education

Exceptional Student Services
Angela Denning
3300 N.Central Avenue
24th Flr
Phoenix, AZ 85007-3280
602-542-4013
E-mail: angela.denning@azed.gov
Web: www.ade.az.gov

State Coordinator for NCLB (No Child Left Behind)

NCLB

(602)364-1842
E-mail: hqtteachers@azed.gov
Web: http://www2.ed.gov/nclb/landing.jhtml

Programs for Infants and Toddlers With Disabilities: Birth–2 Years

Arizona Early Intervention
Program (AzEIP)
Karie Taylor, Part C Coordinator
Department of Economic Security
3839 North 3rd Street, Suite 304
Site Code #801 A-6
Phoenix, AZ 85012
(602) 532-9960
E-mail: KTaylor@azdes.gov
Web: https://www.azdes.gov/main.
aspx?menu=98&id=3026

Programs for Children With Disabilities: 3–5 Years

Exceptional Student Services
Nicol Russell, 619 Coordinator
Arizona Department of Education
1535 West Jefferson, Bin #15
Phoenix, AZ 85007
E-mail: nicol.russell@azed.gov
Web: http://www.azed.gov/early-childhood/
preschool/

State Vocational Rehabilitation Agency

Rehabilitation Services Administration
Department of Economic Security
Skip Bingham, Administrator
1789 W. Jefferson, 2nd Floor,
NW (930A)
Phoenix, AZ 85007
(602) 542-3332; (800) 563-1221
E-mail: sbingham@azdes.gov
*Web: https://www.azdes.gov/rehabilitation_*
services/

Coordinator for Transition Services

Christine Fuller
Rehabilitation Services
Administration
Department of Economic Security
3221 N. 16th Street, Suite 200
Phoenix, AZ 85016
(602) 266-6752
E-mail: cfuller@azdes.org
Web: www.de.state.az.us/rsa

State Mental Health
Representative for Children and Youth

Leslie Schwalbe, Deputy Director
Division of Behavioral Health Services
Department of Health Services
150 N. 18th Avenue, 2nd Floor
Phoenix, AZ 85007
(602) 364-4558
E-mail: lschwal@hs.state.az.us
Web: www.hs.state.az.us/bhs/index.htm

State Developmental Disabilities Program

Department of Economic Security
Division of Developmental Disabilities
Ric Zaharia, Assistant Director
P.O. Box 6123, Site Code (791A)
Phoenix, AZ 85005
(602) 542-0419
Web: https://www.azdes.gov/developmental_
   disabilities/

Council on Developmental Disabilities

Governor's Council on
   Developmental Disabilities
Jami Snyder, Executive Director
3839 North Third Street, Suite 306
Phoenix, Arizona 85012
602-277-4986
E-mail: jsnyder@azdes.gov
Web: http://azmemory.azlibrary.gov/cdm/
   ref/collection/statepubs/id/2393

Protection and Advocacy Agency

Arizona Center for Disability Law
J.J. Rico, Interim Executive Director
5025 E. Washington Street, Suite 202
Phoenix, AZ 85034
(602) 274-6287 (V / TTY)
E-mail: center@azdisabilitylaw.org
Web: www.acdl.com

Native American Protection and Advocacy Project
Therese E. Yanan, Director
3535 E. 30th Street, Suite 201
Farmington, NM 87402
(505) 566-5880; (800) 862-7271
E-mail: tyanan@napap.org
Web: www.dnalegalservices.org

Client Assistance Program

   Contact the Protection and Advocacy agencies listed previously.

Programs for Children With
Special Health Care Needs

Office for Children With Special Health
   Care Needs
Department of Health Services
Cathryn Echeverria, Chief
150 N. 18th Ave. #320
Phoenix, AZ 85007
(602) 542-1860; (800) 232-1676
E-mail: cecheve@hs.state.az.us
Web: http://azdhs.gov/phs/owch/ocshcn/

State CHIP Program (health care for low-income, uninsured children)

KidsCare
920 E. Madison
MD 500
Phoenix, AZ 85034
(602) 417-5437; (877) 764-5437
Web: www.kidscare.state.az.us/English/
   Default.asp

Programs for Children Who
Are Deaf or Hard of Hearing

Arizona Commission for the Deaf
   and the Hard of Hearing
Sherri Collins, Executive Director
100 N. 15th Avenue, Suite 104
Phoenix, AZ 85007
(602) 542-3323 (V); (800) 352-8161 (V/TTY)
(602) 364-0990 (TTY)
E-mail: info@acdhh.az.gov
Web: www.acdhh.org

Telecommunications Relay
Services for Individuals
Who Are Deaf, Hard of Hearing,
or With Speech Impairments

(800) 842-4681 (V)
(800) 367-8939 (TTY); 711 (TTY)
(800) 842-6520 (Speech to Speech)

Programs for Children and Youth
Who Are Blind or Visually Impaired,
Deaf or Hard of Hearing, or Deaf-Blind

Arizona State Schools for the Deaf and the Blind
Dr. Marv Lamer, Interim Superintendent
P.O. Box 88510
Tucson, AZ 85754
(520) 770-3704
E-mail: Mary.Fult@asdb.az.gov
Web: www.asdb.state.az.us

Regional ADA & IT
Technical Assistance Center

Pacific Disability and Business Technical
*   Assistance Center*
Erica C. Jones, Director
Public Health Institute
555 12th Street, Suite 1030
Oakland, CA 94607-4046
(510) 285-5600 (V/TTY); (800) 949-4232 (V/
*   TTY)*
E-mail: adatech@pdbtac.com
Web: http://www.adapacific.org/

University Center for Excellence
in Developmental Disabilities

Institute for Human Development
Richard Carroll, Executive Director
Northern Arizona University
P.O. Box 5630
Flagstaff, AZ 86011
(928) 523-4791
E-mail: ihd.uap@nau.edu
Web: http://nau.edu/sbs/ihd/

Technology-Related Assistance

Arizona Technology Access
*   Program (AZTAP)*
Jill S. Pleasant, Director
Randy Collins, Outreach/
*   Training Coordinator*
Ed Myers, Policy and Funding Specialist
Northern Arizona University
2400 N. Central Avenue, Suite 300
Phoenix, AZ 85004
(602) 728-9534; (602) 728-9536 (TTY)
(800) 477-9921 (toll-free)
E-mail: jill.pleasant@nau.edu
Web: www.nau.edu/ihd/aztap/

State Mediation System

Arizona Department of Education
Exceptional Student Services
Dr. Hugh Pace, Education Program Specialist
400 W. Congress, Suite 241
Tucson, AZ 85701
(520) 628-6616
E-mail: hpace@ade.az.gov
Web: www.ade.az.gov

Special Format Library

Arizona State Library
Archives and Public Records
Braille and Talking Book Division
Linda A. Montgomery, Director
1030 N. 32nd Street
Phoenix, AZ 85008
(602) 255-5578; (800) 255-5578
E-mail: btbl@lib.az.us
Web: www.lib.az.us/braille/

Arizona—Disability-
Specific Organizations

Attention Deficit Disorder

    To identify an ADD group in Arizona, con-
tact either of the following organizations:

Children and Adults With Attention-Deficit/
*   Hyperactivity Disorder (CHADD)*
4601 Presidents Drive, Suite 300
Lanham, MD 20706
(301) 306-7070; (800) 233-4050
*   (Voice mail to request*
*   information packet)*
Web: www.chadd.org

Attention Deficit Disorder Association (ADDA)
P.O. Box 103
Denver PA 17517
(484) 945-2101
Web: www.add.org

Autism

Southwest Autism Research Center
Emily Chappell, Executive Director
1002 E. McDowell, Suite A
Phoenix, AZ 85006
(602) 340-8717; (877) 752-7272
E-mail: sarrc@autismcenter.org
Web: www.autismcenter.org

Blind/Visual Impairments

Foundation for Blind Children
Chris Tompkins, Executive Director
1235 E. Harmont Drive
Phoenix, AZ 85020
(602) 331-1470
E-mail: ctompkins@the-fbc.org
Web: https://www.seeitourway.org/

American Foundation for the Blind–West
Gil Johnson, Director
111 Pine Street, Suite 725
San Francisco, CA 94111
(415) 392-4845
E-mail: sanfran@afb.net
Web: www.afb.org

Brain Injury

Brain Injury Alliance of Arizona
Rebecca Armendariz, President
5025 E. Washington Street, Suite 108
Phoenix, Arizona 85034
(602) 323-9165; (888) 305-0073
E-mail: info@biaaz.phxcoxmail.com
Web: www.biaaz.org

Cerebral Palsy

United Cerebral Palsy of Central
    Arizona
Guy Collison, President
1802 W. Parkside Lane
Phoenix, AZ 85027
(602) 943-5472
E-mail: info@ucpofaz.org
Web: www.ucpofaz.org

Down Syndrome

Down Syndrome Network, Inc.
4025 E. Chandler Boulevard-#70-C3
Phoenix AZ 85048
(480) 759-9150, Fax (480) 759-9180
E-mail: info@dsnetworkaz.org
Web: www.dsnetworkaz.org

Sharing Down Syndrome Arizona, Inc.
Gina Johnson, President/Founder
745 N. Gilbert Road, #124 PMB 273
Gilbert, AZ 85234
(480) 926-6500
(480) 980-3515 (Spanish)
E-mail: gina@sharingds.org
Web: www.sharingds.org

Epilepsy

Epilepsy Foundation of Arizona
Mary Macleish, Executive Director
240 W. Thomas Road, 2nd Floor
Phoenix, Arizona 85013-4407
(602) 406-3581; (888) 768-2690
E-mail: mmaclei@chw.edu
Web: http://www.epilepsy.com/arizona

Learning Disabilities

Learning Disabilities Association of Arizona
18001 N. 79th Avenue, Building E-71
Glendale, AZ 85308
(623) 975-4551
E-mail: dotcrawford@cox.net

Mental Health

Mental Health Association of Arizona
Tiffany Bock, Executive Director
6411 E. Thomas Road
Scottsdale, AZ 85251
(480) 994-4407
E-mail: tbock@mhaarizona.org
Web: www.mhaarizona.org

Arizona Alliance for the Mentally Ill
Sue Davis, Executive Director
NAMI Arizona
5025 E. Washington Street
Suite # 112
Phoenix, AZ 85034
(602) 244-8166; (800) 626-5022
E-mail: azami@azami.org
Web: http://www.namiaz.com/

Mental Retardation

The Arc of Arizona, Inc.
Jon Meyers, Executive Director
PO Box 90714
Phoenix, AZ 85066
(602) 234-2721; (800) 252-9054
E-mail: arc@arcarizona.org
Web: www.arcarizona.org

Speech and Hearing

Arizona Speech-Language-Hearing Association
Tori Micoliczyk, Assistant to ArSHA
P.O. Box 30988
Phoenix, AZ 85046
(602) 354-8062; (800) 705-7510
E-mail: office@arsha.org

Spina Bifida

Arizona Spina Bifida Association Inc.
1001 E. Fairmont Avenue
Phoenix, AZ 85014-4806
(602) 274-3323
E-mail: office@azspinabifida.org
Web: www.azspinabifida.org

Arizona—Organizations Especially for Parents

Parent Training and Information Center (PTI)

Raising Special Kids
Joyce Millard-Hoie, Executive Director
2400 N. Central Avenue, Suite 200
Phoenix, AZ 85004-1313
(602) 242-4366; (800) 237-3007 (in AZ only)
E-mail: info@raisingspecialkids.org
Web: www.raisingspecialkids.org

Pilot Parents of Southern Arizona
Lynn Kallis, Executive Director
2600 N. Wyatt Drive
Tucson, AZ 85712
(520) 324-3150; (877) 365-7220
E-mail: lynn@pilotparents.org
Web: www.pilotparents.org

Parent-to-Parent

Contact Parent Training and Information Center listed previously.

Partners in Policymaking

Pilot Parents of Southern Arizona
Lynn Kallis, Executive Director
2600 N. Wyatt Drive
Tucson, AZ 85712
(520) 324-3150; (877) 365-7220
E-mail: lynn@pilotparents.org
Web: www.pilotparents.org

Parent Teacher Association (PTA)

Arizona Congress of Parents
and Teachers, Inc.
Lucy Ranus, President
2721 N. 7th Avenue
Phoenix, AZ 85007
(602) 279-1811
E-mail: az_office@pta.org
Web: www.azpta.org

Other Parent Organizations

Parent Information Network
Exceptional Student Services
Department of Education
Rita Kenison, Child Find Coordinator
1535 W. Jefferson
Phoenix, AZ 85007
(602) 364-4015; (800) 352-4558
E-mail: Rkeniso@ade.az.gov
Web: http://www.azed.gov/special-
education/deputy-associate-superintendent/
parent-information-network/

Arizona—Other Disability Organizations

Easter Seals Arizona

Michael Fitzgerald, Executive Director
Brian Patchett, Vice President of Programs
2075 S. Cottonwood Drive
Tempe, AZ 85282
(480) 222-4100; (800) 626-6061
E-mail: frontdesk@azseals.org
Web: www.eastersealsarizona.org

Community Information & Referral Services
Adrienne Howell, President
2200 N Central Ave Ste 211
Phoenix, AZ 85004-1431
877-211-8661
E-mail: firstcall@cirs.org
Web: www.cirs.org

VSA Arts of Arizona

Barbara Yorkis, Executive Director
3321 N. Chapel Avenue
Tucson, AZ 85716
(520) 795-6502
E-mail: vsaa@mindspring.com
Web: http://www.vsaaz.org/

Independent Living

For information on the Statewide Independent Living Council (SILC) in Arizona, contact

Independent Living Research Utilization Project
The Institute for Rehabilitation and Research
2323 South Sheppard, Suite 1000
Houston, TX 77019
(713) 520-0232 (V); (713) 520-5136 (TTY)

E-mail: ilru@ilru.org

Web: www.ilru.org

For information on centers for independent living (CILs) in Arizona, contact

National Council on Independent Living
1916 Wilson Boulevard, Suite 209
Arlington, VA 22201
(703) 525-3406; (703) 525-4153 (TTY)
E-mail: ncil@ncil.org
Web: www.ncil.org

ARKANSAS

Arkansas—State Agencies and Organizations

United States Senators
Honorable John Boozman (R)
320 Hart Senate Office Building
Washington, DC 20510
(202) 224-4843
(202) 224-6435 (Fax)
E-mail Web Form: http://lincoln.senate.gov/
   webform.html
Web: http://www.boozman.senate.gov/
   public/index.cfm/e-mail-me

Honorable Mark Pryor (D)
255 Dirksen Senate Office Building
Washington, DC 20510
(202) 224-2353
(202) 228-3973 (Fax)
E-mail: mark_pryor@pryor.senate.gov
Web: http://pryor.senate.gov/

United States Representatives

To find the contact information for your representative in the House of the U.S. Congress, visit the House's Web site at: www.house.gov, or call (202) 225-3121; (202) 225-1904(TTY)

Governor
Honorable Mike Beebe
Governor's Office
State Capitol
500 Woodlane Street, Suite 250
Little Rock, AR 72201
(501) 682-2345
E-mail form available on Governor's Web site.

Web: www.arkansas.gov/governor

Official State Web Site
Web: www.accessarkansas.org/

State Department of Education: Special Education

Special Education
Arkansas Department of Education
Marcia Harding, Associate Director
1401 W. Capitol, Suite 450
Little Rock, AR 72201
(501) 682-4221
E-mail: mharding@arkedu.k12.ar.us
Web: http://www.arkansased.org/

State Coordinator for ESEA (Elementary Secondary Education Act)

Annette Barnes, Assistant Commissioner
Division of Public School Accountability
Arkansas Department of Education
#4 Capitol Mall, Room 205-B
Little Rock, AR 72201
(501) 682-1298
E-mail: annette.barneslewis@arkansas.gov
Web: http://www.arkansased.org/esea-
   flexibility

Programs for Infants and Toddlers With Disabilities: Birth–2 Years

Division of Developmental Disabilities Services
Department of Human Services
Tracy Turner, Part C Coordinator
PO Box 1437, Slot N504
Little Rock, AR 72203-1437
(501) 682-8703
E-mail: tracy.turner@dhs.arkansas.gov
Web: http://humanservices.arkansas.gov/
   ddds/Pages/default.aspx

Programs for Children With Disabilities: 3–5 Years

Preschool Programs, Special
   Education Unit
Sandra K. Reifeiss, Early Childhood
   Program Director
Arkansas Department of Education
1401 W. Capitol, Suite 450
Little Rock, AR 72201-2936
(501) 682-4225

E-mail: sandra.reifeiss@arkansas.gov
Web: http://arksped.k12.ar.us

State Vocational Rehabilitation Agency

Arkansas Rehabilitation Services
Department of Workforce Education
John C. Wyvill, Commissioner
1616 Brookwood Drive
P.O. Box 3781
Little Rock, AR 72203-3781
(501) 296-1616
E-mail: JCWyvill@ARS.state.ar.us
Web: www.arsinfo.org

Department of Human Services
Division of Services for the Blind
James C. Hudson, Director
700 Main Street, S101
P.O. Box 3237
Little Rock, AR 72203
(501) 682-5463; (800) 960-9270
(501) 682-0093 (TTY)
E-mail: jim.hudson@arkansas.gov
Web: www.state.ar.us/dhs/dsb

Coordinator for Transition Services

Arkansas Department of Education
Special Education
Brook Charton, Transition Coordinator
950 Hogan Lane, Suite 5
Conway, AR 72034
(501) 329-7400
E-mail: bcharton@conwaycorp.net
Web: www.acc.k12.ar.us/transition

Office of State Coordinator of Vocational Education for Students With Disabilities

Office of Support for Special Populations
Arkansas Department of Workforce Education
Teresa Dow, Program Manager
#3 Capitol Mall
Little Rock, AR 72201-1083
(501) 682-1800
E-mail: teresa.dow@arkansas.gov
Web: http://dwe.arkansas.gov

State Mental Health Agency

Division of Behavioral Health Services
Pat Dahlgren, Director
4313 W. Markham Street
Little Rock, AR 72205

(501) 686-9164
E-mail: pat.dahlgren@arkansas.gov
Web: www.state.ar.us/dhs/dmhs

State Mental Health Representative for Children and Youth

Anne Wells, Assistant Director
Division of Mental Health Services
4313 W. Markham Street
Little Rock, AR 72205
(501) 686-9489
E-mail: anne.wells@arkansas.gov
Web: www.state.ar.us/dhs/dmhs

State Mental Retardation Program

Division of Developmental Disabilities Services
Department of Human Services
James "Charlie" Green, Director
P.O. Box 1437, Slot N501,
   7th and Main Streets, 5th Floor
Little Rock, AR 72203-1437
(501) 682-8665; (501) 682-1332 (TTY)
E-mail: charlie.green1@arkansas.gov
Web: www.state.ar.us/dhs/ddds

Council on Developmental Disabilities

Governor's Developmental Disabilities Council
Wilma Stewart, Coordinator
Freeway Medical Tower
5800 W. 10th, Suite 805
Little Rock, AR 72204
(501) 661-2589
E-mail: wstewart@healthyarkansas.com
Web: www.ddcouncil.org

Protection and Advocacy Agency

Disability Rights Center
Nan Ellen East, Executive Director
1100 N. University, Suite 201
Little Rock, AR 72207
(501) 296-1775 (V/TTY); (800) 482-1174 (V/TTY)
E-mail: panda@arkdisabilityrights.org
Web: www.arkdisabilityrights.org/

Client Assistance Program

Disability Rights Center
Eddie Miller, CAP Director
1100 N. University, Suite 201
Little Rock, AR 72207

(501) 296-1775 (V/TTY); (800) 482-1174
E-mail: panda@arkdisabilityrights.org
Web: www.arkdisabilityrights.org

Programs for Children With Special Health Care Needs

Children's Medical Services
Gilbert Buchanan, Medical Director
Department of Human Services
P.O. Box 1437, Slot S380
Little Rock, AR 72203-1437
(501) 682-2277; (800) 482-5850, ext. 22277 (in AR)
E-mail: gil.buchanan@arkansas.gov
Web: www.medicaid.state.ar.us

State CHIP Program (health care for low-income, uninsured children)

ARKids
Division of Medical Services
Arkansas Department of Human Services
P.O. Box 1437 (S295)
Little Rock, AR 72203-1437
(888) 474-8275
Web: www.arkidsfirst.com/home.htm

Programs for Children and Youth Who Are Deaf or Hard of Hearing Deaf ACCESS

Arkansas Rehabilitation Services
4601 W. Markham
Little Rock, AR 72205
(501) 686-9680; (501) 686-9836 (TTY)
Web: www.arsinfo.org/deafaccess.html

Telecommunications Relay Services for Individuals Who Are Deaf, Hard of Hearing, or With Speech Impairments

(800) 285-1121 (V)
(800) 285-1131 (TTY); 711 (TTY)
(866) 565-9823 (Speech to Speech)

Programs for Children and Youth Who Are Blind or Visually Impaired or Deaf-Blind

Educational Services for the Visually Impaired
Arkansas Department of Education
2402 Wildwood Avenue, Suite 112
Sherwood, AR 72120
(501) 835-5448
E-mail: jima@esvi.org
Web: www.esvi.org

Regional ADA & IT Technical Assistance Center

Disability Law Resource Project
Wendy Wilkinson, Director
2323 S. Shepard Boulevard, Suite 1000
Houston, TX 77019
(713) 520-0232 (V/TTY); (800) 949-4232 (V/TTY)
E-mail: dlrp@ilru.org
Web: www.dlrp.org

University Center for Excellence in Developmental Disabilities Education, Research and Service

Partners for Inclusive Communities
Mark Swanson, Director
2001 Pershing Circle, Suite 300
North Little Rock, AR 72114-1841
(501) 682-9900; (800) 342-2923
E-mail: swansonmarke@uams.edu
Web: www.uams.edu/UAP/

Technology-Related Assistance

Arkansas Increasing Capabilities Access Network
Barbara Gullett, Project Director
2201 Brookwood, Suite 117
Little Rock, AR 72202
(501) 666-8868 (V/TTY); (800) 828-2799 (in AR)
Web: www.arkansas-ICAN.org

State Mediation System

State Department of Education, Special Education
Tom Hicks, Special Education Program Manager
State Education Building C, Room 105
Little Rock, AR 72201
(501) 682-4221
E-mail: thicks@arkedu.k12.ar.us

Special Format Library

Library for the Blind and Physically Handicapped
John J. D. Hall, Librarian
One Capitol Mall
Little Rock, AR 72201-1081
(501) 682-1155; (866) 660-0885 (in AR)
(501) 682-1002(TTY)
E-mail: nlsbooks@asl.lib.ar.us
Web: http://www.library.arkansas.gov/
libraryForTheBlind/Pages/default.aspx

Arkansas—Disability-Specific Organizations

Attention Deficit Disorder

To identify an ADD group in Arkansas, contact one of the following organizations:

Children and Adults With Attention-Deficit/
    Hyperactivity Disorder (CHADD)
8181 Professional Place, Suite 150
Landover, MD 20785
(301) 306-7070
(800) 233-4050 (Voice mail to request
    information packet)
Web: www.chadd.org

Attention Deficit Disorder Association (ADDA)
P.O. Box 543
Pottstown, PA 19464
(484) 945-2101
Web: www.add.org

Attention Deficit Disorders
    Association–Southern Region
12345 Jones Road, Suite 287-7
Houston, TX 77070
(281) 897-0982
E-mail: addaoffice@pda.net
Web: www.adda-sr.org

Autism

Arkansas Autism Society
2001 Pershing Circle, 3rd Floor
N. Little Rock, AR 72114
(501) 682-9930; (800) 342-2923
E-mail: comments@arautism.org
Web: www.arautism.org

Blind/Visual Impairments

American Foundation for the Blind–Southwest
Judy Scott, Director
11030 Ables Lane
Dallas, TX 75229
(214) 352-7222
E-mail: dallas@afb.net
Web: www.afb.org

Brain Injury

Brain Injury Association of Arkansas
Mary Anne Sullivan, President
525 W. Capitol Avenue, Suite 1533
P. O. Box 26236
Little Rock, AR 72221-6236
(501) 374-3585; (800) 235-2443
E-mail: info@brainassociation.org
Web: www.brainassociation.org

Cerebral Palsy

UCP of Arkansas
Edmond A. Benton, President
9720 N. Rodney Parham Road
Little Rock, AR 72227
(501) 224-6067; (800) 228-6174
E-mail: info@ucpcark.org
Web: www.ucpcark.org

Deaf-Blindness

Arkansas Project for Children With Deaf-Blindness
Lou Kirkpatrick, Project Coordinator
1401 W. Capitol, Suite 450
Little Rock, AR 72201-2936
(501) 682-4222; (501) 682-2380 (TTY)
E-mail: lkirkpatrick@arkedu.k12.ar.us
Web: http://acc.k12.ar.us/ade/db.htm

Deafness/Hard of Hearing

Arkansas Association for Hearing Impaired Children
Karen Lutrick, Executive Director
P.O. Box 2007
Benton, AR 72018-2007
(501) 316-2442; (877) 504-5778
E-mail: aahic@aristotle.net
Web: http://aahic.org

Learning Disabilities

Learning Disabilities Association of Arkansas
7509 Cantrell, Suite 103
Little Rock, AR 72207
(501) 666-8777
E-mail: info@ldaarkansas.org
Web: www.ldaarkansas.org

Mental Health

Mental Health Association
   in NW Arkansas
Abby Selby, President
P.O. Box 1993
Fayetteville, AR 72702
(479) 443-2143; (479) 575-2934
E-mail: akolbse @uark.edu

NAMI Arkansas
Pauline Charton, Executive Director
712 W. 3rd Street, Suite 200
Little Rock, AR 72201
(501) 661-1548; (800) 844-0381
E-mail: nami-ar@nami.org
Web: http://ar.nami.org/

Mental Retardation

The Arc of Arkansas
Steve Hitt, Executive Director
2004 S. Main Street
Little Rock, AR 72206-1597
(501) 375-7770
E-mail: shitt@arcark.org
Web: www.arcark.org

Special HealthCare Needs

Family Voices of Arkansas
Rodney Farley, Regional Coordinator
Tammy Walloch, State Coordinator
110 Louise Street
N. Little Rock, AR 72118
(501) 753-3163; (501) 843-3133
E-mail: refarley@juno.com
Web: www.familyvoices.org

Spina Bifida

Spina Bifida Association of Arkansas
James Rucker, President
P.O. Box 24663
Little Rock, AR 72221
(501) 975-7222
E-mail: sigmondr@sbcglobal.net
Web: www.sbaa.org

Arkansas—Organizations Especially for Parents

Parent Training and Information Centers (PTI)

Arkansas Disability Coalition
Wanda Stovall, Director & Co-Director
1123 S. University Avenue, Suite 225
Little Rock, AR 72204-1605
(501) 614-7020 (V/TTY); (800) 223-1330 (V/TTY)
E-mail: adcwstovall@earthlink.net
Web: www.arkansaspti.org

FOCUS, Inc.
Ramona Hodges, Co-Director
Shelby Knight, Co-Director
2809 Forrest Home Road
Jonesboro, AR 72401
(870) 935-2750; (888) 247-3843
E-mail: focusinc@ipa.net

Arkansas Support Network, Inc.
Lynn Donald, Program Manager
614 E. Emma Avenue, Suite 219
Springdale, AR 72764
(479) 927-1004; (800) 748-9768
E-mail: pti@supports.org
Web: www.supports.org

Partners in Policymaking

Arkansas Governor's Developmental
   Disabilities Council
Mary Edwards, Parent Trainer
Freeway Medical Tower
5800 W. 10th Street, Suite 805
Little Rock, AR 72204
(501) 661-2519; (501) 661-2736 (TTY)
E-mail: medwards@healthyarkansas.com
Web: www.ddcouncil.org

Parent to Parent

The Arc Arkansas
Ashley Rentz, Program Coordinator
2004 S. Main Street
Little Rock, AR 72206-1597
(501) 375-7770
E-mail: arentz@arcark.org
Web: www.arcark.org

Parent Teacher Association (PTA)

Arkansas Congress of Parents and Teachers
Kathy McFetridge, President
P.O. Box 1015
North Little Rock, AR 72115
(501) 753-5247
E-mail: ar_office@pta.org
Web: www.arkansaspta.org

Arkansas—Other Disability Organizations

Easter Seals Arkansas
Sharon Moone-Jochums, President/CEO
3920 Woodland Heights Road
Little Rock, AR 72212
(501) 227-3600
E-mail: info@ar.easter-seals.org
Web: http://ar.easter-seals.org/

Children's Medical Services
Sandi Anderson, President
Rodney Farley, Parent Consultant
Parent Advisory Council, Inc.
P.O. Box 1437, S380
Little Rock, AR 72203-1437
(501) 682-1461
E-mail: Refarley@juno.com

NAMI-Arkansas
Pauline Charton, Executive Director
Family to Family Education Program
712 W. 3rd Street, Suite 200
Little Rock, AR 72201
(501) 661-1548; (800) 844-0381
E-mail: nami-ar@nami.org
Web: http://ar.nami.org/

Independent Living

For information on the Statewide Independent Living Council (SILC) in Arkansas, contact

Independent Living Research Utilization Project
The Institute for Rehabilitation and Research
2323 South Sheppard, Suite 1000
Houston, TX 77019
(713) 520-0232 (V); (713) 520-5136 (TTY)
E-mail: ilru@ilru.org
Web: www.ilru.org

For information on centers for independent
living (CILs) in Arkansas, contact

National Council on Independent Living
1916 Wilson Boulevard, Suite 209
Arlington, VA 22201
(703) 525-3406; (703) 525-4153 (TTY)
E-mail: ncil@ncil.org
Web: www.ncil.org

CALIFORNIA

California—State
Agencies and Organizations

United States Senators

Honorable Dianne Feinstein (D)
331 Hart Senate Office Building
Washington, DC 20510
(202) 224-3841
(202) 228-3954 (Fax)
E-mail Web Form: http://feinstein
    .senate.gov/email.html
Web: http://feinstein.senate.gov

Honorable Barbara Boxer (D)
112 Hart Senate Office Building
Washington, DC 20510
(202) 224-3553
(202) 228-0026 (Fax)
Web: http://boxer.senate.gov

United States Representatives

To find the contact information for your
representative in the House of the U.S.
Congress, visit the House's Web site at: www.
house.gov, or call (202) 225-3121; (202) 225-1904
(TTY).

Governor

Honorable Jerry Brown
State Capitol Building, Suite 1173
Sacramento, CA 95814
(916) 445-2841
(916) 445-4633 (Fax)
E-mail: governor@governor.ca.gov
Web: www.governor.ca.gov/state/govsite/
    gov_homepage.jsp

Official State Web Site
Web: www.state.ca.us/state/portal/
    myca_homepage.jsp

State Department of Education: Special Education

Mary Hudler, Director
Special Education Division
Department of Education
1430 N Street, 2nd Floor
Sacramento, CA 95814
(916) 445-4602
E-mail: mhudler@cde.ca.gov
Web: www.cde.ca.gov/sp/se/

State Coordinator for NCLB (No Child Left Behind)

Tom Torlakson
State Superintendent of Public Instruction
California Department of Education
1430 N Street
Sacramento, CA 95814
(916) 319-0582
E-mail Web Form: http://www.tomtorlakson.
    com/contact
Web: http://www.cde.ca.gov/nclb/

Georgianne Knight, Consultant
Special Education Division
California Department of Education
1430 N Street
Sacramento, CA 95814
(916) 327-0844
E-mail: gknight@cde.ca.gov
Web: www.cde.ca.gov/

Programs for Infants and Toddlers With Disabilities: Birth–2 Years

Azadeh Fares, Part C Coordinator
Children and Family Services Branch
Department of Developmental Services
1600 9th Street, Room 330, MS 3-8
Sacramento, CA 95814
(916) 654-3681; (800) 515-2229
E-mail: azadeh.fares@dds.ca.gov
Web: http://www.dds.ca.gov/EarlyStart/
    Home.cfm

Programs for Children With Disabilities: 3–5 Years

Meredith Cathcart, 619 Coordinator,
    Administrator
Special Education Division
1430 N. Street, Suite 2401
Sacramento, CA 95814
(916) 327-3702
E-mail: mcathcart@cde.ca.gov
Web: http://www.cde.ca.gov/sp/se/fp/
    ecseries.asp

State Vocational Rehabilitation Agency

Catherine Campisi, Director
Department of Rehabilitation
2000 Evergreen Street
Sacramento, CA 95815-3832
(916) 263-8981; (916) 263-7477 (TTY)
Web: www.dor.ca.gov

Coordinator for Transition Services

Robert Snowden, Consultant
Transition Services and Work Ability
Special Education Division
California Department of Education
1430 N Street, Suite 2401
Sacramento, CA 95814
E-mail: bsnowden@cde.ca.gov

Office of State Coordinator of Vocational Education for Students With Disabilities

Patrick Ainsworth, Director
Secondary, Postsecondary and
    Adult Leadership Division
California Department of Education
1430 N Street, Suite 4503
Sacramento, CA 95814
(916) 445-2652
E-mail: painswor@cde.ca.gov
Web: www.cde.ca.gov/re/di/or/division
    .asp?id=spald

State Mental Health Agency

Stephen W. Mayberg, PhD, Director
Department of Mental Health
1600 9th Street, Room 151
Sacramento, CA 95814
(916) 654-2309; (800) 896-4042 (in CA)
E-mail: dmh@dmhhq.state.ca.us
Web: www.dmh.ca.gov

State Mental Health Representative for Children and Youth

Dave Neilsen, Chief
Children and Family Services
California Department of Mental Health
1600 9th Street, Room 100
Sacramento, CA 95814
(916) 654-2952
E-mail: dneilsen@dmhhq.state.ca.us
Web: www.dmh.cahwnet.gov

State Mental Retardation Program

Clifford Allenby, Director
Department of Developmental Services
Health and Human Services Agency
1600 9th Street, Room 240
Sacramento, CA 95814
(916) 654-1897
E-mail: callenby@dds.ca.gov
Web: www.dds.ca.gov

Councils on Developmental Disabilities

Judy McDonald, Director
State Council on Developmental Disabilities
2000 O Street, Room 100
Sacramento, CA 95814
(916) 322-8481
E-mail: council@scdd.ca.gov
Web: www.scdd.ca.gov

Protection and Advocacy Agency

Catherine Blakemore, Executive Director
Protection and Advocacy, Inc.
100 Howe Avenue, Suite 185N
Sacramento, CA 95825-8219
(916) 488-9950; (800) 776-5746 (In CA)
E-mail: legalmail@pai-ca.org
Web: www.pai-ca.org

Client Assistance Program

Sheila Conlon Mentkowski, Chief
Client Assistance Program
Department of Rehabilitation
2000 Evergreen Street, 2nd Floor
Sacramento, CA 95815
(916) 263-7372; (866) 712-0855 (TTY)
(800) 598-3273 (TTY)
E-mail: smentkow@rehab.cahwnet.gov
Web: www.dor.ca.gov

Programs for Children With Special Health Care Needs

Marian Dalsey, MD, MPH, Interim Chief
State Children's Medical Services Branch
Department of Health Services
P.O. Box 942732
Sacramento, CA 94234-7320
(916) 327-1400
E-mail: mdalsey@dhs.ca.gov
Web: www.dhs.ca.gov/pcfh/cms/ccs/

State CHIP Program (health care for low-income, uninsured children)

Healthy Families Program
P.O. Box 138005
Sacramento, CA 95813-8005
(800) 880-5305 (in CA)
Web: www.healthyfamilies.ca.gov/hf/hfhome.jsp

Programs for Children and Youth Who Are Blind or Visually Impaired

Tom Lee, Chief
State Office of Services to the Blind
California Department of Social Services
744 P Street, MS 6-94
Sacramento, CA 95814
(916) 653-8320
E-mail: BlindAccess@dss.ca.gov
Web: http://www.cdss.ca.gov/cdssweb/PG83.htm

Programs for Children and Youth Who Are Deaf or Hard of Hearing

Lisa Bandaccari, Chief
State Office of Deaf Access
Department of Social Services
744 P Street, MS 6-91
Sacramento, CA 95814
(916) 653-8320; (916) 653-7651 (TTY)
E-mail: deaf.access@dss.ca.gov
Web: http://www.cdss.ca.gov/cdssweb/pg145.htm

Telecommunications Relay Services for Individuals Who Are Deaf, Hard of Hearing, or With Speech Impairments

(800) 735-2922 (V)
(800) 735-2929 (TTY); 711 (TTY)
(800) 854-7784 (Speech to Speech)

Programs for Children and Youth Who Are Deaf-Blind

Cathy Kirschner, MS, Regional Representative
Helen Keller National Center for Deaf-Blind Youth & Adults
6160 Cornerstone Court, East
San Diego, CA 92121
(858) 623-2777; (800) 432-7619 (V/TTY)
(858) 646-0784 (TTY)
E-mail: ckirschner@allient.edu
Web: www.hknc.org

Regional ADA & IT
Technical Assistance Center

Erica C. Jones, Director
Pacific Disability and Business
    Technical Assistance Center
Public Health Institute
555 12th Street, Suite 1030
Oakland, CA 94607-4046
(510) 285-5600 (V/TTY); (800)
    949-4232 (V/TTY)
E-mail: adatech@pdbtac.com
Web: www.pacdbtac.org

University Centers
for Excellence in
Developmental Disabilities

Olivia Raynor, PhD, OTR, Co-Director
Andrew Russell, MD, Co-Director
Tarjan Center for Developmental
    Disabilities at UCLA
University of California, Los Angeles
300 UCLA Medical Plaza, Suite 3302
Los Angeles, CA 90095-6967
(310) 825-0170
E-mail: oraynor@mednet.ucla.edu; arussell@
    mednet.ucla.edu
Web: www.tarjancenter.ucla.edu

Robert A. Jacobs, MD, MPH, Director
University of Southern California
University Center for Excellence in
    Developmental Disabilities
Childrens Hospital Los Angeles
4650 Sunset Boulevard
P. O. Box 54700, MS #53
Los Angeles, CA 90054-0700
(323) 669-2300
E-mail: rjacobs@chla.usc.edu
Web: www.uscuap.org

Technology-Related Assistance

Richard Devylder, Project Coordinator
California Assistive Technology System
Department of Rehabilitation
2000 Evergreen Street
Sacramento, CA 95815
(916) 263-8699 (V/TTY)
E-mail: bschlesi@dor.ca.gov
Web: www.dor.ca.gov

State Mediation System

Karen Johnson, ADR Projects Coordinator
Department of Education
Special Education Division
1430 N Street, 2nd Floor
Sacramento, CA 95814
(916) 323-2196
E-mail: kjohnson@cde.ca.gov
Web: www.cde.ca.gov/sp/se/

Special Format Library

Dr. Henry C. Chang, Librarian
Braille Institute Library Services
741 N. Vermont Avenue
Los Angeles, CA 90029-3594
(323) 663-1111, ext. 500; (800) 808-2555
(323) 660-3880 (TTY)
E-mail: bils@braillelibrary.org
Web: www.braillelibrary.org/

California—Disability-Specific Organizations

Attention Deficit Disorder

To identify an ADD group in California, contact either of the following organizations:

Children and Adults With Attention-Deficit/
    Hyperactivity Disorder (CHADD)
8181 Professional Place, Suite 150
Landover, MD 20785
(301) 306-7070
(800) 233-4050 (Voice mail to request
    information packet)
Web: www.chadd.org

Attention Deficit Disorder Association (ADDA)
P.O. Box 543
Pottstown, PA 19464
(484) 945-2101
Web: www.add.org

Autism

To identify an autism group in California, contact

Autism Society of America
7910 Woodmont Avenue, Suite 300
Bethesda, MD 20814
(301) 657-0881; (800) 3-AUTISM
Web: www.autism-society.org

Blind/Visual Impairments

Gil Johnson, Director
American Foundation for the Blind-West
111 Pine Street, Suite 725
San Francisco, CA 94111
(415) 392-4845
E-mail: sanfran@afb.net
Web: www.afb.org

The Center for the Partially Sighted
LaDonna Ringering, PhD, Director
12301 Wilshire Boulevard, Suite 600
Los Angeles, CA 90025
(310) 458-3501; (800) 481-EYES (3937)
E-mail: info@low-vision.org
Web: www.low-vision.org

Cerebral Palsy

United Cerebral Palsy of Greater Sacramento
191 Lathrop Way, Suite N
Sacramento, CA 95815
(916) 565-7700
E-mail: ucp@ucpsacto.org
Web: www.ucpsacto.org

Down Syndrome

Down Syndrome Association of San Diego
Joyce Clark, Program Coordinator
c/o The Exceptional Family Resource Center
9245 Sky Park Court, Suite 130
San Diego, CA 92123
(619) 276-4494
E-mail: jclark@projects.sdsu.edu

Epilepsy

Epilepsy Foundation of San Diego County
Kathy D. West, Executive Director
2055 El Cajon Boulevard
San Diego, CA 92104
(619) 296-0161
E-mail: info@epilepsysandiego.org
Web: www.epilepsysandiego.org

Epilepsy Foundation of Los Angeles, Orange,
    Ventura & San Bernardino Counties
Susan Pietsch-Escueta, Executive Director
5777 W. Century Boulevard
Los Angeles, CA 90045
(310) 670-2870; (800) 564-0445
E-mail: sos@epilepsy-socalif.org
Web: http://www.epilepsy.com/los-angeles

Epilepsy Foundation of Northern California
John Kitto, Executive Director
1624 Franklin Street, Suite 900
Oakland, CA 94612
(510) 893-6272; (800) 632-3532
E-mail: efnca@epilepsynorcal.org
Web: www.epilepsynorcal.org

Learning Disabilities

Learning Disabilities Association of California
Wendy Terry, Executive Secretary
6060 Sunrise Vista Drive, Suite 1550
Citrus Heights, CA 95610
(916) 725-7881; (866) 532-6322
Web: www.LDACA.org

Mental Health
Associations in California

Mental Health
Rusty Selix, Executive Director
1127 11th Street, Suite 925
Sacramento, CA 95814
(916) 557-1167
E-mail: rselix@mhac.org
Web: www.mhac.org

United Advocates for Children of California
Jennifer Clancy, Executive Director
1401 El Camino Avenue, Suite 340
Sacramento, CA 95815-2700
(916) 643-1530; (866) 643-1530
E-mail: information@uacc4families.org
Web: www.uacc4families.org

NAMI California
Grace McAndrews, Executive Director
1111 Howe Avenue, Suite 475
Sacramento, CA 95825
(916) 567-0163
E-mail: Nami@namicalifornia.org
Web: www.NAMICalifornia.org

Mental Retardation

The Arc of California
Tony Anderson, Executive Director
1225 Eighth Street, Suite 210
Sacramento, CA 95814
(916) 552-6619
E-mail: tanderson@arccalifornia.org
Web: www.arccalifornia.org

Speech and Hearing

California Speech-Language-Hearing Association
   (CSHA)
Robert Powell, JD (representing speech-
   language pathologists)
825 University Avenue
Sacramento, CA 95825-6724
(916) 921-1568
E-mail: CSHA@CSHA.org
Web: www.CSHA.org

Spina Bifida

Spina Bifida Association of Greater San Diego
P.O. Box 232272
San Diego, CA 92193-2272
(619) 491-9018
E-mail: sbaofgsd@hotmail.com

California—Organizations Especially for Parents

Parent Training and Information Center (PTI)

Susan Henderson, Director
Disability Rights Education and
   Defense Fund, Inc. (DREDF)
2212 6th Street
Berkeley, CA 94710
(510) 644-2555; (800) 348-4232
E-mail: dredf@dredf.org
Web: www.dredf.org

Exceptional Parents Unlimited
Bobbie Coulbourne, Program Coordinator
4440 N. 1st Street
Fresno, CA 93726
(559) 229-2000
E-mail: bcoulbourne
   @exceptionalparents.org
Web: www.exceptionalparents.org

MATRIX, A Parent Network and Resource Center
Nora Thompson, Executive Director
94 Galli Drive, Suite C
Novato, CA 94949
(415) 884-3535; (800) 578-2592
E-mail: info@matrixparents.org
Web: www.matrixparents.org

Parents Helping Parents of Santa Clara
Mary Ellen Peterson, Chief Executive Officer
3041 Olcott Street
Santa Clara, CA 95054-3222
(408) 727-5775; (408) 748-8339 (TTY)
E-mail: info@php.com
Web: www.php.com

Rowell Family Empowerment of Northern California
Kat Lowrance, Executive Director
1244-B Hartnell Avenue
Redding, CA 96002
(530) 226-5129; (888) 263-1311
E-mail: sklowrance@aol.com
E-mail: sea@sea-center.org
Web: www.rfenc.org

Support for Families of Children With Disabilities
Juno Duenas, Executive Director
2601 Mission Street, Suite 606
San Francisco, CA 94110-3111
(415) 282-7494
E-mail: info@supportforfamilies.org
Web: www.supportforfamilies.org

Team of Advocates for Special Kids (TASK)
Marta Anchondo, Executive Director
Brenda Smith, Deputy Director
100 W. Cerritos Avenue
Anaheim, CA 92805
(714) 533-8275; (866) 828-8275
E-mail: taskca@yahoo.com
Web: www.taskca.org

Team of Advocates for Special Kids
   (TASK), San Diego
Brenda Smith, Director
4550 Kearny Villa Road, Suite 102
San Diego, CA 92123
(858) 874-2386; (858) 874-2387
E-mail: taskd1@yahoo.com
Web: www.taskca.org

Community Parent Resource Center
(serving San Diego and Imperial County)
Sherry Torok, Executive Director
Exceptional Family Resource Center
9245 Sky Park Court, Suite 130
San Diego, CA 92123
(619) 594-7416; (800) 281-8252
Web: www.efronline.org/

Loving Your Disabled Child (LYDC)
(serving most of LA County)
Theresa Cooper, Executive Director
4528 Crenshaw Boulevard
Los Angeles, CA 90043
(323) 299-2925
E-mail: info@lydc.org
Web: www.lydc.org

Parents of Watts
(serving Watts County)
Alice Harris, Executive Director
10828 Lou Dillon Avenue
Los Angeles, CA 90059
(323) 566-7556
E-mail: egertonf@hotmail.com

Sickle Cell Community Health Network
Diana Lee, Director
Oakland PEACE CPRC
1515 Webster
Oakland, CA 94612
(877) 726-2372

Vietnamese Parents of Disabled Children
    Association, Inc.
(serving Orange and Los Angeles County)
Hung Nguyen, President
7526 Syracuse Avenue
Stanton, CA 90680
(310) 370-6704
E-mail: vpdca@aol.com
Web: http://vpdca.org/

Parent Teacher Association (PTA)
Carla Niño, President
California State PTA
930 Georgia Street
P.O. Box 15015
Los Angeles, CA 90015
(213) 620-1100
E-mail: info@capta.org
Web: www.capta.org

California—Other Disability Organizations

California Association of School Psychologists
Suzanne Fisher, Executive Director
1400 K Street, Suite 311
Sacramento, CA 95814
(916) 444-1595
E-mail: memberservices@casponline.org
Web: www.casponline.org

Easter Seals Bay Area
Michael Pelfini, President and CEO
180 Grand Avenue, Suite 300
Oakland, CA 94612
(510) 835-2131, ext. 126
E-mail: mpelfini@esba.org
Web: www.eastersealsbayarea.org

Family Resource Network
(serving Amador, Calaveras, San Joaquin,
    Stanislaus, & Tuolumne Counties)
Ann Cirimele, Executive Director
5250 Claremont Avenue, Suite 239
Stockton, CA 95207
(209) 472-3674; (800) 847-3030
    (in the 5-county region)
E-mail: frnfamilies@aol.com

VSA Arts of California
Leah Goodwin, President
3770 E. Willow Street
Long Beach, CA 90815
(714) 607-8867
E-mail: leahbgood@yahoo.com

Independent Living

For information on the Statewide Independent Living Council (SILC) in California, contact

Independent Living Research
    Utilization Project
The Institute for Rehabilitation
    and Research
2323 South Sheppard, Suite 1000
Houston, TX 77019
(713) 520-0232 (V); (713)
    520-5136 (TTY)
E-mail: ilru@ilru.org
Web: www.ilru.org

For information on centers for independent living (CILs) in California, contact

National Council on Independent Living
1916 Wilson Boulevard, Suite 209
Arlington, VA 22201
(703) 525-3406; (703) 525-4153 (TTY)
E-mail: ncil@ncil.org
Web: www.ncil.org

COLORADO

Colorado—State Agencies and Organizations

United States Senators

Honorable Michael F. Bennet (D)
458 Russell Senate Office Building
Washington, DC 20510
(202) 224-5852
(202) 224-6471 (Fax)
Web: http://www.bennet.senate.gov/contact/

Honorable Mark Udall (D)
730 Hart Senate Office Building
Washington, DC 20510
(202) 224-5941
(202) 228-4609 (Fax)
Web: http://www.markudall.senate.
gov/?p=contact

United States Representatives

To find the contact information for your representative in the House of the U.S. Congress, visit the House's Web site at: www.house.gov, or call (202) 225-3121; (202) 225-1904 (TTY).

Governor

Honorable John W. Hickenlooper
136 State Capitol
Denver, CO 80203-1792
(303) 866-2471
Web: http://www.colorado.gov/cs/Satellite/
GovHickenlooper/CBON/1251592968310

Official State Web Site

Web: www.colorado.gov/

State Department of Education: Special Education

Exceptional Student Services Unit
Colorado Department of Education
201 E. Colfax Avenue
Denver, CO 80203
(303) 866-6694
Web: www.cde.state.co.us

State Coordinator for NCLB (No Child Left Behind)

Trish Boland
Colorado Department of Education
201 E. Colfax Avenue
Denver, CO 80203
(303) 866-6998
Web: http://www.cde.state.co.us/
FedPrograms/ti/parents.asp

Programs for Infants and Toddlers With Disabilities: Birth–2 Years

Ardith Ferguson, Part C Coordinator
CDHS Office of Early Childhood
Division of Community and Family Support
1575 Sherman Street
Denver, CO 80203
(303)866-5468
E-mail: ardith.ferguson@state.co.us
Web: http://www.eicolorado.org

Programs for Children With Disabilities: 3–5 Years

Penny Dell, 619 Coordinator
Exceptional Student Services Unit
1560 Broadway, Suite 1175
Denver, CO 80203
(303) 866-6720
E-mail: dell_p@cde.state.co.us
Web: http://www.cde.state.co.us/early/
PreschoolSpecialED.htm

State Vocational Rehabilitation Agency

Diana Huerta, Director
Division of Vocational Rehabilitation
Department of Human Services
1575 Sherman, 4th Floor
Denver, CO 80203
(303) 866-4150
E-mail: diana.huerta@state.co.us

Susan Schierkolk, Youth Programs Coordinator
Division of Vocational Rehabilitation
Administration Office
Department of Human Services
1575 Sherman, 4th Floor
Denver, CO 80203
(303) 866-4756
E-mail: susan.schierkolk@state.co.us

Coordinator for Transition Services
Barbara Palmer, Consultant
Transition Services
Colorado Department of Education
201 E. Colfax Avenue
Denver, CO 80203
(303) 866-6721
E-mail: palmer_b@cde.state.co.us

**Office of State Coordinator
of Vocational Education
for Students With Disabilities**

Susie Bell, Director
Access to Employment Project
Colorado Community College System
9101 E. Lowry Boulevard
Denver, CO 80230-6011
(303) 595-1611
E-mail: susie.bell@cccs.edu

State Mental Health Agency

Thomas J. Barrett, PhD, Director
Mental Health Services
Colorado Department of Human Services
3824 W. Princeton Circle
Denver, CO 80236
(303) 866-7400
E-mail: tom.barrett@state.co.us
Web: www.cdhs.state.co.us

**State Mental
Health Representative
for Children and Youth**

Claudia Zundel, Unit Manager
Division of Mental Health Services
Department of Human Services
3824 W. Princeton Circle
Denver, CO 80236
(303) 866-7400
E-mail: claudia.zundel@state.co.us

**State Developmental Disabilities
Program for Children and Youth**

Sheila Peil, Program Manager
Division for Developmental Disabilities
3824 W. Princeton Circle
Denver, CO 80236
(303) 866-7467
E-mail: sheila.peil@state.co.us
Web: www.cdhs.state.co.us/ohr/dds/
    dds_center.html

State Developmental Disabilities Program

Fred L. DeCrescentis, Director
Developmental Disabilities Services
3824 W. Princeton Circle
Denver, CO 80236
(303) 866-7450
Web: www.state.co.us/

Councils on Developmental Disabilities

Marcia Tewell, Executive Director
Colorado Developmental Disabilities Council
    (CDDC)
3401 Quebec, Suite 6009
Denver, CO 80207
(720) 941-0176
E-mail: cddpc.email@state.co.us
Web: www.cdhs.state.co.us/opi/cddpc/
    index.htm

Protection and Advocacy Agency

Mary Anne Harvey, Executive Director
The Legal Center for People With Disabilities
    and Older People
455 Sherman Street, Suite 130
Denver, CO 80203
(303) 722-0300; (800) 288-1376 (in CO only)
E-mail: tlcmail@thelegalcenter.org
Web: www.thelegalcenter.org

Client Assistance Program

Contact Protection and Advocacy Agency
Geoffrey Peterson, Coordinator

**Programs for Children With Special
Health Care Needs**

Kathy Watters, Director
Health Care Program For Children With
    Special Needs (HCP)
Department of Public Health and Environment
4300 Cherry Creek Drive South
Denver, CO 80246-1530
(303) 692-2370; (800) 688-7777
E-mail: kathy.watters@state.co.us
Web: www.cdphe.state.co.us

**State CHIP Program (health care
for low-income, uninsured children)**

Child Health Plan Plus
P.O. Box 929
Denver, Colorado 80201-0929
(800) 359-1991
Web: www.cchp.org/

Programs for Children and Youth Who Are Blind or Visually Impaired or Deaf-Blind

Tanni Anthony, Consultant
Colorado Department of Education
201 E. Colfax Avenue
Denver, CO 80203
(303) 866-6681
E-mail: Anthony_T@cde.state.co.us
Web: www.cde.state.co.us

Programs for Children and Youth Who Are Deaf or Hard of Hearing

Cheryl Johnson, Consultant
Colorado Department of Education
201 E. Colfax Avenue
Denver, CO 80203
(303) 866-6960
E-mail: Johnson_C@cde.state.co.us
Web: www.cde.state.co.us

Telecommunications Relay Services for Individuals Who Are Deaf, Hard of Hearing, or With Speech Impairments

(800) 659-3656 (V)
(800) 659-2656 (TTY); 711 (TTY)
(877) 659-4279 (Speech to Speech)

Regional ADA & IT Technical Assistance Center

Patrick Going, Director
Rocky Mountain Disability and Business
   Technical Assistance Center
3630 Sinton Road, Suite 103
Colorado Springs, CO 80907
(719) 444-0268 (V/TTY); (800) 949-4232 (V/
   TTY)
E-mail: rmdbtac@mtc-inc.com
Web: www.adainformation.org

University Center for Excellence in Developmental Disabilities

Cordelia Robinson, Director
JFK Partners
University of Colorado Health Sciences Center
4200 E. 9th Avenue, Suite C-221
Denver, CO 80262
(303) 864-5266
Web: www.jfkpartners.org

Technology-Related Assistance

University of Colorado Health Sciences Center
Cathy Bodine, Project Director
Assistive Technology Partners
Department of Rehabilitation Medicine
1245 E. Colfax Avenue, Suite 200
Denver, CO 80218
(303) 315-1280; (303) 837-8964 (TTY)
(800) 255-3477 (in CO only)
Web: www.uchsc.edu/atp

State Mediation System

Charles Masner, Consultant
Colorado Department of Education
Exceptional Student Services
201 E. Colfax Avenue, Room 300
Denver, CO 80203
(303) 866-6685
E-mail: masner_c@cde.state.co.us
Web: www.cde.state.co.us

Special Format Library

Barbara Goral, Librarian
Colorado Talking Book Library
180 Sheridan Boulevard
Denver, CO 80226-8097
(303) 727-9277; (800) 685-2136
E-mail: ctbl.info@cde.state.co.us
Web: www.cde.state.co.us/ctbl

Colorado—Disability-Specific Organizations

Attention Deficit Disorder

To identify an ADD group in Colorado, contact either of the following organizations:

Children and Adults With Attention-Deficit/
   Hyperactivity Disorder (CHADD)
8181 Professional Place, Suite 150
Landover, MD 20785
(301) 306-7070
(800) 233-4050 (Voice mail to request information packet)
Web: www.chadd.org

Attention Deficit Disorder Association (ADDA)
P.O. Box 543
Pottstown, PA 19464
(484) 945-2101
Web: www.add.org

Autism

Elizabeth Lehman, Executive Director
Autism Society of Colorado
701 S. Logan, Suite 103
Denver, CO 80209
(720) 214-0794
E-mail: asc@autismcolorado.org
Web: www.autismcolorado.org

Blind/Visual Impairments

American Foundation for
    the Blind–Southwest
Judy Scott, Director
11030 Ables Lane
Dallas, TX 75229
(214) 352-7222
E-mail: dallas@afb.net
Web: www.afb.org

Brain Injury

Brain Injury Association of Colorado
Helen Kellogg, Executive Director
4200 W. Conejos Place, Suite 524
Denver, CO 80204
(303) 355-9969; (800)
    955-2443 (in CO only)
E-mail: biacolo@aol.com
Web: www.biacolorado.org

Cerebral Palsy

Cerebral Palsy of Colorado, Inc.
Judith I. Ham, President/CEO
2200 S. Jasmine Street
Denver, CO 80222-5708
(303) 691-9339
E-mail: jham@cpco.org
Web: www.cpco.org

Down Syndrome

Mile High Down Syndrome
    Association, Inc.
Linda K. Barth, Executive Director
1899 Gaylord Street
Denver, CO 80206
(303) 797-1699
E-mail: mhdsa@aol.com
Web: www.mhdsa.org

Epilepsy

Epilepsy Foundation of Colorado, Inc.
Veronica Valdez, Interim Executive Director
234 Columbine Street, Suite 333
Denver, CO 80206-4711
(303) 377-9774; (888) 378-9779 (in CO)
E-mail: efco@msn.com
Web: www.epilepsycolorado.org

Learning Disabilities

Learning Disabilities Association of Colorado
Nina Healy, President
4400 E. Iliff Avenue
Denver, CO 80222-0621
(303) 894-0992
E-mail: info@ldacolorado.com
Web: www.ldacolorado.com

Mental Health

Mental Health Association of Colorado
Jeanne Rohner, Executive Director
6795 E. Tennessee Avenue, Suite 425
Denver, CO 80224
(303) 377-3040
E-mail: mentalhealth@mhacolorado.org
Web: www.mhacolorado.org

NAMI Colorado
David Salsbury, President
1100 Fillmore Street
Denver, CO 80206-3334
(303) 321-3104
E-mail: NAMI-CO@nami.org

Colorado Federation of
Families for Children's Mental Health
Ann L. Schrader, Executive Director
P.O. Box 9086
Englewood, CO 80111
(303) 572-0302; (888) 569-7500
E-mail: a_schrader@coloradofederation.org
Web: www.coloradofederation.org

EMPOWER Colorado
Christiana Humphrey, Director
2200 S. Jasmine Street
Denver, CO 80222-5708
(303) 691-9339
E-mail: policy@cpco.org
Web: http://empowercolorado.org/

Mental Retardation

The Arc of Colorado
Bill Baesman, Executive Director
8000 E. Prentice Avenue, Suite D-1
Greenwood Village, CO 80111
(303) 864-9334; (800) 333-7690
E-mail: bbaesman@thearcofco.org
Web: www.thearcofco.org

Special Health Care Needs

Family Voices
Lorri Park and Christy Blakely, Co-Directors
c/o CP of Colorado
2200 S. Jasmine Street
Denver, CO 80222-5708
(800) 881-8272
E-mail: policy@cpco.org
Web: www.cpco.org; www.FamilyVoices.org

Speech and Hearing

Colorado Speech-Language-Hearing Association
Polly Somers
P.O. Box 345
Sedalia, CO 80135
(720) 733-9097
E-mail: cshassoc@aol.com
Web: www.cshassoc.org

Spina Bifida

Colorado Spina Bifida Association
P.O. Box 22994
Denver, CO 80222
(303) 797-7870
Web: www.coloradospinabifida.org

Colorado—Organizations Especially for Parents

Parent Training and Information Center (PTI)

Barbara Buswell, Executive Director
PEAK Parent Center, Inc.
611 N. Weber, Suite 200
Colorado Springs, CO 80903
(719) 531-9400; (800) 284-0251
E-mail: info@peakparent.org
Web: www.peakparent.org

Parent-To-Parent

Dianne McNamara, Coordinator
Parent to Parent of Colorado
c/o CP of Colorado
2200 S. Jasmine Street
Denver, CO 80222-5708
(877) 472-7201
E-mail: mail@p2p-co.org
Web: www.p2p-co.org

Community Parent Resource Center (serving the City and County of Denver, including Denver Public Schools)

Barbara Buswell, Executive Director
The Denver Outreach Project
1177 Grant Street, Suite 104
Denver, CO 80203
(303) 864-1900; (800) 284-0251
E-mail: bbuswell@peakparent.org
Web: www.peakparent.org

Parent Teacher Association (PTA)

Colorado PTA
Mark Townsend, President
7859 W. 38th Avenue
Wheat Ridge, CO 80033
(303) 420-7820; (888) 225-8234
E-mail: office@copta.org
Web: www.copta.org

Colorado—Other Disability Organizations

Easter Seals Colorado
Lynn Robinson, President
5755 W. Alameda Avenue
Lakewood, CO 80226
(303) 233-1666 (V/TTY); (800) 875-4732
E-mail: hansonn@cess.org
Web: www.eastersealscolorado.org

Rocky Mountain Stroke Association
Esther Fretz, Executive Director
5666 S. Bannock Street
Littleton, CO 80120
(303) 730-8800; (877) 630-7444
E-mail: rmstroke@aol.com
Web: www.strokecolorado.org

VSA Arts Colorado
Damon McLeese, Executive Director
2256 Larimer Street
Denver, CO 80205
(303) 777-0797; (303) 777-0798 (TTY)
E-mail: co@vsarts.org
Web: http://co.vsarts.org

Independent Living

For information on the Statewide Independent Living Council (SILC) in Colorado, contact

Independent Living Research Utilization Project
The Institute for Rehabilitation and Research
2323 South Sheppard, Suite 1000
Houston, TX 77019
(713) 520-0232 (V); (713) 520-5136 (TTY)
E-mail: ilru@ilru.org
Web: www.ilru.org

For information on centers for independent living (CILs) in Colorado, contact

National Council on Independent Living
1916 Wilson Boulevard, Suite 209
Arlington, VA 22201
(703) 525-3406; (703) 525-4153 (TTY)
E-mail: ncil@ncil.org
Web: www.ncil.org

CONNECTICUT

Connecticut—State Agencies and Organizations

United States Senators

Honorable Richard Blumenthal (D)
724 Hart Senate Office Building
Washington, DC 20510
(202) 224-2823
Web: https://www.blumenthal.senate.gov/ contact/

Honorable Christopher Murphy (D)
303 Hart Senate Office Building
Washington, DC 20510
(202) 224-4041; (800) 225-5605 (in CT)
(202) 224-9750 (Fax)
Web: http://www.murphy.senate.gov/contact

United States Representatives

To find the contact information for your representative in the House of the U.S. Congress, visit the House's Web site at: www.house.gov, or call (202) 225-3121; (202) 225-1904 (TTY).

Governor

Honorable Dannel P. Malloy
Executive Office of the Governor
State Capitol
210 Capitol Avenue
Hartford, CT 06106
(860) 566-4840
E-mail: http://www.governor.ct.gov/malloy/ cwp/view.asp?a=3998&q=479082
Web: http://www.governor.ct.gov/malloy/ site/default.asp

Official State Web Site

Web: www.ct.gov/

State Department of Education: Special Education

Dr. Nancy Cappello, Interim Chief
Bureau of Special Education
Department of Education
165 Capitol Avenue, Room 361
Hartford, CT 06106
(860) 713-6912
E-mail: nancy.cappello@ct.gov
Web: www.sde.ct.gov/sde/cwp/view. asp?a=2678&Q=320730

Connecticut was granted an extended waiver from the NCLB program.

State Coordinator for NCLB (No Child Left Behind)

Stefan Pryor, Commissioner
Department of Education
165 Capitol Avenue
Hartford, CT 06106
(860) 713-6500
Web: http://www.sde.ct.gov/sde/site/default. asp

Programs for Infants and Toddlers With Disabilities: Birth–3 Years

Lily Johnson, Birth–3 Part C Coordinator
State Birth to Three System
Department of Developmental Services

460 Capitol Avenue
Hartford, CT 06106-1308
(860) 418-6141
E-mail: lynn.s.johnson@ct.gov
Web: www.birth23.org

Programs for Children With Disabilities: 3–5 Years

Maria Synodi, 3-5 Coordinator,
    State Preschool Program
Bureau of Early Childhood, Career
    and Adult Education
Connecticut Department of Education
165 Capitol Avenue
Hartford, CT 06106
(860) 713-6941
E-mail: maria.synodi@ct.gov
Web: http://www.sde.ct.gov/sde/cwp/view.
    asp?a=2626&q=320750

State Vocational Rehabilitation Program

Brenda L. Moore, Director
Bureau of Rehabilitation Services
Department of Social Services
25 Sigourney Street
Hartford, CT 06106
(860) 424-4848
E-mail: brenda.moore@po.state.ct.us
Web: www.brs.state.ct.us

Coordinator for Transition Services

Karen Halliday, Education Consultant
Bureau of Special Education
Department of Education
165 Capitol Avenue
Hartford, CT 06145-2219
(860) 713-6923
E-mail: karen.halliday@po.state.ct.us

State Adult Mental Health Agency

Thomas A. Kirk, Jr., Commissioner
Department of Mental Health
    and Addiction Services
410 Capitol Avenue
P.O. Box 341431
Hartford, CT 06134
(860) 418-7000; (800) 446-7348
Web: www.dmhas.state.ct.us

State Mental Health Representative for Children

Karen Andersson, PhD, Director of Mental
    Health
Department of Children and Families
505 Hudson Street
Hartford, CT 06106
(860) 550-6683; (800) 842-2288 (in CT)
E-mail: karen.andersson@po.state.ct.us
Web: www.state.ct.us/dcf

State Mental Retardation Program

Peter O'Meara, Commissioner
Department of Mental Retardation
460 Capitol Avenue
Hartford, CT 06106
(860) 418-6000
E-mail: dmrct.co@po.state.ct.us
Web: www.dmr.state.ct.us

Council on Developmental Disabilities

Edward T. Preneta, Director
Connecticut Council on Developmental
    Disabilities
460 Capitol Avenue
Hartford, CT 06106-1308
(860) 418-6160; (800) 653-1154 (in CT)
(860) 418-6172 (TTY)
E-mail: ed.preneta@po.state.ct.us
Web: www.state.ct.us/ctcdd

Protection and Advocacy Agency

James McGaughey, Executive Director
Office of Protection and Advocacy for
    Persons With Disabilities
60 B Weston Street
Hartford, CT 06120-1551
(860) 297-4300; (800) 842-7303 (V/TTY in CT)
(860) 297-4380 (TTY)
E-mail: OPA-Information@po.state.ct.us
Web: www.state.ct.us/opapd/

Client Assistance Program

Susan Werboff, Director
Client Assistance Program
Contact Protection and Advocacy
    Agency listed earlier

**Programs for Children With
Special Health Care Needs**

*Martha Okafor, Director
Family Health Division
Bureau of Community Health
Connecticut Department
    of Public Health
410 Capital Avenue, MS #11 MAT
P.O. Box 340308
Hartford, CT 06134-0308
(860) 509-8066
E-mail: Martha.Okafor@po.state.ct.us
Web: www.dph.state.ct.us*

*Easter Seals Camp Hemlocks
Sunny Ku, Director of Camping and
    Respite Services
85 Jones Street
P.O. Box 198
Hebron, CT 06248-0198
(860) 228-9496; (860) 228-2091 (TTY)
E-mail: Sku@eastersealsct.org
Web: www.ct.easter-seals.org*

**State CHIP Program (health care
for low-income, uninsured children)**

*HUSKY Plan
c/o Department of Social Services
25 Sigourney Street
Hartford, CT 06106-5033
(877) 284-8759; (800) 842-4524 (TTY)
E-mail: webmaster@huskyhealth.com
Web: www.huskyhealth.com/*

**Programs for Children and Youth
Who Are Deaf or Hard of Hearing**

*Stacie Mawson, Executive Director
Connecticut Commission on the Deaf
    and Hearing Impaired
67 Prospect Avenue
Hartford, CT 06106
(860) 231-8756 (V/TTY); (800) 708-6796 (in CT)
(860) 231-8169 (TTY)
E-mail: cdhi@po.state.ct.us
Web: www.state.ct.us/cdhi/index.htm*

**Telecommunications Relay Services
for Individuals Who Are Deaf, Hard
of Hearing, or With Speech Impairments**

(800) 833-8134 (V)

*(800) 942-9710 (TTY); 711 (TTY)
(877) 842-5177 (Speech to Speech)*

**Programs for Children and Youth Who
Are Blind or Visually Impaired or Deaf-Blind**

*Connecticut Board of Education and
    Services for the Blind
Brian Sigmund, Executive Director
184 Windsor Avenue
Windsor, CT 06095
(860) 602-4000; (800) 842-4510
E-mail: BESB@po.state.ct.us
Web: www.besb.state.ct.us*

Regional ADA & IT Technical Assistance Center

*New England ADA and Accessible IT Center
Valerie Fletcher, Executive Director
Oce Harrison, Project Director
Adaptive Environments Center, Inc.
374 Congress Street, Suite 301
Boston, MA 02210
(617) 695-0085 (V/TTY); (800) 949-4232 (V/TTY)
E-mail: adainfo@newenglandada.org
Web: www.newenglandada.org*

**University Center for Excellence in
Developmental Disabilities**

*A. J. Pappanikou Center for
    Developmental Disabilities
Mary Beth Bruder, PhD, Director
University of Connecticut
263 Farmington Avenue, MC6222
Farmington, CT 06030-6222
(860) 679-1500; (860) 679-1502 (TTY)
(866) 623-1315
E-mail: bruder@ns01.uchc.edu
Web: www.uconnucedd.org*

Technology-Related Assistance

*Connecticut Tech Act Project
John M. Ficarro, PhD, Project Director
Department of Social Services
Bureau of Rehabilitation Services
25 Sigourney Street, 11th Floor
Hartford, CT 06106
(860) 424-4881; (800) 537-2549
(860) 424-4839 (TTY)
E-mail: DrJohnF@aol.com
Web: www.techactproject.com/*

State Mediation System

Thomas Badway, Education Consultant
Connecticut Department of Education
Bureau of Special Education
    and Pupil Services
Due Process Unit
165 Capitol Avenue
Hartford, CT 06106-1630
(860) 807-2017
E-mail: tom.badway@po.state.ct.us

Special Format Library

Library for the Blind and Physically Handicapped
Connecticut State Library
Carol A. Taylor, Librarian
198 West Street
Rocky Hill, CT 06067
(860) 566-2151; (800) 842-4516
E-mail: lbph@cslib.org
Web: www.cslib.org/lbph.htm

Connecticut—Disability-Specific Organizations

Attention Deficit Disorder

    To identify an ADD group in Connecticut, contact either of the following organizations:

Children and Adults With Attention-Deficit/
    Hyperactivity Disorder (CHADD)
8181 Professional Place, Suite 150
Landover, MD 20785
(301) 306-7070
(800) 233-4050 (Voice mail to request
    information packet)
Web: www.chadd.org

Attention Deficit Disorder Association (ADDA)
P.O. Box 543
Pottstown, PA 19464
(484) 945-2101
Web: www.add.org

Autism

    To identify an autism group in Connecticut, contact

Autism Society of America
7910 Woodmont Avenue, Suite 300
Bethesda, MD 20814
(301) 657-0881; (800) 3-AUTISM
Web: www.autism-society.org

Blind/Visual Impairments

American Foundation for the Blind
Regina Genwright, Director of
    Information Center
11 Penn Plaza, Suite 300
New York, NY 10001
(212) 502-7600; (212) 502-7662 (TTY)
E-mail: afbinfo@afb.net
Web: www.afb.org

Brain Injury

Brain Injury Association of Connecticut
Julie Peters, Executive Director
1800 Silas Deane Highway, Suite 224
Rocky Hill, CT 06067
(860) 721-8111; (800) 278-8242 (in CT)
E-mail: biacgeneral@biact.org
Web: www.biact.org

Cerebral Palsy

St. Vincents Special Needs Services
Barry Buxbaum, President/CEO
Trumbull Corporate Park
95 Merritt Boulevard
Trumbull, CT 06611
(203) 375-6400
E-mail: feroleto.child.dev@snet.net
Web: www.stvincentsspecialneeds.org

UCP of Eastern Connecticut
Margaret Morrison, Executive Director
42 Norwich Road
Quaker Hill, CT 06375
(860) 447-3889

Epilepsy

Epilepsy Foundation of Connecticut, Inc.
Linda Wallace, Executive Director
386 Main Street
Middletown, CT 06457
(860) 346-1924; (800) 899-3745
E-mail: efct@uol.com
Web: www.epilepsyct.net

Learning Disabilities

Learning Disabilities Association of Connecticut
    (LDA-CT)
999 Asylum Avenue, 5th Floor
Hartford, CT 06105
(860) 560-1711
E-mail: ldact@ldact.org
Web: www.ldact.org

*The Connecticut Association for Children and
    Adults With Learning Disabilities (CACLD)*
Beryl Kaufman, Executive Director
25 Van Zant Street, Suite 15-5
East Norwalk, CT 06855-1719
(203) 838-5010
E-mail: cacld@optonline.net
Web: www.cacld.org

Mental Health

Mental Health Association of Connecticut
Beverly Walton, President and CEO
20-30 Beaver Road, Suite 108
Wethersfield, CT 06109
(860) 529-1970
E-mail: MNTLHLTH@tiac.net
Web: www.mhact.org

NAMI Connecticut
Debra Anderson, Executive Director
30 Jordan Lane, 3rd Floor
Wethersfield, CT 06109
(860) 882-0236; (800) 215-3021
E-mail: namicted@aol.com
Web: www.namict.org

Mental Retardation

The Arc of Connecticut
Margaret Dignoti, Executive Director
1030 New Britain Avenue, Suite 102B
West Hartford, CT 06110
(860) 953-8335
E-mail: arcct@aol.com
Web: http://www.thearcct.org/

*FORConn (Friends of Retarded Citizens
    of Connecticut)*
Robert Wood, President
35 Robinwood Road
Trumbull, CT 06611-4923
(203) 375-1796
E-mail: bob.wood@snet.net
Web: www.forconn.org

Speech and Hearing

*Connecticut Speech-Language-
    Hearing Association*
Vernice Jury, President
213 Back Lane
Newington, CT 06111-4204
(860) 666-6900
E-mail: csha.assoc@snet.net
Web: www.ctspeechhearing.org

Spina Bifida

Spina Bifida Association of Connecticut
Kiley Carlson, President
P.O. Box 2545
Hartford, CT 06146-2545
(800) 574-6274
E-mail: sbac@sbac.org
Web: www.SBAC.org

Connecticut—Organizations Especially for Parents

Parent Training and Information Center (PTI)

Connecticut Parent Advocacy Center (CPAC)
Nancy Prescott, Director
338 Main Street
Niantic, CT 06357
(860) 739-3089; (800) 445-2722 (in CT)
E-mail: cpac@cpacinc.org
Web: www.cpacinc.org

Parent-to-Parent

*PATH Parent to Parent CT
    (Parents Available to Help)*
Nanfi Lubogo, Co-Director
Carmina Cirioli, Co-Director
P.O. Box 117
Northford, CT 06472
(203) 234-9554; (800) 399-7284 (in CT)
E-mail: path03@aol.com

**WeCAHR (Western Connecticut
    Association for Human Rights)**
Pat Tomka, Coordinator
211 Main Street
Danbury, CT 06810
(203) 792-3540
E-mail: advozealot@aol.com
Web: www.wecahr.org

Parent Teacher Association (PTA)

Connecticut Parent-Teachers Association
Kevin Daly, President
Wilbur Cross Commons Building, Suite 12
60 Connolly Parkway
Hamden, CT 06514-2519
(203) 281-6617
E-mail: connecticut.pta@snet.net
Web: www.ctpta.org

Connecticut—Other Disability Organizations

Easter Seals Connecticut
John R. Quinn, President
85 Jones Street
P.O. Box 100
Hebron, CT 06248-0100
(860) 228-9438; (800) 874-7687
E-mail: jquinn@eastersealsofct.org
Web: www.ct.easterseals.com

The Center for Children With Special
* Health Care Needs*
Dr. Leonard Banco, Director
Connecticut Children's Medical Center
282 Washington Street
Hartford, CT 06106
(860) 545-9230; (877) 743-5516 (in CT)
Web: www.ccmckids.org

Arts for All Connecticut
Jane F. Archer, Executive Director
26 Wintonbury Avenue
Bloomfield, CT 06002
(860) 243-9910
E-mail: Artsforallct@msn.com

Independent Living

For information on the Statewide Independent Living Council (SILC) in Connecticut, contact

Independent Living Research Utilization Project
The Institute for Rehabilitation and Research
2323 South Sheppard, Suite 1000
Houston, TX 77019
(713) 520-0232 (V); (713) 520-5136 (TTY)
E-mail: ilru@ilru.org
Web: www.ilru.org

For information on centers for independent living (CILs) in Connecticut, contact

National Council on Independent Living
1916 Wilson Boulevard, Suite 209
Arlington, VA 22201
(703) 525-3406; (703) 525-4153 (TTY)
E-mail: ncil@ncil.org
Web: www.ncil.org

DELAWARE

Delaware—State Agencies and Organizations

United States Senators
Honorable Thomas Carper (D)
513 Hart Senate Office Building
Washington, DC 20510
(202) 224-2441
E-mail Web Form: http://carper.senate.gov/
* email-form.html*
Web: http://carper.senate.gov

Honorable Christopher Coons (D)
127A Russell Senate Office Building
Washington, DC 20510
(202) 224-5042
(202) 224-0139 (Fax)
E-mail: senator@biden.senate.gov
Web: http://biden.senate.gov

United States Representatives

To find the contact information for your representative in the House of the U.S. Congress, visit the House's Web site at: www.house.gov, or call: (202) 225-3121; (202) 225-1904 (TTY).

Governor

Honorable Jack Markell
150 Martin Luther King Jr. Blvd. South
2nd Floor
Dover, DE 19901
(302) 744-4101 (Dover)
(302) 577-3210 (Wilmington)
E-mail Web Form: http://smu.governor.
* delaware.gov/cgi-bin/mail.php?contact*

Official State Web Site

Web: www.de.gov/

State Department of Education: Special Education

Martha Toomey, Director
Exceptional Children and Early Childhood
* Group*
401 Federal Street, Suite 2
Dover, DE 19901-3639
(302) 739-5471
E-mail: mtoomey@doe.k12.de.us
Web: http://www.doe.k12.de.us/infosuites/
* students_family/specialed/default.shtml*

State Coordinator for NCLB (No Child Left Behind)

Susan K. Haberstroh, Associate Secretary
    Education Supports & Innovative Practices
    Branch
Department of Education
The Townsend Building
401 Federal Street, Suite 2
Dover, DE 19901-3639
(302) 735-4159
Email: susan.haberstroh@doe.k12.de.us
Web: http://dedoe.schoolwires.net/site/
    default.aspx?PageID=1

Delaware was granted an extended waiver
from the NCLB program.

Programs for Infants and Toddlers With Disabilities: Birth–2 Years

Susan Campbell, Interim Part C
    Co-Coordinator
Carol Ann Schumann, Interim Part C
    Co-Coordinator
Birth to Three Early Intervention System
Herman M. Holloway, Sr. Campus
Main Administration Building
1901 N. DuPont Highway
New Castle, DE 19720
(302) 255-9137; (302) 255-9136
E-mail: susan.campbell@state.de.us, carolann.
    schumann@state.de.us
Web: http://www.dhss.delaware.gov/dhss/
    dms/epqc/birth3/directry.html

Programs for Children With Disabilities: 3–5 Years

Verna Thompson, 619 Coordinator
Education Specialist, Early Childhood
    Education
Delaware Department of Education
Townsend Building
401 Federal Street, Suite 2
Dover, DE 19901-1402
(302) 735-4295
E-mail: verna.thompson@doe.k12.de.us
Web: http://www.doe.k12.de.us/infosuites/
    students_family/earlychildhood/default.
    shtml

State Division of Vocational Rehabilitation

Andrea S. Guest, Director
Delaware Division of Vocational
    Rehabilitation

4425 N. Market Street
P. O. Box 9969
Wilmington, DE 19809-0969
(302) 761-8275; (302) 761-8336 (TTY)
E-mail: aguest@dvr.state.de.us
Web: www.state.de.us

Coordinator for Transition Services

Mark Chamberlin, Education Associate
Delaware Department of Public Instruction
Secondary Transition
401 Federal Street Suite 2, Townsend Building
P.O. Box 1402
Dover, DE 19903-1402
(302) 739-4667
E-mail: mchamberlin@doe.k12.de.us
Web: www.doe.state.de.us/

Office of State Coordinator of Vocational Education for Students With Disabilities

Adam W. Fisher, PhD, Education Associate
Part B IDEA Funds
Exceptional Children and
    Early Childhood Group
Department of Education
P. O. Box 1402
Dover, DE 19903-1402
(302) 739-4667
E-mail: adfisher@doe.k12.de.us
Web: www.doe.state.de.us/Exceptional_Child/
    ececehome.htm

State Mental Health Agency

Renata J. Henry, Director
Division of Substance Abuse and
    Mental Health
Department of Health and Social Services
Main Administration Building
1901 N. DuPont Highway
New Castle, DE 19720
(302) 255-9398
E-mail: rehenry@state.de.us

State Mental Health Representative for Children

Susan Cycyk, Director
Division of Child Mental Health Services
Department of Services for Children, Youth,
    and Their Families
1825 Faulkland Road
Wilmington, DE 19805-1195

(302) 633-2600
Web: www.state.de.us/kids/cmhs.htm

State Developmental Disabilities Program

Marianne Smith, Director
Division of Developmental Disabilities Services
Delaware Health and Social Services
1056 S. Governors Avenue
Dover, DE 19904
(302) 744-9600
E-mail: dhssinfo@state.de.us
Web: www.state.de.us/dhss/ddds/index.html

Council on Developmental Disabilities

Patricia L. Maichle, Director
Delaware Developmental Disabilities Council
Margaret M. O'Neill Building, 2nd Floor
410 Federal Street, Suite 2
Dover, DE 19904
(302) 739-3333
E-mail: pmaichle@state.de.us
Web: www.state.de.us/ddc

Protection and Advocacy Agency

Brian Hartman, Program Director
Disabilities Law Program
Community Service Building
100 W. 10th Street, Suite 801
Wilmington, DE 19801
(302) 575-0660; (302) 575-0696 (TTY)
(800) 292-7980 (in DE)
Web: www.declasi.org

Client Assistance Program

Melissa Shahan, Director
Client Assistance Program,
    United Cerebral Palsy, Inc.
254 E. Camden-Wyoming Avenue
Camden, DE 19934
(302) 698-9336; (302) 698-9336
E-mail: capucp@magpage.com

Programs for Children With Special Health Care Needs

Dennis L. Rubino, MSW, MPH, Director
CSHCN
Division of Public Health
P.O. Box 637, Jesse Cooper Building
Dover, DE 19903
(302) 744-4553; (800) 464-4357 (Helpline)
E-mail: Dennis.Rubino@state.de.us

State CHIP Program (health care for low-income, uninsured children)

Delaware Healthy Children Program
P.O. Box 950
New Castle, DE 19720-9914
(800) 996-9969
Web: www.state.de.us/dhss/dss/

Programs for Children and Youth Who Are Blind or Visually Impaired

Harry B. Hill, Director
Division for the Visually Impaired
Health and Social Services
1901 N. Dupont Highway, Biggs Building
New Castle, DE 19720
(302) 255-9800
E-mail: Harry.Hill@state.de.us

Programs for Children and Youth Who Are Deaf or Hard of Hearing

Lorretta Sarro, Coordinator
Delaware Office for the Deaf and
    Hard of Hearing
Division of Vocational Rehabilitation
4425 N. Market Street, 3rd Floor
Wilmington, DE 19809
(302) 761-8275 (V/TTY);
    (302) 761-8336 (TTY)
E-mail: LSarro@dvr.state.de.us
Web: www.state.de.us

Telecommunications Relay Services for Individuals Who Are Deaf, Hard of Hearing, or With Speech Impairments

(800) 232-5470 (V)
(800) 232-5460 (TTY); 711 (TTY)
(800) 229-5746 (Speech to Speech–English)
(866) 260-9470 (Speech to Speech–Spanish)

Programs for Children and Youth Who Are Deaf-Blind

Peggy Lashbrook, Coordinator
Delaware Program for
    Deaf-blind Children
620 E. Chestnut Hill Road
Newark, DE 19713
(302) 454-2305

State Education Agency
Rural Representative

Contact State Department of Education: Special Education, listed previously.

**Regional ADA Disability &
Business Technical Assistance Center**

Marian Vessels, Director
ADA and IT Information Center for the
    Mid Atlantic Region
451 Hungerford Drive, Suite 607
Rockville, MD 20850
(301) 217-0124 (V/TTY); (800) 949-4232 (V/
    TTY)
E-mail: adainfo@transcen.org
Web: www.adainfo.org

**Other State Agencies
for Persons With Disabilities**

Kyle Hodges
State Council for Persons With Disabilities
Margaret M. O'Neill Building
P.O. Box 1401
Dover, DE 19903

Wendy Strauss, Executive Director
Governor's Advisory Council for
    Exceptional Citizens (GACEC)
516 W. Loockerman Street
Dover, DE 19904
(302) 739-4553
E-mail: wstrauss@gacec.k12.de.us
Web: http://www.gacec.delaware.gov/

**University Center for Excellence
in Developmental Disabilities**

Michael Gamel-McCormick, Director
University of DE Center for Disabilities Studies
166 Graham Hall
Newark, DE 19716
(302) 831-6974; (302) 831-4689
E-mail: ud-cds@udel.edu
Web: www.udel.edu/cds

Technology-Related Assistance

Beth A. Mineo Mollica, Project Director
Delaware Assistive Technology Initiative
University of DE/Alfred I. duPont Hospital
    for Children
P.O. Box 269
1600 Rockland Road, Room 200
Wilmington, DE 19899
(302) 651-6790; (302) 651-6794 (TTY)
(800) 870-3284 (in DE)
E-mail: dati@asel.udel.edu
Web: www.dati.org

State Mediation System

Martha Toomey, Coordinator
Exceptional Children and Early Childhood Group
Department of Education
P.O. Box 1402
Dover, DE 19903
(302) 739-4667
E-mail: mtoomey@doe.k12.de.us
Web: www.doe.state.de.us

Special Format Library

John Phillos, Librarian
Delaware Division of Libraries
Library for the Blind and Physically Handicapped
43 S. DuPont Highway
Dover, DE 19901
(302) 739-4748; (800) 282-8676 (V/TTY)
E-mail: jphillos@lib.de.us
E-mail: debph@lib.de.us
Web: www.state.lib.de.us

Delaware–Disability-Specific Organizations

Attention Deficit Disorder

    To identify an ADD group in Delaware,
contact

Children and Adults with Attention-Deficit/
    Hyperactivity Disorder (CHADD)
8181 Professional Place, Suite 150
Landover, MD 20785
(301) 306-7070
(800) 233-4050 (Voice mail to request
    information packet)
Web: www.chadd.org

Attention Deficit Disorder Association (ADDA)
P.O. Box 543
Pottstown, PA 19464
(484) 945-2101
Web: www.add.org

Autism

Autism Society of Delaware
Theda M. Ellis, Executive Director
Autism Society of Delaware
5572 Kirkwood Highway
Wilmington, DE 19808
(302) 472-2838
E-mail: theda.ellis@delautism.org
Web: www.delautism.org

Blind/Visual Impairments

American Foundation for the Blind
Regina Genwright, Director of Information Center
11 Penn Plaza, Suite 300
New York, NY 10001
(212) 502-7600; (212) 502-7662 (TTY)
E-mail: afbinfo@afb.net
Web: www.afb.org

Brain Injury

Brain Injury Association of Delaware
Eve Tolley, President
P.O. Box 95
Middletown, DE 19709
(302) 378-3035; (800) 411-0505
Web: http://www.biaofde.org//

Cerebral Palsy

United Cerebral Palsy of Delaware
William J. McCool III, Statewide Executive
   Director
700 A River Road
Wilmington, DE 19809
(302) 764-2400
E-mail: williammccool@ucpde.org

United Cerebral Palsy of Delaware—Kent/Sussex
   County Branch
Carma Carpenter, Director
3249 Midstate Road
Felton, DE 19943
(302) 335-5626

Epilepsy

Epilepsy Foundation of Delaware
Barbara H. Blair, RN, Executive Director
Tower Office Park
240 N. James Street, Suite 208
Newport, DE 19804
(302) 999-9318; (800) 422-3653
E-mail: efd@efd.org
Web: http://www.epilepsy.com/delaware

Mental Health

Mental Health Association in Delaware
James Lafferty, Executive Director
100 W. 10th Street, Suite 600
Wilmington, DE 19801
(302) 654-6833; (800) 287-6423 (In DE)
E-mail: information@mhainde.org
Web: www.mhainde.org

NAMI–Delaware
Rita A. Marocco, Executive Director
2400 W. 4th Street
Wilmington, DE 19805
(302) 427-0787
E-mail: NAMIDE@aol.com
Web: www.namide.org

Mental Retardation

The Arc of Delaware
1016 Centre Road, Suite 1
Wilmington, DE 19805-1234
(302) 996-9400
Web: www.arcde.org

Speech and Hearing

Delaware Speech-Language-
   Hearing Association
Kristen M. Palmer, President
P.O. Box 7383
Newark, DE 19711
E-mail: dshaweb@dshaweb.org

Special Health Care Needs

Delaware Family Voices
   (Contact this organization
   for information about special
   care needs in the state of Delaware.)
Beth A. MacDonald, State and
   Regional Coordinator
2340 Alamo, SE, Suite 102
Albuquerque, NM 87106
(505) 872-4774; (888) 835-5669
E-mail: bmacdonfv@juno.com
Web: www.familyvoices.org/

Delaware–Organizations Especially for Parents

Parent Training and Information Center (PTI)

Parent Information Center of Delaware,
   Inc. (PIC)
Marie-Anne Aghazadian,
   Executive Director
5570 Kirkwood Highway
Wilmington, DE 19808
(302) 999-7394
E-mail: picofdel@picofdel.org
Web: www.picofdel.org

Parent-To-Parent

Contact Parent Training and Information Center listed previously.

Partners in Policymaking

Partners in Policymaking of Delaware
Marsha Mills, Coordinator
Developmental Disabilities Council
Margaret M. O'Neill Building, 2nd Floor
410 Federal Street, Suite 2
Dover, DE 19901
(302) 739-7193
Web: www.state.de.us/ddc/policymaking/

Parent-Teacher Association (PTA)

Delaware Congress of Parents and Teachers
Sarah F. Pierce, President
92 S. Gerald Drive
Newark, DE 19713-3299
(302) 737-4646
E-mail: dpta@delawarepta.org
Web: www.delawarepta.org

Delaware—Other Disability Organizations

American Amputee Soccer Association
Richard Hofman, Executive Director
P.O. Box 9315
Wilmington, DE 19809
(302) 683-0997
E-mail: rgh@ampsoccer.org
Web: www.ampsoccer.org

Delawareans with Special Needs: Medicaid
    Managed Care Panel
Gail Launey, Project Coordinator
102 Glade Circle West
Rehoboth Beach, DE 19971
(302) 226-5232
E-mail: gr8fulgail@bwave.com

Easter Seals Delaware and
    Maryland's Eastern Shore
Sandra Tuttle, President/CEO
61 Corporate Circle
New Castle Corporate Commons
New Castle, DE 19720
(302) 324-4444; (800) 677-3800
E-mail: stuttle@nc.esdel.org
Web: www.de.easterseals.com

Interagency Coordinating Council
Beth MacDonald, Chairperson
Birth to Three Early Intervention System
1901 N. Dupont Highway, 2nd Floor
New Castle, DE 19720
(302) 255-9134; (302) 697-1976
E-mail: bmacdonfv@juno.com

MENTOR ABI Group–New Jersey (Contact this
    organization for information about services
    for people with brain injuries in the state of
    Delaware.)
Rehabilitative and Support Services for Persons
    With Acquired Brain Injury
505 S. Lenola Road
Blason Office Plaza II, Suite 217
Moorestown, NJ 08057
(856) 235-5505

The Leukemia & Lymphoma Society–Delaware
    Chapter
Cindi Romanelli, Team In Training Campaign
    Manager
100 W. 10th Street, Suite 209
Wilmington, DE 19801
(302) 661-7300, ext. 25; (800) 220-1617
E-mail: romanellic@de.leukemia-lymphoma.
    org
Web: www.teamintraining.org/de

VSA Arts of Delaware
Jennifer Gunther, Executive Director
Art Center Gallery, Delaware State University
1200 N. Dupont Highway
Dover, DE 19901
(302) 857-6699
E-mail: jgunther@dsc.edu

Independent Living

To find out the contact information for the Statewide Independent Living Council (SILC) in Delaware, contact

Independent Living Research Utilization Project
The Institute for Rehabilitation and Research
2323 South Sheppard, Suite 1000
Houston, TX 77019
(713) 520-0232 (V); (713) 520-5136 (TTY)
E-mail: ilru@ilru.org
Web: www.ilru.org

To find out the contact information for centers for independent living (CILs) in Delaware, contact

National Council on Independent Living
1916 Wilson Boulevard, Suite 209
Arlington, VA 22201
(703) 525-3406; (703) 525-4153 (TTY)
E-mail: ncil@ncil.org
Web: www.ncil.org

DISTRICT OF COLUMBIA

District of Columbia–Agencies and Organizations

United States House of Representatives
Honorable Eleanor Holmes Norton (D)
1424 Longworth House Office Building
Washington, DC 20515
(202) 225-8050
(202) 225-1904 (TTY)

Official State Web Site

Web: www.dc.gov/index.asp

Department of Education: Special Education

Dr. Marla C. Oakes, Executive Director
Office of Special Education
DC Public Schools
825 N. Capitol Street, N.E. 6th Floor
Washington, DC 20002
(202) 442-5468
E-mail: marla.oakes@k12.dc.us
Web: www.k12.dc.us

State Coordinator for NCLB (No Child Left Behind)

Division of Special Education
DC Public Schools
825 N. Capitol Street, NE, 6th Floor
Washington, DC 20002
(202) 442-4800
Web: www.k12.dc.us

　　Washington, D.C. was granted an extended waiver from the NCLB program.

Programs for Infants and Toddlers With Disabilities: Birth–3 Years

DC Early Intervention Program
Jerri Johnston-Stewart, Program Manager
Office of the State Superintendent of Education (OSSE)
Division of Early Learning
810 First Street, NE, 5th Floor
Washington, DC 20002
(202) 727-5853

E-mail: jerri.johnston-stewart@dc.gov
Web: http://osse.dc.gov/service/strong-start-dc-early-intervention-program-dc-eip

DC Vocational Rehabilitation Agency
Elizabeth Parker, Administrator
DC Rehabilitation Services Administration
Department of Human Services
810 First Street, NE, 10th Floor
Washington, DC 20002
(202) 442-8663

Coordinator for Transition Services

Darlene Gripper, Transition Program Coordinator
DC Rehabilitation Services Administration
810 1st Street, NE, 10th Floor
Washington, DC 20002
(202) 442-8469
E-mail: darlene.gripper@dc.gov

Mental Health Agency

Juanita H. Price, CEO
Community Service Agency
Department of Mental Health
1250 U Street, NW
Washington, DC 20009
(202) 671-4010; (202) 698-2525
(202) 442-4202 (intake office)
E-mail: juanita.price@dc.gov

Mental Retardation Program

Dale E. Brown, Administrator
Mental Retardation/Developmental Disabilities Administration
Department of Human Services
429 O Street, NW, Suite 202
Washington, DC 20001
(202) 673-7657; (202) 673-3580 (TTY)
E-mail: dale.brown@dc.gov

Council on Developmental Disabilities

Mary Brown, Executive Director
DC Developmental Disabilities Council
Department of Human Services
64 New York Avenue, NE, Room 6161
Washington, DC 20001
(202) 671-4990
E-mail: mary.brown@dc.gov
Web: www.dc.gov/agencies

Protection and Advocacy Agency

Jane Brown, Executive Director
University Legal Services:
    Protection and Advocacy
220 I Street, NE, Suite 130
Washington, DC 20002
(202) 547-0198; (202) 547-2657 (TTY)
E-mail: jbrown@uls-dc.com
Web: www.dcpanda.org

Client Assistance Program

Joseph Cooney, Program Director
Client Assistance Program
University Legal Services:
    Protection and Advocacy
220 I Street, NE, Suite 130
Washington, DC 20002
(202) 547-0198 (V); (202) 547-2657 (TTY)
Web: www.dcpanda.org

CHIP Program
(health care for low-
income, uninsured children)

DC Healthy Families Insurance Program
4601 N. Fairfax Drive
Arlington, VA 22203
(888) 557-1116
Web: www.dchealth.dc.gov

Programs for Children
and Youth Who Are
Deaf or Hard of Hearing

Ward 5, CWI Unit & One Stop Center
Jo Constance Bond, Supervisor
DC Rehabilitation Services
    Administration
810 1st Street, NE, 9th Floor
Washington, DC 20002
(202) 442-8629

Telecommunications Relay
Services for Individuals Who
Are Deaf, Hard of Hearing,
or With Speech Impairments

(800) 643-3769 (V)
(800) 643-3768 (TTY); 711 (TTY)
(800) 898-0137 (ASCII)
(800) 898-0740 (Speech to Speech)

(800) 546-7111 (Spanish TTY)
(800) 546-5111 (Spanish Voice)

Programs for Children and Youth
Who Are Blind or Visually Impaired

Marilyn Griffin Clark, Supervisor
Visual Impairment Unit
DC Rehabilitation Services Administration
810 1st Street, NE, 9th Floor
Washington, DC 20002
(202) 442-8628

Regional ADA Technical Assistance Agency

Marian Vessels, Director
ADA and IT Information Center for the
    Mid Atlantic Region
451 Hungerford Drive, Suite 607
Rockville, MD 20850
(301) 217-0124 (V/TTY); (800) 949-4232 (TTY)
E-mail: adainfo@transcen.org
Web: www.adainfo.org

University Center for Excellence
in Developmental Disabilities

Phyllis R. Magrab, Director
Georgetown University Child
    Development Center
3307 M Street, NW, Suite 401
Washington, DC 20007
(202) 687-8837
E-mail: magrabp@georgetown.edu
Web: http://gucchd.georgetown.edu/

Mediation System

Bernadette Bullock, Mediation Coordinator
Office of Mediation and Compliance
Division of Special Education
DC Public Schools
825 N. Capitol Street, NE
Washington, DC 20002
(202) 442-5467
E-mail: bernadette.bullock@k12.dc.us
Web: www.k12.dc.us

Special Format Library

Philip Wong-Cross, Librarian
Head Adaptive Services Division
DC Public Library
901 G Street, NW, Room 215
Washington, DC 20001
(202) 727-2270; (202) 727-2142

(202) 727-2145 (TTY)
E-mail: philip.wong-cross@dc.gov
Web: http://dclibrary.org/lbph/

District of Columbia–
Disability-Specific Organizations

Attention Deficit Disorder

To identify an ADD group in the District of Columbia, contact

Children and Adults with Attention-Deficit/
Hyperactivity Disorder (CHADD)
8181 Professional Place, Suite 150
Landover, MD 20785
(301) 306-7070
(800) 233-4050 (Voice mail to request information packet)
Web: www.chadd.org

Attention Deficit Disorder Association (ADDA)
P.O. Box 543
Pottstown, PA 19464
(484) 945-2101
Web: www.add.org

Autism

To identify an autism group in your state, contact

Autism Society of America
7910 Woodmont Avenue, Suite 300
Bethesda, MD 20814
(301) 657-0881; (800) 3-AUTISM
Web: www.autism-society.org

Blind/Visual Impairments

To locate services in DC, contact

American Foundation for the Blind
Regina Genwright, Director
of Information Center
11 Penn Plaza, Suite 300
New York, NY 10001
(212) 502-7600; (212) 502-7662 (TTY)
E-mail: afbinfo@afb.net
Web: www.afb.org

Cerebral Palsy

United Cerebral Palsy of Washington, DC
Theodore Bergeron, Director
3135 8th Street, NE

Washington, DC 20017-1601
(202) 269-1500
E-mail: tbergeron@ucpdc.org
Web: www.ucpa.org

Epilepsy

Epilepsy Foundation of the Chesapeake Region
LeAnn Kingham, Director
300 E. Joppa Road, Suite 1103
Towson, MD 21286
(410) 828-7700; (800) 492-2523
E-mail: lkingham@epilepsy-
foundation.org
Web: http://www.abilitiesnetwork.org/

Mental Health

Child and Family Community Support Services
Amelia Missieledies, Acting Director
Department of Mental Health
Community Support
821 Howard Road, SE, 1st Floor
Washington, DC 20020
(202) 698-1838
E-mail: amelia.missieledies@dc.gov

Mental Health Association of DC
Dona Bowens, Executive Director
1628 16th Street, NW, 4th Floor
Washington, DC 20009
(202) 265-6363
E-mail: dona.bowens@verizon.net
Web: www.mhadc.org

NAMI DC
Joan Bowser, President
422 8th Street, SE
Washington, DC 20003-2832
(202) 546-0646
Web: http://dc.nami.org

Mental Retardation

The Arc of the District of Columbia, Inc.
Marylou Meccariello, Executive Director
817 Varnum Street, NE, Suite 229
Washington, DC 20017
(202) 636-2950
E-mail: mlmeccariello@arcdc.net
Web: www.arcdc.net

Lt. Joseph P. Kennedy Institute
Rebecca Salon, PhD, Director
801 Buchanan Street, NE

Washington, DC 20017
(202) 281-1338
E-mail: rsalon@kennedyinstitute.org
Web: www.kennedyinstitute.org

Speech and Hearing

DC Speech-Hearing Association (DCSHA)
Suzanne Coyle, President
P.O. Box 29590
Washington, DC 20017
(202) 877-1000

Spina Bifida

Spina Bifida Association of the
    National Capital Area
Jill Hill, President
P.O. Box 523415
Springfield, VA 22152-5415
(703) 455-4900

Tourette Syndrome

Tourette Syndrome Association of
    Greater Washington
Lyn Mox, Executive Director
33 University Boulevard, East
Silver Spring, MD 20901
(301) 681-4133
E-mail: TSAGW@aol.com
Web: www.TSAGW.org

District of Columbia—
Organizations Especially for Parents

Parent Training and Information Center (PTI)

Kim Jones, Executive Director
Advocates for Justice and Education, Inc.
2041 Martin Luther King, Jr. Avenue, SE,
    Suite 301
Washington, DC 20020
(202) 678-8060; (888) 327-8060
E-mail: Bethann.James@aje-dc.org
Web: www.AJE-DC.org

Parent-Teacher Association (PTA)

DC Congress of Parents and Teachers
Linda Hilliard Moody, President

Hamilton School
1401 Brentwood Parkway, NE
Washington, DC 20002
(202) 543-0333
E-mail: dc_pres@pta.org

Other Parent Organization

Parents' Special Education Service Center
P.O. Box 10211
Washington, DC 20018-0211
(202) 471-4272
E-mail: parenttips@shs.net

District of Columbia—Other Disability
Organizations

Disability Rights Council of Greater Washington
11 Dupont Circle, NW, Suite 400
Washington, DC 20036
(202) 234-7550; (202) 234-7590 (TTY)
E-mail: info@disabilityrightscouncil.org
Web: www.disabilityrightscouncil.org

Easter Seals
Programs for Infants and Children
Metropolitan DC, Northern
    Virginia, and Maryland
Lisa Reeves, President/CEO
4041 Powder Mill Road, Suite 100
Calverton, MD 20705
(301) 931-8700
E-mail: lreeves@eseal.org
Web: www.nca-md.easterseals.com

The Quality Trust for Individuals
    With Disabilities
Tina Campanella, Executive Director
5335 Wisconsin Avenue, NW, Suite 825
Washington, DC 20015
(202) 448-1450
E-mail: info@dcqualitytrust.org
Web: www.dcqualitytrust.org

WVSA Arts Connection
L. Lawrence Riccio, President/CEO
1100 16th Street, NW
Washington, DC 20036
(202) 296-9100
E-mail: wvsa@wvsarts.org
Web: www.wvsarts.org

Independent Living

To find out the contact information for the Statewide Independent Living Council (SILC) in the District of Columbia, contact

Independent Living Research Utilization Project
The Institute for Rehabilitation and Research
2323 South Sheppard, Suite 1000
Houston, TX 77019
(713) 520-0232 (V); (713) 520-5136 (TTY)
E-mail: ilru@ilru.org
Web: www.ilru.org

Center for Independent Living (CIL)

DC Center for Independent Living
Richard A. Simms
1400 Florida Avenue, NE
Washington, DC 20002
(202) 388-0033

Anacostia Satellite Office
2110 Mississippi Avenue, SE
Washington, DC 20020
(202) 889-5802

FLORIDA

Florida—State Agencies and Organizations

United States Senators

Honorable Bill Nelson (D)
716 Hart Senate Office Building
Washington, DC 20510
(202) 224-5274; (202) 224-5621 (TTY)
(202) 224-2237 (Fax)
E-mail: http://www.billnelson.senate.gov/
    contact-bill
Web: http://www.billnelson.senate.gov/

Honorable Marco Rubio (R)
284 Russell Senate Office Building
Washington, DC 20510
(202) 224-3041
(202) 224-8022 (Fax)
E-mail Web Form: http://www.rubio.senate.
    gov/public/index.cfm/contact
Web: http://www.rubio.senate.gov/public/
    index.cfm/home

United States Representatives

To find the contact information for your representative in the House of the U.S. Congress, visit the House's Web site at: www.house.gov, or call: (202) 224-3121; (202) 225-1904 (TTY).

Governor

Honorable Rick Scott
Executive Office of the Governor
400 S. Monroe Street
The Capitol
Tallahassee, FL 32399-0001
(850) 488-7146
(850) 487-0801 (Fax)
E-mail: http://www.flgov.com/contact-gov-
    scott/email-the-governor/
Web: http://www.flgov.com/

Official State Web Site

Web: www.myflorida.com/

Florida was granted an extended waiver from the NCLB program.

State Coordinator for NCLB (No Child Left Behind)

Monica Verra-Tirado, Bureau Chief
Exceptional Student Education
Florida Department of Education
325 W. Gaines Street, Suite 614
Tallahassee, FL 32399-0400
(850) 245-0475
E-mail: Monica.Verra-Tirado@fldoe.org
Web: http://www.fldoe.org/academics/
    exceptional-student-edu/

Programs for Infants and Toddlers With Disabilities: Birth–2 Years

Children's Medical Services, Department of Health
Penny Geiger, Bureau Chief for Early Steps
2585 Merchants Row Blvd
Tallahassee, FL 32399-1707
(850) 245-4857
E-mail: penny.geiger@flhealth.gov
Web: http://www.floridahealth.gov/
    AlternateSites/CMS-Kids/families/early_
    steps/early_steps.html

Florida Directory of Early Childhood Services
Lou Ann Long, Director
2807 Remington Green Circle
Tallahasse, FL 32308
(850) 487-6301; (800) 654-4440
E-mail: lalong@centraldirectory.org
Web: www.centraldirectory.org

**Programs for Children
With Disabilities: 3–5 Years**

Florida Partnership for School Readiness
Gladys Wilson, Interim Executive Director
600 S. Calhoun Street
Holland Building, Room 251
Tallahassee, FL 32399-0240
(850) 922-4200; (866) 357-3239
E-mail: gladys.wilson@schoolreadiness.org
Web: www.schoolreadiness.org

Florida Directory of Early Childhood Services
Lou Ann Long, Director
2807 Remington Green Circle
Tallahassee, FL 32308
(850) 487-6301; (800) 654-4440
E-mail: lalong@centraldirectory.org
Web: www.centraldirectory.org

State Vocational Rehabilitation Agency

Loretta Costin, Director
Division of Vocational Rehabilitation
Department of Education
2002 Old St. Augustine Road, Building A
Tallahassee, FL 32301-4862
(850) 488-6210; (800) 451-4327
Web: www.rehabworks.org

Coordinator for Transition Services

The Transition Center
University of Florida
P.O. Box 117050
Gainesville, FL 32611-7050
(352)392-0701, Ext. 267
E-mail: transitioncenter@coe.ufl.edu
Web: www.thetransitioncenter.org

**Career and Technical Education
for Students With Disabilities**

Jane Silveria, State Supervisor
Division of Community Colleges &
    Workforce Education
Department of Education, Turlington Building
325 W. Gaines Street, Room 701
Tallahassee, FL 32399-0400
(850) 245-9022
E-mail: Jane.Silveria@fldoe.org
Web: www.myfloridaeducation.com/comm-
    home

State Mental Health Agency

R. Ed Miles, PhD, Director
Mental Health Programs Office
Department of Children and Families
1317 Winewood Boulevard, Building 6
Tallahassee, FL 32399-0700
(850) 488-8304
E-mail: ed_miles@dcf.state.fl.us
Web: www.state.fl.us/cf_web/

**State Mental Health Representative
for Children and Youth**

Sue Ross, Chief
Mental Health Programs Office
Department of Children and Families
1317 Winewood Boulevard, Building 6, Room 290
Tallahassee, FL 32399-0700
(850) 488-8304
E-mail: Sue_Ross@dcf.state.fl.us
Web: http://www.myflfamilies.com/service-
    programs/mental-health

State Developmental Services

Shelly Brantley, Director
Developmental Disabilities Program
Florida Department of Children and Families
1317 Winewood Boulevard, Building 3,
    Room 325
Tallahassee, FL 32399-0700
(850) 488-4257
E-mail: Shelly_Brantley@dcf.state.fl.us
Web: www.myflorida.com

Council on Developmental Disabilities

Florida Developmental Disabilities Council, Inc.
Debra Dowds, Executive Director
124 Marriott Drive, Suite 203
Tallahassee, FL 32301-2981
(850) 488-4180; (800) 580-7801 (in FL)
Web: www.fddc.org

Protection and Advocacy Agency

Advocacy Center for Persons With Disabilities
Hubert Grissom, Interim Executive Director
2671 Executive Center Circle West,
   Suite 100
Tallahassee, FL 32301-5092
(850) 488-9071; (800) 346-4127 (TTY)
(800) 342-0823; (800) 350-4566 (Spanish- and
   Creole-speaking Clients)
E-mail: info@advocacycenter.org
Web: www.AdvocacyCenter.org

Client Assistance Program

Corey Hinds, CAP Program Director, Contact Protection and Advocacy Agency listed previously.

Programs for Children With Special Health Care Needs

Dr. Phyllis Sloyer, Division Director
Children's Medical Services,
   Department of Health
4052 Bald Cypress Way, Bin A-06
Tallahassee, FL 32399-1707
(850) 245-4200; (800) 654-4440
E-mail: phyllis_sloyer@doh.state.fl.us
Web: www.myflorida.com

State CHIP Program
(health care for low-income, uninsured children)

Florida KidCare
Agency for Healthcare Administration
2727 Mahan Drive
Building 3, Mailstop 20
Tallahassee, FL 32308
(888) 540-5437
Web: www.floridakidcare.org

Programs for Children and Youth Who Are Blind or Visually Impaired

Division of Blind Services
David Newton, Program Specialist
Department of Education
1320 Executive Center Drive
Tallahassee, FL 32399
(850) 245-0322; (800) 342-1828 (in FL)
E-mail: david_newton@dbs.doe.state.fl.us
Web: http://dbs.myflorida.com/

Programs for Children and Youth Who Are Deaf or Hard of Hearing

Deaf and Hard of Hearing Services and
   School-to-Work Transition
Cecil Bradley, VR Administrator
Division of Vocational Rehabilitation
Department of Education
2002 Old St. Augustine Road, Building A
Tallahassee, FL 32301-4862
(850) 245-3353; (850) 245-3403 (V)
(850) 245-3413; (850) 245-3404 (TTY)
E-mail: bradlec@vr.doe.state.fl.us
Web: www.rehabworks.org

Telecommunications Relay for People Who Are Deaf, Hard of Hearing, Deaf/Blind, or Speech Impaired

James Forstall, Executive Director
Florida Telecommunications Relay, Inc.
1820 E. Park Avenue, Suite 101
Tallahassee, FL 32301
E-mail: jforstall@ftri.org
Web: www.ftri.org
Questions or comments: (800) 222-3448 (V);
   (888) 447-5620 (TTY)
To use the relay dial 711 or the
   following toll-free numbers:
(800) 955-8771 (TTY)
(800) 955-8770 (Voice)
(800) 955-3771 (ASCII)
(877) 955-8260 (Voice Carry Over–Direct)
(877) 955-5334 (Speech to Speech)
(877) 955-8773 (Spanish)
(877) 955-8707 (French Cr)

State Education Agency
Rural Representative

Iris Palazesi, Supervisor
Exceptional Student Education Program
    Development and Services
Bureau of Instructional Support and
    Community Services
Florida Department of Education
325 W. Gaines, Suite 601
Tallahaseee, FL 32399-0400
(850) 245-0478
E-mail: iris.palazesi@fldoe.org
Web: www.myfloridaeducation.com/comm-
    home

Regional ADA & IT
Technical Assistance Center

Shelley Kaplan, Project Director
Southeast Disability and Business Technical
    Assistance Center
Center for Assistive Technology and
    Environmental Access
Georgia Tech
490 10th Street
Atlanta, GA 30318
(404) 385-0636; (800) 949-4232 (V/TTY)
E-mail: sedbtac@catea.org
Web: www.sedbtac.org

University Center for Excellence
in Developmental Disabilities

Daniel Armstrong, Director
Mailman Center for Child Development
University of Miami School of Medicine
1601 NW 12th Avenue
Miami, FL 33136
(305) 243-6801
E-mail: darmstrong@miami.edu
Web: http://pediatrics.med.miami.edu

Technology-Related Assistance

Florida Alliance for Assistive Service
    and Technology
Jane E. Johnson, Director
325 John Knox Road, Building B
Tallahassee, FL 32303
(850) 487-3278; (888) 788-9216
(850) 922-5951 (TTY)
E-mail: faast@faast.org
Web: http://faast.org/

State Mediation System

ESE Program Administration and
    Quality Assurance
Eileen Amy, Administrator
Bureau of Instructional
    Support and Community
    Services
Florida Department of Education
325 W. Gaines Street, Suite 614
Tallahassee, FL 32399-0400
(850) 245-0476
E-mail: eileen.amy@fldoe.org
Web: www.myfloridaeducation.com/
    commhome

Special Format Library

Florida Bureau of Braille and
    Talking Book Library Services
Michael Gunde, Bureau Chief
420 Platt Street
Daytona Beach, FL 32114-2804
(386) 239-6000; (800) 226-6075
(800) 955-8771 (TTY)
E-mail: mike_gunde@dbs.doe.state.fl.us
Web: http://dbs.myflorida.com/Talking%20
    Books%20Library/index.html

Florida—Disability-Specific Organizations

Attention Deficit Disorder

To identify an ADD group in Florida, contact

Children and Adults with Attention-Deficit/
    Hyperactivity Disorder (CHADD)
8181 Professional Place, Suite 150
Landover, MD 20785
(301) 306-7070
(800) 233-4050 (Voice mail to request
    information packet)
Web: www.chadd.org

Attention Deficit Disorder
    Association (ADDA)
P.O. Box 543
Pottstown, PA 19464
(484) 945-2101
Web: www.add.org

Autism

Autism Society of Florida, Inc.
P.O. Box 970646
Coconut Creek, FL 33097
(954) 349-2820
Web: www.autismfl.com

Autism Recovery Network
Holly Bortfeld, President
80 Chaney Drive
Casselberry, FL 32707
(407) 695-6092
E-mail: maximom@mindspring.com

Center for Autism and Related Disabilities
(CARD) (One of six regional centers for
autism and related disabilities)
University of Florida
P.O. Box 100234
Gainesville, FL 32610
(352) 846-2761; (800) 754-5891
E-mail: card@mbi.ufl.edu
Web: www.card.ufl.edu

To identify the CARD serving your region,
either call the 800 number above, or visit
www.card.ufl.edu/state.html

Blind/Visual Impairments

Frances Mary D'Andrea, Director
American Foundation for the Blind-National
Literacy Center
100 Peachtree Street, Suite 620
Atlanta, GA 30303
(404) 525-2303
E-mail: literacy@afb.net
Web: www.afb.org

Brain Injury

Elynor Kazuk, Executive Director
Brain Injury Association
of Florida (BIAF)
North Broward Medical Center
201 E. Sample Road
Pompano Beach, FL 33064
(954) 786-2400; (800) 992-3442 (in FL)
E-mail: info@biaf.org
Web: www.biaf.org

Cerebral Palsy

United Cerebral Palsy of Florida
Gloria Wetherington, President of the
Board of Directors
1830 Buford Court
Tallahassee, FL 32308
(850) 878-2141

Down Syndrome

Broward Gold Coast Down Syndrome
Organization
Diane DeBraga, Director
10250 NW 53rd Street
Sunrise, FL 33351
(954) 577-4122
E-mail: jmaia@aol.com
Web: www.bgcdownsyndrome.org

Epilepsy

Epilepsy Services Program
Florida Department of Health
Sheryl Mosley, Program Manager
4052 Bald Cypress Way, Bin A-18
Tallahassee, FL 32399-1744
(850) 245-4330
E-mail: sheryl_mosley@doh.state.fl.us
Web: www.floridaepilepsy.org
Web: http://www.floridahealth.gov/diseas-
es-and-conditions/epilepsy/index.html

Learning Disabilities

Learning Disabilities Association of Florida (LDAF)
Cheryl Kron, Executive Secretary
331 E. Henry Street
Punta Gorda, FL 33950
(941) 637-8957
E-mail: ldaf00@sunline.net
Web: www.lda-fl.org

Mental Health

Center for Child and Adolescent Resources
NAMI-Florida
Lynne Hernandez, Executive Director
911 E. Park Avenue
Tallahassee, FL 32301
(850) 671-4445, ext. 23
E-mail: helpline@namifl.org
Web: www.namifl.org

Mental Retardation/ Developmental Disabilities

ARC/Florida
John Hall, Executive Director
2898 Mahan Drive, Suite 1
Tallahassee, FL 32308
(850) 921-0460
E-mail: arcofflorida@comcast.net
Web: www.arcflorida.org

Speech and Hearing

Florida Association of Speech-
Language Pathologists and
Audiologists (FLASHA)
Tina Kautter, Executive Director
P.O. Box 150127
Altamonte Springs, FL 32715-0127
(407) 774-7880; (800) 243-3574
E-mail: tkautter@kmg.com

Spina Bifida

Spina Bifida Association of Florida of
Jacksonville, Inc.
Stephanie King, Executive Director
807 Children's Way
Jacksonville, FL 32207
(904) 390-3686; (800) 722-6355
E-mail: sbaj@sbaj.org
Web: www.sbaj.org

Florida—Organizations Especially for Parents

Parent Training and Information Center (PTI)

Family Network on Disabilities
of Florida, Inc.
Parent Education Network
Jan LaBelle, Executive Director
Nancy Gonsalves, Project Co-Director
Milagros Pou, Project Co-Director
2735 Whitney Road
Clearwater, FL 33760-1610
(727) 523-1130; (800) 825-5736 (In Fl only)
E-mail: pen@fndfl.org
Web: www.fndfl.org/

Parent-To-Parent

Parent to Parent of Florida
Family Network on Disabilities of Florida, Inc.

Diane Heffernan-Joslin, Director
2735 Whitney Road
Clearwater, FL 33760-1610
(727) 523-1130; (800) 825-5736 (In Fl only)
E-mail: Diane@FNDFL.org
Web: http://fndfl.org/

Parent to Parent of Miami, Inc.
Community Parent Resource Center
Isabel Garcia, Executive Director
7990 SW 117th Avenue, Suite 201
Miami, FL 33183
(305) 271-9797; (800) 527-9552
E-mail: info@ptopmiami.org
Web: www.ptopmiami.org

Parent Teacher Association (PTA)

Pat Lancaster, President
Janice Bailey, Executive Director
Florida Congress of Parents
and Teachers, Inc.
1747 Orlando Central Parkway
Orlando, FL 32809-5757
(407) 855-7604
E-mail: janice@floridapta.org
Web: www.floridapta.org

Other Parent Organization

Parent Resource Organization
(for information and training on
early intervention)
Paula Kendig, Coordinator
2921 Inverness Place
Pensacola, FL 32503
(850) 434-8131; (850) 206-7851 (Cell)
E-mail: PKendig@aol.com

Florida—Other Disability Organizations

Easter Seals Florida
Robert Griggs, President
2010 Mizell Avenue
Winterpark, FL 32792
(407) 629-7881
E-mail: info@fl.easterseals.org
Web: www.fl.easterseals.com

Florida Association of Rehabilitation Facilities, Inc.
Terry R. Farmer, President/CEO
2475 Apalachee Parkway, Suite 205
Tallahassee, FL 32301-4946
(850) 877-4816

E-mail: tfarmer@floridaarf.org
Web: www.floridaarf.org

VSA Arts of Florida
Marian Winters, Executive Director
3500 E. Fletcher Avenue, Suite 234
Tampa, FL 33613
(813) 558-5095
E-mail: mwinters@tempest.coedu.usf.edu
Web: www.vsafl.org

Independent Living

To find out the contact information for the Statewide Independent Living Council (SILC) in Florida, contact

Independent Living Research
   Utilization Project
The Institute for Rehabilitation and Research
2323 South Sheppard, Suite 1000
Houston, TX 77019
(713) 520-0232 (V); (713) 520-5136 (TTY)
E-mail: ilru@ilru.org
Web: www.ilru.org

To find out the contact information for centers for independent living (CILs) in Florida, contact

National Council on Independent Living
1916 Wilson Boulevard, Suite 209
Arlington, VA 22201
(703) 525-3406; (703) 525-4153 (TTY)
E-mail: ncil@ncil.org
Web: www.ncil.org

GEORGIA

Georgia—State Agencies and Organizations

United States Senators

Honorable Saxby Chambliss (R)
416 Russell Senate Office Building
Washington, DC 20510
(202) 224-3521
(202) 224-0072 (Fax)
Web: http://www.chambliss.senate.gov/public/index.cfm/home

Honorable Johnny Isakson (R)
131 Russell Senate Office Building
Washington, DC 20510
(202) 224-3643

(202) 228-2090 (Fax)
E-mail Web Form: http://www.isakson.senate.gov/public/index.cfm/email-me
Web: http://www.isakson.senate.gov/public/index.cfm/home

United States Representatives

To find the contact information for your representative in the House of the U.S. Congress, visit the House's Web site at: www.house.gov, or call: (202) 225-3121; (202) 225-1904 (TTY).

Governor

Honorable Nathan Deal
Office of the Governor
206 Washington Street
111 State Capitol
Atlanta, GA 30334
(404) 656-1776
Web: http://gov.georgia.gov/

Official State Web Site

Web: www.georgia.gov

State Department of Education: Special Education

Nancy O'Hara, Associate Director
Division for Exceptional Students
Georgia Department of Education
1870 Twin Towers East
Atlanta, GA 30334-9048
(404) 656-3963
Web: www.gadoe.org

State Coordinator for NCLB (No Child Left Behind)

Georgia was granted an extended waiver from the NCLB program.

Barbara Lunsford, Associate Superintendent
Federal Programs
Georgia Department of Education
205 Jesse Hill Jr. Drive SE
Atlanta, GA 30334
(404) 657-4209
Email: blunsford@doe.k12.ga.us; TitleI@doe.k12.ga.us
Web: http://www.gadoe.org/School-Improvement/Federal-Programs/Pages/default.aspx

Programs for Infants and Toddlers
With Disabilities: Birth–2 Years

Babies Can't Wait Program
Division of Public Health
Department of Human Resources
Cynthia Bryant, Part C Coordinator
2 Peachtree Street, 11.206
Atlanta, GA 30303-3186
(404) 657-2726
E-mail: cynthia.bryant@dph.ga.gov
Web: http://dph.georgia.gov/Babies-Cant-
    Wait

Programs for Children
With Disabilities: 3–5 Years

Young Children Special Education
Division for Exceptional Students
Georgia Department of Education
Jan Stevenson, 619 Coordinator
1870 Twin Towers East
Atlanta, GA 30334-5060
(404) 657-9965
E-mail: jstevenson@doe.k12.ga.us
Web: http://www.gadoe.org/Curriculum-
    Instruction-and-Assessment/Special-
    Education-Services/Pages/default.aspx

State Vocational Rehabilitation Agency

Jan Cribbs, Workforce Development
    Coordinator
Vocational Rehabilitation Program
Georgia Department of Labor
1700 Century Circle, Suite 300
Atlanta, GA 30345-3020
(404) 235-0156
E-mail: jan.cribbs@dol.state.ga.us
Web: www.vocrehabga.org

Coordinator for Transition Services

    Contact Vocational Rehabilitation Agency
listed above.

Office of State Coordinator of Vocational Education for
Students With Disabilities

Danny Fleming, Education Program Manager
Vocational Education Special Needs Unit
Georgia Department of Education
1752 Twin Towers East

Atlanta, GA 30334
(404) 656-3042
E-mail: dfleming@doe.k12.ga.us

State Mental Health Agency

Frank Berry, Commissioner
Department of Behavioral Health and
    Developmental Disabilities
2 Peachtree Street, NW, 24th Floor
Atlanta, GA 30303-3142
(404) 657-2252
Web: http://dbhdd.georgia.gov/

State Mental Health Representative
for Children and Youth

Linda Henderson-Smith, Director
Office of Children, Young Adults and Families
Department of Behavioral Health and
    Developmental Disabilities
2 Peachtree Street, NW
Atlanta, GA 30303-3171
(404) 657-2157
E-mail: linda.henderson-smith@dbhdd.ga.gov
Web: http://dbhdd.georgia.gov/office-
    children-young-adults-and-families-cyf

State Mental Retardation Program

Dr. Terri Timberlake, Director
Office of Adult Mental Health
Department of Behavioral Health and
    Developmental Disabilities
2 Peachtree Street, NW
Atlanta, GA 30303-3142
(404) 463-7149
E-mail: tetimberlake@dbhdd.ga.gov
Web: http://dbhdd.georgia.gov/adult-mental-
    health

Council on Developmental Disabilities

Eric Jacobson, Executive Director
Governor's Council on Developmental
    Disabilities
2 Peachtree Street, NW, 8.210
Atlanta, GA 30303-3142
(404) 657-2126; (888) 275-4233
E-mail: eejacobson@dhr.state.ga.us
Web: www.gcdd.org

Protection and Advocacy Agency

Georgia Advocacy Office, Inc.
Ruby Moore, Executive Director
100 Crescent Centre Parkway, Suite 520
Tucker, GA 30084
(404) 885-1234 (V/TTY); (800) 537-2329
  (in GA only)
E-mail: info@thegao.org
Web: http://www.thegao.org

Client Assistance Program

Georgia Client Assistance Program
123 N. McDonough Street
Decatur, GA 30030
(404) 373-2040 (V/TTY); (800) 822-9727
  (in GA only)
Web: www.vocrehabga.org/lev3j.html

Programs for Children
With Special Health Care Needs

Office of Children With Special Needs
Department of Human Resources
Department of Public Health,
  Family Health Branch
Justine Strickland, Director
2 Peachtree Street, NW, 11.206
Atlanta, GA 30303
(404) 657-2724; (888) 651-8224
Web: www.dhr.state.ga.us

State CHIP Program (health care for
low-income, uninsured children)

PeachCare for Kids
P.O. Box 2583
Atlanta, GA 30301-2583
(877) 427-3224
Web: www.peachcare.org
Web: www.communityhealth.state.ga.us

Programs for Children and Youth
Who Are Deaf or Hard of Hearing

Georgia Council for the Hearing Impaired, Inc.
Jennifer Whitcomb, Executive Director
4151 Memorial Drive, Suite 103-B
Decatur, GA 30032
(404) 292-5312; (800) 541-0710 (V/TTY)
Web: www.gachi.org

Telecommunications Relay Services
for Individuals Who Are Deaf, Hard of
Hearing, or With Speech Impairments

(800) 255-0135 (V)
(800) 255-0056 (TTY); 711 (TTY)
(800) 229-5746 (Speech to Speech–English)
(866) 260-9470 (Speech to Speech–Spanish)

Programs for Children
and Youth Who Are Blind
or Visually Impaired, Deaf
or Hard of Hearing, or Deaf-Blind

Georgia Sensory Assistance Project
Georgia State University
Department of Educational Psychology
  and Special Education (EPSE)
Dr. Cynthia Vail, Project Director
570 Aderhold Hall
University of Georgia
Athens GA, 30602-7153
(706) 542-5348
E-mail: cvail@uga.edu
Web: http://gsap.coe.uga.edu/

State Education Agency
Rural Representative

Marlene Bryar, Interim Director
Division for Exceptional Students
Georgia Department of Education
1870 Twin Towers East
Atlanta, GA 30334-5060
(404) 656-3963
Web: www.doe.k12.ga.us

Regional ADA & IT
Technical Assistance Center

Southeast Disability and Business Technical
  Assistance Center
Center for Assistive Technology and
  Environmental Access
Georgia Tech
Shelley Kaplan, Project Director
490 10th Street
Atlanta, GA 30318
(404) 385-0636; (800) 949-4232 (V/TTY)
E-mail: sedbtac@catea.org
Web: www.sedbtac.org

University Center for Excellence in Developmental Disabilities

Zolinda Stoneman, Director
Institute on Human
    Development and Disability
Center for Excellence in
    Developmental Disabilities Education,
    Research, and Service
The University of Georgia
850 College Station Road
Athens, GA 30602-4806
(706) 542-3457
Web: www.uap.uga.edu

Technology-Related Assistance

Tools for Life, Georgia Assistive
    Technology Project
Vocational Rehabilitation Program
Georgia Department of Labor
Christopher Lee, Project Manager
1700 Century Circle, Suite 300
Atlanta, GA 30345
(404) 638-0384; (800) 497-8665
(404) 486-6333 (TTY); (866) 373-7778 (TTY)
E-mail: info@gatfl.org
Web: www.gatfl.org

State Mediation System

Nancy O'Hara, Coordinator
Division for Exceptional Students
Georgia Department of Education
1870 Twin Towers East
Atlanta, GA 30334-5060
(404) 657-9959
E-mail: nohara@doe.k12.ga.us
Web: www.doe.k12.ga.us

Special Format Library

Georgia Library for Accessible Services
Linda Stetson, Director/Librarian
1150 Murphy Avenue, SW
Atlanta, GA 30310
(404) 756-4619; (800) 248-6701
E-mail: glass@georgialibraries.org
E-mail: lstetson@georgialibraries.org
Web: http://georgialibraries.org

Georgia—Disability-Specific Organizations

Attention Deficit Disorder

Cherokee/Cobb County, North Atlanta &
    Central Georgia CHADD
Kim McIntosh, Coordinator
350 Weatherstone Place
Woodstock, GA 30188
(770) 517-6963
E-mail: NorthAtlantaCHADD@yahoo.com

Attention Deficit Disorder Association
    (ADDA)
P.O. Box 543
Pottstown, PA 19464
(484) 945-2101
Web: www.add.org

Autism

    To identify an autism group in your state, contact

Autism Society of America
7910 Woodmont Avenue, Suite 300
Bethesda, MD 20814
(301) 657-0881; (800) 3-AUTISM
Web: www.autism-society.org

Blind/Visual Impairments

American Foundation for the Blind—National
    Literacy Center
Frances Mary D'Andrea, Director
100 Peachtree Street, Suite 620
Atlanta, GA 30303
(404) 525-2303
E-mail: literacy@afb.net
Web: www.afb.org

Brain Injury

Mary V. Sloan, Executive Director
Brain Injury Resource Foundation
1841 Montreal Road, Suite 220
Tucker, GA 30084
(678) 937-1555; (888) 334-2424
E-mail: info@birf.info
Web: www.birf.info

Cerebral Palsy

United Cerebral Palsy of Georgia, Inc.
Diane Wilush, Executive Director
3300 Northeast Expressway, Building 9
Atlanta, GA 30341
(770) 676-2000
E-mail: dwilush@ucpga.org
Web: www.ucpga.org

Down Syndrome

Down Syndrome Association of Atlanta
Sue Joe, Executive Director
3232 Cobb Parkway, Suite 213
Atlanta, GA 30339
(404) 320-3233
Web: www.down-syndrome-atlanta.org

Epilepsy

Epilepsy Foundation of Georgia
Melanie Birchfield, Executive Director
2625 Cumberland Parkway, Suite 400
Atlanta, GA*30339
(678) 306-1213; (800) 527-7105 (In GA)
E-mail: epilepsyga@mindspring.com
Web: www.epilepsyga.org

Learning Disabilities

Learning Disabilities Association of Georgia
Christopher Lee, Executive Director
130 W. Wieuca Road, Suite 202
Atlanta, GA 30342
(404) 303-7774
E-mail: services@ldag.org
Web: www.ldag.org

Mental Health

National Mental Health Association of Georgia
Judy Fitzgerald, Executive Director
100 Edgewood Avenue, NE, Suite 502
Atlanta, GA 30303
(404) 527-7175
E-mail: judy@nmhag.org
Web: www.nmhag.org

NAMI–Georgia
Patricia Strode, Interim Executive Director
3050 Presidential Parkway, Suite 202
Atlanta, GA 30340
(770) 234-0855; (800) 728-1052
E-mail: pstrode@nami.org
E-mail: NAMI-GA@nami.org
Web: www.nami.org

Mental Retardation

Arc of Georgia
Julia Bowen, Board of Directors/Chair
    Statewide Education Committee
1900 Century Place, Suite 360
Atlanta, GA 30345
(404) 634-5512
E-mail: beammeupbaby@earthlink.net

Speech and Hearing

Georgia Speech-Language-
    Hearing Association
Jody B. Rosen, APR Executive Director
2020 Howell Mill Road, Suite C-295
Athens, GA 30318
(800) 226-4742
E-mail: exdir@gsha.org
Web: www.gsha.org

Special Health Care Needs

Family Voices of Georgia
Julia Bowen, State Coordinator
2460 LeHaven Drive
Tucker, GA 30084
(770) 256-2988
E-mail: beammeupbaby@earthlink.net
Web: www.familyvoices.org

Spina Bifida

Spina Bifida Association of Georgia, Inc.
William E. Turnipseed, President
1448 B McLendon Drive
Decatur, GA 30033
(770) 939-1044
E-mail: sbag@bellsouth.net

Georgia—Organizations Especially for Parents

Parents Educating Parents
and Professionals, Inc.

(PEPP, Inc.)
Linda Shepard, Executive Director
3680 Kings Highway
Douglasville, GA 30135
(770) 577-7771; (800) 322-7065
E-mail: peppinc@peppinc.org
Web: www.peppinc.org

Georgia Parent Support Network
Sue Smith, Executive Director
1381 Metropolitan Parkway
Atlanta, GA 30310
(404) 758-4500; (800) 832-8645
E-mail: gpsn@mindspring.com
Web: www.gpsn.org

Parent-To-Parent

Parent to Parent of Georgia, Inc.
Esther Sherberger, Executive Director
3805 Presidential Parkway, Suite 207
Atlanta, GA 30340
(770) 451-5484; (800) 229-2038
E-mail: info@parenttoparentofga.org
Web: www.parenttoparentofga.org

Parent Teacher Association (PTA)

Georgia Congress of Parents and Teachers, Inc.
Cherie Eastburn, President
114 Baker Street, NE
Atlanta, GA 30308-3366
(404) 659-0214
E-mail: gapta@bellsouth.net
Web: www.georgiapta.org

Georgia—Other Disability Organizations

Easter Seals North Georgia
Donna Davidson, President/CEO
5600 Roswell Road, Prado North, Suite 100
Atlanta, GA 30342
(404) 943-1070
E-mail: ddavidson@easter-seals-northgeorgia.
  org
Web: www.easter-seals-northgeorgia.org

Georgia Child Care Council
Meghan McNail, Statewide Inclusion Coordinator
2987 Clairmont Road, Suite 220
Atlanta, GA 30329-1687
(888) 295-8912
E-mail: mmcnail@bellsouth.net
Web: www.GAchildcare.org

Georgia Children's Network (GCN)
Carol Sadler, President
1105 Rock Pointe Look
Woodstock, GA 30188
(770) 442-8357
E-mail: sadlerpc@prodigy.net
Web: http://groups.yahoo.com/group/
  GA-ChildrensNetwork

The Foundation for Medically Fragile Children
Dorsa C. McGuire, Executive Director
6666 Powers Ferry Road, Suite 328
Atlanta, GA 30339
(770) 951-6111
E-mail: ffmfc@juno.com
Web: www.care4gakids.org

VSA Arts of Georgia
Jay Tribby, PhD, Executive Director
Healey Building
57 Forsyth Street, NW, Suite R1
Atlanta, GA 30303
(404) 221-1270, ext. 207
E-mail: jay.tribby@vsaartsga.org
Web: www.vsaartsga.org

Independent Living

To find out the contact information for the Statewide Independent Living Council (SILC) in Georgia, contact

Independent Living Research Utilization Project
The Institute for Rehabilitation and Research
2323 South Sheppard, Suite 1000
Houston, TX 77019
(713) 520-0232 (V); (713) 520-5136 (TTY)
E-mail: ilru@ilru.org
Web: www.ilru.org

To find out the contact information for centers for independent living (CILs) in Georgia, contact

National Council on Independent Living
1916 Wilson Boulevard, Suite 209
Arlington, VA 22201
(703) 525-3406; (703) 525-4153 (TTY)
E-mail: ncil@ncil.org
Web: www.ncil.org

GUAM

Guam—Government Representatives

U.S. House of Representatives

Honorable Madeline Bordallo
427 Cannon House Office Building
Washington, DC 20515
(202) 225-1188
Web: www.house.gov/bordallo

Governor

Honorable Eddie Baza Calvo
Executive Chamber
PO Box 2950
Hagatña, GU 96932
(671) 472-8931

Official State Web Site

Web: http://ns.gov.gu/government.html

Disability Agencies and Organizations

Department of Education: Special Education
Katrina Celes Pieper,
*   Associate Superintendent*
Division of Special Education
Guam Department of Education
P.O. Box DE
Hagatña, GU 96932
(671) 475-0554/0549; (671) 475-0550 (TTY)
E-mail: kmceles@gdoe.net

Programs for Infants and Toddlers
With Disabilities: Birth–2 Years

Guam Early Intervention Systems
Division of Special Education
Guam Department of Education
Cathy Tydingco, Part C Administrator
P.O. Box DE
Hagatña, GU 96932
(671) 300-5776; (671) 475-0550 (TTY)
E-mail: cbtydingco@gdoe.net
Web: https://sites.google.com/a/gdoe.net/
*   geis/home*

Programs for Children
With Disabilities: 3–5 Years

Pre-School and Elementary School Programs
Division of Special Education
Guam Department of Education
Cathy Tydingco, Preschool Coordinator
P.O. Box DE
Hagatña, GU 96932
(671) 300-1329
E-mail: cbtydingco@gdoe.net

Programs for Children
With Disabilities: 11–21 Years

Secondary School Programs
Division of Special Education
Guam Department of Education
Judy Quenga, Coordinator
P.O. Box DE
Hagatña, Guam 96932
(671) 475-0575/0563
(671) 475-0550 (TTY)
E-mail: jmquenga@doe.edu.gu

Programs for Children With Disabilities: Child Find/Parent
Services–3–21 Years

Division of Special Education
Guam Department of Education
Sue Williams
P.O. Box DE
Hagatña, Guam 96932
(671) 475-0575/0563
(671) 475-0550 (TTY)
E-mail: doesped1@ite.net

Vocational Rehabilitation Agency

Department of Integrated Services for
*   Individuals With Disabilities*
Rosanna S. Ada, Acting Director
1313 Central Avenue
Tiyan, GU 96913
(671) 475-4646/47; (671) 477-9183 (TTY)

Mental Health Agency

Peter Roberto, Acting Director
Department of Mental Health and
*   Substance Abuse*
790 Governor Carlos G. Camacho Road
Tamuning, GU 96911
(671) 647-5330; (671) 647-5303
E-mail: proberto@mail.gov.gu

Mental Health Representative
for Children and Youth

Contact the Mental Health Agency listed above.

Council on Developmental Disabilities

Guam Developmental Disabilities Council
Joseph T. Flores, Acting Executive Director
130 University Drive, Suite 17
Mangilao, GU 96913
(671) 735-9127; (671) 735-9130 (TTY)
E-mail: guamddc@netpci.com

Protection and Advocacy Agency

GLSC Disability Law Center
Daniel S. Somerfleck, Director
113 Bradley Place
Hagatña, GU 96910
(671) 477-9811; (671) 477-3416 (TTY)
E-mail: glsc@netpci.com

Client Assistance Program

Parent Agencies Networking
Edmund Cruz, CAP Coordinator
P.O. Box 23474
GMF, GU 96921
(671) 649-1948 (V/TTY)

Programs for Children With Special Health Care Needs

Department of Public Health
   and Social Services
Government of Guam
Peter John D. Camacho, M.P.H., Acting
   Director
123 Chalan Kareta
Mangilao, GU 96913
(671) 735-7173
E-mail: director@dphss.govguam.net
Web: http://dphss.guam.gov/

Department of Public Health
   and Social Services
Government of Guam
Janice Yatar, Acting Administrator–BFHNS
123 Chalan Kareta
Mangilao, GU 96913
(671) 735-7173
E-mail: jsyatar@dphss.govguam.net
Web: http://dphss.guam.gov/

Office of Coordinator of Vocational Education for Students With Disabilities

JoAnne Ige, Program Director
Jan Milligan, Academic Counselor

Project AIM
Student Support System—Education,
   Disability Services
Guam Community College
GMF, Guam 96921
(671) 735-5584; (671) 734-8324
E-mail: vdeoro@guamcc.edu

Assistive Technology Project

Guam System for Assistive Technology
Mike Terlaje, Project Coordinator
University Center for Excellence—
   Developmental Disabilities
University of Guam, UOG Station
Mangilao, GU 96923
(671) 735-2490/3; (671) 735-2491 (TTY)
E-mail: mterlaje@ite.net

University Center for Excellence in Developmental Disabilities

Heidi San Nicolas, PhD, Director, Guam
   CEDDERS
University of Guam, Office of Academic Affairs
UOG Station
Mangilao, GU 96923
(671) 735-2481; (671) 734-6531 (TTY)
E-mail: heidisan@ite.net

Mediation System

Jonas Dorego, Coordinator
Department of Education
Division of Special Education
P.O. Box DE
Hagatña, GU 96932
(671) 475-0692; (671) 475-0690
(671) 475-0550 (TTY)
E-mail: jdorego@doe.edu.gu

Independent Living

To find out the contact information for the Statewide Independent Living Council (SILC) for Guam, contact

Independent Living Research Utilization Project
The Institute for Rehabilitation
   and Research
2323 South Sheppard, Suite 1000
Houston, TX 77019
(713) 520-0232 (V); (713) 520-5136 (TTY)
E-mail: ilru@ilru.org
Web: www.ilru.org

HAWAII

Hawaii—State Agencies and Organizations

United States Senators

Honorable Mazie K. Hirono (D)
722 Hart Senate Office Building
Washington, DC 20510
(202) 224-6361
(202) 224-6747 (Fax)
E-mail Web Form: http://www.hirono.senate.
    gov/contact
Web: http://www.hirono.senate.gov/

Honorable Brian Schatz (D)
722 Hart Senate Office Building
Washington, DC 20510
(202) 224-3934
(202) 224-2126 (Fax)
E-mail: http://www.schatz.senate.gov/contact
Web: http://www.schatz.senate.gov/

United States Representatives

To find the contact information for your representative in the House of the U.S. Congress, visit the House's Web site at: www.house.gov, or call: (202) 225-3121; (202) 225-1904 (TTY).

Governor

Honorable Neil Abercrombie
Executive Chambers
State Capitol
Honolulu, HI 96813
(808) 586-0034
E-mail: http://governor.hawaii.gov/
    frequently-requested-numbers/#postbottom
Web: http://governor.hawaii.gov/

Official State Web Site

Web: www.hawaii.gov

State Department of Education: Special Education

Dr. Paul Ban, Director
Special Education Services Branch
Hawaii Department of Education
637 18th Avenue, Room C-102
Honolulu, HI 96816
(808) 733-4400
E-mail: paul_ban@notes.k12.hi.us
Web: www.doe.k12.hi.us

State Coordinator for NCLB (No Child Left Behind)

Hawaii was granted a waiver from the NCLB program.

Kathryn Matayoshi, Superintendent
Hawaii Department of Education
1390 Miller Street
Honolulu, HI 96813
(808) 586-3230
Email Web Form: http://www.
    hawaiipublicschools.org/ConnectWithUs/
    ContactUs/Pages/Home.aspx
Web: http://www.hawaiipublicschools.org/
    Pages/home.aspx

Programs for Infants and Toddlers With Disabilities: Birth–2 Years

Stacy Kong, Quality Assurance & Training Unit
    Supervisor
Clayton Takemoto, Social Work Services Unit
    Supervisor
Department of Health
Early Intervention Section
1350 South King Street, Suite 200
Honolulu, HI 96814
(808) 594-0025; (808) 594-0034
E-mail: stacy.kong@doh.hawaii.gov; clayton.
    takemoto@doh.hawaii.gov
Web: http://health.hawaii.gov/eis/

Programs for Children With Disabilities: 3–5 Years

Patricia Dong, 619 Coordinator
Educational Specialist
OCISS, Special Education Section
Building 302, Room 108B
475 22nd Avenue
Honolulu, HI 96816
(808)203-5560
E-mail: patricia_dong@notes.k12.hi.us
Web: http://www.hawaiipublic-
    schools.org/TeachingAndLearning/
    SpecializedPrograms/SpecialEducation/
    Pages/home.aspx

State Vocational Rehabilitation Agency

Neil Shim, Administrator
Division of Vocational Rehabilitation
Department of Human Services
601 Kamokila Boulevard, Room 515
Kapolei, HI 96707
(808) 692-7719
E-mail: nshim@dhs.state.hi.us

Coordinator for Transition Services

Maxine Nagamine, Coordinator for
    Secondary Transition Services
Office of Special Education
Hawaii Department of Education
637 18th Avenue, Room C-102
Honolulu, HI 96816
(808) 733-4832
E-mail: maxine_nagamine@notes.k12.hi.us
Web: http://sssb.k12.hi.us/

Office of State Director for Career and Technical Education

Karla Jones, State Director
Career and Technical Education
University of Hawaii
Lower Campus Road, Lunalilo Portable 1
Honolulu, HI 96822
(808) 956-7461
E-mail: kjones@hawaii.edu
Web: www.hawaii.edu/cte

State Mental Health Agency

Michelle R. Hill, Deputy Director
Behavioral Health Administration
Department of Health
1250 Punchbowl Street
Honolulu, HI 96813
(808) 586-4416
E-mail: mrhill@mail.health.state.hi.us

Adult Mental Health Division

Dr. Thomas W. Hester, MD Chief
1250 Punchbowl Street, Room 256
Honolulu, HI 96813
(808) 586-4770
E-mail: twhester@amhd.health.state.hi.us
Web: www.amhd.org

State Mental Health Representative for Children

Christina Donkervoet, Chief
Child and Adolescent Mental
    Health Division
Department of Health
3627 Kilauea Avenue, Suite 101
Honolulu, HI 96816
(808) 733-9339
E-mail: cmdonker@camhmis.
    health.state.hi.us

State Mental Retardation Program

David Fray, Chief
Developmental Disabilities Division
P. O. Box 3378
Honolulu, HI 96801
(808) 586-5840
E-mail: DFFray@mail.health.state.hi.us

Council on Developmental Disabilities

Waynette Cabral, Executive Administrator
State Council on Developmental
    Disabilities
919 Ala Moana Boulevard, Suite 113
Honolulu, HI 96814
(808) 586-8100
E-mail: wkcabral@mail.health.state.hi.us
Web: www.hiddc.org

Protection and Advocacy Agency

Gary Smith, President
Hawaii Disability Rights Center
900 Fort Street Mall, Suite 1040
Honolulu, HI 96813
(808) 949-2922 (V/TTY); (800)
    882-1057 (V/TTY) (in HI)
E-mail: info@HawaiiDisabilityRights.org
Web: www.HawaiiDisabilityRights.org

Client Assistance Program

Contact Hawaii Disability Rights Center listed above.

**Programs for Children With
Special Health Care Needs**

Children With Special Health Needs Branch
Department of Health
Patricia Heu, Chief
741 Sunset Avenue
Honolulu, HI 96816
(808) 733-9070
(808) 973-9633 Hawaii Keiki Information Service
(800) 235-5477 (HKISS) Neighbor Islands
E-mail: pat.heu@fhsd.health.state.hi.us

**State CHIP Program (health care
for low-income, uninsured children)**

Med-QUEST Division
P.O. Box 3490
Honolulu, HI 96811-3490
(808) 587-3521
Web: www.med-quest.us/

State Agency for People With Disabilities

Disability and Communication Access Board
Francine Wai, Executive Director
919 Ala Moana Boulevard, Room 101
Honolulu, HI 96814-4920
(808) 586-8121 (V/TTY)
E-mail: accesshi@aloha.net
Web: www.state.hi.us/health/dcab/

**Programs for Children and Youth
Who Are Blind or Visually Impaired**

Vocational Rehabilitation for the Blind
David Eveland, Administrator
P.O. Box 339
Honolulu, HI 96809
(808) 586-5311

**Programs for Children and Youth
Who Are Deaf or Hard of Hearing**

Disability and Communication Access Board
Kristine Puguno, Communication Access
    Specialist
919 Ala Moana Boulevard, Room 101
Honolulu, HI 96814-4920
(808) 586-8121 (V/TTY)
E-mail: accesshi@aloha.net
Web: www.hawaii.gov/health/dcab/

**Telecommunications Relay Services
for Individuals Who Are Deaf, Hard of Hearing, or With
Speech Impairments**

(808) 643-8255 (V)
(808) 643-8833 (TTY); 711 (TTY)
(800) 229-5746 (Speech to Speech)

**State Education Agency
Rural Representative**

Thomas Yamashiro, Assistant Superintendent
Office of Information Technology Services
P.O. Box 2360
Honolulu, HI 96804
(808) 586-3218 (V/TTY)
Web: http://doe.k12.hi.us

**Regional ADA & IT
Technical Assistance Center**

Pacific Disability and Business Technical
    Assistance Center
Erica C. Jones, Director
Public Health Institute
555 12th Street, Suite 1030
Oakland, CA 94607-4046
(510) 285-5600 (V/TTY); (800) 949-4232 (V/
    TTY)
E-mail: adatech@pdbtac.com
Web: www.pacdbtac.org

**University Center for Excellence
in Developmental Disabilities**

Center on Disability Studies
University of Hawaii at Manoa
Robert A. Stodden, Director
1776 University Avenue, UA 4-6
Honolulu, HI 96822
(808) 956-5011
Web: www.cds.hawaii.edu/

Technology-Related Assistance

Assistive Technology Resource Centers of Hawaii
Barbara Fischlowitz-Leong, Executive Director
414 Kuwili Street, Suite 104
Honolulu, HI 96817-5050
(808) 532-7110 (V/TTY); (800) 645-3007
E-mail: atrc@atrc.org
Web: www.atrc.org

*Aloha Special Technology Access
    Center, Inc. (Aloha STAC)*
Eric Arveson, Executive Director
710 Green Street
Honolulu, HI 96813
(808) 523-5547

State Mediation System

Hawaii Department of Education
Special Education Section
637 18th Avenue
Honolulu, HI 96816
(808) 733-4836
Web: http://doe.k12.hi.us

Special Format Library

Hawaii State Library
*Library for the Blind and
    Physically Handicapped*
Fusako Miyashiro, Librarian
402 Kapahulu Avenue
Honolulu, HI 96815
(808) 733-8444; (800) 559-4096
(808) 733-8444 (TTY)
E-mail: olbcirc@librarieshawaii.org
*Web: http://hawaii.sdp.sirsi.net/client/
    default/*

Hawaii — Disability-Specific Organizations

Attention Deficit Disorder

    To identify an ADD group in Hawaii,
contact

*Children and Adults with Attention-Deficit/
    Hyperactivity Disorder (CHADD)*
8181 Professional Place, Suite 150
Landover, MD 20785
(301) 306-7070
*(800) 233-4050 (Voice mail to request
    information packet)*
Web: www.chadd.org

*Attention Deficit Disorder
    Association (ADDA)*
P.O. Box 543
Pottstown, PA 19464
(484) 945-2101
Web: www.add.org

Autism

Autism Society of Hawaii
P.O. Box 2995
Honolulu, HI 96802
(808) 944-4774
Web: www.autismhawaii.org

Blind/Visual Impairments

*American Foundation for the Blind—West (informa-
    tion available here for a large region)*
Gil Johnson, Director
111 Pine Street, Suite 725
San Francisco, CA 94111
(415) 392-4845
E-mail: sanfran@afb.org
Web: www.afb.org

Brain Injury

Brain Injury Association of Hawaii
Kisha Skeen, Program Coordinator
2201 Waimano Home Road, Hale E
Pearl City, HI 96782
(808) 454-0699
E-mail: biahi@verizon.net

Cerebral Palsy

United Cerebral Palsy Association of Hawaii
Donna Fouts, Executive Director
414 Kuwili Street, Suite 105
Honolulu, HI 96817
(808) 532-6744
E-mail: ucpa@DiverseAbilities.org
Web: www.ucpahi.org

Deafness/Hard of Hearing

Hawaii Services on Deafness
Ann K. Reimers, Executive Director
1833 Kalakaua Avenue, Suite 905
Honolulu, HI 96815
(808) 946-7300 (V/TTY)
E-mail: reimers@hsod.org
Web: www.hsod.org

Epilepsy

Epilepsy Foundation of Hawaii, Inc.
Kathryn K. Chung, Executive Director
245 N. Kukui Street, Suite 207
Honolulu, HI 96817
(808) 528-3058; (866) 528-3058
E-mail: EFH@HawaiiEpilepsy.com
Web: http://www.epilepsyhawaii.org/

Gallaudet University Regional Center
Sara Simmons, Executive Director
Kapiolani Community College
4303 Diamond Head Road
Honolulu, HI 96816
(808) 734-9210 (V/TTY)
E-mail: sarasimm@hawaii.edu
Web: http://gurc.gallaudet.edu/
    pacific-gurc.html

Learning Disabilities

Learning Disabilities Association of Hawaii
Jennifer Schember-Lang, Executive Director
200 N. Vineyard Boulevard, Suite 310
Honolulu, HI 96817
(808) 536-9684 (V/TTY); (800) 533-9684 (in HI)
E-mail: LDAH@LDAHawaii.org
Web: www.ldahawaii.org

Mental Health

Mental Health Association in Hawaii
Kennith Wilson, Executive Director
200 N. Vineyard Boulevard, Suite 300
Honolulu, HI 96817
(808) 521-1846
E-mail: mha@i-one.com
Web: www.mhahawaii.org

NAMI-OAHU
Marion Poirier, Executive Director
770 Kapiolani Boulevard, Suite 613
Honolulu, HI 96813
(808) 591-1297
E-mail: mpoir14016@aol.com

Hawaii Families as Allies
Sharon R. Nobriga and Vicky M. Followell,
    Co-Executive Directors
Doran Porter, Managing Director
99-209 Moanalua Road, Suite 305
Aiea, HI 96701
(808) 487-8785; (866) 361-8825
E-mail: hfaa.ohana@verizon.net

Mental Retardation

The Arc in Hawaii
3989 Diamond Head Road
Honolulu, HI 96816
(808) 737-7995
E-mail: info@thearcinhawaii.org
Web: www.thearcinhawaii.org

Speech and Hearing

Hawaii Speech-Language-Hearing Association
Marilyn M. Billingsley, President
P.O. Box 235850
Honolulu, HI 96853-3514
(808) 528-4742

Hawaii—Organizations Especially for Parents

Parent Training and Information Center (PTI)

Assisting With Appropriate Rights
    in Education (AWARE)
Jennifer Schember-Lang, Project Director
200 N. Vineyard Boulevard, Suite 310
Honolulu, HI 96817
(808) 536-9684 (V/TTY);
    (808) 536-2280 (V/TTY)
(800) 533-9684 (in HI)
E-mail: LDAH@LDAHawaii.org
Web: www.ldahawaii.org/aware.htm

Partners in Policymaking

Hawaii Council on Developmental Disabilities
Mary Matsukawa, Program Specialist
54 High Street, 3rd Floor
Wailuku, Maui, HI 96793
(808) 984-8218
E-mail: mauimatsu@yahoo.com
Web: www.hiddc.org

Parent-To-Parent

Special Parent Information Network (SPIN)
Susan Rocco, Coordinator
919 Ala Moana Boulevard, Suite 101
Honolulu, Hawaii 96814
(808) 586-8126 (V/TTY)
E-mail: accesshi@aloha.net
Web: http://spinhawaii.org

Parent Teacher Association (PTA)

Hawaii Congress of Parents, Teachers, and Students
Don Hayman, President
1350 S. King Street
Honolulu, HI 96813
(808) 593-2041; (877) 593-2041
E-mail: hi_office@pta.org
Web: www.hawaiiptsa.org

Hawaii—Other Disability Organizations

Easter Seals Hawaii
John Howell, Chief Executive Officer
710 Green Street
Honolulu, HI 96813
(808) 536-1015 (V/TTY)
Web: www.eastersealshawaii.org

Independent Living

To find out the contact information for the Statewide Independent Living Council (SILC) in Hawaii, contact

Independent Living Research Utilization Project
The Institute for Rehabilitation
   and Research
2323 South Sheppard, Suite 1000
Houston, TX 77019
(713) 520-0232 (V); (713) 520-5136 (TTY)
E-mail: ilru@ilru.org
Web: www.ilru.org

To find out the contact information for centers for independent living (CILs) in your state, contact

National Council on Independent Living
1916 Wilson Boulevard, Suite 209
Arlington, VA 22201
(703) 525-3406; (703) 525-4153 (TTY)
E-mail: ncil@ncil.org
Web: www.ncil.org

IDAHO

Idaho—State Agencies and Organizations

United States Senators

Honorable James E. Risch (R)
483 Russell Senate Office Building
Washington, DC 20510
(202) 224-2752
(202) 228-1067 (Fax)
E-mail Web Form: http://www.risch.senate.
   gov/public/index.cfm/email
Web: http://www.risch.senate.gov/public/

Honorable Michael D. Crapo (R)
239 Dirksen Building
Washington, DC 20510

(202) 224-6142
E-mail Web Form: http://crapo.senate.gov
Web: http://crapo.senate.gov

United States Representatives

To find the contact information for your representative in the House of the U.S. Congress, visit the House's Web site at: www.house.gov, or call: (202) 225-3121; (202) 225-1904 (TTY).

Governor

Honorable C. L. "Butch" Otter
Office of the Governor
700 W. Jefferson, 2nd Floor
P.O. Box 83720
Boise, ID 83720-0034
(208) 334-2100
(208) 334-2175 (Fax)
E-mail Web Form: http://gov.idaho.gov/
   ourgov/contact.html
Web: http://gov.idaho.gov/index.html

Official State Web Site

Web: www.state.id.us/

State Department of Education: Special Education

Jana Jones, Chief
Bureau of Special Education
Idaho Department of Education
P.O. Box 83720
Boise, ID 83720-0027
(208) 332-6910
E-mail: jjones@sde.state.id.us
Web: www.sde.state.id.us/specialed

State Coordinator for NCLB (No Child Left Behind)

Idaho was granted an extended waiver from the NCLB program.

Marcia Beckman, Director
ESEA Programs
Idaho Department of Education
650 West State Street
P.O. Box 83720
Boise, Idaho 83720
(208) 332-6953
Email: mmbeckman@sde.idaho.gov
*Web: http://www.sde.idaho.gov/site/title_*
   one/

**Programs for Infants and Toddlers
With Disabilities: Birth–2 Years**

Children's Developmental Services
Family and Community Services
Department of Health and Welfare
Christy Cronheim, Program Manager
P.O. Box 83720
450 W. State Street, 5th Floor
Boise, ID 83720-0036
(208) 334-5590; (800) 926-2588
E-mail: cronheic@dhw.idaho.gov
Web: http://healthandwelfare.idaho.gov/
default.aspx?TabId=78

Programs for Children With Disabilities: 3–5 Years

Shannon Dunstan, 619 Coordinator
State Department of Education
650 West State Street
P.O. Box 83720
Boise, ID 83720-0027
E-mail: sdunstan@sde.idaho.gov
Web: http://www.sde.idaho.gov/site/special_
edu/

State Vocational Rehabilitation Agency

Dr. Michael Graham, Administrator
Division of Vocational Rehabilitation
P.O. Box 83720
Boise, ID 83720-0096
(208) 334-3390 (V/TTY)
Web: http://www.vr.idaho.gov/index.shtml

Coordinator for Transition Services

Jacque Hyatt, Secondary Transition Specialist
Idaho Department of Education
650 W. State Street
P.O. Box 83720
Boise, ID 83720 0027
(208) 332-6951
E-mail: jhyatt@sde.state.id.us
Web: http://www.sde.idaho.gov/site/special_
edu/

State Division of Professional-Technical Education

State Division of Professional
Technical Education
Mike Rush, Administrator
P.O. Box 83720
Boise, ID 83720-0095

(208) 334-3216
E-mail: mrush@pte.state.id.us
Web: www.pte.state.id.us

State Mental Health Agency

Ray Millar, Program Manager
Adult Mental Health Programs
Division of Family and Community
Services
Department of Health and Welfare
P.O. Box 83720, 5th Floor
Boise, ID 83720-0036
(208) 334-6500
E-mail: millarr@idhw.state.id.us
Web: http://healthandwelfare.idaho.
gov/Medical/MentalHealth/
AdultMentalHealth/tabid/195/Default.aspx

**State Mental Health
Representative for Children**

Chuck Halligan, Program Manager
Children's Mental Health
Division of Family and Community Services
Department of Health and Welfare
P.O. Box 83720
Boise, ID 83720-0036
(208) 334-6559
E-mail: halligan@idhw.state.id.us
Web: http://healthandwelfare.idaho.gov/Medical/
MentalHealth/ChildrensMentalHealth/
tabid/314/Default.aspx

State Mental Retardation Program

Mary Jones, Acting Chief
Bureau of Developmental Disabilities
Division of Family and Community Services
Department of Health and Welfare
P.O. Box 83720
Boise, ID 83720-0036
(208) 334-5523
E-mail: jonesm@idhw.state.id.us
Web: www.idahochild.org

Council on Developmental Disabilities

Idaho Council on Developmental Disabilities
Marilyn Sword, Executive Director
802 W. Bannock Street, Suite 308
Boise, ID 83702
(208) 334-2178
E-mail: msword@icdd.state.id.us
Web: www.state.id.us/icdd/

Protection and Advocacy Agency

Comprehensive Advocacy, Inc. (Co-Ad, Inc.)
James Baugh, Executive Director
4477 Emerald Street, Suite B-100
Boise, ID 83706
(208) 336-5353 (V/TTY); (866) 262-3462
E-mail: coadinc@mcleodusa.net
Web: users.moscow.com/co-ad

Client Assistance Program

Contact Protection and Advocacy Agency listed above.

Programs for Children With Special Health Care Needs

Children's Special Health Program
Brett Harrell, Manager
Bureau of Clinical and Preventive Services
Idaho Department of Health and Welfare
P.O. Box 83720
Boise, ID 83720-0036
(208) 334-5962
E-mail: harrellb@idhw.state.id.us

State CHIP Program (health care for low-income, uninsured children)

Idaho CareLine
Idaho Department of Health and Welfare
P.O. Box 83720
Boise, ID 83720-0026
(800) 926-2588
E-mail: careline@idaho.state.id.us
Web: www.idahocareline.org

Programs for Children and Youth Who Are Blind or Visually Impaired

Angela Roan, Administrator
Commission for the Blind and Visually Impaired
341 W. Washington Street
P.O. Box 83720
Boise, ID 83702-0012
(208) 334-3220; (800) 542-8688
E-mail: aroan@icbvi.state.id.us
Web: www.icbvi.state.id.us

Programs for Children and Youth Who Are Deaf or Hard of Hearing

Pennie Cooper, Executive Director
Idaho Council for the Deaf and
*   Hard of Hearing*

1720 Westgate Drive, Suite A
Boise, ID 83704
(208) 334-0879 (V); (208) 334-0803 (TTY)
(800) 433-1323 (Voice—in ID only)
(800) 433-1361 (TTY—in ID only)
E-mail: cooperp@idhw.state.id.us
Web: www.state.id.us/cdhh/

Telecommunications Relay Services for Individuals Who Are Deaf, Hard of Hearing, or With Speech Impairments

(800) 377-1363 (V)
(800) 377-3529 (TTY/ASCII); 711 (TTY)
(888) 791-3004 (Speech to Speech)
(866) 252-0684 (Spanish)

Project for Children and Youth Who Are Deaf-Blind

Idaho Project for Children and Youth
*   with Deaf-Blindness*
Robin G. Greenfield, PhD
Center on Disabilities
*   and Human Development*
University of Idaho, Boise Center
800 Park Boulevard
Boise, ID 83712
(208) 364-4012
E-mail: rgreen@uidaho.edu
Web: www.idahocdhd.org/

State Education Agency Rural Representative

Jana Jones, EdD, Chief
Bureau of Special Education
Idaho Department of Education
P.O. Box 83720
Boise, ID 83720-0027
(208) 332-6910
E-mail: jjones@sde.state.id.us
Web: www.sde.state.id.us/specialed

Regional ADA & IT Technical Assistance Center

Northwest ADA & IT Center
Oregon Health & Science
*   University-CDRC*
Charles E. Davis, Center Coordinator
P.O. Box 574
Portland, OR 97207-0574
(503) 494-4001; (503) 418-0296 (TTY)
(800) 949-4232 (V/TTY)

E-mail: nwada@ohsu.edu
Web: www.nwada.org

University Center for Excellence in Developmental Disabilities

Center on Disabilities and Human Development
University Center on Excellence/
    University of Idaho
Julie Fodor, Director
129 W. Third Street
Moscow, ID 83843
(208) 885-3559
E-mail: jfodor@uidaho.edu
Web: www.idahocdhd.org

Technology-Related Assistance

Idaho Assistive Technology Project
Ron Seiler, Project Director
129 W. Third Street
Moscow, ID 83843
(208) 885-3573; (800) 432-8324 (V/TTY)
E-mail: rseiler@uidaho.edu
Web: www.educ.uidaho.edu/idatech

State Mediation System

Bureau of Special Education
Larry Streeter, Dispute Resolution Coordinator
Idaho Department of Education
650 W. State Street
P.O. Box 83720
Boise, ID 83720-0027
(208) 332-6914
E-mail: lstreete@sde.state.id.us
Web: www.sde.state.id.us/specialed

Special Format Library

Idaho State Talking Book Library
Sue Walker, Librarian
325 W. State Street
Boise, ID 83702
(208) 334-2117; (800) 233-4931
(800) 377-1363 (TTY)
E-mail: tblbooks@isl.state.id.us
Web: www.lili.org/tbl

Idaho—Disability-Specific Organizations

Attention Deficit Disorder

To identify an ADD group in Idaho, contact either of the following organizations:

Children and Adults with Attention-Deficit/
    Hyperactivity Disorder (CHADD)
8181 Professional Place, Suite 150
Landover, MD 20785
(301) 306-7070
(800) 233-4050 (Voice mail to request
    information packet)
Web: www.chadd.org

Attention Deficit Disorder Association (ADDA)
P.O. Box 543
Pottstown, PA 19464
(484) 945-2101
E-mail: mail@add.org
Web: www.add.org

Autism

Autism Society of America/Treasure Valley Chapter
Paul & Richelle Tierney
7842 Rainbow Place
Nampa, ID 83687
E-mail: jrat@netzero.net

Blind/Visual Impairments

American Foundation for the Blind—West
    (information available for a large region)
Gil Johnson, Director
111 Pine Street, Suite 725
San Francisco, CA 94111
(415) 392-4845
E-mail: sanfran@afb.org
Web: www.afb.org

Brain Injury

Brain Injury Association of Idaho
Michelle Featherston, President
Wendy Cary, Executive Director
P.O. Box 414
Boise, ID 83701-0414
(208) 342-0999; (888) 374-3447 (In ID)
E-mail: info@biaid.org
Web: www.biaid.org

Cerebral Palsy

United Cerebral Palsy of Idaho
Kim Kane, Executive Director
5420 W. Franklin Road, Suite A
Boise, ID 83705
(208) 377-8070; (888) 289-3259
E-mail: info@ucpidaho.org
Web: www.ucpidaho.org

Epilepsy

Epilepsy Foundation of Idaho
David C. Blackwell, Executive Director
310 W. Idaho
Boise, ID 83702
(208) 344-4340; (800) 237-6676 (In ID)
E-mail: efid@epilepsyidaho.org
Web: www.epilepsyidaho.org

Learning Disabilities

Learning Disabilities Association of Idaho
Ginny Hughes
9797 N. Circle Drive
Hayden, ID 83835-9503
(208) 762-2316
E-mail: connect4kids @imbris.com

Mental Health

NAMI-Idaho
Lee Woodland, Executive Director
P.O. Box 68
Albion, ID 83311
(208) 673-6672; (800) 572-9940
E-mail: namiid@atcnet.net
Web: www.nami.org/
    sites/NAMIIDAHO

Office of Consumer Affairs
C. Joseph Drayton, Director
1607 W. Jefferson
Boise, ID 83702
(208) 336-5533
E-mail: oocaata@mindspring.com

Speech and Hearing

Cynthia Olsen, President
Idaho Speech-Language-
    Hearing Association
13352 W. Bluebonnet Drive
Boise, ID 83713-1311
(208) 939-5899
E-mail: ckolsen@cableone.net
Web: ckolsen@cableone.net

Idaho—Organizations Especially for Parents

Parent Training and Information Center (PTI)

Idaho Parents Unlimited, Inc. (IPUL)
Evelyn Mason, Executive Director
600 N. Curtis Road, Suite 145
Boise, ID 83706
(208) 342-5884 (V/TTY); (800) 242-4785
    (in ID only)
E-mail: parents@ipulidaho.org
Web: http://ipulidaho.org

Parent-To-Parent

Contact Parent Training and Information Center listed above.

Partners in Policymaking

Idaho Council on Developmental Disabilities
Christine Pisani, DD Program Specialist
802 W. Bannock, Suite 308
Boise, ID 83702-5840
(208) 334-2178; (800) 544-2433
E-mail: cpisani@icdd.state.id.us
Web: www.state.id.us/icdd
Web: http://idahopartners.state.id.us

Parent Teacher Association (PTA)

Idaho Congress of Parents and Teachers, Inc.
Shirley Block, President
500 W. Washington
Boise, ID 83702-5965
(208) 344-0851; (208) 342-8585
E-mail: idahopta@mindspring.com
Web: www.idahopta.net

Idaho—Other Disability Organizations

VSA Arts of Idaho/Idaho Parents Unlimited
Jose Rodriguez, Program Director
600 N. Curtis Road, Suite 145
Boise, ID 83706
(208) 342-5884
E-mail: jose@ipulidaho.org

Summit Assistance Dogs (information
    available for the region)
Sue Meinzinger, Director
5458 W. Shore Road
Anacortes, WA 98221
(360) 293-5609
E-mail: info@summitdogs.org
Web: www.summitdogs.org/

Washington State Fathers Network
    (information available for the region)
James May, Executive Director
16120 NE 8th Street
Bellevue, WA 98008
(425) 747-4004, ext. 4286; (800) 833-6388
E-mail: jmay@fathersnetwork.org
Web: www.fathersnetwork.org

Independent Living

To find out the contact information for the
Statewide Independent Living Council (SILC)
in Idaho, contact

Independent Living Research Utilization Project
The Institute for Rehabilitation and Research
2323 South Sheppard, Suite 1000
Houston, TX 77019
(713) 520-0232 (V); (713) 520-5136 (TTY)
E-mail: ilru@ilru.org
Web: www.ilru.org

To find out the contact information for
centers for independent living (CILs) in Idaho,
contact

National Council on Independent Living
1916 Wilson Boulevard, Suite 209
Arlington, VA 22201
(703) 525-3406; (703) 525-4153 (TTY)
E-mail: ncil@ncil.org
Web: www.ncil.org

ILLINOIS

Illinois—State Agencies and Organizations

United States Senators

Honorable Richard J. Durbin (D)
711 Hart Senate Office Building
Washington, DC 20510
(202) 224-2152
(202) 228-0400 (Fax)
E-mail: dick@durbin.senate.gov
Web: http://durbin.senate.gov

Honorable Mark Kirk (R)
524 Hart Senate Office Building
Washington, DC 20510
(202) 224-2854
(202) 228-5786 (Fax)
E-mail Web Form: http://www.kirk.senate.
    gov/?p=contact
Web: http://www.kirk.senate.gov/

United States Representatives

To find the contact information for your representative in the House of the U.S. Congress,
visit the House's Web site at: www.house.gov,
or call: (202) 225-3121; (202) 225-1904 (TTY).

Governor

Honorable Pat Quinn
State Capitol
207 Statehouse
Springfield, IL 62706
(217) 782-0244 (V/TTY)
E-mail: governor@state.il.us
Web: www.illinois.gov

Official State Web Site

Web: www.illinois.gov

State Department of Education: Special Education

Christopher Koch, EdD, Director
Department of Special Education
Illinois State Board of Education
100 N. First Street, N-243
Springfield, IL 62777-0001
(217) 782-4870
E-mail: chris.koch@isbe.net
Web: www.isbe.net/spec-ed/

State Coordinator for NCLB (No Child Left Behind)

Illinois was granted a waiver from the
NCLB program.

Melina Wright, NCLB Liaison
Illinois State Board of Education
100 N. 1st Street
Springfield, IL 62777
(312) 814-2804
Email: mewright@isbe.net
Web: http://www.isbe.net/nclb/default.htm

Programs for Infants and Toddlers
With Disabilities: Birth–2 Years

Bureau of Early Intervention
Department of Human Services
Ann Freiburg, Acting Part C Coordinator
823 East Monroe
Springfield, IL 62701
(217) 782-0516
E-mail: ann.freiburg@illinois.gov
Web: http://www.dhs.state.il.us/page.
   aspx?item=32009

Programs for Children
With Disabilities: 3–5 Years

Division of Early Childhood Education
Pam Reising-Rechner
IL State Board of Education
100 N. First Street E-230
Springfield, IL 62777
(217) 524-4835
E-mail: preising@isbe.net
Web: http://www.isbe.net/earlychi/Default.
   htm

Technical Support to Schools on Inclusion

Project CHOICES
Deb Kunz, Statewide Parent Liaison
100 N. First Street, Room N253
Springfield, IL 62777-0001
(217) 782-5589
E-mail: dkunz@isbe.net
Web: www.projectchoices.org

Technical Support to Schools on
Positive Behavior Interventions and Supports

Illinois State Board of Education
EBD/PBIS Network
Lucille Eber, Statewide Coordinator
West 40 ISC #2
928 Barnsdale Road, Suite 254
LaGrange Park, IL 60526
(708) 482-4860
E-mail: lewrapil@aol.com
Web: www.ebdnetwork-il.org/

State Vocational Rehabilitation Agency

Department of Human Services
Robert F. Kilbury, PhD, Director
Division of Rehabilitation Services
100 S. Grand Avenue, East
Springfield, IL 62762

(217) 524-7551 (V/TTY); (800) 843-6154 (V/TTY)
E-mail: ilvr@rehabnetwork.org
Web: www.dhs.state.il.us

Coordinator for
Transition Services

Transition Outreach
   Training for Adult Living
Susan Walter, Training and
   Technical Assistance Coordinator
10 Meadowlark Lane
Highland, IL 62249
(618) 651-9028
E-mail: smwalter@charter.net
Web: www.isbe.net

Illinois State Board of Education

Debra Heckenkamp, Principal
   Education Consultant
Division of Special Education Services
100 N. First Street
Springfield, IL 62777-0001
(217) 782-5589
E-mail: dheckenk@isbe.net
Web: www.isbe.net/spec-ed

Office of State Coordinator of
Vocational Education for
Students With Disabilities

Nancy Harris, Special
   Populations Coordinator
Illinois State Board of Education
100 N. First Street
Springfield, IL 62777-0001
(217) 782-4620
E-mail: nharris@isbe.net
Web: www.isbe.net

State Mental Health Agency

Christopher Fichtener, MD, Director
Division of Mental Health
Department of Human Services
100 S. Grand Avenue, East,
   Harris II, 2nd Floor
Springfield, IL 62762
(217) 785-6023; (800) 843-6154 (Hotline)
(800) 447-6404 (TTY)
E-mail: dhsc1655@dhs.state.il.us
Web: www.dhs.state.il.us/mhdd/mh

State Mental Health Representative for Children and Youth

Christopher Fichtener, MD, Director
Division of Mental Health
Department of Human Services
100 S. Grand Avenue, East, Harris II, 2nd Floor
Springfield, IL 62762
(217) 785-6023; (800) 843-6154 (Hotline)
(800) 447-6404 (TTY)
E-mail: dhsc1655@dhs.state.il.us
Web: www.dhs.state.il.us/mhdd/mh

State Mental Retardation Program

Division of Developmental Disabilities
Department of Human Services
Jeri Johnson, Director
100 S. Grand Avenue, East, 2nd Floor
Springfield, IL 62762
(217) 524-7065
E-mail: dhs9255@dhs.state.il.us
Web: www.state.il.us/agency/dhs

Council on Developmental Disabilities

Illinois Council on Developmental Disabilities
Sheila T. Romano, Executive Director
830 S. Spring Street
Springfield, IL 62704
(217) 782-9696 (V/TTY)
Web: www.state.il.us/agency/icdd/

Protection and Advocacy Agency

Equip for Equality, Inc.
Zena Naiditch, CEO/President
20 N. Michigan, Suite 300
Chicago, IL 60602
(312) 341-0022; (800) 537-2632 (V)
(800) 610-2779 (TTY)
E-mail: contactus@equipforequality.org
Web: www.equipforequality.org

Client Assistance Program

Cathy Meadows, Manager
Illinois Client Assistance Program
100 N. First Street, 1st Floor West
Springfield, IL 62702-5197
(217) 782-5374 (V/TTY); (800) 641-3929 (in IL)
E-mail: dhscap@dhs.state.il.us
Web: www.dhs.state.il.us/ors/cap

Programs for Children With Special Health Care Needs

Division of Specialized Care for Children
University of Illinois at Chicago
Charles N. Onufer, MD, Director
P.O. Box 19481
2815 W. Washington, Suite 300
Springfield, IL 62794-9481
(217) 793-2340; (800) 322-3722
E-mail: cnonufer@uic.edu
Web: www.uic.edu/hsc/dscc/

State CHIP Program (health care for low-income, uninsured children)

All Kids
Illinois Department of Public Aid
201 S. Grand Avenue East
Springfield, IL 62753-0002
(866) 468-7543; (877) 204-1012 (TTY)
Web: http://www.allkids.com/

Programs for Children and Youth Who Are Deaf or Hard of Hearing, or Deaf-Blind

Services for Persons who are Deaf or
    Hard of Hearing
Division of Rehabilitation Services
Department of Human Services
Joseph Parvis, Specialist
100 W. Randolph Street, Suite 8-100
Chicago, IL 60601
(312) 814-2939; (312) 814-3040 (TTY)
Web: www.dhs.state.il.us/ors/sdhh/

Illinois State Board of Education

Barb Sims, Principal Education Consultant
Division of Special Education Services
100 N. First Street
Springfield, IL 62777-0001
(217) 782-5589
E-mail: bsims@isbe.net
Web: www.isbe.net/spec-ed

Telecommunications Relay Services for Individuals Who Are Deaf, Hard of Hearing, or With Speech Impairments

(800) 526-0857 (V)
(800) 526-0844 (TTY); 711 (TTY)
(877) 526-6690 (Speech to Speech)

**Programs for Children and Youth
Who Are Blind or Visually Impaired**

Bureau of the Blind
Bettye Odem-Davis, Bureau Chief
Office of Rehabilitation Services
Department of Human Services
100 W. Randolph Street, Suite 8-100
Chicago, IL 60601
(312) 814-3323
Web: www.dhs.state.il.us/ors/bbs/

Illinois State Board of Education

Paula Stadeker, Principal
    Education Consultant
Division of Special Education Services
100 N. First Street
Springfield, IL 62777-0001
(217) 782-5589
E-mail: pstadeke@isbe.net
Web: www.isbe.net/spec-ed

**State Education Agency
Rural Representative**

Leah Covey, Principal
    Performance Consultant
Department of Rural Education
Southern Illinois Regional Office
Illinois State Board of Education
123 S. Tenth Street, Suite 200
Mt. Vernon, IL 62864
(618) 244-8383
Web: www.isbe.state.il.us

**Regional ADA & IT
Technical Assistance Center**

Great Lakes ADA and Accessible IT Center
University of Illinois/Chicago
Institute on Disability and Human
    Development
Robin Jones, Project Director
1640 W. Roosevelt Road (MC/626)
Chicago, IL 60608-6902
(312) 413-1407 (V/TTY);
    (800) 949-4232 (V/TTY)
E-mail: gldbtac@uic.edu
Web: www.adagreatlakes.org

**University Center for Excellence
in Developmental Disabilities**

Institute on Disability
    and Human Development
Department of Disability and
    Human Development
University of Illinois at Chicago
Tamar Heller, Director
1640 W. Roosevelt Road
Chicago, IL 60608
(312) 413-1647 (V); (312) 413-0453 (TTY)
Web: www.ahs.uic.edu/dhd

Technology-Related Assistance

Illinois Assistive Technology Project
Wilhelmina Gunther, Executive Director
1 W. Old State Capitol Plaza, Suite 100
Springfield, IL 62701
(217) 522-7985 (V/TTY)
(800) 852-5110 (V/TTY, in IL only)
E-mail: wgunther@iltech.org
Web: www.iltech.org

State Mediation System

Sherry Colegrove, Coordinator
Illinois State Board of Education
Division of Special Education Services
100 N. First Street, N-253
Springfield, IL 62777
(217) 782-5589
E-mail: scolegro@isbe.net
Web: www.isbe.net/spec-ed

For a listing of resource centers that provide legal or advocacy services at no or low cost, visit: www.isbe.net/spec-ed/parent%20advocates .htm
For due process information, contact

Illinois State Board of Education
Beth Hanselman, Supervisor
Division of Special Education Services
100 N. First Street
Springfield, IL 62777-0001
(217) 782-5589
Web: www.isbe.net/spec-ed

Special Format Library

Illinois State Library
Talking Book and Braille Service
Sharon Ruda, Associate Director
401 E. Washington
Springfield, IL 62701
(217) 782-9435; (800) 665-5576 ext. 5 (in IL)
(888) 261-5280 (TTY)
E-mail: sruda@ilsos.net
Web: http://www.cyberdriveillinois.com/
    departments/library/TBBS/home.html

Illinois — Disability-Specific Organizations

Attention Deficit Disorder

To identify an ADD group in Illinois, contact either of the following organizations:

Children and Adults with Attention-Deficit/
    Hyperactivity Disorder (CHADD)
8181 Professional Place, Suite 150
Landover, MD 20785
(301) 306-7070
(800) 233-4050 (Voice mail to request
    information packet)
Web: www.chadd.org

Attention Deficit Disorder Association (ADDA)
P.O. Box 543
Pottstown, PA 19464
(484) 945-2101
Web: www.add.org

Autism

To identify an autism group in your state, contact

Autism Society of America
7910 Woodmont Avenue, Suite 300
Bethesda, MD 20814
(301) 657-0881; (800) 3-AUTISM
Web: www.autism-society.org

Illinois Autism/PDD Training
    and Technical Assistance Project
Kathy Gould, Project Director
1301 W. Cossitt Avenue
La Grange, IL 60525
(708) 354-5730
E-mail: kathygould@
    illinoisautismproject.org
Web: www.illinoisautismproject.org

Blind/Visual Impairments

Jay Stiteley, Director
American Foundation for the Blind-Midwest
401 N. Michigan Avenue, Suite 350
Chicago, IL 60611
(312) 396-4420
E-mail: chicago@afb.net
Web: www.afb.org

Brain Injury

Brain Injury Association of Illinois
Philicia L. Deckard, Executive Director
P.O. Box 64420
Chicago, IL 60664-0420
(312) 630-4011; (800) 699-6443 (in IL only)
E-mail: info@biail.org
Web: www.BIAUSA.org/illinois/bia.htm

Cerebral Palsy

United Cerebral Palsy of Illinois
Don Moss, Executive Director
310 E. Adams
Springfield, IL 62701
(217) 528-9681
E-mail: ucpil@sbcglobal.net
Web: www.ucpillinois.com

Epilepsy

Epilepsy Foundation of Greater Chicago
Philip M. Gattone, President/CEO
17 N. State, Suite 1300
Chicago, IL 60602
(312) 939-8622; (800) 273-6027
(312) 628-6027 (TTY)
E-mail: info@epilepsychicago.org
Web: www.epilepsychicago.org

Epilepsy Resource Center (serving central Illinois)
1315 W. Lawrence Avenue
Springfield, IL 62704
(217) 726-1839 (V/TTY); (800) 800-6401
E-mail: epilepsy@spfldsparc.org

Learning Disabilities

Learning Disabilities Association of Illinois
Sandy Zamudio, President
10101 S. Roberts Road, Suite 205
Palos Hills, IL 60465
(708) 430-7532
E-mail: LDAofIL@ameritech.net
Web: www.ldaamerica.org

Illinois Branch of the International
   Dyslexia Association
Carolyn Swallow, PhD, Executive Director
751 Roosevelt Road, Suite 116
Glen Ellyn, IL 60137
(630) 469-6900
E-mail: ilbranch_ida@ameritech.net
Web: www.interdys.org

Mental Health

Mental Health Association in Illinois
188 W. Randolph Street, Suite 2225
Chicago, IL 60601
(312) 368-9070
Web: www.mhai.org

NAMI Illinois
Lora Thomas, Executive Director
218 W. Lawrence
Springfield, IL 62704
(217) 522-1403; (800) 346-4572 (In IL only)
E-mail: namiil@sbcglobal.net;
thomas.lora@sbcglobal.net;
   Web: http://il.nami.org

Mental Retardation/
Developmental Disabilities

The Arc of Illinois
Tony Paulauski, Executive Director
18207-A Dixie Highway
Homewood, IL 60430
(708) 206-1930
E-mail: tony@thearcofil.org
Web: www.thearcofil.org

Speech and Hearing

Illinois Speech-Language-Hearing Association
Cynthia Keillor, Executive Director
230 E. Ohio Street, Suite 400
Chicago, IL 60611-3265
(312) 644-0828, ext. 2210
E-mail: ckeillor@bostrom.com
Web: www.ishail.org

Illinois State Department of Education
Jodi Fleck, Principal Education Consultant
Division of Special Education Services
100 N. First Street
Springfield, IL 62777-0001
(217) 781-5589
E-mail: jfleck@isbe.net
Web: www.isbe.net/spec-ed

Spina Bifida

Illinois Spina Bifida Association
Adam S. Rappaport, Executive Director
3080 Ogden Avenue, Suite 103
Lisle, IL 60532
(630) 637-1050; (773) 581-2426
(800) 969-4722
E-mail: ILSBA1@aol.com
Web: www.illinoisspinabifida
   association.com

Spinal Cord Injury

Spinal Cord Injury Association of Illinois
Mercedes Rauen, Executive Director
1032 S. La Grange Road
LaGrange, IL 60525
(708) 352-6223; (877) 373-0301
E-mail: SCIInjury@aol.com
Web: www.sci-illinois.org

Illinois—Organizations
Especially for Parents

Parent Training and
Information Center (PTI)

Family Resource Center on Disabilities
Charlotte Des Jardins, Director
20 E. Jackson Boulevard, Room 300
Chicago, IL 60604
(312) 939-3513; (312) 939-3519 (TTY)
(800) 952-4199 (In IL)
E-mail: frcdptiil@ameritech.net
Web: www.frcd.org

Designs for Change
Donald Moore, Executive Director
29 E. Madison, Suite 950
Chicago, IL 60602-4404
(312) 236-7252; (312) 236-7944 (TTY)
(800) 851-8728
E-mail: info@designsforchange.org
Web: www.designsforchange.org

Family Matters
Debbie Einhorn, Program Director
2502 S. Veterans Drive
Effingham, IL 62401
(217) 347-0880; (217) 347-5428 (V/TTY)
(866) 436-7842
E-mail: info@fmptic.org
Web: www.fmptic.org

Partners in Policymaking

Phoenix Perth Institute
Ginny Cooke
P.O. Box 5429
Evanston, IL 60401-5429
(847) 425-1967
E-mail: ginnycooke@aol.com

Parent-To-Parent

Family Resource Center on Disabilities
Charlotte Des Jardins, Executive Director
20 E. Jackson Boulevard, Suite 300
Chicago, IL 60604
(312) 939-3513; (312) 939-3519 (TTY)
(800) 952-4199 (In IL)
E-mail: frcdptiil@ameritech.net
Web: www.frcd.org

Family Support Network of Illinois
Charlotte Cronin, Executive Director
5739 W. Martindale Lane
Peoria, IL 61615-9669
(309) 693-8981
E-mail: fsn@familysupportnetwork.org
Web: www.familysupportnetwork.org/

Parent Teacher Association (PTA)

Illinois Congress of Parents and Teachers
Gayla Boomer, President
901 S. Spring Street
Springfield, IL 62704-2790
(217) 528-9617; (800) 877-9617
E-mail: il_office@pta.org

Illinois—Other Disability Organizations

Pathways Awareness Foundation
Kathy O'Brien, Resource Director
150 N. Michigan Avenue, Suite 2100
Chicago, IL 60601
(800) 955-2445; (800) 326-8154 (TTY)
E-mail: friends@pathwaysawareness.org
Web: www.pathwaysawareness.org

Council for Disability Rights
Jo Holzer, Executive Director
205 W. Randolph, Suite 1645
Chicago, IL 60606-1892
(312) 444-9484; (312) 444-1967 (TTY)
E-mail: cdrights@interaccess.com
Web: www.disabilityrights.org

State Advisory Council on the Education
  of Children With Disabilities (ISAC)
Christopher Koch, State Director
  of Special Education
Department of Special Education
Illinois State Board of Education
100 N. First Street, N-243
Springfield, IL 62777-0001
(217) 782-4870
E-mail: chris.koch@isbe.net
Web: www.isbe.net/spec-ed/isac.htm

VSA Arts of Chicago
Amy J. Serpe, Executive Director
Apparel Center
350 N. Orleans, Suite 680
Chicago, IL 60654
(312) 527-2620; (800) 526-0844 (TTY)
E-mail: as@vsachicago.org
Web: www.vsachicago.org

Independent Living

To find out the contact information for the Statewide Independent Living Council (SILC) in Illinois, contact

Independent Living Research
  Utilization Project
The Institute for Rehabilitation and Research
2323 South Sheppard, Suite 1000
Houston, TX 77019
(713) 520-0232 (V); (713) 520-5136 (TTY)
E-mail: ilru@ilru.org
Web: www.ilru.org

To find out the contact information for centers for independent living (CILs) in Illinois, contact

National Council on Independent Living
1916 Wilson Boulevard, Suite 209
Arlington, VA 22201
(703) 525-3406; (703) 525-4153 (TTY)
E-mail: ncil@ncil.org
Web: www.ncil.org

INDIANA

Indiana—State Agencies and Organizations

United States Senators

Honorable Daniel Coats (R)
493 Russell Senate Office Building
Washington, DC 20510
(202) 224-5623
E-mail: http://www.coats.senate.gov/contact/
Web: http://www.coats.senate.gov/

Honorable Joe Donnelly (D)
720 Hart Senate Office Building
Washington, DC 20510
(202) 224-4814
(202) 228-1377 (Fax)
E-mail Web Form: http://www.donnelly.
   senate.gov/contact/email-joe
Web: http://www.donnelly.senate.gov/

United States Representatives

To find the contact information for your representative in the House of the U.S. Congress, visit the House's Web site at: www.house.gov, or call: (202) 225-3121; (202) 225-1904 (TTY).

Governor

Honorable Mike Pence
206 State House
Indianapolis, IN 46204
(317) 232-4567
Web: http://www.in.gov/gov/2752.htm

Official State Web Site

Web: www.in.gov

State Department of Education: Special Education

Becky Bowman, Director
Indiana Department of Education
South Tower, Suite 600
115 W. Washington Street
Indianapolis, IN 46204
E-mail: bbowman@doe.in.gov
Web: http://www.doe.in.gov/specialed

State Coordinator for NCLB (No Child Left Behind)

Indiana was granted an extended waiver from the NCLB program.

Cindy Hurst, Title I Coordinator
Indiana Department of Education
South Tower, Suite 600
115 W. Washington Street
Indianapolis, IN 46204
(317) 234-2145
Email: churst@doe.in.gov
Web: http://www.doe.in.gov/titlei

Programs for Infants and Toddlers With Disabilities: Birth–2 Years

Indiana Family and Social Services Administration
Cathy Robinson, Part C Coordinator
First Steps
Division of Disability Rehabilitation
Bureau of Child Development
402 W. Washington Street, Room W-386
Indianapolis, IN 46204
(317) 234-1527; (800) 441-7837 (in IN)
E-mail: cathy.robinson@fssa.in.gov
Web: http://www.in.gov/fssa/4655.htm

Programs for Children With Disabilities: 3–5 Years

Indiana Department of Education
Christina Furbee, 619 Coordinator
Department of Education
115 W. Washington Street
South Tower, Suite 600
Indianapolis, IN
(317) 232-9142
E-mail: cfurbee@doe.in.gov
Web: http://www.doe.in.gov/specialed

State Vocational Rehabilitation Agency

Indiana Family and Social
   Services Administration
Michael Hedden, Deputy Director
Vocational Rehabilitation Services
Division of Disability, Aging, and
   Rehabilitative Services
402 W. Washington Street, Room W453
P.O. Box 7083
Indianapolis, IN 46207-7083
(317) 232-1319; (800) 545-7763, ext. 1319
E-mail: phedden@fssa.state.in.us
Web: www.IN.gov/fssa/

Coordinator for Transition Services

Indiana Institute on Disability and Community
Teresa Grossi, Director
University Affiliated Program of Indiana
Indiana University
2853 E. 10th Street
Bloomington, IN 47408
(812) 855-6508
E-mail: tgrossi@indiana.edu
Web: http://www.iidc.indiana.edu/index.
   php?pageId=66

Indiana Department of Education
Nancy Zemaitis, Assistant Director
Division of Exceptional Learners
State House, Room 229
Indianapolis, IN 46204-2798
(317) 232-0892
E-mail: zemaitis@doe.state.in.us
Web: www.doe.state.in.us/exceptional/speced

Office of State Coordinator of Vocational Education for Students With Disabilities

Indiana Workforce Development
Terry Fields, State Director
Vocational and Technical Education
10 N. Senate Avenue, Room 212
Indianapolis, IN 46204-2277
(317) 232-1829
E-mail: tfields@dwd.state.in.us
Web: www.IN.gov/dwd/teched/

State Mental Health Agency

Suzanne Clifford, Director
Division of Mental Health and Addiction
Family and Social Services Administration
402 W. Washington Street, Room W353
Indianapolis, IN 46204-2739
(317) 232-7845
E-mail: sclifford@fssa.state.in.us
Web: www.IN.gov/fssa

State Mental Health Representative for Children

Cheryl Shearer, ACSW, LCSW
Children's Services Bureau
Division of Mental Health and Addiction
Family and Social Services Administration
402 W. Washington Street, Room W353
Indianapolis, IN 46204-2739
(317) 232-7934
E-mail: cshearer@fssa.state.in.us
Web: www.IN.gov/fssa

State Developmental Disabilities Agency

Carmella Barrett, Deputy Director
Bureau of Developmental Disabilities Services
P.O. Box 7083
Indianapolis, IN 46207-7083
(317) 232-7842

Council on Developmental Disabilities

The Indiana Governor's Planning
   Council for People with Disabilities
Suellen Jackson-Boner, Director
150 W. Market Street, Suite 628
Indianapolis, IN 46204
(317) 232-7770; (317) 232-7771 (TTY)
E-mail: sjackson@gpcpd.org
Web: www.IN.gov/gpcpd/

Protection and Advocacy Agency

Indiana Protection and Advocacy Services
Thomas Gallagher, Executive Director
4701 N. Keystone Avenue, Suite 222
Indianapolis, IN 46205
(317) 722-5555
(800) 622-4845; (800) 838-1131 (TTY)
E-mail: info@ipas.in.gov
Web: www.in.gov/ipas

Client Assistance Program

Contact Protection and Advocacy Agency listed above.

Programs for Children With Special Health Care Needs

Children's Special Health Care Services
Indiana State Department of Health
Eric Vermeulen, Director
2 N. Meridian Street
Indianapolis, IN 46204
(317) 233-1351; (800) 475-1355
Web: www.in.gov/isdh/programs/cshcs

State CHIP Program (health care for low-income, uninsured children)

Hoosier Healthwise
Children's Health Insurance Program
Department of Health, Family and
   Social Services
402 W. Washington Street, Room 382, MS07
Indianapolis, IN 46204-2739
(800) 889-9949
Web: www.in.gov/fssa/programs/chip

Programs for Children and Youth Who Are Blind or Visually Impaired

Blind and Visually Impaired Services
Indiana Family and Social Services
    Administration
Division of Disability, Aging,
    and Rehabilitative Services
Linda Quarles, Interim Deputy Director
402 W. Washington Street, Room W-453
P. O. Box 7083
Indianapolis, IN 46207-7083
(317) 232-1433; (877) 241-8144
(317) 232-1466 (TTY)
E-mail: lquarles@fssa.state.in.us
Web: www.state.in.us/fssa/servicedisabl/
    blind/index.html

Programs for Children and Youth Who Are Deaf or Hard of Hearing

Indiana Deaf and Hard of Hearing Services
Indiana Family and Social Services
    Administration
Division of Disability, Aging,
    and Rehabilitative Services
James Van Manen, Deputy Director
402 W. Washington Street , Room W-453
P.O. Box 7083
Indianapolis, IN 46207-7083
(317) 232-1143 (V/TTY); (800) 962-8408
    (V/TTY in IN only)
E-mail: jvanmanen@fssa.state.in.us
Web: www.IN.gov/fssa/dhhs

Telecommunications Relay Services for Individuals Who Are Deaf, Hard of Hearing, or With Speech Impairments

(800) 743-3333 (V)
(800) 743-3333 (TTY); 711 (TTY)
(877) 743-8231 (Speech to Speech)

Programs for Children and Youth Who Are Deaf-Blind

The Indiana Deafblind Services Project
Karen Goehl, Director
Blumberg Center, College of Education, Room 502
Indiana State University
Terre Haute, IN 47809
(800) 622-3035; (812) 237-3022 (TTY)
E-mail: kgoehl@indstate.edu
E-mail: lpoff@indstate.edu
Web: www.indstate.edu/soe/blumberg/
    Deafblind.html

Regional ADA & IT Technical Assistance Center

Great Lakes ADA and Accessible IT Center
University of Illinois/Chicago
Department on Disability and
    Human Development
Robin Jones, Project Director
1640 W. Roosevelt Road
Chicago, IL 60608
(312) 413-1407 (V/TTY); (800) 949-4232 (V/TTY)
E-mail: gldbtac@uic.edu
Web: www.adagreatlakes.org

University Centers for Excellence on Developmental Disabilities

Indiana Institute on Disability and Community
David M. Mank, Director
2853 E. 10th Street
Bloomington, IN 47408-2696
(812) 855-6508; (812) 855-9396 (TTY)
E-mail: iidc@indiana.edu
Web: www.iidc.indiana.edu

Riley Child Development Center (RCDC)
John D. Rau, MD, Director
Leadership Education in Neurodevelopmental
    Disabilities (LEND) Program
Indiana University School of Medicine
James Whitcomb Riley Hospital
    for Children
702 Barnhill Drive, Room 5837
Indianapolis, IN 46202-5225
(317) 274-8167
E-mail: jdrau@child-dev.com
Web: www.child-dev.com

Technology-Related Assistance

Attain
Gary R. Hand, Executive Director
32 E. Washington Street
Indianapolis, IN 46204
(317) 486-8808; (800) 528-8246 (in IN)
E-mail: attain@attaininc.org
Web: www.attaininc.org

State Mediation System

Indiana Department of Education
Sally Cook, Mediation Coordinator
Division of Exceptional Learners
State House, Room 229
Indianapolis, IN 46204
(317) 232-0580
E-mail: sacook@doe.state.in.us
Web: www.doe.state.in.us/exceptional/speced

Special Format Library

Indiana State Library Talking Books
Lissa Shanahan, Librarian
140 N. Senate Avenue
Indianapolis, IN 46204
(317) 232-3684; (800) 622-4970
(317) 232-7763 (TTY)
E-mail: lbph@statelib.lib.in.us
Web: www.statelib.lib.in.us/

Indiana—Disability-Specific Organizations

Attention Deficit Disorder

To identify an ADD group in Indiana, contact either of the following organizations:

Children and Adults with Attention-Deficit/
   Hyperactivity Disorder (CHADD)
8181 Professional Place, Suite 150
Landover, MD 20785
(301) 306-7070
(800) 233-4050 (Voice mail to request
   information packet)
Web: www.chadd.org

Attention Deficit Disorder Association (ADDA)
P.O. Box 543
Pottstown, PA 19464
(484) 945-2101
Web: www.add.org

Autism

Indiana Resource Center for Autism (IRCA)
Cathy Pratt, PhD, Director
Indiana Institute on Disability and Community
Indiana's University Center for
   Excellence on Disabilities
Indiana University
2853 E. 10th Street
Bloomington, IN 47408-2696
(812) 855-6508; (812) 855-9396 (TTY)
E-mail: prattc@indiana.edu
Web: www.iidc.indiana.edu/irca

Blind/Visual Impairments

American Foundation for the Blind—Midwest
Jay Stiteley, Director
401 N. Michigan Avenue, Suite 350
Chicago, IL 60611
(312) 396-4420
E-mail: chicago@afb.net
Web: www.afb.org

Brain Injury

Brain Injury Association of Indiana
Lindsay Meyer, Executive Director
9531 Valparaiso Court, Suite A
Indianapolis, IN 46268
(317) 356-7722; (866) 854-4246
E-mail: lindsay.meyer@biai.org
Web: www.biausa.org/indiana/bia.htm

Cerebral Palsy

United Cerebral Palsy Association of
   Greater Indiana, Inc.
Donna Roberts, Executive Director
1915 W. 18th Street, Suite C
Indianapolis, IN 46202
(317) 632-3561; (800) 723-7620
E-mail: donnar@ucpaindy.org
Web: www.ucp.org

Down Syndrome

Indiana Down Syndrome Foundation
Kimberly Pannell, Executive Director
3100 Meridian Parke Drive, Suite N292
Greenwood, IN 46142
(317) 216-6319; (888) 989-9255
E-mail: idsfdirector@insightbb.com
Web: www.indianadsf.org

Down Syndrome Association of Northeast Indiana
Joe Bockerstette, President
1530 Progress Road
Fort Wayne, IN 46808
(260) 471-9964; (877) 713-7264
E-mail: dsani4u@aol.com
Web: www.dsani.org

Epilepsy

Epilepsy Foundation of Greater Cincinnati
Marge Frommeyer, Executive Director
(serving South Eastern Counties)
3 Centennial Plaza, 895 Central Avenue
Cincinnati, OH 45202
(513) 721-2905; (877) 804-2241
E-mail: ecgc@fuse.net
Web: www.ecgc.net

Indiana Epilepsy Services
Kathy S. Forkner, MLS, State Coordinator
Community Health Network Neurosciences
1402 E. County Line Road South
Indianapolis, IN 46227
(317) 355-5824; (800) 642-2608
E-mail: kforkner@ecommunity.com
Web: www.indianaepilepsy.org

Learning Disabilities

Learning Disabilities Association of Indiana
Sharon Harris, Indiana State President
Jan Perzanowski, Conference Director
P.O. Box 20584
Indianapolis, IN 46220
(800) 284-2519 (LD and ADD/HD
Information Request Line)
E-mail: ldain@lda-in.org
Web: www.lda-in.org

Mental Health

Mental Health Association in Indiana, Inc.
Stephen McCaffrey, President
1431 N. Delaware Street
Indianapolis, IN 46202
(317) 638-3501; (800) 555-6424 (in IN only)
E-mail: mha@mentalhealthassociation.com
Web: www.mentalhealthassociation.com

NAMI Indiana
Pamela A. McConey, Executive Director
P.O. Box 22697
Indianapolis, IN 46222-0697
(317) 925-9399; (800) 677-6442
E-mail: nami-in@nami.org
Web: www.namiindiana.org

Mental Retardation

The Arc of Indiana
John Dickerson, Executive Director
107 N. Pennsylvania, Suite 300
Indianapolis, IN 46204
(317) 977-2375
E-mail: jdickerson@arcind.org
Web: www.arcind.org
Web: http://www.arcind.org/

Speech and Hearing

Indiana Speech-Language-Hearing Association
Ann Ninness
1 N. Capitol Avenue, Suite 1111
Indianapolis, IN 46204
(317) 916-4146
E-mail: mail@islha.org
Web: www.islha.org

Spinal Cord Injury

Spinal Cord Injury Association of Illinois
Mercedes Rauen, Executive Director
1032 S. LaGrange Road
LaGrange, IL 60525
(708) 352-6223; (877) 373-0301
E-mail: SCIInjury@aol.com
Web: www.sci-illinois.org

Indiana—Organizations Especially for Parents

Parent Training and Information Center (PTI)

*IN*SOURCE*
Richard Burden, Executive Director
809 N. Michigan Street
South Bend, IN 46601-1036
(574) 234-7101 (V/TTY); (800) 332-4433 (in IN)
E-mail: insource@insource.org
Web: www.insource.org

Partners in Policymaking

UCPA of Greater Indianapolis
1915 W. 18th Street, Suite C
Indianapolis, IN 46202
(317) 632-3561; (800) 821-6708 (in IN)

Parent-To-Parent

Indiana Parent Information Network, Inc.
Rebecca Agness, Executive Director
4755 Kingsway Drive, Suite 105-A
Indianapolis, IN 46205-1545
(317) 257-8683
E-mail: familynetw@ipin.org
Web: www.ipin.org

Parent Teacher Association (PTA)

Indiana Congress of Parents and Teachers, Inc.
Marilyn Jones, President
2525 N. Shadeland Avenue, D-4
Indianapolis, IN 46219
(317) 357-5881
E-mail: in_office@pta.org
E-mail: pta@spitfire.net
Web: www.indianapta.org

Indiana—Other Disability Organizations

Easter Seals Wayne/Union Counties
Pat Bowers, Executive Director
5632 U.S. Highway 40 East
P.O. Box 86
Centerville, IN 47330-0086
(765) 855-2482
E-mail: easterseals@juno.com
Web: http://eastersealswu.tripod.com

Family Voices Indiana
4755 Kingsway Drive, Suite 105A
Indianapolis, IN 46205-1545
(317) 257-8683
E-mail: FamVoicesIn@aol.com

VSA Arts of Indiana

Harrison Centre for the Arts
Jim Nulty, President
1505 N. Delaware Avenue, Suite 100
Indianapolis, IN 46202
(317) 974-4123; (317) 974-4117 (TTY)
E-mail: jnulty@vsai.org
Web: www.vsai.org

Independent Living

To find out the contact information for the *Statewide Independent Living Council (SILC) in Indiana*, contact

Independent Living Research Utilization Project
The Institute for Rehabilitation and Research
2323 South Sheppard, Suite 1000
Houston, TX 77019
(713) 520-0232 (V); (713) 520-5136 (TTY)
E-mail: ilru@ilru.org
Web: www.ilru.org

To find out the contact information for centers for independent living (CILs) in Indiana, contact

National Council on Independent Living
1916 Wilson Boulevard, Suite 209
Arlington, VA 22201
(703) 525-3406; (703) 525-4153 (TTY)
E-mail: ncil@ncil.org
Web: www.ncil.org

IOWA

Iowa—State Agencies and Organizations

United States Senators
Honorable Charles E. Grassley (R)
135 Hart Senate Office Building
Washington, DC 20510
(202) 224-3744
(202) 224-6020 (Fax)
E-mail Web Form: http://grassley.senate.gov/
   webform.html
Web: http://grassley.senate.gov

Honorable Tom Harkin (D)
731 Hart Senate Office Building
Washington, DC 20510
(202) 224-3254
(202) 224-9369 (Fax)
E-mail: tom_harkin@harkin.senate.gov
Web: http://harkin.senate.gov

United States Representatives

To find the contact information for your representative in the House of the U.S. Congress, visit the House's Web site at: www.house.gov, or call: (202) 225-3121; (202) 225-1904 (TTY).

Governor

Honorable Terry Branstad
Office of the Governor
State Capitol
Des Moines, IA 50319
(515) 281-5211
(515) 281-6611 (Fax)
Email Web Form: https://governor.iowa.gov/
   contact/
Web: https://governor.iowa.gov/

Official State Web Site

Web: www.state.ia.us/

**State Department of
Education: Special Education**

Wendy Rickman, Division Administrator
Bureau of Children, Family and
    Community Services
Department of Human Services
DHS - ACFS, 1305 East Walnut
Des Moines, IA 50310-0114
(515) 281-5521
Web: https://www.educateiowa.gov/

**State Coordinator for
NCLB (No Child Left Behind)**

Geri McMahon
NCLB Procedures and Policy
Iowa Department of Education
Grimes State Office Building
Des Moines, IA 50319-0146
(515) 281-3944
E-mail: geri.mcmahon@iowa.gov
Web: www.state.ia.us/educate

**Early Intervention System, Infants and Toddlers With
Disabilities: Birth–2 Years**

Early ACCESS (IDEA, Part C)
Cindy Weigel, State Coordinator
Bureau of Early Childhood Services
400 E. 14th Street
Des Moines, IA 50319
(515) 281-8634
E-mail: cindy.weigel@iowa.gov
Web: https://www.educateiowa.gov/pk-12/
    early-childhood/early-access

**Programs for Children
with Disabilities: Birth–5 Years**

Bureau of Children, Family and
    Community Services

Iowa Department of Education
Dee Gethmann, ESCE Consultant
Grimes State Office Building
400 East 14th Street
Des Moines, IA 50319-0146
(515) 281-5502
E-mail: dee.gethmann@iowa.gov
Web: https://www.educateiowa.gov/pk-12/
    early-childhood/early-childhood-special-ed-
    ucation

State Vocational Rehabilitation

Division of Vocational Rehabilitation Services
Department of Education
Stephen A. Wooderson, Administrator
510 E. 12th Street
Des Moines, IA 50319
(515) 281-6731
E-mail: swooderson@iowa.gov
Web: www.dvrs.state.ia.us

Coordinator for Transition Services

Barbara Guy, State Transition Coordinator
Transition and Work Experience
Department of Special Education
Iowa Department of Education
Grimes State Office Building
400 E. 14th Street
Des Moines, IA 50319-0146
(515) 281-5265
E-mail: Barbara.Guy@ed.state.ia.us
Web: www.state.ia.us/educate/ecese/cfcs/

**Office of State Coordinator of Vocational Education for
Students With Disabilities**

Bureau of Community Colleges & Career and
    Technical Education
Department of Education
Grimes State Office Building
Des Moines, IA 50319-0146
(515) 281-3866
Web: www.state.ia.us/educate/

**Employment Rights for
People With Disabilities**

Division of Persons with Disabilities
Department of Human Rights
Jill Avery, Administrator
Lucas State Office Building
Des Moines, IA 50319
(515) 242-6172; (888) 219-0471 (V/TTY)
E-mail: dhr.disabilities@iowa.gov
Web: www.state.ia.us/dhr

State Mental Health Agency

State Mental Health Agency/State DD Program
Division of Behavioral, Developmental and
    Protective Services for Families, Adults
    and Children
Department of Human Services
Mary Nelson, Administrator
Hoover State Office Building, 5th Floor
1305 E. Walnut Street
Des Moines, IA 50319-0114
(515) 281-5521
E-mail: mnelson1@dhs.state.ia.us
Web: www.dhs.state.ia.us

**State Mental Health Representative
for Children and Youth**

Mary Mohrhauser, Child and Adolescent
    Mental Health Specialist
State Mental Health Agency/State DD Program
Division of Behavioral, Developmental and
    Protective Services for Families, Adults
    and Children
Department of Human Services
Hoover State Office Building, 5th Floor
1305 E. Walnut Street
Des Moines, IA 50319-0114
(515) 242-6845
E-mail: mmohrha@dhs.state.ia.us
Web: www.dhs.state.ia.us

Council on Developmental Disabilities

Becky Harker, Executive Director
Governor's Developmental Disabilities Council
617 E. Second Street
Des Moines, IA 50309
(515) 281-9083
E-mail: bharker@dhs.state.ia.us
Web: http://iddcouncil.idaction.org/

Protection and Advocacy Agency

Sylvia Piper, Executive Director
Iowa Protection and Advocacy Services, Inc.
950 Office Park Road, Suite 221
West Des Moines, IA 50265
(515) 278-2502; (800) 779-2502
(515) 278-0571 (TTY)
E-mail: info@ipna.org
Web: www.ipna.org

Client Assistance Program

Department of Human Rights
Division of Persons with Disability
Client Assistance Program
Harlietta Helland, Consultant
Capitol Complex, Lucas Building
Des Moines, IA 50319
(515) 281-3957; (800) 652-4198 (V/TTY)
E-mail: harlietta.helland@iowa.gov

**Programs for Children With
Special Health Care Needs**

Iowa Child Health Specialty Clinics
Jeffrey G. Lobas, MD, Director
100 Hawkins Drive, Room 247
Iowa City, IA 52242-1011
(319) 356-1118; (866) 219-9119
(866) 236-1423 (TTY)
E-mail: jeffrey-lobas@uiowa.edu
Web: www.medicine.uiowa.edu/chsc

**State CHIP Program (health care
for low-income, uninsured children)**

hawk-i Program
P.O. Box 71336
Des Moines, IA 50325-9958
(800) 257-8563
Web: www.hawk-i.org/

**Programs for Children
and Youth Who Are Blind or
Visually Impaired or Deaf-Blind**

Iowa Department for the Blind
Allen C. Harris, Director
524 Fourth Street
Des Moines, IA 50309-2364
(515) 281-1333; (515) 281-1355 (TTY)
E-mail: harris.allen@blind.state.ia.us
Web: www.blind.state.ia.us

Programs for Children and Youth Who Are Deaf or Hard of Hearing

Kathryn Baumann-Reese, Administrator
Deaf Services Commission of Iowa
Iowa Department of Human Rights
Lucas State Office Building
Des Moines, IA 50319-0090
(515) 281-3164 (V/TTY)
E-mail: dhr.dsci@iowa.gov
Web: www.state.ia.us/government/dhr

Telecommunications Relay Services for Individuals Who Are Deaf, Hard of Hearing, or With Speech Impairments

(800) 735-2943 (V)
(800) 735-2942 (V/TTY); 711 (TTY)
(877) 735-1007 (Speech to Speech)

Regional ADA & IT Technical Assistance Center

Great Plains Disability and
    Business Technical Assistance Center
University of Missouri/Columbia
Jim de Jong, Director
100 Corporate Lake Drive
Columbia, MO 65203
(573) 882-3600; (800) 949-4232 (V/TTY)
E-mail: ada@missouri.edu
Web: www.adaproject.org

University Center for Excellence in Developmental Disabilities

Iowa's University Center for Excellence
    on Disabilities
Center for Disabilities and Development
Robert Bacon, MA, Director
100 Hawkins Drive
Iowa City, IA 52242
(319) 356-1335
E-mail: robert-bacon@uiowa.edu
Web: www.medicine.uiowa.edu/cdd/iuce.asp

Technology-Related Assistance

Iowa Program for Assistive Technology
Center for Disabilities and Development
The University of Iowa
Jane Gay, Director
100 Hawkins Drive, South 295
Iowa City, IA 52242-1011
(319) 353-8777; (800) 331-3027 (V)
(877) 686-0032 (TTY)
E-mail: infotech@uiowa.edu
Web: www.uiowa.edu/infotech/

State Mediation System

Dee Ann Wilson, Consultant
Department of Education
Bureau of Children, Family and
    Community Services
Grimes State Office Building
Des Moines, IA 50319
(515) 281-5766
E-mail: DeeAnn.Wilson@iowa.gov
Web: www.state.ia.us/educate

Special Format Library

Library for the Blind and Physically Handicapped
Iowa Department for the Blind
Karen Keninger, Librarian
524 Fourth Street
Des Moines, IA 50309-2364
(515) 281-1333; (800) 362-2587
(515) 281-1355 (TTY)
E-mail: keninger.karen@blind.state.ia.us
Web: www.blind.state.ia.us/library/

Iowa—Disability-Specific Organizations

Attention Deficit Disorder

To identify an ADD group in Iowa, contact either of the following organizations:

Children and Adults with Attention-Deficit/
    Hyperactivity Disorder (CHADD)
8181 Professional Place, Suite 150
Landover, MD 20785
(301) 306-7070
(800) 233-4050 (Voice mail to request
    information packet)
Web: www.chadd.org

Attention Deficit Disorder Association (ADDA)
P.O. Box 543
Pottstown, PA 19464
(484) 945-2101
E-mail: mail@add.org
Web: www.add.org

Autism

To identify an autism group in your state, contact

Autism Society of America
7910 Woodmont Avenue, Suite 300
Bethesda, MD 20814
(301) 657-0881; (800) 3-AUTISM
Web: www.autism-society.org

Blind/Visual Impairments

American Foundation for the Blind–Midwest
Jay Stiteley, Director
401 N. Michigan Avenue, Suite 350
Chicago, IL 60611
(312) 396-4420
E-mail: chicago@afb.net
Web: www.afb.org

Brain Injury

Brain Injury Association of Iowa
2101 Kimball Avenue, LL7
Waterloo, IA 50702
(319) 272-2312; (800) 475-4442
E-mail: biaia@cedarnet.org
Web: www.biaia.org

Cerebral Palsy

The Arc of Cedar Valley
Peg Eherenman, Executive Director
760 Ansborough Avenue
P.O. Box 4090
Waterloo, IA 50704-4090
(319) 232-0437

Epilepsy

Epilepsy Foundation North/Central Illinois,
*   Iowa & Nebraska*
Victor Verni, Executive Director
321 W. State Street, Suite 208
Rockford, IL 61101-1119
(815) 964-2689; (800) 221-2689
E-mail: efncil@efncil.org
Web: http://www.epilepsy.com/north-central-
*   illinois-iowa-nebraska*

Learning Disabilities

Learning Disabilities Association of Iowa
Kathy Specketer, Coordinator
321 E. Sixth Street
Des Moines, IA 50309
(515) 280-8558; (888) 690-5324
E-mail: kathylda@askresource.org
Web: www.lda-ia.org

Mental Health

Iowa Federation of Families for Children's
*   Mental Health*
Lori Reynolds, Executive Director
P.O. Box 362
Anamosa, IA 52205
(319) 462-2187; (888) 400-6302
E-mail: help@iffcmh.org
Web: www.iffcmh.org

NAMI Iowa
Margaret Stout, Executive Director
5911 Meredith Drive, Suite E
Des Moines, IA 50322-1903
(515) 254-0417; (800) 417-0417
E-mail: namiiowa@aol.com

Mental Retardation

The Arc of Iowa
715 E. Locust
Des Moines, IA 50309
(515) 283-2358; (800) 326-2927
E-mail: arciowa@aol.com

Speech and Hearing

Iowa Speech-Language-Hearing Association
Sheila Dietz, Executive Director
525 SW Fifth Street, Suite A
Des Moines, IA 50309-4501
(515) 282-8192
E-mail: sdietz@assoc-mgmt.com
Web: www.isha.org

Special Health Care Needs

Family Voices/Health Information Center
Paula S. Connolly, Project Director
321 E. Sixth Street
Des Moines, IA 50309
(515) 243-1713; (800) 450-8667
E-mail: f2finfo@askresource.org
Web: www.askresource.org

Spina Bifida

Spina Bifida Association of Iowa
Rod Tressel, President
P.O. Box 1456
Des Moines, IA 50305
(515) 964-8810
E-mail: SpinaBifidaIowa@yahoo.com
Web: www.spinabifidaia.com

Iowa—Organizations Especially for Parents

Access for Special Kids
Parent Training and Information Center (PTI)
Jule Reynolds, Director
321 E. Sixth Street
Des Moines, IA 50309
(515) 243-1713; (800) 450-8667
E-mail: jule@askresource.org
Web: www.askresource.org

Parent-To-Parent

ASK (Access For Special Kids) Resource Center
321 E. Sixth Street
Des Moines, IA 50309
(515) 243-1713; (800) 450-8667
E-mail: info@askresource.org
Web: www.askresource.org

Parent Teacher Association (PTA)

Iowa Congress of Parents and Teachers
Sherry Brown, President
8345 University Boulevard, Suite F-1
Des Moines, IA 50325
(515) 225-4197; (800) 475-4782
E-mail: ia_office@pta.org
Web: www.iowapta.org

Iowa—Other Disability Organizations

Easter Seals Iowa
Donna K. Elbrecht, President/CEO
P.O. Box 4002
Des Moines, IA 50333-4002
(515) 289-1933; (515) 289-4069 (TTY)
E-mail: info@eastersealsia.org
Web: www.eastersealsia.org

Iowa Compass: Information and Referral
Jane Gay, Director
Center for Disabilities and Development
The University of Iowa
100 Hawkins Drive
Iowa City, IA 52242
(319) 353-8777; (800) 779-2001
E-mail: iowa-compass@uiowa.edu
Web: www.medicine.uiowa.edu/iowacompass

Parent Educator Connection
Deb Samson, Parent Coordinator
Department of Education
Grimes State Office Building
Des Moines, IA 50319-0146
(515) 242-5295
E-mail: deb.samson@iowa.gov

VSA Arts of Iowa
Stephanie Dunker, Executive Director
Department of Education
Grimes State Office Building
Des Moines, IA 50319-0146
(515) 281-5839
E-mail: steph.dunker@iowa.gov
Web: http://vsaiowa.org/

Independent Living

To find out the contact information for the Statewide Independent Living Council (SILC) in Iowa, contact

Independent Living Research Utilization Project
The Institute for Rehabilitation and Research
2323 South Sheppard, Suite 1000
Houston, TX 77019
(713) 520-0232 (V); (713) 520-5136 (TTY)
E-mail: ilru@ilru.org
Web: www.ilru.org

To find out the contact information for centers for independent living (CILs) in Iowa, contact

National Council on Independent Living
1916 Wilson Boulevard, Suite 209
Arlington, VA 22201
(703) 525-3406; (703) 525-4153 (TTY)
E-mail: ncil@ncil.org
Web: www.ncil.org

KANSAS

Kansas—State Agencies and Organizations

United States Senators

Honorable Jerry Moran (R)
361A Russell Senate Office Building
Washington, DC 20510
(202) 224-6521
(202) 228-1265 (Fax)
E-mail Web Form: http://www.moran.senate.
gov/public/index.cfm/e-mail-jerry
Web: http://www.moran.senate.gov/public/
index.cfm/home

Honorable Pat Roberts (R)
109 Hart Senate Office Building
Washington, DC 20510
(202) 224-4774
(202) 224-3514 (Fax)
E-mail Web Form: http://roberts.senate.gov/
email.htm
Web: http://roberts.senate.gov

United States Representatives

To find the contact information for your representative in the House of the U.S. Congress, visit the House's Web site at: www.house.gov, or call: (202) 225-3121; (202) 225-1904 (TTY).

Governor

Honorable Sam Brownback
Office of the Governor
Capitol, 300 SW 10th Avenue, Suite 241S
Topeka, KS 66612-1590
(785) 296-3232; (800) 748-4408 (V/TTY)
E-mail: governor@state.ks.us
Web: https://governor.ks.gov/home

Official State Web Site

Web: www.accesskansas.org/

State Department of Education: Special Education
Colleen Riley, Director
Student Support Services
Kansas State Department of Education
120 SE 10th Avenue
Topeka, KS 66612
(785) 291-3097
Web: http://www.ksde.org/Default.
aspx?tabid=101

State Coordinator for NCLB (No Child Left Behind)

Kansas has been granted an extended waiver from the NCLB program.

Colleen Riley, Director
Early Childhood, Special Education, and Title
Services
Kansas Department of Education
900 SW Jackson Street
Topeka, KS 66612
(785) 296-7454
Email: criley@ksde.org
Web: http://www.ksde.org/Default.
aspx?tabid=564

Programs for Infants and Toddlers With Disabilities: Birth–2 Years

Children's Developmental Services
Sarah Walters, Part C Coordinator
State Department of Health and Environment
Curtis State Office Building, Suite 220
Topeka, KS 66612
(785) 296-2245
E-mail: swalters@kdheks.gov
Web: http://www.kdheks.gov/cds/index.html

Programs for Children With Disabilities: 3–5 Years

Kansas State Department of Education
Vera Stroup-Rentier, 619 Coordinator
Early Childhood, Special Education and Title
Services
Landon State Office Building
900 SW Jackson St., Suite 620
Topeka, KS 66612-1212
(785) 296-5081
E-mail: vstroup-rentier@ksde.org
Web: http://www.ksde.org/Default.
aspx?tabid=528

State Vocational Rehabilitation Agency

Kansas Rehabilitation Services
Dale Barnum, Director
Department of Social and
Rehabilitation Services
3640 SW Topeka Boulevard, Suite 150
Topeka, KS 66611
(785) 267-5301
E-mail: dxlb@srskansas.org
Web: www.srskansas.org/rehab/

Coordinator for Transition Services

Wenda Blaauw, Education
   Program Consultant
Student Support Services
Kansas State Department of Education
120 SE 10th Avenue
Topeka, KS 66612
(785) 296-7453
E-mail: wblaauw@ksde.org
Web: www.kansped.org

**Office of State Coordinator
of Vocational Education for
Students With Disabilities**

Technical Education Team
Kansas State Department of Education
Linda Oborny, Assistant Director
120 SE 10th Avenue
Topeka, KS 66612
(785) 296-3048
E-mail: loborny@ksde.org
Web: www.ksde.org

State Mental Health Agency

Health Care Policy Division
Docking State Office Building
915 SW Harrison Street, 10th Floor
Topeka, KS 66612-1570
(913) 296-7272

**State Mental Health
Representative for Children and Youth**

Children's Services, Health
   Care Policy Division
Department of Social and Rehabilitation
   Services
Pam Alger, Team Leader
Docking State Office Building
915 SW Harrison Street, 10th Floor
Topeka, KS 66612-1570
(785) 296-7272
E-mail: PRA@srskansas.org

State Developmental Disabilities Program

Community Supports and Services
Health Care Policy Division
Department of Social and
   Rehabilitation Services

Margaret Zillinger, Director
Docking State Office Building
915 SW Harrison Street, 10th Floor
Topeka, KS 66612-1570
(785) 296-3561
E-mail: mmz@srskansas.org
Web: www.srskansas.org/hcp/

Council on Developmental Disabilities

Kansas Council on Developmental Disabilities
Jane Rhys, Executive Director
Docking State Office Building, Room 141
915 SW Harrison Street
Topeka, KS 66612-1570
(785) 296-2608
E-mail: jrhys@alltel.net
Web: http://nekesc.org/kcdd.html

Protection and Advocacy Agency

Kansas Advocacy and Protective Services
3745 SW Wanamaker Road
Topeka, KS 66610
(785) 273-9661; (877) 776-1541 (in KS only)
E-mail: info@ksadv.org
Web: www.ksadv.org

Client Assistance Program

Client Assistance Program
Rocky Nichols, Director
635 SW Harrison, Suite 100
Topeka, Kansas 66603
(785) 273-9661
(877) 776-1541
E-mail: rocky@drckansas.org
Web: http://www.drckansas.org/publications/
   kansas-client-assistance-program

**Programs for Children With
Special Health Care Needs**

Services for Children with Special Health Care Needs
Heather Smith, Director
Department of Health and Environment
1000 SW Jackson Street, Suite 220
Topeka, KS 66612-1274
(785) 296-1313; (800) 332-6262 (in KS)
E-mail: hsmith@kdheks.gov
Web: http://www.kdheks.gov/shcn/index.
   htm

*State CHIP Program (health care
for low-income, uninsured children)*

Kansas HealthWave
P.O. Box 3599
Topeka, KS 66601
(800) 792-4884
Web: www.kansashealthwave.org/

**Programs for Children and Youth
Who Are Deaf or Hard of Hearing**

Kansas Commission for the Deaf and
    Hard of Hearing
Michael Donnelly, Director
Docking State Office Building, 8th Floor West
915 SW Harrison
Topeka, Kansas 66612
(785) 368-8046 (V/TTY)
(800) 432-0698 (V/TTY)
Web: http://www.dcf.ks.gov/services/RS/
    Pages/KCDHH.aspx

**Telecommunications Relay Services for Individuals Who
Are Deaf, Hard of Hearing, or With Speech Impairments**

(800) 766-3777 (V)
(800) 766-3777 (TTY); 711 (TTY)
(866) 305-1344 (Speech to Speech)

**Programs for Children and Youth Who Are Blind or
Visually Impaired or Deaf-Blind**

William Daugherty, Superintendent
The Kansas State School for the Blind
1100 State Avenue
Kansas City, Kansas 66102
(913) 281-3308; (800) 572-5463 (in KS)
Web: www.kssb.net/

**Regional ADA & IT Technical
Assistance Center**

Great Plains Disability and Business Technical
    Assistance Center
University of Missouri/Columbia
Jim de Jong, Director
100 Corporate Lake Drive
Columbia, MO 65203
(573) 882-3600 (V/TTY); (800) 949-4232
    (V/TTY)
E-mail: ada@missouri.edu
Web: www.adaproject.org

**University Center for Excellence
in Developmental Disabilities**

Kansas University Center on
    Developmental Disabilities
University of Kansas
Michael Wehmeyer, Director
1052 Robert Dole Human
    Development Center
1000 Sunnyside Avenue
Lawrence, KS 66045
(785) 864-4295; (785) 864-5051 (TTY)
E-mail: kucdd@ku.edu
Web: www.lsi.ku.edu

Technology-Related Assistance

Assistive Technology for Kansans Project
Charles Spellman, Director
Sara Sack, Director
2601 Gabriel Avenue
P.O. Box 738
Parsons, KS 67357
(620) 421-8367; (800) 526-3648
E-mail: ssack@ku.edu
Web: http://atk.ku.edu/

State Mediation System

Kansas State Department of Education
Student Support Services Team
Mark Ward, Coordinator
120 SE 10th Avenue
Topeka, KS 66612-1182
(785) 296-5478
E-mail: mward@ksde.org
Web: www.kansped.org

Special Format Library

Kansas State Library Talking Book Service
Toni Harrell, Director/Librarian
ESU Memorial Union
1200 Commercial, Box 4055
Emporia, KS 66801-5087
(620) 343-7124; (800) 362-0699
E-mail: tonih@kslib.info
Web: http://kslib.info/153/Talking-Books

Kansas—Disability-Specific Organizations

Attention Deficit Disorder

To identify an ADD group in Kansas, contact either of the following organizations:

Children and Adults with Attention-Deficit/
Hyperactivity Disorder (CHADD)
8181 Professional Place, Suite 150
Landover, MD 20785
(301) 306-7070
(800) 233-4050 (Voice mail to request
information packet)
Web: www.chadd.org

Attention Deficit Disorder Association (ADDA)
P.O. Box 543
Pottstown, PA 19464
(484) 945-2101
Web: www.add.org

Autism

Autism Society of Kansas
2250 N. Rock Road, Suite 118-254
Wichita, KS 67226
(316) 943-1191
E-mail: askansas@att.net

Autism Asperger Resource Center
Sue Ann Kline, Executive Director
2012 DDC Building
3901 Rainbow Boulevard
Kansas City, KS 66160
(913) 588-5988
E-mail: theaarc@msn.com
Web: www.autismasperger.org

Blind/Visual Impairments

American Foundation for the Blind–Southwest
Judy Scott, Director
11030 Ables Lane
Dallas, TX 75229
(214) 352-7222
E-mail: dallas@afb.net
Web: www.afb.org

Brain Injury

Brain Injury Association of Kansas and
    Greater Kansas City
Leigh Liggett, Executive Director
1100 Pennsylvania
Kansas City, MO 64105-1336
(816) 842-8607; (800) 783-1356
E-mail: leigh@crn.org
Web: www.braininjuryresource.org

Cerebral Palsy

United Cerebral Palsy of Kansas
Dave Jones, Executive Director
5111 E. 21st Street
Wichita, KS 67208
(316) 688-1888
F-mail: Davej@cprf.org
Web: www.ucpa.org

Cerebral Palsy Research Foundation of Kansas, Inc.
Mary Carter, SACT Program Director
School of Adaptive Computer Training
5111 E. 21st Street North
Wichita, KS 67208
(316) 688-1888
E-mail: info@cprf.org
Web: www.cprf.org

Epilepsy

Epilepsy Foundation of Kansas and Western Missouri
Peggy Walls, Executive Director
6550 Troost, Suite B
Kansas City, MO 64131-1272
(816) 444-2800; (800) 972-5163
E-mail: pwalls@efha.org
Web: www.efha.org

Learning Disabilities

Learning Disabilities Association of Kansas
Andrea Blair, President
P.O. Box 4424
Topeka, KS 66604
(785) 273-4505
E-mail: marciasu@aol.com
Web: www.ldakansas.org

Mental Health

Mental Health Association of South Central Kansas
Rose Mary Mohr, President
555 N. Woodlawn, Suite 3105
Wichita, KS 67208
(316) 685-1821
E-mail: rosemary@mhasck.org
Web: www.mhasck.org

NAMI Kansas
Karen Ford Manza, Executive Director
112 SW 6th, Suite 505
P.O. Box 675
Topeka, KS 66601
(785) 233-0755; (800) 539-2660
E-mail: namikansas@nami.org
Web: www.namikansas.org

Mental Retardation

TARC
Mike Purdon, Advocacy Coordinator
2701 SW Randolph
Topeka, KS 66611
(785) 232-0597
E-mail: mpurdon@tarcinc.org
Web: www.tarcinc.org

Speech and Hearing

Kansas Speech-Language-Hearing Association
Dixie Heinrich, KSHA Coordinator
3900 17th Avenue
Great Bend, KS 67530
(620) 793-6550; (800) 248-5742
E-mail: ksha96@aol.com
Web: www.ksha.org

Spina Bifida

Spina Bifida Association of Kansas
Tim Wolke, Co-President
Tammy Wolke, Co-President
4421 W. Harry
Wichita, KS 67209
(316) 516-7225
E-mail: tntwolke@quixnet.net

Kansas—Organizations Especially for Parents

Parent Training and Information Center (PTI)

Families Together, Inc.
Connie Zienkewicz, Executive Director
3033 W. Second, Suite 106
Wichita, KS 67203
(316) 945-7747; (877) 499-5369 (Kansas City)
(888) 815-6364 (Wichita);
    (800) 264-6343 (Topeka)
(888) 820-6364 (Garden City);
    (800) 499-9443 (Espanol)
E-mail: wichita@familiestogetherinc.org
Web: www.familiestogetherinc.org

Community Parent Resource Center (serving
    an urban area within Sedgwick County)
Nina Lomely-Baker, Director/President
Mental Health Association of
    South Central Kansas
555 N. Woodlawn, Suite 3105
Wichita, KS 67208
(316) 685-1821, ext. 256
E-mail: nina@mhasck.org
Web: www.mhasck.org

Partners in Policymaking
Kansas Developmental Disabilities Council
Keith Tatum, Coordinator
Docking State Office Building, Room 141
915 SW Harrison Street
Topeka, KS 66612-1570
(785) 296-2608
E-mail: partnersinpolicy@kcdd.org
Web: http://partnersonlinecourses.com/

Parent Teacher Association (PTA)

Kansas Congress of Parents and Teachers
Peggy Davis, President
715 SW 10th Street
Topeka, KS 66612-1686
(785) 234-5782
E-mail: ks_office@pta.org
Web: www.ptasonline.org

Other Parent Organizations

Keys for Networking
Jane Adams, Executive Director
1301 SW Topeka Boulevard
Topeka, KS 66612-1816
(785) 233-8732; (800) 499-8732 (Parent line)
E-mail: jadams@keys.org
Web: www.keys.org

Kansans for IDEA Compliance
Helle S. Vander Yacht,
    Executive Director
607 E. Republic
Salina, KS 67401
(785) 823-7797
E-mail: helle@cox.net
Web: www.ideacompliance.org

Kansas—Other Disability Organizations

Goodwill Industries Easter Seals of Kansas, Inc.
Marie Mareda, President
3636 North Oliver
P.O. Box 8169
Wichita, KS 67208-0169
(316) 744-9291
Web: www.goodwilleastersealsks.org

Kansas Commission on Disability Concerns
Kansas Department of Commerce
1430 SW Topeka Boulevard
Topeka, KS 66612-1819
(800) 295-5232; (877) 340-5874 (TTY)
Web: http://adabbs.hr.state.ks.us/

Kansas Federation of the Council
    for Exceptional Children
Sue Ann Kline, PhD, President
8930 Foster Lane
Overland Park, KS 66212
E-mail: SAKline101@aol.com

Accessible Arts, Inc.
Martin English, Executive Director
1100 State Avenue
Kansas City, KS 66102
(913) 281-1133
E-mail: accarts@accessiblearts.org
Web: www.accessiblearts.org

Special Olympics Kansas
Chris Hahn, President/CEO
5280 Foxridge Drive
Mission, KS 66202
(913) 236-9290
E-mail: hahnc@ksso.org
Web: www.ksso.org

Independent Living

To find out the contact information for the Statewide Independent Living Council (SILC) in Kansas, contact

Independent Living Research Utilization Project
The Institute for Rehabilitation and Research
2323 South Sheppard, Suite 1000
Houston, TX 77019
(713) 520-0232 (V); (713) 520-5136 (TTY)
E-mail: ilru@ilru.org
Web: www.ilru.org

To find out the contact information for centers for independent living (CILs) in Kansas, contact

National Council on Independent Living
1916 Wilson Boulevard, Suite 209
Arlington, VA 22201
(703) 525-3406; (703) 525-4153 (TTY)
E-mail: ncil@ncil.org
Web: www.ncil.org

KENTUCKY

Kentucky—State Agencies and Organizations

United States Senators

Honorable Mitch McConnell (R)
317 Russell Senate Office Building
Washington, DC 20510
(202) 224-2541
(202) 228-1373 (Fax)
E-mail: senator@mcconnell.senate.gov
Web: http://mcconnell.senate.gov

Honorable Rand Paul (R)
124 Russell Senate Office Building
Washington, DC 20510
(202) 224-4343
(202) 224-2499 (Fax)
E-mail: http://www.paul.senate.gov/?p=contact
Web: http://www.paul.senate.gov/?p=home

United States Representatives

To find the contact information for your representative in the House of the U.S. Congress, visit the House's Web site at: www.house.gov, or call: (202) 225-3121; (202) 225-1904 (TTY).

Governor

Honorable Steve Beshear
700 Capitol Street, Suite 100
Frankfort, KY 40601
(502) 564-2611
E-mail: http://governor.ky.gov/Pages/contact.
    aspx
Web: http://governor.ky.gov/Pages/default.
    aspx

Official State Web Site

Web: http://kentucky.gov/Default.html

State Department of Education: Special Education

R. Larry Taylor, Director
Division of Exceptional Children's Services
Kentucky Department of Education
Capitol Plaza Tower, 8th Floor
500 Mero Street
Frankfort, KY 40601
(502) 564-4970
E-mail: larry.taylor@education.ky.gov
Web: www.education.ky.gov

State Coordinator for NCLB (No Child Left Behind)

Kentucky has been granted an extended waiver from the NCLB program.

Donna Tackett
Next-Generation Schools and Districts
Division of Consolidated Plans and Audits
Kentucky Department of Education
500 Mero Street, 8th Floor CPT
Frankfort, KY 40601
(502) 564 3791
Email: donna.tackett@education.ky.gov
Web: http://education.ky.gov/federal/progs/
    Pages/default.aspx

Programs for Infants and Toddlers With Disabilities: Birth–2 Years

First Steps
Paula Goff, Part C Coordinator
Department for Public Health
Early Childhood Development Branch
275 E. Main Street, HS2G-B
Frankfort, KY 40621
(502) 564-3756; (800) 232-1160
E-mail: paula.goff@ky.gov
Web: http://chfs.ky.gov/dph/firststeps.htm

Programs for Children With Disabilities: 3–5 Years

Division of Early Childhood Development
Department of Education
Sally Shepherd, 619 Coordinator
Office of Next Generation Learners
School Readiness Branch
500 Mero Street, 17th Floor
Frankfort, KY 40601
(502) 564-7056
E-mail: sally.shepherd@education.ky.gov
Web: http://education.ky.gov/specialed/
    Pages/default.aspx

State Vocational Rehabilitation Agency

Beth Smith, Executive Director
Office of Vocational Rehabilitation
Education Cabinet
Department of Workforce Investment
209 St. Clair
Frankfort, KY 40601
(502) 564-4440
E-mail: beth.smith@ky.gov
Web: http://ovr.ky.gov

Coordinator for Transition Services

Preston Lewis, Program Manager
Division for Exceptional Children Services
Kentucky Department of Education
500 Mero Street, CPT 8th Floor
Frankfort, KY 40601
(502) 564-4970
E-mail: plewis@kde.state.ky.us
Web: www.education.ky.gov

Division of Career and Technical Education

Pathways to Careers and Special Programs
Donnalie Stratton, Program Consultant
Capitol Plaza Tower, Room 2113
500 Mero Street
Frankfort, KY 40601
(502) 564-3775
E-mail: dstratto@kde.state.ky.us
Web: www.education.ky.gov

State Mental Health Agency

Pat Wear, II, Commissioner
Department for Mental Health/
    Mental Retardation Services
Cabinet for Health and Family Services
100 Fair Oaks Lane, 4E-B
Frankfort, KY 40621-0001
(502) 564-4527
E-mail: pat.wear@ky.gov
Web: http://mhmr.ky.gov

Department for Mental Health and Substance Abuse

Cabinet for Health and Family Services
Karyn Hascal, Division Director
100 Fair Oaks Lane, 4E-D
Frankfort, KY 40621-0001
(502) 564-2880
E-mail: karyn.hascal@ky.gov
Web: http://mhmr.ky.gov/mh

Early Childhood Mental Health: Birth–5 Years
Beth Jordan, Health Program Administrator
Department for Mental Health and
    Substance Abuse Services
Division of Mental Health
275 E. Main Street, 4WG
Frankfort, KY 40621
(502) 564-4527
E-mail Contact Form: http://dbhdid.ky.gov/
    contact.aspx?p=106
Web: http://dbhdid.ky.gov/dbh/ecmh.aspx

Opportunities for Family Leadership
Susan A. Smith, Coordinator
Department for Mental Health/Mental
    Retardation Services
100 Fair Oaks Lane, 4E-B
Frankfort, KY 40621
(502) 564-4860
E-mail: susana.smith@ky.gov
Web: http://chfs.ky.gov/dbhdid/

State Mental Health Representative for Children and Youth

Randy Oliver, Manager
Children and Youth Services
Division of Mental Health
Department for Mental Health and Mental
    Retardation Services
100 Fair Oaks Lane, 4W-C
Frankfort, KY 40621-0001
(502) 564-7610; (800) 374-9146
E-mail: randy.oliver@ky.gov
Web: http://mhmr.chs.ky.gov/mh/cysb

State Mental Retardation Program

Betsy Dunnigan, Acting Director
Division of Mental Retardation
Department of Mental Health and Mental
    Retardation Services
100 Fair Oaks Lane, 4E-E
Frankfort, KY 40621-0001
(502) 564-7700
Web: http://mhmr.ky.gov/mr

Council on Developmental Disabilities

Pat Seybold, Executive Director
Kentucky Developmental Disabilities Council
Department of Mental Health and
    Mental Retardation Services
100 Fair Oaks Lane, 4E-F
Frankfort, KY 40621-0001
(502) 564-7842
E-mail: pat.seybold@ky.gov
Web: www.kddc.org

Protection and Advocacy Agency

Protection and Advocacy Division
Maureen Fitzgerald, Director
100 Fair Oaks Lane, Third Floor
Frankfort, KY 40601
(502) 564-2967; (800) 372-2988 (V/TTY in KY)
E-mail: info@kypa.net
Web: www.kypa.net

Client Assistance Program

Client Assistance Program
Gerry Gordon-Brown, Director
209 St. Clair, 5th Floor
Frankfort, KY 40601
(502) 564-8035; (800) 633-6283 (in KY)
E-mail: gerry.gordon-brown@ky.gov

Programs for Children With Special Health Care Needs

Commission for Children with Special
  Health Care Needs
Eric Friedlander, Executive Director
982 Eastern Parkway
Louisville, KY 40217
(502) 595-4459, ext. 271; (800) 232-1160
E-mail: eric.friedlander@ky.gov
Web: www.chs.ky.gov/commissionkids

State CHIP Program (health care for low-income, uninsured children)

KCHIP
(877) 524-4718; (877) 524-4719 (TTY)
(800) 662-5397 (Spanish)
Web: www.chs.ky.gov/kchip/

Programs for Children and Youth Who Are Blind or Visually Impaired

Office for the Blind
Department of Workforce Investment
Stephen Johnson, Executive Director
P.O. Box 757
Frankfort, KY 40602-0757
(502) 564-4754; (502) 564-2929 (TTY)
E-mail: stephen.johnson@ky.gov
Web: http://blind.ky.gov

Kentucky School for the Blind
Cathy Johnson, Director
Kentucky Instructional and Diagnostic Services
1867 Frankfort Avenue
Louisville, KY 40206
(502) 897-1583
E-mail: cjohnson@ksb.k12.ky.us
Web: www.ksb.k12.ky.us

Programs for Children and Youth Who Are Deaf or Hard of Hearing

Kentucky Commission on the Deaf and
  Hard of Hearing
Bobbie Beth Scoggins, Executive Director
632 Versailles Road
Frankfort, KY 40601
(502) 573-2604 (V/TTY)
(800) 372-2907 (V/TTY, in KY only)
E-mail: kcdhh@mail.state.ky.us
Web: www.kcdhh.org

Telecommunications Relay Services for Individuals Who Are Deaf, Hard of Hearing, or With Speech Impairments

(800) 648-6057 (V)
(800) 648-6056 (TTY/ASCII); 711 (TTY)
(888) 244-6111 (Speech to Speech)

Programs for Children and Youth Who Are Deaf-Blind

UK Kentucky Deaf-Blind Project
Diane Haynes, Project Director
12 Erikson Hall
Lexington, KY 40506-0050
(859) 257-7732
E-mail: dhaynes@ksb.k12.ky.us

State Education Agency Rural Representative

Kevin Nolan, Deputy Commissioner
  of Operations and Support
Department of Education
500 Mero Street, Capitol Plaza Tower, 1st Floor
Frankfort, KY 40601
(502) 564-4474
E-mail: knolan@kde.state.ky.us
Web: www.education.ky.gov

Regional ADA & IT Technical Assistance Center

Southeast Disability and Business Technical
  Assistance Center
Center for Assistive Technology and
  Environmental Access
Georgia Tech
Shelley Kaplan, Project Director
490 10th Street
Atlanta, GA 30318
(404) 385-0636; (800) 949-4232 (V/TTY)
E-mail: sedbtac@catea.org
Web: www.sedbtac.org

Technology-Related Assistance

Kentucky Assistive Technology Service
  (KATS) Network
Chase Forrester, Director
Charles McDowell Center
8412 Westport Road
Louisville, KY 40242
(502) 327-0022 (V/TTY); (800) 327-5287
  (V/TTY, in KY)
E-mail: katsnet@iglou.com
Web: www.katsnet.org

University Center for Excellence
in Developmental Disabilities

Human Development Institute
Interdisciplinary University
    Center for Excellence
Harold L. Kleinert, Executive Director
University of Kentucky
126 Mineral Industries Building
Lexington, KY 40506-0051
(859) 257-3045
E-mail: haroldk@ihdi.uky.edu

State Mediation System

Pam Goins, Consultant
Division of Exceptional Children Services
Department of Education
Capital Plaza Tower
500 Mero Street, Room 818
Frankfort, KY 40601
(502) 564-4970
E-mail: pgoins@kde.state.ky.us
Web: www.education.ky.gov

Special Format Library

Kentucky Library for the Blind and
    Physically Handicapped
Richard Feindel, Librarian
300 Coffee Tree Road
P.O. Box 818
Frankfort, KY 40602-0818
(502) 564-8300; (800) 372-2968
E-mail: richard.feindel@ky.gov
Web: www.kdla.ky.gov/collectionsktbl.htm

Kentucky—Disability-Specific Organizations

Attention Deficit Disorder

To identify an ADD group in Kentucky, contact either of the following organizations:

Children and Adults with Attention-Deficit/
    Hyperactivity Disorder (CHADD)
8181 Professional Place, Suite 150
Landover, MD 20785
(301) 306-7070
(800) 233-4050 (Voice mail to request
    information packet)
Web: www.chadd.org

Attention Deficit Disorder Association (ADDA)
P.O. Box 543
Pottstown, PA 19464
(484) 945-2101
Web: www.add.org

Autism

To identify an autism group in Kentucky, contact

Autism Society of America
7910 Woodmont Avenue, Suite 300
Bethesda, MD 20814
(301) 657-0881; (800) 3-AUTISM
Web: www.autism-society.org

Blind/Visual Impairments

American Foundation for the Blind–Midwest
Jay Stiteley, Director
401 N. Michigan Avenue, Suite 350
Chicago, IL 60611
(312) 396-4420
E-mail: chicago@afb.net
Web: www.afb.org

Brain Injury

Brain Injury Association of Kentucky
Melinda Mast, Executive Director
4229 Bardstown Road, Suite 330
Louisville, KY 40218
(502) 493-0609; (800) 592-1117 (in KY)
E-mail: melinda.mast@biak.us
Web: www.braincenter.org
Web: www.biak.us

Down Syndrome

Down Syndrome InfoSource, Inc.
Gail T. Lowe, Coordinator
P.O. Box 221316
Louisville, KY 40252-1316
(502) 412-3759; (888) 999-3759
E-mail: GTLowe@aol.com

Epilepsy

Epilepsy Council of Greater Cincinnati, Inc. (this
    organization has information about services
    for people with epilepsy in Kentucky)
Marge Frommeyer, Executive Director
3 Centennial Plaza
895 Central Avenue, Suite 550

Cincinnati, OH 45202
(513) 721-2905; (877) 804-2241
E-mail: ecgc@fuse.net
Web: www.ecgc.net

Epilepsy Foundation of Kentuckiana
Debbie McGrath, Executive Director
501 E. Broadway, Suite 110
Louisville, KY 40202
(502) 584-8817; (866) 275-1078
E-mail: dmcgrath@efky.org
Web: www.efky.org

Learning Disabilities

Learning Disabilities Association of Kentucky, Inc.
Martha Ruth VanCleave, Executive Director
2210 Goldsmith Lane, Suite 118
Louisville, KY 40218
(502) 473-1256
E-mail: ldaofky@aol.com
Web: www.ldaofky.org

Mental Health

Mental Health Association of Kentucky
Sheriall A. Cunningham, Executive Director
120 Sears Avenue, Suite 213
Louisville, KY 40207
(502) 893-0460; (888) 705-0463
E-mail: mhaky@kih.net
Web: www.mhaky.org

Mental Health Association of
    Northern Kentucky
David Olds, Executive Director
605 Madison Avenue
Covington, KY 41011
(859) 431-1077
E-mail: mhnky@aol.com
Web: http://mhanky.org

Kentucky Mental Health Coalition
Sheila Schuster, Executive Director
120 Sears Avenue, Suite 212
Louisville, KY 40207
(502) 894-0222
E-mail: advocacyaction@bellsouth.net
Web: www.kymhc.org

NAMI Kentucky
Dr. Harry G. Mills, Executive Director
10510 LaGrange Road, Building 103
Louisville, KY 40223-1228
(502) 245-5284; (800) 257-5081
E-mail: hmills@nami.org
E-mail: namiky@nami.org
Web: http://ky.nami.org

Kentucky Partnership for Families and Children
207 Holmes Street, First Floor
Frankfort, KY 40601
(502) 875-1320; (800) 369-0533
E-mail: kpfc@kypartnership.org
Web: www.kypartnership.org

Opportunities for Family Leadership
Deborah Anderson, Administrator
Division of Mental Health
100 Fair Oaks Lane, 4E-B
Frankfort, KY 40621
(502) 564-4527
E-mail: deborah.anderson2@ky.gov
Web: http://mhmr.chs.ky.gov

Mental Retardation

The Arc of Kentucky
Patty Dempsey, Executive Director
833 E. Main
Frankfort, KY 40601
(502) 875-5225; (800) 281-1272
E-mail: arcofky@aol.com
Web: http://arcofky.org/

Speech and Hearing

Kentucky Speech-Language-Hearing Association
Patti DeYoung, Executive Director
535 W. Second Street, Suite 103
Lexington, KY 40508
(859) 252-3776; (800) 837-2446
E-mail: KSHAoffice@aol.com
Web: www.kysha.org

Spina Bifida

Spina Bifida Association of Kentucky
982 Eastern Parkway, Box 18
Louisville, KY 40217
(502) 637-7363; (502) 637-1010
E-mail: sbak@sbak.org
Web: www.sbak.org

Kentucky—Organizations Especially for Parents

Parent Training and Information Center (PTI)

Kentucky Special Parent Involvement Network
   (KY-SPIN)
Paulette Logsdon, Director
10301-B Deering Road
Louisville, KY 40272
(502) 937-6894; (800) 525-7746
E-mail: spininc@kyspin.com
Web: www.kyspin.com

Parent-To-Parent

Parent Outreach: Parents Supporting Parents
Susan Lawrence, Parent Outreach Coordinator
1146 S. Third Street
Louisville, KY 40203
(502) 584-1239
E-mail: outreach@councilonmr.org
Web: www.councilonmr.org

Community Parent Resource Center
   (Serving Jefferson County)
FIND of Louisville
Robin Porter, Project Director
1146 S. Third Street
Louisville, KY 40203
(502) 584-1239
E-mail: info@councilonmr.org
Web: www.councilonmr.org

Parent Teacher Association (PTA)

Kentucky PTA
Sharon Barker, President
P.O. Box 654
Frankfort, KY 40602-0654
(502) 564-4378
E-mail: ky_office@pta.org
Web: www.kypta.org

Kentucky—Other Disability Organizations

Directions Disability Link
Dawn Moore, I & R Supervisor
United Way's First Link
United Way of the Bluegrass
2480 Fortune Drive, Suite 250
Lexington, KY 40509
(859) 313-5465, ext. 239
E-mail: dawn.moore@uwbg.org
Web: www.uwbg.org/

Easter Seals Kentucky
Kerry Gillihan, President/CEO
2050 Versailles Road
Lexington, KY 40504
(859) 254-5701; (800) 888-5377
Web: www.cardinalhill.org

Kentucky Disabilities Coalition
Sharon Fields, Executive Director
June Wilson, Office Manager
P.O. Box 1589
Frankfort, KY 40602
(502) 875-1871 (V/TTY); (800) 977-7505 (in KY)
E-mail: kydis@mis.net
Web: www.geocities.com/kydisabilitiescoali-
   tion

Kentucky Education Rights Center, Inc.
Dennie W. Baldwin, Executive Director
106 N. Main Street
Versailles, KY 40383
(859) 879-0411
E-mail: kerc@edrights.com
Web: www.edrights.com

VSA Arts of Kentucky
Ginny Miller, Executive Director
824 Ironwood Drive
Bowling Green, KY 42103
(270) 781-0872 (V/TTY); (877) 417-9594
E-mail: vsaky@bellsouth.net

Independent Living

To find out the contact information for the Statewide Independent Living Council (SILC) in Kentucky, contact

Independent Living Research Utilization Project
The Institute for Rehabilitation and Research
2323 South Sheppard, Suite 1000
Houston, TX 77019
(713) 520-0232 (V); (713) 520-5136 (TTY)
E-mail: ilru@ilru.org
Web: www.ilru.org

To find out the contact information for centers for independent living (CILs) in Kentucky, contact

National Council on Independent Living
1916 Wilson Boulevard, Suite 209
Arlington, VA 22201
(703) 525-3406; (703) 525-4153 (TTY)
E-mail: ncil@ncil.org
Web: www.ncil.org

LOUISIANA

Louisiana—State Agencies and Organizations

United States Senators

Honorable Mary Landrieu (D)
703 Hart Senate Office Building
Washington, DC 20510
(202) 224-5824
(202) 224-9735 (Fax)
E-mail Web Form: http://landrieu.senate.gov/
    webform.html
Web: http://landrieu.senate.gov

Honorable David Vitter (R)
516 Hart Senate Office Building
Washington, DC 20510
(202) 224-4623
(202) 228-2577 (Fax)
E-mail Web Form: http://vitter.senate.gov/
    contact.cfm
Web: http://gov.louisiana.gov/

United States Representatives

To find the contact information for your representative in the House of the U.S. Congress, visit the House's Web site at: www.house.gov, or call: (202) 225-3121; (202) 225-1904 (TTY).

Governor

Honorable Bobby Jindal
Office of the Governor
P.O. Box 94004
Baton Rouge, LA 70804-9004
(225) 342-0991
Web: http://gov.louisiana.gov/

Official State Web Site

Web: http://louisiana.gov/wps/portal

Governor's Office of Disability Affairs

Mary Anne Perault, Executive Director
Governor's Office of Disability Affairs
P.O. Box 94004
Baton Rouge, LA 70804-9004
(225) 219-7550
E-mail: Mary.Perault@la.gov
Web: www.gov.state.la.us/disabilityaffairs/
    default.asp

State Department of Education: Special Education

Dr. Susan Aysene, Director
Division of Educational Improvement and
    Assistance
Louisiana Department of Education
1201 N. 3rd Street
Baton Rouge, LA 70802
(225) 342-3513
Web: www.louisianaschools.net/lde/index.
    html

State Coordinator for NCLB (No Child Left Behind)

Louisiana has been granted a waiver from the NCLB program.

Kimberly Tripeaux, Interim Executive Director
Board of Elementary and Secondary Education
Louisiana State Department of Education
1201 N. 3rd Street
Baton Rouge, LA 70802
(225) 342-5840
Email: Kimberly.Tripeaux@la.gov
Web: http://www.louisianabelieves.com/
    accountability/federal-accountability

Programs for Infants and Toddlers With Disabilities: Birth–2 Years

Louisiana Part C Early Intervention
Louisiana Department of Health & Hospitals
Office of Public Health
Brenda Sharp, Part C Coordinator
628 North Fourth Street, Bin #21
Baton Rouge, LA 70821-3117
(225) 342-0095
E-mail: brenda.sharp@la.gov
Web: http://new.dhh.louisiana.gov/index.
    cfm/page/139/n/139

Programs for Children With Disabilities: 3–7 Years

Division of Special Populations
Louisiana State Department of Education
Ivy Starns, 619 Coordinator
1201 North Third Street
Baton Rouge, LA 70802
(225) 342-3647
E-mail: ivy.starns@la.gov
Web: http://www.louisianabelieves.com/
    early-childhood

State Vocational Rehabilitation Agency

Department of Social Services
Louisiana Rehabilitation Services
James E. Wallace, Director
225 Florida Boulevard
Baton Rouge, LA 70806-4381
(225) 925-4131; (800) 737-2958 (in LA)
E-mail: James.Wallace@dss.state.la.us
Web: www.dss.state.la.us

Coordinator for Transition Services

Virginia Beridon, Director
Division of Special Populations
Louisiana Department of Education
Clairborne Building
1201 North Third Street
Baton Rouge, LA 70802-5243
(225) 342-3633
E-mail: Virginia.Beridon@la.gov
Web: https://www.louisianabelieves.com/
    academics/students-with-disabilities

Office of State Coordinator of Vocational Education for Students With Disabilities

Patricia Merrick, Section Supervisor
Career and Technical Education
P.O. Box 94064
Baton Rouge, LA 70804-9064
(225) 219-9333
E-mail: Patricia.Merrick@la.gov
Web: www.doe.state.la.us

State Mental Health Agency

Office of Mental Health
Department of Health and Hospitals
Cheryll Bowers-Stephens, MD, MBA,
    Assitant Secretary
P.O. Box 4049 - BIN #12
Baton Rouge, LA 70821-4049
(225) 342-9238
E-mail: cstephen@dhh.la.gov
Web: www.dhh.state.la.us

State Mental Health Representative for Children and Youth

J. Richard Bassett, Director
Children's Services
Office of Mental Health
Department of Health and Hospitals
P.O. Box 4049 - BIN #12
Baton Rouge, LA 70821-4049
(225) 342-9238

E-mail: rbassett@dhh.la.gov
Web: www.dhh.state.la.us

State Mental Retardation Program

Mark A. Thomas, Assistant Secretary
Office for Citizens with Developmental
    Disabilities
P.O. Box 3117, Bin 21
Baton Rouge, LA 70821-3117
(225) 342-0095
Email: mark.thomas@la.gov
Web: http://new.dhh.louisiana.gov/index.
    cfm/page/136/n/138

Council on Developmental Disabilities

Louisiana Developmental Disabilities Council
Sandee Winchell, Executive Director
P.O. Box 3455
Baton Rouge, LA 70821-3455
(225) 342-6804; (800) 922-3425 (in LA)
E-mail: swinchel@dhh.state.la.us
Web: www.laddc.org

Protection and Advocacy Agency

The Advocacy Center
Lois V. Simpson, Executive Director
225 Baronne Street, Suite 2112
New Orleans, LA 70112-2112
(504) 522-2337; (800) 960-7705 (in LA only)
E-mail: lsimpson@advocacyla.org
Web: www.advocacyla.org

Client Assistance Program
Diane Mirvis, Director
Client Assistance Program
The Advocacy Center
2620 Centenary Boulevard, Suite 248
Shreveport, LA 71104
(318) 227-1489; (800) 960-7705 (in LA only)
E-mail: dmirvis@advocacyla.org
Web: www.advocacyla.org

Programs for Children With Special Health Care Needs

Children's Special Health Services
Office of Public Health
Department of Health and Hospitals
Linda Pippins, Administrator
P.O. Box 60630, Room 607
New Orleans, LA 70160
(504) 568-5055
E-mail: lpippins@dhh.la.gov
Web: http://www.dhh.state.la.us/index.cfm/
    page/740

State CHIP Program (health care for low-income, uninsured children)

Louisiana Children's Health Insurance Program
LaCHIP Processing Office
P.O. Box 91278
Baton Rouge, LA 70821-9278
(877) 252-2447
Web: http://new.dhh.louisiana.gov/index.
cfm/page/222

Programs for Children and Youth Who Are Blind or Visually Impaired

Blind Services
Department of Social Services
Louisiana Rehabilitation Services
Florence Menard, Executive Director
8225 Florida Boulevard
Baton Rouge, LA 70806-4834
(225) 925-4131; (225) 925-3594
E-mail: fmenard@dss.state.la.us

Louisiana Department of Education
Division of Special Populations
Joyce Russo, Director
P.O. Box 94064
Baton Rouge, LA 70804-9064
(225) 342-3640
E-mail: Joyce.Russo@la.gov
Web: www.doe.state.la.us

Programs for Children and Youth Who Are Deaf or Hard of Hearing

Louisiana Commission for the Deaf
W. Fred Roy, Executive Director
8225 Florida Boulevard
Baton Rouge, LA 70806-4834
(225) 925-4178; (800) 256-1523 (V/TTY)
(800) 543-2099 (TTY)
E-mail: froy1@dss.state.la.us
Web: http://new.dhh.louisiana.gov/index.
cfm/page/318

Telecommunications Relay Services for Individuals Who Are Deaf, Hard of Hearing, or With Speech Impairments

(800) 947-5277 (V)
(800) 846-5277 (TTY); 711 (TTY)
(888) 550-5277 (ASCII)
(888) 272-5530 (Speech to Speech)
(800) 737-1813 (Spanish)

Programs for Children and Youth Who Are Deaf-Blind

Deaf Blind Project
Division of Special Populations
Louisiana Department of Education
Joyce Russo, Director
Shawn Fleming, Educational
Program Coordinator
P.O. Box 94064
Baton Rouge, LA 70804-9064
(225) 342-3640; (877) 453-2721 (in LA)
(225) 219-4588 (TTY)
E-mail: Joyce.Russo@la.gov
E-mail: Shawn.Fleming@la.gov
Web: www.doe.state.la.us

State Education Agency Rural Representative

Bennie McKay, Supervisor
Richland Parish School Board
Special Education
P.O. Box 599
Rayville, LA 71269
(318) 728-5964

Regional ADA & IT Technical Assistance Center

Disability Law Resource Project
Wendy Wilkinson, Director
2323 S. Shepard Boulevard, Suite 1000
Houston, TX 77019
(713) 520-0232 (V/TTY); (800) 949-4232 (V/
TTY)
E-mail: dlrp@ilru.org
Web: www.dlrp.org

University Center for Excellence in Developmental Disabilities

Human Development Center
School of Allied Health Professions
LSU Health Sciences Center
Robert E. Crow, Director
1100 Florida Avenue, Building 138
New Orleans, LA 70119
(504) 942-8200; (504) 942-8380 (TDD/TTY)
E-mail: rcrow@lsuhsc.edu
Web: www.hdc.lsumc.edu

Technology-Related Assistance

Louisiana Assistive Technology Access Network
Julie Nesbit, President/CEO
P.O. Box 14115
Baton Rouge, LA 70898
(225) 925-9500; (800) 270-6185 (V/TTY)
E-mail: cpourciau@latan.org
Web: www.latan.org

State Mediation System

Department of Education
Division of Special Populations
Ellen Dunlap Spears, Coordinator
P.O. Box 94064
Baton Rouge, LA 70804-9064
(225) 342-3661
E-mail: Ellen.Dunlap@la.gov
Web: www.doe.state.la.us

Special Format Library

State Library of Louisiana
Services for the Blind and
    Physically Handicapped
Elizabeth Perkins, Librarian
701 N. Fourth Street
Baton Rouge, LA 70802
(225) 342-4944; (225) 342-4943
(800) 543-4702
E-mail: sbph@state.lib.la.us
Web: http://www.state.lib.la.us/special-
    services

Louisiana—Disability-Specific Organizations

Attention Deficit Disorder

To identify an ADD group in Louisiana, contact either of the following organizations:

Children and Adults with Attention-Deficit/
    Hyperactivity Disorder (CHADD)
8181 Professional Place, Suite 150
Landover, MD 20785
(301) 306-7070
(800) 233-4050 (Voice mail to request
    information packet)
Web: www.chadd.org

Attention Deficit Disorder Association (ADDA)
P.O. Box 543
Pottstown, PA 19464
(484) 945-2101
Web: www.add.org

Autism

Louisiana Department of Education
Shawn Fleming
Division of Special Education
P.O. Box 94064
Baton Rouge, LA 70804-9064
(225) 342-3640
E-mail: shawn.fleming@la.gov
Web: www.doe.state.la.us

Louisiana Center for Excellence in Autism
Bart M. Sevin, Director
Human Development Center
School of Allied Health Professions
LSU Health Sciences Center
1100 Florida Avenue, Building 180
New Orleans, LA 70119
(504) 942-8187; (800) 391-7668
(504) 942-8380 (TTY)
E-mail: bsevin@lsuhsc.edu
Web: www.laautism.org

Louisiana State Autism Chapter
Julie Bourgeois
4425 Annunciation Street
New Orleans, LA 70115
(504) 896-9050; (800) 955-3760
E-mail: jabou@cox.net
Web: www.lastateautism.org

Blind/Visual Impairments

American Foundation for the Blind–Southwest
Judy Scott, Director
11030 Ables Lane
Dallas, TX 75229
(214) 352-7222
E-mail: dallas@afb.net
Web: www.afb.org

Cerebral Palsy

UCP of Baton Rouge—Children's Developmental Center
Janet Ketcham, Executive Director
1805 College Drive
Baton Rouge, LA 70808
(225) 923-3420
E-mail: jketcham@mcmainscdc.org
Web: www.mcmainscdc.org

UCP of Greater New Orleans
Paul Bussell, President/CEO
1000 Leonidas Street and Leake Avenue
New Orleans, LA 70118
(504) 865-0003
E-mail: ucpgno@aol.org
Web: www.ucpgno.org

Epilepsy

Epilepsy Foundation of Southeast Louisiana
Dorothy Martino, LCSW, Executive Director
3701 Canal Street, Suite H
New Orleans, LA 70119
(504) 486-6326; (800) 960-0587
E-mail: epileps@bellsouth.net
Web: http://www.datasync.com/~josw/
    ecsela.htm

Learning Disabilities

Division of Special Populations
Anne Clouatre
Louisiana Department of Education
P.O. Box 94064
Baton Rouge, LA 70804-9064
(225) 342-3640
E-mail: anne.clouatre@la.gov
Web: www.doe.state.la.us

Northwestern State University
Barbara Duchardt, Associate Professor of
    Special Education
Teacher Education Center, Room 103-A, Pod D
Natchitoches, LA 71497
(318) 357-5154
E-mail: duchardt@nsula.edu

Mental Health

Mental Health Association in Louisiana
Yakima Black, Executive Director
263 Third Street, Suite 103
Baton Rouge, LA 70801
(225) 343-1921
E-mail: yblack@mhal.org
Web: www.mhal.org

NAMI Louisiana
Adrian Berry, Executive Director
11762 S. Harrell's Ferry Road, Suite D
Baton Rouge, LA 70816
(225) 292-6928; (888) 343-5864
E-mail: namila@bellsouth.net
Web: http://la.nami.org

Louisiana Federation of Families for
    Children's Mental Health
Verlyn "Vee" Boyd, Executive Director
5627 Superior Drive, Suite A-2
Baton Rouge, LA 70816-6085
(225) 293-3508; (800) 224-4010
E-mail: vboyd@laffcmh.com
Web: www.laffcmh.com

Mental Retardation

The Arc of Louisiana
Julia Kenny, Executive Director
365 N. 4th Street
Baton Rouge, LA 70801
(225) 383-1033
E-mail: jkarcla@bellsouth.net
Web: www.thearcla.org

Special Health Care Needs

Family Voices Louisiana
Phyllis Landry, Executive Director
1539 Jackson Avenue, Suite 200
New Orleans, LA 70130
(504) 299-9175
E-mail: familyla@bellsouth.net
Web: www.familyvoices.org

Speech and Hearing

Louisiana Speech-Language-Hearing Association
8550 United Plaza Boulevard, Suite 1001
Baton Rouge, LA 70809
(225) 922-4512
E-mail: lsha@pncpa.com
Web: www.lsha.org

Spina Bifida

Spina Bifida Association of Greater New Orleans
P.O. Box 1346
Kenner, LA 70063
(504) 737-5181
E-mail: sbagno@email.com
Web: www.sbagno.org

Louisiana—Organizations Especially for Parents

Parent Training and Information Center (PTI)

Project PROMPT
Cindy Arceneaux, Director
4323 Division Street, Suite 110
Metairie, LA 70002-3179
(504) 888-9111; (800) 766-7736 (in LA)
E-mail: fhfgno@ix.netcom.com
Web: www.projectprompt.com

Pyramid Community Parent Resource Center
   (serving the greater New Orleans area)
D.J. and Ursula Markey, Co-Directors
2552 St. Philip Street
New Orleans, LA 70119
(504) 827-0610
E-mail: pyramidcprc@aol.com

Partners in Policymaking

Partners in Policymaking
Sharyn Scheyd, Coordinator
P.O. Box 641642
Kenner, LA 70064
(504) 443-3831
E-mail: sharyn@sharynscheyd.com
Web: www.laddc.org

Parent Teacher Association (PTA)

Louisiana Parent-Teacher Association
Margie Rayburn, President
1543 Del Plaza, Suite 13
Baton Rouge, LA 70815
(225) 927-7382
E-mail: la_office@pta.org
Web: www.lapta.org

Louisiana—Other Disability Organizations

Easter Seals Louisiana
Daniel Underwood, President/CEO
305 Baronne Street, Suite 400
New Orleans, LA 70112-1617
(504) 523-7325 (Voice/TTY)
(800) 695-7325 (Voice/TTY in LA only)
E-mail: DanUnderw1@aol.com
E-mail: essla@aol.com
Web: www.louisiana.easterseals.com

Families Helping Families of Southwest Louisiana
   (part of the statewide network)
Susan Benoit, Executive Director
2927 Hodges Street
Lake Charles, LA 70601
(337) 436-2570; (800) 894-6558
E-mail: fhfswla@xspedius.net
Web: www.fhfla.org

Louisiana Citizens for Action Now (LACAN)
Kay Marcel, Statewide Coordinator
713 N. Lewis Street
New Iberia, LA 70563
(337) 367-7407
E-mail: kamarcel@bellsouth.net
Web: www.lacanadvocates.org

University Center for Excellence in Developmental Disabilities

Direct Support Professional Workforce
   Development Initiatives
Human Development Center
School of Allied Health Professions
LSU Health Sciences Center
Sharon Delvisco, Instructor
1100 Florida Avenue, Building 119
New Orleans, LA 70119
(504) 942-8104; (504) 942-8380 (TTY)
E-mail: sdelvi@lsuhsc.edu
Web: www.hdc.lsumc.edu

Louisiana Occupational Therapy Association
Jessica Broussard, President
Linda Alwood, Club Administrator
P.O. Box 14806
Baton Rouge, LA 70898
(225) 291-4014
E-mail: lotassoc@aol.com
Web: www.lota.org

Louisiana Health and Rehabilitation Center, Inc.
Soundra (Temple) Johnson,
   Chief Executive Officer/CEO
1033 N. Lobdell Avenue
Baton Rouge, LA 70806
(225) 231-2490
E-mail: soundrajt@aol.com
Web: www.lahealthandrehab.org

Louisiana Youth Leadership Forum
Brenda Singelmann, Project Director
4323 Division Street, Suite 110
Metairie, LA 70002
(504) 888-9111; (800) 766-7736
E-mail: bsingelmann@fhfgno.org

VSA Arts of Louisiana
Mazie Malveaux, Executive Director
2758-D Brightside Lane
Baton Rouge, LA 70820
(225) 761-4243 (V/TTY)
E-mail: vsalouisiana@cox.net

Independent Living

To find out the contact information for the Statewide Independent Living Council (SILC) in Louisiana, contact

Independent Living Research Utilization Project
The Institute for Rehabilitation and Research
2323 South Sheppard, Suite 1000
Houston, TX 77019
(713) 520-0232 (V); (713) 520-5136 (TTY)
E-mail: ilru@ilru.org
Web: www.ilru.org

To find out the contact information for centers for independent living (CILs) in Louisiana, contact

National Council on Independent Living
1916 Wilson Boulevard, Suite 209
Arlington, VA 22201
(703) 525-3406; (703) 525-4153 (TTY)
E-mail: ncil@ncil.org
Web: www.ncil.org

MAINE

Maine—State Agencies and Organizations

United States Senators

Honorable Susan M. Collins (R)
413 Dirksen Senate Office Building
Washington, DC 20510
(202) 224-2523
(202) 224-2693 (Fax)
E-mail: senator@collins.senate.gov
Web: http://collins.senate.gov

Honorable Angus S. King, Jr. (I)
359 Dirksen Senate Office Building
Washington, DC 20510
(202) 224-5344
(202) 224-1946 (Fax)
E-mail: http://www.king.senate.gov/contact
Web: http://www.king.senate.gov/

United States Representatives

To find the contact information for your representative in the House of the U.S. Congress, visit the House's Web site at: www.house.gov, or call: (202) 225-3121; (202) 225-1904 (TTY).

Governor

Honorable Paul LePage
Office of the Governor
#1 State House Station
Augusta, ME 04333-0001
(207) 287-3531
E-mail: http://www.maine.gov/governor/
    lepage/citizen_services/ideas-suggestions.
    shtml
Web: http://www.maine.gov/governor/
    lepage/index.shtml

Official State Web Site

Web: www.maine.gov

State Department of Education: Special Education

David Noble Stockford, Director
Department of Education
Office of Special Services
23 State House Station
Augusta, ME 04333-0023
(207) 624-6650; (207) 624-6800 (TTY)
E-mail: david.stockford@maine.gov
Web: www.maine.gov/education/speced/
    specserv.htm

State Coordinator for NCLB (No Child Left Behind)

Maine was granted a waiver from the NCLB program.

Janette Kirk, ESEA Director
Maine Department of Education
23 State House Station
Augusta, ME 04333-0023
(207) 624-6707
Email: janette.kirk@maine.gov
Web: http://www.maine.gov/doe/title-IA/
    index.html

Programs for Infants and Toddlers With Disabilities: Birth–2 Years

Contact Programs for Children With Disabilities: 3–5 Years, below.

*Programs for Children
With Disabilities: 3–5 Years*

Child Development Services
Cindy Brown, CDS State Director
State House Station #146
Augusta, ME 04333
(207) 624-6660
E-mail: cindy.brown@maine.gov
Web: http://www.maine.gov/doe/cds/

State Vocational Rehabilitation Agency

Bureau of Rehabilitation Services
Department of Labor
Jill C. Duson, Executive Director
150 State House Station
Augusta, ME 04333-0150
(207) 624-5954
E-mail: jill.c.duson@maine.gov
Web: www.maine.gov/rehab/

Coordinator for Transition Services

Pam Rosen, CP Coordinator
Office of Special Services
Maine Department of Education
23 State House Station
Augusta, ME 04333
(207) 624-6648
E-mail: pam.rosen@maine.gov
Web: www.maine.gov/education/speced/
    specserv.htm

**Office of State Coordinator of
Career and Technical Education
for Students With Disabilities**

Career and Technical Education Team
Department of Education
Buzz Gamble, Consultant
23 State House Station
Augusta, ME 04333-0023
(207) 624-6747
E-mail: buzz.gamble@maine.gov
Web: www.maine.gov/education/

State Mental Health Agency

Department of Health and Human Services
John R. Nicholas, Commissioner
11 State House Station
Augusta, ME 04333
(207) 287-2736
E-mail: jack.r.nicholas@maine.gov
Web: www.maine.gov/dhs

**State Mental Health Representative
for Children and Youth**

Joan Smyrski, Acting Director
Children's & Youth Services
Department of Behavioral and
    Developmental Services
40 State House Station
Augusta, ME 04333
(207) 287-4251
E-mail: joan.smyrski@maine.gov
Web: www.maine.gov/bds

State Mental Retardation Program

Mental Retardation Services
Department of Behavioral and
    Developmental Services
Jane Gallivan, Program Manager
40 State House Station
Augusta, ME 04333
(207) 287-4242; (207) 287-2000 (TTY)
E-mail: jane.gallivan@maine.gov
Web: www.maine.gov/bds

Council on Developmental Disabilities

Maine Developmental Disabilities Council
Rebecca Weinstein, Executive Director
139 State House Station
225 Western Avenue
Augusta, ME 04333
(207) 287-4213; (800) 244-3990 (in ME only)
E-mail: info@maineddc.org
Web: www.maineddc.org

Protection and Advocacy Agency

Disability Rights Center of Maine
Kimberly A. Moody, Executive Director
P.O. Box 2007
Augusta, ME 04338-2007
(207) 626-2774 (V/TTY);
    (800) 452-1948 (V/TTY in ME)
E-mail: advocate@drcme.org
Web: www.drcme.org

Client Assistance Program

CARES, Inc.
Stephen Beam, Program Director
47 Water Street, Suite 104
Hallowell, ME 04347
(207) 622-7055; (800) 773-7055 (V/TTY)
E-mail: capsite@aol.com
Web: www.caresinc.org

**Programs for Children With
Special Health Care Needs**

Children with Special Health Needs Program
Toni G. Wall, Director
Department of Health and
    Human Services
Key Bank Plaza, 7th Floor
11 State House Station
Augusta, ME 04333-0011
(207) 287-5139, ext. 5350; (800) 698-3624
(207) 287-8015 (TTY)
E-mail: toni.g.wall@maine.gov

**State CHIP Program (health care
for low-income, uninsured children)**

MaineCare
442 Civic Center Drive
Augusta, ME 04333
(207) 624-7539; (800) 321-5557 (option 1)
Web: www.maine.gov/dhs/bfi/cubcare/
    CubCare.htm

**State Education Agency
Rural Representative**

David Noble Stockford, Director
Office of Special Services
Department of Education
23 State House Station
Augusta, ME 04333-0023
(207) 624-6650; (207) 624-6800 (TTY)
E-mail: david.stockford@maine.gov
Web: www.state.me.us/education/speced/
    specserv.htm

**Programs for Children and Youth Who
Are Blind or Visually Impaired or Deaf-Blind**

Division for the Blind and Visually Impaired
Bureau of Rehabilitation Services
Paul Cote, Program Manager
150 State House Station
Augusta, ME 04333-0150
(207) 624-5959
E-mail: paul.e.cote@state.me.us
Web: www.maine.gov/rehab/

Catholic Charities Maine
Jean Small, Program Director
Education Services for Blind and
    Visually Impaired Children
1066 Kenduskeag Avenue
Bangor, ME 04401
(207) 941-2855
E-mail: jsmall@ccmaine.org
Web: http://www.ccmaine.org/a-z-services/
    education-services-for-blind-and-visually-
    impaired-children

**Programs for Children and Youth
Who Are Deaf or Hard of Hearing**

Governor Baxter School for the Deaf
Larry S. Taub, EdD, Superintendent
Mackworth Island
Falmouth, ME 04105
(207) 781-6215 (Newborn to age 5)
(207) 781-6244 (Grades K–12)

**Telecommunications Relay Services for Individuals Who
Are Deaf, Hard of Hearing, or With Speech Impairments**

(800) 457-1220 (V)
(800) 437-1220 (TTY); 711 (TTY)
(800) 229-5746 (Speech to Speech–English)
(866) 260-9470 (Speech to Speech–Spanish)

**Regional ADA & IT
Technical Assistance Center**

New England ADA and Accessible IT Center
Adaptive Environments Center, Inc.
Valerie Fletcher, Executive Director
Oce Harrison, Project Director
374 Congress Street, Suite 301
Boston, MA 02210
(617) 695-0085 (V/TTY);
    (800) 949-4232 (V/TTY)
E-mail: adainfo@newenglandada.org
Web: www.newenglandada.org

*University Center for Excellence
in Developmental Disabilities*

*Center for Community Inclusion
    and Disability Studies, UCEDD
University of Maine
Lucille A. Zeph, Director
5717 Corbett Hall
Orono, ME 04469-5717
(207) 581-1084; (207) 581-3328 (TTY)
E-mail: lu.zeph@umit.maine.edu
Web: www.umaine.edu/cci*

Technology-Related Assistance

*ALLTech
Libby Cohen, Executive Director
The Spurwink Institute
60 Pineland Drive
New Gloucester, ME 04074
(866) 688-4573
E-mail: lcohen@alltech-tsi.org
Web: www.alltech-tsi.org*

*Maine Consumer Information
and Technology Training
Exchange (Maine CITE)*

*Maine CITE Coordinating Center
University of Maine System, University College
Kathleen Powers, Project Director
46 University Drive
Augusta, ME 04330
(207) 621-3195 (V); (207) 621-3482 (TTY)
E-mail: kpowers@maine.edu
Web: www.mainecite.org*

*State Mediation System
Pauline Lamontagne, Coordinator
Office of Special Services, Due Process
23 State House Station
Augusta, ME 04333-0023
(207) 624-6650
E-mail: pauline.lamontagne@maine.gov
Web: www.maine.gov/education/
    speced/specserv.htm*

Special Format Library

*Library Services for the Blind
    and Physically Handicapped
Maine State Library
Melora Ranney Norman, Librarian
64 State House Station
Augusta, ME 04333-0064
(207) 287-5650; (800) 762-7106
E-mail: melora.norman@maine.gov
Web: www.maine.gov/msl/outreach*

Maine—Disability-Specific Organizations

Attention Deficit Disorder

*To identify an ADD group in Maine, contact
either of the following organizations:*

*Children and Adults with Attention-Deficit/
    Hyperactivity Disorder (CHADD)
8181 Professional Place, Suite 150
Landover, MD 20785
(301) 306-7070
(800) 233-4050 (Voice mail to request
    information packet)
Web: www.chadd.org*

*Attention Deficit Disorder Association (ADDA)
P.O. Box 543
Pottstown, PA 19464
(484) 945-2101
Web: www.add.org*

Autism

*Autism Society of Maine
72B Maine Street
Winthrop, ME 04364
(207) 626-2708; (800) 273-5200 (in ME)
E-mail: info@asmonline.org
Web: www.asmonline.org*

Blind/Visual Impairments

*American Foundation for the Blind
Regina Genwright, Director of
    Information Center
11 Penn Plaza, Suite 300
New York, NY 10001
(212) 502-7600; (212) 502-7662 (TTY)
E-mail: afbinfo@afb.net
Web: www.afb.org*

Brain Injury

Brain Injury Association of Maine
Leslie Duval, Director of Operations
325 Main Street
Waterville, ME 04901
(207) 861-9900; (800) 275-1233 (in ME)
E-mail: biaofme@prexar.com
Web: www.biame.org

Cerebral Palsy

United Cerebral Palsy of Northeastern Maine
Bobbie Yeager, Executive Director
700 Mt. Hope Avenue, Suite 320
Bangor, ME 04401
(207) 941-2885; (207) 941-2952 (V/TTY)
E-mail: office@ucpofmaine.org
Web: www.ucpa.org

Deafness/Hard of Hearing

Maine Center on Deafness, MCD
68 Bishop Street, Suite 3
Portland, ME 04103
(207) 797-7656 (V/TTY);
    (800) 639-3884 (V/TTY)
Web: www.mainecenterondeafness.org/
    index.htm

Learning Disabilities

Learning Disabilities Association of Maine
Brenda Bennett, Executive Director
P.O. Box 67
Oakland, ME 04963
(207) 465-7700
E-mail: bbennett@ldame.org
Web: www.ldame.org

New Hampshire Branch of the International
    Dyslexia Association
(also serving Vermont and Maine)
Mike Angwin and Caryl Patten, Co-Presidents
P.O. Box 3724
Concord, NH 03302
(603) 229-7355
E-mail: referralsMaine@nhida.org
Web: www.nhida.org

Mental Health

NAMI Maine
Carol Carothers, Executive Director
P.O. Box 5120
Augusta, ME 04332
(207) 622-5767; (800) 464-5767 (in ME only)
E-mail: clcarothers@gwi.net
Web: http://me.nami.org

Speech and Hearing

Maine Speech-Language-Hearing Association
Waldo County General Hospital
Michael Towey, President
118 Northport Avenue, Box 287
Belfast, ME 04915
(207) 338-9349
E-mail: speech@wcgh.org
Web: www.mslha.org/

Spina Bifida

Spina Bifida Association of Maine
Wendy Bondeson, Director
P. O. Box 11166
Portland, ME 04104
(207) 675-3589

Maine—Organizations Especially for Parents

Parent Training and Information Center (PTI)

Maine Parent Federation
Janice LaChance, Director
P.O. Box 2067
Augusta, ME 04338-2067
(207) 623-2144; (800) 870-7746 (in ME)
E-mail: parentconnect@mpf.org
Web: www.mpf.org
Web: www.linkmaine.org

Community Parent Resource Center
Kimberley L. Megrath, Director
Southern Maine Parent Awareness
886 Main Street, Suite 303
Sanford, ME 04073
(207) 324-2337; (800) 564-9696 (in ME)
E-mail: support@somepa.org
Web: www.somepa.org

Parent-To-Parent

Contact Parent Training and Information Center, listed above.

Parent Teacher Association (PTA)

Maine PTA
Jeffrey M. Pierce, President
28 Webb Road
Windham, ME 04062
(207) 892-5700
E-mail: mainepta@aol.com

Other Parent Organization

Mainely Parents
Pam Marshall, Manager
88 State Street, Suite 400
Portland, ME 04101
(207) 842-2984; (800) 249-5506
E-mail: amandal@day-one.org
Web: www.mainelyparents.org

Maine—Other Disability Organizations

Pine Tree Society
Anne Marsh, Executive Director
Erin Rice, Marketing and
   Communications Director
149 Front Street
Bath, ME 04530
(207) 443-3341 (V/TTY)
E-mail: info@pinetreesociety.org
Web: www.pinetreesociety.org

VSA Arts of Maine
David Webster, Executive Director
P.O. Box 4002
Portland, ME 04101
(207) 761-3861 (V/TTY)
E-mail: me@vsarts.org
Web: www.vsartsmaine.org

Independent Living

To find out the contact information for the Statewide Independent Living Council (SILC) in Maine, contact

Independent Living Research Utilization Project
The Institute for Rehabilitation and Research
2323 South Sheppard, Suite 1000
Houston, TX 77019
(713) 520-0232 (V); (713) 520-5136 (TTY)
E-mail: ilru@ilru.org
Web: www.ilru.org

To find out the contact information for center for independent living (CILs) in Maine, contact

National Council on Independent Living
1916 Wilson Boulevard, Suite 209
Arlington, VA 22201
(703) 525-3406; (703) 525-4153 (TTY)
E-mail: ncil@ncil.org
Web: www.ncil.org

MARYLAND

Maryland—State Agencies and Organizations

United States Senators

Honorable Benjamin L. Cardin (D)
509 Hart Senate Office Building
Washington, DC 20510
(202) 224-4524
(202) 224-1651 (Fax)
E-mail Web Form: http://www.cardin.senate.
   gov/contact/
Web: http://www.cardin.senate.gov/

Honorable Barbara A. Mikulski (D)
503 Hart Senate Office Building
Washington, DC 20510
(202) 224-4654
(202) 224-8858 (Fax)
E-mail: senator@mikulski.senate.gov
Web: http://mikulski.senate.gov

United States Representatives

To find the contact information for your representative in the House of the U.S. Congress, visit the House's Web site at: www.house.gov, or call: (202) 225-3121; (202) 225-1904 (TTY).

Governor

Honorable Martin O'Malley
Office of the Governor
100 State Circle
Annapolis, MD 21401
(410) 974-3901
E-mail: http://www.governor.maryland.gov/
   mail/
Web: www.gov.state.md.us

Official State Web Site

Web: www.maryland.gov/

Department of Disabilities

Kristen Cox, Secretary
Department of Disabilities
One Market Center, Box 10
300 W. Lexington Street
Baltimore, MD 21201-3435
(410) 333-3098 (V/TTY);
   (800) 637-4113 (V/TTY)
E-mail: oid@gov.state.md.us
Web: www.mdtap.org

State Department of Education: Special Education

Carol Ann Baglin, Assistant State
   Superintendent
Maryland State Department of Education
Division of Special Education/
   Early Intervention Services
200 W. Baltimore Street
Baltimore, MD 21201-2595
(410) 767-0238
E-mail: cbaglin@msde.state.md.us
Web: www.msde.state.md.us

State Coordinator for NCLB (No Child Left Behind)

Maryland was granted an extended waiver
from the NCLB act.

Maria E. Lamb, Director
Program Improvement and Family Support
   Branch
Division of Student, Family, and School
   Support
Maryland State Department of Education
200 West Baltimore Street
Baltimore, MD 21201
(410) 767-0286
Email: Maria.Lamb@maryland.gov

Web: http://marylandpublicschools.org/
   msde/programs/titleI.html

Programs for Infants and Toddlers With Disabilities: Birth–2 Years

Maryland Infants and Toddlers Program/
   Preschool Branch
Brian Morrison, Part C Coordinator
State Department of Education
200 West Baltimore Street, 9th Floor
Baltimore, MD 21201
(410) 767-0863
E-mail: bmorrison@msde.state.md.us
Web: http://www.marylandpublicschools.org/
   MSDE/divisions/earlyinterv/infant_toddlers/

Programs for Children With Disabilities: 3–21 Years

Maryland State Department of Education
Division of Special Education/
   Early Intervention Services
Nancy Vorobey, Section Chief
State Department of Education
200 West Baltimore Street
Baltimore, MD 21201
(410) 767-0234
E-mail: nvorobey@msde.state.md.us
Web: http://www.marylandpublicschools.
   org/MSDE/divisions/earlyinterv/infant_
   toddlers/about/preschool_services.htm

State Vocational Rehabilitation Agency

Maryland Division of Rehabilitation Services
Workforce and Technology Center
Maryland State Department of Education
Robert A. Burns, Assistant State Superintendent
2301 Argonne Drive
Baltimore, MD 21218-1696
(410) 554-9385
E-mail: dors@dors.state.md.us
Web: www.dors.state.md.us/

Coordinator for Transition Services

Tom Barkley, Transition Specialist
Division of Special Education
Maryland State Department of Education
200 W. Baltimore Street, 9th Floor
Baltimore, MD 21201
(410) 767-0231
Web: www.msde.state.md.us/
   SpecialEducation/

Office of State Coordinator of Vocational Education for Students With Disabilities

Katharine M. Oliver, Assistant State
    Superintendent
Division of Career Technology and
    Adult Learning
200 W. Baltimore Street
Baltimore, MD 21201
(410) 767-0158
E-mail: koliver@msde.state.md.us
Web: www.msde.state.md.us

State Mental Health Agency

Mental Hygiene Administration
Department of Health and Mental Hygiene
Spring Grove Hospital Center
Brian Hepburn, Director
55 Wade Avenue, Dix Building
Catonsville, MD 21228
(410) 402-8452; (800) 735-2258 (TTY)
E-mail: bhepburn@dhmh.state.md.us
Web: www.dhmh.state.md.us/mha/

**State Mental Health
Representative for Children and Youth**

Albert Zachik, Director
Mental Hygiene Administration
Office of Child and Adolescent Services
Department of Health and Mental Hygiene
Spring Grove Hospital Center
55 Wade Avenue, Mitchell Building
Baltimore, MD 21228
(410) 402-8487
E-mail: azachik@dhmh.state.md.us

State Developmental Disabilities Program

Developmental Disabilities Administration
Department of Health and Mental Hygiene
Diane Coughlin, Director
201 W. Preston Street, Room 422C
Baltimore, MD 21201
(410) 767-5600
E-mail: coughlind@dhmh.state.md.us
Web: www.ddamaryland.org

Council on Developmental Disabilities

Maryland Developmental Disabilities Council
Brian Cox, Executive Director
217 E. Redwood Street, Suite 1300
Baltimore, MD 21202
(410) 333-3688 (V/TTY); (800) 305-6441
    (in MD only)
E-mail: info@md-council.org
Web: www.md-council.org

Protection and Advocacy Agency

Maryland Disability Law Center
Gary Weston, Executive Director
1800 N. Charles, Suite 400
Baltimore, MD 21201
(410) 727-6352; (800) 233-7201
Web: www.mdlcbalto.org

Client Assistance Program

Client Assistance Program
Department of Education
Division of Rehabilitation Services
Beth Lash, Director
2301 Argonne Drive
Baltimore, MD 21218
(410) 554-9358; (800) 638-6243
E-mail: cap@dors.state.md.us
Web: www.dors.state.md.us/

**Programs for Children With
Special Health Care Needs**

Specialty Care Division
Department of Health and Mental Hygiene
Office for Genetics and CSHCN
Dr. Susan Panny, Program Director
201 W. Preston Street, Room 421A
Baltimore, MD 21201
(410) 767-6730; (800) 638-8864
E-mail: pannys@dhmh.state.md.us
Web: http://phpa.dhmh.maryland.gov/
    genetics/SitePages/Home.aspx

**State CHIP Program (health
care for low-income, uninsured children)**

Maryland Children's Health Program
For referral to your local program call:
    (800) 456-8900; (800) 735-2258 (TTY)
Web: www.dhmh.state.md.us/mma/mchp/

Programs for Children and Youth Who Are Blind or Visually Impaired or Deaf-Blind

Maryland School for the Blind
3501 Taylor Avenue
Baltimore, MD 21236
(410) 444-5000
Web: www.mdschblind.org

Programs for Children and Youth Who Are Deaf or Hard of Hearing

Maryland School for the Deaf
James E. Tucker, Superintendent
101 Clarke Place
P.O. Box 250
Frederick, MD 21705-0250
(301) 360.2005 (V/TTY)
Web: www.msd.edu/

Telecommunications Relay Services for Individuals Who Are Deaf, Hard of Hearing, or With Speech Impairments

(800) 201-7165 (V/TTY)
(800) 735-2258 (TTY/HCO); 711 (TTY)
(888) 826-9673 (VCO)
(800) 785-5630 (Speech to Speech)
(877) 735-5151 (ASCII)
(877) 258-9854 (2-Line VCO)
(800) 877-1264 (Spanish)
(900) 344-3323 (pay per call, English)
(900) 344-4889 (pay per call, Spanish)

State Education Agency Rural Representative

Kim Lewis, Program Manager
Program Administration, Support and
    Staff Development
Division of Special Education, Maryland State
    Department of Education
200 W. Baltimore Street, 4th Floor
Baltimore, MD 21201
(410) 767-0249
E-mail: klewis@msde.state.md.us
Web: www.msde.state.md.us

Regional ADA & IT Technical Assistance Center

ADA and IT Information Center for the Mid
    Atlantic Region
Marian Vessels, President
451 Hungerford Drive, Suite 607
Rockville, MD 20850
(301) 217-0124 (V/TTY); (800) 949-4232 (V/TTY)
E-mail: adainfo@transcen.org
Web: www.adainfo.org

University Center for Excellence in Developmental Disabilities

The Kennedy Krieger Institute
Dr. Gary W. Goldstein, President
707 N. Broadway
Baltimore, MD 21205-1890
(443) 923-9300
E-mail: goldstein@kennedykrieger.org
Web: www.kennedykrieger.org

Technology-Related Assistance

Maryland Technology Assistance Program
Workforce and Technology Center
Michael Dalto, Executive Director
2301 Argonne Drive, Room T-17
Baltimore, MD 21218
(800) TECH-TAP (832-4827); (866) 881-7488 (TTY)
E-mail: mdtap@mdtap.org
Web: www.mdtap.org

State Mediation System

Office of Administrative Hearings
Laurie Bennett, Director of Quality Assurance
11101 Gilroy Road
Hunt Valley, MD 21031
(410) 229-4210; (800) 388-8805
E-mail: lbennett@oah.state.md.us

Special Format Books for Children and Youth

Maryland State Library for the Blind and
    Physically Handicapped
Jill Lewis, Director
415 Park Avenue
Baltimore, MD 21201-3603
(410) 230-2424; (800) 964-9209
(410) 230-8679 (TTY); (800) 934-2541
    (TTY outside Metro area)
E-mail: recept@lbph.lib.md.us
Web: www.lbph.lib.md.us

Maryland—Disability-Specific Organizations

Attention Deficit Disorder

To identify an ADD group in Maryland, contact either of the following organizations:

Children and Adults with Attention-Deficit/
  Hyperactivity Disorder (CHADD)
8181 Professional Place, Suite 150
Landover, MD 20785
(301) 306-7070
(800) 233-4050 (Voice mail to request
  information packet)
Web: www.chadd.org

Attention Deficit Disorder Association (ADDA)
P.O. Box 543
Pottstown, PA 19464
(484) 945-2101
Web: www.add.org

Autism

To identify an autism group in Maryland, contact

Autism Society of America
7910 Woodmont Avenue, Suite 300
Bethesda, MD 20814
(301) 657-0881; (800) 3-AUTISM
Web: www.autism-society.org

Blind/Visual Impairments

American Foundation for the Blind
Regina Genwright, Director of
  Information Center
11 Penn Plaza, Suite 300
New York, NY 10001
(212) 502-7600; (212) 502-7662 (TTY)
E-mail: afbinfo@afb.net
Web: www.afb.org

Low Vision Information Center
Amy G. Gabala, Executive Director
7701 Woodmont Avenue, Suite 604
Bethesda, MD 20814
(301) 951-4444
E-mail: lowvisioninfo@lycos.com
Web: www.lowvisioninfo.org/

Brain Injury

Brain Injury Association of Maryland
Diane Triplett, Executive Director
2200 Kernan Drive
Baltimore, MD 21207
(410) 448-2924; (800) 221-6443 (in MD)
E-mail: info@biamd.org
Web: www.biamd.org

Cerebral Palsy

United Cerebral Palsy of Southern Maryland
Mitzi Bernard, Executive Director
211 Chinquapin Round Road
Annapolis, MD 21401
(410) 280-2003
E-mail: ucpinfo@ucpsm.org
Web: www.ucpsm.org

United Cerebral Palsy of Central Maryland
Patricia A. Sandusky, President/CEO
1700 Reisterstown Road, Suite 226
Baltimore, MD 21208
(410) 484-4540; (800) 451-2452
E-mail: psandusky@ucp-cm.org
Web: www.ucp-cm.org

United Cerebral Palsy of Prince George's
  and Montgomery Counties, Inc.
Charles McNelly, PhD, Executive Director
William Irwin Buck Center
4409 Forbes Boulevard
Lanham, MD 20706
(301) 459-0566
E-mail: ucppgmc@aol.com
Web: www.ucppgmc.com
Web: www.high-school-high-tech.com
Web: www.netathon.org

Epilepsy

Abilities Network
Epilepsy Foundation of the Chesapeake Region
Lee Ann Kingham, Executive Director
Hampton Plaza, Suite 1103
300 E. Joppa Road
Towson, MD 21286
(410) 828-7700; (800) 492-2523 (in MD only)
E-mail: lkingham@abilitiesnetwork.org
Web: www.abilitiesnetwork.org

Learning Disabilities

Learning Disabilities Association of Maryland
10339 Southern Maryland Boulevard, Suite 204
Dunkirk, MD 20754
(410) 535-9679; (800) 799-4533
E-mail: LDAMaryland@aol.com
Web: www.ldamaryland.org

Mental Health

Mental Health Association of Maryland
Linda Raines, Executive Director
711 W. 40th Street, Suite 460
Baltimore, MD 21211
(410) 235-1178; (800) 572-6426
E-mail: info@mhamd.org
Web: www.mhamd.org

NAMI Maryland
Barbara Bellack, President
804 Landmark Drive, Suite 122
Glen Burnie, MD 21061
(410) 863-0470; (800) 467-0075
E-mail: amimd@aol.com
Web: http://md.nami.org

Mental Retardation

The Arc of Maryland, Inc.
Cristine Boswell Marchand, Executive Director
49 Old Solomons Island Road, Suite 205
Annapolis, MD 21401
(410) 571-9320; (410) 974-6139 (in Balt.)
E-mail: cmarchand@thearcmd.org
Web: www.thearcmd.org

Speech and Hearing

Maryland Speech-Language-Hearing Association
Nancy Brandenburger, Association Manager
P.O. Box 31
Manchester, MD 21102
(410) 239-7770
E-mail: office@mdslha.org
Web: www.mdslha.org

Spina Bifida

Spina Bifida Association of Maryland
Jeanne Free, President
Susan Whelan, Vice-President (Contact)
2416 Lamp Post Lane
Baltimore, MD 21234
(410) 665-1543
E-mail: susanwhelan1@comcast.net

Tourette Syndrome

Tourette Syndrome Association of Greater Washington
Jennifer Hines, Executive Director
33 University Boulevard East
Silver Spring, MD 20901-2485
(301) 681-4133; (877) 295-2148
E-mail: TSAGW@aol.com
Web: www.TSAGW.org

Maryland—Organizations Especially for Parents

Parent Training and Information Center (PTI)

Parents' Place of Maryland, Inc.
Josie Thomas, Director
801 Cromwell Park Drive, Suite 103
Glen Burnie, MD 21061
(410) 768-9100; (800) 394-5694
E-mail: info@ppmd.org
Web: www.ppmd.org

Community Parent Resource Center
   (Serving Baltimore Metropolitan Area)
Diane Dvoskin Sakwa, Executive Director
Families Involved Together, Inc.
301 N. Charles Street, Suite 901
Baltimore, MD 21201
(410) 235-5222
E-mail: diane@familiesinvolved.org
Web: www.familiesinvolved.org

Parent-To-Parent

Family Support Services, Division of
   Special Education
Early Intervention Services
Maryland State Department of Education
Pam Miller, Education and Resource Specialist
200 W. Baltimore Street, 9th Floor
Baltimore, MD 21201
(410) 767-0557; (800) 535-0182 (in MD only)
E-mail: pmiller@msde.state.md.us
Web: www.msde.state.md.us

Partners in Policymaking

Partners in Policymaking
Mary Baskar, Program Director
49 Old Solomon's Island Road, Suite 205
Annapolis, MD 21401
(410) 974-6139, ext. 26; (888) 272-3449
E-mail: mbaskar@thearcmd.org
Web: www.thearcmd.org

Parent Teacher Association (PTA)

Maryland PTA
Esther Parker, President
5 Central Avenue
Glen Burnie, MD 21061
(410) 761-6221
E-mail: office@mdpta.org
Web: www.mdpta.org

Other Parent Organization

Maryland Coalition of Families for
* Children's Mental Health*
Jane Walker, Executive Director
10632 Little Patuxent Parkway, Suite 119
Columbia, MD 21044
(410) 730-8267; (888) 607-3637
E-mail: info@mdcoalition.org
Web: www.mdcoalition.org

Maryland—Other Disability Organizations

Easter Seals Greater Washington-Baltimore
* Region, Inc.*
Lisa Reeves, President/CEO
4041 Powder Mill Road, Suite 100
Calverton, MD 20705
(301) 931-8700
E-mail: lreeves@eseal.org
Web: www.nca-md.easterseals.com

Family Net Works Program
Stephanie Watkins, Program Director
217 E. Redwood Street, Suite 1300
Baltimore, MD 21202
(301) 834-5427
E-mail: director@family-networks.org
Web: www.family-networks.org

The Coordinating Center (for individuals with
* complex medical needs and disabilities)*
Karen-Ann Lichtenstein, Executive Director
8258 Veterans Highway, Suite 113
Millersville, MD 21108
(410) 987-1048; (301) 621-7830
E-mail: bmccord@coordinatingcenter.org
Web: www.coordinatingcenter.org

The Resource Network (information on
* developmental disability resources)*
A project of Kennedy Krieger Institute
707 N. Broadway
Baltimore, MD 21205
(800) 390-3372; (443) 923-2795 (TTY)
E-mail: info@resourcenetworkatkki.org
Web: www.resourcenetworkatkki.org

Independent Living

To find out the contact information for the State--
* wide Independent Living Council (SILC) in*
* Maryland, contact*

Independent Living Research Utilization Project
The Institute for Rehabilitation and Research
2323 South Sheppard, Suite 1000
Houston, TX 77019
(713) 520-0232 (V); (713) 520-5136 (TTY)
E-mail: ilru@ilru.org
Web: www.ilru.org

*   To find out the contact information for*
centers for independent living (CILs) in Maryland,
contact

National Council on Independent Living
1916 Wilson Boulevard, Suite 209
Arlington, VA 22201
(703) 525-3406; (703) 525-4153 (TTY)
E-mail: ncil@ncil.org
Web: www.ncil.org

MASSACHUSETTS

Massachusetts—State Agencies and Organizations

United States Senators

Honorable Edward J. Markey (D)
218 Russell Senate Office Building
Washington, DC 20510
(202) 224-2742
(202) 224-2417 (Fax)
E-mail: http://www.markey.senate.gov/
* contact*
Web: http://www.markey.senate.gov/

Honorable Elizabeth Warren (D)
317 Hart Senate Office Building
Washington, DC 20510
(202) 224-4543
(202) 224-8525 (Fax)
E-mail: http://www.warren.senate.
gov/?p=email_senator
Web: http://www.warren.senate.gov/

United States Representatives

To find the contact information for your representative in the House of the U.S. Congress, visit the House's Web site at: www.house.gov, or call: (202) 225-3121; (202) 225-1904 (TTY).

Governor

Honorable Deval Patrick
Office of the Governor
State House, Room 105
Boston, MA 02133
(617) 727-6250
E-mail: http://www.mass.gov/governor/
constituentservices/contact/
Web: http://www.mass.gov/governor/

Official State Web Site

Web: www.mass.gov

State Department of
Education: Special Education

Marcia Mittnacht, Director
Special Education Planning and
Policy Development Office
Department of Education
350 Main Street
Malden, MA 02148-5023
(781) 338-3000; (781) 338-3388
E-mail: mmmittnacht@doe.mass.edu
Web: www.doe.mass.edu/sped

State Coordinator for NCLB (No Child Left Behind)

Massachusetts was granted an extended waiver from the NCLB act.

Mitchell D. Chester, Commissioner
Elementary and Secondary
Education
Massachusetts Department of Education
75 Pleasant Street
Malden, MA 02148-4906
(781) 338-3000

Email Web Form: http://www.doe.mass.edu/
contact/qanda.aspx
Web: http://www.doe.mass.edu/apa/titlei/
default.html

Programs for Infants and Toddlers
With Disabilities: Birth–2 Years

Early Childhood Unit
Division for Special Health Needs
Department of Public Health
Ron Benham, Director
250 Washington Street, 5th Floor
Boston, MA 02108
(617) 624-5901
(800) 905-8437 (Early Intervention Programs)
E-mail: ron.benham@state.ma.us
Web: http://www.mass.gov/eohhs/gov/
departments/dph/programs/family-health/
early-intervention/

Programs for Children With Disabilities: 3–5 Years

Early Learning Services
Department of Education
Lauren Viviani, 619 Coordinator
Special Education Planning and Policy
75 Pleasant Street, 4th Floor
Malden, MA 02148
(781) 338-3372
E-mail: lviviani@doe.mass.edu
Web: http://www.doe.mass.edu/sped/

State Vocational Rehabilitation Agency

Massachusetts Rehabilitation Commission
Elmer C. Bartels, Commissioner
Fort Point Place
27 Wormwood Street
Boston, MA 02210-1616
(617) 204-3600; (800) 245-6543 (in MA only)
Web: www.mass.gov/mrc/

Coordinator for Transition Services

Madeline Levine, Assistant Director of Special
Education
Special Education Planning and Policy
Development Office
Massachusetts Department of Education
350 Main Street
Malden, MA 02148
(781) 338-3375
Web: www.doe.mass.edu/sped/

State Department of Education

Career and Technical Education Programs
   for Special Populations
Ramona Foster, Education Specialist
Career and Technical Education
Department of Education
350 Main Street
Malden, MA 02148-5023
(781) 338-3910
Web: www.doe.mass.edu

State Mental Health Agency

Department of Mental Health
Elizabeth Childs, MD, Commissioner
25 Staniford Street
Boston, MA 02114
(617) 626-8123
Web: www.mass.gov/dmh

State Mental Health Representative
for Children and Youth

Child and Adolescent Services
Department of Mental Health
Joan Mikula, Assistant Commissioner
25 Staniford Street
Boston, MA 02114
(617) 626-8086
E-mail: joan.mikula@dmh.state.ma.us
Web: www.mass.gov/dmh

State Mental Retardation Program

Department of Mental Retardation
Gerald J. Morrissey Jr., Commissioner
500 Harrison Avenue
Boston, MA 02118
(617) 727-5608
Web: www.mass.gov/dmr

Council on Developmental Disabilities

Massachusetts Developmental
   Disabilities Council
Daniel Shannon, Executive Director
174 Portland Street, 5th Floor
Boston, MA 02114
(617) 727-6374 ext. 100; (617) 727-1885 (TTY)
E-mail: Dan.Shannon@state.ma.us
Web: www.mass.gov/mddc

Protection and Advocacy Agency

Disability Law Center, Inc.
Christine Griffin, Executive Director
11 Beacon Street, Suite 925
Boston, MA 02108
(617) 723-8455; (800) 872-9992 (V)
(617) 227-9464 (TTY); (800) 381-0577 (TTY)
E-mail: mail@dlc-ma.org
Web: www.dlc-ma.org/

Client Assistance Program

Client Assistance Program
Massachusetts Office on Disability
Barbara Lybarger, Assistant Director
One Ashburton Place, Room 1305
Boston, MA 02108
(617) 727-7440; (800) 322-2020 (in MA)
E-mail: barbara.lybarger@modi.state.ma.us
Web: www.mass.gov/mod

Programs for Children With
Special Health Care Needs

Division for Children with Special
   Health Care Needs
Department of Public Health
250 Washington Street, 4th Floor
Boston, MA 02108-4619
(617) 624-5070; (800) 882-1435
Web: www.mass.gov/dph

State CHIP Program (health care
for low-income, uninsured children)

MassHealth Enrollment Center
Central Processing Unit
P.O. Box 129124
Boston, MA 02112-9124
(888) 665-9993; (888) 665-9997 (TTY)
Web: www.mass.gov/dma

Programs for Children and Youth Who
Are Blind or Visually Impaired or Deaf-Blind

Children's Services
Massachusetts Commission for the Blind
Sandra Daly, Director
48 Boylston Street
Boston, MA 02116
(617) 626-7480; (800) 392-6450
(617) 626-7650 (TTY)
Web: www.mass.gov/mcb

Programs for Children and Youth
Who Are Deaf or Hard of Hearing

Massachusetts Commission for the Deaf and
    Hard of Hearing
Heidi Reed, Commissioner
150 Mt. Vernon Street, Suite 550
Boston, MA 02125
(617) 740-1600; (617) 740-1700 (TTY)
E-mail: MCDHH.office@state.ma.us
Web: www.mass.gov/mcdhh

Telecommunications Relay Services for Individuals Who
Are Deaf, Hard of Hearing, or With Speech Impairments

(800) 439-0183 (V)
(800) 439-2370 (TTY); 711 (TTY)
(800) 439-0183 (Speech to Speech)

Regional ADA & IT
Technical Assistance Center

New England ADA and Accessible IT Center
Adaptive Environments Center, Inc.
Valerie Fletcher, Executive Director
Oce Harrison, Project Director
374 Congress Street, Suite 301
Boston, MA 02210
(617) 695-0085 (V/TTY);
    (800) 949-4232 (V/TTY)
E-mail: adainfo@newenglandada.org
Web: www.newenglandada.org

University Center for Excellence
in Developmental Disabilities

Institute for Community Inclusion
UMASS Boston
William E. Kiernan, Director
100 Morrissey Boulevard
Boston, MA 02125
(617) 287-4300; (617) 287-4350 (TTY)
E-mail: ici@umb.edu
Web: www.communityinclusion.org

UMASS Medical School - E.K. Shriver Center
William McIlvane, Director
Charles Hamad, Associate Center Director
200 Trapelo Road
Waltham, MA 02452-6319
(781) 642-0001; (800) 764-0200 (TTY)
Web: www.umassmed.edu/shriver

Technology-Related Assistance

Massachusetts Assistive Technology Partnership
MATP Center; Children's Hospital
Marylyn Howe, Project Director
1295 Boylston Street, Suite 310
Boston, MA 02215
(617) 355-7820; (800) 848-8867
    (V/TTY, in MA only)
(617) 355-7301 (TTY)
E-mail: MATP@matp.org
Web: www.matp.org

State Mediation System

Bureau of Special Education Appeals
Department of Education
Edward Hermann, Coordinator
350 Main Street
Malden, MA 02148
(781) 338-6443
E-mail: e.hermann@doe.mass.edu
Web: www.doe.mass.edu/bsea

Special Format Library

Braille and Talking Book Library
Perkins School for the Blind
Kim Charlson, Director
175 N. Beacon Street
Watertown, MA 02472
(617) 972-7240; (800) 852-3133
E-mail: library@perkins.org
Web: www.perkinslibrary.org

Massachusetts — Disability-Specific Organizations

Attention Deficit Disorder

    To identify an ADD group in your state
or locality, contact either of the following
organizations:

Children and Adults with Attention-Deficit/
    Hyperactivity Disorder (CHADD)
8181 Professional Place, Suite 150
Landover, MD 20785
(301) 306-7070
(800) 233-4050 (Voice mail to request
    information packet)
Web: www.chadd.org

Attention Deficit Disorder Association (ADDA)
P.O. Box 543
Pottstown, PA 19464
(484) 945-2101
Web: www.add.org

Autism

Autism Society of America - Massachusetts Chapter
789 Clapboard Tree Street
Westwood, MA 02090
(781) 329-4244
E-mail: asamass@gis.net

Blind/Visual Impairments

American Foundation for the Blind
Regina Genwright, Director of
*   Information Center*
11 Penn Plaza, Suite 300
New York, NY 10001
(212) 502-7600; (212) 502-7662 (TTY)
E-mail: afbinfo@afb.net
Web: www.afb.org

Massachusetts Association of Parents of
*   Visually Impaired Children (MAPVI)*
Judy Westgate, President/Treasurer
22 Old Marlboro Road
Maynard, MA 01754
(978) 897-3005
E-mail: judywestgate@comcast.net

Brain Injury

Massachusetts Brain Injury Association
Arlene Korab, Executive Director
484 Main Street, Suite 325
Worcester, MA 01608
(508) 795-0244; (800) 242-0030 (in MA)
E-mail: mbia@mbia.net
Web: www.mbia.net

Cerebral Palsy

United Cerebral Palsy of MetroBoston, Inc.
Todd Kates, Executive Director
71 Arsenal Street
Watertown, MA 02472
(617) 926-5480
E-mail: ucpboston@ucpboston.org
Web: www.ucpboston.org

Down Syndrome

Massachusetts Down Syndrome Congress
Suzanne Shea, President
P.O. Box 866
Melrose, MA 02176
(508) 278-7769; (800) 664-6372
Web: www.MDSC.org

Epilepsy

Epilepsy Foundation of Massachusetts
*   and Rhode Island*
Programs and Services Office
Amy Cole, Information & Referral Coordinator
540 Gallivan Boulevard, 2nd Floor
Boston, MA 02124
(617) 506-6041; (888) 576-9996
E-mail: acole@efmri.org
Web: www.epilepsymassri.org

Learning Disabilities

Learning Disabilities Worldwide
Teresa Citro, Executive Director
P.O. Box 142
Weston, MA 02493
(781) 890-5399
Web: www.ldworldwide.org

Mental Health

NAMI Massachusetts
Toby Fisher, Executive Director
400 W. Cummings Park, Suite 6650
Woburn, MA 01801
(781) 938-4048; (800) 370-9085
E-mail: namimass@aol.com
Web: www.namimass.org

Parent/Professional Advocacy League (PAL)
Donna Welles, Director
59 Temple Place, Suite 664
Boston, MA 02111
(617) 542-7860; (866) 815-8122
E-mail: info@ppal.net
Web: www.ppal.net

Mental Retardation and Related Disabilities

The Arc Massachusetts
Leo Sarkissian, Executive Director
217 South Street
Waltham, MA 02453
(781) 891-6270
E-mail: arcmass@arcmass.org
Web: www.arcmass.org

Greater Boston Arc
Terri Angelone, Executive Director
221 N. Beacon Street, 2nd Floor
Boston, MA 02135
(617) 783-3900
E-mail: gbarc@gbarc.org
Web: www.gbarc.org

The Arc of Northern Bristol County
Michael Andrade, Executive Director
5 Bank Street
Attleboro, MA 02703
(508) 226-1445; (888) 343-3301
E-mail: mandrade@arcnbc.org
Web: www.arcnbc.org

Speech and Hearing

Massachusetts Speech-Language-Hearing
    Association
Mary Ellen Curran, Director
77 Rumford Avenue, Suite 3B
Waltham, MA 02453
(781) 647-7031; (800) 898-8177
E-mail: msha@camihq.com
Web: www.msha-lic.org

Spina Bifida

Massachusetts Spina Bifida Association
Brian Packard, President
733 Turnpike Street, #282
North Andover, MA 01845
(508) 390-5986
E-mail: packard44@comcast.net
Web: www.msbaweb.org

Massachusetts—Organizations Especially for Parents

Parent Training and Information Center (PTI)

Federation for Children with Special Needs
Richard Robison, Executive Director
1135 Tremont Street, Suite 420
Boston, MA 02120-2140
(617) 236-7210 (V/TTY);
    (800) 331-0688 (in MA only)
E-mail: fcsninfo@fcsn.org
Web: www.fcsn.org/

Parent-To-Parent

Family TIES of Massachusetts
Massachusetts Department of Public Health
Mary Castro Aten, Director
Donovan Health Building, 3rd Floor
5 Randolph Street
Canton, MA 02021
(781) 774-6736; (800) 905-TIES
E-mail: mcaten@fcsn.org
Web: www.massfamilyties.org

Massachusetts Families Organizing for Change
P.O. Box 61
Raynham, MA 02768
(800) 406-3632
E-mail: mfofc@tmlp.com
Web: www.mfofc.org

Community Parent Resource Center (serving the city of Boston)

Urban PRIDE
c/o The Boston Foundation
Charlotte R. Spinkston, Project Director
75 Arlington Street, 10th Floor
Boston, MA 02116
(617) 338-4508
E-mail: c.spinkston.urbanpride@att.net

Community Parent Resource Center (serving Martha's Vineyard and Nantucket)

Island Parents Educational Support &
    Training Center (IPEST)
Carol Kennedy, Executive Director
P.O. Box 4081
Vineyard Haven, MA 02568
(508) 693-8612
E-mail: carolkennedy@ipest.org
E-mail: ipest@hotmail.com
Web: www.ipest.org

Parent Teacher Association (PTA)

Massachusetts PTA
Carol Woodbury, President
P.O. Box 710
Fiskdale, MA 01518-0710
(508) 347-7055; (888) 404-4782
E-mail: masspta@aol.com
Web: www.masspta.org

Parent Advisory Council

Massachusetts Association of Special Education
     Parent Advisory Council (MASSPAC)
Suzanne Peyton, Executive Director
P.O. Box 167
Sharon, MA 02067
(671) 962-4558
E-mail: info@masspac.org
Web: www.masspac.org

Massachusetts—Other Disability Organizations

Associated Advocacy Center-Visions
     for the Future, Inc.
Toni Saunders, President
24 Widow Coombs Walk
Sandwich, MA 02563
(508) 420-4356
E-mail: Tonisvision@aol.com
Web: www.aacvisions.org

Easter Seals Massachusetts
(call for info about assistive technology,
     recreation, and therapy)
Kirk Joslin, President
484 Main Street
Worcester, MA 01608
(508) 757-2756; (800) 244-2756
E-mail: kirkj@eastersealsma.org
Web: www.eastersealsma.org

New England INDEX
(Information & referral for people
     with disabilities)
Robert Bass, Director
200 Trapelo Road
Waltham, MA 02452-6319
(781) 642-0248; (800) 642-0249
(800) 764-0200 TTY (in MA)
E-mail: info@disabilityinfo.org
Web: www.disabilityinfo.org

Statewide Head Injury Program
Massachusetts Rehabilitation Commission
Debra S. Kamen, Director
27 Wormwood Street, Fort Point Place, Suite 600
Boston, MA 02210
(617) 204-3852 (V); (617) 204-3817 (TTY)
(800) 223-2559 (MA only)
E-mail: shipu@state.ma.us
Web: http://www.mass.gov/veterans/health-
     and-well-being/tbi/state-tbi-agencies/ship.
     html

Home Modifications
Loan Program for
People With Disabilities

Massachusetts Rehabilitation Commission
27 Wormwood Street
Boston, MA 02210-1616
(617) 204-3600; (800) 245-6543
Web: http://www.mass.gov/eohhs/gov/
     departments/mrc/

VSA Arts of Massachusetts
Charles J. Washburn, Executive Director
China Trade Center
2 Boylston Street, 2nd Floor
Boston, MA 02116-9856
(617) 350-7713 (V); (617) 350-6836 (TTY)
E-mail: cjwashburn@vsamass.org
Web: www.vsamass.org

Independent Living

     To find out the contact information for the
Statewide Independent Living Council (SILC) in
Massachusetts, contact

Independent Living Research Utilization Project
The Institute for Rehabilitation and Research
2323 South Sheppard, Suite 1000
Houston, TX 77019
(713) 520-0232 (V); (713) 520-5136 (TTY)
E-mail: ilru@ilru.org
Web: www.ilru.org

     To find out the contact information for
centers for independent living (CILs) in
Massachusetts, contact

National Council on Independent Living
1916 Wilson Boulevard, Suite 209
Arlington, VA 22201
(703) 525-3406; (703) 525-4153 (TTY)
E-mail: ncil@ncil.org
Web: www.ncil.org

MICHIGAN

Michigan—State Agencies and Organizations

United States Senators

Honorable Carl Levin (D)
269 Russell Senate Office Building
Washington, DC 20510
(202) 224-6221
(202) 224-1388 (Fax)
E-mail: senator@levin.senate.gov
Web: http://levin.senate.gov

Honorable Debbie Stabenow (D)
133 Hart Senate Office Building
Washington, DC 20510
(202) 224-4822
(202) 228-0325 (Fax)
E-mail: senator@stabenow.senate.gov
Web: http://stabenow.senate.gov

United States Representatives

To find the contact information for your representative in the House of the U.S. Congress, visit the House's Web site at: www.house.gov, or call: (202) 225-3121; (202) 225-1904 (TTY).

Governor

Honorable Rick Snyder
Governor's Office
P.O. Box 30013
Lansing, MI 48909
(517) 373-3400
Web: http://www.michigan.gov/snyder

Official State Web Site

Web: www.michigan.gov

State Department of Education: Special Education

Dr. Jacquelyn Thompson, Director
Office of Special Education and Early
    Intervention Services
Michigan Department of Education
P.O. Box 30008
Lansing, MI 48909-7508
(517) 373-0923
E-mail: ThompsonJJ@mi.gov
Web: www.michigan.gov/mde

State Coordinator for NCLB (No Child Left Behind)

Michigan has been granted an extended waiver from the NCLB act.

Venessa Keesler
Deputy Supt for Education Services
Michigan Department of Education
608 W. Allegan Street
P.O. Box 30008
Lansing, MI 48909-7508
(517) 241-3232
Web: www.michigan.gov/mde
Web: http://www.michigan.gov/
    mde/0,1607,7-140-28753-69709--,00.html

Programs for Infants and Toddlers With Disabilities: Birth–2 Years

Office of Special Education and Early
    Intervention Services
Michigan Department of Education
Vanessa Winborne, Part C Coordinator
P.O. Box 30008
Lansing, MI 48909
(517) 335-4865; (800) 327-5966
E-mail: WinborneV@mi.gov
Web: http://www.michigan.gov/
    mde/0,4615,7-140-43092-127141--,00.html

Special Education Funding for Children With Disabilities: Birth–26 Years

Office of Special Education and
    Early Intervention Services
Michigan Department of Education
Lisa Wasacz, Consultant
608 West Allegan, PO Box 30008
Lansing, MI 48909-7508
(517) 241-4520
E-mail: WasaczL@michigan.gov
Web: http://www.michigan.gov/mde/0,4615,7-
    140-6530_6809-127146--,00.html

State Vocational Rehabilitation Agency

Michigan Rehabilitation Services
Office of Special Education and
    Early Intervention Services
Michigan Department of Labor & Economic
    Growth
Jaye Balthazar, Director
P.O. Box 30010
Lansing, MI 48909

(517) 373-3390; (800) 605-6722
E-mail: balthazarj@michigan.gov
Web: www.michigan.gov/mrs

Coordinator for Transition Services

Beth Steenwyk, Deputy Director
Office of Special Education and
*   Early Intervention Services*
Michigan Department of Education
P.O. Box 30008
Lansing, MI 48909-7508
(517) 373-0923
E-mail: steenwykb@mi.gov

Office of State Coordinator
of Vocational Education for
Students With Disabilities

Office of Career and Technical Preparation
Michigan Department of Labor
*   & Economic Growth*
Patty Cantú, Director
201 N. Washington Square
Lansing, MI 48913
(517) 373-3373
E-mail: cantup@michigan.gov
Web: www.michigan.gov/mdcd

State Mental Health Agency

Department of Community Health
Janet Olszewski, Director
Lewis-Cass Building
320 S. Walnut Boulevard
Lansing, MI 48913
(517) 373-3500
Web: www.michigan.gov/mdch

State Mental Health Representative
for Children and Youth

Division of Mental Health Services to
*   Children and Families*
Department of Community Health
Sherida K. Falvay, Director
Lewis Cass Building
320 S. Walnut Street
Lansing, MI 48913
(517) 241-5762
E-mail: Falvay@michigan.gov
Web: www.michigan.gov/mdch

Council on Developmental Disabilities

Michigan Developmental Disabilities Council
Vendella Collins, Executive Director
Lewis-Cass Building
Lansing, MI 48913
(517) 334-6123
E-mail: collinsve@michigan.gov
Web: www.michigan.gov

Protection and Advocacy Agency

Michigan Protection and Advocacy Service, Inc.
Elmer Cerano, Executive Director
4095 Legacy Parkway, Suite 500
Lansing, MI 48911-4263
(517) 487-1755 (V/TTY);
*   (800) 288-5923 (V/TTY)*
E-mail: ecerano@mpas.org
Web: www.mpas.org

Client Assistance Program

Client Assistance Program
Michigan Protection and Advocacy Service, Inc.
Manuela Kress-Shull, Director
4095 Legacy Parkway, Suite 500
Lansing, MI 48911-4263
(517) 487-1755 (V/TTY); (800) 288-5923 (V/
*   TTY)*
E-mail: mkress@mpas.org
Web: www.mpas.org

Programs for Children With
Special Health Care Needs

Children's Special Health Care Services Division
Public Health Administration
Bureau of Family, Maternal Child Health
Department of Community Health
Kathleen A. Stiffler, Director
400 S. Pine
P.O. Box 30479
Lansing, MI 48909-7979
(517) 335-5008; (800) 359-3722
E-mail: stifflerk@michigan.gov
Web: www.michigan.gov/mdch

State CHIP Program (health care for low-income, uninsured children)

MIChild
Capitol View Building
201 Townsend Street
Lansing, Michigan 48913
(888) 988-6300; (888) 263-5897 (TTY)
Web: http://michigan.gov/mdch/0,1607,7-132-2943_4845_4931---,00.html

Programs for Children and Youth Who Are Blind or Visually Impaired or Deaf-Blind

Commission for the Blind
Michigan Department of Labor
& Economic Growth
Patrick Cannon, State Director
201 N. Washington Square
P.O. Box 30652
Lansing, MI 48909
(517) 373-2062
E-mail: cannonp@michigan.gov
Web: www.mcb1.org

Programs for Children and Youth Who Are Deaf or Hard of Hearing

Michigan Coalition for Deaf and Hard of
Hearing People
Michigan Association for Deaf,
Hearing and Speech Services
John Berchtold, Director
2929 Covington Court, Suite 200
Lansing, MI 48912-4939
(517) 487-0066; (800) YOUR EAR (in MI)
E-mail: yourear@madhs.org
Web: www.madhs.org

Telecommunications Relay Services for Individuals Who Are Deaf, Hard of Hearing, or With Speech Impairments

(800) 649-3777 (V/TTY); 711 (TTY)
(866) 656-9826 (Speech to Speech)

Regional ADA & IT Technical Assistance Center

Great Lakes ADA and Accessible IT Center
(contact this organization for information
on ADA and IT technical assistance for
Michigan)
University of Illinois/Chicago
Institute on Disability and Human Development
Robin Jones, Director
1640 W. Roosevelt Road
Chicago, IL 60608-6902
(312) 413-1407 (V/TTY);
(800) 949-4232 (V/TTY)
E-mail: gldbtac@uic.edu
Web: www.adagreatlakes.org

University Center for Excellence in Developmental Disabilities

Developmental Disabilities Institute
Wayne State University
Barbara LeRoy, Director
4809 Woodward Avenue, Suite 268
Detroit, MI 48202
(313) 577-2654
E-mail: B_Le_Roy@wayne.edu
Web: www.wayne.edu/DDI

Technology-Related Assistance

MATR: Michigan's Assistive Technology Resource
Jeff Diedrich, Director
1023 South US 27
St. Johns, MI 48879-2423
(989) 224-0333 (V/TTY);
(800) 274-7426 (nationwide)
E-mail: matr@edzone.net
Web: www.cenmi.org/matr

Michigan's Assistive Technology Project
Michigan Disability Rights Coalition
Kathryn Wyeth and Corrie Bair,
Co-Project Managers
780 W. Lake Lansing Road, Suite 200
East Lansing, MI 48823
(517) 333-2477; (800) 760-4600 (MI only)
E-mail: mdrc@match.org
Web: www.copower.org/AT/index.htm

State Mediation System

Office of Special Education and
   Early Intervention Services
Michigan Department of Education
Joanne Winkleman, Coordinator
P.O. Box 30008
Lansing, MI 48909
(517) 373-0923
E-mail: winkelmanj@mi.gov
Web: www.mi.gov/mde

Special Format Library

Library of Michigan
Service for the Blind and Physically Handicapped
Susan Chinault, Librarian
P.O. Box 30007
Lansing, MI 48909
(517) 373-5614; (800) 992-9012
(517) 373-1592 (TTY)
E-mail: sbph@michigan.gov
Web: www.michigan.gov/sbph

Michigan—Disability-Specific Organizations

Attention Deficit Disorder

   To identify an ADD group in Michigan, contact either of the following organizations:

Children and Adults with Attention-Deficit/
   Hyperactivity Disorder (CHADD)
8181 Professional Place, Suite 150
Landover, MD 20785
(301) 306-7070
(800) 233-4050 (Voice mail to request
   information packet)
Web: www.chadd.org

Attention Deficit Disorder Association (ADDA)
P.O. Box 543
Pottstown, PA 19464
(484) 945-2101
Web: www.add.org

Autism

The Autism Society of Michigan
Dr. Sally Burton-Hoyle, Executive Director
6035 Executive Drive, Suite 109
Lansing, MI 48911
(517) 882-2800; (800) 223-6722
E-mail: autism@autism-mi.org
Web: www.autism-mi.org

Blind/Visual Impairments

American Foundation for the Blind—Midwest
Jay Stiteley, Director
401 N. Michigan Avenue, Suite 350
Chicago, IL 60611
(312) 396-4420
E-mail: chicago@afb.net
Web: www.afb.org

Greater Detroit Agency for the Blind
   and Visually Impaired
Gail McEntee, Interim Executive Director
16625 Grand River Avenue
Detroit, MI 48227
(313) 272-3900
E-mail: webmaster@upshawinst.org
Web: www.upshawinst.org

Blind Vision
(program supporting students with visual
   impairments, IEP advocacy)
Brunhilde Merk-Adam, Founder/
   Executive Director
2501 Pheasant Run
Ortonville, MI 48462
(248) 627-2260
E-mail: bkmabma@worldnet.att.net

Brain Injury

Brain Injury Association of Michigan
Michael Dabbs, President
8619 W. Grand River, Suite I
Brighton, MI 48116-2334
(810) 229-5880; (800) 772-4323 (in MI)
E-mail: info@biami.org
Web: www.biami.org

Cerebral Palsy

United Cerebral Palsy Michigan
Linda Potter, Executive Director
3401 E. Saginaw, Suite 216
Lansing, MI 48912
(517) 203-1200; (800) 828-2714 (V/TTY in MI)
E-mail: ucp@ucpmichigan.org
Web: www.ucpmichigan.org

United Cerebral Palsy of Metro Detroit
James F. Kelly, President/CEO
23077 Greenfield, Suite 205
Southfield, MI 48075
(248) 557-5070; (800) 827-4843
E-mail: ucp@ameritech.net
Web: www.ucp.org

Epilepsy

Epilepsy Foundation of Michigan
Arlene Gorelick, President
25200 Telegraph Road, Suite 110
Southfield, Michigan 48033-7497
(248) 351-7979; (800) 377-6226
E-mail: letters@mail.epilepsymichigan.org
Web: http://www.epilepsy.com/michigan

Learning Disabilities

Learning Disabilities Association of Michigan
Ed Schlitz, President
200 Museum Drive, Suite 101
Lansing, MI 48933-1914
(517) 485-8160; (888) 597-7809
E-mail: ldami@aol.com
Web: www.ldaofmichigan.org

Mental Health

Association for Children's Mental Health
Amy Winans, Executive Director
2465 Woodlake Circle, Suite 140
Okemos, MI 48864
(517) 381-5125; (888) 226-4543 (Parent line)
E-mail: ajwinans@aol.com
Web: www.acmh-mi.org

Michigan Association for Children with
    Emotional Disorders
Susan McParland, Executive Director
30233 Southfield Road, Suite 219
Southfield, MI 48076
(248) 433-2200
E-mail: susan@michkids.org
E-mail: info@michkids.org
Web: www.michkids.org

Mental Health Association in Michigan
Mark Reinstein, PhD, President
30233 Southfield Road, Suite 220
Southfield, MI 48076
(248) 647-1711
E-mail: mhamich@aol.com
Web: www.mha-mi.org

Mental Retardation

The Arc Michigan
1325 S. Washington Avenue
Lansing, MI 48910
(517) 487-5426; (800) 292-7851 (in MI)
E-mail: director@arcmi.org
Web: www.arcmi.org

Speech and Hearing

Michigan Speech-Language-Hearing Association
Dawn Kutney, Administrative Consultant
790 W. Lake Lansing Road, Suite 500A
East Lansing, MI 48823
(517) 332-5691
E-mail: msha@ix.netcom.com
Web: www.michiganspeechhearing.org

Michigan—Organizations Especially for Parents

Parent Training and Information Center (PTI)

Citizens Alliance to Uphold Special Education
    (CAUSE)
Pat Keller, Executive Director
6412 Centurion Drive, Suite 130
Lansing, MI 48917
(517) 886-9167; (800) 221-9105 (in MI)
E-mail: info@causeonline.org
Web: www.causeonline.org

Partners in Policymaking

Michigan Partners in Policymaking
ACA, N.E.W. Center
Jennifer Hill Buehrer, Coordinator
1100 N. Main, Suite 205
Ann Arbor, MI 48104
(734) 662-1256; (800) 890-6084 (in MI)
E-mail: michiganpartners@hotmail.com
Web: www.partnersinpolicymaking.com

Parent-To-Parent

Parent Participation Program
Family Support Network of Michigan
Children's Special Health Care Services
Michigan Department of Community Health
Mary Marin, Executive Director
3056 W. Grand Boulevard, Suite 3-350,
    Cadillac Place
Detroit, MI 48202-6056
(313) 456-4381; (800) 359-3722 (Family
    Phoneline)
Web: www.michigan.gov

Parent Teacher Association (PTA)

Michigan Congress of Parents,
*   Teachers and Students*
Pattie Bayless, President
1011 N. Washington Avenue
Lansing, MI 48906-4897
(517) 485-4345
E-mail: donnar@michiganpta.org
Web: www.michiganpta.org

IDEA Mandated Activities Project

Project PERFORM (Providing Education and
*   Resources to Families and Others Residing*
*   in Michigan)*
Washtenaw Intermediate School District
Kay Moler, Director
1819 S. Wagner Road
Ann Arbor, MI 48103
(734) 994-8100, ext. 6451; (800) 552-4821 (in MI)
E-mail: kmoler@wash.k12.mi.us
Web: www.wash.k12.mi.us/perform/

Michigan—Other Disability Organizations

Division on Deaf and Hard of Hearing
Michigan Department of Labor &
*   Economic Growth*
Christopher Hunter, Director
320 N. Washington Square, Suite 250
Lansing, MI 48913
(517) 334-8000 (V/TTY)
E-mail: hunterc2@michigan.gov
Web: www.mcdc-dodhh.org

Easter Seals Michigan
John Cocciolone, CEO/President
22150 W. 9 Mile Road
Southfield, MI 48034
(248) 386-9600; (800) 757-3257 (in MI)
Web: www.essmichigan.org

Michigan Commission on Disability Concerns
Michigan Department of Labor & Economic
*   Growth*
Duncan Wyeth, Executive Director
320 N. Washington Square, Suite 250
Lansing, MI 48913
(517) 334-8000 (V/TTY)
E-mail: mcdc@michigan.gov
Web: www.mcdc-dodhh.org

University Center for the Development
*   of Language and Literacy*
University of Michigan
Dr. Joanne Marttila Pierson, PhD, CCC-SLP,
*   Associate Director*
Judy Nantau, Assistant Head of
*   Clinical Services*
1111 E. Catherine Street
Ann Arbor, MI 48109-2054
(734) 764-8440
E-mail: ucll@umich.edu
Web: www.languageexperts.org

VSA Arts of Michigan
Lora Frankel, Executive Director
51 W. Hancock
Detroit, MI 48201
(313) 832-3303 (V/TTY)
E-mail: info@vsami.org
Web: www.vsami.org

Independent Living

To find out the contact information for the Statewide Independent Living Council (SILC) in Michigan, contact

Independent Living Research Utilization Project
The Institute for Rehabilitation and Research
2323 South Sheppard, Suite 1000
Houston, TX 77019
(713) 520-0232 (V); (713) 520-5136 (TTY)
E-mail: ilru@ilru.org
Web: www.ilru.org

To find out the contact information for centers for independent living (CILs) in Michigan, contact

National Council on Independent Living
1916 Wilson Boulevard, Suite 209
Arlington, VA 22201
(703) 525-3406; (703) 525-4153 (TTY)
E-mail: ncil@ncil.org
Web: www.ncil.org

MINNESOTA

Minnesota—State Agencies and Organizations

United States Senators

Honorable Al Franken (D)
309 Hart Senate Office Building
Washington, DC 20510
(202) 224-5641
Web: http://www.franken.senate.gov/?p=contact

Honorable Amy Klobuchar (D)
302 Hart Senate Office Building
Washington, DC 20510
(202) 224-3244
(202) 228-2186 (Fax)
Web: http://www.klobuchar.senate.gov/public/

United States Representatives

To find the contact information for your representative in the House of the U.S. Congress, visit the House's Web site at: www.house.gov, or call: (202) 225-3121; (202) 225-1904 (TTY).

Governor

Honorable Mark Dayton
Office of the Governor & Lt Governor
116 Veterans Service Building
20 W 12th Street
St. Paul, MN 55155
651-201-3400; (800) 657-3717
(651) 296-0075 (TTY); (800) 657-3598 (TTY)
E-mail: http://mn.gov/governor/contact-us/
     form/
Web: http://mn.gov/governor/

Official State Web Site

Web: www.state.mn.us/cgi-bin/portal/mn/
     jsp/home.do?agency=NorthStar

State Department of Education: Special Education

Minnesota Department of Education
Special Education Policy
Barbara L. Troolin, Director
1500 Highway 36 West
Roseville, MN 55113-4266
(651) 582-8590; (651) 582-8201 (TTY)
E-mail: barbara.troolin@state.mn.us
Web: http://education.state.mn.us

State Coordinator for NCLB (No Child Left Behind)

Minnesota has been granted an extended waiver from the NCLB act.

John Moorse
Program Accountability & Improvement
     Division
Minnesota Department of Education
1500 Highway 36 West
Roseville, MN 55113
(651) 582-8579
Email: mde.esea@state.mn.us
Web: http://education.state.mn.us/MDE/
     SchSup/ESEA/TitleIPartA/index.html

Programs for Infants and Toddlers With Disabilities: Birth–2 Years

Part C-Infants and Toddlers with Disabilities
Minnesota Department of Education
Kara Tempel, Part C Coordinator
1500 Highway 36 West
Roseville, MN 55113-4266
(651) 582-8495
(800) 728-5420
E-mail: kara.tempel@state.mn.us
Web: http://education.state.mn.us/MDE/
     StuSuc/EarlyLearn/InfTodInterv/index.html

Programs for Children With Disabilities: 3–5 Years

Early Learning Services
Minnesota Department of Education
Jennifer Moses, 619 Coordinator
1500 Highway 36 West
Roseville, MN 55112
(651) 582-8473
E-E-mail: jennifer.moses@state.mn.us
Web: http://education.state.mn.us/MDE/
     StuSuc/EarlyLearn/InfTodInterv/index.html

State Vocational Rehabilitation Agency

Rehabilitation Services Branch
Department of Employment and
     Economic Development
Howard Glad, Director
First National Bank Building
332 Minnesota Street, #E200
St. Paul, MN 55101
(651) 296-7510; (800) 328-9095
E-mail: howard.glad@state.mn.us
Web: www.des.state.mn.us

Coordinator for Transition Services

Jayne Spain, Transition Specialist
Office of Federal Programs/
*   Special Education Policy*
Minnesota Department of Education
1500 Highway 36 West
Roseville, MN 55113
(651) 582-8515
E-mail: jayne.spain@state.mn.us
Web: http://education.state.mn.us

State Mental Health Agency

Department of Human Services
Loren Colman, Assistant Commissioner
*   for Continuing Care*
Human Services Building
444 Lafayette Road
St. Paul, MN 55155-3844
(651) 297-4155
E-mail: Loren.Colman@state.mn.us
Web: www.dhs.state.mn.us

State Mental Health Representative for Children and Youth

Children's Mental Health Division
Department of Human Services
Glenace Edwall, Director
Human Services Building
444 Lafayette Road
St. Paul, MN 55155-3860
(651) 215-1382
E-mail: glenace.edwall@state.mn.us
Web: www.dhs.state.mn.us

State Developmental Disabilities Program

Disabilities Service Division
Department of Human Services
Shirley York, Director
444 Lafayette Road
St. Paul, MN 55155-3872
(651) 582-1805
E-mail: shirley.york@state.mn.us
Web: www.dhs.state.mn.us

Council on Developmental Disabilities

Minnesota Governor's Council on Developmental
*   Disabilities*
Colleen Wieck, Executive Director
370 Centennial Office Building
658 Cedar Street
St. Paul, MN 55155
(651) 296-4018; (877) 348-0505
(651) 297-9962 (TTY)
E-mail: admin.dd@state.mn.us
Web: www.mncdd.org
Web: www.mnddc.org
Web: www.partnersinpolicymaking.com

Protection and Advocacy Agency

Minnesota Disability Law Center
Pamela Hoopes, Legal Director
430 First Avenue, North, Suite 300
Minneapolis, MN 55401-1780
(612) 746-3711; (800) 292-4150
(612) 334-5970 (New Clients)
E-mail: phoopes@midmnlegal.org
Web: www.mndlc.org

Client Assistance Program

*   Contact Protection and Advocacy Agency,*
listed above.

Programs for Children With Special Health Care Needs

Minnesota Children with Special Health Needs
Minnesota Department of Health
John Hurley, Section Manager
85 E. 7th Place, Suite 400
P.O. Box 64882
St. Paul, MN 55164-0882
(651) 215-8956; (800) 728-5420
E-mail: john.hurley@health.state.mn.us
Web: www.health.state.mn.us/mcshn

State CHIP Program (health care for low-income, uninsured children)

MinnesotaCare
P.O. Box 64838
St. Paul, MN 55164-0838
(651) 297-3862; (800) 657-3672
(800) 627-3529 (TTY)
Web: www.minnesotacare411.com

Programs for Children and Youth
Who Are Blind or Visually Impaired

State Services for the Blind
Department of Employment and
    Economic Development
Chuk Hamilton, Director
2200 University Avenue, West, Suite 240
St. Paul, MN 55114-1840
(651) 642-0500; (800) 652-9000
Web: www.mnssb.org

Minnesota Resource Center:
    Blind/Visual Impairments
Minnesota Department of Education
Jean D. Martin, State Specialist
P.O. Box 308
Faribault, MN 55021-0308
(507) 332-5510; (800) 657-3859 (in MN)
E-mail: Jean.Martin@state.mn.us

Programs for Children and Youth Who
Are Deaf or Hard of Hearing or Deaf-Blind

Deaf and Hard of Hearing Services Division
    (also serves people who are deaf/blind)
Department of Human Services
Bruce Hodek, Director
444 Lafayette Road
St. Paul, MN 55155-3814
(651) 296-3980 (V); (651) 297-1506 (TTY)
E-mail: Bruce.Hodek@state.mn.us
Web: www.dhs.state.mn.us
Web: www.dhhsd.org

Minnesota Commission Serving Deaf and
    Hard of Hearing People
Human Services Building
Mary Hartnett, Executive Director
444 Lafayette Road
St. Paul, MN 55155-3814
(612) 297-7305 (V/TTY)
E-mail: mary.hartnett@state.mn.us

Minnesota Resource Center: Deaf/Hard of Hearing
Minnesota Department of Education
Mary Cashman-Bakken, State Specialist
P.O. Box 308
Faribault, MN 55021-0308
(507) 332-5491 (V/TTY);
    (800) 657-3936 (V/TTY)
E-mail: mary.cashman-bakken@state.mn.us

Telecommunications Relay
Services for Individuals
Who Are Deaf, Hard of Hearing,
or With Speech Impairments

(800) 627-3529 (V/TTY/ASCII); 711 (V/TTY/
    ASCII)
(877) 627-3848 (Speech to Speech)
(877) 627-5448 (Spanish)
(900) 246-3323 (900 access)

State Education Agency
Low Incidence Representative

Eric Kloos, Supervisor
Minnesota Department of Education
1500 Highway 36 West
Roseville, MN 55113
(651) 582-8268
E-mail: eric.kloos@state.mn.us
Web: http://education.state.mn.us

Regional ADA & IT
Technical Assistance Center

Great Lakes ADA and Accessible IT Center
Department of Disability and
    Human Development
Robin Jones, Director
1640 W. Roosevelt Road
Chicago, IL 60608
(312) 413-1407 (V/TTY); (800) 949-4232 (V/TTY)
E-mail: gldbtac@uic.edu
Web: www.adagreatlakes.org

University Center
for Excellence in
Developmental Disabilities

Institute on Community Integration (UCE)
David R. Johnson, Director
University of Minnesota, 102 Pattee Hall
150 Pillsbury Drive SE
Minneapolis, MN 55455
(612) 624-6300
E-mail: info@icimail.umn.edu
Web: http://ici.umn.edu/

Technology-Related Assistance

Minnesota STAR Program
Chuck Rassbach, Executive Director
50 Sherburne Avenue, Room 309
St. Paul, MN 55155
(651) 296-2771 (V); (800) 657-3862 (V)
(651) 296-9478 (TTY); (800) 657-3895 (TTY)
E-mail: star.program@state.mn.us
Web: www.admin.state.mn.us/
    assistive technology

State Mediation System

Minnesota Special Education Mediation Service
    (MNSEMS)
Patricia McGinnis, Coordinator
1500 Highway 36 West
Roseville, MN 55113
(651) 582-8222; (866) 466-7367
E-mail: Patricia.Mcginnis@state.mn.us
Web: www.mnsems.state.mn.us

Special Format Library

Minnesota Library for the Blind and Physically
    Handicapped
Catherine Durivage, Librarian
388 SE 6th Avenue
Faribault, MN 55021-6340
(507) 333-4828; (800) 722-0550
E-mail: mn.lbph@state.mn.us
E-mail: catherine.durivage@state.mn.us
Web: www.education.state.mn.us/
    html/intro_mlbph.htm

Minnesota—Disability-Specific Organizations

Attention Deficit Disorder

To identify an ADD group in Minnesota,
contact either of the following organizations:

Children and Adults with Attention-Deficit/
    Hyperactivity Disorder (CHADD)
8181 Professional Place, Suite 150
Landover, MD 20785
(301) 306-7070
(800) 233-4050 (Voice mail to request
    information packet)
Web: www.chadd.org

Attention Deficit Disorder Association (ADDA)
P.O. Box 543
Pottstown, PA 19464
(484) 945-2101
Web: www.add.org

Autism

Autism Society of Minnesota
Mary Powell, Executive Director
2380 Wycliff Street, Suite 102
St. Paul, MN 55114
(651) 647-1083
E-mail: mpowell@goldengate.net
Web: www.ausm.org

Blind/Visual Impairments

National Federation of the Blind of Minnesota
Joyce Scanlan, President
100 E. 22nd Street
Minneapolis, MN 55404-2514
(612) 872-0100
E-mail: info@blindinc.org
Web: www.blindinc.org

American Foundation for the Blind—Midwest
Jay Stiteley, Director
401 N. Michigan Avenue, Suite 350
Chicago, IL 60611
(312) 396-4420
E-mail: chicago@afb.net
Web: www.afb.org

American Council of the Blind of Minnesota
Ken Rodgers, President
P.O. Box 7341
Minneapolis, MN 55407
(612) 730-8100
E-mail: kgr@isd.net
Web: www.acb.org/minnesota

Brain Injury

Brain Injury Association of Minnesota
Tom Gode, Executive Director
34 13th Avenue, NE, Suite B001
Minneapolis, MN 55413
(612) 378-2742; (800) 669-6442 (in MN)
E-mail: info@braininjurymn.org
Web: www.braininjurymn.org

Cerebral Palsy

United Cerebral Palsy of Minnesota
Jo Ann Erbes, Executive Director
Griggs-Midway Building
1821 University Avenue West, Suite 219 South
St. Paul, MN 55104-2892
(651) 646-7588; (800) 328-4827, ext. 1437
E-mail: ucpmn@cpinternet.com

Down Syndrome

Down Syndrome Association of Minnesota
Kathleen Forney, Executive Director
668 Transfer Road
St. Paul, MN 55114
(651) 603-0720; (800) 511-3696
E-mail: dsamn@dsamn.org
Web: www.dsamn.org

Epilepsy

Epilepsy Foundation of Minnesota
Bennie Loro, Executive Director
1600 University Avenue West, Suite 205
St. Paul, MN 55104
(651) 287-2300; (800) 779-0777
E-mail: info@efmn.org
Web: www.efmn.org

Learning Disabilities

Learning Disabilities Program–Children's Home
    Society & Family Service
166 Fourth Street East, Suite 200
St. Paul, MN 55101-1464
(651) 222-0311; (800) 982-2303 (in MN)
E-mail: ajespersen@chsfs.org
Web: www.chsfs.org

Learning Disabilities Association of Minnesota
Kitty Christiansen, Executive Director
4301 Highway 7, Suite 160
Minneapolis, MN 55416
(952) 922-8374
E-mail: info@ldaminnesota.org
Web: www.ldaminnesota.org

Mental Health

Mental Health Association of Minnesota
Sandra Meicher, Executive Director
2021 E. Hennepin Avenue, Suite 412
Minneapolis, MN 55413
(612) 331-6840
E-mail: info@mentalhealthmn.org
Web: www.mentalhealthmn.org

NAMI-Minnesota
Sue Abderholden, Executive Director
800 Transfer Road, Suite 7A
St. Paul, MN 55114
(651) 645-2948; (888) 473-0237
E-mail: nami-mn@nami.org
Web: www.nami.org/namimn

Minnesota Association for Children's
    Mental Health
Deborah Saxhaug, Executive Director
165 Western Avenue, Suite 2
St. Paul, MN 55102
(651) 644-7333; (800) 528-4511 (in MN)
E-mail: info@macmh.org
Web: www.macmh.org

Mental Retardation/ Developmental Disabilities

The Arc of Minnesota
Steve Larson, Executive Director
770 Transfer Road, Suite 26
St. Paul, MN 55114
(651) 523-0823; (800) 582-5256 (in MN)
E-mail: Arcmn115@yahoo.com
Web: www.arcminnesota.com
Web: www.TheArcLink.org

Speech and Hearing

Minnesota Speech-Language-Hearing Association
Frances Laven, Association Executive
P.O. Box 26115
St. Louis Park, MN 55426
(952) 920-0787; (800) 344-8808
E-mail: msha@incnet.com
Web: www.msha.net

Spina Bifida

Spina Bifida Association of Minnesota
Julie Abbot, President
Jim Thayer, Development Director
P.O. Box 29323
Brooklyn Center, MN 55429-0323
(651) 222-6395
E-mail: jscottthayer@msn.com
Web: www.sbaa.org

Tourette Syndrome

Tourette Syndrome Association–Minnesota Chapter
Julie Zabloski, Executive Director
10249 Yellow Circle Drive, Suite 103
Minnetonka, MN 55343
(952) 918-0350
E-mail: director@tsa-mn.org
Web: www.tsa-mn.org

Minnesota–Organizations Especially for Parents

Parent Training and Information Center (PTI)
PACER Center, Inc.
Paula F. Goldberg, Executive Director
Virginia Richardson, PTI Manager
8161 Normandale Boulevard
Minneapolis, MN 55437-1044
(952) 838-9000; (952) 838-0190 (TTY)
(800) 537-2237 (in MN)
E-mail: pacer@pacer.org
Web: www.pacer.org

Parent-To-Parent

Arc Northland
Reenie Engstrom, Family Specialist
and Respite Director
201 Ordean Building
424 W. Superior Street
Duluth, MN 55802
(218) 726-4725; (800) 317-6475
E-mail: arcnorthland.an@charterinternet.net

Community Parent Resource Center (serving St. Paul area)

Discapacitados Abriéndose Caminos
Ana M. Perez de Perez, Executive Director
608 Smith Avenue
St. Paul, MN 55107
(651) 293-1748
E-mail: discapacitados@comcast.net

Partners in Policymaking

Government Training Service
Carol Schoeneck, Program Specialist
2233 University Avenue West, Suite 150
St. Paul, MN 55114
(651) 222-7409, ext. 205
E-mail: cschoeneck@mngts.org
Web: www.mngts.org

Parent Teacher Association (PTA)

Minnesota Congress of Parents,
Teachers and Students
Phil Enke,President
1667 Snelling Avenue, North
St. Paul, MN 55108
(651) 999-7320; (800) 672-0993
E-mail: mnptaofc@mnpta.org
Web: www.mnpta.org

Minnesota—Other Disability Organizations

Courage Center
Eric Stevens, CEO
Sue Warner, Media, Web & Event Manager
3915 Golden Valley Road
Minneapolis, MN 55422
(763) 520-0210; (888) 846-8253
E-mail: courageinfo@courage.org
Web: www.courage.org

Goodwill/Easter Seals
Michael Wirth-Davis, President/CEO
553 Fairview Avenue North
St. Paul, MN 55104
(651) 379-5800 (V/TTY); (800) 669-6719
E-mail: dtretsven@goodwilleasterseals.org
Web: www.goodwilleasterseals.org

Minnesota State Council on Disability
Joan Willshire, Executive Director
121 E. 7th Place, Suite 107
St. Paul, MN 55101
(651) 296-6785 (V/TTY);
(800) 945-8913 (V/TTY)
E-mail: council.disability@state.mn.us
Web: www.disability.state.mn.us

VSA Arts of Minnesota
Craig Dunn, Executive Director
Hennepin Center for the Arts
528 Hennepin Avenue, Suite 305
Minneapolis, MN 55403
(612) 332-3888; (800) 801-3883
E-mail: vsarts@bcmn.com
Web: http://mn.vsarts.org

Independent Living

To find out the contact information for the Statewide Independent Living Council (SILC) in Minnesota, contact

Independent Living Research Utilization Project
The Institute for Rehabilitation and Research
2323 South Sheppard, Suite 1000
Houston, TX 77019
(713) 520-0232 (V); (713) 520-5136 (TTY)
E-mail: ilru@ilru.org
Web: www.ilru.org

To find out the contact information for cen-ters for independent living (CILs) in Minnesota, contact

National Council on Independent Living
1916 Wilson Boulevard, Suite 209
Arlington, VA 22201
(703) 525-3406; (703) 525-4153 (TTY)
E-mail: ncil@ncil.org
Web: www.ncil.org

MISSISSIPPI

Mississippi—State Agencies and Organizations

United States Senators

Honorable Thad Cochran (R)
113 Dirksen Senate Office Building
Washington, DC 20510
(202) 224-5054
E-mail: senator@cochran.senate.gov
Web: http://cochran.senate.gov

Honorable Roger F. Wicker (R)
555 Dirksen Senate Office Building
Washington, DC 20510
(202) 224-6253
(202) 224-2262 (Fax)
E-mail: http://www.wicker.senate.gov/
*   public/index.cfm/contact*
Web: http://www.wicker.senate.gov/public/
*   index.cfm/*

United States Representatives

To find the contact information for your representative in the House of the U.S. Congress, visit the House's Web site at: www.house.gov, or call: (202) 225-3121; (202) 225-1904 (TTY).

Governor

Honorable Phil Bryant
Office of the Governor
P.O. Box 139
Jackson, MS 39205
(601) 359-3150; (877) 405-0733
E-mail Web Form: http://www.
*   governorbryant.com/contact/*
Web: http://www.governorbryant.com/

Official State Web Site

Web: www.ms.gov

State Department of Education: Special Education

Dr. Melody Bounds, Director
Office of Special Education
Department of Education
P.O. Box 771
Jackson, MS 39205-0771
(601) 359-1988
Web: www.mde.k12.ms.us/special_education/

State Coordinator for NCLB (No Child Left Behind)

Mississippi has been granted an extended waiver from the NCLB act.

Kelsey Blumenberg
Division of Program Development and Special
*   Populations*
Mississippi Department of Education
Office of Federal Programs
P.O. Box 771
Jackson, MS 39205-0771
(601) 359-3499
Email: keblumenberg@mde.k12.ms.us
Web: http://www.mde.k12.ms.us/federal-
*   programs/federal-programs---title-i-basic*

Programs for Infants and Toddlers With Disabilities: Birth–2 Years

Stacy Callender, Director
Early Intervention Program (First Steps)
Mississippi State Department of Health
*   (MDSH)*
570 East Woodrow Wilson Boulevard
P.O. Box 1700
(601) 576-7540
E-mail: stacy.callender@msdh.ms.gov
Web: http://www.msdh.state.ms.us/
*   msdhsite/index.cfm/41,0,74,html*

**Programs for Children
With Disabilities: 3–5 Years**

Office of Special Education
Department of Education
Tanya Bradley, Bureau Director II
359 North West Street, P.O. Box 771
Jackson, MS 39201
(601) 359-3498
E-mail: tbradley@mde.k12.ms.us
Web: http://www.mde.k12.ms.us/special-
education

State Vocational Rehabilitation Agency

Mississippi Office of Vocational Rehabilitation
Department of Rehabilitation Services
Gary Neely, Director
P.O. Box 1698
Jackson, MS 39215-1698
(601) 853-5230
Web: www.mdrs.state.ms.us

Office of Vocational Rehabilitation for the Blind
Mississippi Department of Rehabilitation Services
Dr. Michael Gandy, Director
P.O. Box 1698
Jackson, MS 39215-1698
(601) 853-5100; (800) 443-1000
E-mail: mgandy@mdrs.state.ms.us

Coordinator for Transition Services

Trese Evans, Division Director
Office of Special Education
Mississippi Department of Education
P.O. Box 771
Jackson, MS 39205
(601) 359-3498
E-mail: tevans@mde.k12.ms.us
Web: www.mde.k12.ms.us/special_education/

**Office of State Coordinator of Vocational Education for
Students With Disabilities**

Special Vocational Services for the Handicapped
Office of Vocational and Technical Education
Department of Education
Dr. Marion Bihm, Coordinator
P.O. Box 771
Jackson, MS 39205-0771
(601) 359-3089
E-mail: mbihm@mde.k12.ms.us
Web: www.mde.k12.ms.us

State Mental Health Agency

Department of Mental Health
Dr. Albert Randel Hendrix, PhD,
    Executive Director
1101 Robert E. Lee Building
239 N. Lamar Street
Jackson, MS 39201
(601) 359-1288
E-mail: sstokes@msdmh.org
Web: www.dmh.state.ms.us

**State Mental Health Representative
for Children and Youth**

Brenda Scafidi, EdD, Director
Division of Children and Youth Services
Department of Mental Health
1101 Robert E. Lee Building
239 N. Lamar Street
Jackson, MS 39201
(601) 359-1288
E-mail: bscafidi@msdmh.org
Web: www.dmh.state.ms.us

State Mental Retardation Program

Bureau of Mental Retardation
Department of Mental Health
Edwin LeGrand, Deputy Director
1101 Robert E. Lee Building
239 N. Lamar Street
Jackson, MS 39201
(601) 359-1288
Web: www.dmh.state.ms.us

Council on Developmental Disabilities

Council on Developmental Disabilities
Ed Butler, Director
1101 Robert E. Lee Building
239 N. Lamar St.
Jackson, MS 39201
(601) 359-1270
Web: www.dmh.state.ms.us

Protection and Advocacy Agency

Mississippi Protection and Advocacy System
Rebecca Floyd, Executive Director
5305 Executive Place
Jackson, MS 39206
(601) 981-8207; (800) 772-4057
E-mail: info@mspas.com
Web: www.mspas.com

Client Assistance Program

Client Assistance Program
Mississippi Society for Disabilities
Presley Posey, Director
3226 N. State Street
P.O. Box 4958
Jackson, MS 39296-4958
(601) 362-2585
E-mail: presleymsd@bellsouth.net
Web: www.mississippicap.com

Programs for Children With Special Health Care Needs

Children's Medical Program
Board of Health
Larry Clark, Director
P.O. Box 1700
Jackson, MS 39215-1700
(601) 987-3965; (800) 844-0898 (National/
    WATS)

**State CHIP Program (health care
for low-income, uninsured children)**

Mississippi Health Benefits
Division of Medicaid
Robert E. Lee Building, Suite 801
239 N. Lamar Street
Jackson, MS 39201-1399
(877) 870-3110
Web: www.dom.state.ms.us/CHIP/chip.html

**Programs for Children and Youth Who
Are Blind or Visually Impaired or Deaf-Blind**

Mississippi School for the Blind
1252 Eastover Drive
Jackson, MS 39211
(601) 984-8200
Web: www2.mde.k12.ms.us/msb

**Programs for Children and Youth
Who Are Deaf or Hard of Hearing**

Deaf and Hard of Hearing Services
Mississippi Department of
    Rehabilitation Services
Rell Webber, State Coordinator
P.O. Box 1698
Jackson, MS 39215-1698
(601) 853-5310 (V/TTY); (800) 443-1000
E-mail: rwebber@mdrs.state.ms.us
Web: www.mdrs.state.ms.us

**Telecommunications Relay Services for Individuals Who
Are Deaf, Hard of Hearing, or With Speech Impairments**

(800) 582-2233 (V/TTY); 711 (TTY)
(800) 229-5746 (Speech to Speech-English)
(866) 260-9470 (Speech to Speech-Spanish)

**State Education Agency
Rural Representative**

Dr. Melody Bounds
Department of Education
P.O. Box 771
Jackson, MS 39205

**Regional ADA & IT
Technical Assistance Center**

Southeast Disability and Business Technical
    Assistance Center
Center for Assistive Technology and
    Environmental Access
Georgia Tech
Shelley Kaplan, Project Director
490 10th Street
Atlanta, GA 30318
(404) 385-0636; (800) 949-4232 (V/TTY)
E-mail: sedbtac@catea.org
Web: www.sedbtac.org

Toy Library and Technology Learning Center
University of Southern Mississippi
Gulf Park Campus
Sara Jackson, Director
730 E. Beach Boulevard
Long Beach, MS 39560
(228) 867-2636; (228) 214-3286
E-mail: tlc@usm.edu
Web: www.gp.usm.edu/tlc/index.html

**University Center for Excellence
in Developmental Disabilities**

The Institute for Disability Studies
University of Southern Mississippi
Jane Z. Siders, Director
118 College Drive, #5163
Hattiesburg, MS 39406-0001
(601) 266-5163; (888) 671-0051 (V/TTY)
E-mail: jane.siders@usm.edu
Web: www.ids.usm.edu

Technology-Related Assistance

Mississippi Project Start
Stephen Power, Director
P.O. Box 1698
Jackson, MS 39215
(601) 987-4872 (V/TTY);
    (800) 852-8328 (V/TTY in MS)
E-mail: spower@mdrs.state.ms.us
Web: www.msprojectstart.org

State Mediation System

Department of Education
Office of Special Education
Tanya Bradley, Bureau Director
P.O. Box 771
Jackson, MS 39205
(601) 359-3498
E-mail: tbradley@mde.k12.ms.us
Web: www.mde.k12.ms.us

Special Format Library

Mississippi Library Commission
Blind and Physically Handicapped Library
    Services
Rahye Puckett, Director/Librarian
1221 Ellis Avenue
Jackson, MS 39209
(601) 961-4111; (800) 446-0892
E-mail: lbph@mlc.lib.ms.us
E-mail: rahye@mlc.lib.ms.us
Web: www.mlc.lib.ms.us/bphls/

Mississippi — Disability-Specific Organizations

Attention Deficit Disorder

    To identify an ADD group in Mississippi,
contact either of the following organizations:

Children and Adults with Attention-Deficit/
    Hyperactivity Disorder (CHADD)
8181 Professional Place, Suite 150
Landover, MD 20785
(301) 306-7070
(800) 233-4050 (Voice mail to request
    information packet)
Web: www.chadd.org

Attention Deficit Disorder Association (ADDA)
P.O. Box 543
Pottstown, PA 19464
(484) 945-2101
Web: www.add.org

Autism

    To identify an autism group in Mississippi,
contact

Autism Society of America
7910 Woodmont Avenue, Suite 300
Bethesda, MD 20814
(301) 657-0881; (800) 3-AUTISM
Web: www.autism-society.org

TEAAM (Together Enhancing Autism Awareness
    in Mississippi)
Dr. Mark Yeager, President
P.O. Box 213
Newton, MS 39345
(601) 683-4200
E-mail: myeager@cmrc.state.ms.us

Blind/Visual Impairments

Frances Mary D'Andrea, Director
American Foundation for the Blind–National
    Literacy Center
100 Peachtree Street, Suite 620
Atlanta, GA 30303
(404) 525-2303
E-mail: literacy@afb.net
Web: www.afb.org

Brain Injury

Brain Injury Association of Mississippi
P.O. Box 55912
Jackson, MS 39296-5912
(601) 981-1021; (800) 641-6442
E-mail biaofms@aol.com
Web: www.members.aol.com/biaofms/index.
    htm

Cerebral Palsy

Cerebral Palsy Foundation of Mississippi, Inc.
Sheila Pearson, Director
P.O. Box 16924
Jackson, MS 39236-6924
(601) 853-1961; (888) 852-1961 (toll free)
E-mail: cpfofms@aol.com
Web: www.cpfofms.org

Epilepsy

Epilepsy Foundation of Mississippi
Beth Scarbrough, Executive Director
2001 Airport Road, Suite 307
Jackson, MS 39232
(601) 936-5222; (800) 898-0291 (in MS)
E-mail: efm@netdoor.com

Mental Health

Mental Health Association of Mississippi
Brandi H. Clarke, Executive Director
4803 Harrison Circle
Gulfport, MS 39507
(228) 864-6274
E-mail: mhagptms@aol.com

Mental Health Association of the Capital Area, Inc.
Larry Swearengen, Interim Director
411 Briarwood Drive, Suite 401
Jackson, MS 39206
(601) 956-2800
E-mail: mhajxn@aol.com

NAMI Mississippi
Teri Brister, Executive Director
411 Briarwood Drive, Suite 401
Jackson, MS 39206
(601) 899-9058
E-mail: namimiss1@aol.com

Mississippi Families As Allies for
   Children's Mental Health
Tessie Schweitzer, Executive Director
5166 Keele Street, Building A
Jackson, MS 39206
(601) 981-1618; (800) 833-9671
E-mail: tschweitzer@msfaacmh.org
Web: www.msfaacmh.org

Mental Retardation/ Developmental Disabilities

The Arc of Mississippi
Matt Nalker, Executive Director
7 Lakeland Circle, Suite 600
Jackson, MS 39216
(601) 982-1180; (800) 717-1180
E-mail: matt@arcms.org
Web: www.arcms.org

Speech and Hearing

Mississippi Speech-Language-Hearing Association
Deirdre McGowan, CAE, Executive Director
P.O. Box 22664
Jackson, MS 39225-2664
(800) 664-6742
E-mail: mshahelp@mshausa.org
Web: www.mshausa.org

Spina Bifida

Spina Bifida Association of Mississippi
Kelly Wedgeworth, Executive Director
Amy Wilkinson, President
P.O. Box 180594
Richland, MS 39218
(601) 214-1281
E-mail: kgwedge@yahoo.com
E-mail: awsba@yahoo.com

Mississippi—Organizations Especially for Parents

Parent Training and Information Center (PTI) (Mississippians are currently being provided with information and training via the Florida PTI listed here)

Family Network on Disabilities of Florida, Inc.
Parent Education Network
Jan LaBelle, Executive Director
Nancy Gonsalves, Project Co-Director
Milagros Pou, Project Co-Director
2735 Whitney Road
Clearwater, FL 33760-1610
(727) 523-1130; (800) 825-5736
E-mail: pen@fndfl.org
Web: http://fndfl.org

Community Parent Resource Center

EMPOWER Community Resource Center
   (serving Six EMPOWER Counties)
Agnes Johnson, Executive Director
P.O. Box 1733
136 S. Poplar Street
Greenville, MS 38702-1733
(662) 332-4852; (800) 337-4852
E-mail: empower@cox-internet.com
Web: www.msempower.org

Parent Teacher Association (PTA)

Rick Tillotson, President
Mississippi Congress of Parents and
    Teachers, Inc.
P.O. Box 1937
Jackson, MS 39215
(601) 352-7383; (800) 795-6123

Other Parent Organizations

Mississippi SAFE KIDS Campaign
Lori Bezada, Project Coordinator
615 Barksdale Street
Jackson, MS 39202
(601) 969-0669; (877) 706-8741 (V/TTY)
E-mail: MSSAFEKIDS@mscoalition.com
Web: www.mssafekids.com

Parents for Public Schools of Jackson
3252 N. State Street
Jackson, MS 39216
(601) 713-1633
E-mail: dana.larkin@parents4publicschools.com
Web: www.parents4publicschools.com/jackson

Parents United Together
Mandy Rogers, President
P.O. Box 2121
Madison, MS 39130
E-mail: MOM424@aol.com
Web: www.parentsunitedtogether.com

Mississippi—Other Disability Organizations

Coalition for Citizens with Disabilities
Mary G. Troupe, Executive Director
615 Barksdale Street
Jackson, MS 39202
(601) 969-0601 (V/TTY);
    (800) 748-9420 (V/TTY)
Web: www.mscoalition.com

Healthy Futures
Sam Gleese, Project Director
615 Barksdale Street
Jackson, MS 39202
(601) 969-0601; (800) 748-9420 (V/TTY)
E-mail: hfutures@aol.com
Web: www.healthyfuturesms.com

VSA Arts of Mississippi
Leslie Roark Scott, Executive Director
3310 N. State Street, Studio 1

Jackson, MS 39216
(601) 713-3311
E-mail: jacvsa@netdoor.com

Independent Living

To find out the contact information for the Statewide Independent Living Council (SILC) in Mississippi, contact

Independent Living Research Utilization Project
The Institute for Rehabilitation and Research
2323 South Sheppard, Suite 1000
Houston, TX 77019
(713) 520-0232 (V); (713) 520-5136 (TTY)
E-mail: ilru@ilru.org
Web: www.ilru.org

To find out the contact information for centers for independent living (CILs) in Mississippi, contact

National Council on Independent Living
1916 Wilson Boulevard, Suite 209
Arlington, VA 22201
(703) 525-3406; (703) 525-4153 (TTY)
E-mail: ncil@ncil.org
Web: www.ncil.org

MISSOURI

Missouri—State Agencies and Organizations

United States Senators

Honorable Roy Blunt (R)
260 Russell Senate Office Building
Washington, DC 20510
(202) 224-5721; (202) 224-9901 (TTY)
(202) 224-8149 (Fax)
E-mail: http://www.blunt.senate.gov/public/
    index.cfm/contact-form?p=contact-roy
Web: http://www.blunt.senate.gov/public/
    index.cfm/home

Honorable Claire McCaskill (D)
506 Hart Senate Office Building
Washington, DC 20510
(202) 224-6154
(202) 228-0998 (Fax)
E-mail: http://www.mccaskill.senate.gov/
    contact
Web: http://www.mccaskill.senate.gov/

United States Representatives

To find the contact information for your representative in the House of the U.S. Congress, visit the House's Web site at: *www.house.gov*, or call: (202) 225-3121; (202) 225-1904 (TTY).

Governor

Honorable Jay Nixon
Missouri Capitol Building
P.O. Box 720
Jefferson City, MO 65102
(573) 751-3222
E-mail: *https://governor.mo.gov/get-involved/contact-the-governors-office*
Web: *https://governor.mo.gov/*

Official State Web Site

Web: *www.state.mo.us/*

State Department of Education: Special Education

Division of Special Education
Department of Elementary and
    Secondary Education
Melodie Friedebach, Assistant Commissioner
P.O. Box 480
Jefferson City, MO 65102
(573) 751-4444
E-mail: *melodie.friedebach@dese.mo.gov*
Web: *www.dese.mo.gov/divspeced/*

State Coordinator for NCLB (No Child Left Behind)

Missouri has been granted an extended waiver from the NCLB act.

Pat Kaiser, Director
Department of Elementary & Secondary
    Education
Office of Federal Programs
P.O. Box 480, 205 Jefferson Street
Jefferson City, MO 65102
(573) 751-8643
Email: *pat.kaiser@dese.mo.gov*
Web:*http://dese.mo.gov/quality-schools/federal-programs*

Programs for Infants and Toddlers With Disabilities: Birth–2 Years

Special Education Services
Department of Elementary and
    Secondary Education
Pam Thomas, Part C Coordinator
P.O. Box 480
Jefferson City, MO 65102-0480
(573) 751-3559
E-mail: *pam.thomas@dese.mo.gov*
Web: *http://dese.mo.gov/special-education/first-steps*

Programs for Children With Disabilities: 3–5 Years

Effective Practices Section
Department of Elementary and
    Secondary Education
Pam Williams, 619 Coordinator
Special Education Compliance
205 Jefferson Street
PO Box 480
Jefferson City, MO 65102-0480
(573) 751-4909
E-mail: *pam.williams@dese.mo.gov*
Web: *http://dese.mo.gov/special-education/early-childhood-special-education*

State Vocational Rehabilitation Agency

Division of Vocational Rehabilitation
Department of Education
Jeanne Loyd, Assistant Commissioner
3024 Dupont Circle
Jefferson City, MO 65109-0525
(573) 751-3251
Web: *www.vr.dese.mo.gov*

Coordinator for Transition Services

Special Education Effective Practices Section
Department of Elementary and Secondary
    Education
John Bamberg, Assistant Director
P.O. Box 480
Jefferson City, MO 65102-0480
(573) 526-0298
E-mail: *john.bamberg@dese.mo.gov*
Web: *www.dese.mo.gov*

Office of State Coordinator of Vocational Education for Students With Disabilities

Vocational Special Needs
Department of Elementary and
    Secondary Education
Shawn Brice, Director
P.O. Box 480
Jefferson City, MO 65102
(573) 522-1775
E-mail: shawn.brice@dese.mo.gov
Web: www.dese.mo.gov/divcareered/
    special_needs_index.htm

State Mental Health Agency

Department of Mental Health
Dorn Schuffman, Director
1706 East Elm
P.O. Box 687
Jefferson City, MO 65102
(573) 751-3070; (800) 364-9687
Web: www.dmh.mo.gov

State Mental Health Representative for Children and Youth

Department of Mental Health
Linda Roebuck, Deputy Director
1706 E. Elm
P.O. Box 687
Jefferson City, MO 65102
(573) 751-4970
E-mail: linda.roebuck@dmh.mo.gov
Web: www.dmh.mo.gov

State Mental Retardation Program

Division of Mental Retardation and
    Developmental Disabilities
Anne Deaton, Director
1706 E. Elm
P.O. Box 687
Jefferson City, MO 65102
(573) 751-8676; (800) 207-9329
E-mail: anne.deaton@dmh.mo.gov
Web: www.dmh.mo.gov

Council on Developmental Disabilities

Missouri Planning Council for
    Developmental Disabilities
Susan Pritchard-Green, Director
1706 E. Elm
P.O. Box 687
Jefferson City, MO 65102
(573) 751-8611; (800) 500-7878 (in MO)
E-mail: susan.pritchard-green@dmh.mo.gov
Web: www.mpcdd.com

Protection and Advocacy Agency

Missouri Protection and Advocacy Services
Shawn de Loyola, Executive Director
925 S. Country Club Drive
Jefferson City, MO 65109
(573) 893-3333; (800) 392-8667
E-mail: mopasjc@earthlink.com
Web: www.moadvocacy.org

Client Assistance Program

Contact Protection and Advocacy Agency listed above.

Programs for Children With Special Health Care Needs

Special Health Care Needs
Department of Health and Senior Services
Diane Poole, Interim Chief
930 Wildwood Drive
P.O. Box 570
Jefferson City, MO 65102
(573) 751-6246; (800) 451-0669
Web: www.dhss.mo.gov

State CHIP Program (health care for low-income, uninsured children)

MC+ for Children
Missouri Department of Social Services
(888) 275-5908
Web: www.dss.state.mo.us/mcplus/index.htm

Programs for Children and
Youth Who Are Blind or
Visually Impaired or Deaf-Blind

Rehabilitation Services for the Blind
Family Support Division
Michael Fester, Deputy Director
615 Howerton Court
P.O. Box 2320
Jefferson City, MO 65102-2320
(573) 751-4249; (800) 592-6004
E-mail: kimberly.gerlt@dss.mo.gov
Web: www.dss.mo.gov/dfs/rehab/index.htm

Missouri School for the Blind
3815 Magnolia Avenue
St. Louis, MO 63110
(314) 776-4320; (800) 622-5672
E-mail: webmaster@msb.k12.mo.us
Web: www.msb.k12.mo.us

Programs for Children and Youth
Who Are Deaf or Hard of Hearing

Missouri Commission for the Deaf and
Hard of Hearing
Dr. Roy E. Miller, Executive Director
1103 Rear Southwest Boulevard
Jefferson City, MO 65109
(573) 526-5205 (V/TTY)
E-mail: mcdhh@mo.gov
Web: www.mcdhh.state.mo.us

Missouri School for the Deaf
505 E. 5th Street
Fulton, MO 65251-1799
(573) 592-4000
E-mail: webmaster@msd.k12.mo.us
Web: www.msd.k12.mo.us

Telecommunications Relay
Services for Individuals Who
Are Deaf, Hard of Hearing,
or With Speech Impairments

(800) 735-2466 (V)
(800) 735-2966 (TTY); 711 (TTY)
(877) 735-7877 (Speech to Speech)

State Education Agency
Rural Representative

D. Kent King, Commissioner
Department of Elementary and
    Secondary Education
P.O. Box 480
Jefferson City, MO 65102
(573) 751-4212
E-mail: pubinfo@dese.mo.gov
Web: www.dese.mo.gov

Regional ADA & IT
Technical Assistance Center

ADA and IT Center
Great Plains Disability and
    Business Technical Assistance Center
University of Missouri/Columbia
Jim de Jong, Director
100 Corporate Lake Drive
Columbia, MO 65203
(573) 882-3600 (V/TTY); (800) 949-4232 (V/
    TTY)
E-mail: ada@missouri.edu
Web: www.adaproject.org

University Center for
Excellence in Developmental Disabilities

UMKC Institute for Human Development
Carl F. Calkins, Director
Health Sciences Building
2220 Holmes Street, 3rd Floor
Kansas City, MO 64108
(816) 235-1770; (800) 444-0821 (V)
(800) 452-1185 (TTY)
Web: www.ihd.umkc.edu

Technology-Related Assistance

Missouri Assistive Technology
Diane Golden, Project Director
4731 South Cochise, Suite 114
Independence, MO 64055-6975
(816) 373-5193; (800) 647-8557
E-mail: matpmo@swbell.net
Web: www.at.mo.gov

State Mediation System

Special Education Compliance
Missouri Department of Elementary
   and Secondary Education
Pam Williams, Director
P.O. Box 480
Jefferson City, MO 65102
(573) 751-4909
E-mail: pam.williams@dese.mo.gov
Web: www.dese.mo.gov/divspeced/

Special Format Library

Wolfner Library for the Blind and
   Physically Handicapped
Dr. Richard Smith, Librarian
P.O. Box 387
Jefferson City, MO 65102-0387
(573) 751-8720; (800) 392-2614 (in MO)
(800) 347-1379 (TTY/ in MO)
E-mail: wolfner@sos.mo.gov
Web: www.sos.mo.gov/wolfner/

Missouri — Disability-Specific Organizations

Attention Deficit Disorder

To identify an ADD group in Missouri, contact either of the following organizations:

Children and Adults with Attention-Deficit/
   Hyperactivity Disorder (CHADD)
8181 Professional Place, Suite 150
Landover, MD 20785
(301) 306-7070
(800) 233-4050 (Voice mail to request
   information packet)
Web: www.chadd.org

Attention Deficit Disorder
   Association (ADDA)
P.O. Box 543
Pottstown, PA 19464
(484) 945-2101
Web: www.add.org

Autism

Children's Services
Division of Mental Retardation and
   Developmental Disabilities
Julia Kaufmann, Director
1706 E. Elm
P.O. Box 687
Jefferson City, MO 65102
(573) 751-8237
E-mail: julia.kaufman@dmh.mo.gov
Web: www.dmh.mo.gov/mrdd

Blind/Visual Impairments

American Foundation for the Blind–Midwest
Jay Stiteley, Director
401 N. Michigan Avenue, Suite 350
Chicago, IL 60611
(312) 396-4420
E-mail: chicago@afb.net
Web: www.afb.org

Brain Injury

Brain Injury Association of Missouri
Scott Gee, Chief Executive Officer
10270 Page Avenue, Suite 100
St. Louis, MO 63132
(314) 426-4024; (800) 377-6442
E-mail: info@biamo.org
Web: www.biamo.org

Missouri Head Injury Advisory Council
Donna Mueller, Director
P.O. Box 809
Jefferson City, MO 65102
(573) 751-9003
E-mail: donna.mueller@oa.mo.gov
Web: www.tbi.mo.gov

Cerebral Palsy

United Cerebral Palsy Association of Greater St.
   Louis
Richard Forkosh, Executive Director
8645 Old Bonhomme Road
St. Louis, MO 63132-3999
(314) 994-1600
E-mail: forkoshr@ucpstl.org
Web: www.ucpa.org

Epilepsy

Epilepsy Foundation of the St. Louis Region
Darla Templeton, Executive Vice President
7100 Oakland Avenue
St. Louis, MO 63117
(314) 645-6969; (800) 264-6970
E-mail: darla@stl-epil.org
Web: http://www.efmk.org/

Learning Disabilities

Learning Disabilities Association of Missouri
Ginger Johnson, President
1942 E. Meadowmere, Suite104
P.O. Box 3303
Springfield, MO 65804
(417) 864-5110; (800) 473-4965
E-mail: ldamo@cland.net
Web: www.ldamo.org

Mental Health

Mental Health Association of St. Louis
James House, Executive Director
1905 S. Grand Boulevard
St. Louis, MO 63104-1542
(314) 773-1399
E-mail: mhagstl@aol.com
Web: www.mhagstl.org

National Alliances for the Mentally Ill of Missouri
Cindi Keele, Executive Director
1001 Southwest Boulevard, Suite E
Jefferson City, MO 65109
(573) 634-7727; (800) 374-2138
E-mail: namimockj@aol.com
E-mail: namimochildren@aol.com

Missouri Statewide Parent Advisory Network
 (MO-SPAN)
Donna Dittrich, Executive Director
440 Rue St. Francois
Florissant, MO 63031
(314) 972-0600
Web: www.mo-span.org

Speech and Hearing

Missouri Speech-Language-Hearing Association
Central Office
901 Missouri Boulevard, PMB 355
Jefferson City, MO 65109-1759
(888) 729-6742
E-mail: msha@showmemsha.org
Web: www.showmemsha.org

Spina Bifida

Spina Bifida Association of Greater St. Louis
Mark Abbott, Chairperson
8050 Watson Road, Suite 115
St. Louis, MO 63119
(314) 843-2244; (800) 784-0983
E-mail: sbastl@charter.net
Web: www.sbastl.com

Missouri—Organizations Especially for Parents

Parent Training and Information Center (PTI)

Missouri Parents Act (MPACT)
Mary Kay Savage, Executive Director
One W. Armour Boulevard, Suite 302
Kansas City, MO 64111
(816) 531-7070; (800) 743-7634 (V/TTY)
E-mail: msavage@ptimpact.com
Web: www.ptimpact.com

Parent-To-Parent

 Contact Parent Training and Information
Projects listed above.

Partners in Policymaking

Missouri Planning Council for
 Developmental Disabilities
Susan Pritchard-Green, Program Director
P.O. Box 687
Jefferson City, MO 65102
(573) 751-8611; (800) 500-7878 (in MO)
E-mail: susan.pritchard-green@dmh.mo.gov
Web: www.mpcdd.com

Parent Teacher Association (PTA)

Missouri Congress of Parents and Teachers
Tina Zubeck, President
2100 I-70 Drive, SW
Columbia, MO 65203
(573) 445-4161; (800) 328-7330
E-mail: office@mopta.org
E-mail: tinaz@mopta.org
Web: www.mopta.org

Missouri—Other Disability Organizations

Easter Seals Missouri
Craig Byrd, CEO
5025 Northrup Avenue
St. Louis, MO 63110
(314) 664-5025
E-mail: cbyrd@mo.easterseals.com
Web: www.mo.easterseals.com

VSA Arts of Missouri
Lisa Kemper, Executive Director
P.O. Box 1763
Columbia, MO 65205-1763
(573) 875-2872;
*   (866) VSA-ARTS (872-2787)*
E-mail: director@showmevsa.com
Web: www.showmevsa.com

Independent Living

To find out the contact information for the Statewide Independent Living Council (SILC) in Missouri, contact

Independent Living Research Utilization Project
The Institute for Rehabilitation and Research
2323 South Sheppard, Suite 1000
Houston, TX 77019
(713) 520-0232 (V); (713) 520-5136 (TTY)
E-mail: ilru@ilru.org
Web: www.ilru.org

To find out the contact information for centers for independent living (CILs) in Missouri, contact

National Council on Independent Living
1916 Wilson Boulevard, Suite 209
Arlington, VA 22201
(703) 525-3406; (703) 525-4153 (TTY)
E-mail: ncil@ncil.org
Web: www.ncil.org

MONTANA

Montana—State Agencies and Organizations

United States Senators

Honorable Jon Tester (D)
706 Hart Senate Office Building
Washington, DC 20510
(202) 224-2644; (800) 332-6106 (in MT)
(202) 228-3687 (Fax); (202) 224-1998 (TTY)
E-mail Web Form: http://www.tester.senate.
*   gov/?p=email_senator*
Web: http://www.tester.senate.gov/?p=home

Honorable John E. Walsh (D)
511 Hart Senate Office Building
Washington, DC 20510
(202) 224-2651; (202) 224-8616 (TTY)
(202) 224-8594 (Fax)
E-mail Web Form: http://www.walsh.senate.
*   gov/contact.cfm*
Web: http://www.walsh.senate.gov/index.cfm

United States Representatives

To find the contact information for your representative in the House of the U.S. Congress, visit the House's Web site at: www.house.gov, or call: (202) 225-3121; (202) 225-1904 (TTY).

Governor

Honorable Steve Bullock
State Capitol
Helena, MT 59620-0801
(406) 444-3111; (406) 444-3607 (TTY)
Web: http://governor.mt.gov/

Official State Web Site

Web: www.state.mt.us/

State Department of Education: Special Education

Special Education Division
Montana Office of Public Instruction
Robert Runkel, Director
P.O. Box 202501
Helena, MT 59620-2501
(406) 444-4429
E-mail: brunkel@mt.gov
Web: http://www.autism-pdd.net/links/
*   montana.html*

State Coordinator for NCLB (No Child Left Behind)

Denise Juneau, Superintendent
Montana Office of Public Instruction
P.O. Box 202501
Helena, MT 59620-2501
(406) 444-3095
E-mail: OPISupt@mt.gov
Web: http://www.opi.mt.gov/Reports&Data/
     Index.html

Programs for Infants and Toddlers With Disabilities: Birth–2 Years

Developmental Disabilities Program
Department of Public Health and
     Human Services
Jeff Sturm, Director
111 Sanders, Room 305
PO Box 4210
Helena, MT 59604
(406) 444-2695
Web: http://www.dphhs.mt.gov/dsd/
     DevelopmentalDisabililities.aspx

Programs for Children With Disabilities: 3–5 Years

Office of Public Instruction
Danni McCarthy, Compliance Specialist
P.O. Box 202501
Helena, MT 59620-2501
(406) 444-0452
E-mail: dmccarthy@mt.gov
Web: http://opi.mt.gov/Programs/SpecialEd/
     Index.html

State Vocational Rehabilitation Agency

Vocational Rehabilitation Programs
Department of Public Health and Human Services
Joe Mathews, Administrator
P. O. Box 4210
Helena, MT 59604-4210
(406) 444-2590
Web: www.dphhs.state.mt.us/dsd

Coordinator for Transition Services

Dick Trerise, State Transition Contact
     and Coordinator
Division of Special Education
Office of Public Instruction
P.O. Box 202501
Helena, MT 59620
(406) 444-1579

E-mail: dtrerise@state.mt.us
Web: www.opi.state.mt.us

Office of State Coordinator of Vocational Education for Students With Disabilities

Career, Technical and Adult Education
Office of Public Instruction
Jody Messinger, Division Administrator
P.O. Box 202501
Helena, MT 59620-2501
(406) 444-9019
E-mail: jmessinger@state.mt.us
Web: www.opi.state.mt.us

State Mental Health Agency

Addictive and Mental Disorders Division
Department of Public Health and Human
     Services
Glenda Oldenburg, Administrator
100 N. Park, Suite 300
PO Box 202905
Helena MT 59620-2905
(406) 444-3969
Email: goldenburg@mt.gov
Web: http://www.dphhs.mt.gov/amdd.aspx

State Mental Health Program for Children

Children's Mental Health Bureau
Health Resources Division
Department of Public Health and
     Human Services
Pete W. Surdock, Jr., MSW, ACSW,
     Bureau Chief
1400 Broadway—Cogswell Building,
     Room A206
P.O. Box 202951
Helena, MT 59620-2951
(406) 444-1290
E-mail: psurdock@state.mt.us

State Developmental Disabilities Programs

Disability Services Division
Department of Public Health and
     Human Services
Joe Mathews, Administrator
P.O. Box 4210
Helena, MT 59604-4210
(406) 444-2995
Web: www.dphhs.state.mt.us/dsd

Council on Developmental Disabilities

Montana Council on Developmental Disabilities
Deborah Swingley, Executive Director
P.O. Box 526
Helena, MT 59624
(406) 443-4371; (866) 443-4332 (in MT only)
E-mail: deborah@mtcdd.org
Web: www.mtcdd.org

Protection and Advocacy Agency

Montana Advocacy Program
Bernadette Franks Ongoy, Executive Director
P.O. Box 1681
Helena, MT 59624
(406) 449-2344; (800) 245-4743 (V/TTY)
E-mail: bernie@mtadv.org
Web: www.mtadv.org

Client Assistance Program

Montana Advocacy Program
Bernadette Franks-Ongoy, CAP Director
P.O. Box 1681
Helena, MT 59624
(406) 449-2344; (800) 245-4743 (V/TTY)
E-mail: bernie@mtadv.org
Web: www.mtadv.org

**Programs for Children With
Special Health Care Needs**

Children's Special Health Services
Health Care Resources Bureau
Department of Public Health and Human
    Services
Carliss Scott, Outreach Coordinator
P. O. Box 202951
Helena, MT 59620 -2951
(406) 444-3622
E-mail: cscott@state.mt.us

**State CHIP Program health care
(for low-income, uninsured children)**

Montana CHIP
P.O. Box 202951
Helena, MT 59620-2951
(406) 444-4533; (877) 418-4533
E-mail: CHIP@state.mt.us
Web: www.chip.state.mt.us

**Programs for Children and Youth
Who Are Blind or Visually Impaired**

Blind and Low Vision Services
State Vocational Rehabilitation Program for the
    Blind or Visually Impaired
Beverly Berg, Program Administrator
111 Sanders Suite 307
P.O. Box 4210
Helena, MT 59604–4210
(406) 444-2590 (V/TTY); (877) 296-1197

**Programs for Children and Youth Who
Are Deaf or Hard of Hearing or Deaf-Blind**

Montana Deaf and Hard of Hearing
    Services (MDHHS)
Betty Van Tighem, Director
3911 Central Avenue
P.O. Box 6433
Great Falls, MT 59407
(406) 771-9053; (406) 771-9194 (TTY)
E-mail: mdhhsmad@sofast.net

Montana School for the Deaf and the Blind
3911 Central Avenue
Great Falls, MT 59405-1697
(406) 771-6000 (V/TTY); (800) 882-6732
E-mail: bdenoma@sdb.state.mt.us
Web: www.sdb.state.mt.us/

**Telecommunications Relay Services
for Individuals Who Are Deaf, Hard
of Hearing, or With Speech Impairments**

(800) 253-4093 (V)
(800) 253-4091 (TTY); 711 (TTY)
(877) 253-4613 (Speech to Speech)

**State Education Agency
Rural Representative**

Nancy Coopersmith, Assistant Superintendent
Department of Education Services
Office of Public Instruction
P.O. Box 202501
Helena, MT 59620-2501
(406) 444-5541
E-mail: ncoopersmith@state.mt.us
Web: www.opi.state.mt.us

Regional ADA & II
Technical Assistance Center

Rocky Mountain Disability and
    Business Technical Assistance Center
Patrick Going, Director
3630 Sinton Road, Suite 103
Colorado Springs, CO 80907
(719) 444-0268 (V/TTY);
    (800) 949-4232 (V/TTY)
E-mail: rmdbtac@mtc-inc.com
Web: www.adainformation.org

University Center
for Excellence in
Developmental Disabilities

The University of Montana Rural Institute
Center for Excellence in Disability
    Education, Research, and Service
R. Timm Vogelsberg, Executive Director
52 Corbin Hall
Missoula, MT 59812
(406) 243-5467; (800) 732-0322
E-mail: rtvogels@ruralinstitute.umt.edu
Web: http://ruralinstitute.umt.edu

Technology-Related Assistance

MonTECH
The University of Montana, Rural Institute,
    MonTECH Program
Gail McGregor, Director
634 Eddy Avenue
Missoula, MT 59812
(406) 243-5676; (800) 732-0323 (V/TTY)
E-mail: mcgregor@ruralinstitute.umt.edu
Web: http://montech.ruralinstitute.umt.edu/

State Mediation System

Early Assistance Program
Montana Office of Public Instruction
Tim Harris, Program Manager
P.O. Box 202501
Helena, MT 59620-2501
(406) 444-5664
E-mail: tharris@state.mt.us
Web: www.opi.state.mt.us

Special Format Library

Montana Talking Book Library
Christie O. Briggs, Librarian
1515 E. Sixth Avenue
P.O. Box 201800
Helena, MT 59620-1800
(406) 444-2064; (800) 332-3400
(406) 444-3005 (TTY)
E-mail: cbriggs@state.mt.us
Web: http://msl.state.mt.us/tbl/

Montana—Disability-Specific Organizations

Attention Deficit Disorder

To identify an ADD group in Montana,
contact either of the following organizations:

Children and Adults with Attention-Deficit/
    Hyperactivity Disorder (CHADD)
8181 Professional Place, Suite 150
Landover, MD 20785
(301) 306-7070
(800) 233-4050 (Voice mail to request
    information packet)
Web: www.chadd.org

Attention Deficit Disorder Association (ADDA)
P.O. Box 543
Pottstown, PA 19464
(484) 945-2101
Web: www.add.org

Autism

To identify an autism group in Montana,
contact

Autism Society of America
7910 Woodmont Avenue, Suite 300
Bethesda, MD 20814
(301) 657-0881; (800) 3-AUTISM
Web: www.autism-society.org

Blind/Visual Impairments

American Foundation for the Blind–Southwest
Judy Scott, Director
11030 Ables Lane
Dallas, TX 75229
(214) 352-7222
E-mail: dallas@afb.net
Web: www.afb.org

Montana Association for the Blind
P.O. Box 465
Helena, MT 59624-0465
(406) 442-9411

Brain Injury

Ian Elliot, President of the Board of Directors
Brain Injury Association of Montana
University of Montana
52 Corbin Hall, Room 25
Missoula, MT 59812
(406) 243-5973; (800) 241-6442
E-mail: biam@selway.umt.edu
Web: www.biausa.org/Montana

Fragile X Syndrome

Fragile X Resource of Montana
Mary and Dick DeBernardis
12345 Gooch Hill Road
Gallatin Gateway, MT 59730-9707
(406) 763-4268
E-mail: debern@imt.net
Web: www.fragilex.org

Learning Disabilities

Learning Disabilities Association of Montana
Rosie Wathen, President
1438 Cascade Avenue
Billings, MT 59102
(406) 252-7716
E-mail: wathen@mcn.net

Mental Health

Montana Mental Health Association
25 S. Ewing, Suite 206
Helena, MT 59601
(406) 442-4276
E-mail: mmha@qwest.net
Web: www.mhamontana.org/

Family Support Network (FSN)
Barbara Sample, Executive Director
3302 4th Avenue, N., Suite 103
P. O. Box 21366
Billings, MT 59104
(406) 256-7783
E-mail: fsntoo@aol.com

Mental Retardation

Yellowstone Arc
Bev Owens, Arc Treasurer
602 18th Street, W.
Billings, MT 59102
(406) 652-5510

Speech and Hearing

Montana Speech-Language-Hearing Association
Box 215
Miles City, MT 59301
(406) 234-8727
E-mail: info@mshaonline.org
Web: www.mshaonline.org

Montana—Organizations Especially for Parents

Parent Training and Information Center (PTI)

Parents, Let's Unite For Kids (PLUK)
Dennis Moore, Executive Director
516 N. 32nd Street
Billings, MT 59101-6003
(406) 255-0540; (800) 222-7585 (MT only)
E-mail: plukinfo@pluk.org
Web: www.pluk.org

Parent-To-Parent

Contact Parent Training and Information Center (PTI) listed above.

Parent Teacher Association (PTA)

Montana Congress of Parents and Teachers, Inc.
Suzi Ekness, President
P.O. Box 6448
Great Falls, MT 59406
(406) 268-7475
E-mail: montanapta@earthlink.net
Web: www.montanapta.org

IDEA PTA (Individuals with Diverse and
Exceptional Abilities)
Deanna Johnson
P.O. Box 7724
Missoula, MT 59807
(406) 728-1124
E-mail: lotus@bigsky.net

Montana—Other Disability Organizations

Easter Seals–Goodwill Northern Rocky Mountains
Michelle Belknap, President
4400 Central Avenue
Great Falls, MT 59405
(406) 761-3680 (V/TTY); (800) 771-2153
E-mail: michelleb@esgw.org
Web: www.goodwill.org/greatfalls

Montana Center on Disabilities
Montana State University-Billings
Martha Carstensen, Director
1500 University Drive, CEHS Building
Billings, MT 59101
(888) 866-3822 (V/TTY)
E-mail: mcd@msubillings.edu
Web: www.msubillings.edu/mtcd

Support & Techniques for Empowering People
*   (STEP) Inc.*
Sue Dow, Executive Director
1501 14th Street West, Suite 210
Billings, MT 59102
(406) 248-2055; (800) 820-4180
E-mail: suedow@step-inc.org
Web: www.step-inc.org

VSA Arts of Montana
Alayne O. Dolson, Executive Director
200 N. Adams, MCT, Broadway Studio
P.O. Box 7225
Missoula, MT 59807
(406) 549-2984
E-mail: alaynusa@montana.com

Independent Living

To find out the contact information for the Statewide Independent Living Council (SILC) in Montana, contact

Independent Living Research Utilization Project
The Institute for Rehabilitation and Research
2323 South Sheppard, Suite 1000
Houston, TX 77019
(713) 520-0232 (V); (713) 520-5136 (TTY)
E-mail: ilru@ilru.org
Web: www.ilru.org

To find out the contact information for centers for independent living (CILs) in Montana, contact

National Council on Independent Living
1916 Wilson Boulevard, Suite 209
Arlington, VA 22201
(703) 525-3406; (703) 525-4153 (TTY)
E-mail: ncil@ncil.org
Web: www.ncil.org

NEBRASKA

Nebraska—State Agencies and Organizations

United States Senators

Honorable Deb Fischer (R)
383 Russell Senate Office Building
Washington, DC 20510
(202) 224-6551
(202) 224-5213 (Fax)
E-mail: http://www.fischer.senate.gov/
*   public/index.cfm/contact*
Web: http://www.fischer.senate.gov/public/
*   index.cfm/home*

Honorable Mike Johanns (R)
404 Russell Senate Office Building
Washington, DC 20510
(202) 224-4224
(202) 228-0012 (Fax)
E-mail Web Form: http://www.johanns.senate.
*   gov/public/?p=EmailSenatorJohanns*
Web: http://www.johanns.senate.gov/
*   public/?p=Home*

United States Representatives

To find the contact information for your representative in the House of the U.S. Congress, visit the House's Web site at: www.house.gov, or call (202) 225-3121; (202) 225-1904 (TTY).

Governor

Honorable Dave Heineman
Office of the Governor
P.O. Box 94848
Lincoln, NE 68509-4848
(402) 471-2244
(402) 471-6031 (Fax)
E-mail Web Form: http://gov.nol.org/mail/
*   govmail.html*
Web: http://www.governor.nebraska.gov/

Official State Web Site

Web: www.state.ne.us/

**State Department of
Education: Special Education**

Special Populations Office
Nebraska Department of Education
Gary M. Sherman, Administrator
301 Centennial Mall South
P.O. Box 94987
Lincoln, NE 68509-4987
(402) 471-2471 (V/TTY)
E-mail: gary.sherman@nde.ne.gov
Web: http://www.education.ne.gov/sped/
   index.html

**State Coordinator for
NCLB (No Child Left Behind)**

Special Populations Office
Nebraska Department of Education
301 Centennial Mall South
P.O. Box 94987
Lincoln, NE 68509-4987
(402) 471-2471 (V/TTY)
Web: http://www.education.ne.gov/sped/

**Programs for Infants and Toddlers
With Disabilities: Birth–2 Years**

Nebraska Department of Education
Amy Bunnell, Part C Co-Coordinator
301 Centennial Mall South
P.O. Box 94987
Lincoln, NE 68509
(402) 471-5022
E-mail: amy.bunnell@nebraska.gov
Web: http://edn.ne.gov/cms/

Nebraska Department of Health and
   Human Services
Cole Johnson, Part C Co-Coordinator
Early Development Network
NE DHHS - Medicaid & Long-Term Care
301 Centennial Mall South
Lincoln, NE 68509
(402) 471-9092
Email: cole.johnson@nebraska.gov
Web: http://edn.ne.gov/cms/

**Programs for Children
With Disabilities: 3–5 Years**

Special Populations Office
Nebraska Department of Education
Jan Thelen, Coordinator
301 Centennial Mall South
P.O. Box 94987
Lincoln, NE 68509-4987
(402) 471-4319
E-mail: jan.thelen@nebraska.gov
Web: http://www.education.ne.gov/sped/
   contact.html

**Nebraska ChildFind, Rights,
Resources, & Referrals for Children
With Disabilities: Birth–21 Years**

Nebraska ChildFind
Steve Miller, Statewide Coordinator
143 S. 48th Street, Suite C
Lincoln, NE 68516-2204
(402) 471-0734; (888) 806-6287 (in NE)
E-mail: smiller@atp.state.ne.us
Web: www.nde.state.ne.us/ATP/childfind.asp

State Vocational Rehabilitation Agency

Vocational Rehabilitation
Nebraska Department of Education
Frank Lloyd, Director
301 Centennial Mall South, 6th Floor
P. O. Box 94987
Lincoln, NE 68509-4987
(402) 471-3649
Web: www.vocrehab.state.ne.us

**Office of State Coordinator of Vocational Education for
Students With Disabilities**

Career Guidance and Counseling
Nebraska Department of Education
Donna Vrbka, Director
301 Centennial Mall South
P.O. Box 94987
Lincoln, NE 68509-4987
(402) 471-4811
E-mail: dvrbka@nde.state.ne.us
Web: www.nde.state.ne.us/CARED/ career.
   html

Coordinator for Transition Services

Jack Shepard, State Transition Coordinator
Special Populations Office
Nebraska Department of Education
6949 S. 110th Street
Omaha, NE 68128
(402) 595-2171
E-mail: jshepard@nde.state.ne.us
Web: www.nde.state.ne.us/SPED/sped.html

State Mental Health Agency

Nebraska Department of Health and
    Human Services
Richard DeLiberty, Administrator
P.O. Box 98925
Lincoln, NE 68509-8925
(402) 479-5117
E-mail: richard.deliberty@hhss.ne.gov
Web: www.hhs.state.ne.us

**State Mental Health Representative
for Children and Youth**

Susan Adams, Program Specialist
Child and Adolescent
    Project Coordination
Nebraska Department of
    Health and Human Services
P.O. Box 98925
Lincoln, NE 68509-8925
(402) 479-5128
E-mail: susan.adams@hhss.ne.gov
Web: www.hhs.state.ne.us

**State Developmental
Disabilities Programs**

Developmental Disabilities System
Nebraska Department of Health
    and Human Services
René Ferdinand, Administrator
P.O. Box 98925
Lincoln, NE 68509-8925
(402) 479-5110
E-mail: rene.ferdinand@hhss.ne.gov
Web: www.hhs.state.ne.us/

Council on Developmental Disabilities

Nebraska Planning Council on
    Developmental Disabilities
Department of Health and Human Services
Mary Gordon, Program Administrator
301 Centennial Mall South
P.O. Box 95044
Lincoln, NE 68509-5044
(402) 471-2330; (402) 471-9570 (TTY)
E-mail: mary.gordon@hhss.ne.gov
E-mail: lana.erickson@hhss.ne.gov
Web: www.hhs.state.ne.us/ddplanning

Protection and Advocacy Agency

Nebraska Advocacy Services, Inc.
Timothy Shaw, Executive Director
134 South 13th Street, Suite 600
Lincoln, NE 68508
(402) 474-3183; (800) 422-6691
E-mail: nas@nas-pa.org
Web: www.nebraskaadvocacyservices.org

Client Assistance Program

Nebraska Department of Education
Victoria Rasmussen, CAP Director
301 Centennial Mall South
P.O. Box 94987
Lincoln, NE 68509-4987
(402) 471-3656; (800) 742-7594 (in NE)
E-mail: victoria@cap.state.ne.us
Web: www.cap.state.ne.us

**Programs for Children With
Special Health Care Needs**

Aging and Disability Services
Special Services for Children and Adults
Nebraska Department of Health and
    Human Services
Mary Jo Iwan, Deputy Administrator
P.O. Box 95044
Lincoln, NE 68509-5044
(402) 471-9345
E-mail: maryjo.iwan@hhss.ne.gov
Web: www.hhs.state.ne.us

State CHIP Program (health care for low-income, uninsured children)

Nebraska Department of Health and Human
    Services Finance and Support
(Kids Connection)
P.O. Box 85801
Lincoln, NE 68509-85801
Phone: (855) 632-7633; (402) 473-7000 (Lincoln);
    (402) 595-1178 (Omaha)
Web: http://dhhs.ne.gov/medicaid/Pages/
    med_CHIP.aspx

Programs for Children and Youth Who Are Blind or Visually Impaired

Nebraska Commission for the Blind and
    Visually Impaired
Pearl Van Zandt, Executive Director
4600 Valley Road, Suite 100
Lincoln, NE 68510
(402) 471-2891
E-mail: pvanz@ncbvi.state.ne.us
Web: www.ncbvi.state.ne.us

Programs for Children and Youth Who Are Deaf or Hard of Hearing

Programs for Sensory Impairments
Special Populations Office
Nebraska Department of Education
Robert Hill, Director
301 Centennial Mall South
P.O. Box 94987
Lincoln, NE 68509-4987
(402) 471-2471; (800) 311-2065 (Parent Number)
E-mail: roberthill@nde.state.ne.us

Nebraska Commission for the Deaf
    and Hard of Hearing
Tanya Wendel, Executive Director
4600 Valley Road, Suite 420
Lincoln, NE 68510-4844
(402) 471-3593 (V/TTY); (800) 545-6244 (in NE)
E-mail: twendel@ncdhh.state.ne.us
Web: www.nol.org/home/NCDHH

Telecommunications Relay Services for Individuals Who Are Deaf, Hard of Hearing, or With Speech Impairments

(800) 833-0920 (V)
(800) 833-7352 (TTY/ASCII); 711 (TTY)
(888) 696-0629 (Fast ASCII)
(888) 272-5527 (Speech to Speech)
(888) 272-5528 (Spanish)

Programs for Children and Youth Who Are Deaf-Blind

Nebraska Commission for the Blind and
    Visually Impaired
Pearl Van Zandt, Executive Director
4600 Valley Road, Suite 100
Lincoln, NE 68510
(402) 471-2891
E-mail: pvanz@ncbvi.state.ne.us
Web: www.ncbvi.state.ne.us

State Education Agency Rural Representative

Dr. Douglas D. Christensen, Commissioner
Nebraska Department of Education
301 Centennial Mall South
P.O. Box 94987
Lincoln, NE 68509-4987
(402) 471-5025
E-mail: doug_ch@nde.state.ne.us
Web: www.nde.state.ne.us

Regional ADA & IT Technical Assistance Center

ADA and IT Center
Great Plains Disability and Business
    Technical Assistance Center
University of Missouri/Columbia
Jim de Jong, Director
100 Corporate Lake Drive
Columbia, MO 65203
(573) 882-3600 (V/TTY);
    (800) 949-4232 (V/TTY)
E-mail: ada@missouri.edu
Web: www.adaproject.org

University Center for Excellence in Developmental Disabilities

Munroe-Meyer Institute
UCEDD
J. Michael Leibowitz, PhD, Director
985450 Nebraska Medical Center
Omaha, NE 68198-5450
(402) 559-5702
Web: www.unmc.edu/mmi

Technology-Related Assistance

Nebraska Assistive Technology Partnership
Mark Schultz, Director
5143 S. 48th Street, Suite C
Lincoln, NE 68516-2204
(402) 471-0734 (V/TTY);
*   (888) 806-6287 (V/TTY)*
E-mail: atp@atp.state.ne.us
Web: www.nde.state.ne.us/ATP/

Nebraska Educational Assistive Technology
*   (NEAT)*
Pam Brown, Coordinator
1910 Meridian Avenue
Cozad, NE 69130-1159
(308) 784-4525
E-mail: neatcenter@esu10.org
Web: www.neatinfo.net

TechConnectors
Patti Neill, Program Manager
1910 Meridian Avenue
Cozad, NE 69130
(308) 784-4525; (800) 652-0033 (Cozad)
(402) 595-1920; (877) 201-4141 (Omaha)
E-mail: techconnectors@esu10.org
Web: http://www.techconnectors.net

State Mediation System

Special Populations Office
Nebraska Department of Education
John D. Clark, Consultant
301 Centennial Mall South
P.O. Box 94987
Lincoln, NE 68509-4987
(402) 471-4304
E-mail: jclark@nde.state.ne.us
Web: www.nde.state.ne.us/SPED/mediation/
*   index.html*

Special Format Library

Nebraska Library Commission
Talking Book and Braille Service
The Atrium
1200 N Street, Suite 120
Lincoln, NE 68508-2023
(402) 471-4038; (800) 742-7691
E-mail: talkingbook@nlc.state.ne.us
Web: www.nlc.state.ne.us/tbbs/tbbs1.html

Nebraska—Disability-Specific Organizations

Attention Deficit Disorder

*   To identify an ADD group in Nebraska,*
contact either of the following organizations:

Children and Adults with Attention-Deficit/
*   Hyperactivity Disorder (CHADD)*
8181 Professional Place, Suite 150
Landover, MD 20785
(301) 306-7070
(800) 233-4050 (Voice mail to request
*   information packet)*
Web: www.chadd.org

Attention Deficit Disorder Association (ADDA)
P.O. Box 543
Pottstown, PA 19464
(484) 945-2101
Web: www.add.org

Autism

Autism Society of Nebraska
Cynthia Archwamety, President
1407 E. 33rd Drive
Kearny, NE 68847
(402) 484-8003
E-mail: arcofbuffalocounty@frontiernet.net
Web: www.autismnebraska.org

Families for Effective Autism Treatment of
*   Nebraska, Inc.*
Dr. Andrew Lepinski, President
7545 Stevens Ridge Road
Lincoln, NE 68516
(402) 486-1198
E-mail: featofne@neb.rr.com
Web: www.featofnebraska.com

Blind/Visual Impairments

American Foundation for the Blind—Southwest
Judy Scott, Director
1030 Ables Lane
Dallas, TX 75229
(214) 352-7222
E-mail: dallas@afb.net
Web: www.afb.org

Cerebral Palsy

United Cerebral Palsy of Nebraska
Paul Miller, Executive Director
7101 Newport Avenue, Suite 309
Omaha, NE 68152
(402) 572-3686; (800) 729-2556
E-mail: UCPofNE@aol.com
Web: www.ucp.org

Epilepsy

Epilepsy Association of Nebraska, Inc.
Lynne Holmquist, Executive Director
510 S. 51st Avenue
Omaha, NE 68106
(402) 558-7383
E-mail: lynneholmquist@cox.net

Learning Disabilities

Learning Disabilities Association of Nebraska
Stephanie Cain, President
3135 N. 93rd Street
Omaha, NE 68134
(402) 348-1567
E-mail: ldaofneb@yahoo.com

Mental Health

Nebraska Family Support Network
Linda Liebendorfer, Executive Director
3801 Harney Street, 2nd Floor
Omaha, NE 68131
(402) 505-4608; (800) 245-6081
E-mail: nfsn_advocate@yahoo.com

NAMI–Nebraska
Colleen Wuebben, Executive Director
1941 S. 42nd Street, Suite 517
Omaha, NE 68105
(402) 345-8101; (877) 463-6264
E-mail: cwuebben@nami.org
Web: www.nami.org/
Web: http://ne.nami.org/

Mental Retardation/ Developmental Disabilities

The Arc of Nebraska
Deborah Weston, Interim Director
1672 Van Dorn Street
Lincoln, NE 68502
(402) 475-4407
E-mail: arcneb@inebraska.com
Web: www.arc-nebraska.org

Speech and Hearing

Nebraska Speech-Language-Hearing Association
Angie Carman, Executive Assistant
455 S. 11th Street, Suite A
Lincoln, NE 68508-2105
(402) 476-9573
E-mail: angie@ncsa.org
Web: www.nslha.org

Spina Bifida

Spina Bifida Association of Nebraska
7101 Newport Avenue, Suite 206
Omaha, NE 68152-2153
(402) 572-3570

Nebraska—Organizations Especially for Parents

Parent Training and Information Center (PTI)

PTI Nebraska
Glenda Davis, Executive Director
3135 N. 93rd Street
Omaha, NE 68134
(402) 346-0525 (V/TTY); (800) 284-8520 (V/TTY
    in NE only)
E-mail: info@pti-nebraska.org
Web: www.pti-nebraska.org

Parent-To-Parent

Parent to Parent Network
Peggy Vaughn, Executive Director
P.O. Box 1402
504 Prospect Avenue
Norfolk, NE 68702
(402) 379-2268; (877) 379-9926
E-mail: pvaughn@conpoint.com
Web: www.parent-parent.org

The Ollie Webb Center Pilot Parents
Jennifer Varner, Coordinator
1941 S. 42nd Street, Suite 122
Omaha, NE 68105
(402) 346-5220
E-mail: jvarner@olliewebb.org
Web: www.olliewebb.org

Parent Teacher Association (PTA)

Nebraska Congress of Parents and Teachers
Mark Ankersen, President
3534 S. 108th Street
Omaha, NE 68144
(402) 390-3339; (800) 714-3374 (in NE)
E-mail: ne_office@pta.org
Web: www.nebraskapta.org

Nebraska—Other Disability Organizations

Easter Seals Nebraska
Karen C. Ginder, President/CEO
638 N. 109th Plaza
Omaha, NE 68154
(402) 345-2200; (800) 650-9880
E-mail: kginder@ne.easterseals.com
Web: http://ne.easterseals.com

Answers 4 Families
Connie K. Hayek, Director
121 S. 13th Street, Suite 302
Lincoln, NE 68588-0227
(402) 472-9827; (800) 746-8420
E-mail: librarian@answers4families.org
Web: www.answers4families.org

People First of Nebraska
Joe Govier
345 S. G Street
Broken Bow, NE 68822
(308) 872-6490
E-mail: peoplefirstofnebr@lycos.com
Web: www.peoplefirstofnebraska.org

Independent Living

To find out the contact information for the Statewide Independent Living Council (SILC) in Nebraska, contact

Independent Living Research Utilization Project
The Institute for Rehabilitation and Research
2323 South Sheppard, Suite 1000
Houston, TX 77019
(713) 520-0232 (V); (713) 520-5136 (TTY)
E-mail: ilru@ilru.org
Web: www.ilru.org

To find out the contact information for centers for independent living (CILs) in Nebraska, contact

National Council on Independent Living
1916 Wilson Boulevard, Suite 209
Arlington, VA 22201
(703) 525-3406; (703) 525-4153 (TTY)
E-mail: ncil@ncil.org
Web: www.ncil.org

NEVADA

Nevada—State Agencies and Organizations

United States Senators

Honorable Dean Heller (R)
324 Hart Senate Office Building
Washington, DC 20510
(202) 224-6244
(202) 224-7327 (Fax)
E-mail Web Form: http://www.heller.senate.
   gov/public/index.cfm/contact-form
Web: http://www.heller.senate.gov/public/
   index.cfm/home

Honorable Harry Reid (D)
522 Hart Senate Office Building
Washington, DC 20510
(202) 224-3542
(202) 228-2193 (Fax)
E-mail Web Form: http://www.reid.senate.
   gov/contact
Web: http://www.reid.senate.gov/

United States Representatives

To find the contact information for your representative in the House of the U.S. Congress, visit the House's Web site at: www.house.gov, or call (202) 225-3121; (202) 225-1904 (TTY).

Governor

Honorable Brian Sandoval
101 N. Carson Street
Carson City, NV 89701
(775) 684-5670
E-mail Web Form: http://gov.nv.gov/Contact/
   Email-the-Governor/
Web: http://gov.nv.gov/

Official State Web Site

Web: www.nv.gov/

State Department of Education: Special Education

*Office of Special Education, Elementary and
    Secondary Education, and School Improvement
    Programs*
Nevada Department of Education
Frankie McCabe, Director
700 E. Fifth Street, Suite 113
Carson City, NV 89701-5096
(775) 687-9142
E-mail: fmccabe@doe.nv.gov
Web: www.doe.nv.gov

State Coordinator for NCLB (No Child Left Behind)

Nevada was granted an extended waiver from the NCLB program.

Nevada Department of Education
700 E. Fifth Street
Carson City, NV 89701
(775) 687-9200
*Web: http://www.doe.nv.gov/Programs_
    Services/Title_I/*

Programs for Infants and Toddlers With Disabilities: Birth–2 Years

Department of Human Resources, Health Division
Edie King, Part C IDEA Coordinator
1860 E. Sahara Avenue
Las Vegas, NV 89104
(702) 486-5497
E-mail: eking@dhhs.nv.gov
Web: http://health.nv.gov/BEIS.htm

Programs for Children With Disabilities: 3–5 Years

*Office of Special Education, Elementary and Secondary
    Education, and School Improvement Programs*
Nevada Department of Education
Sherry Halley, 619 Coordinator
9890 S. Maryland Parkway, Suite 221
Las Vegas, NV 89183
(702) 486-6460
E-mail: shalley@doe.nv.gov
*Web: http://www.doe.nv.gov/Special_Ed_
    ESCE_Special_Education/*

State Vocational Rehabilitation Agency

Rehabilitation Division
*Department of Employment, Training,
    and Rehabilitation*
Michael Coleman, Administrator
505 E. King Street, Room 502
Carson City, NV 89710
(775) 684-4040
E-mail: detrvr@nvdetr.org
Web: http://detr.state.nv.us/rehab/index.htm

Coordinator for Transition Services

*Tom Venardos, Special Education Consultant
    for Transition*
Nevada Department of Education
Office of Special Education
1820 E Sahara, Suite 208
Las Vegas, NV 89104
(702) 486-6621
E-mail: tvenardos@doe.nv.gov
Web: www.doe.nv.gov/equity/

Office of State Coordinator of Vocational Education for Students With Disabilities

Office of Career, Technical and Adult Education
Department of Education
Phyllis Dryden, State Director
700 E. Fifth Street, Suite 111
Carson City, NV 89701-5096
(775) 687-9144
E-mail: pdryden@nsn.k12.nv.us
Web: www.nde.state.nv.us

State Mental Health Agency

*Division of Mental Health and
    Developmental Services*
Department of Human Resources
Carlos Brandenburg, PhD, Administrator
Kinkead Building, Suite 602
505 E. King Street
Carson City, NV 89701-3790
(775) 684-5943
E-mail: cbrandenburg@dhr.state.nv.us
Web: http://mhds.state.nv.us

State Mental Health Representative for Children and Youth

Jone M. Bosworth, Administrator
Division of Child and Family Services
Department of Human Resources
711 E. Fifth Street
Carson City, NV 89701-5092
(775) 684-4400
E-mail: jbosworth@dcfs.state.nv.us
Web: http://dcfs.state.nv.us

State Mental Retardation Program

Division of Mental Health and
    Developmental Services
Department of Human Resources
Carlos Brandenburg, PhD, Administrator
Kinkead Building, Suite 602
505 E. King Street
Carson City, NV 89701-3790
(775) 684-5943
E-mail: cbrandenburg@dhr.state.nv.us
Web: http://mhds.state.nv.us

State Developmental Disabilities Planning Council

Office of Disability Services
Department of Human Resources
Richard Weathermon, Director
3656 Research Way, Suite 32
Carson City, NV 89706
(775) 687-4452
E-mail: rweathermon@dhr.state.nv.us

Protection and Advocacy Agency

Nevada Disability Advocacy and Law Center
Jack Mayes, Executive Director
6039 Eldora Avenue, Suite C, Box 3
Las Vegas, NV 89146
(702) 257-8150; (888) 349-3843 (toll-free)
(702) 257-8160 (TTY)
E-mail: ndalc@ndalclv.org
Web: www.ndalc.org

Nevada Disability Advocacy and Law Center
1311 N. McCarron Boulevard, Suite 106
Sparks, NV 89431
(775) 333-7878; (775) 788-7824 (TTY)
(800) 992-5715 (toll-free)
E-mail: reno@ndalc.org
Web: www.ndalc.org

Client Assistance Program

Client Assistance Program
Department of Employment, Training and
    Rehabilitation
Rehabilitation Division, Rehabilitation
    Administration
Margaret Moroun, Director
1820 E. Sahata, Suite 109
Las Vegas, NV 89104
(702) 486-6688; (800) 633-9879
E-mail: detrcap@nvdetr.org
Web: http://detr.state.nv.us/rehab/
    reh_cap.htm

Programs for Children With Special Health Care Needs

Family Health Services
Nevada State Health Division
Department of Human Resources
Judith Wright, Bureau Chief
3427 Goni Road, Suite 108
Carson City, NV 89706
(775) 684-4285
E-mail: jwright@nvhd.state.nv.us
Web: www.health2k.state.nv.us/bfhs

State CHIP Program (health care for low-income, uninsured children)

Division of Health Care Financing and Policy
Nevada Check Up
1100 East Williams Street, Suite 119
Carson City, NV 89701
(775) 684-3777; (800) 360-6044
Web: www.nevadacheckup.state.nv.us/

Programs for Children and Youth Who Are Blind or Visually Impaired, Deaf or Hard of Hearing, or Deaf-Blind

Department of Employment, Training and
    Rehabilitation
Rehabilitation Division
Bureau of Services to the Blind and
    Visually Impaired
Birgit Baker, Director
505 East King Street, Room 501
Carson City, NV 89701
(775) 684-4244
Web: www.nvdetr.org/rehab/reh_bvi.htm

Telecommunications Relay Services for Individuals Who Are Deaf, Hard of Hearing, or With Speech Impairments

(800) 326-6888 (V)
(800) 326-6868 (TTY); 711 (TTY)
(888) 326-5658 (Speech to Speech)

State Education Agency
Rural Representative

Rural Clinics Community Mental Health
Charles L. Buel, PhD, Director
503 N. Division Street
Carson City, NV 89703
(775) 687-1000
E-mail: cbuel@ruralclinics.nv.gov

Rural Regional Center, MHDS
Marcia Bennett, PhD, Director
1665 Old Hot Springs Road, Suite 164
Carson City, NV 89706
(775) 687-5162
E-mail: mbennett@dhr.state.nv.us

Regional ADA & IT
Technical Assistance Center

Pacific Disability and Business Technical
Assistance Center
Public Health Institute
Erica C. Jones, Director
555 12th Street, Suite 1030
Oakland, CA 94607-4046
(510) 285-5600 (V/TTY);
(800) 949-4232 (V/TTY)
E-mail: adatech@pdbtac.com
Web: www.pacdbtac.org

University Center for Excellence
in Developmental Disabilities

University Center for Excellence in
Developmental Disabilities
Research and Education Planning Center
JoAnn Johnson, PhD, Director
College of Education/MS285
University of Nevada-Reno
Reno, NV 89557
(775) 784-4921 (V/TTY); (800) 216-7988
E-mail: joannj@unr.edu
Web: http://repc.unr.edu

Technology-Related Assistance

Nevada Assistive Technology Collaborative
Office of Disability Services
Department of Human Resources
Kelleen Preston, MS, CRC, Director
3656 Research Way, Suite 32
Carson City, NV 89706
(775) 687-4452; (775) 687-3388 (TTY)

Nevada Special Education Technology
Assistance Project
Liz Isaacs, Coordinator
P.O. Box 603
Carson City, NV 89702
(775) 283-2315
E-mail: nsetap@aol.com

State Mediation System

Nevada Department of Education
Dr. Keith Allred, Mediation Coordinator
700 E. Fifth Street, Suite 113
Carson City, NV 89701
(775) 687-9170
E-mail: kallred@doe.nv.gov
Web: www.doe.nv.gov

Special Format Library

Nevada Talking Book Services
Keri Putnam, Head of Special Services,
Regional Librarian
100 North Stewart Street
Carson City, NV 89701-4285
(775) 684-3354; (800) 922-9334
(775) 687-8338 (TTY)
Web: www.nevadaculture.org

Nevada—Disability-Specific Organizations

Attention Deficit Disorder

To identify an ADD group in Nevada, contact either of the following organizations:

Children and Adults with Attention-Deficit/
Hyperactivity Disorder (CHADD)
8181 Professional Place, Suite 150
Landover, MD 20785
(301) 306-7070
(800) 233-4050 (Voice mail to request
information packet)
Web: www.chadd.org

Attention Deficit Disorder Association (ADDA)
P.O. Box 543
Pottstown, PA 19464
(484) 945-2101
Web: www.add.org

Autism

To identify an autism group in Nevada, contact

Autism Society of America
7910 Woodmont Avenue, Suite 300
Bethesda, MD 20814
(301) 657-0881; (800) 3-AUTISM
Web: www.autism-society.org

Blind/Visual Impairments

Gil Johnson, Director
American Foundation for the Blind–West
111 Pine Street, Suite 725
San Francisco, CA 94111
(415) 392-4845
E-mail: sanfran@afb.net
Web: www.afb.org

Brain Injury

Nevada Community Enrichment Program
Bob Hogan, Program Director
6375 W. Charleston Boulevard, Suite L200/
    WCL
Las Vegas, NV 89146
(702) 259-1903
E-mail: bobthogan@att.net
Web: www.accessiblespace.org

Northern Nevada Head Injury Association
Roberta L. Johnson, President
P.O. Box 20287
Reno, NV 89515-0287
(775) 853-4019

Cerebral Palsy

United Cerebral Palsy of Northern Nevada
Russ Rougeau, Executive Director
4068 S. McCarran, Suite B
Reno, NV 89502
(775) 331-3323
E-mail: ucpnn@ucpnn.org

Down Syndrome

Down Syndrome Organization of Southern Nevada
Lisa Wright, Board Chairman
5300 Vegas Drive
Las Vegas, NV 89108-2347
(702) 648-1990
E-mail: ceo@dsosn.org
Web: www.dsosn.org

Learning Disabilities

Learning Disabilities Association of America (contact
    this organization for information on services
    for children with learning disabilities in
    Nevada)
4156 Library Road
Pittsburgh, PA 15234
(412) 341-1515; (888) 300-6710
Web: www.ldaamerica.org

Mental Health

NAMI Nevada
Joe Tyler, President
1170 Curti Drive
Reno, NV 89502
(775) 322-1346
Web: www.nami-nevada.org/

Mental Retardation

Opportunity Village
Edward R. Guthrie, Executive Director
6300 W. Oakey Boulevard
Las Vegas, NV 89146
(702) 259-3707
E-mail: Guthrie@opportunityvillage.org
Web: www.opportunityvillage.org

Speech and Hearing

Nevada Speech-Language and Hearing Association
10426 Rockport Lane
Reno, NV 89521
(775) 851-7166
E-mail: info@nvsha.org
Web: www.nvsha.org

Spina Bifida

Spina Bifida and Hydrocephalus Association of Nevada
3106 Laentrada Street
Henderson, NV 89014
(702) 796-7242

Nevada—Organizations Especially for Parents

Parent Training and Information Center (PTI)

Nevada PEP
Karen Taycher, Executive Director
2355 Red Rock, Suite 106
Las Vegas, NV 89146
(702) 388-8899; (800) 216-5188 (in NV)
(775) 448-9950 Satellite Office Reno
E-mail: pepinfo@nvpep.org
Web: www.nvpep.org

Parent-To-Parent

Family TIES of Nevada, Inc.
Nicole Schomberg, Healthcare Specialist
P.O. Box 50815
Sparks, NV 89435-0815
(775) 823-9500; (866) 326-8437
E-mail: info@familytiesnv.org
Web: www.familytiesnv.org/

Parent Teacher Association (PTA)

Nevada Parent-Teacher Association
D. J. Stutz, President
6134 W. Charleston Boulevard
Las Vegas, NV 89146
(702) 258-7885; (800) 782-7201
E-mail: nv_office@pta.org
Web: www.nevadapta.org

Nevada—Other Disability Organizations

Disability Resources, Inc.
Aimee Wittler, Executive Director
155 Glendale Avenue, Suite 11
Sparks, NV 89431
(775) 329-1126
E-mail: awittler@disabilityresourcesonline.org
Web: http://disabilityresourcesonline.org

Easter Seals Sierra Nevada
Donald Stromquist, President
6100 Neil Road, Suite 201
Reno, NV 89511
(775) 322-6555; (800) 228-7102
E-mail: info@eastersealsnv.org
Web: www.easter-seals.org

Easter Seals Southern Nevada
Brian Patchett, President/CEO
6200 W. Oakey Boulevard
Las Vegas, NV 89146
(702) 870-7050
E-mail: bpatchett@eastersealssn.org
Web: www.eastersealssn.org

VSA Arts of Nevada (formerly Very Special Arts Nevada)
Mary Ellen Horan, Executive Director
135 N. Sierra, Suite D
Reno, NV 89501
(775) 826-6100
E-mail: meh@vsan.reno.nv.us
Web: nv.vsarts.org

Independent Living

To find out the contact information for the Statewide Independent Living Council (SILC) in Nevada, contact

Independent Living Research Utilization Project
The Institute for Rehabilitation and Research
2323 South Sheppard, Suite 1000
Houston, TX 77019
(713) 520-0232 (V); (713) 520-5136 (TTY)
E-mail: ilru@ilru.org
Web: www.ilru.org

To find out the contact information for centers for independent living (CILs) in Nevada, contact

National Council on Independent Living
1916 Wilson Boulevard, Suite 209
Arlington, VA 22201
(703) 525-3406; (703) 525-4153 (TTY)
E-mail: ncil@ncil.org
Web: www.ncil.org

NEW HAMPSHIRE

New Hampshire—State Agencies and Organizations

United States Senators

Honorable Kelly Ayotte (R)
144 Russell Senate Office Building
Washington, DC 20510
(202) 224-3324
(202) 228-4131 (Fax)
E-mail: http://www.ayotte.senate.gov/?p=contact
Web: http://www.ayotte.senate.gov/

Honorable Jeanne Shaheen (D)
520 Hart Senate Office Building
Washington, DC 20510
(202) 224-2841
(202) 224-4952 (Fax)
E-mail: http://www.shaheen.senate.gov/
    contact/
Web: http://www.shaheen.senate.gov/

United States Representatives

To find the contact information for your representative in the House of the U.S. Congress, visit the House's Web site at: www.house.gov, or call (202) 225-3121; (202) 225-1904 (TTY).

Governor

Honorable Maggie Hassan
Office of the Governor
107 North Main Street
Concord, NH 03301-4990
(603) 271-2121
Web: http://www.governor.nh.gov/

Governor's Commission on Disability

Governor's Commission on Disability
Carol Nadeau, Executive Director
Maureen Stimpson, Program Specialist
57 Regional Drive
Concord, NH 03301-8518
(603) 271-2773; (800) 852-3405 (in NH)
E-mail: carol.nadeau@nh.gov
E-mail: maureen.stimpson@nh.gov
Web: www.state.nh.us/disability/

Official State Web Site

Web: www.state.nh.us/

State Department of Education: Special Education

Bureau of Special Education
New Hampshire Department of Education
Virginia Irwin, Division Director
101 Pleasant Street
Concord, NH 03301
(603) 271-6693
E-mail: virwin@ed.state.nh.us
Web: www.ed.state.nh.us

State Coordinator for NCLB (No Child Left Behind)

New Hampshire received an extended waiver from the NCLB act.

Mary E. Earick, Administrator
New Hampshire Department of Education
101 Pleasant Street
Concord, NH 03301
(603) 271-6052
Email: Mary.Earick@doe.nh.gov
Web: http://www.education.nh.gov/instruction/integrated/title_i_a_helping.htm

Programs for Infants and Toddlers With Disabilities: Birth–2 Years

New Hampshire Family-Centered
    Early Support and Services
Division of Developmental Services
Carolyn H. Stiles, Part C Coordinator
105 Pleasant Street
Concord, NH 03301
(603) 271-5122; (800) 852-3345 (in NH)
E-mail: cstiles@dhhs.state.nh.us

Programs for Children With Disabilities: 3–5 Years

Bureau of Special Education
New Hampshire Department of Education
Ruth Littlefield, Preschool Education
    Consultant
101 Pleasant Street
Concord, NH 03301
(603) 271-2178
E-mail: rlittlefield@ed.state.nh.us
Web: http://www.education.nh.gov/
    instruction/special_ed/index.htm

State Vocational Rehabilitation Agency

Division of Adult Learning
    and Rehabilitation
New Hampshire Department of Education
Paul K. Leather, Director
21 S. Fruit Street, Suite 20
Concord, NH 03301
(603) 271-3471
E-mail: pleather@ed.state.nh.us
Web: www.ed.state.nh.us/education/

Coordinator for Transition Services

Cate Weir, Transition Consultant
Institute on Disability (UAP)
University of New Hampshire
10 Ferry Street, Suite 14
Concord, NH 03301
(603) 226-2900
E-mail: cweir@cisunix.unh.edu
Web: www.ed.state.nh.us/SpecialEd/
    specia11.htm

Vocational Education for Students With Disabilities

New Hampshire Department of Education
Bureau of Career Development
Constance Manchester-Bonenfant,
    Educational Consultant
21 S. Fruit Street, Suite 20
Concord, NH 03301
(603) 419-0235
E-mail: cmanchester@ed.state.nh.us
Web: www.ed.state.nh.us/education/

State Mental Health Agency

Bureau of Behavioral Health
Department of Health and Human Services
Geoffrey Souther, Director
105 Pleasant Street
Concord, NH 03301
(603) 271-5007
E-mail: gsouther@dhhs.state.nh.us
Web: www.dhhs.state.nh.us/

State Mental Health Representative for Children and Youth

Children's Mental Health Services
Bureau of Behavioral Health
Department of Health and Human Services
Joe Perry, Administrator
State Office Park South
105 Pleasant Street
Concord, NH 03301
(603) 271-5095
E-mail: joeperry@dhhs.state.nh.us
Web: www.dhhs.state.nh.us/

State Mental Retardation Program

Division of Developmental Services
Matthew Ertas, Acting Director
105 Pleasant Street
Concord, NH 03301
(603) 271-5034
E-mail: mertas@dhhs.state.nh.us
Web: www.dhhs.state.nh.us

Council on Developmental Disabilities

New Hampshire Developmental Disabilities Council
Gordon Allen, Executive Director
Walker Building
21 S. Fruit Street, Suite 22
Concord, NH 03301
(603) 271-3236
E-mail: wgallen@dhhs.state.nh.us
Web: www.NHDDC.com

Protection and Advocacy Agency

Disabilities Rights Center, Inc.
Richard Cohen, Executive Director
18 Low Avenue
P.O. Box 3660
Concord, NH 03302-3660
(603) 228-0432; (800) 834-1721 (V/TTY)
E-mail: advocacy@drcnh.org
Web: www.drcnh.org

Client Assistance Program

Client Assistance Program (CAP)
Governor's Commission on Disability
Bill J. Hagy, Ombudsman
57 Regional Drive
Concord, NH 03301-8518
(603) 271-4175/4176; (800) 852-3405 (in NH)
E-mail: bhagy@gov.state.nh.us
Web: www.state.nh.us/disability/
    caphomepage.html

Programs for Children With Special Health Care Needs

Special Medical Services
Office of Medicaid Business and Policy
Judith A. Bumbalo, Bureau Chief
29 Hazen Drive
Concord, NH 03301-6504
(603) 271-4488; (800) 852-3345, ext. 4488 (in NH)
E-mail: jbumbalo@dhhs.state.nh.us
Web: www.dhhs.state.nh.us

State CHIP Program (health care
for low-income, uninsured children)

New Hampshire Healthy Kids
25 Hall Street, Suite 302
Concord, NH 03301
(877) 464-2447
Web: www.nhhealthykids.com/

Programs for Children and Youth
Who Are Blind or Visually Impaired,
Deaf or Hard of Hearing, or Deaf-Blind

Division of Family Assistance
129 Pleasant Street
Concord, NH 03301
(603) 271-4238
Web: www.dhhs.state.nh.us

Telecommunications Relay
Services for Individuals
Who Are Deaf, Hard of
Hearing, or With Speech Impairments

(800) 735-2964 (V/TTY); 711 (TTY)
(877) 735-1245 (Speech to Speech)

State Education
Agency Rural Representative

Virginia Irwin, Division Director
Bureau of Special Education
New Hampshire Department of Education
101 Pleasant Street
Concord, NH 03301
(603) 271-3870
E-mail: virwin@ed.state.nh.us
Web: www.ed.state.nh.us

Regional ADA & IT
Technical Assistance Center

New England ADA and Accessible IT Center
Adaptive Environments Center, Inc.
Valerie Fletcher, Executive Director
Oce Harrison, Project Director
374 Congress Street, Suite 301
Boston, MA 02210
(617) 695-0085 (V/TTY);
   (800) 949-4232 (V/TTY)
E-mail: adainfo@newenglandada.org
Web: www.newenglandada.org

University Center for Excellence
in Developmental Disabilities

Institute on Disability/UCED
University of New Hampshire
Jan Nisbet, Director
10 W. Edge Drive, Suite 101
Durham, NH 03824-3522
(603) 862-4320 (V/TTY); (800) 238-2048 (in NH)
E-mail: institute.disability@unh.edu
Web: www.iod.unh.edu

Technology-Related Assistance

New Hampshire Technology Partnership Project
Institute on Disability/UCED
University of New Hampshire
Sonke Dornblut, Project Coordinator
10 W. Edge Drive, Suite 201
Durham, NH 03824-3522
(603) 862-4320
E-mail: sonke.dornblut@unh.edu
Web: www.iod.unh.edu

State Mediation System

New Hampshire Department of Education
Office of Legislation and Hearings
Stephen W. F. Berwick, Coordinator
101 Pleasant Street
Concord, NH 03301
(603) 271-2299
E-mail: sberwick@ed.state.nh.us
Web: www.ed.state.nh.us/education/laws/
   hearinginfo.htm

Special Format Library

New Hampshire State Library
Library Services to Persons with Disabilities
117 Pleasant Street
Concord, NH 03301-3852
(603) 271-3429; 800-491-4200
Web: http://www.nh.gov/nhsl/talking_books/
   index.html

New Hampshire—Disability-Specific Organizations

Attention Deficit Disorder

   To identify an ADD group in New
Hampshire, contact either of the following
organizations:

Children and Adults with Attention-Deficit/
   Hyperactivity Disorder (CHADD)
8181 Professional Place, Suite 150
Landover, MD 20785
(301) 306-7070
(800) 233-4050 (Voice mail to request
   information packet)
Web: www.chadd.org

Attention Deficit Disorder Association (ADDA)
P.O. Box 543
Pottstown, PA 19464
(484) 945-2101
Web: www.add.org

Autism

Autism Society of New Hampshire
Stacey Shannon, President
P.O. Box 68
Concord, NH 03302
(603) 679-2424
E-mail: nhautism@yahoo.com
Web: www.nhautism.com

Blind/Visual Impairments

American Foundation for the Blind
Regina Genwright, Director of Information Center
11 Penn Plaza, Suite 300
New York, NY 10001
(212) 502-7600; (212) 502-7662 (TTY)
E-mail: afbinfo@afb.net
Web: www.afb.org

Brain Injury

Brain Injury Association of New Hampshire
Steven D. Wade, Executive Director
109 N. State Street, Suite 2
Concord, NH 03301
(603) 225-8400; (800) 773-8400 (in NH only)
E-mail: mail@bianh.org
Web: www.bianh.org

Deafness/Hard of Hearing

Northeast Deaf and Hard of Hearing Services, Inc.
   (NDHHS)
Susan Wolf-Downes, Executive Director
125 Airport Road
Concord, NH 03301
(603) 224-1850; (800) 492-0407
(866) 634-4764 (TTY)
E-mail: info@nhdeaf-hh.org
Web: www.nhdeaf-hh.org

Learning Disabilities

New Hampshire Branch of the International
   Dyslexia Association
Mike Angwin and Caryl Patten, Co-Presidents
P.O. Box 3724
Concord, NH 03302-3724
(603) 229-7355
E-mail: information@nhida.org
Web: www.nhida.org

Mental Health

Granite State Federation of Families for
   Children's Mental Health
c/o ACS
Kathleen Abate, Executive Director
340 Commercial Street, 2nd Floor
Manchester, NH 03101
(603) 785-7948
E-mail: gsffcmh@aol.com

NAMI New Hampshire
Michael Cohen, Executive Director
15 Green Street
Concord, NH 03301
(603) 225-5359; (800) 242-6264 (in NH)
E-mail: info@naminh.org
Web: www.naminh.org

Special Health Care Needs

New Hampshire Family Voices
Terry Ohlson-Martin and Martha-Jean
   Madison, Co-Directors
29 Hazen Drive
Concord, NH 03301
(603) 271-4525; (800) 852-3345, ext. 4525
E-mail: nhfv@yahoo.com
Web: www.nhfv.org

Speech and Hearing

New Hampshire Speech-Language-Hearing
   Association, Inc.
Jessica Bergeron, President
P.O. Box 1538
Concord, NH 03302-1538
(603) 228-5949
E-mail: nhslha@aol.com

New Hampshire—Organizations Especially for Parents

Parent Training and
Information Center (PTI)

Parent Information Center (PIC)
Heather Thalheimer, Executive Director
P.O. Box 2405
Concord, NH 03302-2405
(603) 224-7005 (V/TTY); (800) 232-0986 (in NH)
E-mail: picinfo@parentinformationcenter.org
Web: www.parentinformationcenter.org
Web: www.picnh.org

Parent-To-Parent

Parent to Parent
Philip Eller, Coordinator
P.O. Box 622
Hanover, NH 03755-0622
(603) 448-6393; (800) 698-5465
    (in NH and VT, only)
E-mail: p2pnh@valley.net
Web: www.p2pnh.org

Partners in Policymaking

Institute on Disability/UCE
Mary Schuh, PhD, Program Director
University of New Hampshire,
    The Concord Center
10 Ferry Street, Unit #14, Suite 317
Concord, NH 03301
(603) 228-2084
E-mail: mcschuh@
    cisunix.unh.edu
Web: www.iod.unh.edu/

Parent Teacher Association (PTA)

New Hampshire PTA
Donald Austin, President
47 Kendall Hill Road
Mont Vernon, NH 03057
(877) 701-4PTA
E-mail: nhpta1@aol.com

New Hampshire—Other Disability Organizations

Easter Seals New Hampshire
Larry Gammon, President
555 Auburn Street
Manchester, NH 03103
(603) 623-8863 (V/TTY); (800) 870-8728
E-mail: lgammon@eastersealsnh.org
Web: www.eastersealsnh.org

Education-A-Must (advocacy services for
    children with physical, emotional,
    behavioral, or learning disabilities)
Dorothy French, Director/Founder
P.O. Box 216
East Derry, NH 03041-0216
(603) 437-6286
E-mail: info@education-a-must.com
Web: www.education-a-must.com

New Hampshire Challenge
Janet Krumm, Executive Director
P.O. Box 579
Dover, NH 03820-0579
(603) 742-0500; (800) 758-6430
E-mail: nhchallenge@comcast.net
Web: www.nhchallenge.org

VSA Arts of New Hampshire
Karen Bessette, Executive Director
44 S. Main Street
Concord, NH 03301-4822
(603) 228-4330
E-mail: info@vsaartsnh.org
Web: www.vsarts.org

Independent Living

New Hampshire Statewide Independent
    Living Council
c/o Governor's Commission on Disability
57 Regional Drive
Concord, NH 03301
(603) 271-0476; (800) 852-3405
E-mail: info@silcnh.org
Web: www.silcnh.org

Granite State Independent Living
21 Chenell Drive
Concord, NH 03301
(603) 228-9680; 800-826-3700 (V/TTY)
Web: www.gsil.org

NEW JERSEY

New Jersey—State Agencies and Organizations

United States Senators

Honorable Cory A. Booker (D)
141 Hart Senate Office Building
Washington, DC 20510
(202) 224-3224
(202) 224-8567 (Fax)
E-mail Web Form: http://www.booker.senate.gov/?p=contact
Web: http://www.booker.senate.gov/

Honorable Robert Menendez (D)
528 Hart Senate Office Building
Washington, DC 20510
(202) 224-4744
(202) 224-9707 (Fax)
E-mail Web Form: http://www.menendez.senate.gov/contact/
Web: http://www.menendez.senate.gov/

United States Representatives

To find the contact information for your representative in the House of the U.S. Congress, visit the House's Web site at: www.house.gov, or call (202) 225-3121; (202) 225-1904 (TTY).

Governor (Acting)

Honorable Chris Christie
The State House
P. O. Box 001
Trenton, NJ 08625
(609) 292-6000
E-mail Web Form: http://www.state.nj.us/governor/contact/
Web: www.state.nj.us/governor/

Official State Web Site

Web: www.state.nj.us/

State Department of Education: Special Education

Office of Special Education Programs
New Jersey Department of Education
Roberta Wohle, Acting Director
100 Riverview Plaza
P.O. Box 500
Trenton, NJ 08625
(609) 633-6833
E-mail: Roberta.Wohle@doe.state.nj.uss
Web: http://www.state.nj.us/education/

State Coordinator for NCLB (No Child Left Behind)

New Jersey received a waiver from the NCLB program.

Deborah S. Delisle
Assistant Secretary
Office of Elementary and Secondary Education
Department of Education Building
400 Maryland Ave, SW
Washington, DC 20202
(202) 401-0113
Email: oese@ed.gov
Web: http://www2.ed.gov/parents/academic/involve/nclbguide/parentsguide.html

Programs for Infants and Toddlers With Disabilities: Birth–2 Years

Division of Family Health Services
Early Intervention System
Terry Harrison, Part C Coordinator
50 E. State Street
P. O. Box 364
Trenton, NJ 08625-0364
(609) 777-7739
E-mail: terry.harrison@doh.state.nj.us
Web: http://nj.gov/health/fhs/eis/index.shtml

Programs for Children With Disabilities: 3–5 Years

Office of Special Education Programs
New Jersey Department of Education
Barbara Tkach, Section 619 Coordinator
100 Riverview Plaza
P. O. Box 500
Trenton, NJ 08625-0500
(609) 984-4950
E-mail: btkach@doe.state.nj.us
Web: http://www.state.nj.us/education/specialed/

State Vocational Rehabilitation Agency

Division of Vocational Rehabilitation Services
New Jersey Department of Labor
Thomas G. Jennings, Director
P. O. Box 398
135 E. State Street
Trenton, NJ 08625-0398
(609) 292-5987; (609) 292-2919 (TTY)
E-mail: thomas.jennings@dol.state.nj.us
Web: www.wnjpin.state.nj.us/

Coordinator for Transition Services

Bob Haugh, Transition Coordinator
Office of Special Education Programs
New Jersey Department of Education
P.O. Box 500 Riverview Executive Plaza
Building 100 Route 29
Trenton, NJ 08625
(609) 633-6431
E-mail: robert.haugh@doe.state.nj.us
Web: www.state.nj.us/education

Office of State Coordinator of Vocational Education for Students With Disabilities

Office of Vocational-Technical, Career and
    Adult Programs
New Jersey Department of Education
Michael K. Klavon, Acting Director
P. O. Box 500
Trenton, NJ 08625-0500
(609) 633-0665
E-mail: michael.klavon@doe.state.nj.us
Web: www.state.nj.us/education

State Mental Health Agency

Division of Mental Health Services
New Jersey Department of Human Services
Alan G. Kaufman, Director
50 E. State Street, Capital Center
P. O. Box 727
Trenton, NJ 08625-0727
(609) 777-0702; (800) 382-6717
E-mail: dmhsmail@DHS.state.nj.us
Web: www.state.nj.us/humanservices/dmhs/

State Mental Health Representative for Children and Youth

Lucy C. Keating, Assistant Director
Division of Child Behavioral Health Services
222 S. Warren Street
P.O. Box 700
Trenton, NJ 08625
(609) 777-0740
E-mail: lucy.keating@dhs.state.nj.us
Web: www.njkidsoc.org

State Mental Retardation Program

Division of Developmental Disabilities
New Jersey Department of Human Services
Capital Center
Carol Grant, Acting Director
P.O. Box 726
Trenton, NJ 08625-0726
(609) 292-7260
E-mail: carol.grant@dhs.state.nj.us
Web: www.state.nj.us/humanservices/
    ddd/index.html

Council on Developmental Disabilities

New Jersey Council on Developmental Disabilities
Ethan B. Ellis, Executive Director
20 W. State Street, 7th Floor
P. O. Box 700
Trenton, NJ 08625-0700
(609) 292-3745
E-mail: njddc@njddc.org
Web: www.njddc.org

Protection and Advocacy Agency

New Jersey Protection and Advocacy, Inc.
Sarah W. Mitchell, Executive Director
210 S. Broad Street, 3rd Floor
Trenton, NJ 08608
(609) 292-9742; (609) 633-7106 (TTY)
(800) 922-7233 (in NJ)
E-mail: advocate@njpanda.org
Web: www.njpanda.org

Client Assistance Program

Lillie Lowe-Reid, Coordinator. Contact Protection and Advocacy Agency listed above.

Programs for Children With
Special Health Care Needs

Special Child, Health and Early Intervention Services
New Jersey Department of Health and
    Senior Services
Gloria M. Rodriguez, PhD, Director
50 E. State Street
P.O. Box 364
Trenton, NJ 08625
(609) 984-0755
E-mail: gloria.rodriguez@doh.state.nj.us
Web: www.state.nj.us/health

State CHIP Program (health care
for low-income, uninsured children)

New Jersey Family Care
PO Box 4818
Trenton, NJ 08650-4818
(800) 701-0710
Web: www.njfamilycare.org

Programs for Children and Youth
Who Are Blind or Visually Impaired

Commission for the Blind and Visually Impaired
New Jersey Department of Human Services
Vito DeSantis, Executive Director
153 Halsey Street
Newark, NJ 07101
(973) 648-2324
Web: www.state.nj.us/humanservices/
    cbvi/index.html

Programs for Children and Youth
Who Are Deaf or Hard of Hearing

Division of the Deaf and Hard of Hearing
New Jersey Department of Human Services
Brian Shomo, Director
P. O. Box 074
Trenton, NJ 08625-0074
(609) 984-7281 (V/TTY)
(800) 792-8339 (V/TTY in NJ only)
E-mail: ira.hock@dhs.state.nj.us

Programs for Children
and Youth Who Are Deaf-Blind

New Jersey Association of the Deaf-Blind
Chris Corvino, Executive Director
24K World Fair Drive
Somerset, NJ 08873
(732) 805-1912 (V/TTY)
Web: www.njadb.org

Telecommunications
Relay Services for Individuals
Who Are Deaf, Hard of Hearing,
or With Speech Impairments

(800) 852-7897 (V)
(800) 852-7899 (TTY); 711 (TTY)
(800) 229-5746 (Speech to Speech–English)
(866) 260-9470 (Speech to Speech–Spanish)

State Education Agency
Rural Representative

Special Education
High Point Regional High School
Diane L. Paine, Supervisor
299 Pigeon Hill Road
Sussex, NJ 07461
(973) 875-3102
E-mail: dpaine@hpregional.org

Regional ADA & IT
Technical Assistance Center

Northeast ADA & IT Center
Andrea Haenlin-Mott, Director
Cornell University
331 Ives Hall
Ithaca, NY 14853
(607) 255-6686 (V/TTY/Spanish);
    (800) 949-4232 (V/TTY/Spanish)
E-mail: northeastada@cornell.edu
Web: www.ilr.cornell.edu/ped/northeastada

University Center for Excellence
in Developmental Disabilities

The Elizabeth M. Boggs Center on Developmental
    Disabilities
University of Medicine and Dentistry of
    New Jersey
Deborah Spitalnik, PhD, Executive Director
Robert Wood Johnson Medical School,
    Liberty Plaza
335 George Street, 3rd Floor
P.O. Box 2688
New Brunswick, NJ 08903-2688
(732) 235-9300
E-mail: deborah.spitalnik@umdnj.edu
Web: http://rwjms.umdnj.edu/boggscenter

Technology-Related Assistance

Assistive Technology Advocacy Center
New Jersey Protection and Advocacy, Inc.
Ellen Catanese, Project Director
210 S. Broad Street, Third Floor
Trenton, NJ 08608
(609) 292-9742; (609) 633-7106 (TTY)
(800) 922-7233 (in NJ)
E-mail: advocate@njpanda.org
Web: www.njpanda.org

State Mediation System

Office of Special Education Programs
New Jersey Department of Education
P.O. Box 500
Trenton, NJ 08625-0500
(609) 984-1286
Web: www.state.nj.us/education

Special Format Library

New Jersey Library for the Blind and Handicapped
P. O. Box 501
Trenton, NJ 08625-0501
(609) 530-4000; (800) 792-8322
(800) 582-5945 (Spanish); 800- 882-5593 (TTY)
E-mail: njlbh@njstatelib.org
Web: http://www.njstatelib.org/talking_
   books_and-braille/

New Jersey—Disability-Specific Organizations

Attention Deficit Disorder

To identify an ADD group in New Jersey, contact either of the following organizations:

Children and Adults with Attention-Deficit/
   Hyperactivity Disorder (CHADD)
8181 Professional Place, Suite 150
Landover, MD 20785
(301) 306-7070
(800) 233-4050 (Voice mail to request
   information packet)
Web: www.chadd.org

Attention Deficit Disorder
   Association (ADDA)
P.O. Box 543
Pottstown, PA 19464
(484) 945-2101
Web: www.add.org

Autism

New Jersey Center for Outreach and Services for
   the Autism Community (COSAC)
Paul Potito, Executive Director
1450 Parkside Avenue, Suite 22
Ewing, NJ 08638
(609) 883-8100; (800) 4-AUTISM (in NJ)
E-mail: information@njcosac.org
Web: www.njcosac.org

Blind/Visual Impairments

American Foundation for the Blind
Regina Genwright, Director of Information Center
11 Penn Plaza, Suite 300
New York, NY 10001
(212) 502-7600; (212) 502-7662 (TTY)
E-mail: afbinfo@afb.org
Web: www.afb.org

Parents of Blind Children—New Jersey
Carol Castellano, President
23 Alexander Avenue
Madison, NJ 07940
(973) 625-5999; (973) 377-0976
(888) 625-6066
E-mail: center@webspan.net
Web: www.blindchildren.org

National Federation of the Blind of New Jersey
Joe Ruffalo, President
69 Prospect Place
Belleville, NJ 07109
(973) 759-3622
E-mail: nfbnj@comcast.net

Brain Injury

Brain Injury Association of New Jersey
Barbara Geiger-Parker, Executive Director
1090 King George Post Road, Suite 708
Edison, NJ 08837
(732) 738-1002; (800) 669-4323 (in NJ only)
E-mail: info@bianj.org
Web: www.bianj.org

Cerebral Palsy

Cerebral Palsy of New Jersey
Douglas E. Oberreit, Executive Director
354 S. Broad Street
Trenton, NJ 08608
(609) 392-4004; (888) 322-1918
E-mail: info@cpofnj.org
Web: www.cpofnj.org

Epilepsy

Epilepsy Foundation of New Jersey
Eric M. Joice, Executive Director
429 River View Plaza
Trenton, NJ 08611
(609) 392-4900; (800) 336-5843
E-mail: EMJEFNJ@aol.com
Web: www.efnj.com

Mental Health

Mental Health Association
   in New Jersey
Carolyn Beauchamp, Executive Director
88 Pompton Avenue, Suite 1
Verona, NJ 07044
(973) 571-4100
E-mail: info@mhanj.org
Web: www.mhanj.org

NAMI New Jersey
Sylvia Axelrod, Executive Director
1562 Route 130
North Brunswick, NJ 08902
(732) 940-0991
E-mail: naminj@optonline.net
Web: www.naminj.org/

Mental Retardation/ Developmental Disabilities

The Arc of New Jersey
Tom Baffuto, Executive Director
985 Livingston Avenue
North Brunswick, NJ 08902-1843
(732) 246-2525
E-mail: info@arcnj.org
Web: www.arcnj.org

Special Health Care Needs

Family Voices of New Jersey, at SPAN
Lauren Agoratus, Project Coordinator
35 Halsey Street, 4th Floor
Newark, NJ 07102
(973) 642-8100; (800) 654-SPAN, ext. 110
E-mail: familyvoices@spannj.org
Web: www.spannj.org

Speech and Hearing

New Jersey Speech-Language-Hearing Association
Nancy J. Patterson, President
203 Towne Centre Drive
Hillsborough, NJ 08844
(908) 359-5308
E-mail: info@njsha.org
Web: www.njsha.org

Spina Bifida

Spina Bifida Association of Tri-State Region
Jane Horowitz, Executive Director
84 Park Avenue
Flemington, NJ 08822
(908) 782-7475
E-mail: sbatsr@sbatsr.org
Web: www.sbatsr.org

Tourette Syndrome

Tourette Syndrome Association of New Jersey, Inc.
Faith Warner Rice, President
198 W. High Street
Somerville, NJ 08876
(732) 972-4459
E-mail: NJTSA@aol.com
Web: www.tsanj.org

New Jersey—Organizations Especially for Parents

Parent Training and Information Center (PTI)

Statewide Parent Advocacy Network (SPAN)
Diane Autin, Executive Co-Director
Deborah Jennings, Co-Director
35 Halsey Street, 4th Floor
Newark, NJ 07102
(973) 642-8100; (800) 654-7726 (in NJ)
E-mail: span@spannj.org
Web: www.spannj.org

Parent-To-Parent

New Jersey Statewide Parent-to-Parent
Malia Corde, Program Coordinator
35 Halsey Street
Newark, NJ 07102
(908) 537-4673; (800) 372-6510
E-mail: Parent2Parent@spannj.org
Web: www.spannj.org/familywrap/
   parent2parent.htm

Parent Teacher Association (PTA)

New Jersey Congress of Parents and Teachers
Lynn Morris, President
900 Berkeley Avenue
Trenton, NJ 08618-5322
(609) 393-5004
E-mail: njpta@dca.net
Web: www.njpta.org

Other Parent Organization

Special Parent Assistance & Resource
    Center (SPARC)
UCP of Hudson County, Inc.
Michelle Evans, Co-Founder and Director of
    Support and Family Relations
721 Broadway
Bayonne, NJ 07002
(201) 656-3779
E-mail: SPARKLEOFUCP@yahoo.com
Web: www.geocities.com/sparcofucp

New Jersey—Other
Disability Organizations

Alliance for the Betterment of Citizens with
    Disabilities
Lowell Arye, Executive Director
127 Route 206, Suite 18
Hamilton, NJ 08610
(609) 581-8375
E-mail: lowell@abcdnj.org
Web: www.abcdnj.org

Easter Seals New Jersey
Brian J. Fitzgerald, President/CEO
1 Kimberly Road
East Brunswick, NJ 08816-1076
(732) 25/-6662; (800) 486-0027
E-mail: essnj@nj.easter-seals.org
Web: www.eastersealsnj.org

Family Support Center of New Jersey
Veronica Trathen, Director
2516 Route 35 North
Manasquan, NJ 08736
(732) 528-8080; (800) 372-6510 (in NJ)
E-mail: FSCNJ@familysupportnj.com
Web: www.familysupportnj.com

New Jersey Mentor
Rehabilitative and Support Services for
    Persons with Acquired Brain Injury
505 S. Lenola Road
Blason Office Plaza II, Suite 217
Moorestown, NJ 08057
(856) 235-5505
E-mail: scott.patrick@thementornetwork.com
Web: www.thementornetwork.com

New Jersey Self-Help Group Clearinghouse
(free help to those seeking to find or start a
    local or national support group)
Edward Madara, Director
100 Hanover Avenue, Suite 202
Cedar Knolls, NJ 07927-2020
(973) 326-6789; (800) 367-6274 (in NJ)
E-mail: njshc@cybernex.net
Web: www.njgroups.org

Division of Disability Services
William A. B. Ditto, Executive Director
P.O. Box 700
Trenton, NJ 08625-0700
(609) 292-7800; (609) 292-1210 (TTY)
(888) 285-3036
E-mail: william.ditto@dhs.state.nj.us
Web: www.state.nj.us/humanservices/dds

VSA Arts New Jersey
Vanessa Young, Executive Director
703 Jersey Avenue
New Brunswick, NJ 08901
(732) 745-3885; (732) 745-3913 (TTY)
E-mail: info@vsanj.org
Web: www.vsanj.org

Independent Living

To find out the contact information for the
Statewide Independent Living Council (SILC) in
New Jersey, contact

Independent Living Research Utilization Project
The Institute for Rehabilitation and Research
2323 South Sheppard, Suite 1000
Houston, TX 77019
(713) 520-0232 (V); (713) 520-5136 (TTY)
E-mail: ilru@ilru.org
Web: www.ilru.org

To find out the contact information for centers for independent living (CILs) in New Jersey,
contact

National Council on Independent Living
1916 Wilson Boulevard, Suite 209
Arlington, VA 22201
(703) 525-3406; (703) 525-4153 (TTY)
E-mail: ncil@ncil.org
Web: www.ncil.org

NEW MEXICO

New Mexico—State Agencies and Organizations

United States Senators

Honorable Martin Heinrich (D)
702 Hart Senate Office Building
Washington, DC 20510
(202) 224-5521; (202) 224-3844 (TTY)
E-mail Web Form: http://www.heinrich.
   senate.gov/contact
Web: http://www.heinrich.senate.gov/

Honorable Tom Udall (D)
110 Hart Senate Office Building
Washington, DC 20510
(202) 224-6621; (800) 443-8658 (in NM)
(202) 224-1792 (TTY)
(202) 224-2852 (Fax)
E-mail Web Form: http://www.tomudall.
   senate.gov/?p=contact
Web: http://www.tomudall.senate.gov/

United States Representatives

To find the contact information for your representative in the House of the U.S. Congress, visit the House's Web site at: www.house.gov, or call (202) 225-3121; (202) 225-1904 (TTY).

Governor

Honorable Susana Martinez
Office of the Governor
State Capitol, Room 400
Santa Fe, NM 87501
(505) 476-2200
Web: www.governor.state.nm.us/

Governor's Commission on Disabilities
Mary K. Beresford, PhD, Director
Lamy Building, Room 117
491 Old Santa Fe Trail
Santa Fe, NM 87501

(505) 476-0412; (877) 696-1470 (in NM)
(505) 476-0413 (TTY)
Web: www.nmgcd.org

Governor's Behavioral Health Planning Council
Theta Nyein, Block Grant Coordinator
P.O. Box 26110
Santa Fe, NM 87502-6110
(505) 827-2601
Web: www.nmcares.org

Official State Web Site

Web: www.state.nm.us/

State Department of Education: Special Education

Public Education Department
Denise Koscielniak, Director
Special Education Bureau
120 S. Federal Place, Room 206
Santa Fe, NM 87501
(505) 927-1457
E-mail: denise.koscielniak@state.nm.us
Web: www.ped.state.nm.us

State Coordinator for NCLB (No Child Left Behind)

New Mexico received a waiver from the NCLB program.

Sam Ornelas, Director
Title I Program
Public Education Department
300 Don Gaspar Avenue
Santa Fe, NM 87501-2786
(505) 827-7592
Email: sam.ornelas@state.nm.us
Web: http://ped.state.nm.us/ped/Title1index.
   html
E-mail: dwatson@ped.state.nm.us
Web: www.ped.state.nm.us

Programs for Infants and Toddlers With Disabilities: Birth–2 Years

Family Infant Toddler Program
New Mexico Department of Health
Andy Gomm, Part C Coordinator
810 San Mateo
Santa Fe, NM 87506
(505) 476-8975
E-mail: andrew.gomm@state.nm.us
Web: http://nmhealth.org/about/ddsd/
   cpb/fit/

BubyNet
(information about medical and support
   services for pre-natal, infants, and toddlers)
Sandra Skaar, Health Educator
2300 Menaul, NE
Albuquerque, NM 87107
(505) 272-8549; (800) 552-8195 (in NM)
E-mail: infonet@unm.edu
E-mail: sskaar@salud.unm.edu

Programs for Children With Disabilities: 3–5 Years

Early Childhood Special Education
Ida Tewa, 619 Coordinator
Special Education Bureau
Public Education Department
120 South Federal Place, Room 206
Santa Fe, NM 87501
(505) 827-1466
E-mail: idam.tewa@state.nm.us
Web: http://www.ped.state.nm.us/seb/

State Vocational Rehabilitation Agency

Division of Vocational Rehabilitation
Catherine Cross Maple, PhD, Assistant Secretary
435 St. Michaels Drive, Building D
Santa Fe, NM 87505
(505) 954-8500; (505) 954-8511 (V/TTY)
(800) 224-7005
Web: www.dvrgetsjobs.com/

Coordinator for Transition Services

Sue Gronewald, Director of Transition Services
Public Education Department
300 Don Gaspar Avenue
Santa Fe, NM 87501
(505) 827-6553
E-mail: sgronewold@ped.state.nm.us
Web: www.ped.state.nm.us/seo/index.htm

Office of State Coordinator of Vocational Education for Students With Disabilities

Public Education Department
Career-Technical and Workforce Education
   Bureau
Lena Trujillo-Chavez, Special Projects Coordinator
300 Don Gaspar Avenue
Santa Fe, NM 87501
(505) 827-6512
E-mail: ltrujillo@ped.state.nm.us
Web: www.ped.state.nm.us

State Mental Health Agency

Behavioral Health Services Division
New Mexico Department of Health
Richard Tavares, Acting Division Director
1190 St. Francis Drive, Room N3300
Santa Fe, NM 87502
(505) 827-2601
Web: www.nmcares.org

State Mental Health Representative for Children and Youth

Marg Elliston, Director
New Mexico Children, Youth
   and Families Department
Family Services
P.O. Box 5160
Santa Fe, NM 87502-5160
(505) 827-9988
Web: www.state.nm.us/cyfd

State Mental Retardation Program

Long-Term Services Division
New Mexico Department of Health
Sam Howarth, Director
1190 St. Francis Drive, Room N. 3050
P.O. Box 26110
Santa Fe, NM 87502-6110
(505) 827-2574
E-mail: sam.howarth@health.state.nm.us

Council on Developmental Disabilities

New Mexico Developmental
   Disabilities Planning Council
Patrick Putnam, Director
810 W. San Mateo Road, Suite C
Santa Fc, NM 87505-4144
(505) 476-7321
E-mail: pputnam@state.nm.us
Web: www.nmddpc.com

Protection and Advocacy Agency

Protection and Advocacy System, Inc.
James Jackson, Executive Director
1720 Louisiana Boulevard, NE, Suite 204
Albuquerque, NM 87110
(505) 256-3100; (800) 432-4682 (in NM)
E-mail: info@nmpanda.org
Web: www.nmpanda.org

Native American Protection and Advocacy Project
3535 E. 30th Street, Suite 201
Farmington, NM 87402
(505) 566-5880; (800) 862-7271
    (intake and client only)
E-mail: cjohn@napap.org

Client Assistance Program

Bernadine Chavez, CAP Coordinator. Contact Protection and Advocacy System, Inc. listed above.

Programs for Children With
Special Health Care Needs

Family Health Bureau
Public Health Division
New Mexico Department of Health
Jane Peacock, Bureau Chief
2040 S. Pacheco, Room 103
Santa Fe, NM 87505
(505) 476-8901

Children's Medical Services
Family Health Bureau
Public Health Division
New Mexico Department of Health
Lynn Christiansen, Program Manager
2040 S. Pacheco, Room 226B
Santa Fe, NM 87505
(505) 476-8868; (877) 890-4692
E-mail: LChristiansen@Doh.state.nm.us

State CHIP Program
(health care for low-income,
uninsured children)

New Mexi Kids
New Mexico Human Services Department–
    Medical Assistance Division
P.O. Box 2348
Santa Fe, NM 87504-2348
(888) 997-2583
Web: www.state.nm.us/hsd/mad/
    OtherDocs/NewMexikids.htm

Programs for Children and Youth
Who Are Blind or Visually Impaired

New Mexico Commission for the Blind
Greg Trapp, Director
2905 Rodeo Park Drive East, Building 4,
    Suite 100
Santa Fe, NM 87505
(505) 476-4479; (888) 513-7968
E-mail: greg.trapp@state.nm.us
Web: www.state.nm.us/cftb

Programs for Children and Youth
Who Are Deaf or Hard of Hearing

New Mexico Commission for Deaf and
    Hard of Hearing Persons
Thomas Dillon, Executive Director
1435 S. St. Francis Drive, Suite 101
Santa Fe, NM 87505-4083
(505) 827-7584 (V/TTY); (800) 489-8536
    (V/TTY, in NM only)
E-mail: NMCDHHA@doh.state.nm.us
Web: www.nmcdhh.org

New Mexico School for the Deaf
Outreach Department
Joyce Horvath, Coordinator
1060 Cerrillos Road
Santa Fe, NM 87503
(505) 476-6400 (V/TTY);
    (800) 841-6699 (V/TTY)
E-mail: Joyce.Horvath@nmsd.k12.nm.us

Telecommunications Relay Services for Individuals Who
Are Deaf, Hard of Hearing, or With Speech Impairments

(800) 659-1779 (V)
(800) 659-8331 (TTY); 711 (TTY)
(888) 659-3952 (Speech to Speech)

State Education Agency
Rural Representative

Steven Oldroyd, Director
Office of Special Education
Public Education Department
300 Don Gaspar Avenue
Santa Fe, NM 87501-2786
(505) 827-6541
E-mail: soldroyd@ped.state.nm.us
Web: www.ped.state.nm.us

Regional ADA & IT
Technical Assistance Center

Disability Law Resource Project
Wendy Wilkinson, Director
2323 S. Shepard Boulevard, Suite 1000
Houston, TX 77019
(713) 520-0232 (V/TTY); (800) 949-4232 (V/TTY)
E-mail: dlrp@ilru.org
Web: www.dlrp.org

University Center for Excellence
in Developmental Disabilities

Center for Development and Disability (CDD)
Dr. Catherine McClain, Director
University of New Mexico
2300 Menaul Boulevard, NE
Albuquerque, NM 87107
(505) 272-3000
E-mail: cmcclain@salud.unm.edu
Web: http://cdd.unm.edu

Technology-Related Assistance

New Mexico Technology Assistance Program
Andy Winnegar, Project Director
435 St. Michael's Drive, Building D
Santa Fe, NM 87505
(505) 954-8539 (V/TTY); (800) 866-2253 (V)
(800) 659-4915 (TTY)
E-mail: awinnegar@state.nm.us
Web: www.nmtap.com

State Mediation System

Office of Special Education
Public Education Department
Duane Ellis, Parent Liaison
300 Don Gaspar Avenue
Santa Fe, NM 87501-2786
(505) 827-6541
E-mail: dellis@ped.state.nm.us
Web: www.ped.state.nm.us

Special Format Library

New Mexico Library for the Blind and
    Physically Handicapped
1209 Camino Carlos Rey
Santa Fe, NM 87507-5166
(505) 476-9770; 800-456-5515
E-mail: talkingbooks@stlib.state.nm.us
Web: http://www.nmstatelibrary.org/direct-
    and-rural-services/lbph

New Mexico—Disability-Specific Organizations

Attention Deficit Disorder

    To identify an ADD group in New Mexico,
contact either of the following organizations:

Children and Adults with Attention-Deficit/
    Hyperactivity Disorder (CHADD)
8181 Professional Place, Suite 150
Landover, MD 20785
(301) 306-7070
(800) 233-4050 (Voice mail to request
    information packet)
Web: www.chadd.org

Attention Deficit Disorders Association–Southern
    Region (ADDA)
12345 Jones Road, Suite 287
Houston, TX 77070
(281) 897-0982
Web: www.adda-sr.org

Autism

New Mexico Autism Society
P.O. Box 30955
Albuquerque, NM 87190
(505) 332-0306
E-mail: nmautism@nmautismsociety.org
Web: www.nmautismsociety.org

Blind/Visual Impairments

American Foundation for the Blind–Southwest
Judy Scott, Director
11030 Ables Lane
Dallas, TX 75229
(214) 352-7222
E-mail: dallas@afb.net
Web: www.afb.org

Brain Injury

Brain Injury Association of New Mexico
Miryam Miller, Director
121 Cardenas, NE
Albuquerque, NM 87108
(505) 292-7414; (888) 292-7415 (in NM)
E-mail: info@braininjurynm.org
Web: www.braininjurynm.org

Learning Disabilities

Patty Useem
New Mexico Learning Disabilities Association
6301 Menaul NE, #556
Albuquerque, NM 87110
(505) 821-2545
E-mail: nmlda2003@yahoo.com

Mental Health

NAMI-New Mexico
Dale Johnson, President
P.O. Box 3086
Albuquerque, NM 87190-3086
(505) 260-0154; (800) 953-6745
E-mail: naminm@aol.com
Web: http://nm.nami.org

Mental Retardation/ Developmental Disabilities

The Arc of New Mexico
Rebecca Shuman, Executive Director
3655 Carlisle, NE
Albuquerque, NM 87110
(505) 883-4630; (800) 358-6493 (in NM)
E-mail: arcnm@arcnm.com
Web: www.arcnm.com

Speech and Hearing

New Mexico Speech-Language-Hearing Association
P.O. Box 66085
Albuquerque, NM 87193-6085
(505) 899-6674; (800) 292-8465
E-mail: nmsha@qwest.com
Web: www.nmsha.net

New Mexico—Organizations Especially for Parents

Parent Training and Information Center (PTI)

Parents Reaching Out (PRO)
Sallie Van Curen, Executive Director
1920 B Columbia, SE
Albuquerque, NM 87106
(505) 247-0192; (800) 524-5176 (In NM)
E-mail: vancurren@parentsreachingout.org
Web: www.parentsreachingout.org

STEP*HI Parent/Infant Program
Early Childhood Programs
New Mexico School for the Deaf
Rosemary Gallegos, Director
1060 Cerrillos Road
Santa Fe, NM 87505
(505) 476-6418 (V/TTY); (800) 841-6699
E-mail: Rosemary.Gallegos@nmsd.k12.nm.us

Abrazos Family Support Services
Education for Parents of Indian Children with
    Special Needs (EPICS) Project
Martha J. Gorospe-Charlie, Project Director
P.O. Box 788
Bernalillo, NM 87004
(505) 867-3396 (V/TTY)
E-mail: info@abrazosnm.org
Web: www.abrazosnm.org

Parent-To-Parent

Parents Reaching Out (PRO)
Sallie Van Curen, Executive Director
1920 B Columbia, SE
Albuquerque, NM 87106
(505) 247-0192; (800) 524-5176 (in NM)
E-mail: vancurren@parentsreachingout.org
Web: www.parentsreachingout.org

Community Parent Resource Center (serving the
    22 tribes of New Mexico)

Abrazos Family Support Services
Education for Parents of Indian Children with
    Special Needs (EPICS) Project
Martha J. Gorospe-Charlie, Project Director
P.O. Box 788
Bernalillo, NM 87004
(505) 867-3396 (V/TTY)
E-mail: info@abrazosnm.org
Web: www.abrazosnm.org

Parent Teacher Association (PTA)

New Mexico Congress of Parents and Teachers
Leslie Boggs, President
3315 Louisiana NE
Montgomery Complex
Albuquerque, NM 87110
(505) 881-0712
E-mail: nmpta@aol.com
Web: www.nmpta.org

New Mexico—Other Disability Organizations

Easter Seals New Mexico
2819 Richmond Drive, NE
Albuquerque, NM 87107
(505) 888-3811; (800) 279-5261
E-mail: esnmcontact@aol.com
Web: www.nm.easterseals.com

Information Center for New Mexicans with
    Disabilities/BabyNet
Sandra Skaar, Health Educator
2300 Menaul, NE
Albuquerque, NM 87107
(505) 272-8549; (800) 552-8195 (in NM)
E-mail: infonet@unm.edu
E-mail: sskaar@salud.unm.edu

Parents for Behaviorally Different Children
Delfy Roach, Executive Director
1101 Cardenas, NE, Suite 202
Albuquerque, NM 87110
(505) 265-0430; (800) 273-7232
E-mail: pbdc2000@aol.com

VSA Arts of New Mexico
Marjorie Neset, Executive Director
4904 4th, NW
Albuquerque, NM 87107
(505) 345-2872
E-mail: info@vsartsnm.org

Independent Living

To find out the contact information for the Statewide Independent Living Council (SILC) in New Mexico, contact

Independent Living Research Utilization Project
The Institute for Rehabilitation and Research
2323 South Sheppard, Suite 1000
Houston, TX 77019
(713) 520-0232 (V); (713) 520-5136 (TTY)
E-mail: ilru@ilru.org
Web: www.ilru.org

To find out the contact information for centers for independent living (CILs) in New Mexico, contact

National Council on Independent Living
1916 Wilson Boulevard, Suite 209
Arlington, VA 22201
(703) 525-3406; (703) 525-4153 (TTY)
E-mail: ncil@ncil.org
Web: www.ncil.org

NEW YORK

State Agencies and Organizations

United States Senators

Honorable Kirsten E. Gillibrand (D)
478 Russell Senate Office Building
Washington, DC 20510
(202) 224-4451
(202) 228-0282 (Fax)
(202) 224-6821 (TTY)
E-mail Web Form: http://www.gillibrand.
    senate.gov/contact/
Web: http://www.gillibrand.senate.gov/

Honorable Charles E. Schumer (D)
322 Hart Senate Office Building
United States Senate
Washington, DC 20510
(202) 224-6542
(202) 228-3027 (Fax)
E-mail Web Form: http://schumer.senate.gov/
    webform.html
Web: http://schumer.senate.gov

United States Representatives

To find the contact information for your representative in the House of the U.S. Congress, visit the House's Web site at: www.house.gov, or call (202) 225-3121; (202) 225-1904 (TTY).

Governor

Honorable Andrew Cuomo
State Capitol
Albany, NY 12224
(518) 474-8390
E-mail form available
    on Governor's Web site.
Web: http://www.governor.ny.gov/

Official State Web Site

Web: www.state.ny.us

State Department of Education: Special Education

Office of Vocational and Educational Services for
Individuals with Disabilities (VESID)
State Education Department
Dr. Rebecca Cort, Deputy Commissioner
1 Commerce Plaza, Room 1606
Albany, NY 12234
(518) 474-2714
Web: www.nysed.gov

State Coordinator for NCLB (No Child Left Behind)

New York received an extended waiver
from the NCLB act.

Mr. Roberto Reyes, Director
Title I School and Community Services
New York State Education Department
89 Washington Avenue, Room 365 EBA
Albany, NY 12234
(518) 473-0295
Web: http://www.p12.nysed.gov/irs/account-
ability/home.html

Programs for Infants and Toddlers With Disabilities: Birth–2 Years

Early Intervention Program
Brenda Knudson Chouffi, Co-Director
Donna Noyes, Co-Director
Bureau of Early Intervention
State Department of Health
Corning Tower Building, Room 287
Empire State Plaza
Albany, NY 12237
(518) 473-7016
E-mail: brenda.knudsonchouffi@health.ny.gov
donna.noyes@health.ny.gov
Web: http://www.health.ny.gov/community/
infants_children/early_intervention/

Programs for Children With Disabilities: 3–5 Years

Special Education Policy and Professional
Development
Patricia Geary, Coordinator
Office of Special Education
Education Department
89 Washington Avenue
Albany, NY 12234
(518) 473-2878
E-mail: pgeary@mail.nysed.gov
Web: http://www.p12.nysed.gov/specialed/
preschool/home.html

State Vocational Rehabilitation Agency

Office of Vocational and Educational Services for
Individuals with Disabilities (VESID)
New York State Education Department
Dr. Rebecca Cort, Deputy Commissioner
1 Commerce Plaza, Room 1606
Albany, NY 12234
(518) 474-2714
Web: www.nysed.gov

Coordinator for Transition Services

Doris Jamison, Manager
Planning and Research
Office of Vocational and Educational Services
for Individuals with Disabilities
One Commerce Plaza, Room 1624
Albany, NY 12234
(518) 474-7566; (800) 222-5627
E-mail: djamison@mail.nysed.gov
Web: www.vesid.nysed.gov

State Mental Health Agency

Office of Mental Health
Sharon Carpinello, Commissioner
44 Holland Avenue
Albany, NY 12229
(518) 474-4403
E-mail: colejxw@omh.state.ny.us
Web: www.omh.state.ny.us

State Mental Health Representative for Children and Youth

David Woodlock, Deputy Commissioner
Children and Families
Office of Mental Health
44 Holland Avenue
Albany, NY 12229
(518) 473-6328
E-mail: cocodjw@omh.state.ny.us

State Mental Retardation Program

New York State Office of
Mental Retardation and
Developmental Disabilities
Thomas Maul, Commissioner
44 Holland Avenue
Albany, NY 12229
(518) 473-1997
Web: www.omr.state.ny.us

Council on Developmental Disabilities

New York State Developmental Disabilities
    Planning Council
Sheila Carey, Executive Director
155 Washington Avenue, 2nd Floor
Albany, NY 12210
(518) 486-7505; (800) 395-3372
E-mail: scarey@ddpc.state.ny.us
Web: www.ddpc.state.ny.us

Protection and Advocacy Agency

New York State Commission on Quality of Care
Marcel Chaine, Director Advocacy
    Services Bureau
401 State Street
Schenectady, NY 12305-2397
(518) 388-2892; (800) 624-4143
E-mail: marcelc@cqc.state.ny.us
Web: www.cqc.state.ny.us

New York State Office of Advocate for
    Persons with Disabilities
Richard Warrender, State Advocate
1 Empire State Plaza, Suite 1001
Albany, NY 12223-1150
(518) 474-5567 (V); (518) 473-4231 (TTY)
(800) 522-4369 (V/TTY/Spanish, in NY only)
Web: www.oapwd.org

Client Assistance Program

New York State Commission on Quality of Care
Michael Peluso, CAP Director
401 State Street
Schenectady, NY 12305-2397
(518) 388-2892; (800) 624-4143
E-mail: michaelp@cqc.state.ny.us
Web: www.cqc.state.ny.us

Programs for Children With
Special Health Care Needs

Children with Special Health Care Needs
New York State Department of Health
Susan Slade, Program Director
ESP-Corning Tower Building, Room 208
Albany, NY 12237-0618
(518) 474-2001
E-mail: sjs11@health.state.ny.us
Web: www.health.state.ny.us

State CHIP Program
(health care for low-income,
uninsured children)

Child Health Plus
New York State Health Department
Box 2000
Albany, NY 12220
(800) 698-4543; (877) 898-5849 (TTY)
Web: www.health.state.ny.us/nysdoh/
    chplus/index.htm

Programs for Children
and Youth Who Are Blind
or Visually Impaired, or Deaf-Blind

Commission for the Blind and Visually
    Handicapped
Office of Children and Family Services
Thomas Robertson, Associate Commissioner
Capital View Office Park
52 Washington Street, Room 201,
    South Building
Rensselaer, NY 12144-2796
(518) 473-1801
Web: www.dfa.state.ny.us/cbvh

Programs for Children and Youth
Who Are Deaf or Hard of Hearing

Office of Vocational and
    Educational Services for
    Individuals with Disabilities (VESID)
Dorothy Steele, Coordinator, Deaf Services
One Commerce Plaza, Room 1623
Albany, NY 12234
(518) 474-5652 (V); (518) 486-3773 (TTY)
(800) 222-5627 (V/TTY)
E-mail: dsteele@mail.nysed.gov
Web: www.vesid.nysed.gov/

Telecommunications Relay
Services for Individuals Who
Are Deaf, Hard of Hearing,
or With Speech Impairments

(800) 421-1220 (V)
(800) 662-1220 (TTY); 711 (TTY)
(877) 662-4234 (Speech to Speech)

Regional ADA & IT Technical Assistance Center

Northeast ADA & IT Center
Andrea Haenlin-Mott, Director
Cornell University
331 Ives Hall
Ithaca, NY 14853
(607) 255-6686 (V/TTY/Spanish);
　　(800) 949-4232 (V/TTY/Spanish)
E-mail: northeastada@cornell.edu
Web: www.ilr.cornell.edu/ped/northeastada

University Centers for Excellence in Developmental Disabilities

Developmental Disabilities Center
Dr. Steven Wolf, Director
St. Lukes–Roosevelt Hospital Center
1000 10th Avenue
New York, NY 10019
(212) 523-6230

Westchester Institute for
　　Human Development/UCE
Ansley Bacon, Executive Director
Cedarwood Hall
Valhalla, NY 10595-1689
(914) 493-8204
E-mail: Ansley_Bacon@NYMC.edu
Web: www.nymc.edu/wihd

University Center for Excellence
　　in Developmental Disabilities
　　Education, Research and Service
Herbert J. Cohen, MD, Director
Rose F. Kennedy Center
Albert Einstein College of Medicine/
　　Yeshiva University
1410 Pelham Parkway South
Bronx, NY 10461
(718) 430-8522
E-mail: hcohen@aecom.yu.edu

Strong Center for Developmental Disabilities
Dr. Philip Davidson, Director
University of Rochester Medical Center
601 Elmwood Avenue
P.O. Box 671
Rochester, NY 14642
(585) 275-2986
E-mail: phil_davidson@urmc.rochester.edu
Web: www.urmc.rochester.edu/strong/scdd

Technology-Related Assistance

New York State TRAID Project
New York State Office of Advocate for
　　Persons with Disabilities
Lisa Rosano-Kaczkowski, Project Director
One Empire State Plaza, Suite 1001
Albany, NY 12223-1150
(518) 474-2825 (V); (518) 473-4231 (TTY);
(800) 522-4369 (V/TTY/Spanish, in NY only)
E-mail: traid@oapwd.org
Web: www.oapwd.org

State Mediation System

Office of Vocational and Educational Services for
　　Individuals with Disabilities (VESID)
Elaine Gervais, Associate in Special Education
1 Commerce Plaza, Room 1619
Albany, NY 12234
(518) 486-7462
E-mail: egervais@mail.nysed.gov
Web: www.vesid.nysed.gov/lsn

Special Format Books

New York State Talking Book & Braille Library
　　(serving upstate New York for Children
　　and Youth From 3–19 Years)
Jane Somers, Director
Sharon B. Phillips, School and Youth Services
　　Librarian
New York State Library
Cultural Education Center, Empire State Plaza
Albany, NY 12230
(518) 474-5935; (800) 342-3688
E-mail: tbblkids@mail.nysed.gov (school/
　　youth services)
E-mail: tbbl@mail.nysed.gov (adult services)
Web: www.nysl.nysed.gov/talk.htm

Andrew Heiskell Library for the Blind & Physically
　　Handicapped (serving New York City and
　　Long Island)
Robert McBrien, Head Librarian
New York Public Library
40 West 20th Street
New York, NY 10011
(212) 206-5400; (212) 206-5425
　　(24 hour Voicemail)
E-mail: ahlbph@nypl.org
Web: http://talkingbooks.nypl.org

New York—Disability-Specific Organizations

Attention Deficit Disorder

To identify an ADD group in New York, contact either of the following organizations:

Children and Adults with Attention-Deficit/
    Hyperactivity Disorder (CHADD)
8181 Professional Place, Suite 150
Landover, MD 20785
(301) 306-7070
(800) 233-4050 (Voice mail to request
    information packet)
Web: www.chadd.org

Attention Deficit Disorder Association (ADDA)
P.O. Box 543
Pottstown, PA 19464
(484) 945-2101
Web: www.add.org

Autism

To identify an autism group in New York, contact

Autism Society of America
7910 Woodmont Avenue, Suite 300
Bethesda, MD 20814
(301) 657-0881; (800) 3-AUTISM
Web: www.autism-society.org

Blind/Visual Impairments

American Foundation for the Blind
Regina Genwright, Director of Information
    Center
11 Penn Plaza, Suite 300
New York, NY 10001
(212) 502-7600; (212) 502-7662 (TTY)
E-mail: afbinfo@afb.org
Web: www.afb.org

Brain Injury

Brain Injury Association of New York State
Judith Avner, Executive Director
10 Colvin Avenue
Albany, NY 12206
(518) 459-7911; (800) 228-8201 (in NY)
E-mail: info@bianys.org
Web: www.bianys.org

Cerebral Palsy

Cerebral Palsy Associations of New York State
Susan Constantino, Executive Director
330 W. 34th Street
New York, NY 10001
(212) 947-5770, ext. 201
E-mail: nysucpa@aol.com
Web: www.cerebralpalsynys.org

Epilepsy

Epilepsy Foundation of Long Island
Thomas Hopkins, President
1500 Hempstead Turnpike
East Meadow, NY 11554
(516) 739-7733
Email Web Form: http://efli.org/contact-us
Web: www.efli.org

Epilepsy Foundation Northeastern New York
Jeannine Garab, Executive Director
3 Washington Sq
Albany, NY, 12205-5523
(518) 456-7501; (800) 894-3223
Email: jgarab@epilepsyneny.org
Web: http://old.epilepsyfoundation.org/local/
    efneny/#.VJGn7NLF8R0

Epilepsy Foundation Rochester-Syracuse-Binghamton
Jeff Sinsebox, President
2 Townline Circle
Rochester, NY 14623
(585) 442-6420 x236
Email: jsinsebox@epiny.org
Web: http://epiny.org/index.php

Epilepsy Foundation New York City
65 Broadway, Ste. 505
New York, NY 10006
(212) 677-8550
Email: info@efmny.org
Web: http://www.efmny.org/

Learning Disabilities

Learning Disabilities Association of New York State
Michael Helman, President
1202 Troy-Schenectady Road, Building 1
Latham, NY 12110
(518) 608-8992
E-mail: statelda@ldanys.org
Web: www.ldanys.org

Mental Health

Mental Health Association of New York State
Glenn Liebman, CEO
194 Washington Avenue, Suite 415
Albany, NY 12210
(518) 434-0439; (800) 766-6177
E-mail: info@mhanys.org
Web: www.mhanys.org

National Alliance for the Mentally Ill of
    New York State
Ione Christian, President
260 Washington Avenue
Albany, NY 12210-1312
(518) 462-2000; (800) 950-3228
E-mail: info@naminys.org
Web: www.naminys.org

Families Together in New York State, Inc.
Paige Macdonald, Executive Director
15 Elk Street
Albany, NY 12207
(518) 432-0333; (888) 326-8644 (in NY)
E-mail: info@ftnys.org
Web: www.ftnys.org

Mental Retardation

NYSARC, Inc.
Marc Brandt, Executive Director
393 Delaware Avenue
Delmar, NY 12054
(518) 439-8311; (800) 724-2094
E-mail: brandtm@nysarc.org
Web: www.nysarc.org

Speech and Hearing

New York State Speech-Language-Hearing
    Association, Inc.
Tricia Shaw, Executive Assistant
1 Northway Lane
Latham, NY 12110
(518) 786-0947
E-mail: info@nysslha.org
Web: www.nysslha.org

Spina Bifida

Spina Bifida Association: Albany/Capital District
Vanessa and Kevin Chamberlain, Co-Presidents
109 Spring Road
Scotia, NY 12302
(518) 399-9151
E-mail: SBAALBANY102@aol.com
Web: www.SBAAlbany.org

New York—Organizations Especially for Parents

Parent Training and Information Center (PTI)

The Advocacy Center
Paul Shew, Executive Director
590 South Avenue
Rochester, NY 14620
(585) 546-1700; (800) 650-4967 (in NY)
E-mail: info@advocacycenter.com
Web: www.advocacycenter.com

Advocates for Children of New York
    (New York City)
Jill Chaifetz, Executive Director
151 W. 30th Street, 5th Floor
New York, NY 10001
(212) 947-9779
E-mail: jchaifetz@advocatesforchildren.org
Web: www.advocatesforchildren.org
Web: www.insideschools.org

Resources for Children with Special Needs, Inc.
Karen Thoreson Schlesinger, Executive Director
116 E. 16th Street, 5th Floor
New York, NY 10003
(212) 677-4650
E-mail: info@resourcesnyc.org
Web: www.resourcesnyc.org

Sinergia/Metropolitan Parent Center
Donald Lash, Executive Director
15 W. 65th Street, 6th Floor
New York, NY 10023
(212) 496-1300
E-mail: intake@Sinergiany.org
Web: www.sinergiany.org

Community Parent Resource Center (serving Green Point and Williamsburg)

United We Stand of New York
Lourdes Rivera-Putz, Program Director
202 Union Avenue, Suite L
Brooklyn, NY 11211
(718) 302-4313/4314
E-mail: uwsofny@aol.com
Web: www.taalliance.org/ptis/uws/

Partners in Policymaking

The Advocacy Center
Joyce Steel, Program Director
590 South Avenue
Rochester, NY 14620
(585) 546-1700, ext. 234

E-mail: steel@advocacycenter.com
Web: www.advocacycenter.com

Parent-To-Parent

Parent to Parent of New York State
Janice Fitzgerald, Executive Director
500 Balltown Road
Schenectady, NY 12304
(518) 381-4350; (800) 305-8817
Web: www.parenttoparentnys.org

Parent Teacher Association (PTA)

New York State Congress of Parents and Teachers, Inc.
Penny Leask, President
One Wembley Square
Albany, NY 12205-3830
(518) 452-8808; (877) 5NYSPTA
E-mail: office@nypta.com
Web: www.nypta.com/

Other Parent Organizations

Early Childhood Direction Centers (information
    about resources serving children aged from
    birth to 5 years and their families)
Office of Vocational and Educational Services
    for Individuals with Disabilities (VESID)
Elaine Gervais, Associate in Special Education
One Commerce Plaza, Room 1619
Albany, NY 12234
(518) 486-7462
E-mail: egervais@mail.nysed.gov
Web: www.vesid.nysed.gov

The Family Resource Network, Inc. (serving
    Otsego, Chenango, Delaware, Broome,
    Tioga, and Tompkins counties)
46 Oneida Street
Oneonta, New York 13820
(607) 432-0001; (800) 305-8814
E-mail: familyrn@dmcom.net
Web: www.geocities.com/familyrn/

New York—Other Disability Organizations

Easter Seals New York
Christine McMahon, Chief Operating Officer
11 W. 42nd Street, 30th Floor
New York, NY 10036
(518) 456-4880; (800) 727-8785 (in NY)
E-mail: essofny@aol.com
Web: www.ny.easter-seals.org

MENTOR ABI Group–New Jersey
Rehabilitative and Support Services for
    Persons with Acquired Brain Injury
505 S. Lenola Road
Blason Office Plaza II, Suite 217
Moorestown, NJ 08057
(856) 235-5505
Web: http://nj.thementornetwork.com/
    state/index.asp

New York State Occupational Therapy Association
Caroline Alterio, President
119 Washington Avenue, 2nd Floor
Albany, NY 12210
(518) 462-3717
E-mail: info@nysota.org
Web: www.nysota.org

VSA Arts of New York City
Dr. Bebe Bernstein, Director
18-05 215 Street, Suite 15N
Bayside, NY 11360
(718) 225-6305 (V/TTY)
E-mail: Bbvsanyc@msn.com

Family Empowerment Council, Inc.
Joseph O'Connell, Executive Director
225 Dolson Avenue, Suite 403
Middletown, NY 10940
(845) 343-8100
E-mail: joconnell@familyempowerment.org
Web: www.familyempowerment.org

Independent Living

To find out the contact information for the
Statewide Independent Living Council (SILC) in
New York, contact

Independent Living Research Utilization Project
The Institute for Rehabilitation and Research
2323 South Sheppard, Suite 1000
Houston, TX 77019
(713) 520-0232 (V); (713) 520-5136 (TTY)
E-mail: ilru@ilru.org
Web: www.ilru.org

To find out the contact information for centers for independent living (CILs) in New York,
contact

National Council on Independent Living
1916 Wilson Boulevard, Suite 209
Arlington, VA 22201
(703) 525-3406; (703) 525-4153 (TTY)
E-mail: ncil@ncil.org
Web: www.ncil.org

NORTH CAROLINA

North Carolina—State Agencies and Organizations

United States Senators

Honorable Richard Burr (R)
217 Russell Office Building
Washington, DC 20510
(202) 224-3154
(202) 224-1100 (Fax)
E-mail Web Form: http://www.burr.senate.
gov/public/index.cfm?FuseAction=Contact.
ContactForm
Web: http://www.burr.senate.gov/public/
index.cfm?FuseAction=Home.Home

Honorable Kay R. Hagan (D)
521 Dirksen Senate Office Building
Washington, DC 20510
(202) 224-6342
(202) 228-1374 (Fax)
E-mail Web Form: http://www.hagan.senate.
gov/contact/
Web: http://www.hagan.senate.gov/

United States Representatives

To find the contact information for your representative in the House of the U.S. Congress, visit the House's Web site at: www.house.gov, or call (202) 225-3121; (202) 225-1904 (TTY).

Governor

Honorable Pat McCrory
Office of the Governor
20301 Mail Service Center
Raleigh, NC 27699-0301
(919) 733-5811
(800) 662-7952 (in NC)
E-mail Web Form: http://www.governor.state.
nc.us/contact/email-pat
Web: www.governor.state.nc.us

Official State Web Site

Web: www.ncgov.com/

State Department of Education: Special Education

Exceptional Children Division
Department of Public Instruction
Mary Watson, Director

6356 Mail Service Center
Raleigh, NC 27699-6356
(919) 807-3969/3971
E-mail: mwatson@dpi.state.nc.us
Web: www.ncpublicschools.org/ec

State Coordinator for NCLB (No Child Left Behind)

North Carolina received an extended waiver from the NCLB act.

The North Carolina Department of Public Instruction
301 North Wilmington Street
Raleigh, NC 27601
(919) 807-3300
Email: Information@dpi.nc.gov
Web: http://www.ncpublicschools.org/nclb/

Programs for Infants and Toddlers With Disabilities: Birth–3 Years

Early Intervention Program,
Division of Public Health
Sherry Franklin, Quality Improvement Unit Manager
Women's and Children's Health Section
5605 Six Forks Road
1916 Mail Service Center
Raleigh, NC 27699
(919) 218-2786
E-mail: sherry.franklin@dhhs.nc.gov
Website: http://www.beearly.nc.gov/index.
php/

Programs for Children With Disabilities: 3–5 Years

Vivian James, 619 Preschool Coordinator
State Department of Public Instruction and Exceptional Children's Program
NC Office of Early Learning
2075 Mail Service Center
Raleigh, NC 27699
(919) 218-8384
E-mail: vivian.james@dpi.nc.gov
Web: http://www.earlylearning.nc.gov/
PreKindergarten/PreschoolEC/
indexNEW08.asp

State Vocational Rehabilitation Agency

Division of Vocational Rehabilitation Services
Department of Health and Human Services
George McCoy, Director
2801 Mail Service Center

Raleigh, NC 27699-2801
(919) 855-3500; (919) 855-3579 (TTY)
E-mail: George.McCoy@ncmail.net
Web: http://dvr.dhhs.state.nc.us

Coordinator for Transition Services

Freda Lee, Consultant for Mental Disabilities,
    Transition Services and Secondary Education
Exceptional Children Division
North Carolina Department of Public
    Instruction
6356 Mail Service Center
Raleigh, NC 27699-6356
(919) 807-3989
E-mail: flee@dpi.state.nc.us
Web: www.ncpublicschools.org/ec/

Office of State Coordinator of Vocational Education for Students With Disabilities

Career–Technical Education
Department of Public Instruction
Helena Hendrix-Frye, Coordinator
6359 Mail Service Center
Raleigh, NC 27699-6359
(919) 807-3891
E-mail: hhendrix@dpi.state.nc.us
Web: www.dpi.state.nc.us/workforce_
    development

State Mental Health Agency

Developmental Disabilities and
    Substance Abuse Services
Division of Mental Health
Mike Moseley, Director
Department of Health and Human Services
    MSC: 3001
Raleigh, NC 27699-3001
(919) 733-7011
E-mail: mike.moseley@ncmail.net
Web: www.dhhs.state.nc.us/mhddsas/

State Mental Health Representative for Children and Youth

Flo Stein, Chief
Community Policy Management
Division of Mental Health
Developmental Disabilities and Substance
    Abuse Services
Department of Health and Human Services

3007 Mail Service Center
Raleigh, NC 27699-3007
(919) 733-4670
E-mail: flo.stein@ncmail.net
Web: www.dhhs.state.nc.us/mhddsas

State Developmental Disabilities Program

Best Practice Team
Developmental Disability Services Team
Division of Mental Health
Developmental Disabilities
    and Substance Abuse Services
Department of Health and Human Services
Vivian Leon, Program Consultant
3005 Mail Service Center
Raleigh, NC 27699-3005
(919) 715-2774
E-mail: vivian.leon@ncmail.net
Web: www.dhhs.state.nc.us/mhddsas

Council on Developmental Disabilities

North Carolina Council on
    Developmental Disabilities
Holly Riddle, Executive Director
3801 Lake Boone Trail, Suite 250
Raleigh, NC 27607
(919) 420-7901 (V/TTY); (800) 357-6916
E-mail: hriddle@nc-ddc.org
Web: www.nc-ddc.org

Protection and Advocacy Agency

Governor's Advocacy Council for
    Persons with Disabilities
Allison Bowen, Interim Executive Director
1314 Mail Service Center
Raleigh, NC 27699-1314
(919) 733-9250; (800) 821-6922 (in NC)
E-mail: allison.bowen@ncmail.net
Web: www.gacpd.com

Client Assistance Program

Client Assistance Program
Kathy Brack, Director
2806 Mail Service Center
Raleigh, NC 27699-2806
(919) 855-3600 (V/TTY)
E-mail: Kathy.Brack@ncmail.net
Web: http://dvr.dhhs.state.nc.us/DVR/
    CAP/caphome.htm

**Programs for Children
With Special Health Care Needs**

Children and Youth Branch
Women's and Children's Health Section
Division of Public Health
Department of Health and Human Services
Carol Tant, Chief
1928 Mail Service Center
Raleigh, NC 27699-1928
(919) 715-3808
E-mail: carol.tant@ncmail.net
Web: www.dhhs.state.nc.us

**State CHIP Program
(health care for low-
income, uninsured children)**

North Carolina Health Choice
P.O. Box 30111
Durham, NC 27702-3111
(800) 422- 4658
Web: www.dhhs.state.nc.us/dma/cpcont.htm

**Programs for Children and Youth Who
Are Blind or Visually Impaired, Deaf
or Hard of Hearing, or Deaf-Blind**

Office of Education Services
Department of Health and Human Services
Cyndie Bennett, Director
2302 Mail Service Center
Raleigh, NC 27699-2302
(919) 855-4430
E-mail: cyndie.bennett@ncmail.net

**Programs for Children and Youth
Who Are Blind or Visually Impaired**

Division of Services for the Blind
Department of Health and Human Services
Debbie Jackson, Director
2601 Mail Service Center
Raleigh, NC 27699-2601
(919) 733-9822
E-mail: debbie.jackson@ncmail.net
Web: www.dhhs.state.nc.us/dsb

**Programs for Children and Youth
Who Are Deaf or Hard of Hearing**

Division of Services for the
    Deaf and Hard of Hearing
Department of Health and Human Services
Linda Harrington, Director
319 Chapanoke Road, Suite 108
Raleigh, NC 27603
(919) 773-2970; (919) 773-2969 (TTY)
E-mail: linda.harrington@ncmail.net
Web: http://dsdhh.dhhs.state.nc.us

**Telecommunications Relay
Services for Individuals
Who Are Deaf, Hard of Hearing,
or with Speech Impairments**

(800) 735-8262 (V)
(800) 735-2962 (TTY); 711 (TTY)
(877) 735-8261 (Speech to Speech)

**Programs for Children and
Youth Who Are Deaf-Blind**

Margaret Richardson, Chairperson
Deaf-Blind Multihandicapped Association
    of North Carolina
2435 Thomashire Court
Charlotte, NC 28262
(704) 549-5775
E-mail: info@NCKIDS-DB.org

**Regional ADA & IT
Technical Assistance Center**

Southeast Disability and Business Technical
    Assistance Center
Center for Assistive Technology and
    Environmental Access
Shelley Kaplan, Project Director
Georgia Tech
490 10th Street
Atlanta, GA 30318
(404) 385-0636; (800) 949-4232 (V/TTY)
E-mail: sedbtac@catea.org
Web: www.sedbtac.org

**University Center for Excellence
in Developmental Disabilities**

Clinical Center for the Study of
    Development and Learning
Melvin Levine, Director
CB# 7255
University of North Carolina
Chapel Hill, NC 27599-7255
(919) 966-5171
E-mail: mel.levine@cdl.unc.edu
Web: www.cdl.unc.edu

Technology-Related Assistance

North Carolina Assistive Technology Program
Ricki Hiatt, Director
Department of Health and Human Services
Division of Vocational Rehabilitation Services
1110 Navaho Drive, Suite 101
Raleigh, NC 27609-7322
(919) 850-2787 (V/TTY)
E-mail: rhiatt@ncatp.org
Web: www.ncatp.org

State Mediation System

Exceptional Children Division
North Carolina Department of
    Public Instruction
Brenda Winston, Section Chief
6356 Mail Service Center
Raleigh, NC 27699-6356
(919) 807-3976
E-mail: bwinston@dpi.state.nc.us
Web: www.ncpublicschools.org/ec/

Special Format Library

North Carolina Library for the Blind and
    Physically Handicapped
State Library of North Carolina
Department of Cultural Resources
Francine I. Martin, Librarian
1811 Capital Boulevard
Raleigh, NC 27635
(919) 733-4376; (888) 388-2460
(919) 733-1462 (TTY)
E-mail: nclbph@ncmail.net
Web: http://statelibrary.ncdcr.gov/lbph/
    index.html

North Carolina—Disability-Specific Organizations

Attention Deficit Disorder

To identify an ADD group in North Carolina, contact either of the following organizations:

Children and Adults with Attention-Deficit/
    Hyperactivity Disorder (CHADD)
8181 Professional Place, Suite 150
Landover, MD 20785
(301) 306-7070
(800) 233-4050 (Voice mail to request
    information packet)
Web: www.chadd.org

Attention Deficit Disorder Association (ADDA)
P.O. Box 543
Pottstown, PA 19464
(484) 945-2101
Web: www.add.org

Autism

Jill Hinton Keel, Director
Autism Society of North Carolina
505 Oberlin Road, Suite 230
Raleigh, NC 27605-1345
(919) 743-0204; (800) 442-2762 (in NC)
E-mail: jhkeel@autismsociety-nc.org
Web: www.autismsociety-nc.org

Blind/Visual Impairments

American Foundation for the Blind—National
    Literacy Center
Frances Mary D'Andrea, Director
100 Peachtree Street, Suite 620
Atlanta, GA 30303
(404) 525-2303
E-mail: literacy@afb.net
Web: www.afb.org

Brain Injury

Brain Injury Association of North Carolina
P.O. Box 748
Raleigh, NC 27602
(919) 833-9634; (800) 377-1464 (in NC)
E-mail: info@bianc.net
Web: www.bianc.net

Cerebral Palsy

Easter Seals UCP North Carolina
Connie Cochran, President
2315 Myron Drive
Raleigh, NC 27607-3357
(919) 783-8898; (800) 662-7119
E-mail: ccochran@eastersealsucp.com
Web: http://nc.eastersealsucp.com

Epilepsy

Epilepsy Foundation of North Carolina, Inc.
Epilepsy Foundation North Carolina
Piedmont One 1920 W. First Street, Suite 5541A
Winston Salem, North Carolina 27104-4220
United States
(336) 716-2320
(800) 451-0694
Email: info@epilepsync.org
Web: http://www.epilepsync.org/

Learning Disabilities

Learning Disabilities
    Association of North Carolina
Jonathan Jones and Pat Lillie, Co-Presidents
9650 Strickland Road, Suite 103-224
Raleigh, NC 27615-1937
(919) 493-5362
E-mail: ldanc@mindspring.com
Web: www.ldanc.org

Mental Health

Mental Health Association in North Carolina
John Tote, Executive Director
3820 Bland Road
Raleigh, NC 27609-6239
(919) 981-0740
E-mail: johntote3@aol.com
Web: www.mha-nc.org

NAMI–North Carolina
Chris Aycock, Executive Director
309 W. Millbrook Road, Suite 121
Raleigh, NC 27609
(919) 788-0801; (800) 451-9682 (in NC)
E-mail: mail@naminc.org
Web: www.naminc.org

Mental Retardation

The Arc of North Carolina
Dave Richard, Executive Director
4200 Six Forks Road, Suite 100
Raleigh, NC 27609
(919) 782-4632; (800) 662-8706
E-mail: dave@arcnc.org
Web: www.arcnc.org

Speech and Hearing

North Carolina Speech, Hearing and
    Language Association
G. Peyton Maynard, Executive Director
P.O. Box 28359
Raleigh, NC 27611-8359
(919) 833-3984
E-mail: ncshla@bellsouth.net
Web: www.ncshla.org

Spina Bifida

Spina Bifida Association of North Carolina
3915 Grace Court
Indian Trail, NC 28079
(800) 847-2262
E-mail: sbanc@mindspring.com
Web: www.sbanc.org

North Carolina—Organizations Especially for Parents

Parent Training and Information Center (PTI)

ECAC, Inc. (Exceptional Children's Assistance Center)
Connie Hawkins, Executive Director
Mary LaCorte, PTI Project Director
907 Barra Row, Suite 102/103
Davidson, NC 28036
(704) 892-1321(V/TTY);
    (800) 962-6817 (in NC only)
E-mail: ecac@ecacmail.org
Web: www.ECAC-parentcenter.org

Parent-To-Parent

Family Support Network of North Carolina
Irene Zipper, Director
Central Directory of Resources, CB #7340
University of North Carolina at Chapel Hill
Chapel Hill, NC 27599-7340
(919) 966-2841; (800) 852-0042
E-mail: cdr@med.unc.edu
Web: www.familysupportnetworknc.org

Community Parent Resource Center

FSN/HOPE (serving Burke,
*   Caldwell, Catawba, McDowell*
*   and Alexander Counties)*
Vickie Dieter, Executive Director
300 Enola Road
Morganton, NC 28655
(828) 438-6540
E-mail: vbdieter@charter.net

FIRST (serving Buncombe, Henderson,
*   Madison and Yancey Counties)*
Janet Price-Ferrell, Director
P.O. Box 802
Asheville, NC 28802
(828) 277-1315; (877) 633-3178
E-mail: firstwnc@aol.com

Parent Teacher Association (PTA)

North Carolina Congress
*   of Parents and Teachers*
Clarie Y. White, President
3501 Glenwood Avenue
Raleigh, NC 27612-4934
(919) 787-0534; (800) 255-0417
E-mail: office@ncpta.org
Web: www.ncpta.org

Other Parent Organizations

First in Families of North Carolina
Karen E. Barbour, Technical Assistant
3924 Browning Place, Suite 5
Raleigh, NC 27609
(919) 571-8092, ext. 18; (866) 740-4135
E-mail: kbarbour@ecacmail.org
Web: www.firstinfamiliesofnc.org

North Carolina Families United
c/o ECAC, Inc.
Pat Solomon, Coordinator
907 Barra Row, Suite 102/103
Davidson, NC 28036
(910) 895-9392
E-mail: phsolomon@earthlink.net
Web: www.ncfamiliesunited.org

North Carolina—Other Disability Organizations

TelAbility (medical information and community
*   resources for children with special needs in*
*   North Carolina)*
Dr. Joshua Alexander, Program Director
1101 Weaver Dairy Road, Suite 202
Chapel Hill, NC 27514
(919) 843-0427
E-mail: pdrehab@med.unc.edu
Web: www.TelAbility.org

Independent Living

To find out the contact information for the Statewide Independent Living Council (SILC) in North Carolina, contact

Independent Living Research Utilization Project
The Institute for Rehabilitation and Research
2323 South Sheppard, Suite 1000
Houston, TX 77019
(713) 520-0232 (V); (713) 520-5136 (TTY)
E-mail: ilru@ilru.org
Web: www.ilru.org

To find out the contact information for centers for independent living (CILs) in North Carolina, contact

National Council on Independent Living
1916 Wilson Boulevard, Suite 209
Arlington, VA 22201
(703) 525-3406; (703) 525-4153 (TTY)
E-mail: ncil@ncil.org
Web: www.ncil.org

NORTH DAKOTA

North Dakota—State Agencies and Organizations

United States Senators

Honorable Heidi Heitkamp (D)
502 Hart Senate Office Building
Washington, DC 20510
(202) 224-2043
E-mail Web Form: http://www.heitkamp.
*   senate.gov/public/index.cfm/email-heidi*
Web: http://www.heitkamp.senate.gov/
*   public/index.cfm/home*

Honorable John Hoeven (R)
338 Russell Senate Office Building
Washington, DC 20510
(202) 224-2551
(202) 224-1193 (Fax)
E-mail: http://www.hoeven.senate.gov/
    public/index.cfm/email-the-senator
Web: http://www.hoeven.senate.gov/public/
    index.cfm/home

United States Representatives

To find the contact information for your representative in the House of the U.S. Congress, visit the House's Web site at: www.house.gov, or call (202) 225-3121; (202) 225-1904 (TTY).

Governor

Honorable Jack Dalrymple
Governor's Office
600 E. Boulevard Avenue, Department 101
Bismarck, ND 58505-0001
(701) 328-2200; (701) 328-2205 (Fax)
E-mail: http://governor.nd.gov/contact-us
Web: http://governor.nd.gov/

Official State Web Site

Web: http://discovernd.com/

State Department of Education: Special Education

Office of Special Education
Department of Public Instruction
Robert Rutten, Director
600 E. Boulevard Avenue, Department 201
Bismarck, ND 58505-0440
(701) 328-2277; (701) 328-4920 (TTY)
E-mail: brutten@state.nd.us
Web: www.dpi.state.nd.us/speced/index.shtm

State Coordinator for NCLB (No Child Left Behind)

Kirsten Baesler, State Superintendent
Department of Public Instruction
600 E. Boulevard Avenue, Department 201
Bismarck, ND 58505-0440
(701) 328-2260
E-mail: dpi@nd.gov
Web: www.dpi.state.nd.us

Programs for Infants and Toddlers With Disabilities: Birth–2 Years

Developmental Disabilities Unit
North Dakota Department of Human Services
Amanda Carlson, Part C Coordinator
1237 West Divide Avenue, Suite 1A
Bismarck, ND 58501
(701) 328-8936; (800) 755-8529 (in ND)
E-mail: arcarlson@nd.gov
Web: http://www.nd.gov/dhs/services/
    disabilities/earlyintervention/

Programs for Children With Disabilities: 3–5 Years

Office of Special Education
Gerry Teevens, Director
Nancy Skorheim, 619 Coordinator
Department of Public Instruction
600 East Boulevard Avenue
Bismarck, ND 58505
(701) 328-2277
E-mail: gteevens@nd.gov, nskorheim@nd.gov
Web: http://www.dpi.state.nd.us/speced1/

State Vocational Rehabilitation Agency

Disability Services Division
Gene Hysjulien, Director
North Dakota Department of Human Services
600 S. 2nd Street, Suite 1B
Bismarck, ND 58504-5729
(701) 328-8950; (701) 328-8968 (TTY)
(800) 755-2745 (in ND)
E-mail: sohysg@state.nd.us

Coordinator for Transition Services

Geraldine Teevens, Transition Coordinator
Office of Special Education
North Dakota Department of Public Instruction
600 E. Boulevard Avenue
Bismarck, ND 58505-0440
(701) 328-2277
E-mail: gsteevens@state.nd.us
Web: www.dpi.state.nd.us/transitn/

State Board of Career and Technical Education

State Board of Career and Technical Education
Garry Freier, Supervisor of Special Needs
15th Floor, Capitol Tower
600 E. Boulevard Avenue
Bismarck, ND 58505-0610
(701) 328-3178
E-mail: GFreier@state.nd.us
Web: www.state.nd.us/cte

State Mental Health Agency

Division of Mental Health and Substance
  Abuse Services
JoAnne Hoesel, Administrator
Department of Human Services
600 S. 2nd Street, Suite 1E
Bismarck, ND 58504
(701) 328-8924; (800) 755-2719 (in ND)
E-mail: sohoej@state.nd.us
Web: www.state.nd.us/humanservices

State Mental Health Representative for Children and Youth

Children's Mental Health Services
Division of Mental Health and Substance
  Abuse Services
Children and Family Services Division
State Capitol–Judicial Wing
600 E. Boulevard Avenue, Room 302
Bismarck, ND 58505
(701) 328-8924
Web: www.state.nd.us/humanservices/
  services/mentalhealth/children.html

State Mental Retardation Program

Disability Services Division
Gene Hysjulien, Director
North Dakota Department of Human Services
600 S. 2nd Street, Suite 1A
Bismarck, ND 58504-5729
(701) 328-8930; (800) 755-8529 (in ND)
E-mail: dhsds@state.nd.us

Council on Developmental Disabilities

State Council on Developmental Disabilities
Tom Wallner, Director
Department of Human Services
600 S. 2nd Street, Suite 1B
Bismarck, ND 58504-5729
(701) 328-8953
E-mail: sowalt@state.nd.us
Web: www.ndcd.org/ndcpd/uapdis

Protection and Advocacy Agency

North Dakota Protection and Advocacy Project
Teresa Larson, Executive Director
400 E. Broadway, Suite 409
Bismarck, ND 58501-4071
(701) 328-2950; (800) 472-2670 (in ND)
(ND Relay 711)
E-mail: panda@state.nd.us
Web: www.ndpanda.org

Client Assistance Program

Client Assistance Program
Dennis Lyon, Director
Department of Human Services
600 S. 2nd Street, Suite 1B
Bismarck, ND 58504-5729
(701) 328-8964; (800) 207-6122 (in ND)
E-mail: cap@state.nd.us
Web: www.state.nd.us/cap

Programs for Children With Special Health Care Needs

Children's Special Health Services
Department of Human Services
State Capitol
Tamara Gallup-Millner, Unit Director
600 E. Boulevard Avenue, Department 325
Bismarck, ND 58505-0269
(701) 328-2436; (800) 755-2714 (in ND)
E-mail: dhscshs@state.nd.us
Web: www.state.nd.us/humanservices

State CHIP Program (health care for low-income, uninsured children)

Healthy Steps
Department 325
600 E. Boulevard Avenue
Bismarck, ND 58505-0250
(800) 755-2604
E-mail: somooa@state.nd.us
Web: www.state.nd.us/childrenshealth/

Programs for Children and Youth Who Are Deaf or Hard of Hearing

North Dakota School for the Deaf
Rocklyn Cofer, Superintendent
1401 College Drive North
Devils Lake, ND 58301
(701) 662-9000
E-mail: rocklyn.cofer@sendit.nodak.edu
Web: www.discovernd.com/ndsd

Telecommunications Relay Services for Individuals Who Are Deaf, Hard of Hearing, or With Speech Impairments

(800) 366-6889 (V)
(800) 366-6888 (TTY); 711 (TTY)
(877) 366-3709 (Speech to Speech)

Programs for Children and Youth Who Are Blind or Visually Impaired

North Dakota Vision Services–School for the Blind
Carmen Grove-Suminski, Superintendent
500 Stanford Road
Grand Forks, ND 58203
(701) 795-2708; (800) 421-1181
Web: www.ndvisionservices.com

Programs for Children and Youth Who Are Deaf-Blind

North Dakota Deaf-Blind Project
Linda Marsh, Project Coordinator
1401 College Drive North
Devils Lake, ND 58301
(701) 662-9001
E-mail: linda.marsh@sendit.nodak.edu
Web: www.state.nd.us/deafblind

State Education Agency Rural Representative

North Dakota Department of Public Instruction
Patricia A. Laubach, Programs Administrator
State Capitol
600 E. Boulevard Avenue, Department 201
Bismarck, ND 58505-0440
(701) 328-4525
E-mail: plaubach@state.nd.us
Web: www.dpi.state.nd.us

Regional ADA & IT Technical Assistance Center

Rocky Mountain Disability and Business Technical
*   Assistance Center*
Patrick Going, Director
3630 Sinton Road, Suite 103
Colorado Springs, CO 80907
(719) 444-0268 (V/TTY); (800) 949-4232 (V/
*   TTY)*
E-mail: rmdbtac@mtc-inc.com
Web: www.adainformation.org

University Center for Excellence in Developmental Disabilities

North Dakota Center for Persons with Disabilities
Minot State University
Bryce Fifield, Director
500 University Avenue West
Minot, ND 58707
(701) 858-3580; (800) 233-1737
E-mail: ndcpd@minotstateu.edu
Web: www.ndcpd.org

Technology-Related Assistance

North Dakota Interagency Program
*   for Assistive Technology*
Judie Lee, Project Director
3509 Interstate Boulevard
Fargo, ND 58103
(701) 265-4807 (V/TTY);
*   (800) 265-4728 (V/TTY)*
E-mail: jlee@polarcomm.com
Web: www.ndipat.org

State Mediation System

Department of Public Instruction
Office of Special Education
Teresa Monicken, Coordinator
State Capitol
600 E. Boulevard Avenue
Bismarck, ND 58505-0440
(701) 328-2277
E-mail: tmonicken@state.nd.us
Web: www.dpi.state.nd.us

Special Format Library

North Dakota State Library
Talking Book Services
Stella Cone, Librarian
604 E. Boulevard Avenue, Department 250
Bismarck, ND 58505-0800
(701) 328-1408; (800) 843-9948 (in ND)
(800) 892-8622 (TTY, in ND)
E-mail: tbooks@state.nd.us
Web: http://www.library.nd.gov/talkingbooks.
*   html*

North Dakota—Disability-Specific Organizations

Attention Deficit Disorder

To identify an ADD group in North Dakota, contact either of the following organizations:

Children and Adults with Attention-Deficit/
  Hyperactivity Disorder (CHADD)
8181 Professional Place, Suite 150
Landover, MD 20785
(301) 306-7070
(800) 233-4050 (Voice mail to request
  information packet)
Web: www.chadd.org

Attention Deficit Disorder Association (ADDA)
P.O. Box 543
Pottstown, PA 19464
(484) 945-2101
Web: www.add.org

Autism

To identify an autism group in North Dakota, contact

Autism Society of America
7910 Woodmont Avenue, Suite 300
Bethesda, MD 20814
(301) 657-0881; (800) 3-AUTISM
Web: www.autism-society.org

Blind/Visual Impairments

American Foundation for the Blind–Midwest
Jay Stiteley, Director
401 N. Michigan Avenue, Suite 350
Chicago, IL 60611
(312) 396-4420
E-mail: chicago@afb.net
Web: www.afb.org

Brain Injury

Brain Injury Association of North Dakota
Mary Simonson, Executive Director
Open Door Center
209 2nd Street SE
Valley City, ND 58072
(701) 845-1124

Epilepsy

To identify an epilepsy group in North Dakota, contact

Epilepsy Foundation of Minnesota
Bennie Loro, Executive Director
1600 University Avenue, Suite 205
St. Paul, MN 55104
(651) 287-2300; (800) 779-0777
E-mail: info@efmn.org
Web: www.efmn.org

Learning Disabilities

Learning Disabilities Association of North Dakota
Mary Ann M. Anderson, Co-President
409 3rd Avenue, NW
Mandan, ND 58554
(701) 663-1949

Learning Disabilities Association of North Dakota
Henri Heidt, Co-President
7840 Arcata Drive
Bismarck, ND 58503-6333
(701) 222-1490

Mental Health

Mental Health Association in North Dakota
Allan Stenehjem, Director
1051 E. Interstate Avenue
P.O. Box 4106
Bismarck, ND 58502-4106
(701) 255-3692; (800) 472-2911
E-mail: astenehjem@mhand.org
Web: www.mhand.org

Mental Retardation

The Arc, Upper Valley
The Arc of North Dakota
Dianne Sheppard, CEO
2500 DeMers Avenue
P.O. Box 12420
Grand Forks, ND 58208-2420
(701) 772-6191; (877) 250-2022
E-mail: thearc@arcuv.com
Web: www.thearcuppervalley.com

Special Health Care Needs

Family Voices of North Dakota, Inc.
Donene Feist, Director
312 2nd Avenue
P.O. Box 163
Edgeley, ND 58433
(701) 493-2634; (888) 522-9654
E-mail: feist@daktel.com
Web: www.geocities.com/ndfv

Speech and Hearing

North Dakota Speech-Language-Hearing
Association
Vicki Riedinger, President
1405 15th Avenue East
West Fargo, ND 58078
(701) 433-0880
E-mail: vicki.riedinger
@aegistherapies.com

North Dakota—Organizations Especially for Parents

Parent Training and Information Center (PTI)

Pathfinder Family Center
Kathryn Erickson, Director
1600 2nd Avenue, SW, Suite 19
Minot, ND 58701-3459
(701) 837-7500; (701) 837-7501 (TTY)
(800) 245-5840 (in ND)
E-mail: ndpath01@ndak.net
Web: www.pathfinder.minot.com

Parent-To-Parent

Family to Family Support Network
University of North Dakota School
of Medicine and Health Sciences
Center for Rural Health
Kathy Twite, Program Coordinator
P.O. Box 9037
Grand Forks, ND 58202-9037
(701) 777-2359; (888) 434-7436
E-mail: NDF2F@medicine.nodak.edu
Web: http://medicine.nodak.edu/crh

Partners in Policymaking

North Dakota Partners in Policymaking
Joyce Smith, Program Coordinator
Dakota CIL
3111 E. Broadway Avenue
Bismarck, ND 58501
(701) 222-3636; (800) 489-5013
E-mail: joyces@dakotacil.org
Web: www.dakotacil.org

North Dakota—Other Disability Organizations

Easter Seals Goodwill of North Dakota, Inc.
Gordon Hauge, Chief Executive Officer

211 Collins Avenue
P.O. Box 1206
Mandan, ND 58554
(701) 663-6828; (800) 247-0698
E-mail: ghauge@esgwnd.org

Independent Living

To find out the contact information for the Statewide Independent Living Council (SILC) in North Dakota, contact

Independent Living Research Utilization Project
The Institute for Rehabilitation and Research
2323 South Sheppard, Suite 1000
Houston, TX 77019
(713) 520-0232 (V); (713) 520-5136 (TTY)
E-mail: ilru@ilru.org
Web: www.ilru.org

To find out the contact information for centers for independent living (CILs) in North Dakota, contact

National Council on Independent Living
1916 Wilson Boulevard, Suite 209
Arlington, VA 22201
(703) 525-3406; (703) 525-4153 (TTY)
E-mail: ncil@ncil.org
Web: www.ncil.org

OHIO

Ohio—State Agencies and Organizations

United States Senators

Honorable Sherrod Brown (D)
713 Hart Senate Office Building
Washington, DC 20510
(202) 224-2315
(202) 228-1382 (Fax)
E-mail Web Form: http://www.brown.senate.
gov/contact/
Web: http://www.brown.senate.gov/

Honorable Rob Portman (R)
448 Russell Senate Office Building
Washington, DC 20510-3503
(202) 224-3353
(202) 224-6519 (Fax)
Web: http://www.portman.senate.gov/
public/index.cfm/home

United States Representatives

To find the contact information for your representative in the House of the U.S. Congress, visit the House's Web site at: www.house.gov, or call (202) 225-3121; (202) 225-1904 (TTY).

Governor

Honorable Bob Taft
77 S. High Street, 30th Floor
Columbus, OH 43215-6117
(614) 466-3555
E-mail Web Form: http://governor.ohio.gov/
   contactinfopage.asp
Web: http://governor.ohio.gov/

Official State Web Site

Web: http://ohio.gov/

State Department of Education: Special Education

Office for Exceptional Children
Ohio Department of Education
Thomas Scheid, Director
25 S. Front Street, 2nd Floor
Columbus, OH 43215
E-mail: thomas.scheid@ode.state.oh.us
Web: www.ode.state.oh.us

State Coordinator for NCLB (No Child Left Behind)

Ohio was granted an extended waiver from the NCLB act.

Jeremy S. Marks
Federal Programs
Ohio Department of Education
25 South Front Street
Columbus, Ohio
43215-4183
(614) 466-5834
Email: jeremy.marks@education.ohio.gov
Web: http://education.ohio.gov/Topics/
   School-Improvement/Federal-Programs

Programs for Infants and Toddlers With Disabilities: Birth–2 Years

Bureau of Early Intervention Services
Wendy Grover, Part C Coordinator
State Department of Health
246 North High Street, 5th Floor
P.O. Box 118
Columbus, OH 43266
(614) 728-9152
E-mail: wendy.grove@odh.ohio.gov
Web: http://www.helpmegrow.ohio.gov/
   en/Early%20Intervention/Early%20
   Intervention.aspx

Programs for Children With Disabilities: 3–5 Years

Office of Early Learning and School Readiness
Barbara Weinberg, 619 Coordinator
Ohio Department of Education
25 S. Front Street, Mail Stop 305
Columbus, OH 43215
(614) 387-2239; (614) 466-0224
E-mail: barbara.weinberg@ode.state.oh.us
Web: http://education.ohio.gov/Topics/Early-
   Learning/Preschool-Special-Education

State Vocational Rehabilitation Agency

Rehabilitation Services Commission
John M. Connelly, Executive Director
400 E. Campus View Boulevard, SW3
Columbus, OH 43235-4604
(614) 438-1210 (V/TTY)
E-mail: john.connelly@rsc.state.oh.us
Web: www.state.oh.us/rsc

Coordinator for Transition Services

Lawrence Dennis, Educational
   Consultant/Project Life
Ohio Department of Education
Office for Exceptional Children
25 S. Front Street, 2nd Floor
Columbus, OH 43215-4183
(614) 466-2650
E-mail: lawrence.dennis@ode.state.oh.us
Web: http://education.ohio.gov/Topics/
   Special-Education/Federal-and-State-
   Requirements/Secondary-Transition-
   Planning-for-Students-with-Di

**Office of State Coordinator
of Vocational Education
for Students With Disabilities**

Office for Exceptional Children
Joyce Brouman, Educational Consultant
Ohio Department of Education
Office of Career-Technical and Adult Education
25 S. Front Street, Suite 202
Columbus, OH 43235
(614) 728-1105
E-mail: joyce.brouman@ode.state.oh.us
Web: www.ode.state.oh.us

State Mental Health Agency

Ohio Department of Mental Health
Michael F. Hogan, PhD, Director
30 E. Broad Street, 8th Floor
Columbus, OH 43215-3430
(614) 466-2596
E-mail: hoganm@mh.state.oh.us
Web: www.mh.state.oh.us

**State Mental Health
Representative for
Children and Youth**

Kay Rietz, Assistant Deputy Director
Sharon Aungst, Assistant Deputy Director
Office of Children's Services and Prevention
Ohio Department of Mental Health
30 E. Broad Street, 8th Floor
Columbus, OH 43215-3430
(614) 466-1984
E-mail: rietzk@mh.state.oh.us
E-mail: aungsts@mh.state.oh.us
Web: www.mh.state.oh.us

State Mental Retardation Program

Ohio Department of Mental Retardation/
   Developmental Disabilities
Kenneth W. Ritchey, Director
1810 Sullivant Avenue
Columbus, OH 43223-1239
(614) 466-5214
Web: www.state.oh.us/dmr

Council on Developmental Disabilities

Ohio Developmental Disabilities Council
David Zwyer, Executive Director
8 E. Long Street, Atlas Building, 12th Floor
Columbus, OH 43215
(614) 466-5205
E-mail: david.zwyer@dmr.state.oh.us
Web: www.ddc.ohio.gov

Protection and Advocacy Agency

Ohio Legal Rights Services
Carolyn S. Knight, Executive Director
8 E. Long Street, 5th Floor
Columbus, OH 43215-2999
(614) 466-7264; (614) 728-2553 (TTY)
(800) 282-9181 (in OH)
E-mail: WebMaster@olrs.state.oh.us
Web: www.state.oh.us/olrs/

Client Assistance Program

Ohio Legal Rights Services
Carolyn S. Knight, Executive Director
8 E. Long Street, 5th Floor
Columbus, OH 43215-2999
(614) 466-7264; (614) 728-2553 (TTY)
(800) 282-9181 (in OH)
E-mail: WebMaster@olrs.state.oh.us
Web: www.state.oh.us/olrs/

**Programs for Children With
Special Health Care Needs**

Bureau for Children with Medical Handicaps
James Bryant, MD, Chief
Ohio Department of Health
246 N. High Street
P.O. Box 118
Columbus, OH 43215
(614) 466-1549; (800) 755-4769 (parents only)
E-mail: JBryant@odh.ohio.gov
Web: www.odh.state.oh.us

**State CHIP Program (health care
for low-income, uninsured children)**

Healthy Start Healthy Families
(800) 324-8680; (800) 292-3572 (TTY)
   Consumer Hotline
Web: http://medicaid.ohio.gov/
   FOROHIOANS/Programs.aspx#62373-
   children-families-and-women

Programs for Children and Youth Who Are Blind or Visually Impaired, Deaf or Hard of Hearing, or Deaf-Blind

Rehabilitation Services Commission
John Connelly, Executive Director
400 E. Campus View Boulevard
Columbus, OH 43235-4604
(614) 438-1200; (800) 282-4536 (in OH)
Web: www.state.oh.us/rsc

Telecommunications Relay Services for Individuals Who Are Deaf, Hard of Hearing, or With Speech Impairments

(800) 750-0750 (V)
(216) 476-6001 (V/TTY); 711 (TTY)
(877) 750-9097 (Speech to Speech)

State Education Agency Rural Representative

Michael Armstrong, Director
Office for Exceptional Children
Ohio Department of Education
25 S. Front Street, 2nd Floor
Columbus, OH 43215
(614) 466-2650
E-mail: mike.armstrong@ode.state.oh.us
Web: www.ode.state.oh.us/ exceptional_children/

Regional ADA & IT Technical Assistance Center

Great Lakes ADA and Accessible IT Center
Robin Jones, Director
University of Illinois/Chicago
Institute on Disability and Human Development
1640 W. Roosevelt Road
Chicago, IL 60608-6902
(312) 413-1407 (V/TTY); (800) 949-4232 (V/TTY)
E-mail: gldbtac@uic.edu
Web: www.adagreatlakes.org

University Center for Excellence in Developmental Disabilities

Division of Developmental Disabilities
Sonya Oppenheimer, MD, Director
Cincinnati Children's Hospital Medical Center
3333 Burnet Avenue
Cincinnati, OH 45229-3939
(513) 636-8383
E-mail: sonya.oppenheimer@cchmc.org
Web: www.cincinnatichildrens.org/svc/ dept-div/disabilities/default.htm

University Center for Excellence in Developmental Disabilities

Steven Reiss, Director
Ohio State University
357B McCampbell Hall
1581 Dodd Drive
Columbus, OH 43210
(614) 292-2390
Web: http://nisonger.osu.edu

Technology-Related Assistance

Assistive Technology of Ohio
Bill Darling, Interim Director
445 E. Dublin-Granville Road, Building L
Worthington, OH 43085
(614) 293-9134; (800) 784-3425 (V/TTY, in OH)
E-mail: atohi003@osu.edu
Web: www.atohio.org

State Mediation System

Office for Exceptional Children
Nabil Sharabi, Coordinator
Ohio Department of Education
25 S. Front Street, 2nd Floor
Columbus, OH 43215
(614) 466-2650
E-mail: bill.sharabi@ode.state.oh.us
Web: www.ode.state.oh.us

Special Format Library

Library for the Blind and Physically Handicapped
Donna Foust, Librarian
The Public Library of Cincinnati and Hamilton County
800 Vine Street, Library Square
Cincinnati, OH 45202-2071
(513) 369-6999; (800) 582-0335
(513) 369-3372 (TTY)
E-mail: lfb@cincinnatilibrary.org
Web: www.cincinnatilibrary. org/main/lb.asp

Ohio—Disability-Specific Organizations

Attention Deficit Disorder

To identify an ADD group in Ohio, contact either of the following organizations:

Children and Adults with Attention-Deficit/
Hyperactivity Disorder (CHADD)
8181 Professional Place, Suite 150
Landover, MD 20785
(301) 306-7070
(800) 233-4050 (Voice mail to request
information packet)
Web: www.chadd.org

Attention Deficit Disorder Association (ADDA)
P.O. Box 543
Pottstown, PA 19464
(484) 945-2101
Web: www.add.org

Autism

To identify an autism group in Ohio, contact

Autism Society of America
7910 Woodmont Avenue, Suite 300
Bethesda, MD 20814
(301) 657-0881; (800) 3-AUTISM
Web: www.autism-society.org

Blind/Visual Impairments

American Foundation for the Blind—Midwest
Jay Stiteley, Director
401 North Michigan Avenue, Suite 350
Chicago, IL 60611
(312) 396-4420
E-mail: chicago@afb.net
Web: www.afb.org

Brain Injury

Brain Injury Association of Ohio
Suzanne Minnich, Executive Director
1335 Dublin Road, Suite 217D
Columbus, OH 43215-1000
(614) 481-7100; (866) 644-6242 (in OH)
E-mail: help@biaoh.org
Web: www.biaoh.org

Cerebral Palsy

Cerebral Palsy Association of Ohio, Inc.
Beverly Johnson, Executive Director
4550 Indianola Avenue
Columbus, OH 43214-2246
(614) 267-5071; (800) 796-8498
E-mail: cpo@iwaynet.net

Down Syndrome

Down Syndrome Association of Central Ohio
2879 Johnstown Road
Columbus, OH 43219
(614) 475-6440, ext. 311
E-mail: office@dsaco.net
Web: www.dsaco.net

Epilepsy

Epilepsy Association
Kelley Needham, Executive Director
2800 Euclid Avenue, Room 450
Cleveland, OH 44115
(216) 579-1330; (800) 653-4300
E-mail: info@epilepsyinfo.org
Web: www.epilepsyinfo.org

Mental Health

NAMI Ohio
Terry Russell, Executive Director
747 E. Broad Street
Columbus, OH 43205
(614) 224-2700; (800) 686-2646
(866) 924-1478 (TTY)
E-mail: amiohio@amiohio.org
Web: www.namiohio.org

Mental Retardation/ Developmental Disabilities

The Arc of Ohio
Gary Tonks, Executive Director
1335 Dublin Road, Suite 205-C
Columbus, OH 43215
(614) 487-4720; (800) 875-2723
E-mail: Info@TheArcofOhio.org
Web: www.thearcofohio.org

Speech and Hearing

Ohio Speech-Language-Hearing Association
Nancy Bailey, Executive Director
P.O. Box 309
Germantown, OH 45327
(800) 866-6742
E-mail: OSLHAoffice@donet.com
Web: www.ohioslha.org

Tourette Syndrome

Tourette Syndrome Association of Ohio
P.O. Box 28345
Columbus, OH 43228
(614) 272-1824; (800) 543-2675 (in OH)
E-mail: admin@tsaohio.org
Web: www.tsaohio.org

Ohio—Organizations Especially for Parents

Parent Training and Information Center (PTI)

Ohio Coalition for the Education of
    Children with Disabilities
Margaret Burley, Executive Director
Bank One Building
165 W. Center Street, Suite 302
Marion, OH 43302-3741
(740) 382-5452
(800) 374-2806
E-mail: ocecd@gte.net
Web: www.ocecd.org

Parent Teacher Association (PTA)

Ohio Congress of Parents and Teachers
Barbara Sprague, Executive Director
40 Northwoods Boulevard, Suite A
Columbus, OH 43235
(614) 781-6344
E-mail: oh_office@pta.org
Web: www.ohiopta.org

Other Parent Organization

Educational Advocacy Services Memorial Inc.
Cathy Heizman, Director
3000 Vernon Place
Cincinnati, OH 45219
(513) 621-3032
E-mail: cheizman@memorialinc.com
Web: www.memorialinc.com

Ohio—Other Disability Organizations

Easter Seals Northeast Ohio
Sheila M. Dunn, President
1929A E. Royalton Road
Cleveland, OH 44147
(440) 838-0990 (V/TTY); (888) 325-8532
E-mail: info@eastersealsneo.org
Web: www.eastersealsneo.org

Easter Seals Central and Southeast Ohio
Karen Zuckerman, CEO
565 Children's Drive West
P.O. Box 7166
Columbus, OH 43205
(614) 228-5523
Web: www.eastersealscentralohio.org

Ohio Association of Pupil Services
    Administrators (OAPSA)
Dr. John Opperman, Communications Officer
3880 Ridge Road
Medina, OH 44256
(330) 239-1901, ext. 1226
E-mail: opperman@highlandschools.org
Web: www.highlandschools.org/oapsa

Ohio Family and Children First Initiative
Jessie Cannon, Chief of Staff
30 E. Broad Street, 34th Floor
Columbus, OH 43215
(614) 752-4044
E-mail: info@ohiofcf.org
Web: www.ohiofcf.org

VSA Arts of Ohio
Kimberly Murray, Executive Director
77 S. High Street, 2nd Floor
Riffe Center for Government and the Arts
Columbus, OH 43215
(614) 241-5325
E-mail: info@vsao.org
Web: www.vsao.org

Independent Living

To find out the contact information for the
Statewide Independent Living Council (SILC)
in Ohio, contact

Independent Living Research Utilization Project
The Institute for Rehabilitation and Research
2323 South Sheppard, Suite 1000
Houston, TX 77019
(713) 520-0232 (V); (713) 520-5136 (TTY)
E-mail: ilru@ilru.org
Web: www.ilru.org

To find out the contact information for centers for independent living (CILs) in Ohio, contact

National Council on Independent Living
1916 Wilson Boulevard, Suite 209
Arlington, VA 22201
(703) 525-3406; (703) 525-4153 (TTY)
E-mail: ncil@ncil.org
Web: www.ncil.org

OKLAHOMA

Oklahoma—State Agencies and Organizations

United States Senators

Honorable Tom Coburn (R)
172 Russell Senate Office Building
Washington, DC 20510
(202) 224-5754
(202) 224-6008 (Fax)
Web: http://coburn.senate.gov/

Honorable James M. Inhofe (R)
205 Russell Senate Office Building
Washington, DC 20510-3603
(202) 224-4721
(202) 228-0380 (Fax)
E-mail Web Form: http://inhofe.senate.gov/
contactus.htm
Web: http://inhofe.senate.gov

United States Representatives

To find the contact information for your representative in the House of the U.S. Congress, visit the House's Web site at: *www.house.gov*, or call (202) 225-3121; (202) 225-1904 (TTY).

Governor

Honorable Mary Fallin
Governor's Office
State Capitol Building
2300 N. Lincoln Boulevard, Suite 212
Oklahoma City, OK 73105
(405) 521-2342; (405) 521-3353 (Fax)
E-mail: governor@gov.state.ok.us
Web: http://www.ok.gov/governor/

Official State Web Site

Web: www.ok.gov

State Department of Education: Special Education

Special Education Services
Department of Education
Misty Kimbrough, Assistant State
Superintendent
2500 N. Lincoln Boulevard, Suite 412
Oklahoma City, OK 73105-4599
(405) 521-4873
E-mail: misty_kimbrough@sde.state.ok.us
Web: www.sde.state.ok.us

State Coordinator for NCLB (No Child Left Behind)

School Improvement, Office of Standards and
Curriculum
Liz Young, Executive Assistant to the
Superintendent
Department of Education
2500 N. Lincoln Boulevard, Suite 315
Oklahoma City, OK 73105-4599
(405) 521-3301
E-mail: Liz.young@sde.ok.gov
Web: www.sde.state.ok.us

Programs for Infants and Toddlers With Disabilities: Birth–2 Years

Sooner Start/Early Intervention Services
Mark Sharp, Associate Director
Special Education Services
Department of Education
Oliver Hodge Memorial Education Building,
4th Floor
2500 N. Lincoln Boulevard
Oklahoma City, OK 73105-4599
(405) 521-4880
E-mail: mark_sharp@sde.state.ok.us
Web: http://ok.gov/sde/soonerstart

**Programs for Children
With Disabilities: 3–5 Years**

Sooner Start/Early Intervention Services
Michelle Reeves, 619 Coordinator
Special Education Services
State Department of Education
2500 North Lincoln Boulevard
Oklahoma City, OK 73105
(405) 522-4513
E-mail: michelle.reeves@sde.ok.gov
Web: http://ok.gov/sde/early-childhood-
    special-education

State Vocational Rehabilitation Agency

Department of Rehabilitation Services
Linda S. Parker, Director
3535 NW 58th, Suite 500
Oklahoma City, OK 73112
(405) 951-3400; (800) 845-8476
E-mail: lparker@drs.state.ok.us

Coordinator for Transition Services

Jodi Hanson, Associate Director
Special Education Services
Department of Education
2500 N. Lincoln Boulevard, Suite 412
Oklahoma City, OK 73105-4599
(405) 522-1464
E-mail: jodi_hanson@sde.state.ok.us
Web: www.sde.state.ok.us

**Oklahoma Department of
Career and Technology Education**

Department of Career and Technology
Denise North, Disabilities Services Specialist
1500 W. 7th Avenue
Stillwater, OK 74074-4364
(405) 377-2000 (Ext. 138); (405) 743-5138
(800) 522-5810, ext. 138; (405) 743-6816 (TTY)
E-mail: dnort@okcareertech.org
Web: http://okcareertech.org

State Mental Health Agency

Department of Mental Health and
    Substance Abuse Services
Terry L. Cline, PhD, Commissioner
P.O. Box 53277
Oklahoma City, OK 73152-3277
(405) 522-3878
E-mail: tcline@odmhsas.org
Web: www.odmhsas.org

**State Mental Health Representative
for Children and Youth**

Children Services
Jackie Shipp, Coordinator
Department of Mental Health and Substance
    Abuse Services
P.O. Box 53277
Oklahoma City, OK 73152
(405) 522-4142
E-mail: jshipp@odmhsas.org

State Mental Retardation Program

Developmental Disabilities Services
Jim Nicholson, Division Director
Department of Human Services
P.O. Box 25352
Oklahoma City, OK 73125
(405) 521-3571
E-mail: james.nicholson@okdhs.org
Web: www.okdhs.org/ddsd

Council on Developmental Disabilities

Oklahoma Developmental Disabilities Council
Ann Trudgeon, Director
2401 NW 23rd Street, Suite 74
Oklahoma City, OK 73107
(405) 521-4984; (800) 836-4470
E-mail: OPCDD@aol.com
Web: www.okddc.ok.gov

Protection and Advocacy Agency

Oklahoma Disability Law Center, Inc.
Kayla A. Bower, JD, Executive Director
2915 Classen Boulevard
300 Cameron Building
Oklahoma City, OK 73106
(405) 525-7755 (V/TTY);
    (800) 880-7755 (V/TTY, in OK)
E-mail: kayla@justice.com
Web: www.oklahomadisabilitylaw.org
Web: www.redlands-partners.org
Web: www.idea-504.info

Oklahoma Disability Law Center, Inc.
Kayla A. Bower, JD, Executive Director
2828 E. 51st Street, Suite 302
Tulsa, OK 74105
(918) 743-6220 (V/TTY); (800) 226-5883
(V/TTY, in OK)
E-mail: kayla@justice.com
Web: www.oklahomadisabilitylaw.org
Web: www.redlands-partners.org
Web: www.idea-504.info

Client Assistance Program

Client Assistance Program
Office of Handicapped Concerns
James O. Sirmans, Director
2401 NW 23rd, Suite 90
Oklahoma City, OK 73107
(405) 521-3756; (800) 522-8224
(800) 522-8506 Relay: 711 (TTY)
Web: www.ohc.state.ok.us/

Programs for Children With Special Health Care Needs

Family Support Services
Mary Stalnacker, Director
Department of Human Services
P.O. Box 25352
Oklahoma City, OK 73125
(405) 521-3076
Web: http://okdhs.org

State CHIP Program health care for low-income, uninsured children)

Oklahoma Health Care Authority
(405) 522-6205; (800) 522-0114
Web: http://www.okhca.org/individuals.
aspx?id=124

Programs for Children and Youth Who Are Blind or Visually Impaired

Oklahoma School for the Blind
Department of Rehabilitation Services
Karen Kizzia, Superintendent
3300 Gibson
Muskogee, OK 74403
(918) 781-8200
E-mail: kekizzia@drs.state.ok.us

Programs for Children and Youth Who Are Deaf or Hard of Hearing

Oklahoma School for the Deaf
Department of Rehabilitation Services
Larry Hawkins, Superintendent
1100 E. Oklahoma Street
Sulphur, OK 73086-3108
(580) 622-4900; (888) 685-3323
E-mail: lhawkins@osd.k12.ok.us
Web: www.osd.k12.ok.us

Programs for Children and Youth Who Are Deaf-Blind

Oklahoma Deaf-Blind Technical Assistance Project
Jan Watts, Project Coordinator
University of Oklahoma
820 Van Vleet Oval
Norman, OK 73072
(405) 325-0441
E-mail: jwatts@ou.edu
Web: www.ou.edu/okdbp

Programs for Children and Youth Who Are Deaf or Hard of Hearing

Oklahoma School for the Deaf
Larry Hawkins, Superintendent
1100 E. Oklahoma Street
Sulphur, OK 73086-3108
(580) 622-4200
E-mail: lhawkins@osd.k12.ok.us

Telecommunications Relay Services for Individuals Who Are Deaf, Hard of Hearing, or With Speech Impairments

(800) 522-8506 (V/TTY)
(800) 722-0353 (V/TTY); 711 (TTY)
(877) 722-3515 (Speech to Speech)

Regional ADA & IT Technical Assistance Center

Disability Law Resource Project
Wendy Wilkinson, Director
2323 S. Shepard Boulevard, Suite 1000
Houston, TX 77019
(713) 520-0232 (V/TTY);
(800) 949-4232 (V/TTY)
E-mail: dlrp@ilru.org
Web: www.dlrp.org

University Center for Excellence in Developmental Disabilities

Center for Learning and Leadership/UCEDD
Valerie N. Williams, Director
University of Oklahoma
    Health Sciences Center
College of Medicine
P.O. Box 26901, ROB 342
Oklahoma City, OK 73190-3042
(405) 271-4500, ext 41017; (405) 271-1464 (TTY)
E-mail: valerie-williams@ouhsc.edu
Web: http://w3.ouhsc.edu/thecenter

Projects of National Significance in Family Support

Oklahoma Family Support Partnership Project
Vyonda G. Martin, Project Director
Center for Learning and Leadership/UCEDD
University of Oklahoma Health Sciences Center
College of Medicine
P.O. Box 26901, ROB 342
Oklahoma City, OK 73190
(405) 271-4500, ext. 41005; (405) 271-1464 (TTY)
E-mail: vyonda-martin@ouhsc.edu

Oklahoma Family 360 Project
Tara Lozano, Project Coordinator
Center for Learning and Leadership/UCEDD
University of Oklahoma
    Health Sciences Center
College of Medicine
P.O. Box 26901, ROB 342
Oklahoma City, OK 73190
(504) 271-4500, ext 41006; (405) 271-1464 (TTY)
E-mail: tara-lozano@ouhsc.edu

Technology-Related Assistance

Oklahoma ABLE Tech
Oklahoma State University,
    Seretean Wellness Center
Linda Jaco, Project Manager
1514 W. Hall of Fame
Stillwater, OK 74078-2026
(405) 744-9864; (800) 257-1705 (V/TTY)
(888) 885-5588 (ABLE Tech Info-line)
E-mail: mljwell@okstate.edu
Web: http://okabletech.okstate.edu

State Mediation System

Administrative Office of the Supreme Court of
    Oklahoma
Sue Darst Tate, Director
1915 N. Stiles, Suite 305
Oklahoma City, OK 73105
(405) 522-7876
E-mail: sue.tate@oscn.net
Web: www.oscn.net/static/adr/start.asp

Special Format Library

Oklahoma Library for the Blind and Physically
    Handicapped
Geraldine Adams, Librarian
Department of Rehabilitation Services
300 NE 18th Street
Oklahoma City, OK 73105
(405) 521-3514; (405) 522-0516
(800) 523-0288; (405) 521-4672 (TTY)
E-mail: olbph@oltn.odl.state.ok.us
Web: www.library.state.ok.us

Oklahoma—Disability-Specific Organizations

Attention Deficit Disorder

    To identify an ADD group in Oklahoma,
contact either of the following organizations:

Children and Adults with Attention-Deficit/
    Hyperactivity Disorder (CHADD)
8181 Professional Place, Suite 150
Landover, MD 20785
(301) 306-7070
(800) 233-4050 (Voice mail to request
    information packet)
Web: www.chadd.org

Attention Deficit Disorder Association (ADDA)
P.O. Box 543
Pottstown, PA 19464
(484) 945-2101
Web: www.add.org

Autism

    To identify an autism group in Oklahoma
contact

Autism Society of America
7910 Woodmont Avenue, Suite 300
Bethesda, MD 20814
(301) 657-0881; (800) 3-AUTISM
Web: www.autism-society.org

Blind/Visual Impairments

American Foundation for the Blind–Southwest
Judy Scott, Director
11030 Ables Lane
Dallas, TX 75229
(214) 352-7222
E-mail: dallas@afb.net
Web: www.afb.org

Brain Injury

Brain Injury Association of Oklahoma, Inc.
Tracy Grammer, Chair
P.O. Box 88
Hillsdale, OK 73743-0088
E-mail: biaok@earthlink.net
Web: www.braininjuryoklahoma.org

Cerebral Palsy

United Cerebral Palsy of Oklahoma
Jim Rankin, Executive Director
5208 W. Reno Street, Suite 275
Oklahoma City, OK 73127
(405) 917-7080
E-mail: oklahoma@ucpok.org
Web: www.ucpok.org

Developmental Disabilities

TARC
John Gajda, Executive Director
16 E. 16th Street, Suite 405
Tulsa, OK 74119-4447
(918) 582-8272; (800) 688-8272
(outside Tulsa only)
E-mail: tarc@ddadvocacy.net
Web: www.ddadvocacy.net

Epilepsy

Epilepsy Association of Oklahoma
711 Stanton L. Young Boulevard, Suite 550
Oklahoma City, OK 73104
(405) 271-3232
E-mail: epilepsy-ok@prodigy.net
Web: http://www.okepilepsy.org/

Learning Disabilities

Learning Disabilities Association of Oklahoma
Joy Modenbach, President
P.O. Box 1134
Jenks, OK 74037
(918) 298-1600; (800) 532-6365 (in OK)
E-mail: ldao@sbcglobal.net
Web: www.epilepsy-ok.org

Mental Health

Mental Health Association in Oklahoma County
Charlotte New, Executive Director
5104 N. Francis, Suite B
Oklahoma City, OK 73118
(405) 843-9900
E-mail: mentalhealth@coxinet.net

NAMI Oklahoma
500 N. Broadway, Suite 100
Oklahoma City, OK 73102
(405) 230-1900; (800) 583-1264 (in OK)
E-mail: nami-ok@swbell.net
Web: http://ok.nami.org/

Oklahoma Parents as Partners
Melody Ruth Andrews, Executive Director
132 NW 13th Street
Oklahoma City, OK 73103
(405) 232-2796; (866) 492-KIDS
E-mail: parentsaspartners@coxinet.net
Web: www.ffcmh-ok.org/

Special Health Care Needs

Family Voices
Lyn Thoreson Land, State Coordinator
P.O. Box 32255
Oklahoma City, OK 73123
(405) 271-9444, ext. 56910; (800) 766-2223,
ext. 56910 (in OK)
E-mail: okvoices@aol.com
Web: http://OKVoices.org

Speech and Hearing

Oklahoma Speech-Language-Hearing Association
Jeannie McEachin Long, President
P.O. Box 53217
Oklahoma City, OK 73152-3217
(405) 769-7329
E-mail: oslha@hotmail.com
Web: www.oslha.org

Spina Bifida

Spina Bifida Association of Oklahoma
P.O. Box 271675
Oklahoma City, OK 73137
(405) 789-7056
E-mail: victoryonthethirdday@cox.net

Oklahoma—Organizations Especially for Parents

Parent Training and Information Center (PTI)

Oklahoma Parents Center
Sharon Bishop, Executive Director
4600 SE 29th, Suite 115
Del City, OK 73115-4224
(405) 619-0500; (877) 553-4332
E-mail: okparentctr@aol.com
Web: www.okparents.org

Parent Teacher Association (PTA)

Oklahoma Congress of Parents and Teachers, Inc.
Lois Breedlove, President
2801 N. Lincoln Boulevard, Suite 214
Oklahoma City, OK 73105
(405) 681-0750
E-mail: ok_office@pta.org
Web: www.okpta.org

State Information and Referral Service

Oklahoma Areawide Service Information System
    (OASIS)
Madalyn McCollom, Director
University of Oklahoma Health Sciences Center
1122 NE 13th, Room EB-102
Oklahoma City, OK 73118
(405) 271-6302 (V/TTY; 800-42-OASIS (V/TTY)
E-mail: madalyn-mccollom@ouhsc.edu
Web: http://oasis.ouhsc.edu

Other Parent Organizations

Oklahoma Family Network
Joni Bruce, Executive Director
P.O. Box 21072
Oklahoma City, OK 73156-1072
(405) 203-8745
E-mail: jbruceofn@sbcglobal.net
Web: www.oklahomafamilynetwork.org

Oklahoma—Other Disability Organizations

Easter Seals Oklahoma
Patricia Filer, President
701 NE 13th Street
Oklahoma City, OK 73104
(405) 239-2525
E-mail: esok1@coxinet.net
Web: www.eastersealsoklahoma.org

J. D. McCarty Center for Children with
    Developmental Disabilities
Curt Peters, Director & CEO
2002 E. Robinson Street
Norman, OK 73071
(405) 307-2800
E-mail: curt@jdmc.org
Web: www.jdmc.org

Oklahoma Office of Handicapped Concerns
Steve Stokes, Director
2401 NW 23rd, Suite 90
Oklahoma City, OK 73107
(405) 521-3756; (800) 522-8224
Web: www.ohc.state.ok.us/

Independent Living

To find out the contact information for the Statewide Independent Living Council (SILC) in Oklahoma, contact

Independent Living Research Utilization Project
The Institute for Rehabilitation and Research
2323 South Sheppard, Suite 1000
Houston, TX 77019
(713) 520-0232 (V); (713) 520-5136 (TTY)
E-mail: ilru@ilru.org
Web: www.ilru.org

To find out the contact information for centers for independent living (CILs) in Oklahoma, contact

National Council on Independent Living
1916 Wilson Boulevard, Suite 209
Arlington, VA 22201
(703) 525-3406; (703) 525-4153 (TTY)
E-mail: ncil@ncil.org
Web: www.ncil.org

OREGON

Oregon—State Agencies and Organizations

United States Senators

Honorable Jeff Merkley (D)
313 Hart Senate Office Building
Washington, DC 20510
(202) 224-3753
(202) 224-3997 (Fax)
E-mail Web Form: http://www.merkley.
*   senate.gov/contact/*
Web: http://www.merkley.senate.gov/

Honorable Ron Wyden (D)
221 Dirksen Senate Office Building
Washington, DC 20510
(202) 224-5244
(202) 228-2717 (Fax)
E-mail Web Form: http://wyden.senate.gov/
*   contact.html*
Web: http://wyden.senate.gov

United States Representatives

To find the contact information for your representative in the House of the U.S. Congress, visit the House's Web site at: www.house.gov, or call (202) 225-3121; (202) 225-1904 (TTY).

Governor

Honorable John Kitzhaber
160 State Capitol
900 Court Street
Salem, OR 97301-4047
(503) 378-4582; (503) 378-6827 (Fax)
Web: http://www.oregon.gov/Gov/Pages/
*   about.aspx*

Official State Web Site

Web: www.oregon.gov/

State Department of Education: Special Education

Office of Student Learning and Partnerships
Nancy J. Latini, PhD, Associate Superintendent
Department of Education
255 Capitol Street NE
Salem, OR 97310-0203
(503) 947-5600
E-mail: nancy.latini@state.or.us
Web: www.ode.state.or.us

State Coordinator for NCLB (No Child Left Behind)

Oregon was granted an extended waiver from the NCLB act.

Dave Cook, Interim Director
Federal Systems
Oregon Department of Education
255 Capitol Street NE
Salem, OR 97310-0203
(503) 947-5915
Email: dave.cook@ode.state.or.us
Web: http://www.ode.state.or.us/search/
*   results/?id=95*

Programs for Infants and Toddlers With Disabilities: Birth–5 Years

Early Intervention/Early Childhood Special
*   Education Department*
Nancy Johnson-Dorn, Part C Coordinator
Office of Special Education
Department of Education
255 Capitol Street NE
Salem, OR 97310-0203
(503) 947-5703; (503) 378-2892 (TTY)
E-mail: nancy.johnson-dorn@state.or.us
Web: http://www.ode.state.or.us/search/
*   results/?id=252*

State Vocational Rehabilitation Agency

Office of Vocational Rehabilitation Services
Stephaine Parrish-Taylor, Administrator
Department of Human Services, Children,
*   Adults & Families*
500 Summer Street NE, E87
Salem, OR 97301-1120
(503) 945-5880 (V); (503) 945-5894 (TTY)
E-mail: eugenia.cox@state.or.us
Web: www.dhs.state.or.us/vr

Coordinator for Transition Services

Jackie Burr, Transition Specialist
Office of Special Education
Department of Education
255 Capitol Street NE
Salem, OR 97310
(503) 378-3600, ext. 2335
E-mail: jackie.burr@state.or.us
Web: www.ode.state.or.us

State Mental Health Agency

Office of Mental Health and Addiction Services
Bob Nikkel, Administrator
500 Summer Street, NE, E86
Salem, OR 97301-1118
(503) 945-9704
Web: www.dhs.state.or.us/mentalhealth

State Mental Health Representative for Children and Youth

Bill Bouska, MPA, Team Leader
Children's Treatment System
Office of Mental Health and Addiction Services
500 Summer Street, NE, E86
Salem, OR 97301-1118
(503) 945-9717
E-mail: bill.bouska@state.or.us
Web: www.dhs.state.or.us/mentalhealth

State Mental Retardation Program

Seniors and People with Disabilities
James D. Toews, Deputy Assistant Director
Department of Human Services
500 Summer Street NE, Suite E02
Salem, OR 97301-1073
(503) 945-6478
E-mail: james.d.toews@state.or.us
Web: www.dhs.state.or.us/seniors/

Council on Developmental Disabilities

Oregon Council on Developmental Disabilities
Bill Lynch, Executive Director
540 24th Place NE
Salem, OR 97301-4517
(503) 945-9941; (800) 292-4154 (in OR)
E-mail: OCDD@ocdd.org
Web: www.ocdd.org

Protection and Advocacy Agency

Oregon Advocacy Center
Robert Joondeph, Executive Director
620 SW 5th Avenue, Suite 500
Portland, OR 97204-1428
(503) 243-2081; (503) 323-9161 (TTY)
(800) 452-1694
E-mail: welcome@oradvocacy.org
Web: www.oradvocacy.org/

Client Assistance Program

Oregon Disabilities Commission
Danielle Knight, Executive Director

1257 Ferry Street SE
Salem, OR 97301
(503) 378-3142 (V/TTY); (800) 358-3117
E-mail: danielle.knight@state.or.us
Web: www.odc.state.or.us

Programs for Children With Special Health Care Needs

Child Development and Rehabilitation Center
Brian Rogers, MD, Director
Oregon Health & Science University
P.O. Box 574
Portland, OR 97207-0574
(503) 494-8362
Web: http://cdrc.ohsu.edu/

State CHIP Program (health care for low-income, uninsured children)

Oregon SCHIP
Oregon Department of Human Services
Health Services: Office of Medical Assistance
    Programs
500 Summer Street, NE E49
Salem, OR 97301
(503) 945-5772; (800) 527-5772
(800) 375-2863
Web: www.dhs.state.or.us/healthplan/
    app_benefits/schip.html

Programs for Children and Youth Who Are Blind or Visually Impaired or Deaf-Blind

Regional Programs for Low Incidence Disabilities
Jay Gense, Director
Department of Education
255 Capitol Street, NE
Salem, OR 97310-0203
(503) 378-3600, ext. 2325
Web: www.ode.state.or.us

Vocational Rehabilitation Programs for Youth and Adults Who Are Blind, Visually Impaired or Deaf-Blind

Oregon Commission for the Blind
Linda Mock, Administrator
535 SE 12th Avenue
Portland, OR 97214
(503) 731-3221; (888) 202-5463
E-mail: ocbmail@state.or.us
Web: www.CFB.state.or.us

Programs for Children and Youth Who Are Deaf or Hard of Hearing

Deaf and Hard of Hearing Access Program
Nancy Groff, Program Coordinator
Oregon Disabilities Commission
1257 Ferry Street SE
Salem, OR 97301-4278
(503) 378-3142 (V/TTY); (503) 378-5478 (TTY)
(800) 358-3117 (V/TTY, in OR)
(800) 521-9615 (V/TTY, in OR)
E-mail: nancy.groff@state.or.us
Web: www.odc.state.or.us/dhhap/index.htm

Telecommunications Relay Services for Individuals Who Are Deaf, Hard of Hearing, or With Speech Impairments

(800) 735-1232 (V)
(800) 735-3250 (VCO)
(800) 735-2900 (TTY); 711 (TTY)
(800) 735-0644 (ASCII)
(800) 735-7525 (Speech to Speech)
(800) 735-3896 (Spanish)
(900) 568-3323 (900 Services)

Regional ADA & IT Technical Assistance Center

Northwest ADA & IT Center
Charles E. Davis, Center Coordinator
Oregon Health & Science University-CDRC
P.O. Box 574
Portland, OR 97207-0574
(503) 494-4001; (503) 418-0296 (TTY)
(800) 949-4232 (V/TTY)
E-mail: nwada@ohsu.edu
Web: www.nwada.org

University Centers for Excellence in Developmental Disabilities

Center on Human Development
Hill M. Walker, Co-Director
Jeff Sprague, Co-Director
University of Oregon
901 E. 18th Avenue, Room 350
Eugene, OR 97403
(541) 346-3591
Web: http://darkwing.uoregon.edu/~ivdb

Oregon Institute on Disability and Development
Gloria L. Krahn, Director
Oregon Health & Science University
P.O. Box 574
Portland, OR 97207-0574
(503) 494-8364; (800) 452-3563
(503) 494-8095 (TTY)
E-mail: krahng@ohsu.edu
Web: www.oidd.org

Technology-Related Assistance

Access Technologies, Inc.
(Technology Access for Life Needs)
Laurie Brooks, President
3070 Lancaster Drive NE
Salem, OR 97305
(503) 361-1201; (800) 677-7512 (V/TTY)
E-mail: info@accesstechnologiesinc.org
Web: www.accesstechnologiesinc.org

State Mediation System

Office of Student Learning and Partnerships
Valerie Miller, Coordinator
Department of Education
255 Capitol Street NE
Salem, OR 97310-0203
(503) 378-3600 ext. 2340
E-mail: valerie.miller@state.or.us
Web: www.ode.state.or.us/

Special Format Library

Oregon State Library
Talking Book and Braille Services
250 Winter Street NE
Salem, OR 97301-3950
(503) 378-3849; (800) 452-0292 (in Portland)
(503) 378-4276 (TTY)
E-mail: tbabs@sparkie.osl.state.or.us
Web: http://oregon.gov/OSL/TBABS/

Oregon—Disability-Specific Organizations

Attention Deficit Disorder

To identify an ADD group in Oregon, contact either of the following organizations:

Children and Adults with Attention-Deficit/
   Hyperactivity Disorder (CHADD)
8181 Professional Place, Suite 150
Landover, MD 20785
(301) 306-7070
(800) 233-4050 (Voice mail to request
   information packet)
Web: www.chadd.org

Attention Deficit Disorder Association (ADDA)
P.O. Box 543
Pottstown, PA 19464
(484) 945-2101
E-mail: mail@add.org
Web: www.add.org

Autism

   To identify an autism group in Oregon,
contact

Autism Society of America
7910 Woodmont Avenue, Suite 300
Bethesda, MD 20814
(301) 657-0881; (800) 3-AUTISM
Web: www.autism-society.org

Regional Programs for Low Incidence Disabilities
State Services for Autism
Department of Education
Jay Gense, Director
255 Capitol Street, NE
Salem, OR 97310-0203
(503) 378-3600, ext. 2338
Web: www.ode.state.or.us

Blind/Visual Impairments

American Foundation for the Blind–West
Gil Johnson, Director
111 Pine Street, Suite 725
San Francisco, CA 94111
(415) 392-4845
E-mail: sanfran@afb.net
Web: www.afb.org

Brain Injury

Brain Injury Association of Oregon
Sherry Stock, Director
Wayne Eklund, RN, President
2145 NW Overton Street
Portland, OR 97210
(503) 413-7707; (800) 544-5243 (in OR)
E-mail: biaor@biaoregon.org
Web: www.biaoregon.org

The Oregon Brain Injury Resource Network
345 N. Monmouth Avenue
Monmouth, OR 97361
(503) 413-7707; (800) 544-5243
E-mail: tbi@wou.edu
Web: www.tr.wou.edu/tbi

Cerebral Palsy

United Cerebral Palsy of Oregon and Southwest
   Washington
Bud Thoune, Executive Director
7830 SE Foster Road
Portland, OR 97206
(503) 777-4167
E-mail: bthoune@ucpaorwa.org
Web: www.ucpaorwa.org

Epilepsy

Epilepsy Foundation of Northwest
Joel Neier, President
619 SW 11th Avenue, Suite 225
Portland, OR 97205-2646
(503) 228-7651; (888) 828-7651
E-mail: jforeman@epilepsynw.org
Web: www.epilepsyoregon.org

Learning Disabilities

Learning Disabilities Association of Oregon
Myrna Soule, President
P.O. Box 1221
Portland, OR 97207
(503) 626-4622
E-mail: woodmontsch00199@yahoo.com
Web: www.ldaor.org

Mental Health

Mental Health Association of Oregon
Steve Weiss, President
812 SW Washington Street, Suite 640
Portland, OR 97205
(503) 222-6438
E-mail: mhao@quik.com

NAMI-Oregon
Dave Gallison, Executive Director
3550 SE Woodward
Portland, OR 97202-1552
(503) 230-8009; (800) 343-6264
E-mail: namioregon@qwest.net
Web: www.nami.org/MSTemplate.cfm?
   Site=NAMI_Oregon

Oregon Family Support Network, Inc.
Jeanne Schulz, Executive Director
15544 S. Clackamas River Drive
Oregon City, OR 97045
(503) 656-5440; (800) 323-8521
E-mail: OFSN@Open.org

Mental Retardation

The Arc of Oregon
Marcie Ingledue, Acting Executive Director
1745 State Street
Salem, OR 97301
(503) 581-2726; (877) 581-2726 (toll-free)
E-mail: info@arcoregon.org
Web: www.arcoregon.org/

Speech and Hearing

Oregon Speech and Hearing Association
Robert Buckendorf, President
P.O. Box 523
Salem, OR 97308
(503) 370-7019
E-mail: assoc@wvi.com
Web: www.oregonspeechandhearing.org/

Oregon—Organizations Especially for Parents

Parent Training and Information Center (PTI)

Oregon Parent Training and Information Center
(formerly known as COPE)
Janice Richards, Executive Director
2295 Liberty Street, NE
Salem, OR 97303
(503) 581-8156; (888) 505-2673 (in OR)
E-mail: info@orpti.org
Web: www.orpti.org

Parent-To-Parent

Contact Parent Training and Information Center listed above.

Parent Teacher Association (PTA)

Oregon PTA
Diana Oberbarnscheidt, President
P.O. Box 4569
Portland, OR 97208-4569
(503) 234-3928
E-mail: or_office@pta.org
E-mail: or_pres@pta.org
Web: www.oregonpta.org

Oregon—Other Disability Organizations

Easter Seals Oregon
J. David Cheveallier, President/CEO
5757 SW Macadam Avenue
Portland, OR 97239
(503) 228-5108
E-mail: info@or.easterseals.com
Web: www.or.easterseals.com

Independent Living

To find out the contact information for the Statewide Independent Living Council (SILC) in Oregon, contact

Independent Living Research Utilization Project
The Institute for Rehabilitation and Research
2323 South Sheppard, Suite 1000
Houston, TX 77019
(713) 520-0232 (V); (713) 520-5136 (TTY)
E-mail: ilru@ilru.org
Web: www.ilru.org

To find out the contact information for centers for independent living (CILs) in Oregon, contact

National Council on Independent Living
1916 Wilson Boulevard, Suite 209
Arlington, VA 22201
(703) 525-3406; (703) 525-4153 (TTY)
E-mail: ncil@ncil.org
Web: www.ncil.org

PENNSYLVANIA

Pennsylvania—State Agencies and Organizations

United States Senators

Honorable Robert P. Casey Jr. (D)
393 Russell Senate Office Building
Washington, DC 20510
(202) 224-6324
(202) 228-1229 (Fax)
E-mail: http://www.casey.senate.gov/contact/
Web: http://www.casey.senate.gov/

Honorable Patrick J. Toomey (R)
248 Russell Senate Office Building
Washington, DC 20510
(202) 224-4254
(202) 228-0604 (Fax)
Web: http://www.toomey.senate.gov/?p=home

United States Representatives

To find the contact information for your representative in the House of the U.S. Congress, visit the House's Web site at: www.house.gov, or call (202) 225-3121; (202) 225-1904 (TTY).

Governor

Honorable Tom Corbett
225 Main Capitol Building
Harrisburg, PA 17120
(717) 787-2500
E-mail Web Form: http://sites.state.pa.us/
   PA_Exec/Governor/govmail.html
Web: www.governor.state.pa.us/

Official State Web Site

Web: www.pa.gov

State Department of Education: Special Education

Bureau of Special Education
John J. Tommasini, Director
Department of Education
333 Market Street, 7th Floor
Harrisburg, PA 17126
(717) 783-6913
Special Education Consultline: (800) 879-2301
   (V/TTY)
Web: www.pde.state.pa.us

Pennsylvania was granted a waiver from the NCLB act. Web: http://www2.ed.gov/nclb/landing.jhtml?src=ft

Programs for Infants and Toddlers With Disabilities: Birth–2 Years

Office of Child Development
Bureau of Early Intervention Services
James Coyle, Part C Coordinator
Department of Education and Welfare
333 Market Street, 6th Floor
Harrisburg, PA 17126
(717) 783-7213
E-mail: jecoyle@pa.gov
Web: http://www.dpw.state.pa.us/
   forchildren/earlyinterventionservices/
   index.htm

Programs for Children With Disabilities: 3–5 Years

Division of Early Intervention and Support Services
Bureau of Early Intervention Services
James Coyle, Part C Coordinator
Department of Education and Welfare
333 Market Street, 6th Floor
Harrisburg, PA 17126
(717) 783-7213
E-mail: jecoyle@pa.gov
Web: http://www.education.state.pa.us/
   portal/server.pt/community/early_
   intervention/8710

State Vocational Rehabilitation Agency

Office of Vocational Rehabilitation
Tom Washic, Executive Director
Department of Labor and Industry
1521 N. 6th Street
Harrisburg, PA 17102
(717) 787-5244
E-mail: twashic@state.pa.us

Coordinator for Transition Services

Pennsylvania Training and Technical Assistance
   Network
Dr. Ellen Romett, Director
3190 William Pitt Way
Pittsburgh, PA 15238
(412) 826-2336; (800) 446-5607
E-mail: eromett@pattan.k12.pa.us
Web: www.pattan.k12.pa.us/

Office of State Liaison of Career and Technical Education for Students With Disabilities

Bureau of Career and Technical Education
Lee Burket, Acting Director
Division of Field Support
Department of Education
333 Market Street, 6th Floor
Harrisburg, PA 17126-0333
(717) 787-8022
E-mail: jofoster@state.pa.us
Web: www.pde.state.pa.us

State Mental Health Agency

Office of Mental Health and Substance Abuse
 Services
Joan Ernie, Deputy Secretary
Department of Public Welfare
Health and Welfare Building, Room 502
P.O. Box 2675
Harrisburg, PA 17105-2675
(717) 787-6443
E-mail: joernie@state.pa.us
Web: www.dpw.state.pa.us

State Mental Health Representative for Children and Youth

Bureau of Children's Services
Stanley J. Mrozowski, PhD, Director
Beechmont Building
P.O. Box 2675
Harrisburg, PA 17105
(717) 772-7763
E-mail: smrozowski@state.pa.us

State Mental Retardation Program

Department of Public Welfare
Kevin Casey, Deputy Secretary
 for Mental Retardation
Health and Welfare Building, Room 512
P.O. Box 2675
Harrisburg, PA 17105-2675
(717) 787-3700
Web: www.dpw.state.pa.us

Council on Developmental Disabilities

Developmental Disabilities Council
Graham Mulholland, Executive Director
561 Forum Building, Commonwealth Avenue
Harrisburg, PA 17120
(717) 787-6057
E-mail: gmulholland@dpw.state.pa.us
Web: www.paddc.org

Protection and Advocacy Agency

Pennsylvania Protection and Advocacy Inc.
Eilene Shane, Executive Director
1414 N. Cameron Street, Suite C
Harrisburg, PA 17103
(717) 236-8110; (800) 692-7443 (in PA)
(717) 346-0293; (877) 375-7139 (TTY)
E-mail: ppa@ppainc.org
Web: www.ppainc.org

Client Assistance Program

Center for Disability Law and Policy
Stephen Pennington, Statewide Director
1617 JFK Boulevard, Suite 800
Philadelphia, PA 19103
(215) 557-7112 (V/TTY)
E-mail: info@equalemployment.org
Web: www.equalemployment.org

Programs for Children With Special Health Care Needs

Division of Child and Adult Health Services
Carolyn Cass, Director
Department of Health, 7th Floor, East Wing
P.O. Box 90
Harrisburg, PA 17108
(717) 772-2762
(800) 986-4550–Special Kids Networks
E-mail: ccass@state.pa.us
Web: www.state.pa.us

State CHIP Program (health care for low-income, uninsured children)

Pennsylvania's Children's Health Insurance
 Program
333 Market Street
Harrisburg, PA 17120
(800) 986-5437
Web: www.ins.state.pa.us

**Programs for Children and Youth
Who Are Blind or Visually Impaired**

Bureau of Blindness and Visual Services
Office of Vocational Rehabilitation
Department of Labor and Industry
Pamela Shaw, Director
1521 N. 6th Street
Harrisburg, PA 17102
(717) 787-6176; (800) 622-2842 (in PA)
E-mail: pashaw@state.pa.us
Web: www.state.pa.us

**Programs for Children
and Youth Who Are
Deaf or Hard of Hearing**

Office for the Deaf and Hard of Hearing
Ken Puckett, Director
1521 N. 6th Street
Harrisburg, PA 17102
(717) 783-4912 /V/TTY
(800) 233-3008 (V/TTY in PA only)
E-mail: kpuckett@state.pa.us
Web: www.dli.state.pa.us

**Telecommunications Relay
Services for Individuals Who
Are Deaf, Hard of Hearing, or
With Speech Impairments**

(800) 654-5988 (V)
(800) 654-5984 (TTY); 711 (TTY)
(800) 229-5746 (Speech to Speech–English)
(866) 260-9470 (Speech to Speech–Spanish)

**Programs for Children
and Youth Who Are Deaf-Blind**

Pennsylvania Deaf-Blind Project
Julie Baumgartner
6340 Flank Drive, Suite 600
Harrisburg, PA 17112-2764
(717) 541-4960; (800) 360-7282 (in PA only)
Web: www.pattan.k12.pa.us

**State Education Agency
Rural Representative**

Bureau of Special Education
Department of Education
333 Market Street, 7th Floor
Harrisburg, PA 17126-0333
(717) 783-6913
Web: www.pde.state.pa.us

**Regional ADA & IT
Technical Assistance Center**

ADA and IT Information Center for the
    Mid Atlantic Region
Marian Vessels, Director
451 Hungerford Drive, Suite 607
Rockville, MD 20850
(301) 217-0124 (V/TTY); (800) 949-4232 (V/TTY)
E-mail: adainfo@transcen.org
Web: www.adainfo.org

**University Center for Excellence
in Developmental Disabilities**

Institute on Disabilities–UCEDD
Diane Nelson Bryen, Director
Temple University, Ritter Annex, Room 423
1301 Cecil B. Moore Avenue
Philadelphia, PA 19122
(215) 204-1356 (V/TTY)
E-mail: dianeb@temple.edu
Web: http://disabilities.temple.edu

Leadership Education in Neurodevelopmental
    Disabilities (LEND)
Nathan Blum, MD, Director
Children's Seashore House of the Children's
    Hospital of Philadelphia
3405 Civic Center Boulevard, Room 210
Philadelphia, PA 19104-4388
(215) 590-7681
E-mail: blum@email.chop.edu

Technology-Related Assistance

Pennsylvania's Initiative on Assistive Technology
Institute on Disabilities/UCEDD
Amy S. Goldman, Associate Director
1301 Cecil B. Moore Avenue
Ritter Hall Annex 423
Philadelphia, PA 19122
(215) 204-3862 (V); (215) 204-1356 (V/TTY)
(800) 204-PIAT (V)
E-mail: piat@temple.edu
Web: http://disabilities.temple.edu

State Mediation System

Office for Dispute Resolution
Linda McKay, Coordinator
6340 Flank Drive, Suite 600
Harrisburg, PA 17112
(717) 541-4960
Web: www.pattan.k12.pa.us/isp/odr

Special Format Library

Library for the Blind and Physically Handicapped
Free Library of Philadelphia
Vickie L. Collins, Librarian
919 Walnut Street
Philadelphia, PA 19107
(215) 683-3213; 800-222-1754
E-mail: flpblind@library.phila.gov
Web: www.library.phila.gov/lbh/lbh.htm

Pennsylvania — Disability-Specific Organizations

Attention Deficit Disorder

To identify an ADD group in Pennsylvania, contact either of the following organizations:

Children and Adults With Attention-Deficit/
Hyperactivity Disorder (CHADD)
8181 Professional Place, Suite 150
Landover, MD 20785
(301) 306-7070
(800) 233-4050 (Voice mail to request
information packet)
Web: www.chadd.org

Attention Deficit Disorder Association (ADDA)
P.O. Box 543
Pottstown, PA 19464
(484) 945-2101
E-mail: mail@add.org
Web: www.add.org

Autism

ABOARD (Advisory Board on
Autism and Related Disorders)
35 Wilson Street, Suite 100
Pittsburgh, PA 15223
(412) 781-4116; (800) 827-9385
E-mail: info@aboard.org
Web: www.aboard.org

To identify an autism group in Pennsylvania, contact

Autism Society of America
7910 Woodmont Avenue, Suite 300
Bethesda, MD 20814
(301) 657-0881; (800) 3-AUTISM
Web: www.autism-society.org

Blind/Visual Impairments

American Foundation for the Blind
Regina Genwright, Director of
Information Center
11 Penn Plaza, Suite 300
New York, NY 10001
(212) 502-7600; (212) 502-7662 (TTY)
E-mail: afbinfo@afb.org
Web: www.afb.org

National Federation of the
Blind of Pennsylvania
James Antonacci, President
42 S. 15th Street, Suite 222
Philadelphia, PA 19102
(215) 988-0888
E-mail: nfbofpa@att.net
Web: www.nfbp.org

Cerebral Palsy

United Cerebral Palsy of Pennsylvania
Joan W. Martin, Executive Director
1902 Market Street
Camp Hill, PA 17011
(717) 761-6129; (717) 761-6950 (TTY)
(866) 761-6129
E-mail: info@ucpofpa.org
Web: www.ucpofpa.org

Epilepsy

Epilepsy Foundation Western/
Central Pennsylvania
Judy Painter, Executive Director
Vocational Rehabilitation Center
1323 Forbes Avenue, Suite 102
Pittsburgh, PA 15219
(412) 261-5880; (800) 361-5885
E-mail: pbeem@efwp.org
E-mail: jpainter@efwp.org
Web: www.efwp.org

Epilepsy Foundation of Eastern Pennsylvania
Jeanette K. Chelius, Executive Director
919 Walnut Street, Suite 700
Philadelphia, PA 19107-5237
(215) 629-5003; (800) 887-7165 (in PA)
E-mail: efsepa@efsepa.org
Web: www.efepa.org

Learning Disabilities

Learning Disabilities Association of Pennsylvania
Debbie Rodes, President
Toomey Building
P.O. Box 208
Uwchland, PA 19480
(610) 458-8193

Mental Health

NAMI Pennsylvania
James W. Jordan, Jr., Executive Director
2149 N. Second Street
Harrisburg, PA 17110
(717) 238-1514; (800) 223-0500
Web: http://namipa.nami.org

Parents Involved Network of Pennsylvania
    (PIN of Pennsylvania)
Child and Adolescent and Family Division
    of the Mental Health Association of
    Southeastern Pennsylvania
Catherine Tanzarella, Director
1211 Chestnut Street, 11th Floor
Philadelphia, PA 19107
(215) 751-1800; (800) 688-4226
E-mail: ctanzarella@mhasp.org
Web: www.pinofpa.org

Mental Retardation

The Arc of Pennsylvania
Stephen H. Suroviec, Executive Director
2001 N. Front, Building 2, Suite 221
Harrisburg, PA 17102-2104
(717) 234-2621; (800) 692-7258
E-mail: ssuroviec@thearcpa.org
Web: www.thearcpa.org

Speech and Hearing

Pennsylvania Speech-Language-Hearing
    Association
Diane Yenerall, Business Manager
800 Perry Highway, Suite 3
Pittsburgh, PA 15229-1128
(412) 366-9858
E-mail: psha@psha.org
Web: www.psha.org

Spina Bifida

Spina Bifida Association
Patricia Fulvio, Executive Director
209 E. State Street
Quarryville, PA 17566-1242
(717) 786-9280; (888) 770-7272 (in PA)
E-mail: SBAofPA@aol.com
Web: www.geocities.com/SBAofgpa

Tourette Syndrome

Pennsylvania Tourette Syndrome Association
Laura Umbrell, LPN, Advocacy Specialist
132 W. Middle Street
Gettysburg, PA 17325
(717) 337-1134; (800) 990-3300 (in PA)
E-mail: laura@patsainc.org
Web: www.patourettesyndrome.org

Pennsylvania—Organizations Especially for Parents

Parent Training and Information Center (PTI)

Parent Education Network
Louise Thieme, Director
2107 Industrial Highway
York, PA 17402
(717) 600-0100; (800) 522-5827 (V/TTY) (in PA);
(800) 441-5028 (Spanish)
E-mail: pen@parentednet.org
Web: www.parentednet.org

Parent-To-Parent

Parent to Parent of Pennsylvania
Wendy Hoke Witmer, Program Director
6340 Flank Drive, Suite 600
Harrisburg, PA 17112-2764
(717) 540-4722; (800) 986-4550 (in PA)
E-mail: info@parenttoparent.org
Web: www.parenttoparent.org

Community Parent Resource Center

Mentor Parent Program (serving Northwest
    Rural Pennsylvania)
Gail Walker, Program Director
P.O. Box 47
Pittsfield, PA 16340
(814) 563-3470; (888) 447-1431 (in PA)
E-mail: gwalker@westpa.net
Web: www.mentorparent.org

Hispanos Unidos para Ninos Excepcionales
   (Philadelphia HUNE, Inc.)
(serving American Street Empowerment Zone
   and providing intense training sessions
   to parents of children with disabilities in
   Philadelphia)
Luz Hernandez, Program Director
Buena Vista Plaza
166 W. Lehigh Avenue, Suite 400
Philadelphia, PA 19133-3838
(215) 425-6203
E-mail: huneinc@aol.com
Web: http://huneinc.org

Partners in Policymaking

Institute on Disabilities/University Center for
   Excellence
Kathy Miller, Program Director
Temple University
Ritter Annex, Room 423
1301 Cecil B. Moore Avenue
Philadelphia, PA 19122
(215) 204-9395
E-mail: millerk@temple.edu

Parent Teacher Association (PTA)

Pennsylvania Congress of Parents and Teachers, Inc.
Carol Ritter, President
4804 Derry Street
Harrisburg, PA 17111
(717) 564-8985
E-mail: info@papta.org
Web: www.papta.org

Pennsylvania—Other Disability Organizations

Easter Seals South Central Pennyslvania
Debra L. Noel, Executive Director
2201 S. Queen Street
York, PA 17402
(717) 741-3891; (888) 273-7251
E-mail: DNoe13@aol.com
Web: www.visiteasterseals.org

Easter Seals of Southeastern Pennsylvania
Carl G. Webster, Executive Director/CEO
3975 Conshohocken Avenue
Philadelphia, PA 19131
(215) 879-1000
E-mail: cwebster@easterseals-sepa.org
Web: www.easterseals-sepa.org

Easter Seals Society of Western Pennsylvania
Larry Rager, President
632 Fort Duquesne Boulevard
Pittsburgh, PA 15222
(412) 281-7244
(800) 587-3257
E-mail: lmeinert@westernpa.easterseals.com
Web: www.westernpa.easterseals.com

MENTOR ABI Group–New Jersey (also a
   resource for Pennsylvania)
Rehabilitative and Support Services for Persons
   with Acquired Brain Injury
505 S. Lenola Road
Blason Office Plaza II, Suite 217
Moorestown, NJ 08057
(856) 235-5505
Web: http://nj.thementornetwork.com/state/
   index.asp

Neurofibromatosis Clinics Association
P.O. Box 14185
Pittsburgh, PA 15239
(412) 795-3029
E-mail: info@nfpittsburgh.org
Web: www.nfpittsburgh.org

Pennsylvania Parents and Caregivers Resource
   Network
Sue Scott Dolan, Director
P.O. Box 4336
Harrisburg, PA 17111-0336
(717) 561-0098; (888) 572-7368 (in PA)
E-mail: ppcrn@ppcrn.org
Web: www.ppcrn.org

Independent Living

   To find out the contact information for the
Statewide Independent Living Council (SILC) in
Pennsylvania, contact

Independent Living Research Utilization Project
The Institute for Rehabilitation and Research
2323 South Sheppard, Suite 1000
Houston, TX 77019
(713) 520-0232 (V); (713) 520-5136 (TTY)
E-mail: ilru@ilru.org
Web: www.ilru.org

   To find out the contact information for
centers for independent living (CILs) in
Pennsylvania, contact

National Council on Independent Living
1916 Wilson Boulevard, Suite 209
Arlington, VA 22201
(703) 525-3406; (703) 525-4153 (TTY)
E-mail: ncil@ncil.org
Web: www.ncil.org

PUERTO RICO

Puerto Rico—Agencies and Organizations

United States House of Representatives

Honorable Pedro Pierluisi
1213 Longworth HOB
Washington, DC 20515
(202) 225-2615; (202) 225-2154 (Fax)
Web: http://pierluisi.house.gov/

Governor

Honorable Luis Fortuño
La Fortaleza
P. O. Box 9020082
San Juan, PR 00902-0082
(787) 721-7000

Official State Web Site

Web: www.pr.gov

Department of Education: Special Education

Department of Education
Dr. Ernesto Perez
Assistant Secretary of Special Education
P.O. Box 190759
San Juan, PR 00919-0759
E-mail: rosario_so@de.gobierno.pr

Programs for Infants and Toddlers With Disabilities: Birth–2 Years

Infants and Toddlers Program
Dr. Naydamar Perez de Otero, Director
Department of Health
P. O. Box 70184
San Juan, PR 00936-8184
(787) 274-5659, 5661; (787) 274-3301 (Fax)
E-mail: naydamar@salud.gov.pr
Web: http://www.salud.gov.pr/Pages/
default.aspx

Programs for Children With Disabilities: 3–5 Years

Special Education Programs
Timothy Garcial Maldonado, 619 Coordinator
Department of Education
P.O. Box 100759
San Juan, PR 00919-0759
(939) 642-6208
E-mail: garviasti@de.gobierno.pr
Web: http://www.de.gobierno.pr/educacion-
especial-menu/602-servicios

Vocational Rehabilitation Agency

Vocational Rehabilitation Administration
Ms. María Rosa Iturregui, Administrator
P.O. Box 191118
San Juan, PR 00919-1118
(787) 729-0160, ext. 2301; (787) 728-8070 (Fax)
E-mail: norma@vra.gobierno.pr

Office of Coordinator of Vocational Education for Students With Disabilities

Technical Education Programs
José O. Berdecia, Assistant Secretary
P.O. Box 190759
Hato Rey, PR 00919
(787) 758-4132

Mental Health Agency

Mental Health and Anti-Addiction Services
Administration
Carmen Graulau, Administrator
Ave Barbosa 414
P.O. Box 21414
San Juan, PR 00928-1414
(787) 764-3670; (787) 764-3795
(787) 765-5888 (Fax)

Mental Health Representative for Children and Youth

Dr. Pedro J. Morales, Assistant Administrator
Treatment of Children and Adolescents
Mental Health Representative for
Children and Youth
Ave Barbosa 414
P.O. Box 21414
San Juan, PR 00928-1414
(787) 763-7575, ext. 2393/2371/2310

Mental Retardation Program

Mental Retardation Program
Ana Garcia Huertas, Director
Department of Health
P.O. Box 70184
San Juan, PR 00936
(787) 721-3374; (787) 725-4487 (Fax)

Council on Developmental Disabilities

Puerto Rico Developmental Disabilities Council
Mr. Vincente Sanabria Acevedo, President
P.O. Box 9543
San Juan, PR 00908
(787) 722-0595; (787) 722-0590
E-mail: prced@prtc.net

Protection and Advocacy Agency

Office of the Ombudsman for Persons With
    Disabilities
Jose R. Ocasio, Esq., Ombudsman
P.O. Box 41309
San Juan, PR 00940-1309
(787) 729-4299, ext. 2004/2005; (787) 725-2333
(787) 725-4014 (TTY); (787) 721-2455 (Fax)
E-mail: jrocasio@oppi.gobierno.pr

Client Assistance Program

Office of the Ombudsman for Persons With
    Disabilities
Maria Rosa, Coordinator
P.O. Box 41309
San Juan, PR 00940-1309
(787) 725-2333, ext. 2049, 2050
(787) 725-4014 (TTY)
E-mail: mrosa@oppi.gobierno.pr

Programs for Children With Special Health Care Needs

Maternal and Child Health
Crippled Children's Programs
Dr. Naydamar Pérez de Otero
Department of Health
P. O. Box 70184
San Juan, PR 00936-8184
(787) 274-5659 or 5660; (787) 274-3301
E-mail: nperez@salud.gov.pr

Telecommunications Relay Services for Individuals Who Are Deaf, Hard of Hearing, or With Speech Impairments

(800) 229-5746 (Speech to Speech English)
(866) 260-9470 (Speech to Speech Spanish)

Regional ADA & IT Technical Assistance Center

Northeast ADA & IT Center
Cornell University
Andrea Haenlin-Mott, Director
331 Ives Hall
Ithaca, NY 14853
(607) 255-6686 (V/TTY/Spanish);
    (800) 949-4232 (V/TTY/Spanish)
E-mail: northeastada@cornell.edu
Web: www.ilr.cornell.edu/ped/northeastada

FILI US Institute–Assistive Technology Project at
    Puerto Rico
University of Puerto Rico
María I. Miranda, Project Director
Jardin Botanico Sur #1187 calle Flamboyan
San Juan, PR 00926-1117
(787) 758-2525, ext. 4406; (800) 496-6035
(800) 981-6033 (in PR)
Web: http://pratp.upr.edu

Mediation System

Puerto Rico Department of Education
Marta Colon-Rivera, Coordinator
P.O. Box 190759
San Juan, PR 00919
(787) 754-8926

Puerto Rico—Disability-Specific Organizations

Attention Deficit Disorder

To identify an ADD group in Puerto Rico, contact

Children and Adults With Attention-Deficit/
    Hyperactivity Disorder (CHADD)
8181 Professional Place, Suite 150
Landover, MD 20785
(301) 306-7070
(800) 233-4050 (Voice mail to request
    information packet)
Web: www.chadd.org

Autism

Parents Society for Children and Adults With
   Autism in Puerto Rico
Autism Society of America Puerto Rico Chapter
Mrs. Milagros Rodríguez, Director
P.O. Box 190594
San Juan, PR 00919-0594
(787) 723-4566

Blind/Visual Impairments

American Foundation for the Blind–Southeast
Frances Mary D'Andrea, Director
100 Peachtree Street, Suite 620
Atlanta, GA 30303
(404) 525-2303
E-mail: atlanta@afb.net
Web: www.afb.org

Epilepsy

Sociedad Puertorriqueña De Epilepsia
Sonia de Jesus Ortiz, Executive Director
1100 Ruiz Soler
Calle Marginal
Bayamon, PR 00959-7365
(787) 782-6200; (787) 782-6254
(787) 782-3991 (Fax)
E-mail: sociedadepilepsiapr@excite.com

Learning Disabilities

Learning Disabilities Association of Puerto Rico
Elisa Blum, President
Box #003
Calle Loiza 1750, esquina Taft
San Juan, PR 00911
(787) 728-5166
E-mail: ElisaBlum@yahoo.com

Speech and Hearing

Organización Puertorriqueña de Patologia del
   Habla, Lenguaje y Audiología, Inc.
Iris Mañosa Santiago, President
P.O. Box 20147
San Juan, PR 00928-0147
(787) 268-0273
E-mail: opphla@prw.net

Special Format Library

Puerto Rico Regional Library for the Blind and
   Physically Handicapped
Ms. Igri Enriquez, Director/Librarian
520 Ponce de Leon Avenue, Suite 2
San Juan, PR 00901
(787) 723-2519; (800) 981-8008
(787) 721-8177 (Fax)
E-mail: bibciego@tld.net

Spina Bifida

Asociación de Espina Bifida e Hydrocefalia
Isolina Laboy Arroyo, Director
P.O. Box 8262
Bayamon, PR 00960-8032
(787) 740-6695 or (787) 740-0033
(787) 787-1377 (Fax)
E-mail: asoc_espina_bifida@hotmail.com

Puerto Rico—Organizations Especially for Parents

Parent Training and Information Center (PTI)

APNI, Inc. (Asociación de Padres Pro Bienestar de
   Niños con Impedidos de Puerto Rico, Inc.)
Carmen Sélles de Vilá, Executive Director
P.O. Box 21280
San Juan, PR 00928-1280
(787) 763-4665; (787) 753-7185 (TTY)
(800) 981-8492; (800) 981-8393
(787) 763-4665 (Fax)
E-mail: centroinfo@apnipr.org
Web: www.apnipr.org

Puerto Rico—Other Disability Organizations

Easter Seals Puerto Rico
Nilda M. Morales, Executive Director
P.O. Box 360325
San Juan, PR 00936-0325
(787) 767-6710
E-mail: info@serpr.org

Independent Living

To find out the contact information for the
Statewide Independent Living Council (SILC) in
Puerto Rico, contact

Independent Living Research Utilization Project
The Institute for Rehabilitation and Research
2323 South Sheppard, Suite 1000
Houston, TX 77019
(713) 520-0232 (V); (713) 520-5136 (TTY)
E-mail: ilru@ilru.org
Web: www.ilru.org

To find out the contact information for centers for independent living (CILs) in Puerto Rico, contact

National Council on Independent Living
1916 Wilson Boulevard, Suite 209
Arlington, VA 22201
(703) 525-3406; (703) 525-4153 (TTY)
E-mail: ncil@ncil.org
Web: www.ncil.org

RHODE ISLAND

Rhode Island—State Agencies and Organizations

United States Senators

Honorable Jack Reed (D)
728 Hart Senate Office Building
Washington, DC 20510
(202) 224-4642
(202) 224-4680 (Fax)
E-mail: http://reed.senate.gov/
form-opinion.htm
Web: http://reed.senate.gov

Honorable Sheldon Whitehouse (D)
530 Hart Senate Office Building
Washington, DC 20510
(202) 224-2921; (800) 662-5188 (in RI)
(202) 224-7746 (TTY)
E-mail Web Form: http://www.whitehouse.
senate.gov/contact/
Web: http://www.whitehouse.senate.gov/

United States Representatives

To find the contact information for your representative in the House of the U.S. Congress, visit the House's Web site at: www.house.gov, or call (202) 225-3121; (202) 225-1904 (TTY).

Governor

Honorable Lincoln Chafee
Office of the Governor
82 Smith Street
Providence, RI 02903-1196
(401) 222-2080
E-mail: governor@governor.ri.gov
Web: http://www.governor.ri.gov/

Official State Web Site

Web: www.ri.gov/index.php

Governor's Commission on Disabilities

Governor's Commission on Disabilities
Bob Cooper, Executive Secretary
John O. Pastore Center
41 Cherry Dale Court
Cranston, RI 02920
(401) 462-0100; (401) 462-0101 (TTY)
Web: www.disabilities.ri.gov

State Department of Education: Special Education

Office of Special Populations
Kenneth G. Swanson, Director
Rhode Island Department of Elementary and
Secondary Education
255 Westminster Street, Room 400,
Shepard Building
Providence, RI 02903-3400
(401) 222-3505
Web: www.ride.ri.gov

Rhode Island received an extended waiver from the NCLB program.

Colleen Hedden
Student, Community & Academic Supports
Rhode Island Department of Elementary and
Secondary Education
255 Westminster Street
Providence, RI 02903
(401) 222-8939
Email: Colleen.Hedden@ride.ri.gov
Web: http://www.ride.ri.gov/
InstructionAssessment/
InstructionalResources/
TitleIImprovingAcademicAchievement.aspx

Programs for Infants and Toddlers
With Disabilities: Birth–2 Years

Executive Office of Health and Human Services
Brenda DuHamel, Part C Coordinator
Center for Child and Family Health
74 West Road, Building 74
Cranston, RI 02920
(401) 462-0318
E-mail: brenda.duhamel@ohhs.ri.gov
Web: http://www.eohhs.ri.gov/Consumer/
    ConsumerInformation/Healthcare/
    PeoplewithSpecialNeedsandDisabilities/
    Children/EarlyIntervention.aspx

Programs for Children With Disabilities: 3–5 Years

Office of Instruction, Assessment and Curriculum
Ruth Gallucci, Early Childhood Educational
    Specialist
Department of Elementary and Secondary
    Education
255 Westminster Street
Providence, RI 02903
(401) 222-8947
E-mail: ruth.gallucci@ride.ri.gov
Web: http://www.ride.ri.gov/Instruction
    Assessment/EarlyChildhoodEducation/
    EarlyChildhoodSpecialEducation.aspx

State Vocational Rehabilitation Agency

Office of Rehabilitation Services
Raymond A. Carroll, Administrator
Department of Human Services
40 Fountain Street
Providence, RI 02903
(401) 421-7005, Ext. 301; (401) 421-7016 (TTY)
E-mail: rcarroll@ors.ri.gov
Web: www.ors.ri.gov

Coordinator for Transition Services

J. David Sienko, Educational Specialist/
    Secondary Transition
Rhode Island Department of Elementary and
    Secondary Educaton
Independence Employment
UCE/ Rhode Island College
255 Westminister Street, Shepard Building
Providence, RI 02903-3400
(401) 222-4600, Ext. 2216
E-mail: rid03249@ride.ri.net
Web: www.ridoe.net/special_needs/
    transition.htm

State Department of Education: Vocational Education for
Students With Disabilities

Rhode Island Department of Elementary and
    Secondary Education
J. David Sienko, Educational Specialist/
    Secondary Transition
255 Westminster Street, Shepard Building
Providence, RI 02903-3400
(401) 222-4600, Ext. 2216
E-mail: rid03249@ride.ri.net
Web: www.ridoe.net

State Mental Health Agency

Department of Mental Health, Retardation
    and Hospitals
Kathleen M. Spangler, Acting Director
14 Harrington Road
Cranston, RI 02920
(401) 462-3201
E-mail: kspangler@mhrh.ri.gov
Web: www.mhrh.state.ri.us

State Mental Health
Agency for Children and Youth

Division of Children's Behavioral Health
Janet L. Anderson, EdD, Assistant Director
Department of Children, Youth and Families
101 Friendship Street
Providence, RI 02903
(401) 528-3756
E-mail: janet.anderson@dcyf.state.ri.gov
Web: www.dcyf.state.ri.us

State Mental Retardation Program

Division of Developmental Disabilities
Lynda Kahn, Executive Director
Department of Mental Health, Retardation and
    Hospitals
14 Harrington Road, Barry Hall
Cranston, RI 02920
(401) 462-3234
E-mail: lkahn@mhrh.ri.gov

Council on Developmental Disabilities

Rhode Island Developmental Disabilities Council
Marie Citrone, Executive Director
400 Bald Hill Road, Suite 515
Warwick, RI 02886
(401) 737-1238
E-mail: riddc@riddc.org
Web: www.riddc.org

Protection and Advocacy Agency

Rhode Island Disability Law Center
Raymond L Bandusky, Executive Director
349 Eddy Street
Providence, RI 02903
(401) 831-3150; (401) 831-5335 (TTY)
(800) 733-5332 (in RI)
E-mail: rbandusky@ridlc.org

Client Assistance Program

Contact Protection and Advocacy Program,
listed above.

Programs for Children With
Special Health Care Needs

Office for Families Raising Children with Special
    Health Care Needs
Deborah Garneau, Chief
Rhode Island Department of Health
3 Capitol Hill, Room 302
Providence, RI 02908-5097
(401) 222-5929; (401) 222-2312
E-mail: debg@doh.state.ri.us
Web: www.health.state.ri.us

State CHIP Program
(health care for low-income,
uninsured children)

RIte Care
(401) 462-5300(V); (401) 462- 3363 (TTY)
(401) 462-1500 (Spanish)
Web: http://www.eohhs.ri.gov/Consumer/
    ConsumerInformation/Healthcare/
    FamilieswithChildren.aspx

Programs for Children and Youth
Who Are Blind or Visually Impaired

Services for the Blind and Visually Impaired
Gary Wier, Deputy Administrator
Department of Human Services
40 Fountain Street
Providence, RI 02903
(401) 222-2300
(401) 272-8090 (Hispanic telephone line)
Web: www.ors.ri.gov

Programs for Children
and Youth Who Are Deaf
or Hard of Hearing or Deaf-Blind

Rhode Island Commission on the Deaf and Hard of
    Hearing
Steven A. Florio, Executive Director
One Capitol Hill, Ground Level
Providence, RI 02908-5850
(401) 222-1204 (V); (401) 222-1205 (TTY)
E-mail: cdhh@cdhh.ri.gov
Web: www.cdhh.ri.gov

Telecommunications Relay
Services for Individuals Who
Are Deaf, Hard of Hearing, or
With Speech Impairments

(800) 745-6575 (V)
(800) 745-5555 (TTY); 711 (TTY)
(800) 745-1570 (ASCII)
(866) 355-9213 (Speech to Speech)
(866) 355-9214 (Spanish)

State Education Agency
Rural Representative

Thomas DiPaola, PhD, Director
Office of Special Populations
Rhode Island Department of
    Elementary and Secondary Education
255 Westminster Street, Room 400,
    Shepard Building
Providence, RI 02903-3400
(401) 222-3505
Web: www.ridoe.net

Regional ADA & IT
Technical Assistance Center

New England ADA and Accessible IT Center
Valerie Fletcher, Executive Director
Oce Harrison, Project Director
Adaptive Environments Center, Inc.
374 Congress Street, Suite 301
Boston, MA 02210
(617) 695-0085 (V/TTY); (800) 949-4232 (V/TTY)
E-mail: adaptive@adaptenv.org
Web: www.adaptenv.org

University Center for Excellence
in Developmental Disabilities

The Paul V. Sherlock Center on Disabilities
A. Anthony Antosh, Director
Rhode Island College
600 Mount Pleasant Avenue
Providence, RI 02908
(401) 456-8072; (401) 456-8773 (TTY)
E-mail: aantosh@ric.edu
Web: www.sherlockcenter.org

Technology-Related Assistance

Rhode Island Assistive Technology Access
    Partnership
Regina Connor, Project Director
Office of Rehabilitation Services
40 Fountain Street
Providence, RI 02903-1898
(401) 421-7005, ext. 390; (401) 421-7016 (TTY)
(800) 752-8088, ext. 2608 (in RI)
E-mail: reginac@ors.ri.gov
Web: www.atap.ri.gov

State Mediation System

Rhode Island Department of Elementary and
    Secondary Education
Susan Wood, PhD
255 Westminster Street, Shephard Building
Providence, RI 02903
(401) 222-4600, ext. 2309
E-mail:rid00870@ride.ri.net

Special Format Library

Talking Books Plus
Andrew Egan, Librarian
Office of Library and Information Services
One Capitol Hill
Providence, RI 02908
(401) 222-5800; (800) 745-5555 (TTY)
E-mail: tbplus@lori.state.ri.us
Web: http://lorinet.info/tbp/

Rhode Island—Disability-Specific Organizations

Attention Deficit Disorder

    To identify an ADD group in Rhode Island,
contact either of the following organizations:

Children and Adults with Attention-Deficit/
    Hyperactivity Disorder (CHADD)
8181 Professional Place, Suite 150
Landover, MD 20785
(301) 306-7070
(800) 233-4050 (Voice mail to request
    information packet)
Web: www.chadd.org

Attention Deficit Disorder Association (ADDA)
P.O. Box 543
Pottstown, PA 19464
(484) 945-2101
Web: www.add.org

Autism

    To identify an autism group in Rhode
Island, contact

Autism Society of America
7910 Woodmont Avenue, Suite 300
Bethesda, MD 20814
(301) 657-0881; (800) 3-AUTISM
Web: www.autism-society.org

Blind/Visual Impairments

American Foundation for the Blind
Regina Genwright, Director of Information
    Center
11 Penn Plaza, Suite 300
New York, NY 10001
(212) 502-7600; (212) 502-7662 (TTY)
E-mail: afbinfo@afb.net
Web: www.afb.org

National Federation of the Blind of Rhode Island
Richard Gaffney, President
P.O. Box 154564
Riverside, RI 02915
(401) 433-2606
E-mail: info@nfbri.org
Web: www.nfbri.org

Brain Injury

Brain Injury Association of Rhode Island
Sharon Brinkworth, Executive Director
935 Park Avenue, Suite 8
Cranston, RI 02910
(401) 461-6599; (888) 824-8911
E-mail: braininjuryctr@biaofri.org
Web: www.biaofri.org

Cerebal Palsy

United Cerebral Palsy of Rhode Island
200 Main Street, Suite 210
P.O. Box 36
Pawtucket, RI 02862
(401) 728-1800
E-mail: ucprisupport@ucpri.org
Web: www.ucpri.org

Down Syndrome

Down Syndrome Society of Rhode Island, Inc.
Claudia M. Lowe
99 Bald Hill Road
Cranston, RI 02920
(401) 463-5751; (800) 745-5555 (TDD for RI relay)
E-mail: coordinator@dssri.org
Web: www.dssri.org

Epilepsy

Epilepsy Foundation of Massachusetts
   and Rhode Island
Leslie G. Brody, PhD, Chief Executive Officer
540 Gallivant Boulevard, 2nd Floor
Boston, MA 02124
(617) 506-6041; (888) 576-9996
Web: www.efmri.org

Mental Health

Mental Health Association of Rhode Island
Cynthia A. Barry, Executive Director
500 Prospect Street
Pawtucket, RI 02860
(401) 726-2285
E-mail: cynbarry@hotmail.com
Web: www.mhari.org

Parent Support Network of Rhode Island
Cathy Ciano, Executive Director
400 Warwick Avenue, Suite 12
Warwick, RI 02888
(401) 467-6855; (800) 483-8844 (in RI)
E-mail: cathyciano@aol.com
Web: www.psnri.org

NAMI Rhode Island
Nicki Sahlin, PhD, Executive Director
Dorian Parker, Assistant Director
82 Pitman Street
Providence, RI 02906
(401) 331-3060; (800) 749-3197
E-mail: nicknami@aol.com
E-mail: dorianparker@minister.com
Web: www.namiri.org

Mental Retardation

Rhode Island Arc
James Healey, Executive Director
99 Bald Hill Road
Cranston, RI 02920
(401) 463-9191
E-mail: riarc@compuserve.com

Special Health Care Needs

Family Voices of the Rhode Island Parent
   Information Network
Dawn Wardyga, Program Director
175 Main Street
Pawtucket, RI 02860
(401) 727-4144, ext. 158; (800) 464-3399,
   ext. 158 (in RI)
E-mail: familyvoices@ripin.org
Web: http://ripin.org/

Speech and Hearing

Rhode Island Speech-Language-Hearing Association
Sheryl C. Amaral, President
P.O. Box 9241
Providence, RI 02940
(401) 455-7472
Web: www.risha.info

Rhode Island—Organizations Especially for Parents

Parent Training and Information Center (PTI)

Rhode Island Parent Info Network (RIPIN)
Cheryl Collins, Program Director
175 Main Street
Pawtucket, RI 02860
(401) 727-4144, ext. 152; (800) 464-3399 (in RI)
E-mail: collins@ripin.org
Web: www.ripin.org

Parent-To-Parent

Family to Family of Rhode Island
Family Voices at the Rhode Island Parent
   Information Network
Cindy Montero, Outreach Coordinator
175 Main Street
Pawtucket, RI 02860
(401) 727-4144, ext. 141; (800) 401-3399 (in RI)
E-mail: montero@ripin.org
Web: www.rifamilytofamily.net

Parent Teacher Association (PTA)

Rhode Island Congress of Parents and Teachers
Mary Anne Roll, President
RIC East Campus-Building 6
600 Mount Pleasant Avenue
Providence, RI 02908
(401) 272-6405
E-mail: ri_office@pta.org

Rhode Island—Other Disability Organizations

Advocates in Action
P.O. Box 41528
Providence, RI 02940-1528
(401) 785-2028; (800) 745-5555
    (TTY, via RI relay)
E-mail: aina@aina-ri.org
Web: www.aina-ri.org

Exeter/West Greenwich Individuals Needs
    Advisory Committee
c/o Special Services Office
930 Nooseneck Hill Road
West Greenwich, RI 02817
E-mail: EWGINAC@att.net
Web: http://EWGINAC.home.att.net

VSA Arts of Rhode Island
Jeannine Chartier, Executive Director
500 Prospect Street
Pawtucket, RI 02860
(401) 725-0247; (800) 745-5555 (TTY/Relay)
E-mail: ri@vsarts.org
Web: http://ri.vsarts.org/

Independent Living

To find out the contact information for the *Statewide Independent Living Council (SILC) in Rhode Island, contact*

Independent Living Research Utilization Project
The Institute for Rehabilitation and Research
2323 South Sheppard, Suite 1000
Houston, TX 77019
(713) 520-0232 (V); (713) 520-5136 (TTY)
E-mail: ilru@ilru.org
Web: www.ilru.org

To find out the contact information for centers for independent living (CILs) in Rhode Island, contact

National Council on Independent Living
1916 Wilson Boulevard, Suite 209
Arlington, VA 22201
(703) 525-3406; (703) 525-4153 (TTY)
E-mail: ncil@ncil.org
Web: www.ncil.org

SOUTH CAROLINA

South Carolina—State Agencies and Organizations

United States Senators

Honorable Lindsey Graham (R)
290 Russell Senate Office Building
Washington, DC 20510
(202) 224-5972
(202) 224-1189 (Fax)
E-mail Web Form: http://www.
    lgraham.senate.gov/public/
    index.cfm?FuseAction=contact.
    emailsenatorgraham

Honorable Tim Scott (R)
167 Russell Senate Office Building
Washington, DC 20510
(202) 224-6121; (800) 922-8503 (in SC)
(202) 224-4293 (Fax)
E-mail Web Form: http://www.scott.senate.
    gov/contact/email-me
Web: http://www.scott.senate.gov/

United States Representatives

To find the contact information for your representative in the House of the U.S. Congress, visit the House's Web site at: *www.house.gov*, or call (202) 225-3121; (202) 225-1904 (TTY).

Governor

Honorable Nikki Haley
Office of the Governor
1205 Pendleton Street
Columbia, SC 29201
(803) 734-2100; (803) 734-5167 (Fax)
E-mail Web Form: http://www.governor.
    sc.gov/ContactUs/Pages/index.aspx
Web: http://www.governor.sc.gov/Pages/
    default.aspx

Official State Web Site

Web: www.sc.gov

State Department of Education: Special Education

Office of Exceptional Children
State Department of Education
John Payne, Director
1429 Senate Street, Room 808
Columbia, SC 29201
(803) 734-2738
E-mail: JRPayne@ed.sc.gov
Web: http://ed.sc.gov/agency/ac/Special-
   Education-Services/

   SC was granted an extended waiver from the NCLB act.

Roy Stehle, Director
Office of Federal and State Accountability
1429 Senate Street Suite 502
Columbia, SC 29201
(803) 734-8118
E-mail: RStehle@ed.sc.gov
Web: http://ed.sc.gov/agency/programs-
   services/77/

Programs for Infants and Toddlers With Disabilities: Birth–2 Years

South Carolina First Steps to School Success
Kristie Musick, Part C Coordinator
1300 Sumter Street, Suite 100
Columbia, SC 29201
(803) 734-8068
E-mail: KMusick@scfirststeps.org
Web: http://scfirststeps.org/

Programs for Children With Disabilities: 3–5 Years

Office of Exceptional Children
State Department of Education
Norma Donaldson-Jenkins, 619 Coordinator
Rutledge Building
1429 Senate Street
Columbia, SC 29201
(803) 734-4824
E-mail: njenkins@ed.sc.gov
Web: http://ed.sc.gov/agency/ac/Special-
   Education-Services/

State Vocational Rehabilitation Agency

South Carolina Vocational Rehabilitation
   Department
Larry C. Bryant, Commissioner
410 Boston Avenue
P.O. Box 15
West Columbia, SC 29171-0015
(803) 896-6500
Web: www.scvrd.net

Coordinator for Transition Services

Joy Ivester, Coordinator
Office of Exceptional Children
South Carolina Department of Education
1429 Senate Street, Room 503-A
Columbia, SC 29201
(803) 734-8483
E-mail: ivesterj@cdd.sc.us
Web: www.scdcdt.org/

Office of State Coordinator of Vocational Education for Students With Disabilities

Office of Career and Technology Education
Dr. James R. Couch, Director
912A Rutledge Building
Columbia, SC 29201
(803) 734-8410
E-mail: jcouch@sde.state.sc.us
Web: www.state.sc.us/sde

State Mental Health Agency

Department of Mental Health
George P. Gintoli, Director
P. O. Box 485
Columbia, SC 29202
(803) 898-8319
E-mail: gpg97@scdmh.org
Web: www.state.sc.us/dmh

State Mental Health Representative for Children and Youth

Division of Children, Adolescents and
   Their Families
Louise Johnson, Director
Department of Mental Health
2414 Bull Street, Room 304
Columbia, SC 29201
(803) 898-8350
E-mail: lkj40@sc.dmh.org

State Department of Disabilities and Special Needs

Department of Disabilities and Special Needs
Stanley J. Butkus, Director
3440 Harden Street Extension
P.O. Box 4706
Columbia, SC 29240
(803) 898-9769
E-mail: jterry@ddsn.state.sc.us
Web: www.state.sc.us/ddsn

Council on Developmental Disabilities

Developmental Disabilities Council
Charles Lang, Executive Director
Office of the Governor
Edgar A. Brown Building
1205 Pendleton Street, Suite 453
Columbia, SC 29201
(803) 734-0465
E-mail: clang@govoepp.state.sc.us
Web: www.scddc.state.sc.us

Protection and Advocacy Agency

Protection and Advocacy for People with Disabilities
Gloria M. Prevost, Executive Director
3710 Landmark Drive, Suite 208
Columbia, SC 29204
(803) 782-0639; (866) 275-7273
E-mail: info@protectionandadvocacy-sc.org
Web: www.protectionandadvocacy-sc.org

Client Assistance Program

Client Assistance Program
Larry Barker, PhD, Director
Office of the Governor
1205 Pendelton Street, Room 447
Columbia, SC 29201
(803) 734-0285; (800) 868-0040 (in SC)
(803) 734-1147 (TTY)
E-mail: lbarker@govoepp.state.sc.us
Web: www.govoepp.state.sc.us/cap/

Programs for Children With Special Health Care Needs

Division of Children with Special Health Care Needs
Department of Health and Environmental Control
P.O. Box 101106
Columbia, SC 29211
(803) 898-0789
E-mail: priceld@dhec.sc.gov

State CHIP Program (health care for low-income, uninsured children)

Partners for Healthy Children
P.O. Box 100101
Columbia, SC 29202
(888) 549-0820
Web: www.dhhs.state.sc.us/InsideDHHS/
   Bureaus

SCDHHS P.O. Box 8206
Columbia, SC 29202-8206
Web:http://www.medicaid.gov/Medicaid-
   CHIP-Program-Information/By-State/
   south-carolina.html

Programs for Children and Youth Who Are Blind or Visually Impaired

South Carolina Commission for the Blind
Dr. Nell C. Carney, Commissioner
P.O. Box 79
Columbia, SC 29202-0079
(803) 898-8822
E-mail: ljohnston@sccb.state.sc.us

State School for the Deaf and the Blind
Dr. Sheila S. Breitweiser, President
South Carolina School for the
   Deaf and the Blind
355 Cedar Springs Road
Spartanburg, SC 29302-4699
(864) 585-7711
E-mail: sbreitweiser@scsdb.k12.sc.us
Web: www.scsdb.k12.sc.us

Telecommunications Relay Services for Individuals Who Are Deaf, Hard of Hearing, or With Speech Impairments

(800) 735-2905 (V)
(800) 735-7293 (ASCII); 711 (TTY)
(877) 735-7277 (Speech to Speech)
(800) 735-8583 (SC Relay)
(877) 225-8337 (SC TEDP)

State Education Agency
Rural Representative

Gail Redford, Education Associate
State Department of Education
Office of Exceptional Children
1429 Senate Street, 8th Floor
Columbia, SC 29201-3730
(803) 734-3266
E-mail: gredford@sde.state.sc.us
Web: www.sde.state.sc.us

Regional ADA & IT
Technical Assistance Center

Southeast Disability and Business Technical
   Assistance Center
Shelley Kaplan, Project Director
Center for Assistive Technology and
   Environmental Access
Georgia Tech
490 10th Street
Atlanta, GA 30318
(404) 385-0636; (800) 949-4232 (V/TTY)
E-mail: sedbtac@catea.org
Web: www.sedbtac.org

University Center for Excellence
in Developmental Disabilities

Center for Disability Resources (UCEDD)
Richard R. Ferrante, PhD, Director
University of South Carolina
USC School of Medicine
Department of Pediatrics
Columbia, SC 29208
(803) 935-5248
E-mail: richardf@cdd.sc.edu
Web: www.cdd.sc.edu

Technology-Related Assistance

South Carolina Assistive Technology Project
Evelyn Evans, Project Director
USC School of Medicine–Department of
   Pediatrics
Center for Disability Resources
8301 Farrow Road
Columbia, SC 29203
(803) 935-5263; (803) 935-5340
E-mail: youngs@cdd.sc.edu
E-mail: evelyne@cdd.sc.edu

State Mediation System

Office of General Counsel
Department of Education
Barbara Drayton, Coordinator
Rutledge Building, Room 1015
1429 Senate Street
Columbia, SC 29201
(803) 734-8783
E-mail: bdrayton@sde.state.sc.us
Web: www.myscschools.com

Special Format Library

Talking Book Services
Guynell Williams, Librarian
South Carolina State Library
P.O. Box 821
Columbia, SC 29202-0821
(803) 734-4611; (800) 922-7818
(803) 734-7298 (TTY)
E-mail: lbphbooks@leo.scsl.state.sc.us
Web: http://sctalkingbook.org/

South Carolina—Disability-Specific Organizations

Attention Deficit Disorder

   To identify an ADD group in South Carolina,
contact either of the following organizations:

Children and Adults With Attention-Deficit/
   Hyperactivity Disorder (CHADD)
8181 Professional Place, Suite 150
Landover, MD 20785
(301) 306-7070
(800) 233-4050 (Voice mail to request
   information packet)
Web: www.chadd.org

Attention Deficit Disorder Association (ADDA)
P.O. Box 543
Pottstown, PA 19464
(484) 945-2101
Web: www.add.org

Autism

South Carolina Autism Society
Craig Stoxen, Executive Director
652 Bush River Road, Suite 203
Columbia, SC 29210
(803) 750-6988; (800) 438-4790
E-mail: scas@scautism.org
Web: www.scautism.org

Blind/Visual Impairments

American Foundation for the Blind–National
   Literacy Center
Frances Mary D'Andrea, Director
100 Peachtree Street, Suite 620
Atlanta, GA 30303
(404) 525-2303
E-mail: literacy@afb.net
Web: www.afb.org

Brain Injury

Brain Injury Alliance of South Carolina
Phil Clarkson, President
Dr. Robert Brabham, Executive Director
920 St. Andrews Road
Columbia, SC 29210
(803) 731-9823
E-mail: scbraininjury@mindspring.com
Web: www.biausa.org/sc

Epilepsy

Epilepsy Foundation South Carolina
Barbara Brothers, Executive Director
652 Bush River Road, Suite 211
Columbia, SC 29210
(803) 798-8502
E-mail: foundationepilep@bellsouth.net
Web: https://www.scepilepsy.org/

Mental Health

Federation of Families of South Carolina
Diane Revels-Flashnick, Executive Director
P.O. Box 1266
Columbia, SC 29202
(803) 779-0402; (866) 779-0402
E-mail: fedfamsc@yahoo.com
Web: www.midnet.sc.edu/ffsc/

Mental Health Association in South Carolina
Joy Jay, Executive Director
1823 Gadsden Street
Columbia, SC 29201
(803) 779-5363
E-mail: mha-sc@mha.org
Web: www.mha-sc.org

NAMI of South Carolina
J. David Almeida, Executive Director
P.O. Box 1267
Columbia, SC 29202
(803) 733-9591/9592; (800) 788-5131
E-mail: namiofsc@logicsouth.com
Web: www.namisc.org

Mental Retardation

The Arc of South Carolina
Redick Loring, Executive Director
P.O. Box 8707
Columbia, SC 29202
(803) 935-5266; (866) 300-9331
E-mail: TheArcSC@aol.com
Web: www.arcsc.org

Speech and Hearing

South Carolina Speech-Language-Hearing
   Association
Deborah Arnold, President
701 Gervais Street, Suite 150-206
Columbia, SC 29201
(888) 729-3717
E-mail: scsha@scsha.com
Web: www.scsha.com

South Carolina—Organizations Especially for Parents

Parent Training and Information Center (PTI)

PRO-Parents of South Carolina
Mary Eaddy, Director
652 Bush River Road, Suite 218
Columbia, SC 29210
(803) 772-5688 (V/TTY); (800) 759-4776 (in SC)
E-mail: PROParents@aol.com
Web: www.proparents.org

Parent Teacher Association (PTA)

South Carolina Congress of Parents and Teachers
Chuck Saylors, President
1826 Henderson Street
Columbia, SC 29201-2619
(800) 743-3782; (803) 765-0806
E-mail: sc_office@pta.org
Web: www.scpta.org

South Carolina—Other Disability Organizations

Center for Disability Resources Library
Roz McConnaughy, Coordinator
School of Medicine Library
University of South Carolina
Columbia, SC 29208
(803) 733-3310
E-mail: roz@med.sc.edu
Web: http://uscm.med.sc.edu/CDR/index.
   htm

Easter Seals South Carolina
Tom McGee, President/CEO
3020 Farrow Road
Columbia, SC 29203
(803) 256-0735; (800) 951-4090
Web: www.sc.easter-seals.org

South Carolina Services Information System
Denise Rivers, Director
Bureau of Senior Services
1801 Main Street
P.O. Box 8206
Columbia, SC 29202-8206
(803) 898-8878 (Admin. Number Only)
E-mail: riversd@dhhs.state.sc.us
Web: www.scsis.org

Family Connection of South Carolina, Inc.
Connie Ginsberg, Executive Director
2712 Middleburg Drive, Suite 103-B
Columbia, SC 29204
(803) 252-0914; (800) 578-8750 (in SC)
(864) 331-1340 (in Greenville)
(843) 662-0675 (in Florence)
(864) 560-1476 (in Spartanburg)
E-mail: info@familyconnectionsc.org
Web: www.familyconnectionsc.org

Independent Living

Disability Action Center, Inc.
Amy Mayne, Program Director
1115 Belleview Street
Columbia, SC 29201
(803) 779-5121 (V); (803) 779-0949 (TTY)
Web: www.dacsc.org

Independent Living Research Utilization Project
The Institute for Rehabilitation and Research
2323 South Sheppard, Suite 1000
Houston, TX 77019
(713) 520-0232 (V); (713) 520-5136 (TTY)
E-mail: ilru@ilru.org
Web: www.ilru.org

SOUTH DAKOTA

South Dakota—State Agencies and Organizations

United States Senators

Honorable Tim Johnson (D)
136 Hart Senate Office Building
Washington, DC 20510
(202) 224-5842
(202) 228-5765 (Fax)
E-mail: tim@johnson.senate.gov
Web: http://johnson.senate.gov

Honorable John Thune (R)
511 Dirksen Senate Office Building
Washington, DC 20510
(202) 224-2321
(202) 224-2047 (Fax)
E-mail Web Form: http://www.thune.senate.
  gov/public/index.cfm/contact
Web: http://www.thune.senate.gov/public/
  index.cfm/home

United States Representatives

To find the contact information for your representative in the House of the U.S. Congress, visit the House's Web site at: www.house.gov, or call (202) 224-3121; (202) 225-1904 (TTY).

Governor

Honorable Dennis Daugaard
500 E. Capitol Avenue
Pierre, SD 57501-5070
(605) 773-3212
E-mail: http://sd.gov/governor/contact.aspx
Web: http://sd.gov/governor/Default.aspx

State Department of Education: Special Education

Special Education Programs
Michelle Powers, Director
Department of Education Offices
Office of Educational Services and Supports
800 Governors Drive
Pierre, SD 57501-2291
(605) 773-3134
E-mail: michelle.powers@state.sd.us
Web: http://doe.sd.gov/oess/sped.aspx

South Dakota was granted an extended waiver from the NCLB program.

Office of Educational Support and Services
South Dakota Department of Education
800 Governors Drive
Pierre, SD 57501
(605) 773-6400
Web: http://doe.sd.gov/oess/TitleI.aspx

Programs for Infants and Toddlers
With Disabilities: Birth–2 Years

Special Education Programs
Sarah Carter, Director and Part C Coordinator
Birth to Three Connections
State Department of Education
800 Governors Drive
Pierre, SD 57501
(605) 773-4478
E-mail: sarah.carter@state.sd.us
Web: https://doe.sd.gov/oess/Birthto3.aspx

Programs for Children
With Disabilities: 3–5 Years

Special Education Programs
Wendy Trujillo, 619 Coordinator
Department of Education
800 Governors Drive
Pierre, SD 57501
(605) 773-8071; (800) 305-3064 (in SD)
E-mail: wendy.trujillo@state.sd.us
Web: https://doe.sd.gov/oess/sped_
    earlyIntervention619.aspx

State Vocational Rehabilitation Agency

Division of Rehabilitation Services
Grady Kickul, Director
Department of Human Services
Hillsview Plaza, East Highway 34
c/o 500 E. Capitol
Pierre, SD 57501-5070
(605) 773-3195
E-mail: grady.kickul@state.sd.us
Web: www.state.sd.us/dhs/drs/

Office of State Coordinator of Vocational Education for
Students With Disabilities

Office of Career and Technical Education
Tiffany Sanderson, Director
Department of Education Programs
800 Governors Drive
Pierre, SD 57501-2291
(605) 773-3423
E-mail: tiffany.sanderson@state.sd.us
Web: http://www.doe.sd.gov

State Mental Health Agency

Division of Mental Health
Kim Malsam-Rysdon, Director
Department of Human Services
Hillsview Plaza, East Highway 34
c/o 500 E. Capitol
Pierre, SD 57501-5070
(605) 773-5991; (605) 773-5990 (TTY)
E-mail: kim.malsam-rysdon@state.sd.us
Web: www.state.sd.us/dhs

State Mental Health
Representative for Children and Youth

Amy Iversen Pollreisz, Community Mental
    Health Manager
Department of Human Services
Division of Mental Health
Hillsview Plaza, East Highway 34
c/o 500 E. Capitol
Pierre, SD 57501-5070
(605) 773-5991; (605) 773-5990 (TTY)
E-mail: amy.iversen-pollreisz@state.sd.us
Web: www.state.sd.us/dhs

State Developmental Disabilities Program

Division of Developmental Disabilities
Wanda Seiler, Division Director
Department of Human Services
Hillsview Plaza, East Highway 34
c/o 500 E. Capitol
Pierre, SD 57501
(605) 773-3438; (800) 265-9684
E-mail: wanda-seiler@state.sd.us
Web: www.state.sd.us/dhs/dd/

State Developmental Disabilities Representative for
Children and Youth

Division of Developmental Disabilities
Donna Olivier, Program Specialist
Department of Human Services
Hillsview Plaza, East Highway 34
c/o 500 E. Capitol
Pierre, SD 57501-5070
(605) 773-3438; (800) 265-9684
(605) 773-5990 (TTY)
E-mail: donna.olivier@state.sd.us
Web: www.state.sd.us/dhs/dd/

Council on Developmental Disabilities

South Dakota Council on Developmental
  Disabilities
Arlene Poncelet, Executive Director
Hillsview Plaza, East Highway 34
c/o 500 E. Capitol
Pierre, SD 57501-5070
(605) 773-6369; (800) 265-9684
E-mail: arlene.poncelet@state.sd.us
Web: www.state.sd.us/dhs/ddc/

Protection and Advocacy Agency

South Dakota Advocacy Services
Robert J. Kean, Executive Director
221 S. Central Avenue
Pierre, SD 57501
(605) 224-8294; (800) 658-4782 (in SD)
E-mail: sdas@sdadvocacy.com
Web: www.sdadvocacy.com

Client Assistance Program

   Contact Protection and Advocacy Agency,
listed above.

**Programs for Children
With Special Health Care Needs**

Children's Special Health Services
Nancy Hoyme, Director
Health and Medical Services
Department of Health
615 E. Fourth Street
Pierre, SD 57501
(605) 773-3737; (800) 305-3064
E-mail: Nancy.Hoyme@state.sd.us
Web: www.state.sd.us/doh

**Programs for Children and Youth
Who Are Blind or Visually Impaired**

Service to the Blind and Visually Impaired
Gaye Mattke, Director
Hillsview Plaza
500 E. Capitol
Pierre, SD 57501
(605) 773-4644
E-mail: infosbvi@state.sd.us
Web: www.state.sd.us/dhs/sbvi/

**Programs for Children and Youth
Who Are Deaf or Hard of Hearing**

Communication Services for the Deaf, Inc. (CSD)
Benjamin Soukup, CEO
102 N. Krohn Place
Sioux Falls, SD 57103
(605) 367-5760 (V); (800) 642-6410 (V/in SD)
(605) 367-5761 (TTY); (866) 273-3323 (TTY)
E-mail: bsoukup@c-s-d.org
Web: www.c-s-d.org

**Telecommunications Relay
Services for Individuals Who
Are Deaf, Hard of Hearing, or
With Speech Impairments**

(800) 877-1113 (V/TTY); 711 (TTY)
(877) 981-9744 (Speech to Speech)

State Respite Care Program

Respite Care Program
Kathy Olson, Program Specialist
Department of Human Services
Hillsview Plaza, East Highway 34
c/o 500 E. Capitol
Pierre, SD 57501-5070
(605) 773-3438; (800) 265-9684
E-mail: Kathy.Olson@state.sd.us
Web: www.state.sd.us/dhs/dd/respite/
  index.htm

**State Education Agency
Rural Representative**

   Contact State Department of Education:
Special Education, listed above.

**Regional ADA & IT
Technical Assistance Center**

Rocky Mountain Disability and
  Business Technical Assistance Center
Patrick Going, Director
3630 Sinton Road, Suite 103
Colorado Springs, CO 80907
(719) 444-0268 (V/TTY);
  (800) 949-4232 (V/TTY)
E-mail: rmdbtac@mtc-inc.com
Web: www.adainformation.org

University Center for Excellence
in Developmental Disabilities

Center for Disabilities
Judy Struck, Executive Director
Health Science Center
1400 W. 22nd Street
Sioux Falls, SD 57105
(605) 357-1439; (800) 658-3080 (V/TTY)
Web: www.usd.edu/cd

Technology-Related Assistance

DakotaLink
Dave Vogel, Project Director
221 S. Central
Pierre, SD 57501
(605) 224-5336; (800) 224-5336
E-mail: dvogel@tie.net
Web: http://dakotalink.tie.net

State Mediation System

Special Education Programs
Department of Education Programs
Michelle Powers, Director
700 Governors Drive
Pierre, SD 57501-2291
(605) 773-3678
E-mail: michelle.powers@state.sd.us
Web: www.state.sd.us/deca/Special/index.htm

South Dakota—Disability-Specific Organizations

Attention Deficit Disorder

To identify an ADD group in South Dakota, contact either of the following organizations:

Children and Adults With Attention-Deficit/
   Hyperactivity Disorder (CHADD)
8181 Professional Place, Suite 150
Landover, MD 20785
(301) 306-7070
(800) 233-4050 (Voice mail to request
   information packet)
Web: www.chadd.org

Attention Deficit Disorder Association (ADDA)
P.O. Box 543
Pottstown, PA 19464
(484) 945-2101
Web: www.add.org

Autism

To identify an autism group in South Dakota, contact

Autism Society of America
7910 Woodmont Avenue, Suite 300
Bethesda, MD 20814
(301) 657-0881; (800) 3-AUTISM
Web: www.autism-society.org

Blind/Visual Impairments

American Foundation for the Blind—Midwest
Jay Stiteley, Director
401 N. Michigan Avenue, Suite 350
Chicago, IL 60611
(312) 396-4420
E-mail: chicago@afb.net
Web: www.afb.org

Learning Disabilities

LDA of South Dakota
James Huff, President
P.O. Box 9760
Rapid City, SD 57709-9760
1-888-388-5553 (in SD only)
E-mail: dthom@rapidnet.com
Web: www.geocities.com/Athens/Ithaca/
   8835/AboutLDA-SD.html

Mental Health

NAMI South Dakota
P.O. Box 1204
Huron, SD 57350-1204
(800) 551-2531
E-mail: namisd@santel.net
Web: http://sd.nami.org

Speech and Hearing

South Dakota Speech-Language-Hearing
   Association
Shirley Hauge, President
P.O. Box 308
Sioux Falls, SD 57101
(605) 331-2927
Web: www.sdslha.org

South Dakota—Organizations Especially for Parents

Parent Training and Information Center (PTI)

South Dakota Parent Connection
Lynn Boettcher Fjellanger, Director
3701 W. 49th Street, Suite 200B
Sioux Falls, SD 57106
(605) 361-3171 (V/TTY); (800) 640-4553 (in SD)
E-mail: sdpc@sdparent.org
Web: www.sdparent.org

Parent Teacher Association (PTA)

South Dakota Congress of Parents and Teachers
Betty Ochsner, President
411 E. Capitol
Pierre, SD 57501-3194
(605) 224-0144
E-mail: sd_office@pta.org
Web: www.southdakotapta.org

No Child Left Behind–Parent Information & Resource Center

South Dakota Parent Resource Network
Mary Baumeister, Director
P.O. Box 218
Sturgis, SD 57785
(800) 219-6247; (605) 347-6260
E-mail: llaughlin@bhssc.tie.net
E-mail: maryb@bhssc.tie.net
Web: www.tie.net/prn

South Dakota—Other Disability Organizations

Easter Seals South Dakota
Patricia K. Miller, CEO/Executive Director
1351 N. Harrison Avenue
Pierre, SD 57501
(605) 224-5879; (800) 592-1852
E-mail: administrator@sd.easter-seals.org
Web: www.sd.easterseals.com

South Dakota Family Support Council
Teri Suss, Chair
14828 482nd Avenue
Milbank, SD 57252
(605) 432-4203

South Dakota Coalition of Citizens with Disabilities
Shelly Pfaff, Executive Director
221 South Central Avenue
Pierre, SD 57501
(800) 210-0143 (V/TTY);
    (605) 945-2207 (V/TTY)
E-mail: shellyp@sd-ccd.org
Web: www.sd-ccd.org

Independent Living

To find out the contact information for the Statewide Independent Living Council (SILC) in South Dakota, contact

Independent Living Research Utilization Project
The Institute for Rehabilitation and Research
2323 South Sheppard, Suite 1000
Houston, TX 77019
(713) 520-0232 (V); (713) 520-5136 (TTY)
E-mail: ilru@ilru.org
Web: www.ilru.org

To find out the contact information for centers for independent living (CILs) in South Dakota, contact

National Council on Independent Living
1916 Wilson Boulevard, Suite 209
Arlington, VA 22201
(703) 525-3406; (703) 525-4153 (TTY)
E-mail: ncil@ncil.org
Web: www.ncil.org

TENNESSEE

Tennessee—State Agencies and Organizations

United States Senators

Honorable Lamar Alexander (R)
455 Dirksen Senate Office Building
Washington, DC 20510
(202) 224-4944; (202) 224-1911 (TTY)
(202) 228-1264 (Fax)
E-mail Web Form: http://www.alexander.
    senate.gov/public/index.cfm/email
Web: http://www.alexander.senate.gov/
    public/index.cfm/home

Honorable Bob Corker (R)
455 Dirksen Senate Office Building
Washington, DC 20510
(202) 224-3344
(202) 228-3398 (Fax)
E-mail Web Form: http://www.corker.senate.
gov/public/index.cfm?p=ContactMe
Web: http://www.corker.senate.gov/public/
index.cfm/

United States Representatives

To find the contact information for your representative in the House of the U.S. Congress, visit the House's Web site at: www.house.gov, or call (202) 225-3121; (202) 225-1904 (TTY).

Governor

Honorable Bill Haslam
Governor's Office
Tennessee State Capitol
Nashville, TN 37423-0001
(615) 741-2001
(615) 532-9711 (Fax)
E-mail: http://www.tn.gov/governor/contact.
shtml
Web: http://www.tn.gov/governor/

Official State Web Site

Web: www.state.tn.us/

State Department of Education: Special Education

Division of Special Education
Joey Hassell, Assistant Commissioner
Department of Education
Andrew Johnson Tower, 5th Floor
710 James Robertson Parkway
Nashville, TN 37243-0380
(615) 253-2112
E-mail: Joey.Hassell@tn.gov
Web: www.state.tn.us/education/speced/

State Coordinator for NCLB (No Child Left Behind)

Tennessee was granted an extended waiver from the NCLB act.

Katina Grays, Executive Director Consolidated
Planning and Monitoring
710 James Robertson Parkway
Nashville, TN 37243
(615) 253-3786

Email: Katina.Grays@tn.gov
Web: http://www.tn.gov/education/districts/
cpm/ESEA.shtml

**Programs for Infants and
Toddlers With Disabilities: Birth–2 Years**

Tennessee Early Intervention System (TEIS)
Joan Kennedy, Part C Coordinator
State Department of Education
Andrew Johnson Tower, 7th Floor
710 James Robertson Parkway
Nashville, TN 37243
(615) 741-9873
E-mail: joan.kennedy@tn.gov
Web: http://www.tn.gov/education/early_
learning/TEIS.shtml

**Programs for Children
With Disabilities: 3–5 Years**

Office of Early Childhood
Gary Smith, 619 Coordinator
State Department of Education
Andrew Johnson Tower, 7th Floor
710 James Robertson Parkway
Nashville, TN 37243
(615) 741-9871
E-mail: wendy.trujillo@state.sd.us
Web: http://www.tn.gov/education/early_
learning/index.shtml

State Vocational Rehabilitation Agency

Division of Rehabilitation Services
Carl Brown, Assistant Commissioner
Department of Human Services
400 Deaderick Street, 15th Floor
Nashville, TN 37248-0060
(615) 313-4714
E-mail: carl.w.brown@state.tn.us
Web: www.state.tn.us/humanserv

Coordinator for Transition Services

Tennessee Department of Education
710 James Robertson Parkway
Andrew Johnson Tower, 5th Floor
Nashville, TN 37243
(615) 741-7790
E-mail: Joe.Fisher@state.tn.us
Web: www.state.tn.us/education/speced/

Office of State Coordinator of Vocational Education for Students With Disabilities

Division of Vocational Education
Andrew Johnson Tower, 4th Floor
710 James Robertson Parkway
Nashville, TN 37243-0383
(615) 532-2834
Web: www.state.tn.us/education/

State Mental Health Agency

Department of Mental Health and
Developmental Disabilities
Virginia Trotter-Betts, Commissioner
Cordell Hull Building, 3rd Floor
425 5th Avenue North
Nashville, TN 37243
(615) 532-6500
E-mail: Shawn.Cook@state.tn.us
Web: www.state.tn.us/mental

State Mental Health Representative for Children and Youth

Office of Children and Adolescent Services
Pam Sylakowski, Director
Department of Mental Health and
Developmental Disabilities
Cordell Hull Building, 3rd Floor
425 5th Avenue North
Nashville, TN 37243
(615) 532-6758; (615) 532-6612 (TTY)
E-mail: Pam.Sylakowski@state.tn.us
Web: www.state.tn.us/mental

State Mental Retardation Program

Division of Mental Retardation Department of
Finance and Administration
Richard Kellogg, Acting Deputy Commissioner
Andrew Jackson Building
500 Deaderick Street, 15th Floor
Nashville, TN 37243
(615) 532-6530
E-mail: Richard.Kellogg@state.tn.us
Web: www.state.tn.us/mental/mrs.html

Council on Developmental Disabilities

Tennessee Council on Developmental Disabilities
Wanda Willis, Executive Director
Andrew Jackson Building
500 Deaderick Street, 13th Floor, Suite 1310

Nashville, TN 37243-0228
(615) 532-6615
E-mail: tnddc@state.tn.us
Web: www.state.tn.us/cdd

Protection and Advocacy Agency

Tennessee Protection and Advocacy, Inc.
Shirley Shea, Executive Director
P.O. Box 121257
Nashville, TN 37212
(615) 298-1080; (800) 342-1660
   (Toll-free in TN only)
(615) 298-2471 (TTY)
E-mail: shirleys@tpainc.org
Web: www.tpainc.org

Client Assistance Program

   Contact Protection and Advocacy Agency,
listed above.

Programs for Children With Special Health Care Needs

Children's Special Services
Department of Health
Title 5 Children with Special Health Care Needs
Margaret Major, Acting Director
Cordell Hull Building, 5th Floor
425 5th Avenue North
Nashville, TN 37247-4750
(615) 741-8530
E-mail: Margaret.Major@.state.tn.us
Web: www.state.tn.us/health/MCH/css.htm

State CHIP Program (health care for low-income, uninsured children)

TennCare
(800) 669-1851
Web: www.state.tn.us/tenncare/

State Education Agency Rural Representative

Division of Special Education
Ann Hampton, CSPD Coordinator
Department of Education
Andrew Johnson Tower, 5th Floor
710 James Robertson Parkway
Nashville, TN 37243-0380
(615) 741-2851
E-mail: ahampton@state.tn.us
Web: www.state.tn.us/education/

Programs for Children and Youth
Who Are Deaf or Hard of Hearing

Tennessee Council for the Deaf and Hard of Hearing
Thom Roberts, Director
Citizens Plaza Building, 11th Floor
400 Deaderick Street
Nashville, TN 37248-6000
(615) 313-4918; (615) 313-5695 (TTY)
(800) 270-1349 (in TN)
Web: www.state.tn.us/humanserv

Telecommunications Relay Services
for Individuals Who Are Deaf, Hard
of Hearing, or With Speech Impairments

(800) 848-0299 (V)
(800) 848-0298 (V/TTY); 711 (TTY)
(866) 503-0264 (Speech to Speech)
(866) 503-0263 (V/TTY/ASCII)

Programs for Children and Youth Who
Are Blind or Visually Impaired or Deaf-Blind

Project TREDS
Lisa Cushing, Program Coordinator
Vanderbilt University
Peabody Box 328
230 Appleton Place
Nashville, TN 37203-5701
(615) 322-8279; (615) 322-8280 (V/TTY)
(800) 288-2266 (V/TTY)
E-mail: lisa.cushing@vanderbilt.edu
Web: www.vanderbilt.edu/kennedy/treds/
    index.html

Services for the Blind and Visually Impaired
Cathy Steger, Deaf-Blind Coordinator
Division of Rehabilitation Services
Citizens Plaza State Office Building
400 Deaderick Street, Suite 1100
Nashville, TN 37248-6200
(615) 313-4917; (800) 628-7818
(615) 313-6601 (TTY); (800) 270-1349 (TTY)
E-mail: Cathy.Steger@state.tn.us
Web: www.state.tn.us/humanserv/
    vis-home.html

State Department for Children
and Youth in State Custody

Tennessee Department of Children's Services
Michael Miller, Commissioner
Tricia Henwood, Director of Medical Services
Cordell Hull Building, 7th Floor
436 6th Avenue North
Nashville, TN 37243-1290
(615) 741-9699
E-mail: tricia.henwood@state.tn.us
Web: www.state.tn.us/youth

Regional ADA & IT
Technical Assistance Center

Southeast Disability and Business Technical
    Assistance Center
Shelley Kaplan, Project Director
Center for Assistive Technology and
    Environmental Access
Georgia Tech
490 10th Street
Atlanta, GA 30318
(404) 385-0636; (800) 949-4232 (V/TTY)
E-mail: sedbtac@catea.org
Web: www.sedbtac.org

University Center for Excellence
in Developmental Disabilities

Boling Center for Developmental Disabilities
Frederick B. Palmer, Director
The University of Tennessee Health Science
    Center
711 Jefferson Avenue
Memphis, TN 38105
(901) 448-6512; (888) 572-2249
(901) 448-4677 (TTY)
E-mail: fpalmer@utmem.edu
Web: www.utmem.edu/bcdd/boling.html

Technology-Related Assistance

Tennessee Technology Access Project
Kevin R. Wright, Executive Director
Citizens Plaza State Office Building, 11th Floor
400 Deaderick Street
Nashville, TN 37248
(615) 532-3122 (V); (615) 741-4566 (TTY)
(800) 732-5059 (Toll-free in TN only)
E-mail: Kevin.R.Wright@state.tn.us
Web: www.state.tn.us/humanserv/
    ttap_index.htm

State Mediation System

Division of Special Education
Bill Ward, Legal Consultant
Department of Education
Andrew Johnson Tower
710 James Robertson Parkway, 5th Floor
Nashville, TN 37243-0380
(615) 741-2422
E-mail: Bill.Ward@state.tn.us
Web: www.state.tn.us/education/msped.htm

Special Format Library

Tennessee Library for the Blind and
    Physically Handicapped
Tennessee State Library and Archives
Ruth Hemphill, Librarian
403 Seventh Avenue North
Nashville, TN 37243-0313
(615) 741-3915; (800) 342-3308
E-mail: tlbph@state.tn.us
Web: http://www.tennessee.gov/tsla/lbph/

Tennessee—Disability-Specific Organizations

Attention Deficit Disorder

To identify an ADD group in Tennessee, contact either of the following organizations:

Children and Adults with Attention-Deficit/
    Hyperactivity Disorder (CHADD)
8181 Professional Place, Suite 150
Landover, MD 20785
(301) 306-7070
(800) 233-4050 (Voice mail to request
    information packet)
Web: www.chadd.org

Attention Deficit Disorder Association (ADDA)
P.O. Box 543
Pottstown, PA 19464
(484) 945-2101
Web: www.add.org

Autism

To identify an autism group in Tennessee, contact

Autism Society of America
7910 Woodmont Avenue, Suite 300
Bethesda, MD 20814

(301) 657-0881; (800) 3-AUTISM
Web: www.autism-society.org

Blind/Visual Impairments

American Foundation for the Blind–National
    Literacy Center
Frances Mary D'Andrea, Director
100 Peachtree Street, Suite 620
Atlanta, GA 30303
(404) 525-2303
E-mail: literacy@afb.net
Web: www.afb.org

Cerebral Palsy

UCP of the Mid South, Inc.
Diana Reid, Executive Director
4189 Leroy Avenue
Memphis, TN 38108
(901) 761-4277
E-mail: dreid@ucpmemphis.org

Epilepsy

Epilepsy Foundation of West Tennessee
Jean Dodds, Executive Director
70 Timber Creek, Suite 1
Cordova, TN 38018
(901) 854-0114
E-mail: jeanmdodd@hotmail.com

Learning Disabilities

Learning Disability Advocacy Center (LDAC)
7516 Enterprise Avenue, Suite 1
Germantown, TN 38138
(901) 755-0244
E-mail: IEPHelp@aol.com

Mental Health

Mental Health Association of Middle Tennessee
Angie Thompson, Executive Director
2416 21st Avenue South, Suite 201
Nashville, TN 37212
(615) 269-5355
E-mail: forinfo@mhamt.org
Web: www.ichope.com

NAMI-Tennessee
Thelma Vaughan, President
5410 Homberg Drive, Suite 4
Knoxville, TN 37919-5029

(865) 602-7900; (800) 467-3589 (in TN)
E-mail: nami-tn@nami.org
Web: http://namitn.nami.org

Tennessee Voices for Children
Charlotte Bryson, Executive Director
1315 8th Avenue South
Nashville, TN 37203
(615) 269-7751; (800) 670-9982
E-mail: TVC@TNVoices.org
Web: www.tnvoices.org

Tennessee Respite Network
Kim Gustin, Respite Project Coordinator
1315 8th Avenue South
Nashville, TN 37203
(615) 269-7855; (800) 269-7855
E-mail: kgustin@tnvoices.org
Web: www.tnvoices.org

Mental Retardation

The Arc of Tennessee
Walter Rogers, Executive Director
44 Vantage Way, Suite 550
Nashville, TN 37228
(615) 248-5878
E-mail: wrogers@thearctn.org
E-mail: walterrogersarc@aol.com
Web: www.thearctn.org

Speech and Hearing

Tennessee Association of Audiologists
and Speech-Language Pathologists
John and Nelia Westenberger, Executive
Directors
P.O. Box 70
Spring Hill, TN 37174
(931) 487-9871
E-mail: wmijohn@aol.com
Web: www.taaslp.org

Spina Bifida

Spina Bifida Association of Tennessee
Lynn Hess, Executive Director
P.O. Box 23056
Nashville, TN 37202-3056
E-mail: spinabifTN@aol.com

Tennessee—Organizations Especially for Parents

Parent Training and Information Center (PTI)

Nancy Diehl, Executive Director
Support and Training for Exceptional
Parents, Inc. (STEP)
712 Professional Plaza
Greeneville, TN 37745
(423) 639-0125; (800) 280-7837 (English &
Spanish Toll-free in TN only)
(423) 636-8217 (TTY)
E-mail: Nancy.Diehl@tnstep.org
E-mail: information@tnstep.org
Web: www.tnstep.org

Parent-To-Parent

Parents Encouraging Parents (PEP) Program
Dusti Williams, Nursing Consultant
Children's Special Services
Tennessee Department of Health
Cordell Hull Building, 5th Floor
425 5th Avenue North
Nashville, TN 37247-4750
(615) 741-0353
E-mail: dusti.williams@state.tn.us
Web: www2.state.tn.us/health/mch/css.htm

Community Parent Resource Center

The Arc of Davidson County (serving Nashville/
Davidson County)
Norman Tenenbaum, Executive Director
111 N. Wilson Boulevard
Nashville, TN 37205
(615) 321-5699
E-mail: ntenenbaum@arcdc.org
Web: www.thearctn.org

Parent Teacher Association (PTA)

Tennessee Congress of Parents and Teachers, Inc.
Lucy Spurgeon, President
1905 Acklen Avenue
Nashville, TN 37212-3788
(615) 383-9740
E-mail: tn_office@pta.org
Web: www.pta.org

Tennessee—Other Disability Organizations

Easter Seals
Jayne Perkins, President/CEO
2001 Woodmont Boulevard
Nashville, TN 37215
(615) 292-6640; (800) 264-0078
E-mail: jperkins@eastersealstn.com
Web: www.tn.easter-seals.org

March of Dimes Birth Defects Foundation
Leslie Ladd, State Director
1101 Kermit Drive, Suite 201
Nashville, TN 37217
(615) 399-3200; (888) 399-3272
Web: http://marchofdimes.com/

Tennessee Disability Coalition
Carol Westlake, Executive Director
480 Craighead Street, Suite 200
Nashville, TN 37204
(615) 383-9442; (615) 292-7790 (TTY)
E-mail: coalition@tndisability.org
Web: www.tndisability.org

Tennessee Disability Pathfinder
Carole Moore-Slater, Program Director
Vanderbilt Kennedy Family Outreach Center
* and Clinics*
1810 Edgehill Avenue
Nashville, TN 37212
(615) 322-8529; (800) 640-4636
* (English/Spanish line)*
(615) 322-7830 (Nashville line)
(800) 273-9595 (TTY)
E-mail: carole.moore-slater@vanderbilt.edu
Web: www.familypathfinder.org

Independent Living

To find out the contact information for the Statewide Independent Living Council (SILC) in Tennessee, contact

Independent Living Research Utilization Project
The Institute for Rehabilitation and Research
2323 South Sheppard, Suite 1000
Houston, TX 77019
(713) 520-0232 (V); (713) 520-5136 (TTY)
E-mail: ilru@ilru.org
Web: www.ilru.org

To find out the contact information for centers for independent living (CILs) in Tennessee, contact

National Council on Independent Living
1916 Wilson Boulevard, Suite 209
Arlington, VA 22201
(703) 525-3406; (703) 525-4153 (TTY)
E-mail: ncil@ncil.org
Web: www.ncil.org

TEXAS

Texas—State Agencies and Organizations

United States Senators

Honorable John Cornyn (R)
517 Hart Senate Office Building
Washington, DC 20510
(202) 224-2934
(202) 228-2856 (Fax)
E-mail Web Form: http://cornyn.senate.gov/
* contact/index.html*
Web: http://cornyn.senate.gov

Honorable Ted Cruz (R)
185 Dirksen Senate Office Building
Washington, DC 20510
(202) 224-5922; (202) 224-5903 (TTY)
(202) 224-0776 (Fax)
E-mail Web Form: http://www.cruz.senate.
* gov/?p=email_senator*
Web: http://www.cruz.senate.gov/

United States Representatives

To find the contact information for your representative in the House of the U.S. Congress, visit the House's Web site at: www.house.gov, or call: (202) 225-3121; (202) 225-1904 (TTY).

Governor

Honorable Rick Perry
Office of the Governor
P.O. Box 12428
Austin, TX 78711–2428
(512) 463-2000; (800) 252-9600 (in TX)
E-mail Web Form: www.governor.state.tx.us/
* contact*
Web: www.governor.state.tx.us/

Governor's Committee on People With Disabilities

Committee on People with Disabilities
Pat Pound, Executive Director

P.O. Box 12428
Austin, TX 78711
(512) 463-5742; (512) 463-5746 (TTY)
711 (Relay Service)
E-mail: ppound@governor.state.tx.us
Web: www.governor.state.tx.us/disabilities

Official State Web Site

Web: www.texas.gov

State Department of Education: Special Education

Special Programs, Monitoring, and Interventions
Mario Acosta, Deputy Associate Commissioner
Texas Education Agency
1701 N. Congress Avenue
Austin, TX 78701-1494
(512) 463-9734; (800) 252-9668
E-mail: teainfo@tea.state.tx.us
Web: http://www.tea.state.tx.us/index2.
    aspx?id=2147491399

Texas was granted an extended waiver from the NCLB program.

Division of Federal and State Education Policy
Texas Education Agency
1701 N. Congress Avenue
Austin, Texas, 78701
(512) 463-9414
Email: nclb@tea.texas.gov
Web: http://tea.texas.gov/About_TEA/
    Laws_and_Rules/NCLB_and_ESEA/No_
    Child_Left_Behind_and_Elementary_and_
    Secondary_Education_Act/

**Programs for Infants and Toddlers
With Disabilities: Birth–3 Years**

Early Childhood Intervention
Kim Wedel, Assistant Commissioner
Department of Assistive and Rehabilitative
    Services
Brown-Heatly State Office Building
4900 North Lamar
Austin, TX 78751
(512) 424-6754
Email: kim.wedel@dars.state.tx.us
Website: http://www.dars.state.tx.us/ecis/
    index.shtml

Programs for Children With Disabilities: 3–5 Years

Terrie Breeden, 619 Coordinator
Texas Education Agency

1701 North Congress Avenue
Austin, TX 78701
(512) 463-9560
E-mail: terrie.breeden@tea.state.tx.us
Web: http://www.tea.state.tx.us/index4.
    aspx?id=2147494988

State Vocational Rehabilitation Agencies

Department of Assistive
    and Rehabilitative Services
Terry Murphy, Commissioner
4900 N. Lamar
Austin, TX 78751-2399
(512) 424-4001
Web: www.dars.state.tx.us

Department of Aging
    and Disability Services
Jim Hine, Commissioner
701 W. 51st Street
Austin, TX 78751
(512) 438-3011; (800) 874-9426 (TTY)
E-mail: mail@dads.state.tx.us
Web: www.dads.state.tx.us

Coordinator for Transition Services

Division of IDEA Coordination
Susan Rose, Interagency Coordinator
Texas Education Agency
1701 N. Congress Avenue
Austin, TX 78701
(512) 463-9414
E-mail: susan.rose@tea.state.tx.us
Web: www.tea.state.tx.us/special.ed/

Career and Technology Education

Division of Curriculum
Texas Education Agency
Karen Batchelor
1701 N. Congress Avenue, Room 3–121
Austin, TX 78701
(512) 463-9581
Web: www.tea.state.tx.us/Cate

Department of State Health Services

Department of State Health Services
Eduardo J. Sanchez, MD, MPH, Commissioner
1100 W. 49th Street
Austin, TX 78756
(512) 458-7375
Web: www.dshs.state.tx.us

**State Mental Health Representative
for Children and Youth**

*Debbie Berndt, Director
Children's Services
Department of State Health Services
P.O. Box 12668
Austin, TX 78711-2668
(512) 206-4722
E-mail: debbie.berndt@mhmr.state.tx.us
Web: www.dshs.state.tx.us*

Council on Developmental Disabilities

*Texas Council for Developmental Disabilities
Roger A. Webb, Executive Director
6201 E. Oltorf, Suite 600
Austin, TX 78741-7509
(512) 437-5432; (800) 262-0334
(512) 437-5431 (TTY)
E-mail: tcdd@tcdd.state.tx.us
Web: www.txddc.state.tx.us*

Protection and Advocacy Agency

*Advocacy, Inc.
Mary Faithfull, Executive Director
7800 Shoal Creek Boulevard, Suite 171-E
Austin, TX 78757
(512) 454-4816; (800) 252-9108 (in TX)
E-mail: infoai@advocacyinc.org
Web: www.advocacyinc.org*

Client Assistance Program

*Client Assistant Program
Karen Stanfill, CAP Coordinator
Advocacy, Inc.
7457 Harwin, Suite 100
Houston, TX 77036
(713) 974-7691; (800) 252-9108 (in TX)
E-mail: kstanfill@advocacyinc.org
Web: www.advocacyinc.org*

**Programs for Children With
Special Health Care Needs**

*Children with Special Health Care Needs (CSHCN)
    Services Program
Sam B. Cooper III, MSW, LMSW, Manager
Purchased Health Services Unit
Department of State Health Services
1100 W. 49th Street
Austin, TX 78756-3179
(512) 458-7355
E-mail: cshcn@dshs.state.tx.uss
Web: www.dshs.state.tx.us/cshcn/*

**State CHIP Program (health care
for low-income, uninsured children)**

*TexCare
(800) 647-6558
Web: http://www.benefits.gov/benefits/
    benefit-details/1613*

**Programs for Children and Youth
Who Are Blind or Visually Impaired**

*Department of Assistive and Rehabilitative Services
Terry Murphy, Commissioner
4900 N. Lamar
Austin, TX 78751-2399
(512) 424-4001
Web: www.dars.state.tx.us*

**Programs for Children and Youth Who
Are Blind or Visually Impaired or Deaf-Blind**

*Texas School for the Blind and Visually Impaired
Dr. Phil Hatlen, Superintendent
1100 W. 45th Street
Austin, TX 78756
(512) 454-8631; (800) 872-5273
    (to leave a message)
(512) 206-9451 (TTY)
Web: www.tsbvi.edu*

**Programs for Children and Youth
Who Are Deaf or Hard of Hearing**

*Texas School for the Deaf
Claire Bugen, Superintendent
1102 S. Congress Avenue
Austin, TX 78704-1728
(512) 462-5300 (V/TTY)
Web: www.tsd.state.tx.us*

*Education Resource Center on Deafness (ERCOD)
Statewide Information at Texas
    School for the Deaf
1102 S. Congress Avenue
Austin, TX 78704-1728
(512) 462-5329; (800) 332-3873 (V/TTY)
E-mail: ercod@tsd.state.tx.us
Web: www.tsd.state.tx.us*

*Division of IDEA Coordination, Deaf Services
Don Curran, Program Specialist
Texas Education Agency
1701 N. Congress Avenue
Austin, TX 78701
(512) 463-9424 (V); (512) 475-3540 (TTY)
E-mail: deafed@tea.state.tx.us
Web: www.tea.state.tx.us/deaf*

Department of Assistive and Rehabilitative Services
David Myers, Executive Director
P. O. Box 12904
Austin, TX 78711–2904
(512) 407-3250 (V); (512) 407-3251 (TTY)
E-mail: david.myers@dars.state.tx.us
Web: www.dars.state.tx.us

**Telecommunications Relay Services
for Individuals Who Are Deaf, Hard of Hearing, or With
Speech Impairments**

(800) 735-2988 (V)
(800) 735-2989 (TTY); 711 (TTY)
(800) 735-2991 (ASCII)
(877) 826-6607(Speech to Speech)

**State Education Agency
Rural Representative**

Special Programs, Monitoring, and Interventions
Gene Lenz, Deputy Associate Commissioner
Texas Education Agency
Division of Special Education
1701 N. Congress Avenue
Austin, TX 78701-1494
(512) 463-9414
E-mail: sped@tea.state.tx.us
Web: www.tea.state.tx.us/special.ed

**Regional ADA & IT
Technical Assistance Center**

Disability Law Resource Project
Wendy Wilkinson, Director
2323 S. Shepard Boulevard, Suite 1000
Houston, TX 77019
(713) 520-0232 (V/TTY); (800) 949-4232 (V/TTY)
E-mail: dlrp@ilru.org
Web: www.dlrp.org

**University Center for Excellence
in Developmental Disabilities**

Center for Disability Studies
Dr. Penny Seay, Executive Director
University of Texas at Austin
4030 W. Braker Lane
Building 2, Suite 220
Austin, TX 78759
(512) 232-0740; (800) 828-7839
(512) 232-0762 (TTY)
E-mail: pseay@mail.utexas.edu
Web: http://tcds.edb.utexas.edu

Technology-Related Assistance

Texas Technology Access Project
John Moore, Project Director
University of Texas at Austin
4030 W. Braker Lane
Building 2, Suite 220
Austin, TX 78759
(512) 232-0740; (800) 828-7839
(512) 232-0762 (TTY)
E-mail: john.moore@mail.utexas.edu
Web: http://techaccess.edb.utexas.edu

State Mediation System

Mediation Coordinator
Carlos Gonzales, Program Administrator
Texas Education Agency
1701 N. Congress Avenue
Austin, TX 78701
(512) 463-9290
E-mail: cgonzales@tea.state.tx.us
Web: www.tea.state.tx.us

Special Format Library

Talking Book Program
Ava Smith, Division Director
Texas State Library and Archives Commission
P.O. Box 12927
Austin, TX 78711–2927
(512) 463-5458; (800) 252-9605
E-mail: tbp.services@tsl.state.tx.us
Web: www.texastalkingbooks.org

Texas—Disability-Specific Organizations

Attention Deficit Disorder

To identify an ADD group in Texas, contact either:

Children and Adults with Attention-Deficit/
    Hyperactivity Disorder (CHADD)
8181 Professional Place, Suite 201
Landover, MD 20785
(301) 306-7070
(800) 233-4050 (Voice mail to request information packet)
Web: www.chadd.org

*Attention Deficit Disorders Association–Southern
    Region (ADDA-SR)*
Pam Esser, Executive Director
12345 Jones Road, Suite 287–7
Houston, TX 77070
(281) 897-0982
E-mail: addaoffice@pdq.net
Web: www.adda-sr.org

Autism

To identify an autism group in Texas, contact

Autism Society of America
7910 Woodmont Avenue, Suite 300
Bethesda, MD 20814
(301) 657-0881; (800) 3-AUTISM
Web: www.autism-society.org

Blind/Visual Impairments

*American Foundation for the
    Blind–Southwest*
Judy Scott, Director
11030 Ables Lane
Dallas, TX 75229
(214) 352-7222
E-mail: dallas@afb.net
Web: www.afb.org

Brain Injury

Brain Injury Association of Texas
Brack Collier, President
1339 Lamar Square Drive, Suite 103
Austin, TX 78704
(512) 326-1212; (800) 392-0040 (in TX)
E-mail: info@biatx.org
Web: www.biatx.org

Cerebral Palsy

United Cerebral Palsy of Texas
Jean Langendorf, Executive Director
5555 N. Lamar, Suite L139
Austin, TX 78751
(512) 472-8696; (800) 798-1492 (in TX)
E-mail: info@ucptexas.org
Web: www.ucptexas.org

Epilepsy

*Epilepsy Foundation Texas-Houston/Dallas-Fort
    Worth/West Texas*
Donna Stahlhut, Executive Director
2630 Fountain View, Suite 210
Houston, TX 77057
*(713) 789-6295; (888) 548-9716
    (in certain service areas)*
E-mail: dstahlhut@efset.org
Web: http://eftx.org/

Epilepsy Foundation, Central and South Texas
Sindi Rosales, Executive Director
10615 Perrin Beitel, Suite 602
San Antonio, TX 78217
*(210) 653-5353; (888) 606-5353 (in certain
    service areas)*
E-mail: sindi@efcst.org
Web: www.efcst.org

Learning Disabilities

Learning Disabilities Association of Texas
Ann Robinson, Coordinator
1011 W. 31st Street
Austin, TX 78705
(512) 458-8234; (800) 604-7500 (in TX)
E-mail: contact@ldat.org
Web: www.ldat.org

Mental Health

Mental Health Association in Texas
Lynn Lasky Clark, President & CEO
1210 San Antonio, Suite 200
Austin, TX 78701
(512) 454-3706
E-mail: Lynn@mhatexas.org
Web: www.mhatexas.org

NAMI Texas
Diane Bisig, Executive Director
III Fountain Park Plaza
2800 South IH 35, Suite 140
Austin, TX 78704
(512) 693-2000; (800) 633-3760
Web: www.namitexas.org

Texas Federation of Families for
    Children's Mental Health
Patti Derr, Director
7701 N. Lamar, Suite 518
Austin, TX 78752
(512) 407-8844; (866) 893-3264
E-mail: info@txffcmh.org
Web: www.txffcmh.org

Mental Retardation

The Arc of Texas
Mike Bright, Executive Director
8001 Centre Park Drive
Austin, TX 78754
(512) 454-6694; (800) 252-9729
E-mail: secretary@thearcoftexas.org
Web: www.thearcoftexas.org

Speech, Language, and Hearing

Texas Speech-Language-Hearing Association
Roy K. Bohrer, Executive Director
P. O. Box 140647
Austin, TX 78714–0647
(512) 452-4636; (888) 729-8742
E-mail: tsha@assnmgmt.com
Web: www.txsha.org

Texas—Organizations Especially for Parents

Parent Training and Information Centers (PTI)

Partners Resource Network, Inc. (serving
    San Antonio, Houston, and the
    Lower Rio Grande Valley)
Debbie Schultz, Program Manager
Team Project
3311 Richmond, Suite 334
Houston, TX 77098
(713) 524-2147; (877) 832-8945 (in TX)
E-mail: prnteam@sbcglobal.net
Web: www.partnerstx.org

PATH Project (serving Dallas, Fort Worth, Austin,
    Wichita Falls, Southeast and East Texas)
Alice Robertson, Program Manager
1090 Longfellow Drive, Suite B
Beaumont, TX 77706-4819
(409) 898-4684; (800) 866-4726 (in TX)
E-mail: partnersresource@sbcglobal.net
Web: www.partnerstx.org

PEN Project (Serving Amarillo, Lubbock,
    Abilene, San Angelo, and El Paso)
Jon Howell, Program Manager
1001 Main Street, Suite 804
Lubbock, TX 79401
(806) 762-1434; (877) 762-1435 (in TX)
E-mail: wtxpen@sbcglobal.net

Parent-To-Parent

Texas Parent to Parent
Laura J. Warren, Executive Director
Tammy Mann, Outreach and Training Director
3710 Cedar Street, Box 12
Austin, TX 78705
(512) 458-8600; (866) 896-6001
E-mail: txp2p@sbcglobal.net
Web: www.main.org/txp2p

Community Parent Resource Centers

The Arc of Texas in the Rio Grande Valley
Parents Supporting Parents Network
Leticia Padilla, Coordinator
601 N. Texas Boulevard
Weslaco, TX 78596
(956) 447-8408; (888) 857-8668
E-mail: lpadilla@rgv.rr.com
Web: www.thearcoftexas.org

Partners in Policymaking

Partners in Policymaking
Laura Buckner, Program Coordinator
P.O. Box 5905
Katy, TX 77491-5905
(903) 291-1990; (866) 291-1990
E-mail: txpartners@cablelynx.com
Web: www.familytofamilynetwork.org

Parent Teacher Association (PTA)

Texas PTA
Craig Tounget, President
408 W. 11th Street
Austin, TX 78701-2113
(512) 476-6769; (800) 825-5782
E-mail: txpta@txpta.org
Web: www.txpta.org

Other Parent Organization

Family to Family Network
Eve Cugini, Executive Director
13150 FM 529, Suite 106
Houston, TX 77041
(713) 466-6304
E-mail: f2fnetwork@sbcglobal.net
Web: www.familytofamilynetwork.org

Texas—Other Disability Organizations

Easter Seals of Greater Dallas
Elizabeth A. Hart, President/CEO
3820 W. Northwest Highway, Suite 100
Dallas, TX 75220
(214) 366-4201; (800) 580-4718
Web: www.easterseals.com

Easter Seals Epilepsy Services
Easter Seals Greater Northwest Texas
508 S. Adams Street, Suite 200
Ft. Worth, TX 76104
(817) 536–8693; (888) 288–8324 (in TX)
E-mail: mail@easterseals-fw.org
Web: www.easterseals-fw.org

Texas Advocates Supporting Kids with Disabilities
(TASK)
P.O. Box 162685
Austin, TX 78716
(512) 336-0897 (V or Fax)
E-mail: ASKTASK@aol.com
Web: www.main.org/task/index.htm

Disability Policy Consortium
7800 Shoal Creek Boulevard, Suite 171-E
Austin, TX 78757
(512) 454-4816 (V/TTY)
E-mail: dpctexas@advocacyinc.org
Web: www.dpctexas.org

Independent Living

Texas State Independent Living Council (SILC)
Ted Thayer, Executive Director
5555 N. Lamar, Suite K103
P.O. Box 9879
Austin, TX 78766
(512) 371-7353; (817) 371-7353
E-mail: texsilc@texas.net
Web: www.texsilc.org

UTAH

Utah—State Agencies and Organizations

United States Senators

Honorable Orrin G. Hatch (R)
104 Hart Senate Office Building
Washington, DC 20510
(202) 224-5251
(202) 224-6331 (Fax)
E-mail Web Form: www.senate.gov/ ~hatch/
index.cfm?Fuseaction= Offices.Contact
Web: www.senate.gov/~hatch

Honorable Mike Lee (R)
316 Hart Senate Office Building
Washington, DC 20510
(202) 224-5444
E-mail: http://www.lee.senate.gov/public/
index.cfm/contact
Web: http://www.lee.senate.gov/public/
index.cfm/home

United States Representatives

To find the contact information for your representative in the House of the U.S. Congress, visit the House's Web site at: www.house.gov, or call (202) 225-3121; (202) 225-1904 (TTY).

Governor

Honorable Gary Herbert
Utah State Capitol Complex
350 North State Street, Suite 200
P.O. Box 142220
Salt Lake City, UT 84114-2220
(801) 538-1000
(801) 538-1528 (Fax)
Web: www.utah.gov/governor

Official State Web Site

Web: http://www.utah.gov/index.html

State Department of Education: Special Education

At Risk and Special Education Services
Karl A. Wilson, Director
State Office of Education
250 East 500 South
P.O. Box 144200
Salt Lake City, UT 84111-4200
(801) 538-7509
E-mail: kawilson@usoe.k12.ut.us
Web: www.usoe.k12.ut.us/sars

Utah was granted an extended waiver from the NCLB program.

Ann White, Director
Special and Federal Programs
250 East 500 South | PO Box 144200
Salt Lake City, UT | 84114-4200
(801) 538-7509
Email: ann.white@schools.utah.gov
http://schools.utah.gov/fsp/

Programs for Infants and Toddlers With Disabilities: Birth–2 Years

BabyWatch
Early Intervention Program
Susan Ord, EIP Director
Utah Department of Health
P.O. Box 144720
Salt Lake City, UT 84114-4720
(801) 584-8226; (800) 961-4226
E-mail: sord@utah.gov
Web: www.utahbabywatch.org

Programs for Children With Disabilities: 3–5 Years

Utah State Office of Education
Betsy Sutherland, 619 Coordinator
250 East 500 South
P.O. Box 144200
Salt Lake City, UT 84114
(801) 538-7948
E-mail: betsy.sutherland@schools.utah.gov
Web: http://www.schools.utah.gov/sars/
    Preschool.aspx

State Vocational Rehabilitation Agency

Utah State Office of Rehabilitation
Blaine Petersen, Executive Director
P.O. Box 144200
Salt Lake City, UT 84114-4200
(801) 538-7530 (V/TTY)
E-mail: bpetersen@utah.gov
Web: www.usor.utah.gov

Coordinator for Transition Services

Susan Loving, Specialist in Transition
Utah State Office of Education
Special Education Services Unit
250 East 500 South
P.O. Box 144200

Salt Lake City, UT 84114-4200
(801) 538-7645
E-mail: sloving@usoe.k12.ut.us
Web: www.usoe.k12.ut.us/

State Mental Health Agency

Division of Substance Abuse and Mental Health
Randall W. Bachman, Director
Department of Human Services
120 North 200 West, Room 209
Salt Lake City, UT 84103
(801) 538-3939
E-mail: rbachman@utah.gov
Web: www.hsmh.utah.gov

State Mental Health Representative for Children and Youth

Ming Wang, LCSW, Program Coordinator
Child Mental Health, Rural, and Cultural
    Competency Programs
Utah Division of Substance Abuse
    and Mental Health
120 North 200 West, Room 209
Salt Lake City, UT 84103
(801) 538-4276; (801) 550-2451 (Cell)
E-mail: mwang@utah.gov
Web: www.hsmh.state.ut.us

State Mental Retardation Program

Division of Services for People With Disabilities
Department of Human Services
Dr. Fran Morse, Director
120 North 200 West, Suite 411
Salt Lake City, UT 84103
(801) 538-4200
E-mail: fmorse@utah.gov
Web: www.hsdspd.state.ut.us

Council on Developmental Disabilities

Utah Governor's Council for People With Disabilities
Dr. Alison Lozano, Executive Director
155 South 300 West, Suite 100
Salt Lake City, UT 84101
(801) 533-3965
E-mail: alozano@utah.gov
Web: www.gcpd.org

Protection and Advocacy Agencies

Disability Law Center
Fraser Nelson, Executive Director
205 North 400 West
Salt Lake City, UT 84103
(801) 363-1347; (800) 662-9080 (in UT) (V/TTY)
E-mail: info@disabilitylawcenter.org
Web: www.disabilitylawcenter.org

Native American Protection and Advocacy Project
Therese E. Yanan, Director
3535 E. 30th Street, Suite 201
Farmington, NM 87402
(505) 566-5880; (800) 862-7271
E-mail: cjohn@dnalegalservices.org
Web: www.dnalegalservices.org

Native American Protection and Advocacy Project
P.O. Box 3539
Tuba City, AZ 86045
(928) 283-3208; (877) 283-3208
E-mail: franl@dnalegalservices.org
Web: www.dnalegalservices.org

Client Assistance Program

Client Assistance Program
Nancy Friel, Director
Contact Disability Law Center, under Protection
and Advocacy Agencies, listed above.

Programs for Children With Special Health Care Needs

Children with Special Health Care Needs
Dr. Fan Tait, Bureau Director
Utah Department of Health
Community and Family Health Services
44 North Medical Drive
P.O. Box 144610
Salt Lake City, UT 84114-4610
(801) 584-8240; (800) 829-8200
E-mail: ftait@utah.gov
Web: http://health.utah.gov/cfhs

State CHIP Program (health care for low-income, uninsured children)

Utah CHIP
P.O. Box 143107
Salt Lake City, UT 84114-3107
(877) KIDS-NOW
Email: chip@utah.gov
Web: http://health.utah.gov/chip/

Services for Children With Birth Defects

Utah Birth Defect Network
Amy Nance, Study Coordinator
Department of Health
P.O. Box 144697
Salt Lake City, UT 84114-4697
(801) 257-0566, ext. 201
E-mail: aenance@utah.gov
Web: http://health.utah.gov/birthdefect

Programs for Children and Youth Who Are Blind or Visually Impaired

Division of Services for the Blind and Visually
*   Impaired*
Bill Gibson, Director
250 North 1950 West, Suite B
Salt Lake City, UT 84116-7902
(801) 323-4343
E-mail: bgibson@utah.gov
Web: www.usor.state.ut.us/services.html

Programs for Children and Youth Who Are Deaf-Blind

Utah Schools for the Deaf and the Blind
742 Harrison Boulevard
Ogden, UT 84404
(801) 629-4700 (V); (801) 624-4701 (TTY)
Web: www.usdb.org

State Deafblind Project
Darla Fowers, Project Director
742 Harrison Boulevard
Ogden, UT 84404
(801) 629-4732; (801) 629-4701 (TTY)
E-mail: darlaf@usdb.org
Web: www.usdb.org/dbs/home.htm

Programs for Individuals Who Are Deaf or Hard of Hearing

Utah Community Center of the Deaf
*   and Hard of Hearing*
Marilyn Call, Executive Director
Utah State Office of Rehabilitation
5709 South 1500 West
Salt Lake City, UT 84123
(801) 263-4860 (V/TTY)
(800) 860-4860 (V/TTY, in UT only)
Web: www.usor.state.ut.us/dsdhh/dsdhh.html

*Telecommunications Relay
Services for Individuals Who
Are Deaf, Hard of Hearing, or
With Speech Impairments*

*(888) 735-5906 (V)
(800) 346-4128 (V/TTY); 711 (TTY)
(800) 346-4128 (TTY)
(888) 346-5822 (Speech to Speech)*

*Regional ADA & IT
Technical Assistance Center*

*Rocky Mountain Disability and Business
    Technical Assistance Center
Patrick Going, Director
3630 Sinton Road, Suite 103
Colorado Springs, CO 80907
(719) 444-0268 (V/TTY); (800) 949-4232 (V/
    TTY)
E-mail: rmdbtac@mtc-inc.com
Web: www.adainformation.org*

*University Center
for Excellence in
Developmental Disabilities*

*Center for Persons with Disabilities
Dr. Sarah Rule, Director
Utah State University
6800 Old Main Hill
Logan, UT 84322-6800
(435) 797-1987
E-mail: sarah.rule@usu.edu
Web: www.cpd.usu.edu*

Technology-Related Assistance

*Utah Assistive Technology Program
Center for Persons with Disabilities
Martin E. Blair, Program Director
Utah State University
6855 Old Main Hill
Logan, UT 84322-6855
(435) 797-3824
E-mail: meblair@cc.usu.edu
Web: www.uatpat.org*

*Utah Center for Assistive Technology
500 South 1595 West
Salt Lake City, UT 84104-5238
(801) 887-9500 (V/TTY); (888) 866-5550
Web: www.usor.state.ut.us*

State Mediation System

*Utah State Office of Education
Karen Kowalski
250 East 500 South
P.O. Box 144200
Salt Lake City, UT 84114
(801) 538-7568
E-mail: kkowalsk@usoe.k12.ut.us
Web: www.usoe.k12.ut.us*

Special Format Library

*Program for the Blind and Disabled
Utah State Library Division
Gerald A. Buttars, Librarian
250 North 1950 West, Suite A
Salt Lake City, UT 84116-7901
(801) 715-6789; (800) 662-5540 (in UT)
(800) 453-4293 (all states, except Utah)
(801) 715-6721 (TTY)
E-mail: blind@utah.gov
Web: http://blindlibrary.utah.gov/index.html*

Utah — Disability-Specific Organizations

Attention Deficit Disorder

To identify an ADD group in Utah, contact
either of the following organizations:

*Children and Adults with Attention-Deficit/
    Hyperactivity Disorder (CHADD)
8181 Professional Place, Suite 150
Landover, MD 20785
(301) 306-7070
(800) 233-4050 (Voice mail to request
    information packet)
Web: www.chadd.org*

*Attention Deficit Disorder Association (ADDA)
P.O. Box 543
Pottstown, PA 19464
(484) 945-2101
Web: www.add.org*

Autism

*Autism Information Resources at the Utah Parent
    Center
Kim Moody, Executive Director
2290 East 4500 South, Suite 110
Salt Lake City, UT 84117
(801) 272-1051; (800) 468-1160 (V/TTY)
Web: www.utahparentcenter.org*

Blind/Visual Impairments

American Foundation for the Blind–West
Gil Johnson, Director
111 Pine Street, Suite 725
San Francisco, CA 94111
(415) 392-4845
E-mail: sanfran@afb.net
Web: www.afb.org

Brain Injury

Brain Injury Association of Utah, Inc.
Ron Roskos, Executive Director
1800 South West Temple, Suite 203
Salt Lake City, UT 84115
(801) 484-2240; (800) 281-8442 (in UT)
E-mail: biau@sisna.com
Web: www.biau.org

Cerebral Palsy

United Cerebral Palsy of Utah
Shelly Petty, Executive Director
3550 South 700 West
Salt Lake City, UT 84119
(801) 266-8031; (888) UCP-UTAH
E-mail: shellyp@ucputah.org
Web: www.ucputah.org

Epilepsy

Epilepsy Association of Utah
275 E. South Temple, Suite 200
Salt Lake City, UT 84111
(801) 534-0210
E-mail: info@epilepsyut.org
Web: www.epilepsyut.org

Learning Disabilities

Learning Disabilities Association of Utah
Debbie McInelly, President
P. O. Box 900726
Sandy, UT 84090-0726
(801) 553-9156
E-mail: rdmcinelly@emcity.net

Mental Health

Mental Health Association in Utah
Dr. Mack Gift, Executive Director
1800 South West Temple, Suite 501
Salt Lake City, UT 84115
(801) 596-3705
E-mail: mhaut@xmission.com

Allies with Families
Lori Cerar, Executive Director
450 E. 1000 N., Suite 311
North Salt Lake, UT 84054
(801) 292-2515; (877) 477-0764
E-mail: awfamilies@msn.com

NAMI-Utah
Vickie Cottrell, Executive Director
309 East 100 South
Salt Lake City, UT 84111
(801) 323-9900
E-mail: vicki@namiut.org
Web: www.namiut.org

Mental Retardation

The Arc of Utah
Donna Gleaves, Executive Director
155 South 300 West, Suite 201
Salt Lake City, UT 84101
(801) 364-5060; (800) 371-5060 (in UT)
E-mail: donna@arcutah.org
Web: www.arcutah.org

Special Health Care Needs

Family Voices of Utah
Gina Pola-Money, State Coordinator
2290 East 4500 South #110
Salt Lake City, UT 84117
(801) 631-1609
E-mail: utahfamilyvoices@juno.com
Web: www.familyvoices.org

Speech and Hearing

Utah Speech-Language-Hearing Association
Cheryl Orme, President
1379 31st Street
Ogden, UT 84403
(801) 402-5477
Web: www.ushaonline.net/

Spina Bifida

Spina Bifida Association of Utah
P.O. Box 27801
Salt Lake City, UT 84127
(801) 561-5268

Utah — Organizations Especially for Parents

Parent Training and Information Center (PTI)

Utah Parent Center
Helen Post, Executive Director
Jennie Gibson, Associate Director
2290 East 4500 South, Suite 110
Salt Lake City, UT 84117
(801) 272-1051 (V/TTY); (800) 468-1160 (in UT)
E-mail: info@utahparentcenter.org
Web: www.utahparentcenter.org

Parent Teacher Association (PTA)

Utah Congress of Parents and Teachers
JoAnn Neilson, President
5192 S. Greenpine Drive
Salt Lake City, UT 84123
(801) 261-3100; (866) 782-8824
E-mail: kids@utahpta.org
Web: www.utahpta.org

Other Parent Organization

State Family Council of Utah
Phoebe Blackham, Executive Director
698 Ridge Lane
Alpine, UT 84004
(877) 352-2221
E-mail: information@statefamilycouncil.org
Web: www.statefamilycouncil.org

Utah — Other Disability Organizations

Access Utah Network (statewide information
   and referral for disability issues)
Mark Smith, Information Specialist
155 South 300 West, Suite 100
Salt Lake City, UT 84102
(801) 533-4636 (SLC area); (800) 333-8824
   (outside SLC)
E-mail: accessut@utah.gov
Web: www.accessut.org

Easter Seals Utah
Richard O. Starley, President/CEO
638 E. Wilmington Avenue
Salt Lake City, UT 84106
(801) 486-3778 (V/TTY); (800) 388-1991
   (in UTAH)
E-mail: rstarley@eastersealsutah.org
Web: www.eastersealsutah.org

Legislative Coalition for People with Disabilities
Linda Smith and Kris Fawson, Co-Directors
275 East South Temple, Suite 201
Salt Lake City, UT 84111-1268
(801) 363-3300
E-mail: lcpd1@riseinc.net
Web: http://lcpdutah.org

Art Access/VSA Arts of Utah
Ruth Lubbers, Executive Director
339 W. Pierport Avenue
Salt Lake City, UT 84101
(801) 328-0703 (V/TTY)
E-mail: ruth@accessart.org

Independent Living

To find out the contact information for the
Statewide Independent Living Council (SILC)
in Utah, contact

Independent Living Research Utilization Project
The Institute for Rehabilitation and Research
2323 South Sheppard, Suite 1000
Houston, TX 77019
(713) 520-0232 (V); (713) 520-5136 (TTY)
E-mail: ilru@ilru.org
Web: www.ilru.org

To find out the contact information for
centers for independent living (CILs) in Utah,
contact

National Council on Independent Living
1916 Wilson Boulevard, Suite 209
Arlington, VA 22201
(703) 525-3406; (703) 525-4153 (TTY)
E-mail: ncil@ncil.org
Web: www.ncil.org

VERMONT

Vermont—State Agencies and Organizations

United States Senators

Honorable Patrick J. Leahy (D)
437 Russell Senate Office Building
Washington, DC 20510
(202) 224-4242; (800) 642-3193 (in VT)
E-mail Web Form: http://leahy.senate.gov/
    contact.html
Web: http://leahy.senate.gov

Honorable Bernard Sanders (I)
332 Dirksen Senate Office Building
Washington, DC 20510
(202) 224-5141; (800) 835-5500 (V/TTY)
E-mail Web Form: http://www.sanders.senate.
    gov/contact/
Web: http://www.sanders.senate.gov/

United States Representatives

To find the contact information for your representative in the House of the U.S. Congress, visit the House's Web site at: www.house.gov, or call (202) 225-3121; (202) 225-1904 (TTY).

Governor

Honorable Peter Shumlin
Office of the Governor
109 State Street
Montpelier, VT 05609
(802) 828-3333; (802) 828-3339
(800) 649-6825 (in VT only)
E-mail Web Form: http://governor.vermont.
    gov/contact-us/opinion
Web: http://governor.vermont.gov/

Official State Web Site

Web: www.vermont.gov/

State Department of Education: Special Education

Student Support Services
Dennis Kane, Director
120 State Street, State Office Building
Montpelier, VT 05620-2501
(802) 828-2755
Web: www.state.vt.us/educ/sped.htm

State Coordinator for NCLB (No Child Left Behind)

Carol Duley, VT DOE, Independent & Federal
    Programs
120 State Street, State Office Building
Montpelier, VT 05620-2501
(802) 479-1279
E-mail: carol.duley@state.vt.us
Web: http://education.vermont.gov/laws/
    no-child-left-behind

Programs for Infants and Toddlers With Disabilities: Birth–2 Years

Children's Integrated Services
Danielle Howes, Part C Coordinator
Child Development Division
103 South Main Street, DCF -2 North
Waterbury, VT 05671
(802) 769-6174
E-mail: danielle.howes@state.vt.us
Web: http://dcf.vermont.gov/cdd/cis/IDEA_
    Part_C_early_intervention

Programs for Children With Disabilities: 3–5 Years

Special Education Unit
Department of Education
Kate Rogers, 619 Coordinator
120 State Street
Montpelier, VT 05620-2501
(802) 828-5115
E-mail: kate.rogers@state.vt.us
Web: http://education.vermont.gov/special-
    education

State Vocational Rehabilitation Agency

Vocational Rehabilitation Division
Diane Dalmasse, Director
Department of Aging and Disabilities
Agency of Human Services
103 S. Main Street
Waterbury, VT 05671-2303
(802) 241-2186
E-mail: diane@dad.state.vt.us
Web: www.vocrehabvermont.org

Coordinator for Transition Services

K. Michael Ferguson, Special Education
   Consultant BEST Team
Vermont State Department of Education
120 State Street
Montpelier, VT 05620
(802) 828-5110
E-mail: mlferguson@doe.state.vt.us
Web: www.state.vt.us/educ/new/html/
   pgm_sped.html#links

Office of State Coordinator of Vocational Education for Students With Disabilities

Vocational Education for Disadvantaged and
   Handicapped Programs
Department of Education
Ruth Durkee, Special Needs Consultant
120 State Street
Montpelier, VT 05620
(802) 828-3101
Web: www.state.vt.us/educ

State Developmental & Mental Health Services

Department of Developmental and
   Mental Health Services
Agency of Human Services
Susan Besio, Commissioner
103 S. Main Street, Weeks Building
Waterbury, VT 05671-1601
(802) 241-2610
E-mail: sbesio@ddmhs.state.vt.us
Web: www.state.vt.us/dmh/

State Mental Health Representative for Children and Youth

Charles Biss, Director of the Child,
   Adolescent and Family Unit
Division of Mental Health
103 S. Main Street, Weeks Building
Waterbury, VT 05671-1601
(802) 241-2650
E-mail: cbiss@ddmhs.state.vt.us
Web: www.state.vt.us/dmh/

State Developmental Services Program

Division of Developmental Services
Department of Developmental and
   Mental Health Services
Theresa Wood, Director
103 S. Main Street, Weeks Building
Waterbury, VT 05671-1601
(802) 241-2648; (802) 241-2614
E-mail: twood@ddmhs.state.vt.us
Web: www.state.vt.us/dmh

Council on Developmental Disabilities

Vermont Developmental Disabilities Council
103 S. Main Street, North 1
Waterbury, VT 05671-0206
(802) 241-2612 (V/TTY)
E-mail: vtddc@ahs.state.vt.us
Web: www.ahs.state.vt.us/vtddc

Protection and Advocacy Agency

Disability Law Project
Nancy Breiden, Director
57 N. Main Street
Rutland, VT 05701
(802) 775-0021; (800) 769-7459 (V/TTY)
(800) 889-2047 (state office)
E-mail: nbreiden@vtlegalaid.org
Web: www.vtlegalaid.org

Vermont Protection and Advocacy, Inc.
Ed Paquin, Executive Director
141 Main Street, Suite 7
Montpelier, VT 05602
(802) 229-1355; (800) 834-7890 (in VT)
E-mail: info@vtpa.org
Web: www.vtpa.org

Client Assistance Program

Client Assistance Program
Karen Colgrove, Director
1111 Main Street, Suite B
St. Johnsbury, VT 05819
(802) 748-4611; (802) 769-6728
E-mail: kcolgrove@vtlegalaid.org
Web: www.vtlegalaid.org

**Programs for Children
With Special Health Care Needs**

Children with Special Health Needs
Department of Health
Carol Hassler, MD, Director
108 Cherry Street
P.O. Box 70
Burlington, VT 05402
(802) 863-7338
E-mail: chassle@vdh.state.vt.us
Web: www.state.vt.us/health/hi/cshn/cshn.htm

**State CHIP Program (health care
for low-income, uninsured children)**

Dave Yacovone, Commissioner
103 S. Main Street
Waterbury, VT 05671
(802) 871-3385
Web: http://dcf.vermont.gov/esd/ltc_medicaid

**Programs for Children and Youth
Who Are Blind or Visually Impaired**

Division for the Blind and Visually Impaired
Department of Aging and Disabilities
Agency of Human Services
Fred Jones, Director
103 S. Main Street
Waterbury, VT 05671-2304
(802) 241-2132
E-mail: fredj@dad.state.vt.us
Web: www.dad.state.vt.us/dbvi/

**Programs for Children and Youth
Who Are Deaf or Hard of Hearing**

Division of Vocational Rehabilitation
Rene' Pellerin, Coordinator of Services for
   the Deaf
103 S. Main Street, Osgood II
Waterbury, VT 05671-2303
(802) 241-2186 (V/TTY); (802) 241-2199 (TTY)
E-mail: rene@dad.state.vt.us
Web: www.vocrehabvermont.org

Vermont Center for the Deaf and Hard of Hearing
Ed Peltier, Executive Director
209 Austine Drive, Suite 310
Brattleboro, VT 05301
(802) 258-9500 (V/TTY)
Web: www.austine.pvt.k12.vt.us

**State Education Agency
Rural Representative**

Leane Page Garland
Department of Education
Special Education Unit
120 State Street
Montpelier, VT 05602
(802) 828-0555
Web: www.state.vt.us/educ

**Telecommunications Relay
Services for Individuals Who
Are Deaf, Hard of Hearing,
or With Speech Impairments**

(800) 253-0195 (V)
(800) 253-0191 (TTY); 711 (TTY)
(800) 229-5746 (Speech to Speech-English)
(866) 260-9470 (Speech to Speech-Spanish)

**Regional ADA & IT
Technical Assistance Center**

New England ADA and Accessible IT Center
Adaptive Environments Center, Inc.
Valerie Fletcher, Executive Director
Oce Harrison, Project Director
374 Congress Street, Suite 301
Boston, MA 02210
(800) 949-4232 (V/TTY)
E-mail: adaptive@adaptenv.org
Web: www.adaptenv.org

**University Center
for Excellence in
Developmental Disabilities**

Center on Disability and
   Community Inclusion
University Center for Excellence in
   Developmental Disabilities Education,
   Research, and Service
Chigee Cloninger, Executive Director
University of Vermont
208 Colchester Avenue
Burlington, VT 05405-1757
(802) 656-4031 (V/TTY)
E-mail: chigee.cloninger@uvm.edu
Web: www.uvm.edu/~cdci

Technology Related Assistance

Vermont Assistive Technology Project
Julie Tucker, Director
103 South Main Street, Weeks Building
Waterbury, VT 05671-2305
(802) 241-2620 (V/TTY)
E-mail: jtucker@dad.state.vt.us
Web: www.vocrehabvermont.org

State Mediation System

Vermont Department of Education
Susan Boyd, Coordinator
120 State Street
Montpelier, VT 05620-2501
(802) 828-3136
E-mail: Sboyd@doe.state.vt.us
Web: www.state.vt.us/educ/

Special Format Library

Vermont Department of Libraries
Special Services Unit
S. Francis Woods, Librarian
578 Paine Turnpike North
Berlin, VT 05602
(802) 828-3273; (800) 479-1711
E-mail: ssu@dol.state.vt.us

Vermont—Disability-Specific Organizations

Attention Deficit Disorder

To identify an ADD group in Vermont, contact either of the following organizations:

Children and Adults with Attention-Deficit/
Hyperactivity Disorder (CHADD)
8181 Professional Place, Suite 150
Landover, MD 20785
(301) 306-7070
(800) 233-4050 (Voice mail to request
information packet)
Web: www.chadd.org

Attention Deficit Disorder Association (ADDA)
P.O. Box 543
Pottstown, PA 19464
(484) 945-2101
Web: www.add.org

Autism

Autism Society of Vermont
Lisa W. Lawlor, Director
P.O. Box 978
White River Junction, VT 05001
(802) 457-3764; (800) 559-7398
Web: www.autism-info.org

Blind/Visual Impairments

American Foundation for the Blind
Regina Genwright, Director of
Information Center
11 Penn Plaza, Suite 300
New York, NY 10001
(212) 502-7658; (212) 502-7662 (TTY)
E-mail: afbinfo@afb.net
Web: www.afb.org

Vermont Association for the Blind
and Visually Impaired
Steve Pouliot, Executive Director
37 Elmwood Avenue
Burlington, VT 05401
(802) 863-1358; (800) 639-5861
E-mail: general@vabvi.org
Web: www.vabvi.org/

Brain Injury

Brain Injury Association of Vermont
James Vyhnak, Executive Director
8 Mountain Street
Bristol, VT 05443
(802) 453-6456
E-mail: biavt@aol.com
Web: www.biavt.org

Cerebral Palsy

Association for Cerebral Palsy
James Lund, Executive Director
73 Main Street, Room 17
Montpelier, VT 05602
(802) 223-5161

Down Syndrome

Down Syndrome Network of Vermont
Jeneane Lunn
7 Center Street
Montpelier, VT 05602
(802) 223-0113; (802) 223-6149
E-mail: cvarc@adelphia.net

Epilepsy

Epilepsy Foundation of Vermont
Audrey Butler, Executive Director
P.O. Box 6292
Rutland, VT 05702
(802) 775-1686
E-mail: epilepsy@sover.net

Learning Disabilities

Learning Disabilities Association of Vermont
Christina Thurston
P.O. Box 1041
Manchester Center, VT 05255
(802) 362-3127
E-mail: chthurston@juno.com

New Hampshire Branch of the International
*   Dyslexia Association*
(also serving Vermont and Maine)
Mike Angwin and Caryl Patten, Co-Presidents
P.O. Box 3724
Concord, NH 03302
(603) 229-7355
E-mail: referralsVermont@nhida.org
Web: www.nhida.org

Mental Health

*   To identify an NMHA chapter in Vermont*
contact

National Mental Health Association (NMHA)
1021 Prince Street
Alexandria, VA 22314-2971
(800) 969-6642
Web: www.nmha.org

NAMI Vermont
Clare Munat, President
132 S. Main Street
Waterbury, VT 05676
(802) 244-1396; (800) 639-6480
E-mail: namivt@adelphia.net
Web: www.namivt.org

Vermont Federation of Families for Children's
*   Mental Health*
Lisa Conlan, Executive Director
P.O. Box 607
Montpelier, VT 05601-0607
(802) 223-4917; (800) 639-6071 (Families only)
E-mail: VFFCMH@together.net

Mental Retardation/ Developmental Disabilities

ARC of Vermont
David Wallace, Executive Director
346 Shelburne Road
Burlington, VT 05401
(802) 846-7291
E-mail: info@arcvermont.org
Web: www.arcvermont.org

Central Vermont Arc
James Lund, Executive Director
73 Main Street, Suite 17
Montpelier, VT 05602
(802) 223-6149
E-mail: cvarc@adelphia.net

Speech and Hearing

Vermont Speech-Language-Hearing Association
Patti Taffel, President
64 West Road
Barre, VT 05641
(802) 479-2109
E-mail: ptaffel@helicon.net

Vermont—Organizations Especially for Parents

Parent Training and Information Center (PTI)

Vermont Parent Information Center
Connie Curtin, Director
Chace Mill
1 Mill Street, Suite 310
Burlington, VT 05401
(802) 658-5315 (V/TTY); (800) 639-7170 (in VT)
E-mail: vpic@vtpic.com
Web: www.vtpic.com

Parent-To-Parent

Parent-to-Parent Program of Vermont
Nancy DiVenere, Director
600 Blair Park Road, Suite 240
Williston, VT 05495
(800) 800-4005, ext. 26
E-mail: p2pvt@partoparvt.org
Web: www.partoparvt.org

Parent Teacher Association (PTA)

Vermont Congress of Parents and Teachers
Holly Hall, President
P.O. Box 284
Richmond, VT 05477
(802) 893-0782
E-mail: vt_office@pta.org
Web: www.vermontpta.org

Vermont—Other Disability Organizations

Addison County Parent Child Center
Donna Bailey and Susan Harding, Co-Directors
P.O. Box 646
Middleburg, VT 05753
(802) 388-3171
Web: www.sover.net/~thepcc

Vermont Coalition for Disability Rights
Peter Youngbaer, Executive Director
73 Main Street, Suite 402
Montpelier, VT 05602
(802) 223-6140
E-mail: VCDR@sover.net

VSA Arts of Vermont
Alex Chirelstein, Executive Director
The Woolen Mill
20 W. Canal Street, Suite 7
Winooski, VT 05404
(802) 655-7772
E-mail: info@vsavt.org
Web: www.vsavt.org

Independent Living

Vermont Center for Independent Living
Deborah Lisi-Baker, Executive Director
11 E. State Street
Montpelier, VT 05602
(802) 229-0501; (800) 639-1522 (V/TTY)
E-mail: vcil@vcil.org
Web: www.vcil.org

To find out the contact information for centers for independent living (CILs) in Vermont, contact

National Council on Independent Living
1916 Wilson Boulevard, Suite 209
Arlington, VA 22201
(703) 525-3406; (703) 525-4153 (TTY)
E-mail: ncil@ncil.org
Web: www.ncil.org

VIRGIN ISLANDS

Virgin Islands—Agencies and Organizations

U.S. House of Representatives

Honorable Donna Christian-Christensen
1711 Longworth House Office Building
Washington, DC 20515
(202) 225-1790
Web: www.house.gov/
    christian-christensen/

Governor

John P. de Jongh, Jr.
Government House
21-22 Kongens Gade
Charlotte Amalie
St. Thomas, VI 00802
(340) 774-0001
Web: www.vinow.com/

Department of Education:
Special Education

State Office of Special Education
Belinda W. O'Neal, State Director
Special Education/Department of Education
44-46 Kongens Gade
Charlotte Amalie
St. Thomas, VI 00802
(340) 774-4399
E-mail: bwoneal@usviosep.org

Programs for Infants
and Toddlers With
Disabilities: Birth–3 Years

Infant and Toddlers Program
Nona McCray, Acting Part C Coordinator
Department of Health
Elaineco Complex #78-1, 2, 3
St. Thomas, VI 00802
(340) 777-8804
E-mail: nona.mccray@doh.vi.gov; nona.
    mccray@usvi-doh.org
Web: http://www.healthvi.org/programs/
    family-health/infants-toddlers/index.html

Programs for Children
With Disabilities: 3–5 Years

State Office of Special Education
Jill Singer, Director
Office of Special Education
1834 Kongens Gade
St. Thomas, VI 00802
(340) 776-5802
E-mail: jsinger@doe.vi
Web: http://www.healthvi.org/programs/
   family-health/infants-toddlers/index.html

Vocational Rehabilitation Agency

Division of Disabilities and Vocational
   Rehabilitation Services
Beverly Plaskett, Administrator
Department of Human Services
Knud Hansen Complex, Building A
1303 Hospital Ground
Charlotte Amalie
St. Thomas, VI 00802
(340) 774-0930, ext. 4190

Office of Coordinator of Vocational Education for
Students With Disabilities

Vocational, Technical and Adult Education
Anna L. Lewis, State Director
Department of Education
44-46 Kongens Gade
Charlotte Amalie
St. Thomas, VI 00802
(340) 776-3484; (340) 776-3488 (Fax)

Mental Health Agency

Division of Mental Health, Alcoholism and
   Drug Dependency Services
Dr. Celia Victor, Director
Barbel Plaza South, 2nd Floor
St. Thomas, VI 00801
(340) 774-4882

Mental Health Representative
for Children and Youth

Division of Mental Health, Alcoholism and
   Drug Dependency Services
Dr. Celia Victor, Director
Barbel Plaza South, 2nd Floor
St. Thomas, VI 00801
(340) 774-4882

Monitoring and Improvement Planning

Office of Special Education
Department of Education
Dolores Clendinen, Disabilities Compliance
   Manager
44-46 Kongens Gade
Charlotte Amalie
St. Thomas, VI 00802
(340) 774-4399
E-mail: dclendinen@usviosep.org

Council on Developmental Disabilities

Division of Disabilities and Vocational
   Rehabilitation Services
Department of Human Services
Beverly Plaskett, Administrator
Knud Hansen Complex, Building A
1303 Hospital Ground
Charlotte Amalie
St. Thomas, VI 00802
(340) 774-0930, ext. 4190

Protection and Advocacy Agency

Virgin Islands Advocacy, Inc.
Amelia Headley-LaMont, Executive Director
63 Estate Carlton
Fredericksted, St. Croix, VI 00840
(340) 772-1200; (340) 772-4641 (TTY)
(340) 772-0609 (Fax)
E-mail: info@viadvocacy.org
Web: www.viadvocacy.org

Client Assistance Program

   Contact Protection and Advocacy Agency
listed above.

Programs for Children With
Special Health Care Needs

Maternal Child Health and Children with
   Special Health Care Needs Program
C. Patricia Penn, RN, Assistant Director
Department of Health
Estate Contant, Elainco Building
Charlotte Amalie
St. Thomas, VI 00802
(340) 776-3580
E-mail: cppenn@earthlink.net

Programs for Children and Youth
Who Are Deaf or Hard of Hearing

State Office of Special Education
Belinda W. O'Neal, State Director
Special Education/Department of Education
44-46 Kongens Gade
Charlotte Amalie
St. Thomas, VI 00802
(340) 774-4399
E-mail: bwoneal@usviosep.org

Telecommunications Relay Services for Individuals Who
Are Deaf, Hard of Hearing, or With Speech Impairments

711 (TTY)
(800) 229-5746 (Speech to Speech-English)
(866) 260-9470 (Speech to Speech-Spanish)

Regional ADA Technical Assistance Agency

Northeast ADA & IT Center
Andrea Haenlin-Mott, Director
Cornell University
331 Ives Hall
Ithaca, NY 14853
(607) 255-6686 (V/TTY/Spanish);
    (800) 949-4232 (V/TTY/Spanish)
E-mail: northeastada@cornell.edu
Web: www.ilr.cornell.edu/ped/northeastada

University Center for Excellence
in Developmental Disabilities

Virgin Islands University Center for Excellence in
    Developmental Disabilities
Dr. Yegin Habtes, PhD, Executive Director
University of the Virgin Islands
2 John Brewers Bay
St. Thomas, VI 00802-9990
(340) 693-1323
E-mail: yhabtes@uvi.edu

Mediation System

State Office of Special Education
Special Education/Department of Education
Belinda W. O'Neal, State Director
44-46 Kongens Gade
Charlotte Amalie
St. Thomas, VI 00801
(340) 774-4399
E-mail: bwoneal@usviosep.org

Virgin Islands—Organizations Especially for Parents

Parent Training and
Information Centers (PTI)

VIFIND
Catherine Rehema Glenn, Executive Director
2 Nye Gade
St. Thomas, VI 00802
(340) 774-1662
E-mail: vifind@islands.vi
Web: www.taalliance.org/ptis/vifind/

Virgin Islands Coalition of Citizens
    with Disabilities
Rosemary J. Sumas, Executive Director
P.O. Box 9500
St. Thomas, VI 00801
(340) 776-1277
E-mail: DAR@viaccess.net

Assistive and Adaptive Computer
    Technology for the Disabled
Shirley Joseph, Executive Director
Virgin Islands Resource Center for the
    Disabled, Inc.
P.O. Box 308427
St. Thomas, VI 00803-8427
(340) 777-2253
E-mail: VIRCD@islands.vi
Web: www.vircd.org

Community Parent Resource Center

Country/Hills Project
Catherine Rehema Glenn, Program Director
#2 Nye Gade
St. Thomas, VI 00802
(340) 774-1662
E-mail: vifind@islands.vi
Web: www.taalliance.org/ptis/vifind/

Parent Information
Resource Center (PIRC)

Virgin Islands Parents Uniting Schools and Home
Sandra G. Phaire, Project Director
P.O. Box 24325
Christiansted, St. Croix, VI 00824
(340) 692-2323
(340) 714-1395 (St. Thomas)
E-mail: vipush2002@yahoo.com
E-mail: vipush@vipowernet.com

Virgin Islands—Other Disability Organizations

Independent Living

To find out the contact information for the Statewide Independent Living Council (SILC) in the Virgin Islands, contact

Independent Living Research Utilization Project
The Institute for Rehabilitation and Research
2323 South Sheppard, Suite 1000
Houston, TX 77019
(713) 520-0232 (V); (713) 520-5136 (TTY)
E-mail: ilru@ilru.org
Web: www.ilru.org

To find out the contact information for centers for independent living (CILs) in the Virgin Islands, contact

National Council on Independent Living
1916 Wilson Boulevard, Suite 209
Arlington, VA 22201
(703) 525-3406; (703) 525-4153 (TTY)
E-mail: ncil@ncil.org
Web: www.ncil.org

VIRGINIA

Virginia—State Agencies and Organizations

United States Senators

Honorable Tim Kaine (D)
388 Russell Senate Office Building
Washington, DC 20510
(202) 224-4024
(202) 224-6295 (Fax)
E-mail Web Form: http://warner.senate.gov/
    contact/contactme.cfm
Web: http://warner.senate.gov

Honorable George Allen (R)
204 Russell Senate Office Building
Washington, DC 20510
(202) 224-4024; (202) 224-6755 (TTY)
(202) 224-5432 (Fax)
E-mail Web Form: http://www.kaine.senate.
    gov/contact
Web: http://www.kaine.senate.gov/

United States Representatives

To find the contact information for your representative in the House of the U.S. Congress, visit the House's Web site at: www.house.gov, or call (202) 225-3121; (202) 225-1904 (TTY).

Governor

Honorable Terry McAuliffe
State Capitol, 3rd Floor
Richmond, VA 23219
(804) 786-2211; (804) 371-6351 (Fax)
(804) 371-8015 (TTY)
E-mail Web Form: https://governor.virginia.
    gov//constituent-services/Communicating-
    with-the-governors-office
Web: www.governor.virginia.gov/

Official State Web Site

Web: www.vipnet.org/cmsportal/

State Department of Education: Special Education

Division of Special Education
    and Student Services
Department of Education
John Eisenberg, Assistant Superintendent
P.O. Box 2120
Richmond, VA 23218-2120
(804) 786-8079; (800) 292-3820
E-mail: John.Eisenberg@doe.virginia.gov
Web: http://www.pen.k12.va.us/special_ed/
    index.shtml

State Coordinator for NCLB (No Child Left Behind)

Virginia was granted an extended waiver from the NCLB program.

Dr. Sandra E. Ruffin, Director
Division of Special Education & Student Services
Virginia Department of Education
P.O. Box 2120, Richmond, VA 23218
(804) 225-2768
Email: Sandra.Ruffin@doe.virginia.gov
Web: http://www.doe.virginia.gov/federal_
    programs/index.shtml

Programs for Infants and Toddlers
With Disabilities: Birth–3 Years

Office of Mental Retardation Services
Department of Behavioral Health and
*   Developmental Services*
David K. Mills, Manager
P.O. Box 1797
Richmond, VA 23218
(804) 371-6593
(800) 234-1448 (Central Directory for Early
*   Intervention Services)*
E-mail: david.mills@dbhds.virginia.gov
Web: www.infantva.org

Office of Mental Retardation Services
Department of Behavioral Health and
*   Developmental Services*
Catherine Hancock, Part C Coordinator
P.O. Box 1797
Richmond, VA 23218
(804) 371-6592
E-mail: Catherine.Hancock@dbhds.virginia.gov
Web: www.infantva.org

Programs for Children
With Disabilities: 2–5 Years

Division of Special Education and Instructional
*   Services*
Department of Education
Phyllis Mondak
P.O. Box 2120
Richmond, VA 23218-2120
(804) 225-2675; (800) 292-3820
E-mail: pmondak@mail.vak12ed.edu
Web: www.pen.k12.va.us/VDOE/sess

State Vocational Rehabilitation Agency

Virginia Department of Rehabilitative Services
James A. Rothrock, Commissioner
Erica A. Lovelace, Education Services Manager
8004 Franklin Farms Drive
P. O. Box K300
Richmond, VA 23288-0300
(804) 662-7000; (804) 662-7081
(800) 552-5019; (800) 464-9950 (TTY)
E-mail: drs@drs.state.va.us
E-mail: lovelaea@drs.state.va.us
Web: www.vadrs.org

Office of State Coordinator
of Vocational Education for
Students With Disabilities

Office of Career and Technical Education Services
Winona Barnstein, Division Secretary
Department of Education
P.O. Box 2120
Richmond, VA 23218-2120
(804) 225-2757
E-mail: Winona.Barnstein@doe.virginia.gov
Web: http://www.doe.virginia.gov/
*   instruction/career_technical/*

Office of Career and Technical Education Services
Lan Neugent, Assistant Superintendent
Department of Education
P.O. Box 2120
Richmond, VA 23218-2120
(804) 225-2757
E-mail: Lan.Neugent@doe.virginia.gov
Web: http://www.doe.virginia.gov/
*   instruction/career_technical/*

State Mental Health Agency

Department of Mental Health, Mental Retardation
*   and Substance Abuse Services*
Debra Ferguson, PhD, MD, Commissioner
P.O. Box 1797
Richmond, VA 23219
(804) 786-3921
E-mail: jreinhard@dmhmrsas.state.va.us
Web: www.dmhmrsas.state.va.us

State Mental
Health Representative
for Children and Youth

Child and Adolescent Services
Department of Mental Health, Mental
*   Retardation and Substance Abuse Services*
Pamela Fitzgerald Cooper, Director
P.O. Box 1797
Richmond, VA 23218-1797
(804) 371-2183
E-mail: pcooper@dmhmrsas.state.va.us
Web: www.dmhmrsas.state.va.us

State Health Department:
Child and Adolescent Health

Division of Child and Adolescent Health
Joanne S. Boise, Director
Virginia Department of Health
109 Governor Street, Eighth Floor
Richmond, VA 23219
(804) 864-7688
E-mail: joanne.boise@vdh.virginia.gov
Web: www.vahealth.org/childadoles
    centhealth/index.htm

State Mental Retardation Program

Office of Mental Retardation Services
Department of Mental Health, Mental
    Retardation and Substance Abuse Services
Frank L. Tetrick, III, Associate Commissioner
P.O. Box 1797
Richmond, VA 23219
(804) 786-1746
E-mail: FTetrick@dmhmrsas.state.va.us
Web: www.dmhmrsas.state.va.us

Council on Developmental Disabilities

Virginia Board for People with Disabilities
Heidi Lawyer, Director
Ninth Street Office Building
202 N. Ninth Street, 9th Floor
Richmond, VA 23219
(804) 786-0016 (V/TTY); (800) 846-4464 (in VA)
Web: www.vaboard.org

Protection and Advocacy Agency

Virginia Office for Protection and Advocacy
    (VOPA)
V. Colleen Miller, Director
1910 Byrd Avenue, Suite 5
Richmond, VA 23230
(804) 225-2042 (V/TTY); (800) 552-3962 (in VA)
Web: www.vopa.state.va.us/

Client Assistance Program

   Contact Protection and Advocacy Agency
listed above.

Programs for Children With
Special Health Care Needs

Children with Special Health Care Needs Program
Nancy Bullock, RN, MPH, Director
Division of Child and Adolescent Health
Virginia Department of Health
109 Governor Street
Richmond, VA 23219
(804) 864-7685
E-mail: nancy.bullock@vdh.virginia.gov
Web: www.vahealth.org/specialchildren/
    index.htm

State CHIP Program (health care
for low-income, uninsured children)

FAMIS
P.O. Box 1820
Richmond, VA 23218-1820
(866) 873-2647
Web: www.famis.org

Programs for Children and Youth Who
Are Blind or Visually Impaired or Deaf-Blind

Virginia Department for the Blind and Vision
    Impaired
Joseph A. Bowman, Commissioner
Glen R. Slonneger, Director, Education Services
397 Azalea Avenue
Richmond, VA 23227-3600
(804) 371-3140
E-mail: slonnegr@dbvi.state.va.us
Web: www.vdbvi.org

Programs for Children and Youth
Who Are Deaf or Hard of Hearing

Virginia Department for the Deaf and Hard of
    Hearing
Ronald L. Lanier, Director
Ratcliffe Building, Suite 203
1602 Rolling Hills Drive
Richmond, VA 23229-5012
(804) 662-9502 (V/TTY); (800) 552-7917 (V/
    TTY)
E-mail: DDHHInfo@ddhh.state.va.us
Web: www.vddhh.org

Telecommunications Relay Services for Individuals Who Are Deaf, Hard of Hearing, or With Speech Impairments

(800) 828-1140 (V)
(800) 828-1120 (TTY); 711 (TTY)
(800) 229-5746 (Speech to Speech-English)
(866) 260-9470 (Speech to Speech-Spanish)

Regional ADA & IT Technical Assistance Center

ADA and IT Information Center
Marian Vessels, Director
451 Hungerford Drive, Suite 607
Rockville, MD 20850
(301) 217-0124 (V/TTY); (800) 949-4232 (V/TTY)
E-mail: adainfo@transcen.org
Web: www.adainfo.org

University Center for Excellence in Developmental Disabilities

Partnership for People with Disabilities
Dr. Fred P. Orelove, Executive Director
Virginia Commonwealth University
700 E. Franklin Street, 10th Floor
P.O. Box 843020
Richmond, VA 23284-3020
(804) 828-3876 (V/TTY); (800) 828-1120
E-mail: forelove@mai11.vcu.edu
Web: www.vcu.edu/partnership

Technology-Related Assistance

Virginia Assistive Technology System
Kenneth Knorr, Project Director
8004 Franklin Farms Drive
P.O. Box K300
Richmond, VA 23288-0300
(804) 662-9990; (800) 552-5019 (in VA only)
E-mail: knorrkh@drs.state.va.us
Web: www.vats.org

State Mediation System

Mediation
Arthur Stewart, Coordinator
Virginia Department of Education
P.O. Box 2120
Richmond, VA 23218-2120
(804) 786-0711
E-mail: astewart@mail.vak12ed.edu
Web: www.pen.k12.va.us/VDOE/sess

Special Format Library

Virginia Library and Resource Center
Virginia Department for the Blind and Vision Impaired
Barbara McCarthy, Director
395 Azalea Avenue
Richmond, VA 23227-3633
(804) 371-3661 (V/TTY); (800) 552-7015 (V/TTY)
E-mail: mccartbn@dvh.state.va.us
Web: www.vdbvi.org/

Virginia—Disability-Specific Organizations

Attention Deficit Disorder

To identify an ADD group in Virginia, contact either of the following organizations:

Children and Adults with Attention-Deficit/ Hyperactivity Disorder (CHADD)
8181 Professional Place, Suite 150
Landover, MD 20785
(301) 306-7070
(800) 233-4050 (Voice mail to request information packet)
Web: www.chadd.org

Attention Deficit Disorder Association (ADDA)
P.O. Box 543
Pottstown, PA 19464
(484) 945-2101
Web: www.add.org

Autism

Commonwealth Autism Service
John Toscano, Executive Director
2201 W. Broad Street, Suite 107
Richmond, VA 23220
(804) 355-0300; (800) 649-8481
E-mail: information@autismva.org
Web: www.autismva.org

Virginia Autism Resource Center
Carol Schall, Executive Director
P.O. Box 2500
Winchester, VA 22604
1-877-667-7771; (540) 542-1723
E-mail: info@varc.org
Web: www.varc.org

Blind/Visual Impairments

American Foundation for the Blind-National
    Literacy Center
Frances Mary D'Andrea, Director
100 Peachtree Street, Suite 620
Atlanta, GA 30303
(404) 525-2303
E-mail: literacy@afb.net
Web: www.afb.org

Brain Injury

Brain Injury Association of Virginia
Harry Weinstock, Executive Director
3212 Cutshaw Avenue, Suite 315
Richmond, VA 23230
(804) 355-5748; (800) 334-8443 (in VA)
E-mail: info@biav.net
Web: www.biav.net

Cerebral Palsy

Cerebral Palsy of Virginia
Kathy Prendergast, Executive Director
5825 Arrowhead Drive, Suite 201
Virginia Beach, VA 23462
(757) 497-7474
E-mail: cerebralpalsy@cerebralpalsyofvirginia.org
Web: www.cerebralpalsyofvirginia.org/

Deafness/Hard of Hearing

Virginia Association of the Deaf
Bennie Lacks, President
2521 Malden Avenue
Norfolk, VA 23518
(757) 587-9555; (757) 587-9729 (Video phone)
E-mail: lacksb@cox.net
Web: www.vad.org

Epilepsy

Epilepsy Foundation of Virginia
Suzanne Bischoff, Executive Director
UVA Medical Center
P.O. Box 800659
Charlottesville, VA 22908
(434) 924-8669 (Charlottesville); (804) 796-9935
    (Richmond)
(757) 478-0983 (Tidewater); (800) 332-1000
    (National Answer Place line)
E-mail: epi@avenue.org
Web: www.efva.org

Epilepsy Foundation of the Chesapeake Region
Robin Lincoln, Education Coordinator
107 S. West Street, PMB #141
Alexandria, VA 22314
(703) 862-7549
E-mail: rlincoln@epilepsy-foundation.org
Web: www.epilepsy-foundation.org

Learning Disabilities

Learning Disabilities
    Association of Virginia
Anna Marie Johnson, President
4324 Fordham Road
Richmond, VA 23236
(804) 745-9325
E-mail: info@ldavirginia.org
Web: www.ldavirginia.org

Mental Health

Mental Health Association of Virginia
Vickie Fisher, Executive Director
530 E. Main Street, Suite 707
Richmond, VA 23219
(804) 225-5591
E-mail: mhav@mhav.org
Web: www.mhav.org

NAMI Virginia
Valerie Marsh, Executive Director
P.O. Box 1903
Richmond, VA 23218-1903
(804) 225-8264; (888) 486-8264
E-mail: vaami@aol.com
Web: www.namivirginia.org

Parents and Children Coping Together
Joyce Kube, Executive Director
P.O. Box 26691
Richmond, VA 23261-6691
(804) 559-6833; (800) 477-0946 (in VA)
E-mail: pacct@infionline.net
Web: www.pacct.net/

Mental Retardation

The Arc of Virginia
Teja Stokes, Executive Director
2025 E. Main Street, Suite 120
Richmond, VA 23223
(804) 649-8481; (888) 604-2677
E-mail: tstokes@arcofva.org
Web: www.arcofva.org

Speech and Hearing

Speech-Language-Hearing Association
of Virginia, Inc.
Mary Jo Grote, President
P.O. Box 76
Basye, VA 22810
(540) 856-2111; (800) 487-4637
E-mail: gnmm@lbjlimited.com
Web: www.shav.org

Tourette Syndrome

Tourette Syndrome Association of
Greater Washington
Lyn Mox, Executive Director
33 University Boulevard East
Silver Spring, MD 20901-2485
(301) 681-4133; (877) 295-2148
E-mail: TSAGW@aol.com
Web: www.TSAGW.org

Virginia—Organizations Especially for Parents

Parent Training and
Information Center (PTI)

Parent Educational Advocacy Training
Center (PEATC)
Cherie Takemoto, Executive Director
6320 Augusta Drive, Suite 1200
Springfield, VA 22150
(703) 923-0010; (800) 869-6782 (in VA)
(804) 819-1999 (Richmond)
(703) 569-6200 (en Español)
E-mail: partners@peatc.org
Web: www.peatc.org/

Community Parent Resource Center

PADDA Community Parent Resource
Center (serving the Hampton
Roads and Tidewater Area)
Mark Jacob, Executive Director
813 Forrest Drive, Suite 3
Newport News, VA 23606
(888) 337-2332; (757) 591-9119
E-mail: hmathews@padda.org
Web: www.padda.org

Parent Resource Center

Division of Special Education and Student Services
Virginia Department of Education
Judy Hudgins, Specialist
Sandra Peterson, Specialist
P.O. Box 2120
Richmond, VA 23218-2120
(800) 422-2083; (804) 371-7420/7421
E-mail: jhudgins@mail.vak12ed.edu
E-mail: speterso@mail.vak12ed.edu
Web: www.pen.k12.va.us/VDOE/sess

Parent-To-Parent

Parent to Parent of Virginia
Dana Yarbrough, Executive Director
P.O. Box 38341
Richmond, VA 23231
(804) 222-1945
E-mail: PTPofVA@aol.com

Parent Teacher Association (PTA)

Virginia PTA
Ramona Morrow, President
1027 Wilmer Avenue
Richmond, VA 23227
(804) 264-1234
E-mail: info@vapta.org
Web: www.vapta.org

Virginia—Other Disability Organizations

Easter Seals Virginia
Melissa Hays-Smith, President
201 E. Main Street
Salem, VA 24153
(540) 777-7325; (800) 365-1656 (in VA)
E-mail: info@va.easter-seals.org
Web: www.va.easterseals.com

VSA Arts of Virginia
Nancy M. Gray, Executive Director
P.O. Box 27862
Richmond, VA 23861
(804) 230-0246
E-mail: Ngray.vsav@plantzero.com

Independent Living

To find out the contact information for the Statewide Independent Living Council (SILC) in Virginia, contact

Independent Living Research Utilization Project
The Institute for Rehabilitation and Research
2323 South Sheppard, Suite 1000
Houston, TX 77019
(713) 520-0232 (V); (713) 520-5136 (TTY)
E-mail: ilru@ilru.org
Web: www.ilru.org

To find out the contact information for centers for independent living (CILs) in Virginia, contact

National Council on Independent Living
1916 Wilson Boulevard, Suite 209
Arlington, VA 22201
(703) 525-3406; (703) 525-4153 (TTY)
E-mail: ncil@ncil.org
Web: www.ncil.org

WASHINGTON

Washington—State Agencies and Organizations

United States Senators

Honorable Maria Cantwell (D)
311 Hart Senate Office Building
Washington, DC 20510
(202) 224-3441
(202) 228-0514 (Fax)
E-mail Web Form: http://cantwell.senate.gov/
    contact/index.html
Web: http://cantwell.senate.gov/

Honorable Patty Murray (D)
154 Russell Senate Office Building
Washington, DC 20510
(202) 224-2621
(202) 224-0238 (Fax)
E-mail Web Form: http://murray.senate.gov/
    email/index.cfm
Web: http://murray.senate.gov

United States Representatives

To find the contact information for your representative in the House of the U.S. Congress, visit the House's Web site at: www.house.gov, or call (202) 225-3121; (202) 225-1904 (TTY).

Governor

Honorable Jay Inslee
Office of the Governor
P.O. Box 40002
Olympia, WA 98504-0002
(360) 902-4111; (360) 753-4110 (Fax)
E-mail Web Form: http://www.governor.
    wa.gov/contact/default.asp
Web: www.governor.wa.gov/

Official State Web Site

Web: http://access.wa.gov/

State Department of Education: Special Education

Special Education Section
Office of Superintendent of Public Instruction
600 Washington Street SE
Olympia, WA 98504
(360) 725-6075
E-mail Web Form: https://www.k12.wa.us/
    SpecialEd/ContactUs.aspx
Web: https://www.k12.wa.us/SpecialEd/
    default.aspx

State Coordinator for NCLB (No Child Left Behind)

Pat Eirish, Program Supervisor, Consolidated
    Federal Programs
Office of Superintendent of Public Instruction
P.O. Box 47200
Olympia, WA 98504-7200
(360) 725-6234
Web: http://www.k12.wa.us/

Programs for Infants and Toddlers With Disabilities: Birth–2 Years

Infant Toddler Early Intervention Program
Department of Early Learning
Early Support for Infant and Toddlers Program
Karen Walker, Program Administrator
PO Box 40970
Olympia, WA 98504
(360) 725-3516
E-mail: karen.walker@del.wa.gov
Web: http://del.wa.gov/development/esit/
    Default.aspx

Programs for Children With Disabilities: 3–5 Years

Early Childhood Services
Office of Superintendent of Public Instruction
Valerie Arnold, 619 Coordinator
Special Education Department
Old Capitol Building, 600 Washington Street S.E.
PO Box 47200
(360) 725-6075
E-mail: valerie.arnold@k12.wa.us
Web: http://www.k12.wa.us/specialed/

State Vocational Rehabilitation Agency

Division of Vocational Rehabilitation
Department of Social and Health Services
Michael O'Brien, Director
P.O. Box 45340
Olympia, WA 98504-5340
(360) 438-8008; (800) 637-5627 (V/TTY)
E-mail: obriemd@dshs.wa.gov
Web: www1.dshs.wa.gov/dvr

Coordinator for Transition Services

Cinda Johnson, EdD, Director
Center for Change in Transition Services
Seattle University
901 12th Avenue P.O. Box 222000
Seattle, WA 98122
(206) 296-6494
E-mail: cinda@seattleu.edu
Web: http://www.seattleu.edu/ccts/#.
     VE-4RlfXeUl

Office of State Coordinator of Vocational Education for Students With Disabilities

Career and Technical Education
Rob Fieldman, Director
P.O. Box 47200
Olympia, WA 98504-7200
(360) 725-6242; (360) 664-3631 (TTY)
E-mail: rfieldman@ospi.wednet.edu
Web: www.k12.wa.us/careerteched

State Mental Health Agency

Mental Health Division
Department of Social and Health Services
Karl Brimner, Director
P.O. Box 45320
Olympia, WA 98504-5320
(360) 902-0790
Web: http://www.dshs.wa.gov/dbhr/mh_
   information.shtml

State Developmental Disabilities Program

Division of Developmental Disabilities
Department of Social and Health Services
Linda Rolfe, Director
P.O. Box 45310
Olympia, WA 98504-5310
(360) 902-8484
Web: www1.dshs.wa.gov/ddd

Council on Developmental Disabilities

Developmental Disabilities Council
Ed Holen, Director
2600 Martin Way East, Suite F
P.O. Box 48314
Olympia, WA 98504-8314
(360) 586-3558; (800) 634-4473 (V/TTY)
E-mail: EdH@cted.wa.gov
Web: www.ddc.wa.gov

Protection and Advocacy Agency

Washington Protection and Advocacy System
Mark Stroh, Executive Director
315 Fifth Avenue South, Suite 850
Seattle, WA 98104
(206) 324-1521; (800) 562-2702
E-mail: info@dr-wa.org
Web: http://www.disabilityrightswa.org

Client Assistance Program

Client Assistance Program
Jerry Johnsen, Director
2531 Rainier Avenue South
Seattle, WA 98144
(206) 721-5999; (800) 544-2121 (in WA)
(888) 721-6072 (TTY)
E-mail: CAPSeattle@att.net

Programs for Children With Special Health Care Needs

Children with Special Health Care Needs
Community and Family Health
Department of Health
Maria Nardella, Manager
P.O. Box 47880
Olympia, WA 98504-7880
(360) 236-3573
E-mail: maria.nardella@doh.wa.gov

State CHIP Program (health care for low-income, uninsured children)

The CHIP Program
Washington State Department of Social and
    Health Services
(877) 543-7669
Web: http://fortress.wa.gov/dshs/maa/
    CHIP/Index.html

Programs for Children and Youth Who Are Blind or Visually Impaired

Department of Services for the Blind
Bill Palmer, Executive Director
P.O. Box 40933
Olympia, WA 98504-0933
(360) 725-3830
E-mail: info@dsb.wa.gov
Web: www.dsb.wa.gov

Programs for Children and Youth Who Are Deaf or Hard of Hearing

Office of Deaf and Hard of Hearing Services
Eric Raff, Director
P.O. Box 45300
Olympia, WA 98504-5300
(360) 902-8000 (V/TTY); (800) 422-7930 (V/TTY)
E-mail: rafferic@dshs.wa.gov
Web: www.dshs.wa.gov/hrsa/odhh/index.shtml

Telecommunications Relay Services for Individuals Who Are Deaf, Hard of Hearing, or With Speech Impairments

(800) 833-6384 (V)
(800) 833-6388 (TTY); 711 (TTY)
(800) 833-6385 (Tele-Braille)
(877) 833-6341 (Speech to Speech)

Programs for Children and Youth Who Are Deaf-Blind

Washington State Services for Children with
    Deaf-Blindness
Kathee K. Scoggin, Co-Director
Nancy Hatfield, Co-Director
400 SW 152nd Street
Burien, WA 98166-2209
(206) 439-6937 (V/TTY); (800) 572-7000 (in WA)
    (V/TTY)
E-mail: wsds@psesd.org
Web: www.wsdsonline.org

Regional ADA & IT Technical Assistance Center

Northwest ADA & IT Center
Charles E. Davis, Center Coordinator
Oregon Health & Science University-CDRC
P.O. Box 574
Portland, OR 97207-0574
(503) 494-4001; (503) 418-0296 (TTY)
(800) 949-4232 (V/TTY)
E-mail: nwada@ohsu.edu
Web: www.nwada.org

University Center for Excellence in Developmental Disabilities

Center on Human Development and Disability
Michael Guralnick, Director
University of Washington
Box 357920
Seattle, WA 98195-7920
(206) 543-7701
E-mail: chdd@u.washington.edu
Web: http://depts.washington.edu/chdd/

Technology-Related Assistance

Washington Assistive Technology Alliance
Debbie Cook, Project Director
UWCTDS/University of Washington
P.O. Box 357920
Seattle, WA 98195-7920
(206) 685-4181; (800) 214-8731 (I&R)
(206) 616-1396 (TTY)
E-mail: uwat@u.washington.edu
Web: http://wata.org

Eastern Assistive Technology Resource Center
West 606 Sharp
Spokane, WA 99201
(509) 328-9350 (V/TTY); (800) 214-8731 (V/TTY)
E-mail: Spokane@wa.easter-seals.org
Web: http://wata.org/wata/eatrc/index.htm

State Mediation System

Sound Options Group, LLC
Greg Abell, Coordinator
197 Parfitt Way, Suite 220
Bainbridge Island, WA 98110
(206) 842-2298; (800) 692-2590
E-mail: grega@somtg.com
Web: www.soundoptionsgroup.com

Special Format Library

Washington Talking Book and Braille Library
Gloria Leonard, Director
2021 9th Avenue
Seattle, WA 98121-2783
(206) 615-0400; (800) 542-0866
(206) 615-0419 (TTY)
E-mail: wtbbl@wtbbl.org
Web: http://www.wtbbl.org/

Washington—Disability-Specific Organizations

Attention Deficit Disorder

To identify an ADD group in Washington, contact either of the following organizations:

Children and Adults with Attention-Deficit/
Hyperactivity Disorder (CHADD)
8181 Professional Place, Suite 150
Landover, MD 20785
(301) 306-7070; (800) 233-4050 (Voice mail to
request information packet)
Web: www.chadd.org

Attention Deficit Disorder Association (ADDA)
P.O. Box 543
Pottstown, PA 19464
(484) 945-2101
E-mail: mail@add.org
Web: www.add.org

Autism

To identify an autism group in Washington, contact

Autism Society of America
7910 Woodmont Avenue, Suite 300
Bethesda, MD 20814
(301) 657-0881; (800) 3-AUTISM
Web: www.autism-society.org

Blind/Visual Impairments

American Foundation for the Blind–West
Gil Johnson, Director
111 Pine Street, Suite 725
San Francisco, CA 94111
(415) 392-4845
E-mail: sanfran@afb.net
Web: www.afb.org

Scott Birdwell, Marketing &
    Communications Assistant
Community Services for the Blind &
    Partially Sighted
9709 Third Avenue NE, Suite 100
Seattle, WA 98115-2027
(206) 525-5556, ext. 208
Web: www.csbps.com
Web: www.sightconnection.com
    (Adaptive Aids Store)

Brain Injury

Brain Injury Association of Washington
16315 NE 87th Street, Suite B-4
Redmond, WA 98052-3537
(425) 895-0047; (800) 523-5438 (in WA)
E-mail: biawa@biawa.org
Web: www.biawa.org

Head Injury Support Group
Wanda Godin
St. Peter Hospital
413 Lilly Road NE
Olympia, WA 98506

Developmental Disabilities/Mental Retardation

Family Educator Partnership Project
The Arc of Washington State
Susan Atkins and Sue Elliott, Co-Directors
2600 Martin Way East, Suite D
Olympia, WA 98506
(360) 357-3279; (888) 754-8798 (in WA)
E-mail: info@arcwa.org
Web: www.arcwa.org

PROVAIL
Michael Hatzenbeler, CEO
3670 Stoneway North
Seattle, WA 98103
(206) 363-7303; (206) 440-2206 (TTY)
Web: www.provail.org

Epilepsy

Epilepsy Foundation of Washington
Brent Herrmann, President/CEO
2311 N 45th St #134
Seattle, Washington 98103-6905
United States
(206) 547-4551
(800) 752-3509
E-mail: mail@epilepsynw.org
Web: http://www.epilepsynw.org/

Learning Disabilities

Learning Disabilities Association of Washington
Lee Kueckelhan, President
7819 159th Place NE
Redmond, WA 98052-7301
(425) 882-0792; (800) 536-2343 (Information and
*   referral, in WA)*
(425) 882-0820 (Business Line)
Web: www.ldawa.org

Speech and Hearing

Washington Speech-Language-Hearing Association
Jennette Barrow, President
2150 N. 107th Street, Suite 204
Seattle, WA 98133-9009
(206) 367-8704
E-mail: office@wslha.org
Web: www.wslha.org

Washington—Organizations Especially for Parents

Parent Training and Information Center (PTI)

Parents Are Vital in Education (PAVE)
Joanne Butts, Executive Director
6316 S. 12th Street, Suite B
Tacoma, WA 98465
(253) 565-2266 (V/TTY); (800) 572-7368 (V/TTY)
E-mail: wapave9@washingtonpave.com
Web: www.washingtonpave.org

Parent-To-Parent

Washington State P2P Programs
Susan Atkins, Coordinator
State Coordinating Office
4738 172nd Court, SE
Bellevue, WA 98006
(425) 641-7504; (800) 821-5927
E-mail: statep2p@earthlink.net
Web: www.arcwa.org

Community Parent Resource Center

Parent to Parent Power (serving Pierce,
*   North King County and vicinity)*
Yvone Link, Program Director
1118 S. 142nd Street
Tacoma, WA 98444
(253) 531-2022; (253) 531-1146
E-mail: yvone_link@yahoo.com
E-mail: support@p2ppower.org
Web: http://p2ppower.org

Partners in Policymaking

Washington Developmental Disabilities Council
Donna Patrick, Program Director
2600 Martin Way E, Suite F
Olympia, WA 98504
(360) 586-3566
E-mail: donnap@cted.wa.gov

Parent Teacher Association (PTA)

Washington State PTA
Jean Carpenter, Executive Director
2003 65th Avenue West
Tacoma, WA 98466-6215
(253) 565-2153; (800) 562-3804 (in WA only)
E-mail: wapta@wastatepta.org
Web: www.wastatepta.org

Other Parent Organization

Specialized Training of Military Parents (STOMP)
PAVE
Heather Hebdon, Program Coordinator
6316 S. 12th Street, Suite B
Tacoma, WA 98465
(253) 565-2266 (V/TTY); (800) 572-7368
*   (V/TTY)*
E-mail: stomp@washingtonpave.comm
Web: www.washingtonpave.org

Washington—Other Disability Organizations

Easter Seals Washington
Garry Wyckoff, President/CEO
521 Second Avenue West
Seattle, WA 98119
(206) 281-5700 (V/TTY);
*   (800) 678-5708*
E-mail: esw@seals.org
Web: www.seals.org

The FAS (Fetal Alcohol Syndrome)
*   Family Resource Institute*
Jocie Devries, Director
P.O. Box 2525
Lynwood, WA 98036
(253) 531-2878; (800) 999-3429
E-mail: vicfas@hotmail.com
Web: http://fetalalcoholsyndrome.org

Infant/Toddler Early Intervention Program
Washington PAVE
Cassie Johnston, Parent Participation
  Coordinator
6316 S. 12th Street
Tacoma, WA 98465
(360) 701-7012 (V/TTY); (800) 572-7368
(253) 565-2266 (V/TTY)
E-mail: weecare@olywa.net
Web: www.washingtonpave.org

Summit Assistance Dogs
Sue Meinzinger, Director
5458 W. Shore Road
Anacortes, WA 98221
(360) 293-5609
E-mail: info@summitdogs.org
Web: www.summitdogs.org

VSA Arts of Washington
Daniel Schmitt, Executive Director
305 Harrison Street, Suite 303
Seattle, WA 98109
(206) 443-1843
E-mail: info@vsaaw.org
Web: www.vsaaw.org

Washington State Fathers Network
James May, Executive Director
Kindering Center
16120 NE 8th Street
Bellevue, WA 98008-3937
(425) 747-4004, ext. 4286
E-mail: jmay@fathersnetwork.org
Web: www.fathersnetwork.org

Independent Living

To find out the contact information for the Statewide Independent Living Council (SILC) in Washington, contact

Independent Living Research Utilization Project
The Institute for Rehabilitation and Research
2323 South Sheppard, Suite 1000
Houston, TX 77019
(713) 520-0232 (V); (713) 520-5136 (TTY)
E-mail: ilru@ilru.org
Web: www.ilru.org

To find out the contact information for centers for independent living (CILs) in Washington, contact

National Council on Independent Living
1916 Wilson Boulevard, Suite 209
Arlington, VA 22201
(703) 525-3406; (703) 525-4153 (TTY)
E-mail: ncil@ncil.org
Web: www.ncil.org

WEST VIRGINIA

West Virginia—State Agencies and Organizations

United States Senators

Honorable Joe Manchin III. (D)
306 Hart Senate Office Building
Washington, DC 20510
(202) 224-3954; (202) 224-4849 (TTY)
E-mail: http://www.manchin.senate.gov/
  public/index.cfm/contact-form
Web: http://www.manchin.senate.gov/
  public/index.cfm/home

Honorable John D. Rockefeller IV (D)
531 Hart Senate Office Building
Washington, DC 20510
(202) 224-6472; (202) 224-7665 (Fax)
E-mail: senator@rockefeller.senate.gov
Web: http://rockefeller.senate.gov

United States Representatives

To find the contact information for your representative in the House of the U.S. Congress, visit the House's Web site at: www.house.gov, or call (202) 225-3121; (202) 225-1904 (TTY).

Governor

Honorable Earl Ray Tomblin
State Capitol Complex
1900 Kanawha Boulevard
Charleston, WV 25305
(304) 558-2000; (888) 438-2731
E-mail Web Form: http://www.
  governor.wv.gov/Pages/
  SubmitaCommenttotheGovernor.aspx
Web: http://www.governor.wv.gov/Pages/
  default.aspx

Governor's Cabinet on Children and Families
  (Community Voices)
Elizabeth Lovas, Special Assistant
210 Brooks Street, Lee Building, Suite 300
Charleston, WV 25301
(304) 558-0600
Web: www.state.wv.us

Official State Web Site

Web: www.wv.gov/

State Department of Education: Special Education

Office of Special Programs
Patricia Homberg, Executive Director
1900 Kanawha Boulevard East
Building 6, Room 304
Charleston, WV 25305-0330
(304) 558-2696
E-mail: phomberg@access.k12.wv.us
Web: http://wvde.state.wv.us

State Coordinator for NCLB (No Child Left Behind)

West Virginia was granted a waiver from the NCLB program.

Gayle C. Manchin, President
West Virginia Board of Education
1900 Kanawha Boulevard East
Charleston, WV 25305
Web: http://wvde.state.wv.us/waiver/

Programs for Infants and Toddlers With Disabilities under Part C of IDEA: Birth–3 Years

West Virginia Birth to Three
Office of Maternal, Child and Family Health
Bureau of Public Health
Pamela Roush, Director
350 Capitol Street, Room 427
Charleston, WV 25301
(304) 558-5388; (866) 321-4728
E-mail: pam.s.roush@wv.gov
Web: www.wvdhhr.org/birth23

Programs for Children With Disabilities: 3–5 Years

Office of Special Education
Ginger Huffman, Coordinator
1900 Kanawha Boulevard East

Building 6, Room 304
Charleston, WV 25305-0330
(304) 558-2696
E-mail: vhuffman@k12.wv.us
Web: http://wvde.state.wv.us/osp/

State Vocational Rehabilitation Agency

Division of Rehabilitation Services
Janice Holland, Interim Director
State Capitol Complex
P.O. Box 50890
Charleston, WV 25305-0890
(304) 766-4601
E-mail: janiceh@mail.drs.state.wv.us
Web: www.wvdrs.org

Coordinator for Transition Services

Shana Clay
Office of Special Education
West Virginia Department of Education
1900 Kanawha Boulevard East
Building 6, Room 243
Charleston, WV 25305-0330
(304) 558-3075
E-mail: sdclay@k12.wv.us
Web: http://wvde.state.wv.us/ose/

Office of State Coordinator of Vocational Education for Students With Disabilities

Division of Technical and Adult Education Services
West Virginia Department of Education
Dr. Stanley Hopkins, Assistant State
  Superintendent of Schools
1900 Kanawha Boulevard East
Building 6, Room B-221
Charleston, WV 25305-0330
(304) 558-2349
E-mail: shopkins@access.k12.wv.us
Web: http://wvde.state.wv.us

State Mental Health Agency

Bureau for Behavioral Health and Health Facilities
Department of Health and Human Resources
Nancy Exline, Acting Commissioner
350 Capitol Street, Room 350
Charleston, WV 25301-3702
(304) 356-4521
Web: http://www.wvdhhr.org/

State Mental Health Representative for Children and Youth

Division of Children's Mental Health Services
Bureau for Behavioral Health and Health
   Facilities
Department of Health and Human Resources
Beth Morrison, Director
350 Capitol Street, Room 350
Charleston, WV 25301-3702
(304) 558-0627
E-mail: beth.j.morrison@wv.gov
Web: http://www.wv.gov/

State Mental Retardation Program

Division of Developmental Disabilities
Bureau for Behavioral Health and
   Health Facilities
Department of Health and Human Resources
Frank Kirkland, Director
350 Capitol Street, Room 350
Charleston, WV 25301-3702
(304) 558-0627
E-mail: fkirkland@wvdhhr.org
Web: http://www.wv.gov/

Council on Developmental Disabilities

West Virginia Developmental Disabilities Council
Clarice Hausch, Executive Director
110 Stockton Street
Charleston, WV 25387
(304) 558-0416; (304) 558-2376 (TTY)
E-mail: swiseman@wvdhhr.org
Web: http://www.wv.gov/

Protection and Advocacy Agency

West Virginia Advocates
1207 Quarrier Street, 4th Floor
Charleston, WV 25301
(304) 346-0847 (V/TTY); (800) 950-5250 (in WV)
E-mail: WVAinfo@wvadvocates.org
Web: www.wvadvocates.org

Client Assistance Program

West Virginia Advocates
1207 Quarrier Street, 4th Floor
Charleston, WV 25301
(304) 346-0847 (V/TTY); (800) 950-5250 (in WV)
E-mail: WVAinfo@wvadvocates.org
Web: www.wvadvocates.org

Programs for Children With Special Health Care Needs

Children's Specialty Care
Janet Lucas, Director
Office of Maternal Child and Family Health
Bureau for Public Health
West Virginia Department of Health and
   Human Resources
350 Capitol Street, Room 427
Charleston, WV 25301
(304) 558-5388
E-mail: janetlucas@wvdhhr.org
Web: http://www.wv.gov/

State CHIP Program (health care for low-income, uninsured children)

WV CHIP
(877) 982-2447
Web: www.wvchip.org

Programs for Children and Youth Who Are Deaf or Hard of Hearing or Deaf-Blind

West Virginia Commission for the Deaf and Hard of
   Hearing
Ruth Ann King, Coordinator
Annette Carey, Coordinator
State Capitol Complex
1900 Kanawha Boulevard East
Building 6, Room 863
Charleston, WV 25305-0330
(304) 558-1675; (866) 461-3578
E-mail: wvcdhh@wvdhhr.org
Web: http://www.wv.gov/

Telecommunications Relay Services for Individuals Who Are Deaf, Hard of Hearing, or With Speech Impairments

(800) 982-8772 (V)
(800) 982-8771 (TTY); 711 (TTY)
(800) 229-5746 (Speech to Speech-English)
(866) 260-9470 (Speech to Speech-Spanish)

*Programs for Children
and Youth Who Are
Blind or Visually Impaired*

Department of Education
Annette Carey, Coordinator
Office of Special Education
900 Kanawha Boulevard East
Building 6, Room 304
Charleston, WV 25305-0330
(304) 558-2696; (800) 642-8541 (in WV)
E-mail: acarey@access.k12.wv.us
Web: http://wvde.state.wv.us/ose/

*Regional ADA & IT
Technical Assistance Center*

ADA and IT Information Center for the
    Mid Atlantic Region
Marian Vessels, Director
451 Hungerford Drive, Suite 607
Rockville, MD 20850
(301) 217-0124 (V/TTY); (800) 949-4232 (V/
    TTY)
E-mail: adainfo@transcen.org
Web: www.adainfo.org

*University Center
for Excellence in
Developmental Disabilities*

West Virginia University Center for
    Excellence in Disabilities
Ashok S. Dey, Director
955 Hartman Run Road
Morgantown, WV 26505
(304) 293-4692
E-mail: wvuced@hsc.wvu.edu
Web: www.cedwvu.org/

Technology-Related Assistance

Rehab Technology Department
Division of Rehabilitation Services
Dale Castilla, Manager
P.O. Box 1004
Institute, WV 25112
(304) 766-4600
Web: www.wvdrs.org

State Mediation System

West Virginia Department of Education
Office of Special Education
Ghaski Lee Browning, Coordinator
1900 Kanawha Boulevard East
Building 6, Room 304
Charleston, WV 25305-0330
(304) 558-2696
E-mail: glee@access.k12.wv.us
Web: http://wvde.state.wv.us/ose/

Special Format Library

West Virginia Library Commission
Special Libraries-Blind and Physically
    Handicapped Cultural Center
Donna B. Calvert, Librarian
1900 Kanawha Boulevard East
Charleston, WV 25305-0330
(304) 558-4061; (800) 642-8674
E-mail: calvertd@mail.wv1c.lib.wv.us
Web: http://www.librarycommission.wv.gov/
    Pages/default.aspx

West Virginia—Disability-Specific Organizations

Attention Deficit Disorder

West Virginia CHADD
Holly H. Graff, Coordinator
Email: virtualchapter@chadd.net
Web: http://www.chadd.org/Support/
    Directory-Details/id/7D5A7872-3B2D-E311-
    B849-0050569C00A7.aspx

Autism

West Virginia Autism Training Center
Dr. Barbara Becker-Cottrill, Director
Marshall University
One John Marshall Drive
Huntington, WV 25755-2430
(304) 696-2332; (800) 344-5115 (in WV)
Web: www.marshall.edu/coe/atc

Blind/Visual Impairments

American Foundation for the Blind–National
    Literacy Center
Frances Mary D'Andrea, Director
100 Peachtree Street, Suite 620
Atlanta, GA 30303
(404) 525-2303
E-mail: literacy@afb.net
Web: www.afb.org

Brain Injury

Brain Injury Association of West Virginia, Inc.
Peggy Brown, Executive Director
P.O. Box 574
Institute, WV 25112
(304) 766-4892; (800) 356-6443 (in WV)
E-mail: BIAWV@aol.com
Web: www.BIAUSA.org/WVirginia

Learning Disabilities

Learning Disabilities Association
   of West Virginia
Lori Dubrawka, President
1003 Highland Road
Charleston, WV 25302
(866) 985-3211 (in WV)
E-mail: dubrawka@aol.com

Mental Health

Mental Health Association in the
   Greater Kanawha Valley, Inc.
Ellen Ward, Executive Director
One United Way Square
Charleston, WV 25301-1098
(304) 340-3512
E-mail: mha@wvinter.net
Web: http://mha-kanawha.org

NAMI-West Virginia
Michael Ross, Executive Director
P.O. Box 2706
Charleston, WV 25330-2706
(304) 342-0497
E-mail: NAMIWV@aol.com

Mountain State Parents-CAN
Teri Toothman, Executive Director
P.O. Box 6658
Wheeling, WV 26003
(304) 233-5399; (800) 244-5385
E-mail: ttoothman@mspcan.org
Web: www.mspcan.org

West Virginia Health Consumers Association
Lorie Roberts, Executive Director
910 Quarrier Street, Suite 414
Charleston, WV 25301
(304) 345-7312; (800) 598-8847
E-mail: lorieroberts@contac.org
Web: www.wvmhca.org

Speech and Hearing

West Virginia Speech-Language-Hearing Association
Brian K. Reed, President
2103 36th Street
Parkersburg, WV 26101
(304) 420-9563
E-mail: breed1975@aol.com

Tourette Syndrome

Tourette Syndrome Association of Greater
   Washington
Lyn Mox, Executive Director
33 University Boulevard East
Silver Spring, MD 20901
(301) 681-4133; (877) 295-2148
E-mail: TSAGW@aol.com
Web: www.TSAGW.org

West Virginia—Organizations Especially for Parents

Parent Training and Information Center (PTI)

West Virginia Parent Training and Information
   Project (WVPTI)
Pat Haberbosch, Director
371 Broaddus Avenue
Clarksburg, WV 26301
(304) 624-1436 (V/TTY); (800) 281-1436 (in WV)
E-mail: wvpti@aol.com
Web: www.wvpti.org

Parent-To-Parent

West Virginia Parent-Educator Resource Center
   (PERC) Project
Lynn Reichard, Educator
Ty Strauch, Parent
509 W. Martin Street
Martinsburg, WV 25401
(304) 263-5717
E-mail: bcperc@yahoo.com

Parent Teacher Association (PTA)

West Virginia Congress of Parents and Teachers
Jenny Raber, President
P.O. Box 3557
Parkersburg, WV 26103-3557
(304) 420-9576; (304) 420-9577
E-mail: wv_office@pta.org
Web: www.wvpta.net/

Parent-Educator Resource Center

West Virginia Parent-Educator Resource Center
(PERC) Project
Nancy Drake, Parent Coordinator
West Virginia Department of Education
Office of Special Education
1900 Kanawha Boulevard E, Building 6,
Room 304
Charleston, WV 25305-0330
(304) 558-2696
E-mail: ndrake@access.k12.wv.us
Web: http://wvde.state.wv.us

West Virginia—Other Disability Organizations

Easter Seals West Virginia
Lori Untch, President/CEO
1305 National Road
Wheeling, WV 26003-5780
(304) 242-1390 (V/TTY); (800) 677-1390
E-mail: ateaster@comcast.net
Web: www.wv.easter-seals.org

SOPHIA'S PLACE
Amy L. Brooks, Founder
50 Fenwick Drive
Martinsburg, WV 25401
E-mail: wifeof1motherof3@cs.com

West Virginia Family Support Program
Scott Miller, State Coordinator
350 Capitol Street, Room 350
Charleston, WV 25301-3702
(304) 558-0627
E-mail: smiller@wvdhhr.org

VSA Arts West Virginia
John Hunter, Jr., Executive Director
Marshall University
400 Hal Greer Boulevard
Huntington, WV 25755
(304) 696-6384
E-mail: vsaartswv@charter.net

Independent Living

To find out the contact information for the Statewide Independent Living Council (SILC) in West Virginia, contact

Independent Living Research Utilization Project
The Institute for Rehabilitation and Research
2323 South Sheppard, Suite 1000
Houston, TX 77019
(713) 520-0232 (V); (713) 520-5136 (TTY)
E-mail: ilru@ilru.org
Web: www.ilru.org

To find out the contact information for centers for independent living (CILs) in West Virginia, contact

National Council on Independent Living
1916 Wilson Boulevard, Suite 209
Arlington, VA 22201
(703) 525-3406; (703) 525-4153 (TTY)
E-mail: ncil@ncil.org
Web: www.ncil.org

WISCONSIN

Wisconsin—State Agencies and Organizations

United States Senators

Honorable Tammy Baldwin (D)
717 Hart Senate Office Building
Washington, DC 20510
(202) 224-5653
(202) 224-9787 (Fax)
E-mail Web Form: http://www.baldwin.
senate.gov/contact
Web: http://www.baldwin.senate.gov/

Honorable Ron Johnson (R)
328 Hart Senate Office Building
Washington, DC 20510
(202) 224-5323
(202) 224-2725 (Fax)
E-mail Web Form: http://www.ronjohnson.
senate.gov/public/index.cfm/contact
Web: http://www.ronjohnson.senate.gov/
public/index.cfm/home

United States Representatives

To find the contact information for your representative in the House of the U.S. Congress, visit the House's Web site at: www.house.gov, or call (202) 225-3121; (202) 225-1904 (TTY).

Governor

Honorable Scott Walker
State Capitol
P.O. Box 7863
Madison, WI 53707
(608) 266-1212
E-mail Web Form: http://walker.wi.gov/
  contact-us
Web: http://walker.wi.gov/

Official State Web Site

Web: www.wisconsin.gov/state/home/

Governor's Committee for People With Disabilities

Governor's Committee for People with Disabilities
Malika Monger, Staff Support
One W. Wilson Street, Room 518
Madison, WI 53703
(608) 261-7816
Web: http://www.dhs.wisconsin.gov/
  disabilities/physical/gcpd.htm

State Department of Education: Special Education

Division for Learning Support: Equity and
  Advocacy
Carolyn Stanford Taylor, Assistant State
  Superintendent
Stephanie Petska, Director of Special
  Education Team
125 S. Webster Street
P.O. Box 7841
Madison, WI 53707-7841
(608) 266-1649; (800) 441-4563
E-mail: carolyn.stanford.taylor@dpi.state.wi.us
Web: http://dls.dpi.wi.gov/

State Coordinator for NCLB (No Child Left Behind)

Wisconsin was granted an extended waiver
from the NCLB program.

Aundrea Kerkenbush
Wisconsin Department of Public Instruction
125 S. Webster Street
P.O. Box 7841
Madison, WI 53707-7841
(608) 261-6322
Email Web Form: http://focus-schools.dpi.
  wi.gov/user/1196/contact
Web: http://focus-schools.dpi.wi.gov/

Programs for Infants and Toddlers With Disabilities: Birth–3 Years

Division of Disability and Elder Services
Department of Health and Family Services
Terri Enters, Supervisor/Part C Coordinator
P.O. Box 7851
Madison, WI 53707-7851
(608) 267-3270; (800) 642-7837
E-mail: Terri.Enters@dhs.wisconsin.gov
Web: http://www.dhs.wisconsin.gov/
  children/birthto3/index.htm

Programs for Children With Disabilities: 3–5 Years

Division for Learning Support:
  Equity and Advocacy
Department of Public Instruction
Jenny Giles, Early Childhood Consultant
125 South Webster Street
Madison, WI 53707-7841
(608) 267-9172; (800) 441-4563
E-mail: jenny.giles@dpi.wi.gov
Website: http://ec.dpi.wi.gov/ec_ecspedhm

State Vocational Rehabilitation Agency

Division of Vocational Rehabilitation
Department of Workforce Development
Charlene Dwyer, Administrator
201 E. Washington Avenue, Room A100
P.O. Box 7852
Madison, WI 53707-7852
(608) 261-0050; (800) 442-3477
(608) 266-0283 (TTY)
Web: www.dwd.state.wi.us/dvr

Coordinator for Transition Services

Wendi Dawson, Director
Wisconsin Department of Public Instruction
125 South Webster Street
Madison, WI 53703
(608) 266-1146
E-mail: wendid@witig.org
Web: www.wsti.org

Vocational Education for Students With Disabilities

Division for Academic Excellence
Shiela J. Briggs, PhD, Assistant State
    Superintendent
Department of Public Instruction
P.O. Box 7841
Madison, WI 53707-7841
(608) 266-3361; (800) 441-4563
Web: http://dae.dpi.wi.gov/

State Mental Health Agency

Bureau of Mental Health and Substance
    Abuse Services
Division of Disability and Elder Services
Department of Health and Family Services
Joyce Bohn-Allen, Director
P.O. Box 7851
Madison, WI 53707-7851
(608) 266-2717
E-mail: Joyce.Allen@wisconsin.gov
Web: www.dhfs.state.wi.us

State Children's Services

Division of Children and Family Services
Department of Health and Family Services
William Fiss, Deputy Administrator
P.O. Box 8916
Madison, WI 53708-8916
(608) 267-3905
E-mail: fisswr@dhfs.state.wi.us
Web: www.dhfs.wisconsin.gov

State Mental Health Representative for Children and Youth

Bureau of Mental Health and
    Substance Abuse Services
Brad Schlough, M.S., LPC, Director of Clinical
    Programs
Brad Schlough, M.S., LPC, Director of Clinical
    Programs
Department of Health and Family Services
P.O. Box 7851
Madison, WI 53707-7851
(608) 280-2700
Web: http://www.journeymhc.org/

State Developmental Disabilities Program

Bureau of Developmental Disabilities Services
Camille Rodriguez, Director
One W. Wilson Street, Room 418

Madison, WI 53707-7851
(608) 266-8560
E-mail: Camille.Rodriguez@dhs.wisconsin.gov
Web: http://www.dhs.wisconsin.gov/

Councils on Developmental Disabilities

Wisconsin Board for People With Developmental
    Disabilities
Beth Swedeen, Executive Director
101 East Wilson Street, Rm. 219
Madison, WI 53703
(608) 266-7826; (888) 332-1677
E-mail: beth.swedeen@wisconsin.gov;
    bpddhelp@wi-bpdd.org
Web: http://www.wi-bpdd.org/

Protection and Advocacy Agency

Disability Rights Wisconsin
Dan Idzikowski, Executive Director
131 W. Wilson Street, Suite 700
Madison, WI 53703
(608) 267-0368; (800) 928-8778 (in WI only)
E-mail Web Form: http://www.
    disabilityrightswi.org/contact-us/secure-email
Web: http://www.disabilityrightswi.org/

Client Assistance Program

Client Assistance Program
Linda Vegoe, Director
Department of Agriculture
Trade and Consumer Protection
2811 Agriculture Drive
P.O. Box 8911
Madison, WI 53708-8911
(608) 224-5070; (800) 362-1290 (in WI)
E-mail: linda.vegoe@datcp.state.wi.us
Web: www.datcp.state.wi.us/

Programs for Children With Special Health Care Needs

Children's Special Health Care Needs Supervisor
Peggy Helm-Quest, MSEd, MHA
Bureau of Community Health and Prevention
Division of Public Health
1 W. Wilson Street
P.O. Box 2659
Madison, WI 53701-2659
(608) 267-2945
E-mail: helmqp@dhfs.state.wi.us
Web: www.dhfs.wisconsin.gov

State CHIP Program (health care
for low-income, uninsured children)

Wisconsin BadgerCare
P.O. Box 6678
Madison, WI 53716
(800) 362-3002
Web: http://www.medicaid.gov/Medicaid-
    CHIP-Program-Information/By-State/
    wisconsin.html

Programs for Children and Youth
Who Are Blind or Visually Impaired

Wisconsin Center for the Blind and
    Visually Impaired
Sue H. Enoch, Director
1700 W. State Street
Janesville, WI 53546
(608) 758-6100; (800) 832-9784 (in WI)
Web: www.wcbvi.k12.wi.us/index.html

Programs for Children and Youth Who
Are Deaf or Hard of Hearing or Deaf-Blind

Office for the Deaf and Hard of Hearing
Department of Health and Family Services
Linda Huffer, Director
One W. Wilson Street, Room 451
P.O. Box 7851
Madison, WI 53707-7851
(608) 266-3118; (608) 266-5641 (V/TTY)
E-mail: hufferl@dhfs.state.wi.us
Web: www.dhfs.wisconsin.gov

Wisconsin Educational Services Program for
    Deaf and Hard of Hearing (WESPDHH)
Alex Slappey, Director
Marcy Dicker Dropkin, Director of Outreach
19601 W. Bluemound Road, #200
Brookfield, WI 53045
(262) 787-9540 (V/TTY)
E-mail: marcy.dropkin@wesp-dhh.wi.gov
Web: www.wesp-dhh.wi.gov

Wisconsin School for the Deaf
309 W. Walworth Avenue
Delavan, WI 53115
(262) 728-7120 (V/TTY); (877) 973-3323 (V/TTY)
E-mail: alex.slappey@dpi.state.wi.us
Web: www.wsd.k12.wi.us

Telecommunications Relay Services
for Individuals Who Are Deaf, Hard
of Hearing, or With Speech Impairments

(800) 947-6644 (V)
(800) 947-3529 (TTY); 711 (TTY)
(800) 272-1773 (ASCII);
    (800) 267-8867 (Fast ASCII)
(800) 833-7637 (Speech to Speech)
(866) 833-7813 (Spanish)

State Education Agency
Rural Representative

David Carlson, Director
School Financial Services
Department of Public Instruction
125 S. Webster Street
P.O. Box 7841
Madison, WI 53702
(608) 266-6968
E-mail: david.carlson@dpi.state.wi.us
Web: www.dpi.state.wi.us

Regional ADA & IT
Technical Assistance Center

Great Lakes ADA and Accessible IT Center
Robin Jones, Project Director
University of Illinois/Chicago
Institute on Disability and
    Human Development
1640 W. Roosevelt Road
Chicago, IL 60608
(312) 413-1407 (V/TTY);
    (800) 949-4232 (V/TTY)
E-mail: gldbtac@uic.edu
Web: www.adagreatlakes.org

University Center for Excellence
in Developmental Disabilities

Waisman Center
Daniel Bier, Associate Director
University of Wisconsin-Madison
1500 Highland Avenue
Madison, WI 53705-2280
(608) 263-5254
E-mail: bier@waisman.wisc.edu
Web: www.waisman.wisc.edu/index.htmlx

Technology-Related Assistance

Wistech
Susan Abbey, Director
Division of Disability and Elder Services
1 W. Wilson, Room 450
P.O. Box 7851
Madison, WI 53707-7851
(608) 266-1794; (608) 267-9880 (TTY)
Web: http://dhfs.wisconsin.gov/disabilities/
   wistech

Center for Dispute Resolution Education
State Mediation System
Eva Soeka, Director
Marquette University
106 Wehr Physics
P.O. Box 1881
Milwaukee, WI 53201-1881
(888) 298-3857
Web: www.marquette.edu/wsems

Special Format Library

Wisconsin Regional Library for the Blind and
   Physically Handicapped
Marsha Valance, Librarian
813 W. Wells Street
Milwaukee, WI 53233-1436
(414) 286-3045; (800) 242-8822
(414) 286-3548 (TTY)
E-mail: lbph@mpl.org
Web: http://talkingbooks.dpi.wi.gov/

Wisconsin—Disability-Specific Organizations

Attention Deficit Disorder

To identify an ADD group in Wisconsin, contact either of the following organizations:

Children and Adults with Attention-Deficit/
   Hyperactivity Disorder (CHADD)
8181 Professional Place, Suite 150
Landover, MD 20785
(301) 306-7070
(800) 233-4050 (Voice mail to request
   information packet)
Web: www.chadd.org

Attention Deficit Disorder Association (ADDA)
P.O. Box 543
Pottstown, PA 19464
(484) 945-2101
Web: www.add.org

Autism

Autism Society of Wisconsin
103 W. College Avenue, Suite 709
Appleton, WI 54911-5744
(920) 993-0279; (888) 4-AUTISM (in WI)
Web: www.asw4autism.org

Blind/Visual Impairments

American Foundation for the Blind–Midwest
Jay Stitely, Director
401 N. Michigan Avenue, Suite 350
Chicago, IL 60611
(312) 396-4420
E-mail: chicago@afb.net
Web: www.afb.org

Brain Injury

Brain Injury Association of Wisconsin
Caroline Feller, Executive Director
2900 N. 117th Street, Suite 100
Wauwatosa, WI 53222
(414) 778-4144; (800) 882-9282
   (Family Helpline, in WI)
E-mail: biaw@execpc.com
Web: www.biaw.org

Cerebral Palsy

Cerebral Palsy of Mideast Wisconsin
Judith Britton, Executive Director
36 Broad Street, Suite 120
P.O. Box 1241
Oshkosh, WI 54903-1241
(920) 424-4071; (800) 261-1895 (in WI)
(920) 424-4076 (TTY)
E-mail: cpmideastwi@vbe.com
Web: www.cpmideastwis.org

United Cerebral Palsy of Southeastern
   Wisconsin, Inc.
Fred Hesselbein, Executive Director
7519 W. Oklahoma Avenue
Milwaukee, WI 53219
(414) 329-4500; (414) 329-4511 (TTY)
(888) 482-7739
E-mail: ucpofsew@execpc.com
Web: www.ucpa.org

Down Syndrome

Down Syndrome Association of Wisconsin, Inc.
The Cambridge Office Center
9401 W. Beloit Road, Suite 112
Milwaukee, WI 53227-4357
(414) 327-3729; (866) 327-3729
E-mail: info@dsaw.org
E-mail: dsaw@globaldialog.com
Web: www.dsaw.org

Learning Disabilities

Learning Disabilities Association of Wisconsin
LeAnn Knoeck, President
13035 W. Bluemound Road, Suite 100
Brookfield, WI 53005
(414) 299-9002; (866) 532-9472
E-mail: ldawisconsin@hotmail.com
Web: www.ldawisconsin.com

Mental Health

Mental Health Association in Milwaukee County
Martha Rasmus, President
734 N. 4th Street, Suite 200
Milwaukee, WI 53203-2102
(414) 276-3122; (866) 642-4630
E-mail: mha@mhamilw.org
Web: www.mhamilw.org

NAMI Wisconsin
Francisco J. Mesa, Executive Director
4223 W. Beltline Highway
Madison, WI 53711
(608) 268-6000; (800) 236-2988
E-mail: namiwisc@choiceonemail.com
Web: www.namiwisconsin.org

Wisconsin Family Ties
Hugh Davis, Executive Director
16 N. Carroll Street, Suite 640
Madison, WI 53703
(608) 267-6888; (800) 422-7145
E-mail: info@wifamilyties.org
Web: www.wifamilyties.org

Mental Retardation

The Arc-Wisconsin Disability Association, Inc.
Jim Hoegemeier, Executive Director
600 Williamson Street, Suite J
Madison, WI 53703
(608) 251-9272; (877) 272-8400
E-mail: arcw@chorus.net
Web: www.arc-wisconsin.org

Speech and Hearing

Wisconsin Speech-Language-Pathology and
    Audiology Association, Inc.
P.O. Box 1109
Madison, WI 53701-1109
(608) 283-5489; (800) 545-0640
E-mail: wsha@wismed.org
Web: www.wisha.org

Spina Bifida

Spina Bifida Association of Wisconsin
Rita Flores, Executive Director
830 N. 109th Street, Suite 6
Wauwatosa, WI 53226
(414) 607-9061
E-mail: sbawi@sbawi.org
Web: www.sbawi.org

Wisconsin—Organizations Especially for Parents

Parent Training and Information Center (PTI)

Wisconsin FACETS Parent Resource Center
Janis M. Serak and Charlotte Price,
    Co-Directors
2714 N. Dr. Martin Luther King Drive
Milwaukee, WI 53212
(414) 374-4645; (414) 374-4635 (TTY)
(877) 374-4677
E-mail: wifacets@execpc.com
Web: www.wifacets.org

Native American Family Empowerment Center
Great Lakes-Inter-Tribal Council, Inc.
Don Rosin, Executive Director
2932 Highway 47 North
P.O. Box 9
Lac du Flambeau, WI 54538
(715) 588-3324; (800) 472-7207
E-mail: drosin@glitc.org
Web: www.glitc.org/

Parent-To-Parent

MUMS-National Parent to Parent Network
Julie Gordon, Executive Director
150 Custer Court
Green Bay, WI 54301-1243
(920) 336-5333; (877) 336-5333
E-mail: mums@netnet.net
Web: www.netnet.net/mums/

Parent Projects
Liz Hecht, Coordinator
Waisman Center for Excellence in
    Developmental Disabilities
1500 Highland Avenue
Madison, WI 53705-2280
(608) 263-5022
E-mail: hecht@waisman.wisc.edu
Web: www.waisman.wisc.edu/birtht03/
    index.htmlx

Community Parent Resource Center

Wisconsin FACETS (serving Milwaukee only)
Sue Endress, Program Director
2714 N. Dr. Martin Luther King Drive
Milwaukee, WI 53212
(414) 374-4645; (414) 374-4635 (TTY)
(877) 374-4677
E-mail: wifacets@execpc.com
Web: www.wifacets.org

Parent Teacher Association (PTA)

Wisconsin Congress of Parents & Teachers, Inc.
Cynthia DiCamelli, President
4797 Hayes Road, Suite 102
Madison, WI 53704-3256
(608) 244-1455
E-mail: wi_office@pta.org
Web: www.wisconsinpta.org/

Wisconsin—Other Disability Organizations

Prader-Willi Syndrome Association
    of Wisconsin, Inc.
Mary Lynn Larson, Program Director
2701 N. Alexander Street
Appleton, WI 54911
(920) 882-6371; (866) 797-2947
E-mail: wisconsin@pwsausa.org
Web: www.pwsausa.org/wi

Easter Seals Wisconsin
Christine Fessler, President/CEO
101 Nob Hill Road, Suite 301
Madison, WI 53713
(608) 277-8288 (V); (608) 277-8031 (TTY)
(800) 422-2324
E-mail: chrisf@wi-easterseals.org
Web: www.wi-easterseals.org

Wisconsin First Step
c/o Gundersen Lutheran
Mary Mundt-Reckase,
    Executive Director
FHO-004
1900 South Avenue
LaCrosse, WI 54601
(800) 642-7837
Web: www.mch-hotlines.org

VSA Arts of Wisconsin, Inc.
Kathie Wagner, President
4785 Hayes Road, Suite 201
Madison, WI 53704
(608) 241-2131
E-mail: vsawis@vsawis.org
Web: www.vsawis.org

Independent Living

To find out the contact information for the Statewide Independent Living Council (SILC) in Wisconsin, contact

Independent Living Research Utilization Project
The Institute for Rehabilitation and Research
2323 South Sheppard, Suite 1000
Houston, TX 77019
(713) 520-0232 (V); (713) 520-5136 (TTY)
E-mail: ilru@ilru.org
Web: www.ilru.org

To find out the contact information for centers for independent living (CILs) in Wisconsin, contact

National Council on Independent Living
1916 Wilson Boulevard, Suite 209
Arlington, VA 22201
(703) 525-3406; (703) 525-4153 (TTY)
E-mail: ncil@ncil.org
Web: www.ncil.org

WYOMING

Wyoming—State Agencies and Organizations

United States Senators

Honorable John Barrasso (R)
307 Dirksen Senate Office Building
Washington, DC 20510
(202) 224-6441
(202) 228-0359 (Fax)
E-mail Web Form: http://www.
    barrasso.senate.gov/public/index.
    cfm?FuseAction=ContactUs.ContactForm
Web: http://www.barrasso.senate.gov/public/
    index.cfm?FuseAction=Home.Home

Honorable Michael B. Enzi (R)
379A Russell Senate Office Building
Washington, DC 20510
(202) 224-3424
(202) 224-1724 (Fax)
E-mail Web Form: http://www.enzi.senate.
    gov/public/index.cfm/contact?p=e-mail-
    senator-enzi
Web: http://www.enzi.senate.gov/public/
    index.cfm/home

United States Representatives

To find the contact information for your representative in the House of the U.S. Congress, visit the House's Web site at: www.house.gov, or call (202) 225-3121; (202) 225-1904 (TTY).

Governor

Honorable Matt Mead
Office of the Governor
State Capitol Building, Room 124
Cheyenne, WY 82002
(307) 777-7434
E-mail Web Form: http://governor.wy.gov/
    contactus/Pages/default.aspx
Web: http://governor.wy.gov/Pages/default.
    aspx

Official State Web Site

Web: http://wyoming.gov/

State Department of Education: Special Education

Special Programs Unit
Leslie Bechtel Van Orman, Director
Department of Education
320 W. Main Street
Riverton, WY 82501
(307) 857-9250
Email: leslie.vanorman@wyo.gov
Web: www.k12.wy.us

State Coordinator for NCLB (No Child Left Behind)

Assessment & Accountability
Department of Education
Sean McInerney, Accountability Supervisor
2300 Capitol Avenue, 2nd Floor
Cheyenne, WY 82001
(307) 777-8752
E-mail: Sean.McInerney@wyo.gov
Web: www.k12.wy.us

Programs for Infants and Toddlers With Disabilities: Birth–2 Years

Developmental Disabilities Division
Christine Demers, Part C Coordinator
Department of Health
186 E. Qwest Building
6101 Yellowstone Road
Cheyenne, WY 82002
(307) 777-5246
E-mail: christine.demers@wyo.gov
Web: http://health.wyo.gov/ddd.html

Programs for Children With Disabilities: 3–5 Years

Developmental Disabilities Division
Department of Health
Nicholas Whynott, Part B/619 Coordinator
186 E. Qwest Building
6101 Yellowstone Road
Cheyenne, WY 82002
(307) 777-8762
E-mail: nicholas.whynott@wyo.gov
Web: http://www.health.wyo.gov/ddd/
    earlychildhood/index.html

State Vocational Rehabilitation Agency

Division of Vocational Rehabilitation
Department of Employment
Jim McIntosh, Administrator
1100 Herschler Building
Cheyenne, WY 82002
(307) 777-7389
E-mail: jmcint@state.wy.us
Web: www.wyomingworkforce.org/

Coordinator for Transition Services

Mary Brown, Transition Coordinator
Wyoming State Department of Education
320 W. Main
Riverton, WY 82501
(307) 777-2564
E-mail: mbrown3@educ.state.wy.us
Web: www.k12.wy.us/

State Director for
Career Technical Education

Career and Technical Education
Department of Education
Teri Wigert, Director
Hathaway Building, 2nd Floor
2300 Capital Avenue
Cheyenne WY 82002-0050
(307) 777-7708
Web: www.k12.wy.us

State Mental Health Agency

Mental Health Division
Department of Health
Chris Newman, Administrator
Division of Behavioral Health
6101 Yellowstone Road, Room 259B
Cheyenne, WY 82002-0480
(307) 777-7094
Web: wdbh.state.wy.us/index.html

State Mental Retardation Program

Division of Developmental Disabilities
Department of Health
Robert Clabby, Administrator
Herschler Bldg., 1st Floor West
122 West 25th St.
Cheyenne, WY 82002
(307) 777-7115; (307) 777-5578 (TTY)
E-mail: jnaran@state.wy.us
Web: ddd.state.wy.us

Council on Developmental Disabilities

Governor's Planning Council on Developmental
  Disabilities
Shannon Buller, Executive Director
122 W. 25th Street
Herschler Building, 1st West
Cheyenne, WY 82002
(307) 777-7332 (TTY); (800) 438-5791 (in WY)
E-mail: shannon.butler@wyo.gov
Web: http://ddcouncil.state.wy.us

Protection and Advocacy Agency

Protection and Advocacy System, Inc.
Jeanne Thobro, Chief Executive Officer
7344 Stockman Street
Cheyenne, WY 82009
(307) 632-3496; (307) 332-8268
E-mail: wypandl@wypanda.com
Web: http://www.wypanda.com/

Client Assistance Program

Client Assistance Program
Protection and Advocacy System, Inc.
Kristine M. Smith, Sr. Program Administrator
320 W. 25th Street, 2nd Floor
Cheyenne, WY 82001
(307) 638-7668; (800) 821-3091 (in WY)
E-mail: wypanda@vcn.com
Web: http://wypanda.vcn.com/

Programs for Children With
Special Health Care Needs

UPLIFT (Wyoming Family Voices)
Michelle Heinen
4007 Greenway St., Ste 201
Cheyenne, WY 82001
(307) 778-8686; (888) 875-4383
E-mail: mheinen@upliftwy.org

Children's Special Health Program
Linda McElwain, BSN, Maternal Child Health
  Unit
Wyoming Department of Health
6101 Yellowstone Road, Suite 420
Cheyenne, WY 82002
(307) 777-6921; (800) 438-5795
Web: http://health.wyo.gov/familyhealth/
  csh/index.html

State CHIP Program (health care
for low-income, uninsured children)

Kid Care CHIP
Thomas O. Forslund, Director
Wyoming Department of Health
Children's Insurance Programs
6101 Yellowstone Road, Ste 210
Cheyenne, WY 82002
(855) 294-2127
Web: health.wyo.gov/chip

Programs for Children and Youth Who
Are Deaf or Hard of Hearing or Deaf-Blind

Division of Vocational Rehabilitation
Lori Cielinski, TRS/Deaf Services Program
    Consultant
851 Werner Court, Suite 120
Casper, WY 82601
(307) 577-0539; (800) 452-1408(V/TTY)
E-mail: lcieli@state.wy.us
Web: http://dwsweb.state.wy.us/vr/
    deafservices.asp

Programs for Children
and Youth Who Are Blind
or Visually Impaired

Services for the Visually Impaired
Wyoming Department of Education
Gary Olson, Supervisor
2300 Capitol Avenue
Hathaway Building, First Floor
Cheyenne, WY 82002-0050
307-777-6257
E-mail: golson@edu.state.wy.us
Web: www.k12.wy.us/

State Education
Agency Rural Representative

Department of Education
Bruce Hayes, Facilities & School Consultant
Hathaway Building, 2nd Floor
2300 Capitol Avenue
Cheyenne, WY 82002
(307) 777-6198
E-mail: bhayes1@state.wy.us
Web: www.k12.wy.us

Regional ADA & IT
Technical Assistance Center

Rocky Mountain Disability and Business Technical
    Assistance Center
Patrick Going, Director
3630 Sinton Road, Suite 103
Colorado Springs, CO 80907
(719) 444-0268 (V/TTY); (800) 949-4232 (V/
    TTY)
E-mail: rmdbtac@mtc-inc.com
Web: www.adainformation.org

University Center
for Excellence in
Developmental Disabilities

Wyoming Institute for Disabilities
Keith A. Miller, Director
University of Wyoming, Department 4298
1000 E. University Avenue
Laramie, WY 82071
(307) 766-2761
E-mail: WIND.UW@uwyo.edu
Web: wind.uwyo.edu/

Technology-Related Assistance

Wyoming New Options in
    Technology (WYNOT)
Keith A. Miller, Director
Wyoming Institute for Disabilities
University of Wyoming, Department 4298
1000 E. University Avenue
Laramie, WY 82071
(307) 766-2761; (800) 861-4312
E-mail: wynot.uw@uwyo.edu
Web: http://wind.uwyo.edu/wynot

State Mediation System

Special Education Unit
Carolee Buchanan, Mediation Program
    Manager
Department of Education
320 W. Main
Riverton, WY 82501
(307) 777-3562
E-mail: cbucha@educ.state.wy.us
Web: www.k12.wy.us

Special Format Library

Utah State Library Division (serving
    Wyoming also)
Program for the Blind and Disabled
250 North 1950 West, Suite A
Salt Lake City, UT 84116-7901
(801) 715-6789; (800) 662-5540 (in Utah)
(800) 453-4293 (all states, except Utah)
(801) 715-6721 (TTY)
E-mail: blind@utah.gov
Web: http://www.wyomingtalkingbooks.org/

Wyoming—Disability-Specific Organizations

Attention Deficit Disorder

To identify an ADD group in Wyoming,
contact either of the following organizations:

Children and Adults with Attention-Deficit/
    Hyperactivity Disorder (CHADD)
8181 Professional Place, Suite 150
Landover, MD 20785
(301) 306-7070
(800) 233-4050 (Voice mail to request
    information packet)
Web: www.chadd.org

Attention Deficit Disorder Association (ADDA)
P.O. Box 543
Pottstown, PA 19464
(484) 945-2101
Web: www.add.org

Autism

Autism Society of America
7910 Woodmont Avenue, Suite 300
Bethesda, MD 20814
(301) 657-0881; (800) 3AUTISM
Web: www.autism-society.org

Blind/Visual Impairments

American Foundation for the Blind–Southwest
Judy Scott, Director
11030 Ables Lane
Dallas, TX 75229
(214) 352-7222
E-mail: dallas@afb.net
Web: www.afb.org

Brain Injury

Brain Injury Association of Wyoming
Dorothy Cronin, Executive Director
111 W. 2nd Street, Suite 106
Casper, WY 82601
(307) 473-1767; (800) 643-6457
E-mail: biaw@trib.com
Web: www.biausa.org/Wyoming/

Epilepsy

Wyoming Epilepsy Association
Richard Leslie, Executive Director
1612 Central Avenue, #3
Cheyenne, WY 82001
(307) 634-5329
E-mail: richleslie66@hotmail.com
Web: www.wyomingepilepsy.org/

Mental Health

NAMI Wyoming
Theresa Bush, President
100 W. B Street, Suite 211
Casper, WY 82604
(307) 234-0440; (888) 882-4968
E-mail: nami-wyo@qwest.net
Web: www.nami.org/sites/NAMIWyoming

UPLIFT, Inc.
Peggy Nikkel, Executive Director
P.O. Box 664
Cheyenne, WY 82003
(888) 875-4383; (307) 778-8686
E-mail: pnikkel@upliftwy.org
Web: www.upliftwy.org

Mental Retardation

The Arc of Natrona County
Toni Hutchison, Executive Director
P.O. Box 393
Casper, WY 82602
(307) 577-4913

Wyoming—Organizations Especially for Parents

Parent Training and Information Center (PTI)

Parent Information Center
Terri Dawson, Director
5 N. Lobban
Buffalo, WY 82834
(307) 684-2277; (800) 660-9742 (in WY)
E-mail: tdawson@wpic.org
Web: www.wpic.org

Parent-To-Parent

WIND Family Support Network, Inc.
Wyoming Institute for Disabilities
Lynda Baumgardner, Project Director
1110 E. 5th Avenue
Cheyenne, WY 82001
(307) 632-0839; (800) 567-9376
(866) 231-6586 (Español)
E-mail: carlawfsn@aol.com
E-mail: lynda@uwyo.edu
Web: http://wind.uwyo.edu/wfsn

Parent Teacher Association (PTA)

Wyoming Congress of Parents and Teachers
Jeanne Scheneman, President
1821 Spruce Drive
Cheyenne, WY 82001
(307) 630-1007
E-mail: Jmschnmn@aol.com

Wyoming—Other Disability Organizations

Easter Seals-Goodwill
Northern Rocky Mountain, Inc.
Jodi Smith, Executive Director
991 Joe Street
Sheridan, WY 82801
(307) 672-2816
E-mail: jodis@fiberpipe.net
Web: http://esgw-nrm.easterseals.com/

VSA Arts of Wyoming
Judy Bower, Executive Director
239 W. First Street
Casper, WY 82601
(307) 237-8618
E-mail: vsaarts@trib.com
Web: http://vsawyo.org

Independent Living

To find out the contact information for the Statewide Independent Living Council (SILC) in Wyoming, contact

Independent Living Research Utilization Project
The Institute for Rehabilitation and Research
2323 South Sheppard, Suite 1000
Houston, TX 77019
(713) 520-0232 (V); (713) 520-5136 (TTY)
E-mail: ilru@ilru.org
Web: www.ilru.org

To find out the contact information for centers for independent living (CILs) in Wyoming, contact

National Council on Independent Living
1916 Wilson Boulevard, Suite 209
Arlington, VA 22201
(703) 525-3406; (703) 525-4153 (TTY)
E-mail: ncil@ncil.org
Web: www.ncil.org

Additional Resources

BULLYING AND BEHAVIOR ISSUES

Bullying

Preventing Bullying

- *Do interventions work to reduce bullying in school?*

  www.education.unisa.edu.au/bullying/ intervention.htm

  This 66-page report from the the University of South Australia focuses on reducing bullying in preschool and early primary grades. The evaluation examined 13 studies from more than 8 countries. Similarities were noted in how to stop and reduce bullying. The report discusses the successes and failures of these different attempts.

- *The lowdown on bullying*

  www.nmha.org/pbedu/backtoschool/bullying .cfm

  What's bullying and what do we do about it? This article from the National Mental Health Association tells the story, quick and to the point.

- *Untangling the myths: What the research tells us*

  www.nwrel.org/request/dec01/untangling .html

  Find out what is and isn't true about bullies. Learn how to identify a bully and a bullying victim. Get suggestions on how to stop bullying.

- *Want to create an antibullying program at your school?*

  www.nwrel.org/request/dec01/choosing creating.htm

  Learn how to avoid potential pitfalls when starting a schoolwide antibullying program. Find out how to choose a bullying prevention program that is right for your school. Print out the worksheet on creating an antibullying plan.

- *Quick training aids for the prevention of bullying*

  http://smhp.psych.ucla.edu/qf/bully_qt

  Planning on giving your staff training on bullying? Check out these talking points for conducting an inservice workshop. You'll

353

find links to various research studies and papers on bullying. Get overviews, factsheets, tools, handouts, model programs, and additional resources. You'll also find overheads to use in your presentation.

- What's a parent to do?

www.pacer.org/publications/bully.htm

Find out, and tell others, with Is Your Child a Target of Bullying? Intervention Strategies for Parents of Children With Disabilities, a publication of the PACER Center. It's available on CD-ROM or on overhead color transparencies with a printed script ($15 CD-ROM / $165 Color Transparencies with Script). This link will tell you all about it.

- A discussion and activity kit to use with children

www.thebullybook.com/

"The Bully" tells the story of a character most of our children will recognize. It's designed to be used to stimulate discussion and problem solving with children. Originally published as an ebook and still available online in that form, it is now also available in print form. Find out more at this link.

- And when youth with disabilities are bullied . . .

www.ncset.org/publications/viewdesc.asp?id=1332

Consult this Issue Brief from NCSET (National Center for Secondary Education and Transition), called Bullying and Teasing of Youth With Disabilities: Creating Positive School Environments for Effective Inclusion.

- Newsletter on bullying

www.aboutourkids.org/aboutour/parent_letter/

You won't wont to miss this newsletter from New York University (NYU) Child Study Center. The October 2003 issue is dedicated to "Bullies and Victims: What a Parent Can Do." It is available in English, Spanish, Chinese, and Korean.

- Bullying Prevention Initiative

www.mentalhealth.samhsa.gov/15plus/aboutbullying.asp

The Substance Abuse and Mental Heath Services Administration's (SAMHSA's) Center for Mental Health Services (CMHS) is offering new, online publications that focus on bullying as part of its Bullying Prevention Initiative. The initiative is supported by prime time television, public service messages, and bullying prevention educational materials. This ongoing, multimedia communications initiative is titled 15+ Make Time To Listen, Take Time To Talk . . . About Bullying. Download the publications at this link.

- And last but not least—Take a Stand. Lend a Hand. Stop Bullying Now!

www.stopbullyingnow.hrsa.gov/index.asp

The team of adults who developed this Stop Bullying campaign worked very closely with members of a youth expert panel made up of 9- through 13-year-olds who made sure the campaign reflected the real life impact of bullying in middle school and beyond. Find a wealth of information and resources on bullying and how to stop it.

Behavior Assessment Plans and Positive Support

Behavior as Communication

- Why does my kid do that?

http://smhp.psych.ucla.edu/qf/behaviorprob_qt/assessing_motivation.pdf

This document helps you find the reasons behind misbehavior in children.

- What does defiant behavior mean?

www.pbs.org/parents/issuesadvice/inclusivecommunities/challenging_behavior.html

PBS offers many resources for parents of children with disabilities, including this brief called *Challenging Behavior in Children.*

- *Behavior serves a purpose.*

  http://cecp.air.org/familybriefs/

  The Center for Effective Collaboration and Practice (CECP) offers a number of family briefs on behavior, but if you want to know more about how behavior is a form of communication and why some children choose inappropriate behaviors as a way of communicating, try CECP's brief called *Functional Communication Training to Promote Positive Behavior.* A natural follow-up is CECP's brief called *Planned Ignoring as an Intervention Strategy for Parents and Family Members.*

- *What are children trying to tell us?*

  http://csefel.uiuc.edu/briefs/wwb9.pdf

  What Works briefs from the Center on the Social and Emotional Foundations for Early Learning summarize effective practices for supporting children's social-emotional development and preventing challenging behaviors. This 4-page paper talks about functional behavior assessment and how it's used to figure out the purpose or function of a child's problem behavior—in effect, what the child is trying to say.

- *More on the function of behavior: Achieving the purpose in appropriate ways*

  The Early Childhood Behavior Project offers many materials on challenging behavior, including this Introduction. Also extremely interesting—and useful—is the project's page on ways to provide the child with an appropriate communication alternative that will achieve the original purpose of the problem behavior. Find this latter information at http://ici2.umn.edu/preschoolbehavior/strategies/default.html

- *Is this behavior normal, a phase, a development issue, or something more serious?*

  www.nlm.nih.gov/medlineplus/childbehavior disorders.html

  Family members and teachers may see a range of behaviors from children and still not be sure if a particular behavior indicates a childhood behavior disorder. Medline Plus's page connects with various resources to help you decide, including *Development and Behavior; You and Your Child's Behavior; Children's Threats: When Are They Serious?;* and specific aspects, such as aggressive behavior, children who won't go to school, conduct disorders, fighting and biting, helping the child who is expressing anger, and know when to seek help for your child.

Behavior Assessment

- *So what exactly is a functional behavioral Assessment?*

  www.air.org/cecp/fba/default.htm

  This page answers the basic questions of "FBA: What is it?" It covers how to conduct an FBA and how to use the results to create a positive behavioral intervention plan and supports. The information is broken down into digestible sizes and is easy to read and consume.

- *Details about the process involved in FBA*

  www.aboutourkids.org/aboutour/letter/novdec02.pdf

  This 6-page newsletter defines the process of FBA. It gives clear descriptions and specific examples. A great, reader-friendly overview!

- *Here's another reader-friendly overview.*

  http://www.fape.org/

  FAPE is the Families & Advocates Partnership for Education. Although the project is no longer in operation, its 8-page brief on functional behavioral assessment and positive behavioral interventions is still available online.

- Take a look at this review of research: Functional Analysis of Problem Behavior.

  http://www.armstrong.edu/images/ psychology/FA_of_prob_beh.pdf?AASU STID=556f57945edc327c00c5d12179d7486e

  This research review was originally published in Applied Behavior Analysis in Summer 2003.

- What is "multimodal behavior analysis"?

  http://mfba.net/index.html

  The Duquesne University School Psychology Program provides a thorough description of the process of conducting a functional behavioral assessment and writing a behavior intervention plan.

- What does "strength-based assessment" mean?

  www.air.org/cecp/interact/expertonline/ strength/empower/1.htm

  This method of assessment empowers children by building on their personal strengths and resources rather than focusing on their problems.

- The IEP team is definitely involved!

  The IEP team might find these two resources helpful in understanding FBA and what comes next: (1) An IEP Team's Introduction To Functional Behavioral Assessment And Behavior Intervention Plans (available at http://cecp.air.org/fba/problembehavior/ main.htm); and (2) Conducting a Functional Behavioral Assessment (available at http://cecp.air.org/fba/problembehavior/ conducting.htm).

Behavior Intervention Plans

- What is the link between functional behavior assessments and behavior intervention plans?

  http://ericec.org/digests/e592.html

  Research has demonstrated that FBAs can lead to the development of effective, proactive

BIPs. Find out more in this digest from the ERIC system.

- How do you go about developing a behavioral intervention plan?

  www.ldonline.org/ld_indepth/behavior/ behavioral_intervention.html

  This article explains the requirements of IDEA regarding addressing problem behavior. It provides a step-by-step guide to conducting a functional behavioral analysis and writing a behavior plan.

- Writing the plan for school involves the IEP team

  http://cecp.air.org/familybriefs/

  The Center for Effective Collaboration and Practice (CECP) offers a number of family briefs on behavior. Two were mentioned earlier under "Behavior as Communication." If you'd like to know more about how to write a BIP, read CECP's Behavioral Planning Meetings, which describes what BIPs are and how parents and the school system work together to write one.

- Suppose the IEP team doesn't know much about behavior, FBA, or BIPs?

  http://cecp.air.org/fba/problembehavior/ main.htm

  If the IEP team isn't sure how to address a student's problem behavior, then members might find this CECP resource helpful: Addressing Student Problem Behavior, Part I: An IEP Team's Introduction to Functional Behavioral Assessment and Behavior Intervention Plans. It's available at this link. Also to the point is Creating Positive Behavioral Intervention Plans and Supports, available at www.air.org/cecp/fba/problembehavior3/ main3.htm

Positive Behavior Support

- What exactly is positive behavior support?

  www.nau.edu/ihd/positive/ovrvw.html

This excellent, reader-friendly guide to positive behavior support is provided by Institute for Human Development at Northern Arizona University. A Spanish version is available at www.nau.edu/ihd/positive/sumario. html

- *What are the components of behavioral support?*

  www.state.ky.us/agencies/behave/home page.html

  This site offers information on a 3-tier model of behavior support: (a) schoolwide, (b) small group, and (c) individual. It gives information on what all students need to be successful.

- *Positive behavior support and functional assessment*

  http://eric.ed.gov/?q=positive+behavior+ support+&ff1=pubERIC+Digests+in+ Full+Text&id=ED434437

  This digest from the ERIC system looks at the research on positive behavior support and schoolwide behavior change, then it briefly discussions functional assessment of young children.

- *Positive behavioral interventions and supports*

  www.ldonline.org/ld_indepth/behavior/ positive_behavioral_intervention.html

  This article from LDOnline explains why PBIS is important and outlines key principles of practice.

- *More about PBS and its individualized approach to managing challenging behavior*

  http://csefel.vanderbilt.edu/resources/ wwb/wwb10.html

  This What Works brief from the Center on the Social and Emotional Foundations for Early Learning summarizes PBS and talks about how it works, factors that will limit its effectiveness, and whether it's really just "giving in" to the child. A Spanish version is available at http://csefel.vanderbilt.edu/ briefs/wwb10-sp.pdf

- *Tips for parents: How to get behavior supports into the IEP*

  https://www.pbis.org/resource/268/tips-for-parents-incorporating-positive-behavior-support-pbs-into-the-iep

  This guide, a collaboration between the Beach Center on Disabilities and the Center for Positive Behavioral Interventions and Supports, contains a wealth of suggestions for parents.

- *Need training materials for parents on positive behavioral interventions?*

  http://www.fastfamilysupport.org/ fasttraining/index.asp

  These training materials, subtitled What Every Parent Needs to Know. The set is also available in Spanish.

Yet More Resources

- *There's a center focusing exclusively on PBIS*

  http://www.pbis.org/

  The Center on Positive Behavioral Interventions and Supports is funded by the Office of Special Education Programs (OSEP) to provide information, training, support, and guidance to the nation on addressing behavior problems in research-based and effective ways. They offer information in English and in Spanish.

- *Check out this one-stop shop on behavior!*

  www.bridges4kids.org/PBS/PBS.html

  This site has info for both families and teachers on FBAs, behavior intervention plans, bullying, and discipline issues.

- *Don't forget to check out the other NICHCY A-Z pages on behavior.*

  http://www.parentcenterhub.org/nichcy-resources/

  They're listed and linked at the beginning of this resource, and they offer quick connections and resources on other behavior-related issues.

Behavior at Home

*Using Positive Methods
for Change at Home*

- *Help your children develop self-control.*

  http://www.aboutourkids.org/

  Using real-life stories, this Web site (from the New York University Child Study Center) illustrates the warning signs of problem behavior, do's and don'ts of discipline, and references to related articles and books.

- *How might you address your child's challenging behavior?*

  www.pbs.org/parents/issuesadvice/inclusive communities/challenging_behavior.html

  This reader-friendly site is well organized. It has facts about all aspects of working with children who have challenging behavior. Links to information on assessment and special education are provided. The information is also available in Spanish, at www.pbs. org/parents/issuesadvice/inclusivecommu nities/challenging_behavior_sp.html

- *More on teaching kids self-control skills*

  www.naspcenter.org/pdf/behavior%20 template.pdf

  Written by the National Association of School Psychologists, this 4-page document gives ways to help children identify their feelings and learn to recognize the connection between feelings and behaviors. It also offers specific techniques to teach your child how to handle anger.

- *Yet more on teaching children to manage their own behavior*

  http://csefel.vanderbilt.edu/resources/ what_works.html

  What Works briefs from the Center on the Social and Emotional Foundations for Early Learning summarize effective practices for supporting children's social and emotional development and preventing challenging behaviors. This 4-page paper describes prac- *tical strategies for helping children learn to manage their own behavior and provides references to more information. A Spanish version is available at http://csefel.uiuc.edu/ briefs-sp/wwb7.html*

- *Get behavior in shape at home*

  http://www.pbis.org/

  How do you create a positive behavioral support system in your home? This Web site gives easy-to-implement suggestions. Learn the reasoning behind different techniques and how to use them to achieve your behavior goals. Specific examples include eating dinner, asking for things while grocery shopping, and budgeting to teach children the value of money. (Also available in Spanish at www.pbis.org/files/behshapespanish.doc)

- *Learn practical solutions to common behavior problems.*

  http://cecp.air.org/familybriefs

  This Web page links to 12 different publications on various topics, including promoting resilience in children, encouraging good behavior, and how to get your children involved in addressing their own challenging behaviors.

- *Your parent-friendly guide to functional assessment and support*

  www.uoregon.edu/~ttobin/parent.pdf

  This 21-page guide describes what a functional assessment is and what it can do to help your child. Parents can use this information to help children at home and also work with school staff to put plans into place at school.

- *Functional behavioral assessment (FBA) and positive interventions:
  What parents need to know*

  http://www.wrightslaw.com/info/discipl. fba.jordan.pdf

  This publication will help you find out what is causing your child's problem behaviors.

After you find the cause, you can create a game plan to support and encourage the behaviors you want and get rid of the ones you don't want. Also available in Spanish and Hmong.

Improving Family Life

• *Why does my kid do that?*

http://www.beachcenter.org/resource_library/default.aspx

Want to know why your child engages in problem behavior? Check out this guide to family-friendly resources from the Beach Center. Find out how to determine why a person with a disability engages in problem behavior and ways to support the individual in learning other ways to act. Read articles, personal stories, tip lists, and find out about other Web sites, books, manuals, and reports on solving behavior problems.

• *Fact sheets! Get your fact sheets here!*

http://www.mentalhealthamerica.net/faqs

This site is a fact sheet treasure chest. You'll find information on a wide range of topics such as anxiety disorders, bullying, ADHD, and autism. Also get tips for making transitions back to school after vacations go smoothly.

• *How to get help for your child*

www.uoregon.edu/~ttobin/Finding.htm

Having trouble getting what your child needs? This reader-friendly site offers communication tips to use when seeking help. You'll learn techniques for keeping things in perspective, focusing on the problem at hand, and what info you should be prepared to provide when you are asking for help. Plus you can print out a handy checklist to help keep track of the information you gather.

• *How to get help for yourself*

www.conductdisorders.com/

This link leads you to a group of parents who are raising challenging children. They invite you in and offer their site as a "soft place to land for the battle-weary parent."

• *Mental Health Fact Sheets*

www.aacap.org/publications/factsfam/index.htm

This Web site has 87 fact sheets on various issues, including ADHD, depression, conduct disorders, oppositional defiance disorder, and violent behavior. These up-to-date, well-written publications are available in English, Español, Deutsch, Français, Polish, and Icelandic.

• *Learn what really works!*

http://cecp.air.org/familybriefs/

This Web page links to 12 different research-based publications on various topics, including promoting resilience in children, encouraging good behavior, and ways to get children involved in addressing their own challenging behaviors.

• *What's temperament and personality got to do with it?*

http://familyfun.go.com/raisingkids/child/skills/feature/FGP_personality/FGP_personality .html

This 4-page excerpt from the Field Guide to Parenting by Shelley Butler and Deb Kratz discusses temperament and behavior. Bonus: This Web site is rich in links to many parenting tips and other Web sites.

• *More about temperament and its affect on behavior*

http://www.greatschools.org/special-education/health/788-temperament-traits.gs?content=788

Schwab Learning introduces you to 9 temperament traits: activity level, sensitivity, regularity, approach/withdrawal, adaptability, mood, intensity, persistence, and distractibility. Find out how to pinpoint your child's traits and how they can affect behavior.

- *Working with your child's temperament*

  http://www.greatschools.org/parenting/ behavior-discipline/tips-for-handling- problematic-temperament-traits. gs?content=787

  Get ideas on helping children in ways that match their natural tendencies. This site offers suggestions for managing extreme behaviors. Click on the link to the Parent to Parent message board to read tips from other parents.

Behavior at School

Using Positive Methods for Change in the Classroom

- *Don't miss this quick training on behavior problems in school.*

  http://smhp.psych.ucla.edu/qf/behavior prob_qt

  You'll love the brief overviews on topics such as "Behavior Problems. What's a School to do?" Check out the fact sheets on behaviors like oppositional defiance disorder (ODD), and conduct disorder. You'll also find tools and handouts, model programs, and additional resources.

- *Teachers! Arm yourself with this knowledge and stop problem behaviors before they start!*

  http://smhp.psych.ucla.edu/pdfdocs/rhythms .pdf

  This 65-page guide helps teachers anticipate common problems throughout the year and plan prevention and early intervention to minimize them. Suggestions are provided on a monthly basis.

- *Play at being good: The good behavior game*

  www.colorado.edu/cspv/publications/fact sheets/blueprints/FS-BPP01.html

  This is one fun way to involve the whole class in supporting positive behavior. It's especially good for elementary students demonstrating early high-risk behavior.

- *Time-outs*

  http://www.ky.gov/agencies/behave/bi/ to.pdf

  This guide helps teachers, educators, and other practitioners implement time-out procedures appropriately and effectively.

- *Discipline: What works, what doesn't*

  www.naspcenter.org/factsheets/effdiscip_fs .html

  This guide discusses the failure of punitive disciplinary practices and promotes supportive discipline strategies. It provides great tips on research-based approaches to positive behavior change.

- *Dodging the power struggle trap: Ideas for teachers*

  http://www.interventioncentral.org/ behavioral-intervention-modification

  A conflict requires two people. If a teacher remains cool and calm, a conflict can often be avoided. This guide offers practical advice for disengaging, interrupting, and deescalating problem behavior and gives specific examples of how to react in different scenarios.

- *Tips for classroom management*

  http://www.pbis.org/common/cms/files/ pbisresources/B8_Newcomer.pdf

  Here you'll find ideas for developing classroom systems of positive behavioral support. These are tried and true management practices that have proven effective over years of use.

- *A LOT on classroom management*

  http://edglossary.org/classroom- management/

  The Classroom Management at the Glossary of Education Reform points to exemplary, free, and fee-based digital content on research- based classroom management practices that can help administrators, policy makers, and educators plan for and implement programs that result in effective learning and teaching.

- More on teaching children to manage their own behavior

  http://csefel.vanderbilt.edu/briefs/wwb7.pdf

  What Works briefs from the Center on the Social and Emotional Foundations for Early Learning summarize effective practices for supporting children's social and emotional development and preventing challenging behaviors. This 4-page paper describes practical strategies for helping children learn to manage their own behavior and provides references to more information. A Spanish version is available at http://csefel.uiuc.edu/ briefs-sp/wwb7.html

- What about early childhood settings and the social development of young children with their peers?

  http://www.wbpress.com/index.php?main_page=product_book_info&cPath=75&products_id=231

  This research synthesis from the Research and Training Center (RTC) on Early Childhood Development tells early childhood practitioners what types of toys and play materials are most associated with young children's social play with peers.

Behavior and Specific Disabilities

- Creating a behavior plan? Need some ideas?

  www.albany.edu/psy/autism/pbsplan.html

  Check out this sample behavioral support plan template. It is clearly written, well thought out, and easy to follow.

- Watch out for these behavior plan pitfalls.

  www.schoolbehavior.com/Files/pitfalls.PDF

  This 3-page guide gives descriptions of 12 common mistakes in implementing behavior plans, then offers solutions.

- Do you have a moody student?

  www.schoolbehavior.com/Files/tips_mood.pdf

  Read about accommodations for medication side-effects, sleep disturbances, impaired concentration, focus, memory, testing, homework and more.

- Behavior and students with AD/HD

  www.chadd.org

  If you have a student with attention-deficit/hyperactivity disorder (AD/HD), you'll find a lot of useful info at CHADD (Children and Adults with AD/HD), especially this fact sheet on managing and modifying behavior.

- Behavior and students with learning disabilities

  www.ldonline.org/ld_indepth/behavior/behavior_modification.html

  This article, available at LDOnline, comes from the book published by Paul H. Brookes, titled Learning Disabilities and Challenging Behaviors: A Guide to Intervention and Classroom Management.

- Working with students with ODD/conduct disorder

  http://www.beachcenter.org/resource_library/search_beach_resources.aspx

  This site provides real-life stories and tip lists for encouraging cooperation from students with ODD and conduct disorders.

- Students with autism

  http://www.autism-society.org/living-with-autism/autism-through-the-lifespan/school-age/

  From the Autism Society of America, learn more about children with autism.

- What does the research say about pivotal response training (PRT) for young children with autism?

  http://www.hindawi.com/journals/aurt/2012/709861/

This research synthesis focuses on the effectiveness of Pivotal Response Training (PRT) as a behavioral intervention for young children with disabilities.

- Students with autism, MR, or other developmental disabilities

http://daddcec.org/ArticleDetails/tabid/76/ArticleID/18/Books-DADD-Prism-Volume-1-Within-Our-Reach-Behavior-Prevention-and-Intervention-Strategies-for-Learners-with-Mental-Retardation-and-Autism.aspx

Within Our Reach: Behavior Prevention and Intervention Strategies for Learners with Mental Retardation and Autism, the first book in the DDD Prism Series, provides practical ways to resolve behavioral concerns of students with mental retardation, autism, and other developmental disabilities and focuses on responding to the communicative intent of various behavior problems. (Product #D5250, $11.95/CEC Members $9.00.) To order, call toll-free 1.888.232.7733.

- Down syndrome and behavior

http://www.ndsccenter.org/about-ndsc/position-statements/

This "Position Statement on the Management of Challenging Behaviors" from the National Down Syndrome Congress (NDSC) identifies key features consistent with quality programs for individuals with Down syndrome. Presented as guidelines, the statement is derived from several sources: (a) the research literature on behavior management,(b) model programs that implement state-of-the-art procedures and deliver effective services for people with disabilities, and (c) values about the rights of individuals with disabilities and their place in society.

What Does the Law Require of Schools?

The Individuals with Disabilities Education Act (IDEA) has well-specified requirements of how schools must address behavior issues with respect to students with disabilities. Find out more about those requirements via the following resources:.

- Start at NICHCY

http://www.specialed.us/discoveridea/idealist.htm

This link leads you to what we call the "vetted" list—meaning, publications reviewed and approved by the Office of Special Education Programs (OSEP) on the IDEA and its regulations. Click on "Behavior/Discipline," and you'll jump to authoritative documents on what IDEA requires when disciplining students with disabilities.

- Disciplining students with disabilities: A very thorough overview from NASP

http://www.nasponline.org/publications/booksproducts/hchs3_samples/s4h18_discipline.pdf

Visit all the bases in this article from the National Association of School Psychologists: positive learning environments, the IEP as a vehicle to manage behavior problems, addressing and preventing challenging behaviors, weapons and drugs, and an explanation of what IDEA requires schools to do.

- What are the school's obligations?

http://www.wrightslaw.com/advoc/ltrs/behavior_obligate.htm

Wrightslaw answers questions from school personnel about obligations to "students who may be dangerous to us."

- Discipline: Suspensions, expulsions, and IEPs

www.wrightslaw.com/info/discipl.suspend.crabtree.htm

Parent attorney Bob Crabtree describes the school's responsibilities under IDEA, including provision of FAPE, alternative educational placements, functional behavioral assessments, and behavior intervention plans.

Using Positive Methods for Change in the Whole School

- Good behavior for the whole school

http://www.specialed.us/discoveridea/topdocs/schoolwidebeh.pdf

This family-friendly guide gives a quick overview on why positive behavior programs work even better when implemented on a schoolwide basis. Contact information on further resources is provided.

- *Schoolwide positive behavior support helps individual students with disabilities.*

  http://www.beachcenter.org/research/
  FullArticles/PDF/PBS19_Blueprint%20
  for%20Schoolwide%20PBS.pdf

  This 26-page how-to guide provides a case study of an eighth grader with autism and gives concrete examples of how to implement PBS at the universal, group, and individual levels. Implementing PBS on a schoolwide basis positively affected this student with autism, on an individual level.

- *What challenges do urban schools face when applying schoolwide positive behavior supports?*

  www.beachcenter.org/research/
  FullArticles/PDF/PBS23_Urban%20applica-
  tions.pdf

  This high-level publication discusses the unique issues that urban, lower socioeconomic areas deal with when implementing schoolwide positive behavior plans and the lessons that have been learned through trial and error. In addition to the general discussion, this publication highlights a particular student and follows him through several years of school.

- *Positive behavioral support and the whole school*

  https://www.pbis.org/resource/713/
  school-wide-positive-behavior-support-
  implementers%E2%80%99-blueprint-and-
  self-assessment

  This publication breaks down the process of developing a schoolwide PBS system, giving specific examples of how these systems are designed and implemented. It answers FAQs regarding schoolwide PBS systems and provides links to other sites. A Spanish version

is also available at www.pbis.org/Spanish/default.htm

- *A whole-school model of behavior reform*

  www.ldonline.org/ld_indepth/behavior/
  special_edge_behavior.pdf

  This article describes a proactive approach to schoolwide discipline, the differences between behavior management and behavioral support, and the individual behavior support planning required by federal law, illuminating the discussion with real-life examples.

- *What Works! Interventions for chronic behavior problems*

  https://www.supportforfamilies.
  org/disabilitypackets/
  interventionschronicbehavior.pdf

  This publication gives an overview on what research says about promising interventions for students with a history of behavior problems. Plus it's chock full of resources for further information.

- *Principals! Don't miss this! Defusing Violent Behavior in Young Children: An Ounce of Prevention*

  www.naspcenter.org/pdf/violent_handout.
  pdf

  This excellent 4-page document from the National Association of School Psychologists addresses how to handle violent outbursts in young elementary students.

- *Fight hate and promote tolerance!*

  www.tolerance.org

  This site has sections for teachers, parents, teens, and kids.

- *Enhancing school staff understanding of mental health and psychosocial concerns*

  http://smhp.psych.ucla.edu/pdfdocs/
  enhancingschoolstaff.pdf

This 73-page publication offers ways to address barriers for all students. It has been written by the UCLA Center for Mental Health in Schools.

- Hear ye! Hear ye! Read all about it!

  www.specialednews.com/behavior/behavior.html

  The best part of this site is the news list. You'll also find links to behavior-related news articles, a reading list on behavior materials, and links to other behavior-related Web sites.

- Especially for elementary and middle schools

  www.emstac.org/resources/social_skills.htm

  Don't miss this site! It is dedicated to social skills and discipline. Check out the links to information, organizations, and other Web sites.

Behavior Expertise

Centers and Projects

Researchers are hard at work trying to pinpoint the reason or reasons for a problem behavior and how to provide a resolution. The following groups' primary purpose is helping students improve their behavior.

- The Technical Assistance Center on Positive Behavior Interventions and Supports

  www.pbis.org/english

  This site is great for administrators and school personnel who are working to put a schoolwide system in place for dealing with disciplinary issues. You'll find info on functional behavioral assessment (FBA), schoolwide support, classroom support, individual support, family support, conferences, presentations, newsletters, tools, and links to further info. Truly a great site, it is also available in Spanish from the home page. Check it out!

- Beach Center on Disability

  http://www.beachcenter.org/

Want to know why your child engages in problem behavior? Check out this guide to family-friendly resources from the Beach Center. Find out how to determine why a person with a disability engages in problem behavior and ways to support the individual in learning other ways to act. Read articles, personal stories, tip lists, and find out about other Web sites, books, manuals, and reports on solving behavior problems.

- Cambridge Center for Behavioral Studies

  www.behavior.org/

  Did you know that the number and quality of words children hear in the early years of life have a tremendous impact on the development of their brains? Vocabulary development is closely tied to early language experiences and to the ability to think rationally, solve problems, and reason abstractly. Wow! This site can teach you how to help improve your child's language abilities. Specific information is available on autism, applied behavioral analysis (ABA), behavior in everyday life, and parenting.

- Center for Effective Collaboration and Practice

  http://cecp.air.org/

  This site has a "mini Web site" on FBA, Prevention Strategies that Work, Prevention and Early Intervention, Promising Practices in Children's Mental Health, and Strength-Based Assessment. You'll find numerous publictions. Some are also available in Spanish.

- The Center for Evidence-Based Practice: Young Children With Challenging Behavior

  http://challengingbehavior.fmhi.usf.edu

  The mission of the Center is to promote the use of evidence-based practice to meet the needs of young children who have, or are at risk for, problem behavior. Find research syntheses on effective intervention procedures, presentation and workshop materials, training opportunities, and a wide variety of useful links.

- *The Council for Children with Behavioral Disorders (CCBD)*

  www.ccbd.net/

  This site offers monthly updates on legislation affecting children with behavioral disorders. It offers publications, message boards, an advocacy section, links to other sites, and a quarterly newsletter (available online, free of charge). CCBD is a membership organization, composed of educators, parents, mental health personnel, and a variety of other professionals.

- *Kentucky Behavior Page*

  www.state.ky.us/agencies/behave/home page.html

  To help a child make a change in behavior for the better, you first need to identify the causes of the misbehavior. Check out the Behavior Home Page Discussion Forum to see what experts in the field are saying. Get resources for supporting behavior on the schoolwide, group, and individual levels. Check out links to state and federal legislation. Read about professional resources.

- *Mental health*

  http://www.samhsa.gov/

  Take a good look at this site. It has info on children's mental health, a mental health dictionary, a listing of Indian mental health resources, and a toll-free number to call for help and information. You'll also find pubs on autism, ADD, anxiety, depression, conduct disorder, anger management, and more. Selected publications are in Spanish.

- *National Association on Mental Illness (NAMI)*

  www.nami.org/

  You'll find a ton of info on this site. Check out the reader-friendly overview on mental illness. Join an online discussion group for family members. Read personal stories of children and teens with mental illness. Print out fact sheets, brochures, and reading lists.

Follow links to other children and adolescent sites. Some resources are available in Spanish.

- *Research and Training Center on Family Support and Children's Mental Health (RTC)*

  http://rtc.pdx.edu/

  The RTC's activities focus on improving services to children and youth who have mental, emotional, or behavioral disorders. This friendly, well-organized Web site hosts monthly online family discussions. Keep up to date on relevant political and policy news. Browse through dozens and dozens of recent publications.

- *SchoolBehavior.com*

  www.schoolbehavior.com

  This site is run by Leslie E. Packer, PhD, a psychologist who treats children and adolescents with Tourette's syndrome and its associated conditions. Read succinct overviews of different disorders, including Tourette's syndrome, Asperger's syndrome, attention deficit disorder, mood disorder, depression, sleep disorders, bipolar disorder, obsessive compulsive disorder. Read classroom tips on how to deal with various behavior issues.

- *School Violence Prevention Initiative*

  http://www.samhsa.gov/sites/default/ files/samhsa-school-violence-resources-national_0.pdf

  Families, communities, and schools need to work together to conquer disruptive behavior disorders. This site offers tips for dealing with anger, managing conflict, and dealing with bullies. Learn the warning signs for violence. Read about successful research-based programs that build resilience to behavior disorders.

Behavior Journals

These journals publish peer-reviewed articles about behavior research. Some content is available online at no charge. Other content requires a paid subscription.

- *From AAMR*

  *http://www.aamr.org/Periodicals/index.
  shtml*

  *The AAMR publishes (1) The American Journal
  on Mental Retardation, a scholarly research
  journal; (2) Mental Retardation, a practitioners'
  journal of research, reviews, and opinions;
  and (3) AAMR FYI, an online newsletter, published 6 times a year.*

- *Behavior Modification*

  www.sagepub.com/journal.aspx?pid=152

  *Formerly titled the Behavior Modification
  Quarterly, this journal is for researchers,
  academics, and practitioners in clinical
  psychology. It covers a wide range of topics,
  including problem behavior, learning disabilities, and phobias. Check out a sample issue.*

- *Behavioral Interventions*

  *www3.interscience.wiley.com/cgi-bin/
  jhome/24375*

  *Get a sample copy of this journal for clinical
  psychologists, psychiatrists, nurses, therapists, and researchers. It reports research and
  practices of the use of behavior techniques.*

- *British Journal of Developmental Psychology*

  www.bps.org.uk/publications/jDP_1.cfm

  *This journal publishes discussion papers and
  brief reports on all aspects of developmental
  psychology. You can order it online.*

- *British Journal of Educational Psychology*

  www.bps.org.uk/publications/jEP_1.cfm

  *This journal publishes research on the under-
  standing and practice of education.*

- *Child Development*

  www.srcd.org/cd.html

  *This bimonthly journal covers topics in child
  development, from the fetal period through
  adolescence.*

- *Developmental Psychology*

  *www.apa.org/journals/dev/description.
  htm*

  *This journal publishes articles that advance
  knowledge and theory about human development across the life span. View the current
  and past table of contents online.*

- *Journal for Developmental and Behavioral
  Pediatrics*

  www.jrnldbp.com

  *Written for physicians, clinicians, psycholo-
  gists, and researchers, this journal covers developmental and psychosocial aspects of pediatric
  health care. Topics include learning disorders;
  developmental disabilities; and emotional,
  behavioral, and psychosomatic problems.*

- *Journal for the Education of Students Placed at
  Risk (JESPAR)*

  www.csos.jhu.edu/jespar/past.htm

  *JESPAR publishes literature and report
  reviews, research articles on promising reform
  programs, and case studies on "schools that
  work." Selected articles are available free of
  charge. Read the table of contents for the current issue as well as issues back to 1996.*

- *Journal for the Experimental Analysis of Behavior*

  http://seab.envmed.rochester.edu/jeab

- *Journal of Applied Behavior Analysis*

  http://seab.envmed.rochester.edu/jaba

- *Journal of Autism and Developmental Disorders*

  www.kluweronline.com/issn/0162-3257

  *Get a free issue of this journal. View table of
  contents of past journals back to 1997. Read
  abstracts. View PDFs of articles.*

- *Journal of Behavior Therapy and Experimental
  Psychiatry*

  *www.sciencedirect.com/science/journal/
  00057916*

  *View abstract, full text, and links of articles in
  current issue and all issues back to 1970.*

- *Journal of Behavioral Education*

  www.kluweronline.com/ISSN/1053-0819

  Get a free issues of this journal. View articles from the current issue and past issues back to 1997.

- *Journal of Positive Behavioral Interventions*

  www.education.ucsb.edu/autism/jpbi.html

  This journal publishes research articles, discussions, literature reviews, and conceptual papers on programs and practices, family support and family perspectives, and reviews of published materials. Read table of contents and abstracts on issues back to 1999.

- *Journal of School Psychology*

  www.elsevier.com/locate/jschpsyc

  In this journal, you'll find original articles on empirical research and practice relevant to the development of school psychology as both a scientific and an applied specialty.

- *The Behavior Analyst*

  www.abainternational.org/tbajournal

  You can order this online. View the table of contents of the current issue and previous issue. Search journal abstracts. Read selected article reprints.

Professionals Who Can Help

Teachers

- *American Federation of Teachers*
  555 New Jersey Avenue, NW, Washington, DC 20001
  (202) 879-4400 (phone)
  online@aft.org (e-mail)
  www.aft.org/ (Web)

- *National Education Association*
  1201 16th Street NW, Washington, DC 20036
  (202) 833-4000 (phone)
  (202) 822-7974 (fax)
  www.nea.org/ (Web)

Psychologists

- *American Psychological Association*
  750 First Street, NE, Suite 700, Washington, DC 20002-4241
  (202) 336-5500 (phone)
  www.apa.org/ (Web)

- *National Association of School Psychologists*
  4340 East West Highway, Suite 402, Bethesda, MD 20814
  (301) 657-0270 (phone)
  (301) 657-0275 (fax)
  (301) 657-4155 (tty)
  nasp@naspweb.org (e-mail)
  www.nasponline.org/index2.html (Web)

Medical Doctors, Including Psychiatrists

- *American Academy of Pediatrics*
  141 Northwest Point Boulevard, Elk Grove Village, IL 60007
  (847) 228-5005 (phone)
  www.aap.org/ (Web)

- *American Association of Psychiatric Services for Children*
  Child Welfare League of America, 440 First Street, NW, 3rd Floor
  Washington, DC 20001-2085
  (202) 942-0295 (phone)
  www.cwla.org/ (Web)

- *American Psychiatric Association*
  1400 K Street, NW, Washington, DC 20005
  (202) 682-6220 (phone)
  www.psych.org (Web)

- *American Society for Adolescent Psychiatry*
  P.O. Box 570218, Dallas, TX 75357-0218
  (972) 686-6166 (phone)
  (972) 613-5532 (fax)
  info@adolpsych.org (e-mail)
  www.adolpsych.org/ (Web)

- *American Academy of Child and Adolescent Psychiatry*
  Child, Adolescent and Family Branch Center for Mental Health Services

5600 Fishers Lane, Room 18-49, Bethesda, MD
20857
(301) 443-1333 (phone)
(800) 789-2647 (toll-free phone)
www.mentalhealth.org/child (Web)
www.aacap.org/ (Web)

- Center for the Advancement of Children's
Mental Health
Division of Child and Adolescent Psychiatry,
Columbia University
(212) 543-6066 (phone)
(212) 543-5260 (fax)
www.kidsmentalhealth.org/ (Web)

Counselors

- School Social Worker Association of America
PO Box 2072, Northlake IL 60164
(847) 289-4527; (847) 289-4642 (phone)
sswaa@aol.com (e-mail)
www.sswaa.org/ (Web)

- American School Counselor Association
1101 King Street, Suite 625, Alexandria, VA
22314
(703) 683-ASCA; (800) 306-4722
(toll-free phone)
(703) 683-1619 (Fax)
E-mail: asca@schoolcounselor.org
Web: www.schoolcounselor.org/

- American Counseling Association
5999 Stevenson Avenue, Alexandria, VA
22304
(703) 823-0252; (800) 347-6647
(703) 823-6862 (TTY)
(800) 473-2329 (Fax)
Web: www.counseling.org/

What Do They Mean By . . . ?

Need help understanding all of those jar-
gony terms you're encountering as you delve
more deeply into behavior concerns? With these
glossaries, dictionaries, and cheat sheets, you
can sound like an expert yourself.

- *Behavior terms*

www.coedu.usf.edu/abaglossary/main.asp

This online database houses over 2,000
behavior-related terms. Whew! Who would've
thought there could be so many?

- *More behavior terms*

www.thecol.org/guide/glossary.html

This site provides a well-written glossary of
general behavior terms.

- *Behavioral health terms*

www.uihealthcare.com/depts/uibehavioral
health/patiented/glossary.html

This behavioral health glossary gives definitions of mental health conditions, particularly
personality disorders.

- *Behavior intervention terms*

www.usu.edu/teachall/text/behavior/
BEHAVglos.htm

This glossary, from Utah Students at Risk, covers
behavioral intervention terms. At the bottom of
each defined term is a PDF link to more information regarding that behavioral intervention.

- *Treatment descriptions*

www.aacap.org/publications/factsfam/
continum.htm

Read these brief descriptions of different
programs, settings, or treatments that children with mental illness may receive.

INDIVIDUALS WITH DISABILITIES EDUCATION IMPROVEMENT ACT (IDEA) AND INDIVIDUALIZED EDUCATION PROGRAMS (IEPs)

Individuals With Disabilities Education Improvement Act of 2004

The Law Itself

- The "slip law" is the Public Law (PL) print of
P.L. 108-446, the Individuals with Disabilities
Education Improvement Act of 2004. It's
available in PDF format and is 162 pages

long. The PDF file is available online through NICHCY, at http://www.parentcenterhub. org/wp-content/uploads/repo_items/ PL108-446.pdf

- And a text-only version of the law can be accessed at

  http://thomas.loc.gov/cgibin/query/ z?c108:h.1350.enr:

From the Feds

From Congress:

- IDEA: Guide to Frequently Asked Questions discusses key definitions, new provisions with respect to highly qualified teachers, funding, private schools, charter schools, new state policies, IEPs, procedural safeguards, discipline, and monitoring and enforcement. Find the guide on the U. S. House of Representatives Web site at http://edwork force.house.gov/issues/109th/education/ idea/ideafaq.pdf

- Issues page provides links to such documents as the Bipartisan House-Senate Conference Report on H.R. 1350; a summary of the bill; and four fact sheets on the bill, titled (a) Special Education Reform: Supporting Teachers & Schools, Providing New Choices for Parents & Students; (b) Making Special Education Stronger for Students & Parents; (c) Reducing Unnecessary Lawsuits and Litigation in Special Education; and (d) Building on Historic Funding Increases for Special Education. Find the issues page at http://edworkforce.house.gov/issues/

From OSERS and OSEP:

For authoritative input on the law, look to the Office of Special Education and Rehabilitative Services (OSERS) and the Office of Special Education Programs (OSEP), both within the Department of Education. These are the agencies within the federal government responsible for overseeing IDEA's implementation. They've established a dedicated IDEA 2004 page, at www.ed.gov/policy/speced/guid/idea/idea 2004.html

OSERS and OSEP have also made the following 1-page summaries available on changes from the IDEA 97 to IDEA 2004:

- Alignment with the No Child Left Behind Act

  http://www2.ed.gov/policy/speced/guid/ idea/tb-nclb-align.pdf

- Changes in Initial Evaluations and Reevaluations

  http://www2.ed.gov/policy/speced/guid/ idea/tb-init-eval.pdf

- Children Enrolled by Their Parents in Private Schools

  http://www2.ed.gov/policy/speced/guid/ idea/tb-priv-school.pdf

- Discipline

  http://www2.ed.gov/policy/speced/guid/ idea/tb-discipline.pdf

- Disproportionality and Overidentification

  http://www2.ed.gov/policy/speced/guid/ idea/tb-overident.pdf

- Early Intervening Services

  http://www2.ed.gov/policy/speced/guid/ idea/tb-early-intervent.pdf

- Highly Qualified Teachers

  http://www2.ed.gov/policy/speced/guid/ idea/tb-qual-teachers.pdf

- Individualized Education Program (IEP)

  http://idea.ed.gov/object/fileDownload/ model/TopicalBrief/field/PdfFile/primary_ key/10

- Individualized Education Program (IEP) Team Meetings and Changes to the IEP

  http://www2.ed.gov/policy/speced/guid/ idea/tb-iep-meetings.pdf

- Local Funding

  https://www.google.com/url?sa=t&rct= j&q=&esrc=s&source=web&cd=1&cad=

rja&uact=8&ved=0CB4QFjAA&url=http%
3A%2F%2Fwww2.ed.gov%2Fpolicy%
2Fspeced%2Fguid%2Fidea%2Ftb-local-fund.
doc&ei=r2FqVPWzCoqNuASSiID4Bg&
usg=AFQjCNF_tFirnQ8NkhqIbY8
ZuqhjM3glmg

- Part C Option: Age 3 to Kindergarten Age

  http://www2.ed.gov/policy/speced/guid/
  idea/tb-partc-opt.pdf

- I. Procedural Safeguards Regarding Surrogates, Notice and Consent

  http://www2.ed.gov/policy/speced/guid/
  idea/tb-safeguards-1.pdf

- II. Procedural Safeguards Regarding Mediation and Resolution Sessions

  http://www2.ed.gov/policy/speced/guid/
  idea/tb-safeguards-2.pdf

- III. Procedural Safeguards Regarding Due Process Hearings

  http://www2.ed.gov/policy/speced/guid/
  idea/tb-safeguards-3.pdf

- Secondary Transition

  http://www2.ed.gov/policy/speced/guid/
  idea/tb-second-trans.pdf

- Statewide and Districtwide Assessments

  http://www.nj.gov/education/specialed/
  idea/reauth/1pagers/assessments.pdf

General Summaries

It goes without saying, or surprise, that reauthorization of a law of IDEA's incredible power would generate a multitude of comments, analyses, and summaries. What's new? What's different? What's the same? Here is a long list of what has already hit the streets for all of us to use to understand the new law's requirements.

- IDEA 2004: Overview, Explanation & Comparison

  www.wrightslaw.com/idea/idea.2004.all.
  pdf

Courtesy of Wrightslaw, this 56-page article describes the substantive changes to the five key statutes of IDEA 2004 by section and subsection. Text added to IDEA 2004 is in italics. Text deleted from IDEA 97 has been struck through.

- IDEA: Analysis of Change Made by P.L. 108-446

  www.cec.sped.org/pp/docs/
  CRSAnalysisofNewIDEAPL108-446.pdf

The Congressional Research Service, the part of the Library of Congress that serves as the research arm of Congress, has published a 47-page analysis of the new IDEA law.

- A User's Guide

  www.c-c-d.org/IdeaUserGuide.pdf

The Consortium for Citizens with Disabilities (CCD) offers this 63-page guide on additions and deletions to IDEA brought about by the 2004 reauthorization. It includes relevant information from the Conference Report, which articulates Congressional intent.

- More from Wrightslaw

  www.wrightslaw.com/idea/index.htm

Wrightslaw also makes available a number of other articles on IDEA 2004, including How Will IEPs Change Under IDEA 2004?; IDEA 2004: IEP Team Members & IEP Team Attendance; Requirements for Highly Qualified Special Ed Teachers, and Transition Services for Education, Work, Independent Living.

- And from the Thompson Publishing Group

  IDEA: New Expectations for Schools and Students is hot off the press at Thompson. For a mere $149 introductory offer (with discounts for multiple copies), this book is designed as a tool for educators, administrators, school attorneys, school board members, and parents seeking to understand and implement the new law. Call 1.(800) 964-5815 to order, or read about the book online at *www.thompson.com/libraries/education/idea/index.html*

- Summary of the 2004 IDEA

  www.ndsccenter.org/events.asp#summary

  Courtesy of the National Down Syndrome Congress (NDSC), this summary looks at the IEP process, due process, and discipline.

- Summary of the new IDEA provisions *www.napas.org/publicpolicy/*

  Brief_Summary_of_Individuals_with_Disabilities_Education_Improvement_Act_of_2004_with_Current_Law.pdf

  This summary is provided courtesy of NAPAS, the National Association of Protection and Advocacy Systems, Inc.

- Summary of the new law

  http://www.nationalparentcenters.org/idea/summary.htm

  This one is offered courtesy of the National Committee of Parents and Advocates Organized to Protect IDEA.

- CEC's summary

  www.cec.sped.org/pp/IDEA_120204.pdf

  And this one is available through the courtesy of the Council for Exceptional Children.

- Let's go section by section

  www.copaa.org/news/idea04.html

  Take a look at the Comparison of H.R. 1350 (Individuals with Disabilities Education Improvement Act of 2004) and IDEA '97, courtesy of the Council of Parent Attorneys and Advocates (COPAA). You can download the entire comparison in PDF format or look at individual comparisons of Parts A, B, C, or D of the law and the new provisions for the National Center for Special Education Research.

- A side-by-side analysis of transition requirements

  ncset.org/publications/related/ideatransition.asp

  provided courtesy of NCSET, the National Center on Secondary Education and Transition, this side-by-side analysis identifies major changes between IDEA 1997 and H.R. 1350 (IDEA 2004) concerning transition services for youth with disabilities.

- And 200 pages from NASDSE

  www.nasdse.org/

  NASDSE, the National Association of State Directors of Special Education, offers a 200-page side-by-side version that compares current law to the amended law signed by President Bush on December 3, 2004. Individual copies are $15 each; bulk orders of 100 copies or more receive a 15% discount. To order your copy, send a check or purchase order to NASDSE, 1800 Diagonal Road, Suite 320, Alexandria, VA 22314, Attention: C. Burgman. The document is not available in electronic format.

Individualized Education Programs

IDEA and the IEP

- Want a brief description of the IEP process under IDEA?

  http://www.parentcenterhub.org/repository/lg1/

  Try NICHCY's Questions Often Asked by Parents about Special Education Services. For the same information in Spanish, read Preguntas Comunes de los Padres sobre los Servicios de Educación Especial at *http://www.parentcenterhub.org/repository/lg1sp/*. You can also read The Arc's brief question and answer on the subject at *http:// thearc.org/faqs/qa-idea.html*

- How about a more detailed description?

  http://www.parentcenterhub.org/repository/qa2/

  Questions and Answers About IDEA tells you what the IEP must contain, who must be on the IEP team, and much more. For the same information in Spanish, read *Preguntas y Respuestas sobre IDEA,* at

- *The Federal regulations and official Federal guidance on IEPs*

  http://www.ldonline.org/article/6337/

  NICHCY's *Individualized Education Programs* is a verbatim reprinting of (a) federal regulations about IEPs, and (b) Appendix A (formerly Appendix C) to IDEA '97, a series of questions and answers about IDEA's requirements on the IEP.

- *More official IEP guidance from the Feds*

  www.ed.gov/parents/needs/speced/iep guide/index.html

  The Office of Special Education Programs (OSEP), at the U.S. Department of Education, issued *A Guide to the Individualized Education Program* in 2000 as a resource for parents and teachers.

- *Did you know the IDEA may be changed in the near future?*

  The Congress is currently discussing amending the IDEA. When this happens, there will likely be changes in IEPs. Keep on top of the emerging story through NICHCY's reauthorization page, at http://www.parentcenterhub.org/repository/reauth-esea/

Especially for Parents

- *Want to be a full participant in developing your child's IEP?*

  http://www.parentcenterhub.org/repository/pa12/

  Take a look at NICHCY's *Developing Your Child's IEP* and learn how to effectively work with schools to meet the needs of your child. For the same information in Spanish, read *Desarrollando el IEP de su Hijo,* at http://www.parentcenterhub.org/wp-content/uploads/repo_items/spanish/pa12sp.pdf

- *And your child can be involved, too!*

  http://www.parentcenterhub.org/repository/st1script/

NICHCY offers a *Student's Guide to the IEP,* a booklet designed to help students become active participants in their own IEP development. This is especially important when the IEP team focuses on transition planning. The guide comes with an audiotape or CD of students with disabilities talking about how they've been involved. There's also a guide for parents and school personnel, called *Helping Students Develop Their IEPs,* available online at http://www.parentcenterhub.org/repository/ta2script/

- *What to do before the meeting*

  www.nolo.com

  Nolo: Law for All offers *Preparing for the IEP Meeting: What you need to know before you meet with the representatives of your school district.* From the home page, search using the term "IEP." This brief will be among the results. (You'll find other resources you'll probably like, too.)

- *Want to know more about what to do before, during, and after the IEP meeting?*

  www.fape.org/pubs/index.htm

  Planning Your Child's Individualized Education Program (IEP): Some Suggestions to Consider offers suggestions for the IEP meeting. This publication from FAPE (Families and Advocates Partnership for Education) is also available in Spanish at the link provided.

- *What do you say when THEY say ... ?*

  www.nclid.unco.edu/HVoriginals/Advocacy/Popup/popup.html

  The *IEP Pop-Up* gives you responses to common "hurdle talk" (words and attitudes that keep an IEP meeting from being successful).

- *And don't forget to talk about the "special factors" IDEA mentions.*

  www.ericec.org/digests/e578.html

  New IDEA '97 Requirements: Factors to Consider in Developing an IEP looks only at the "special factors" you may need to consider when working on your child's IEP.

- *Need more information on Individualized Education Programs (IEPs)?*

  www.ericec.org/minibibs/eb27.html

  ERIC offers a minibibliography on IEPs that will lead you to yet more resources on this important topic.

Especially for Professionals

In addition to parents, many school professionals will be involved on the IEP team developing a student's IEP. This includes administrators, educators, special educators, and, often, related services personnel.

- *IEP basics and the importance of the IEP team*

  www.ericec.org/digests/e600.html

  Creating Useful Individualized Education Programs (IEPs) takes a brief look at why it's so important for the professionals on the IEP team to understand what the IEP is all about.

- *What's the role of the regular education teacher on the IEP team?*

  www.ed.gov/policy/speced/leg/idea/brief3.html

  The Office of Special Education Programs, at the U.S. Department of Education, answers this critical question by looking at what IDEA has to say on the subject.

- *How to get* **parents** *involved in the IEP process*

  http://www.parentcenterhub.org/repository/ta2script/

  Learn how to work effectively with parents in creating the IEP, during the IEP meeting, and in times of disagreement.

- *How to get* **students** *involved in the IEP process*

  www.nichcy.org/stuguid.asp

  Helping Students Develop Their IEPs, available at this link, is a guide for school personnel and parents to help support student involvement in IEP development. The

guide comes as a set and includes A Student's Guide to the IEP and an audiotape or CD program featuring students with disabilities talking about this very subject.

Transition and the IEP

- *What's transition planning, and why is it important?*

  IDEA emphasizes that students with disabilities are to be prepared for employment and independent living and that specific attention is to be paid to planning how they will transition from secondary school to the adult world. Learn what IDEA requires in terms of transition planning, who is involved, and what types of activities and services are important, in

  - *Designing Individualized Education Program (IEP) Transition Plans*

    http://ericec.org/digests/e598.html

  - *IDEA 1997 Transition Issues: The IEP for Transition-Aged Students*

    www.ncset.org/publications/default .asp#parent

  - *Transition Requirements: A Guide for States, Districts, Schools, Universities and Families*

    http://interact.uoregon.edu/wrrc/ trnfiles/trncontents.htm

- *How to involve all the resources in communities, not just the agencies that have traditionally been involved*

  http://ecac-parentcenter.org/userfiles/PTI/ Resource%20pages/Transition%20to%20 Adulthood/Transition%20Planning%20 A%20Team%20Effort%20NICHCY.pdf

  NICHCY's Transition Planning: A Team Effort has a wealth of useful ideas about who to involve and what role they might play.

- *And the students themselves should be involved!*

  resource not transferred to CPIR but audio transcript available http://www. parentcenterhub.org/repository/st1script/

NICHCY's Student Guide to the IEP set, which includes Helping Students Develop Their IEPs, was mentioned earlier and is particularly appropriate for students planning their transitions to the adult world.

- Here's another resource for helping students take part in transition planning.

  www.ericec.org/digests/e593.html

  Planning Student-Directed Transitions to Adult Life helps teachers with skills students need to know to participate in transition planning.

Resources from Commercial Publishers

- What Every Parent Needs to Know about Special Education

  www.lrp.com

  Available from LRP Publications; order online or call 1 (800) 341-7874.

- The Complete IEP Guide: How to Advocate for Your Special Education Child

  www.nolo.com

  Available from Nolo Press; order online or call 1 (800) 728-3555.

- My Future My Plan: A Transition Planning Resource for Life After High School

  www.myfuturemyplan.com

  This resource includes a 30-minute video, video discussion guide, a planning and resource notebook for students, and a guide to the notebook for family members and teachers. It's available from State of the Art, Inc., 4455 Connecticut Avenue, NW, Suite B-200, Washington, DC 20008, (202) 537-0818.

- Guide to Writing Quality Individualized Education Programs: What's Best for Students with Disabilities?

  www.ablongman.com/

  Order this Allyn & Bacon book from www.amazon.com

- Better IEPs: How to Develop Legally Correct and Educationally Useful Programs

  Order this book from www.amazon.com

Other Resources of Interest

- The IEP: A Synthesis of Current Literature Since 1997

  www.nasdse.org/forum.htm

  This is available online at Project FORUM, a project of the National Association of State Directors of Special Education (NASDSE).

- The IEP: A Tool for Realizing Possibilities

  www.peakparent.org

  These training materials are used to teach parents how to take an active role in their child's Individualized Education Program (IEP). The tool kit includes a complete script, a video, and a book that discusses all the components of an IEP. The video and book are also available in Spanish, El IEP: Un Instrumento Valioso para Realizar las Posibilidades, and Planes de Educación Individuales: Padres Activos y Efectivos. Both are available from: PEAK Parent Center, Inc., 611 North Weber Suite 200, Colorado Springs, CO 80903, (719) 531-9400, 1(800) 284-0251 (Hotline), info@peakparent.org

INCLUDING STUDENTS WITH DISABILITIES IN STATE AND DISTRICT ASSESSMENTS

What's Required—and Why?

- Frequently asked questions—and answers

  www.education.umn.edu/nceo/TopicAreas/Participation/participation_FAQ.htm

  The participation of students with disabilities in state and district assessments is a special topic area of the National Center on Educational Outcomes (NCEO). If this topic is new to you, you'll want to start your investigation with NCEO's FAQ (Frequently

Asked Questions). What do you want to know? NCEO tries to answer the questions most people start with.

- *All Kids Count: Including students with disabilities in statewide assessment programs*

  http://fcsn.org/peer/assess.htm

  The guide you'll find at this link is a product of the PEER Project, a technical assistance project formerly funded by the U.S. Department of Education, Office of Special Education Programs. All Kids Count is intended as a basic primer on the participation of students with disabilities in statewide assessment systems. Its purpose is to give parents, parent leaders, professionals, and other interested parties basic guidelines and points of reference for participating in discussions around policies and practices related to the inclusion of students with disabilities in large-scale assessment programs.

- *Assessing students with disabilities: Issues and evidence*

  www.cse.ucla.edu/reports/TR587.pdf

  This 2003 report discusses major issues raised by the inclusion of students with disabilities in large-scale assessments and summarizes pertinent research.

- *Any guidance from the feds?*

  www.dssc.org/frc/fed/OSEP01-06.FF Assessment.pdf

  Guidance on Including Students With Disabilities in Assessment Programs is available from the Office of Special Education Programs (OSEP), U.S. Department of Education. Find the family version at this link. The same information, prepared for state directors of special education, is available at

  www.dssc.org/frc/AssessmentQ%26A.html

- *What are the positive aspects of including students with disabilities in assessment programs?*

  www.education.umn.edu/nceo/OnlinePubs/ Synthesis51.html

When investigators document the consequences of high-stakes assessments for students with disabilities, many negative consequences are cited. The National Center on Educational Outcomes (NCEO) examined both empirical and anecdotal evidence for positive consequences of large-scale high-stakes assessments for students with disabilities. This report synthesizes their findings.

Test Accommodations

- *Accommodations: Making it possible for students to show you "what they got"*

  www.education.umn.edu/nceo/ TopicAreas/Accommodations/Accom_topic. htm

  And we're back at the National Center on Educational Outcomes (NCEO), because they're the experts. Check out their resources on testing accommodations, which are "changes in testing materials or procedures that enable students to participate in assessments in a way that allows abilities to be assessed rather than disabilities." This NCEO special topic area includes, among other things, an Introduction to Accommodations (at this link) and an FAQ (Frequently Asked Questions). Find out what accommodations are, what categories they fall into, and when you'd want to make one (or two . . .) for a student with a disability.

- *When you make a change to the test, what happens?*

  www.ihdi.uky.edu/msrrc/PDF/Tindal& Fuchs.PDF

  If you make an accommodation, does it make the student's test results any less valid? This 1999 summary addresses the issue of validity with primary consideration on using this research to implement sound testing practices and to make appropriate educational decisions.

- *A summary of research on test changes*

  http://education.umn.edu/nceo/onlinepubs/ Technical34.htm

  This 2002 paper, titled A Summary of Research on the Effects of Test Accommodations: 1999 through 2001, summarizes research on the effects of test accommodations, including: type of assessment, content area assessed, number of research participants, types of disabilities included in the sample, grade level of the participants, research design, research findings, limitations of the study, and recommendations for future research.

• Try the Online Accommodations Bibliography.

http://education.umn.edu/nceo/AccomStudies.htm

The Online Accommodations Bibliography, at the National Center on Educational Outcomes (NCEO), allows users to search a compilation of empirical research studies on the effects of various testing accommodations for students with disabilities. Convenient, eh? The research you'll find is the same as what's summarized in the article cited and linked in the previous item, plus additional research studies presented or published in more recent years.

• Need a tool kit or staff development tool on assessment accommodations?

www.cec.sped.org/bk/catalog2/assessment.html

Making Assessment Accommodations: A Toolkit For Educators 2000 [and Videotape] is a product of the ASPIIRE and ILIAD IDEA Partnership Projects, formerly funded by OSEP. An introductory section provides an overview of the tool kit. A 15-minute videotape looks at commonly used assessment accommodations from the perspectives of practitioners, policymakers, administrators, and parents. The "Practitioner's Guide" section briefly describes the most commonly used accommodations in five areas: timing, scheduling, setting, presentation, and response. The "Administrator's Guide" section includes a discussion of implementation along with examples of schools that have made assessment accommodations for students with disabilities. A pamphlet to share with family members is also included in this section. The final section presents suggestions and ideas for using the tool kit in staff development sessions for small study groups. To order, call The Council for Exceptional Children, 1 (888) 232-7733, or e-mail service@cec.sped.org

• State policies: Assessment and accommodations

www.education.umn.edu/nceo/TopicAreas/Accommodations/StatesAccomm.htm

Want to know what your state's policy is about including students with disabilities in standardized assessments? Take a look at this link, courtesy of the National Center on Educational Outcomes (NCEO), which has been tracking and analyzing state policies on participation in assessments and accommodations for more than a decade now.

• And then you include the scores of students with disabilities in the state's accountability system, right? No matter what they are?

www.education.umn.edu/nceo/OnlinePubs/Technical33.htm

States want to have good scores on their tests, just like any student does. If the students in the state do well on these large-scale tests, that means the state's education system is working. But what if the scores turn out lousy? No one wants to hear that bad news! Nonetheless, states have to tell us how students are doing (and, by extension, how the state's system is doing). But are they really including students with disabilities in the overall performance picture? This study, "Are We There Yet? Accountability for the Performance of Students With Disabilities," identifies and describes the accountability systems that states are using and discusses the degree to which publicly available documents clearly articulate whether students with disabilities are included in accountability calculations.

• Want more resources? Try NICHCY's TA&D Resource Library

http://www.tadnet.org/pages/513-products

This link provides a list of all the publications and products available on the subject that are available from the TA&D (Technical Assistance and Dissemination) network funded by the Office of Special Education Programs (OSEP) at the U.S. Department of Education.

Alternate Assessments

- *What we know and need to know about alternate assessment*

  http://journals.sped.org/ec/archive_articles/ VOLUME70NUMBER1Fall2003_EC_ Browder70-1.pdf

  This 2003 journal article appeared in Exceptional Children, Vol. 70, No. 1, pp. 45-61.

  It reviews promises, practices, and provisos of using alternate assessments to measure progress of students with disabilities in state-wide assessment programs.

- *Alternate assessment: Q & A*

  www.usu.edu/mprrc/infoserv/pubs. cfm#aa

  This document was created as a tool for state staff, local educators, and other stakeholders who have vested interests in creating an alternative assessment process for states and local districts. Alternative assessment is defined and examples are offered.

- *Here's a ton of info on alternate assessment—all in one place.*

  http://education.umn.edu/nceo/TopicAreas/ AlternateAssessments/alt_assess_topic.htm

  You'll notice how often this A-Z page takes you to the National Center on Educational Outcomes (NCEO)—that's because they're the experts! They offer a gratifying number of resources on alternate assessment, which is "designed to measure the performance of students who are unable to participate in general large-scale assessments used by districts and states." This NCEO special topic area includes, among other things, an Introduction (at this link), an FAQ (Frequently Asked Questions), and connection to resources on the subject.

- *What are your state's alternate assessment policies?*

  http://education.umn.edu/nceo/TopicAreas/ AlternateAssessments/StatesAlt Assess.htm

If you want to know what your state is up to, take a look at this link, again courtesy of the National Center on Educational Outcomes (NCEO), which has been tracking and analyzing state policies on participation in assessments and accommodations for more than a decade now.

- *A standard setting method for alternate assessments for students with significant disabilities.*

  www.education.umn.edu/NCEO/Online Pubs/Synthesis47.html

  Exploration of the rationale and design of the alternate portfolio assessment.

- *Want more resources? Try NICHCY's TA&D Resource Library*

  http://www.tadnet.org/pages/513-products

  This link provides a list of all the publications and products available on the subject available from the TA&D (Technical Assistance and Dissemination)network funded by the Office of Special Education Programs (OSEP) at the U.S. Department of Education.

LEARNING DISABILITIES

Quick Intros to Learning Disabilities

- *Want a quick overview?*

  http://www.ccisd.net/docs/special-education-services-documents/learning_ disabilities.pdf?sfvrsn=0

  Read NICHCY's 4-page fact sheet on LD.

- *LD at a glance*

  www.ld.org/LDInfoZone/InfoZone_Fact Sheet_LD.cfm

  The National Center for Learning Disabilities (NCLD) is an excellent source of information. Read about LD in this fact sheet: how to tell if someone has a learning disability, what causes LD, how common LDs are, and what can be done.

- If you're new to LD . . .

  http://www.ldaamerica.org/new_to_ld/index.asp

  . . . then the *Learning Disabilities Association of America* has written this intro for you.

- The ABCs of LD

  www.ldonline.org/abcs_info/articlesinfo.html

  You'll find *LD Online* a rich source of info. Start here for a quick intro.

- Definitions and overviews

  www.schwablearning.org/resources.asp?g=1&s=1&t=1

  Schwab Learning will give you LD fast facts, an overview, and definitions.

Diagnosing LD

The diagnosis of learning disabilities is often a sticky issue. Of particular concern are the various methods used to test children suspected of having learning disabilities and the differing eligibility criteria that states apply to decide whether or not a child qualifies for special education and related services. A lot rides on those decisions. Depending on the diagnostic process used, the resulting picture may vary as to the child's abilities and difficulties. And based upon the picture that emerges of the child, decisions are made about the education and special assistance that the child will receive (or not) and the resources that the state will commit to provide the child with special education (or not).

- What's the primary approach to diagnosing LD? Here's an overview of the discrepancy approach.

  Fletcher, J. M., Francis, D. J., Shaywitz, S. E., Lyon, G. R., Foorman, B. R., Stuebing, K. K.,

Shaywitz, B. A. (1998, Fall). Intelligent testing and the discrepancy model for children with learning disabilities. *Learning Disabilities Research & Practice, 13(4)*, 186-203.

This article isn't available online, but it's worthwhile pursuing at a library, resource room, or from the publisher itself. It reviews the historical basis and rationale for identifying children as learning disabled on the basis of a discrepancy between scores on measures of intelligence and achievement. In addition to a historical perspective, recent studies that address the validity of classifications of children with LD according to the presence or absence of discrepancies between IQ and achievement are reviewed.

"Throughout this article, the role of IQ testing in the designation of children as learning disabled for research and public policy is addressed. The authors conclude that IQ tests have limited utility for the identification of children with LD. Alternative approaches to classification that incorporate the idea of a discrepancy between aptitude and achievement are discussed." (ERIC: Authors)

- What else is possible? Alternate approaches

  Torgesen, J. K., & Wagner, R. K. (1998, Fall). Alternative diagnostic approaches for specific developmental reading disabilities. *Learning Disabilities Research & Practice, 13(4)*, 220-232.

  "Research on reading disabilities conducted within the . . . two decades [prior to the article's publication] provides evidence in support of new approaches to the diagnoses of reading disabilities in children and adults. This article summarizes recently acquired information about a specific set of linguistic-cognitive markers for reading disabilities, and it also describes efforts to develop measures of these markers in the areas of phonological awareness, rapid automatic naming, and verbal short-term memory. In addition, implications of this new information for the diagnosis of reading disabilities are considered." (ERIC: Authors)

- *The official policy of the Educational Testing Service (ETS)*

  Office of Disability Policy, Educational Testing Service. (1999, June). *Policy statement for documentation of a learning disability in adolescents and adults (Rev.)*. Princeton, NJ: Author. Available online at www.ets.org/ disability/ldpolicy.html

  This document provides individuals, schools, professional diagnosticians, and service providers with a common understanding and knowledge base of those components of documentation that are necessary to validate a learning disability and the need for reasonable accommodations for candidates seeking to register with various Educational Testing Service testing programs.

- *What the states use: The situation in 2000*

  Schrag, J. A. (2000, October). *Discrepancy approaches for identifying learning disabilities (Quick Turn Around)*. Alexandria, VA: Project FORUM. Available online at www.nasdse .org/FORUM/PDF%20files/identifying_ learning_disabilities.PDF

  This report is a brief review of recent trends, issues, and changes within the states related to the use of discrepancy formulas and other approaches for determining eligibility of students with LD for special education and related services. This document was reviewed by the U.S. Office of Special Education Programs for consistency with the Individuals with Disabilities Education Act Amendments of 1997.

- *Where to go from here? Recommendations from the National Center for Learning Disabilities*

  National Center for Learning Disabilities. (2004). *Keep kids learning: A new model to identify students with learning disabilities before they fail*. Available online at www.ld.org/ Advocacy/kids_learning.cfm

This document provides background on the use of the discrepancy approach to diagnosis, summarizes what we know from research and practice, and makes policy recommendations about where we need to go from here.

- *And last but not least . . . the Center's that looking into it all*

  http://nrcld.org/index.html

The National Research Center on Learning Disabilities (NRCLD) has been funded by OSEP to address the complex issues surrounding the proper identification of students with LD who need special education services. Specifically, the Center is analyzing existing methods of identifying students with learning disabilities. It is also studying state and local policies to determine factors that explain the differences in the number and characteristics of students identified with learning disabilities from state to state, from district to district within a state, and even from school to school within a district. On NRCLD's Web site, you can access the results of these efforts, including

- *Reschly, D. J., Hosp, J. L., & Schmied, C. M. (2003, August). And miles to go . . . State SLD requirements and authoritative recommendations. Nashville, TN: National Research Center on Learning Disabilities.* This paper focuses on the major events leading to the widespread rejection of the discrepancy criterion and an analysis of current state specific learning disabilities (SLD) requirements in relation to proposed changes in SLD classification criteria. Possibilities for and barriers to change are addressed in this analysis. Available online at http://nrcld.org/html/research/states/index .html

- *Symposium on responsiveness to intervention. (2003, December).* NRCLD hosted a 2-day symposium focusing on issues regarding responsiveness to intervention (RTI). (RTI refers to individual, comprehensive student-centered assessment models that focus on applying a problem-solving framework to identify and address a student's difficulties. For an overview of RTI's core concepts, visit http://nrcld.org/html/research/rti/concepts.html.) The assembled speakers, discussants, and participants represented the wide diversity of individuals with a vested interest in LD determination issues. Sessions were organized around critical questions, ranging from "How should screening for secondary intervention occur?" to "What are alternative models to LD identification other than RTI?" To access the papers presented during the symposium, PowerPoint presentations used by the presenters, and videos of the symposium sessions, when available, visit

http://nrcld.org/html/symposium2003/index.html

LD in More Detail

- While you're at NICHCY, might as well read the longer piece on reading and learning diabilities.

http://www.ldaofky.org/Reading%20&%20 Learning%20Disabilities.pdf

NICHCY offers a 16-page paper on reading and learning disabilities that talks in greater depth about LD in children, what to do if you're an adult who suspects you might have a learning disability, and how parents can help their children with LD at home and in school. Find lists of reading materials for families, for adults, and for educators and connect with LD organizations, government agencies, and literacy groups.

- LD Online takes a deeper look.

www.ldonline.org/ld_indepth/resource-guide.html

LD OnLine is the official Web site of the National Joint Committee on Learning Disabilities. This link leads you its "LD in Depth" page, where you can select the topic you want to go deeper into—adult issues, behavior, giftedness, the IEP, parenting . . . it's up to you. There's lots of detail here.

- Delve into the treasure chest at LDA.

www.ldaamerica.org/index.asp

LDA stands for the Learning Disabilities Association of America. From their home page (at this link), you can pick the type of information you need on LD. Are you a parent? A teacher? A professional needing to understand the characteristics of LD and associated conditions, such as attention deficit hyperactivity disorder (ADHD), in order to provide effective services and assistance? Are you an adult with LD? Pick your pleasure and go straight to tailored info on LD.

- And find treasures at NCLD.

http://www.ld.org/LDInfoZone/index.cfm

Visit the InfoZone at NCLD (National Center for Learning Disabilities). It's divided into 3 sections: resource locator, fact sheets, and research news.

- Use the Resource Locator to find organizations in your state.
- Go to Research News if you're interested in seeing the results of the 1999 Summit on Research in Learning Disabilities.
- Go to Fact Sheets if you want information about specific learning disabilities, such as dyslexia (learning disabilities in reading), dysgraphia (writing), dyscalculia (math), dyspraxia (motor skills), information processing disorders (including the different types of auditory and visual processing disorders), visual processing disorders, or AD/HD.

- And while we're on the subject of dyslexia, dysgraphia, dyscalculia . . .?

www.schwablearning.org/resources. asp?g=1&s=1&t=1

If you scroll down this page at Schwab-Learning, you'll find overviews of each of the "dys" aspects of LD. You'll also find info on auditory processing disorder and central *auditory processing disorder and a discussion of whether or not they're the same thing.*

- *LDA also offers quick overviews of dyslexia, dysgraphia, dyscalculia.*

  www.ldaamerica.org/index.asp

  At the home page of LDA (Learning Disabilities Association of America), the first paragraph states, "Typical learning difficulties include dyslexia, dyscalculia, and dysgraphia." Each "dys" is linked to a list of the signs and symptoms of that disorder and a quick list of strategies to use to offset its effects.

- *And for the authoritative specialist on dyslexia . . .*

  www.interdys.org

  The International Dyslexia Association's name speaks for itself.

National Organizations That Can Help

The organizations that offer the previously listed publications are the same ones that offer a wide range of other information, assistance, and services. But to make life a little easier, here's a quick, consolidated list in alphabetical order:

- *Council for Learning Disabilities (CLD)*

  www.cldinternational.org

- *Division for Learning Disabilities (DLD)*

  www.dldcec.org

- *International Dyslexia Association*

  www.interdys.org

- *LDOnline*

  www.ldonline.org

- *Learning Disabilities Association of America (LDA)*

  www.ldaamerica.org

- *National Association of School Psychologists (NASP)*

  www.nasponline.org

- *National Center for Learning Disabilities*

  www.ld.org
  www.getreadytoread.org

- *Recording for the Blind and Dyslexic*

  www.rfbd.org

- *Schwab Learning*

  www.schwablearning.org

Find an LD Group in Your State

Several of the national groups just listed have chapters throughout the United States. You can often find out where your state chapter is located by visiting online. And often, the state chapter can put you in touch with local chapters. We've provided the names and links of organizations that offer this type of info, support, and connection:

- *Council for Learning Disabilities (CLD)*

  Find your regional CLD chapter at

  www.cldinternational.org/c/@rmLS9PNU-Gukig/Pages/chapters.html

- *International Dyslexia Association*

  www.interdys.org/jsp/branch/structure.jsp

- *Learning Disabilities Association of America (LDA)*

  www.ldaamerica.org/state_chapters/index.asp

- *National Center for Learning Disabilities*

  www.ld.org/LDInfoZone/InfoZone_Resource Locator.cfm

- *Schwab Learning*

  Confession: Schwab doesn't really have state or local chapters, per se, but you can use their online resources page to make state and local connections of all kinds. For example,

    - *Using a drop-down menu, you can select your state and be given the contact info for a wide variety of groups and agencies in that state addressing issues related to learning disabilities.*

www.schwablearning.org/resources.asp?
g=4&s=5

- If you're looking to discuss concerns
and experiences of parenting a child
with a learning or attention problem,
try their Parent to Parent message board
at www.schwablearning.org/resources.
asp?g=3

- Before you leap into a message board,
though,you might want to read an
interesting article about Online Parent
Groups at www.schwablearning.org/
articles.asp?r=62&g=3

LD Research

• *Summarizing LD research*

Lyon, R. (1997). Report on learning disabilities research. Adapted from testimony given
by Dr. Reid Lyon before the Committe on
Education and the Workforce in the U.S.
House of Representatives on July 10, 1997.
Available online at www.ldonline.org/ld_
indepth/reading/nih_report.html

At the time of this testimony, Dr. Lyon
was the Acting Chief of the Child Development
and Behavior Branch at the National Institute
of Child Health and Human Development
(NICHD), National Institutes of Health (NIH).
His testimony begins with a summary of what is
known about how children learn to read, including understanding how sounds are connected
to print, how reading fluency develops, and
how meaning is constructed from print, as
well as other factors that influence learning to
read. Next, an overview is provided on why
so many children are having difficulty learning to read (deficits in phoneme awareness and
developing the alphabetic principle, deficits in
acquiring reading comprehension strategies and
applying them to the reading of text, deficits in
developing and maintaining the motivation to learn
to read, limitations in effectively preparing teachers). The testimony also includes a summary of
what we can do help children learn to read.

• *What have we learned from the last two decades of
the 20th century of LD research?*

Two Decades of Research in Learning Disabilities:
Reading Comprehension, Expressive Writing,
Problem Solving, Self-Concept. Keys to Successful
Learning: A National Summit on Research in
Learning Disabilities. (1999). (ERIC Document
Reproduction Service No. ED 430 365)

This document presents four brief papers that
review and synthesize the research on intervention with students who have LD:

- "Can School-Based Interventions Enhance
the Self-Concept of Students With
Learning Disabilities?" (Elbaum, B., &
Vaughn, S.). This review finds that school-
based interventions of either the skill
development or skill enhancement types
can lead to beneficial changes in students'
self-perceptions and thatmiddle school
students appeared most responsive to
such interventions. Executive summary is
available at www.ld.org/research/ncld_
self_concept.cfm

- "Reading Comprehension Instruction for
Students With Learning Disabilities"
(Gersten, R., & Baker, S.). Findings
indicated the effectiveness of reading
comprehension interventions, instruction in self-monitoring techniques,
and peer-assisted learning strategies.
Continuing difficulties with teaching
students to generalize new skills were
also found. Executive summary is available at www.ld.org/research/ncld_read-
ing_comp.cfm

- "Teaching Expressive Writing to Students
With Learning Disabilities" (Gersten, R.,
& Baker, S.). Instructional writing interventions were found to lead to significant improvements in students' writing
and that common features of successful
instruction included explicit instruction in
the phases of writing, teacher demonstration, and teacher and/or peer feedback.
Executive summary is available at www.
ld.org/research/ncld_writing.cfm

- *"Intervention Research for Adolescents With Learning Disabilities" (Swanson, H. L.). "This paper reports on a meta-analysis of 58 interventions. It found that direct instruction and strategy instruction were the most effective techniques." (ERIC: DB) Executive summary is available at www.ld.org/research/ncld_high_order.cfm*

• *Instructionally, what works with students with LD? More from the National Summit on Research Improving Instruction for Students with Learning Disabilities: The Results of Three Research Syntheses. Keys to Successful Learning: A National Summit on Research in Learning Disabilities. (1999). (ERIC Document Reproduction Service No. ED 430 367)*

This booklet presents three brief papers that summarize three meta-analytic research syntheses of instruction for students with learning disabilities:

- *"Intervention Research for Students With Learning Disabilities" (Swanson, H. L.). Findings that resulted from a review of 272 studies are grouped into those on most effective forms of instruction, subject areas most affected by different instructional strategies, and other factors that influence achievement. Executive summary is available at www.ld.org/research/osep_swanson.cfm*

- *"The Effect of Instructional Grouping Format on the Reading Outcomes of Students With Disabilities" (Elbaum, B., Vaughn, S., Hughes, M., Moody, S. W., & Schumm, J. S.). This analysis of 20 studies presents conclusions on results of students tutoring each other; effects of small group instruction; the outcomes of multiple grouping formats; and effects of length of time during which alternative formats are implemented. Executive summary is available at www.ld.org/research/osep_reading.cfm*

- *"Effective Instruction for Learning Disabled or At-Risk English-Language Learners?" (Gersten, R., Baker, S., Marks, S. U., & Smith, S. B.). "Recommendations address components of an effective English-language development program, the value of adapted forms of the instructional approaches identified in the effective teaching research with this population, and effective ways to merge content area instruction with English-language development instruction." (ERIC: DB) Executive summary is available at www.ld.org/research/osep_at_risk.cfm*

• *Findings from 13 studies about expressive writing: A meta-analysis*

Baker, S., & Gersten, R. (2001, January). Teaching expressive writing to students with learning disabilities: A meta-analysis. Elementary School Journal, 101(3), 251-72. (An article by the same title, but a publication date of 1999, is available through the ERIC system, EDRS Reproduction Service No. ED 439 532, and online at www.ericdigests.org/2000-4/writing.htm)

The 2001 article: "Presents analysis of 13 studies designed to teach students with learning disabilities to write better expository or narrative text. Notes the success of these interventions and details three components for any comprehensive instructional program: instruction in writing process, critical dimensions of different writing genres, and structures for feedback." (ERIC: JPB)

The 1999 article: "Summarizes research on effective instruction in writing for students with learning disabilities. It finds that three components stand out as methods that reliably and consistently lead to improved outcomes in teaching expressive writing to these students. These components are: (1) adhering to a basic framework of planning, writing, and revision; (2) explicitly teaching critical steps in the writing process; and (3) providing feedback guided by the information explicitly taught. The paper also notes two specific teaching methodologies that incorporate these three principles: first, self-regulated strategy development, which involves self-directed prompts, and second, cognitive *strategy instruction in writing, which focuses on prewriting strategies. Emerging issues in writing instruction are identified, including the mechanics versus the content of writing, dictation as a means of eliminating mechanical difficulties of expressive writing, and transfer of writing skills and related strategies to other subject-matter areas." (Contains 10 references.) (ERIC: DB)*

- *The Collaborative Strategic Reading (CSR) model, the Strategic Instruction Model (SIM), and high school students..*

  Bremer, C. D., Clapper, A. T., & Kachgal, M. M. (2000). Never too late: Approaches to reading instruction for secondary students with disabilities. Research to Practice Brief: Improving Secondary Education and Transition Services through Research. (ERIC Document Reproduction Service No. ED 466 913) (Available online at www.ncset.org/publications/viewdesc.asp? id=274)

  "This research brief discusses two reading instruction models for teaching secondary school students with disabilities. The first, Collaborative Strategic Reading (CSR), is designed specifically for students with learning disabilities and students who are at risk of reading failure. This strategy adapts reciprocal reading and incorporates cooperative learning. CSR utilizes four strategies: preview, click, and clunk (students identify parts of a passage that are hard to understand, then using four 'fix-up' strategies, get the gist and wrap up). Students are also taught to use the following cooperative group roles: leader, clunk expert, gist expert, announcer, and encourager. The second strategy, Strategic Instruction Model (SIM), consists of a package of components for use by students with learning disabilities, as well as instructional tools for use by teachers. The reading strategies portion of SIM includes: paraphrasing, self-questioning, visual imagery, and word identification. The Content Enhancement Routines in SIM help teachers manage and present the content of their classes in ways that help all students learn. A concept anchoring table is presented. The article closes with a description of other approaches and suggestions for selecting and implementing the appropriate model." (Contains 19 references.) (ERIC: CR)

Find out in detail about the SIM at www. ku-crl.org/iei/sim/index.html. You may also be interested in another Research to Practice Brief at NCSET, "Collaborative Strategic Reading (CSR): Improving Secondary Students' Reading Comprehension Skills," by Bremer, C. D., Vaughn, S., Clapper, A. T., & Kim, A.-H. Find it at www.ncset.org/publications/viewdesc.asp? id=424

What About School?

- *Look up—at the section on LD research*

  The section just prior, on LD research, connects you with what research has to say about teaching students with LD. Take a look, if you haven't already—and put these research insights into practice when you're looking for interventions that work.

- *What is dysgraphia? What to do when children have trouble with writing.*

  www.vtpic.com/Dysgraphia.pdf

  This 2-page paper, available online at PIC (the Vermont Parent Training and Information Center), concisely discusses what kinds of accommodations and adjustments at school help children with writing difficulties.

- *Help students learn to strategically process what they read.*

  www.ericdigests.org/2001-4/reading.html

  Williams, J. P. (2000). Strategic processing of text: Improving reading comprehension of students with learning disabilities (ERIC/OSEP Digest #599). (ERIC Document Reproduction Service No. ED 449 596). This digest, based on a book of the same title, summarizes relevant research and promising practices in the strategic processing of text, both narrative and expository, by students with learning disabilities. The digest stresses the importance of training teachers in strategy instruction.

- *Visit the Teacher's Homepage at LD Online.*

  www.ldonline.org/teaching/index.html

  This page showcases ideas and strategies for teaching students with learning disabilities from outstanding and experienced teachers. Find out what to do if you suspect a student has a learning disability; how to handle assessment issues, inclusion, and parent conferences; and what teaching strategies and techniques work.

- *Working with paraeducators*

  www.ldonline.org/ld_indepth/teaching_ techniques/work_with_paraeducator.html

- *Check out LDA's materials for teachers.*

  www.ldaamerica.org/aboutld/teachers/ index.asp

- *Schwab Learning has a boatload of info on managing LD in the school setting.*

  www.schwablearning.org/index.asp

  Behavior, assistive technology, learning strategies, homework . . . roam around Schwab's site, use the "select a topic to search" dropdown menu at the top, or enter a keyword and search, or click on the tabs "managing" or "connecting" to find the info on school you're looking for.

- *Current Practice Alerts*

  www.teachingld.org/ld_resources/alerts/ default.htm

  Click this link, and you'll access a library of previous alerts about research in learning disabilities. The Alerts series is a joint initiative sponsored by two divisions of the Council for Exceptional Children: the Division for Learning Disabilities (DLD) and the Division for Research (DR). Alerts provide timely and informed judgments regarding professional practices in the field. Based on the adequacy of the current knowledge base and practice experience, each Alert makes a recommendation of "Go For It" (practices for which there is solid research evidence of effectiveness), or "Use Caution" (practices for which the research evidence is incomplete, mixed, or negative).

What About Home?

- *Check out LDA's materials for parents.*

  www.ldaamerica.org/aboutld/parents/index. asp

- *Parents, LD, and designing educational services for your child*

  http://ncld.org/LDInfoZone/InfoZone_ FactSheetIndex.cfm

  NCLD (National Center for Learning Disabilities) offers 2 separate guides to help parents and guardians get help and services if they believe their preschool or school-aged child has a learning disability. Scroll down the page until you see "LD Advocacy." You'll find the links to the guides there.

- *"I have homework . . . "*

  www.vtpic.com/Homework.pdf

  Homework can be a constant source of trouble for parents and students alike. If you're finding it so, this 2-page brief was written for you! It's available online, courtesy of VPIC (the Vermont Parent Training and Information Center).

- *Homework tool kits for parents*

  www.ldonline.org/article.php?id=1040& loc=89

- *More on homework—and four basic principles for enhancing study skills*

  www.ldonline.org/article.php?max- =20&id=832&loc=15

- *Assistive technology and learning disabilities*

  www.ldonline.org/ld_indepth/technology/ technology.html

  Find out what assistive technology may help your child with learning disabilities.

- *Enhancing self-concept: What works*

  Elbaum, B., & Vaughn, S. (2003, March/April). For which students with learning disabilities are self-concept interventions effective? Journal of Learning Disabilities, 36(2), 101-108. (Note: This article is drawn from the same work that resulted in an article noted in the Two Decades of Research document listed under "LD Research" above. An executive summary for that article can be found at www.ld.org/research/ncld_self_concept.cfm)

"This meta-analysis looked at outcomes of school-based interventions aimed at enhancing the self-concept of students with learning disabilities, specifically effect sizes in relation to students' self-concepts prior to the intervention. Results indicated that only students with documented low self-concept benefited significantly from intervention. For these students effect sizes were quite large." (Contains references.) (ERIC: Author/DB)

- SparkTop.org is not just for anybody.

  www.sparktop.org/intro.html

  SparkTop.org—where no two brains spark alike—is for 8-12 year-olds who learn differently. If that's you, you might want to go there to learn about your LD, recognize strengths, showcase your creativity, and connect with other kids who have LD.

- For students themselves: Being your own advocate

  http://ncld.org/LDInfoZone/InfoZone_FactSheetIndex.cfm

  NCLD (National Center for Learning Disabilities) pairs its 2 parent guides (noted earlier) with one called "Being Your Own Advocate." This introductory guide is designed to help teens and adults with learning disabilities become familiar with the rights and responsibilities they have in school, college, and the workplace. Scroll down the page until you see "LD Advocacy." You'll find the links to the guide there.

- Going on to postsecondary schooling, financial aid, and more

  www.heath.gwu.edu/FactSheets.htm

  Visit the HEATH Resource Center—it's not a college, and it doesn't offer financial aid itself, but you can learn about both there. HEATH is the national center on postsecondary education for individuals with disabilities. At this link, you'll find publica-tions such as "Financial Aid for Individuals with Learning Disabilities" and "Selecting A College for Students With Learning Disabilities or Attention Deficit Hyperactivity Disorder (ADHD)."

Ongoing Sources of Research Info

- Annals of Dyslexia

  www.interdys.org/jsp/member/index.jsp

  Annals of Dyslexia is an interdisciplinary peer-reviewed journal published by The International Dyslexia Association. Articles appearing in Annals are written by researchers, scientists, educators, and clinicians concerned with dyslexia and related language disabilities. Annals is a benefit of membership in IDA. Read more about it and subscribe via this link. To learn more about Annals and view the list of contributors to the journal, visit www.interdys.org/bs/web-cart_default1.asp?prod_type=IDA&cat=Annals+of+Dyslexia

- Current Practice Alerts

  www.teachingld.org/ld_resources/alerts/default.htm

  Click this link, and you'll access a library of previous alerts about research in learning disabilities. The Alerts series is a joint initiative sponsored by two divisions of the Council for Exceptional Children: the Division for Learning Disabilities (DLD) and the Division for Research (DR). Alerts provide timely and informed judgments regarding professional practices in the field. Based on the adequacy of the current knowledge base and practice experience, each Alert makes a recommendation of "Go For It" (practices for which there is solid research evidence of effectiveness), or "Use Caution" (practices for which the research evidence is incomplete, mixed, or negative).

- Intervention in School and Clinic

  Includes hands-on tips, techniques, methods, and ideas from top authorities for improving the quality of assessment, instruction, and management. Published five times a year, it's a publication of Pro-Ed, 8700 Shoal Creek Boulevard, Austin, TX 78757-6897.

Telephone: (800) 897-3202; (512) 451-3246. Web: www .proedinc.com/journals.html

- *Journal of Learning Disabilities*

  www.sagepub.com/journal.aspx?pid=251

  The Journal of Learning Disabilities provides information about best practice and research, in learning disabilities. Read more about it and subscribe via this link.

- *Another Journal of Learning Disabilities? Yes.*

  www.proedinc.com/jld.html

  This Journal of Learning Disabilities provides in-depth coverage of specific topics or issues in the field of learning disabilities, extensive literature reviews, theoretical papers, position papers, reports of empirical research, intervention articles, and overviews of successful interventions that can be replicated with other individuals with learning disabilities. Read more about it and subscribe via this link.

- *Journal of Special Education*

  The Journal of Special Education is a research journal in the field of special education for individuals with disabilities ranging from mild to severe. Published quarterly, it's a publication of Pro-Ed, 8700 Shoal Creek Boulevard, Austin, TX 78757-6897. Telephone: (800) 897-3202; (512) 451-3246. Web: www.proedinc.com/journals .html

- *Learning Disabilities—A Multidisciplinary Journal*

  A publication of the Learning Disabilities Association of America, 4156 Library Road, Pittsburgh, PA 15234, it's published twice yearly. (412) 341-1515. Web: www.ldaamerica .org

- *Learning Disabilities Research & Practice*

  The Learning Disabilities Research & Practice journal presents current research in the field of learning disabilities and disseminates information important to practitioners in the field. Members of the Division for Learning Disabilities (a special interest division of the

Council for Exceptional Children) receive the Journal series as part of their membership. To find out how to join DLD, visit www. teachingld.org/become/default.htm

- *Learning Disability Quarterly*

  The Learning Disability Quarterly reports research on the many facets of learning disabilities. It's published 4 times per year by the Council for Learning Disabilities. Membership in the Council for Learning Disabilities includes a complimentary subscription, but a subscription is also available without membership. To subscribe, visit www.cldinternational.org/c/ @nbz2w2jsbn8KE/Pages/ldqinfo.html

- *Reading & Writing Quarterly—Overcoming Learning Difficulties*

  This journal provides critical information to improve instruction for regular and special education students who have difficulty learning to read and write, for university-based instructors and researchers, learning consultants, school psychologists, and teachers. It's published quarterly by Taylor & Francis, Inc., 325 Chestnut Street, Suite 800, Philadelphia, PA 19106. Web: www.tandf.co.uk/journals/ titles/10573569.asp

- *Remedial and Special Education*

  This journal emphasizes interpretation of research and specific recommendations for practice. It's a bimonthly publication of Pro-Ed, 8700 Shoal Creek Boulevard, Austin, TX 78757-6897. Telephone: (800) 897-3202; (512) 451-3246. Web: www.proedinc.com/journals. html

Information on Specific Disabilities

- *NICHCY offers disability fact sheets on the following disabilities at*

  http://www.parentcenterhub.org/repository/ specific-disabilities/

  AD/HD, autism/PDD, cerebral palsy, deafness/ hearing impairments, Down syndrome, emotional disorders, epilepsy, learning disabilities, mental retardation, pervasive developmental disorders (PDD), severe/multiple disabilities, speech/language impairments, spina bifida, traumatic brain injury (TBI), visual impairments.

- How does your state define these disabilities?

www.nasdse.org/FORUM/PDF%20files/
disability_categories.pdf

Find out your state's policies in Project FORUM's report, *Disability Categories: State Terminology, Definitions & Eligibility Criteria (2004)*, available at this link.

- Information in Spanish?

Yes!. Visit the disability information page in Spanish, located at http://www.parentcenterhub.org/lista-espanol/. Also visit the 2 new Spanish-language resource pages that'll connect you to Spanish materials about (a) specific disabilities and (b) disability topics. These pages are available in both English and Spanish.

- Didn't find what you were looking for?

If you're looking for information on a disability NOT covered by one of the fact sheets, please do write (malizo@spannj.org) or call in English or in Spanish. There is a lot of information to share on other disabilities.

- Looking for information on a rare disorder? Contact
  - the National Organization for Rare Disorders (NORD) at 1 (800) 999-6673, and www.rarediseases.org
  - the Office of Rare Disorders at the National Institutes of Health at http://rarediseases. info.nih.gov/index.html
  - the Genetic and Rare Diseases Information Center, which is a part of the Office of Rare Disorders and which answers questions from the general public, including patients and their families, health care professionals, and biomedical researchers. Call toll-free at 1 (888) 205-2311 (Voice), 1 (888) 205-3223 (TTY).
  - DiseaseInfoSearch, for information on specific genetic conditions at www.genetical liance. org/ws_display.asp?filter=diseases

Disability Organizations

- Looking for an organization focusing on a specific disability?

Visit the "Quick Find/NICHCY Resources" page at http://www.parentcenterhub.org/nichcy-resources/# to see if there's an organization specializing in that disability. (Hint: If you can't find one, give a call at 1 (800) 695-0285.)

- Just want to know what's out there?

There's a National Resources list to help you find disability information and disability organizations. It can be accessed from http://www.parentcenterhub.org/nichcy-resources/#

- Try the government's resource list.

DisabilityInfo.gov is the comprehensive federal Web site of disability-related government resources. You can find out about government disability programs and benefits, the Americans with Disabilities Act (ADA), the 2002 Red Book on Work Incentives and Employment Supports, Career One-Stops, Employment, Education, Housing, Transportation, Health, Income Support, Technology, Community Life, and Civil Rights.

The TA&D Network—at Your Service!

The TA&D Network refers to the Technical Assistance and Dissemination network funded by the U.S. Department of Education, Office of Special Education Programs (OSEP). There are more than 40 information centers set up to offer assistance on special education and disability topics.

NICHCY is one such center. Others focus on early childhood, special education finance, learning disabilities, mediation, minorities, outcomes, transition, IDEA, and on and on.

- Would a fast guide to the TA&D centers help?

The Federal Resource Center on Special Education (FRC) has a list of all the centers, their contact information, and Web site addresses. Find this handy guide online at www.dssc.org/frc/oseptad.htm

- Publications, publications, publications!

  NICHCY offers online access to the TA&D resource library, with descriptions of all TA&D publications, CDs, videos, research articles, and disability briefs. Search the library at http://www.tadnet.org/pages/513-products

Disability Awareness

- What do parents experience?

  http://www.familyvoices.org/admin/work_caring/files/nd20.pdf

  NICHCY offers a 16-page publication called Parenting a Child With Special Needs. A Spanish version, called Cómo Criar un Niño con Necesidades Especiales, is also available. The publication is written primarily for parents new to the disability experience and shines a light upon emotional reactions that parents may experience and the lessons others have learned. You don't have to be a parent of a child with disabilities, though, to find this document illuminating. If you're working with parents, this publication opens a window into what it means to have a child with a disability.

- Need others to be more aware of what it means to have a disability?

  http://www.parentcenterhub.org/repository/awareness/

  Classrooms, day care centers, scout troops, clubs—any place children come together may benefit from this resource. NICHCY's Disability Awareness can connect you with curriculum, books, children's books, videos, and posters or other merchandise developed specifically to foster disability awareness.

Accessibility

- Key concepts of accessibility

  www.nod.org/

  The National Organization on Disability (NOD) sheds light on the many dimensions of accessibility: economic, social, medical/ health care, religious, political, housing—these are just a few areas of concern to individuals with disabilities.

- What does the ADA require?

  The ADA is the Americans with Disabilities Act, a law which requires that persons with disabilities have access to public accommodations, including hotels, restaurants, theaters, retail stores, parks, zoos, transportation terminals, and other facilities open to the public. The 10 regional centers on the ADA exist to provide information about the law and its accessibility requirements. These are known as DBTACs: Disability and Business Technical Assistance Centers. Enter the DBTAC network with a phone call to 1 (800) 949-4232 (V/TTY) or visit www.adata .org/ index.html

- Removing physical barriers to accessibility

  The Architectural Barriers Act of 1968 requires that facilities designed, constructed, or altered with federal funds comply with certain accessibility standards. Find out more by visiting the Access Board at www.access-board.gov

- Addressing barriers to employment

  If you're an employer and need information on the practical steps employers can take to make accommodations for the functional limitations of employees and applicants with disabilities, you'll love JAN, the Job Accommodations Network. JAN's services are free and numerous and very helpful. Visit JAN at www.jan.wvu.edu

- Access to educational curriculum and learning

  Heard of the universal design for learning (UDL)? If not, take the Universal Design for

Learning Web Tour, brought to you by the National Center on Accessing the General Curriculum. The tour's available at www. cast.org/ncac

- A research synthesis on Universal Design for Learning

"What is All the Buzz about Universal Design for Learning?" is available online at www.ihdi. uky.edu/msrrc/PDF/UDL%20Synthesis.pdf

- Web site accessibility

What makes a Web site accessible to visitors with disabilities? How is an accessible Web site created and maintained? Learn from the experts, the World Wide Web Consortium (W3C), whose Web Accessibility Initiative (WAI) includes substantial resources and guidance online. Go to: www.w3.org/WAI / about.html

- Section 508

The W3C is a great place to begin, but there's more to the story (naturally). Section 508 of the Rehabilitation Act, as amended, requires that federal agencies' electronic and information technology is accessible to people with disabilities. You'll need to know Section 508 requirements and strategies for compliance, which you can easily find out at the official 508 Web site: www. section508.gov

- Bobby, the helpful accessibility cop

Bobby is a free online service that allows you to test Web pages and identify and repair barriers to accessibility within existing accessibility guidelines, such as Section 508 and the W3C. Go under Bobby's scrutiny at http://bobby.watchfire.com/bobby/html/ en/index.jsp

- There are so many types of access!

This list of connections to accessibility information and strategies could go on and on

and on. Here are a few last, quick links, for accessibility to . . .

- . . . higher education: The Association on Higher Education And Disability (AHEAD) exists to upgrade the quality of services and support available to persons with disabilities in higher education. Take advantage of their resources and services at www.ahead. org
- . . . housing: Visit HUD, U.S. Department of Housing and Urban Development at www.hud.gov/groups/disabilities.cfm
- . . . information technology in education: Visit the National Center on Accessible Information Technology in Education (AccessIT) at www.washington.edu/ accessit/index.php
- . . . recreation: Visit the National Center on Accessibility, which promotes access for people with disabilities in recreation, at www.ncaonline.org/index.shtml
- . . . transportation: Who better than the U.S. Department of Transportation to tell you about accessible transportation, at www .dot.gov/citizen_services/disability/ disability.html
- . . . worship: Benefit from the Religion and Disability Program of the National Organization on Disability (NOD), described at www.nod.org/religion/index. cfm. Download a 50-page guide, called Accessible Faith: A Technical Guide for Accessibility in Houses of Worship, from www .rrf.org/noteworthy/accessible.html47

Parent Groups

- Wondering what kind of parent groups are out there?

https://ia802608.us.archive.org/27/items/ ERIC_ED370272/ERIC_ED370272.pdf

Here's a quick read on the subject: Accessing Parent Groups, and its Spanish version, Acceso a los Grupos de Padres.

- *Sometimes only another parent can help.*

  To talk with another parent whose child has the same disability as yours, let Parent to Parent connect you. Find them at www. p2pusa.org. (Wondering what Parent to Parent is? Read Parent to Parent Support and find out what this program has to offer. In Spanish, this publication is called Apoyo Padre a Padre. Both can be accessed from: http://www.parentcenterhub. org/repository/parentgroups/

- *Looking for a nearby parent group on your child's disability?*

  There are lots of parent groups organized around specific disabilities. If you're looking for one in your neck of the woods, take a look under "Disability-Specific Organizations" in the state resource sheets at www.nichcy.org/ states.htm

- *The special expertise of your state's PTI is at your fingertips.*

  Give your state's PTI (that stands for Parent Training and Information Center) a call when you want to (a) find out about education rights in your state, (b) learn how to advocate for your child, (c) find local resources, or (d) get expert advice on parenting a child with a disability. Find your state's PTI by looking at the state resource sheets or by checking out the PTI listings on the central PTI site at the Alliance at www.taalliance. org/Centers/ PTIs.htm. And read all about what PTIs do for parents and children in the publication, Parent Training and Information Centers, at http://www.twu.edu/ downloads/family-sciences/Parent_Training_ and_Information_Centers.pdf

- *How about the PTA?*

  The National Parent Teacher Association (PTA) offers both information and local organizations to help parents stay involved in the lives of their children—those with disabilities, too! To find your state's PTA, visit the national site at www.pta.org or look at the state resource sheets under "Organizations Especially for Parents."

- *For adoptive parents, there's . . .*
  - *the National Adoption Information Clearinghouse at http://naic.acf.hhs.gov/index .cfm*
  - *the National Adoption Center at www. adopt .org*
  - *the National Resource Center on Special Needs Adoption at www.spaulding.org/nrc/ index.htm*

Groups for Kids

- *Electronic connections*

  Try NICHCY's Zigawhat! site, where children with disabilities can learn about their disability (and others), connect with other kids, read tips just for them, have fun and play games, and tell their stories. Zig into Zigawhat at www.nichcy.org/kids/index.htm

- *Sibling support*

  Kids who have brothers and sisters with special needs have needs of their own. Want to know more?

  - *Read about sibs' special needs in the ERIC Clearinghouse's Siblings of Children With Disabilities at http://ericec.org/faq/ siblings.html*

  - *And then there's Soda Pop Online, which stands for: Siblings of Disabled (Kids) and Peers Offering Promise. This online space is made for kids and teenagers who have a sibling or friend with a disability. Take a sip at www.sodapoponline.org/*

  - *Visit the Arc's Sibling Support Project page. The Sibling Support Project is a national program dedicated to the interests of brothers and sisters of people with special health and developmental needs. Find out more about holding a Sibshop and search the database of over 350 existing Sibshops and other sibling programs across the United States, Canada and beyond, all at www.thearc.org/sibling support/*

Disability Stats

Looking for statistics related to disability? Here are some sources!

- *For general disability statistics*

    Contact the Disability Statistics Rehabilitation, Research and Training Center (DSRRTC) at (415) 502-5210, distats@itsa.ucsf .edu, or visit their Web site at www.dsc.ucsf.edu

    The DSRRTC has the most recent published sources of statistical data on disability, including such products as Disability Statistics Reports and Disability Statistics Abstracts. Data cover demography; epidemiology; health services use, costs, and coverage; employment and earnings; and social services and benefits. Data are also available on the following national programs: vocational rehabilitation; Medicaid and Medicare; veterans programs; Social Security (SSDI and SSI); and special education.

- *For health statistics*

    Here are two resources: (a) The National Center for Health Statistics, which offers "fast stats" on disability at www.cdc.gov/nchs/fastats/disable.htm and (b) the Maternal and Child Health Information Resource Center (MCHIRC) at (202) 842-2000, mchirc@hsrnet .com, www.mchirc.net. For statistics on many child-related topics, go to "View Child Health USA 2002" at www.mchirc.net/HTML/CHUSA-02/

- *For disability-related education statistics*

    Every year, the U.S. Department of Education, Office of Special Education Programs (OSEP), prepares a report for Congress on the implementation of the nation's special education law, the Individuals with Disabilities Education Act. These reports always come with impressive data tables about the numbers of students with disabilities served under IDEA, their disabilities, their educational placements, their teaching staff, and so on. Find OSEP's annual reports to Congress online at www.ed.gov/about/reports/annual/osep/ index.html

- *For diverse education statistics*

    The National Center for Education Statistics collects and analyzes data related to education in the United States. This includes children with disabilities. Visit the NCES site at http://nces.ed.gov/ and search using the term "disability," for example. Search results will include how many children with disabilities are being served under federal disability programs, how many exit from high school, the numbers that enroll in postsecondary education, and more.

- *For statistics on the participation of people with disabilities in American life*

    The National Organization on Disability (NOD.), in cooperation with the Harris Poll, is a source of timely survey research data on people with disabilities in American life. Visit the "stats" part of NOD's site at www.nod.org/ stats/

TEACHING STRATEGIES AND MATERIALS

Curriculum

General Education Curriculum Web Sites

- **Federal Resources for Educational Excellence (Free)**

    www.ed.gov/free/

    This site lists resources from the U.S. government for various age levels and subject areas

- **The Gateway to Educational Materials (GEM)**

    www.thegateway.org/

    This is a searchable database of general education curriculum materials sponsored by the U.S. Department of Education.

- **The Educator's Reference Desk**

    www.eduref.org/

    This database of lesson plans (formerly known as the AskERIC Lesson Plans) is

*searchable by grade, subject area, and key-
word. The lessons are mainly from the general curriculum, but many can be adapted for
children with disabilities.*

- **E-subjects: Curriculum and Lesson Plans**

www.esubjects.com/

*The site is broken into areas for students, par-
ents, and teachers. Some materials can only be
accessed with a subscription to the site.*

- **DiscoverySchool.com**

http://school.discovery.com/

*DiscoverySchool.com provides innovative
teaching materials for teachers and is con-
stantly reviewed for educational relevance
by practicing classroom teachers in elementary school, middle school, and high school.
You can browse lesson plans by grade and
by subject. The Curriculum Center also offers
activities, worksheets, puzzles, quizzes, and
more to help you teach science.*

- **Sites for Teachers**

www.sitesforteachers.com/

*Sitesforteachers.com provides only links to
sites that contain teacher's resource and educational material. Sites are ranked by popularity.*

- **A to Z for Teachers**

www.atozteacherstuff.com/

*A to Z Teacher Stuff provides access to thou-
sands of lesson plans through theme and
lesson plan pages, as well as Lesson Planz.
com.*

Special Education Curriculum Web Sites

- **About.com's Links to Special Education
Lesson Plans**

*http://specialed.about.com/education/
specialed/cs/lessonplans/index.htm*
- *About.com's Links to Mainstreaming/
Inclusion Information & Strategies*

*http://7-12educators.mining co.com/msub81
mainstreaming.htm*

- **Instructional Strategies on the Internet**

*http://interact.uoregon.edu/wrrc/InstStrat.
htm*

*This site links to curriculum and teaching
technique sites reviewed by the Western
Regional Resource Center.*

- **Intervention Techniques**

*http://curry.edschool.virginia.edu/go/cise/
ose/information/interventions.html*

*Special education majors at the UVA review
journal articles on teaching techniques for
students with disabilities.*

- **Preschool Zone: Resources for Early
Childhood Special Education**

*www.mcps.k12.md.us/curriculum/pep/pz
.html*

- **Teachers Helping Teachers**

*www.pacificnet.net/~mandel/
SpecialEducation.html*

*This site has available Special Education les-
son plans submitted by teachers.*

- **TeacherVision.com Search Engine**

www.teachervision.com/tv/tvsearch.php

*Searching under the word "Curriculum,"
"Disabilities," or the phrase "Special Education" brings up a list of articles and Web
resources on that subject, broken down into
subtopics.*

Books and Articles

- *Curricular accommodations can really help
students with disabilities.*

*http://www.csus.edu/indiv/b/brocks/
Courses/EDS%20245/EDS245%20
Outline%20Folder/bib1.pdf*

*Learn more about curricular accommoda-
tions in this NICHCY document, Resources
You Can Use, on making adaptations for
students with disabilities.*

- What does the research have to say about useful enhancements or adaptations to curriculum for students with disabilities?

  www.cast.org/ncac/

  The National Center on Accessing the General Curriculum (NCAC) offers, among other valuable resources, several in-depth articles on effective classroom practices, based upon a review of the literature. Read online what research reveals about explicit instruction, differentiated instruction, curriculum-based evaluations, and peer-mediated instruction and intervention.

- Universal design for learning

  Universal design for learning is a way of building curricular adaptations into teaching tools that draws on new brain research and new media technologies to respond to individual learner differences. Find out more about universal design for learning (UDL) in the topical brief, A Curriculum Every Student Can Use: Design Principles for Student Access, and Research Connections in Special Education on universal design (RC#5) at www.ericec.org/osep-sp. Visit the National Center on Accessing the General Curriculum (NCAC) Web site, where extensive materials on universal design are offered at www.cast .org/ncac/WhatisUDL372.cfm

- LD Online

  http://www.ldonline.org/ld_indepth/ teaching_techniques/strategies.html

  LD Online provides a wealth of materials for and about students with learning disabilities. You'll find articles about specific instructional strategies and techniques for this population, including

  - General classroom instruction accommodations
  - Teaching phonological awareness, reading
  - Teaching spelling
  - Teaching oral and written language
  - Teaching organization, active reading and listening, and study skills

  - Teaching mathematics
  - Teaching social behavior skills

- **ERIC EC Digests** (Available at least until December 31st, 2006)

  http://ericec.org/digests/prodfly.html

  A variety of digests are available at this site with information on curriculum and adaptations divided into the following subcategories: Cultural Diversity, Early Childhood, Gifted, Instruction & Management, Learning Disabilities/Attention Deficit Disorder, and Other Disabilities.

Foreign Language Materials

- Culturally and Linguistically Appropriate Services (CLAS) Early Childhood Research Institute

  www.clas.uiuc.edu/

  The CLAS Early Childhood Research Institute collects and describes early childhood/early intervention resources that have been developed across the United States for children with disabilities and their families and the service providers who work with them.

- The Foreign Language Teacher's Guide to Learning Disabilities

  www.fln.vcu.edu/ld/ld.html

  This Web address links to sites and articles with information pertaining to teaching foreign languages to students with various disabilities. Some information is specifically on curriculum, adaptations, and activities, but most of the information is on general resources.

- NCELA, the National Clearinghouse for English Language Acquisition and Language Instruction Educational Programs

  www.ncela.gwu.edu

  NCELA provides links to state-by state policies and resources as well as compiled information on meeting the educational needs of linguistically and culturally diverse students in the United States. Curriculum standards, information on accommodations for state-wide assessments, and state policy information available in foreign languages are linked to if available.

Research Basics

- Visit NIFL, an authoritative source for literacy information.

www.nifl.gov/nifl/index.html

NIFL is the National Institute for Literacy, and its site overflows with resources. Search NIFL's national database of literacy programs to find one in your neck of the woods. Access NIFL's many publications, including a 58-page teacher's guide for using the findings of the National Reading Panel in the classroom (called Put Reading First: The Research Building Blocks for Teaching Children to Read); a Parent's Guide called Helping Your Child Learn to Read; and a series of adult literacy publications titled Bridges to Practice.

- What does the research have to say about what works in literacy?

www.ciera.org/index.html

Center for the Improvement of Early Reading Achievement (CIERA) offers technical reports that have the latest research findings of different literacy studies. You'll also find publications on reading, appropriate for both teachers and parents. Don't miss the series of instructional resources.

- And then there's the National Reading Panel and its research reports

www.nationalreadingpanel.org/Publications/publications.htm

In April 2000, the National Reading Panel (NRP) released its research-based findings

in two reports and a video titled, Teaching Children to Read. The first report is an excellent resource for anyone interested in learning about reading instruction research. The second report (a more technically written document) reviews the reports of subgroups that assessed the status of research-based knowledge on the effectiveness of various approaches to teaching children to read.

- What has NICHD found out about reading development, reading disorders, and reading instruction?

www.ld.org/research/keys99_nichd.cfm

During the past 33 years, scientists at NICHD (the National Institute of Child Health and Human Development) have studied the reading development of 34,501 children and adults. This includes 12,641 individuals with reading difficulties, many of whom have been studied for as long as 12 years. This link leads to a synthesis online at the National Center for Learning Disabilities (NCLD) and authored by Reid Lyon, which is derived from an analysis of over 2,500 publications generated by NICHD scientists since 1965.

- What do we know about preventing reading difficulties in young children?

stills.nap.edu/html/prdyc/

Teachers and researchers may wish to read this 1998 report of the National Research Council that synthesizes the research on early reading development. It paints an integrated picture of how reading develops and how reading instruction should be provided.

- What about the Reading First program?

www.nasdse.org/FORUM/reading_first.pdf

The Reading First program is a focused effort to improve reading skills of students in kindergarten through the third grade. This link connects you to Project FORUM's synthesis of information shared by the Department of Education at the Reading

Research Symposium for the Council of Great City Schools, in March 2002.

- What types of parent involvement help children learn to read?

  www.gse.harvard.edu/hfrp/projects/fine/ resources/digest/literacy.html

  This Research Digest investigates (a) what types of parenting practices are related to children's early literacy in reading, math, and general knowledge performance at the end of the kindergarten year, and (b) how does the relationship between parent involvement and early literacy vary for children from different racial/ethnic and income backgrounds?

- And for parents—here's something written just for you about the research on reading.

  www.reading.org/pdf/1055.pdf

  The International Reading Association offers What is Evidence-based Reading Instruction? to help parents understand the research in reading, including how to identify literacy instruction methods that are likely to lead to high student achievement. Download the brochure at this link.

- More about the research base on reading— and PowerPoint slides!

  www.nichd.nih.gov/crmc/cdb/approach.pdf

  In 28 pages, find out about Reading: A Research-Based Approach, available online (at this link) at the NICHD, the National Institute of Child Health and Human Development at the National Institutes of Health. You may also be interested in NICHD's PowerPoint slides on the subject at *www.nichd.nih.gov/ crmc/cdb/reading/index.htm*

- Summarizing the knowledge base

  http://www.ncrel.org/litweb/knowlb.htm

  NCREL (the North Central Regional Educational Laboratory) provides summaries, syntheses, and links to literacy resources on its site.

- Research-based literacy materials from the U.S. Department of Education and the projects it funds

  http://pplace.org/Litguidepage.html

  See our federal tax dollars at work! Download the Literacy Resource Guide for Families and Educators, and connect with current research-based literacy resources available through the U.S. Department of Education and its funded projects. The guide lists whether the resources are available in print, online, CD-rom, or videotape. The description of each item also includes information about cost (many are free!), ordering (including bulk copies), and the relevance for specific audiences (e.g., older students, students with disabilities, and English-language learners).

- To teach phonics or not?

  Here are two resources addressing this question.

  www.aera.net/pubs/rer/abs/rer7132.htm

  Systematic Phonics Instruction Helps Students Learn to Read: Evidence from the National Reading Panel's Meta-Analysis is a 2001 article appearing in Review of Educational Research (Vol. 71, No. 3, 393–447). This link takes you to the article's abstract.

  www.nichd.nih.gov/publications/nrp/report. htm

  The National Reading Panel's report Teaching Children to Read includes reports of the Panel's subgroups. This link will lead you to the Table of Contents for the subgroups' reports. Chapter 2 focuses on Alphabetics and includes closer looks at phonemic awareness and phonics instruction.

NCLB and Reading

- The law speaks to reading improvement.

  www.NoChildLeftBehind.gov/

This Web site includes an easy-to-read overview of the No Child Left Behind Act (NCLB), tips for helping children learn to read, school reform news, lists of state education contacts, FAQs on reading, testing, accountability, safe schools, and much more.

- Find helpful materials on the NCLB Web site.

www.ed.gov/parents/landing.jhtml

Parents, caregivers, teachers, and others will find useful publications on the NCLB Web site. Check out: School-Home Links Reading Kit, A Compact for Reading Guide, the READ*WRITE*NOW series, Helping Your Child Become a Reader, and many more! Some are available in Spanish, too.

Teaching Reading–Is it Rocket Science?

- Yes, it is! See why in this report.

www.aft.org/edissues/rocketscience.htm

Teaching Reading IS Rocket Science: What Expert Teachers of Reading Should Know and Be Able to Do reviews the reading research. It also describes the knowledge base essential for teacher candidates and practicing teachers to master if they are to be successful in teaching all children to read well. Finally, the report makes recommendations for improving the system of teacher education and professional development.

- Interested in an online workshop?

www.cec.sped.org/pd/reading.html

The Council for Exceptional Children offers this online workshop in Beginning Reading Instruction. Educators, paraeducators, administrators, and teachers-in-training can take the online course whenever it best fits their schedule. The workshop focuses on research-based strategies to strengthen students' phonemic awareness, decoding, fluency, word recognition, and comprehension skills.

- To the point: A quick read

www.sedl.org/pubs/sedl-letter/v14n03/welcome.html

The Southwest Educational Development Laboratory (SEDL) focuses an edition of its SEDL Letter on Putting Reading First. Find out about 10 myths of reading instruction, the importance of phoneme awareness, and activities teachers can use in their classrooms.

- What teaching strategies help?

www.vanderbilt.edu/CASL/outreach.html

Teachers! You'll find reports on teaching strategies on this Web site of the Center on Accelerating Student Learning (CASL). Topics include reading, writing, handwriting, math, spelling, phonological awareness, and reading comprehension. Also available are CASL newsletters, manuals, and videotapes.

- Looking for instructional materials?

www.teachers.net/4blocks/

The Four Blocks Literacy Center provides information and support to teachers and parents based upon the Four Blocks Literacy program. You can find instructional materials, books, and information on training seminars on this site.

- More on teaching strategies

cela.albany.edu/publication/ilu.htm

Visit the site Improving Literary Understanding Through Classroom Conversation. Teachers will find their publications on literacy and teaching strategies very useful.

- NCITE is the National Center to Improve the Tools of Educators.

idea.uoregon.edu/~ncite/programs/read.html

Visit NCITE's site to get an information kit, principles for learning to read, tips for teaching reading to children with learning disabilities, and tips for parents on how to strengthen reading skills.

- Attend a teacher prep and professional development conference virtually.

www.connectlive.com/events/learning summit/

Watch the video from the 1999 conference, the National Summit: Revealing Keys to Learning Success for All Children. Focusing on teacher preparation and ongoing professional development, this conference highlighted successful examples of teachers incorporating research into practice—in particular, taking learning disability research findings and applying them to teaching methods for all students.

- *Useful information if you're training teachers*

www.texasreading.org/utcrla/default.asp

Anyone who is involved with training teachers will find lots of useful information at the site of the Texas Center for Reading and Language Arts (TCRLA). Read about research efforts, get a booklet on coteaching, and access a series of professional development guides. TCRLA is developing a national training model for kindergarten through second-grade teachers in effective early reading instruction.

- *Read, write, think: Free standards-based lesson plans and online resources*

www.readwritethink.org/

The Read-Write-Think Web site connects theory to practice and was developed by the International Reading Association in partnership with NCTE (the National Council of Teachers of English). A wide range of lessons are available to help teachers work with students to learn language, learn about language, and learn through language.

Beginning Reading Instruction

- *What are the developmental milestones for reading and writing?*

www.ed.gov/pubs/CheckFamilies/

Read Checkpoints for Progress in Reading and Writing for Families and Communities to find out the developmental milestones for kids from birth through Grade 12. Also find out what most children will be able to read and write within those milestone periods. Print out the reading suggestions for each age group to take with you to the library. Read about strategies and resources parents can use to assist their children.

- *Building early literacy skills of preschool children*

getreadytoread.org/index.html

The Get Ready to Read site is friendly, colorful, and chock-full of ideas for building the early literacy skills of preschool children. Information is broken down into helpful categories for parents, educators, health care professionals, and advocates. Use the 20-question, easy-to-use, research-based screening tool to determine your child's progress in building the skills needed to learn to read and write.

- *Dynamic indicators of early literacy skills*

idea.uoregon.edu/

The acronym is IDEA but on this Web site, it stands for the Institute for the Development of Educational Achievement. Educators, this site is especially for you! You'll find lots of useful reading and literacy materials. Don't miss the links to Dynamic Indicators of Basic Early Literacy Skills and Big Ideas in Beginning Reading.

- *Check out the Early Literacy Network.*

http://literacy.edreform.net/

The Early Literacy Network at the Education Reform Network connects you to resources promoting early literacy. The materials are organized by the following categories: phonemic awareness, phonics and spelling, fluency, comprehension, vocabulary, writing, motivation, family literacy, struggling readers, English language learners, professional development, and instructional approaches.

- *Match the books you use to the literacy goals you have.*

www.uth.tmc.edu/circle/

Visit the Center for Improving the Readiness of Children for Learning and Education (CIRCLE). There, you'll find a terrific list of children's books (in both English and Spanish) categorized by different literacy goals (e.g., "Motivation to Read" "Phonological Awareness"). Don't miss the fun activities to help children learn letters, sounds, and more. Also available is a list of publications produced from research studies.

- Try this early childhood learning kit.

www.ed.gov/inits/americareads/RSRkit.html

Ready Set Read! was developed to help every child in the United States read well, on their own, by the end of the third grade. The kit includes activity guides for families and caregivers, a growth chart, and an activity calendar filled with helpful tips and special activities to promote reading and language skills for young children. A Spanish version is also available.

- Getting children started on the right track

bob.nap.edu/readingroom/books/sor/

Starting Out Right: A Guide to Promoting Children's Reading Success is reader-friendly. It explains how children learn to read and how adults can help them. It provides realistic tips and ideas that parents, educators, policy makers, and others can use to help young children get on the right track for reading.

- For parents

A Child Becomes a Reader: Proven Ideas for Parents from Research-Birth to Preschool: This booklet offers advice for parents of children from birth to preschool on how to support reading development at home and how to recognize preschool and day care activities that start children on the road to becoming readers. It's available online at www.nifl.gov/partnershipforreading/publications/pdf/low_res_child_reader_B-K.pdf. A separate booklet looks at kindergarten through Grade 3, available at www.nifl.gov/partnershipforreading/publications/pdf/low_res_child_reader_K-3.pdf

- A cautionary note about applying research findings

www.aera.net/pubs/er/arts/29-06/taylor01.htm

Discretion in the Translation of Research to Policy: A Case From Beginning Reading. sounds the caution bell about how research can be misapplied or misinterpreted when it comes time to make policy. Offered as an example of this unfortunate possibility is one recent, and uncommonly influential, reading methods study that the authors claim has been overly promoted by the media and misused by some policy makers and educational leaders to support a simple solution to the complex problem of raising the literacy of young children in high-poverty neighborhoods. As a counterpoint to this caution, you may also wish to read a response to the article, called Response to Taylor et al.: Misrepresentation of Research by Other Researchers, at www.aera.net/pubs/er/arts/29-06/forman01.htm

Reading With Older Children

- Adolescent literacy workshops

www.nifl.gov/partnershipforreading/adolescent/

A series of workshops was held to review and summarize the critical issues relevant to adolescent literacy. Results are summarized on the Partnership for Reading's Web site at this link, and they include a Video Summary of the Second Adolescent Literacy Workshop: Practice Models for Adolescent Literacy Success.

- Need high interest/low reading level materials?

www.accessiblebookcollection.org/default.htm

Try the Accessible Book Collection. Here you can find age-appropriate reading materials for students reading below their grade level (often called high interest/low reading level materials). Qualified students can borrow digital copies or e-books from the vast collection. These are great for students who are prevented from reading standard print due to visual, perceptual, or physical disability, such as blindness, physical disability, visual impairment, learning disabilities, and dyslexia.

- For middle schoolers and up

www.literacymatters.org/

The goal of the Literacy Matters project is to improve the literacy development of middle grade and secondary school students, especially those students who are struggling to succeed. Find helpful resources for teachers, parents, and students themselves. Electronic workshops are available, too!

- When secondary students struggle

www.sedl.org/pubs/sedl-letter/v14n03/5.html

The Southwest Educational Development Laboratory (SEDL) offers insight into and suggestions for addressing reading instruction with students in high school.

- For 15 elements of effective adolescent literacy programs

www.all4ed.org/publications/ReadingNext/

Written by five of the nation's leading researchers, Reading Next: A Vision for Action and Research in Middle and High School Literacy, charts an immediate route to improving adolescent literacy.

- Adolescent Literacy Learning Link

www.med.unc.edu/ahs/clds/projects.html

Called ALL-Link, Adolescent Literacy Learning Link is a field-initiated research and development project. Currently being field tested by adolescents with severe speech and physical disabilities across the country, ALL-Link is a comprehensive, integrated, Web-delivered set of reading and writing instructional materials at the beginning levels.

Spanish is coming soon, according to the Center for Literacy and Disability Studies (CLDS).

- Heard of the SIM, the Strategic Instruction Model?

www.ku-crl.org/index.html

The University of Kansas Center for Research on Learning has developed the SIM, which is a comprehensive approach to adolescent literacy that addresses the need of students to be able to read and understand large volumes of complex reading materials as well as to be able to express themselves effectively in writing. Visit the Center (use this link) and take a look at their available materials on the SIM—and more!

Don't-Miss Resources

- Reading Is Fundamental—a Web site, an organization, and a statement of fact

www.rif.org/

Reading Is Fundamental (RIF) offers guides that parents love on how to start the habit of reading in your family. Teachers can use the variety of book lists, Internet resources, articles, teacher tips, and student activities. In addition, you can find out general information about RIF and how to start a program in your area.

- Reading Rockets—more than a TV program

www.readingrockets.org/

This friendly site has reading information for both parents and teachers. Keep up on reading and literacy issues through the world news headlines (updated daily). Chat with others on the two lively online bulletin boards: "Reading with Your Child" and "Teaching Reading." Spanish information is available, too.

- It's all online

www.readingonline.org/

Reading Online is a journal of K–12 practice and research published by the International Reading Association. Visit the "Electronic Classroom" for ideas and information about applying technology in literacy instruction, find out about literacy practices all over the world, and read peer-reviewed articles about all aspects of literacy.

- *Connecting to literacy through your doctor*

www.reachoutandread.org/

Reach Out and Read (ROR) promotes early literacy by making books a routine part of pediatric care. ROR trains doctors and nurses to advise parents about the importance of reading aloud and to give books to children at pediatric check-ups from 6 months to 5 years of age, with a special focus on children growing up in poverty. Currently, there are more than 1,800 program sites based on the ROR model, all located at clinics, hospitals, office practices, or other primary care sites. To find where programs exist in your area, visit www.reachoutandread.org/about_find. html

- *Volunteering to help children learn to read*

http://nationalserviceresources.org/

The National Service Resource Center (NSRC) can connect you with resources related to community service and volunteering. The NSRC's online publications include connections to such literacy topics as tutoring (student to student and cross-aged tutoring), guidebooks, volunteer tutor programs, and more. See what's available at http://nationalservice resources.org/resources/online_pubs/ #literacy

- *It's a family thing*

www.barbarabushfoundation.com/

The Barbara Bush Foundation for Family Reading works to promote literacy within the family and to break the intergenerational cycle of illiteracy.

Literacy and Children With Disabilities

- *Ever tried accessible books?*

In addition to the Accessible Book Collection mentioned earlier under "Reading with Older Students," there are a number of notable sources of materials specially designed for individuals with reading or physical disabilities that impede their use of print text. Try:

- *the National Library Service for the Blind & Physically Handicapped at the Library of Congress at www.loc.gov/nls*
- *Recording for the Blind and Dyslexic at www.rfbd.org*
- *bookshare.org, a Web-based system supplying accessible books in digital formats designed for people with disabilities at www.bookshare.org*

- *A ground-breaking center working on literacy and children with disabilities*

www.med.unc.edu/ahs/clds/

The Center for Literacy and Disabilities Studies (CLDS) promotes literacy learning and use for individuals of all ages with disabilities. This site describes their ongoing literacy projects and connects you with upcoming events in your area.

- *Need to know about Braille and literacy?*

www.afb.org/

Visit the American Foundation for the Blind and find an overview of literacy, Braille literacy resources for parents, resources for teachers of Braille, discussions of electronic books, a newsletter on Braille literacy, a Braille e-mail discussion group, and more.

- *Looking for embossed Braille resources?*

www.bookshare.org

Braille books originating from the bookshare .org's digital Braille files can be ordered in embossed Braille form and mailed directly to you or as a gift.

- *For children with learning disabilities*

  The materials available on literacy for children with LD are a splendid resource for all of us. The problem is—where to begin? Here is an obviously short list that will lead you into a universe of more . . .

  - *LDonline at: www.ldonline.org/*
  - *National Center for Learning Disabilities (NCLD) at www.ld.org, and its generous sister-site at www.getreadytoread.org*
  - *the Learning Disabilities Association of America (LDA) at www.ldaamerica. org/*

- *For deaf and hard of hearing children*

  ncam.wgbh.org/cornerstones

  Cornerstones: A New Approach to Literacy Development for Deaf and Hard of Hearing Children has a great tool for teachers of children who are deaf and hard of hearing: A Cornerstones teaching unit based on an episode of "Between the Lions," the award-winning PBS literacy series for beginning readers. Included are clear lesson plans as well as supportive material.

- *For children with Down syndrome*

  www.woodbinehouse.com

  Woodbine House makes available Teaching Reading to Children With Down Syndrome: A Guide for Parents and Teachers. For more information about the book, its cost, and how to order, visit this Web site.

- *For children with mental retardation*

  www.cec.sped.org/bk/catalog2/autism.html

  This link connects you to the Council for Exceptional Children's (CEC) catalog. Scroll down until you reach the description of The Quest for Literacy: Curriculum and Instructional Procedures for Teaching Reading and Writing to Students with Mental Retardation. Order this 80-page book online by calling CEC's toll-free number, 1 (888) 232-7733, or by e-mail at service@cec.sped.org

Reading and English Language Learners

- *What works with students learning English as a second language?*

  www.csos.jhu.edu/crespar/techReports/ Report66.pdf

  Off the press in December 2003, Effective Reading Programs for English Language Learners: A Best-Evidence Synthesis is available from the Center for Research on the Education of Students Placed at Risk (CRESPAR).

- *What works with adults learning English?*

  www.cal.org/ncle/readingbib/

  Find out in Research on Reading Development of Adult English Language Learners: An Annotated Bibliography, available at this link from NCLE, the National Center for ESL Literacy Education.

Teaching Students With Rett Syndrome

- *Lots of education-related info and guidance on IRSA's site*

  www.rettsyndrome.org/main/toc-education .htm

  The International Rett Syndrome Association (IRSA) offers a lengthy table of contents on education issues that will take you to individual articles. Find out about inclusion, accessing the general education curriculum, finding the right school placement, testing methods, and scads of info on how to design an IEP for a student with Rett's.

- *The importance of the IEP*

  www.autism-society.org/site/PageServer ?pagename=IEP

  The Individualized Education Program (IEP) is a written document that outlines a child's education. For students with autism, it's a cornerstone of the educational services they will receive and needs to be carefully planned. Parents and teachers alike will find this article on the IEP helpful.

- If you want to know more about special education, IEPs, and educational rights under the law, be sure to take a look at NICHCY's materials.

  http://www.parentcenterhub.org/

  NICHCY publications are now available for free on their affiliate, CPIR's Web site. You can also call at 1 (800) 695-0285 for copies or to talk over personal questions and concerns.

- IRSA also offers, for low cost, a book for parents, teachers, and therapists.

  www.rettsyndrome.org/main/understanding_rett_syndrome.htm

  Find out more about Understanding Rett Syndrome: A Practical Guide for Parents, Teachers and Therapists at the International Rett Syndrome Association (IRSA). The foreword of the book is written by Dr. Andreas Rett, the discoverer of the syndrome.

  Again, from the perspective that Rett Syndrome is a disorder on the autism spectrum, the following autism-related information may be useful to you.

- Educating Children With Autism and Pervasive Developmental Disorder

  www.autismweb.com/education.htm

  Courtesy of Autism Web.

- Educating Children With Autism

  www.nap.edu/catalog/10017.html

  The Committee on Educational Inverventions for Children With Autism, National Research Council, offers Educating Students With Autism, which examines the scientific knowledge underlying educational practices, programs, and strategies for children with this disability. Read the book online, order online, or call 1 (888) 624-8373.

- A special resource: The Professional Development in Autism Center

  http://depts.washington.edu/pdacent/

  The Professional Development in Autism Center (PDA) provides training and support for school districts, families, and communities to ensure that students with ASD have access to high-quality, evidence-based educational services in their local school districts. Visit online or call (206) 543-4011.

Spanish Materials

- El Síndrome de Rett, a fact sheet from NINDS, the National Institute of Neurological Disorders and Stroke.

  www.ninds.nih.gov/health_and_medical/pubs/el_sindrome_de_rett.htm

- Translate IRSA's site.

  www.rettsyndrome.org/

  On the top left menu of the International Rett Syndrome Association's Web site, you'll see a tab titled "Translate." Babel Fish is used to render the site into Spanish, 150 words at a time!

- For low cost, you can buy The Rett Syndrome Handbook in Spanish.

  www.rettsyndrome.org/main/rett_syndrome_handbook.htm

  The Rett Syndrome Handbook is written by IRSA founder and President, Kathy Hunter, and covers all areas of Rett Syndrome you can think of. It's available in Spanish. Find out more and order it online via this link.

- The Spanish version of When your child is diagnosed with an autism spectrum disorder

  www.iidc.indiana.edu/irca/fspanish.html

  Cuando su niño/niña es diagnosticado con alguno de los desórdenes en la gama del autismo is the Spanish title of this publication from the Indiana Resource Center for Autism.

- *Looking at the genetics of autism (in Spanish), including Rett's*

  www.exploringautism.org/spanish/autism/evaluation.htm

- *¿Qué es el Síndrome Rett?, from the Rett Syndrome Association of Argentina*

  www.rett.com.ar/sindrome_rett.htm

- *Síndrome de Rett: Revisión y actualización deconceptos, from Venezuela*

  http://ceril.cl/P41_s_rett.htm

SUMMER CAMPS FOR CHILDREN WITH DISABILITIES

General

Camps 2005: A Directory of Camps and Summer Programs for Children and Youth With Special Needs and Disabilities in the Metro New York Area

Resources for Children With Special Needs Publications/Department B
116 E. 16th Street, 5th Floor
New York, NY 10003
(212) 677-4650
E-mail: Info@resourcesnyc.org
Web: www.resourcesnyc.org
$33.00 including shipping and handling (available in English & Spanish)

Easter Seals Camping and Recreation List
Easter Seals-National Office
230 West Monroe Street, Suite 1800
Chicago, IL 60606
(800) 221-6827; (312) 726-6200 (Voice)
(312) 726-4258 (TTY)
E-mail: info@easterseals.com, or rgarza@easterseals.com
Web: www.easterseals.com
Free (some "camperships" are available)

Guide to Summer Camps and Summer Schools (29th edition)
Porter Sargent Publishers, Inc., c/o IDS
300 Bedford Street, Building B, Suite 213
Manchester, NH 03101

(800) 342-7470
E-mail: info@portersargent.com
Web: www.portersargent.com
$45.00 hard-cover; $27.00 soft-cover (plus shipping and handling)

Guide to ACA Accredited Camps 2004
American Camping Association (ACA), Inc.
5000 State Road 67 North
Martinsville, IN 46151-7902
(800) 428-2267; (765) 342-8456
E-mail: bookstore@acacamps.org
Web: www.acacamps.org
$12.95 (includes shipping and handling)
(You can search ACA's database of camps online free of charge.)

National Camp Association, Inc.
610 Fifth Avenue
P.O. Box 5371
New York, NY 10185
(800) 966-CAMP (2267); (212) 645-0653
E-mail: info@summercamp.org
Web: www.summercamp.org
(CampQuest, an online camp selection guide, is available on the NCA Web site.)

Summer Opportunities for Kids & Teenagers
Peterson's
Princeton Pike Corporate Center
2000 Lenox Drive
Lawrenceville, NJ 08648
(800) 338-3282
E-mail: info@petersons.com
Web: http://e-catalog.thomsonlearning.com/ 326
$29.95 (plus shipping and handling)

Disability-specific

Camp List for Children With Cancer
The Candlelighters Childhood Cancer Foundation
National Office
P.O. Box 498
Kensington, MD 20895-0498
(301) 962-3520; (800) 366-2223
E-mail: info@candlelighters.org
Web: www.candlelighters.org/supportcamps.stm

Camps for Children With Spina Bifida
Spina Bifida Association of America
4590 MacArthur Boulevard, NW, Suite 250

Washington, DC 20007-4226
(800) 621-3141; (202) 944-3285
E-mail: sbaa@sbaa.org
Web: www.sbaa.org
Call for a state-by-state listing.

Web Sites

- *Association of Independent Camps: Summer Camp Directory & Resource*
  www.independentcamps.com/intercamp

- *Brave Kids: Camps and Resources for Children With Chronic, Life-threatening Illnesses or Disabilities*
  www.bravekids.org

- *Camp Channel: Bringing Summer Camps to the Internet*
  www.campchannel.com/docs/camp search.html

- *The CampPage Guide to Summer Camps*
  www.camppage.com

- *The Camp & Conference Homepage*
  www.camping.org

- *Camps for Children With Diabetes*
  www.childrenwithdiabetes.com/camps

- *CampResource.com: Special Needs Camps*
  www.campresource.com/camps/spec_ needs_camps.cfm

- *Camp Search: The Search Engine for Camps*
  www.campsearch.com/

- *Children's Hemiplegia and Stroke Association (CHASA)*
  www.chasa.org/summercamps.htm

- *Children's Oncology Camping Association*
  www.coca-intl.org

- *Diabetes Camping Association: Diabetes Camp Directory—U.S. Camps*
  www.diabetescamps.org/uscamps.html

- *Grown-Up Camps*
  www.grownupcamps.com

- *Kids' Camps*
  www.kidscamps.com

- *National Center on Physical Activity & Disability (NCPAD) Summer Camps Fact Sheet*
  www.ncpad.org/fun/fact_sheet.php ?sheet=88&view=all

- *Special Needs Camps*
  www.mysummercamps.com/camps/ Special_Needs_Camps/index.html

- *Summer Camps for Amputees and Children With Limb Differences*
  www.amputee-coalition.org/fact_ sheets/Kidscamps.html

- *Summer Camps for Children Who Are Deaf or Hard of Hearing*
  http://clerccenter.gallaudet.edu/ InfoToGo/142.html

- *Summer Camps for Kids With Learning and Attention Problems*
  www.schwablearning.org/camp/index .asp

- *Summer Camp Search*
  http://summercamps.com/cgi-bin/ summercamps/search.cgi

- *Thomson & Peterson's Listing of Special Needs Summer Programs*
  www.petersons.com/summerop/select/ t004se.html